AF674908

THE NEXT ENLIGHTENMENT

THE NEXT ENLIGHTENMENT

Reimagining Consciousness, Wealth, and the Future of Humanity

WILLIAM NANDA BISSELL

with ROLANDO MONTECALVO

First published in 2020 by Hachette India
(Registered name: Hachette Book Publishing India Pvt. Ltd)
An Hachette UK company
www.hachetteindia.com

1

ISBN 978-93-5195-139-1

Hachette Book Publishing India Pvt. Ltd
4th & 5th Floors, Corporate Centre,
Plot No. 94, Sector 44, Gurugram – 122003, India

Typeset in Adobe Garamond 11.5/15
by InoSoft Systems, Noida

Printed and bound in India by
Manipal Technologies Limited, Manipal

To my parents, John and Bim,
two kind and generous souls
who cared deeply about the world around them.

And to my children, Sara and John,
in the hope that their generation
will fashion a future built on a higher consciousness.

Acknowledgements

I began work on this project in 2009, right after completing my first book, *Making India Work*. Throughout the ten years of working on *The Next Enlightenment* I kept coming back to the same question: is it possible to create a new blueprint for society to realise our highest ideals as human beings?

During this journey, I have been assisted by a number of friends and colleagues who have believed in this transformational project and have argued for and against its many aspects.

This book would not have been written if not for my co-author, Rolando Montecalvo. I thank him for his intellectual rigour, enthusiasm, perseverance, hard work, and especially his conviction that the ideas in this book needed to be heard. For the last several years he has been my sounding board, meticulously scrutinising all the original thoughts and policy proposals that I threw at him and forcing me to consider their every implication and iron out every kink in their logic. He helped me turn a collection of distinct ideas into a coherent ideology. He carefully rewrote large portions of the manuscript to reflect more accurately the fundamental principles that I wanted to convey. Thank you, Rolando.

My thanks go to Atul Mishra, Ameya Nagarajan, Cyriac George, Tanuj Kumar, and Kate Grayson, who all helped me put together the early drafts of several chapters and gathered much of the necessary information; and to the readers of preliminary drafts of the manuscript, who contributed to refining many of the ideas presented here: Anna da Costa, Richard Celeste, Professor Bina Agarwal, and Madhukar Khera. And to our stellar editor, Ashok Chandran, whose attentive line editing gave the book a shape worthy of publication, and whose perceptive critique of content forced me to rethink and improve some of the book's concepts.

I am grateful to Katherine Allen for all her support to this project and for her affection and commitment to my family; to Anita Duggal for providing the organisational support that was necessary to bring this project to fruition and for always being a rock in our lives; and to Kim Vaiphei for her thoughtfulness, ability to anticipate so much that happened while writing the manuscript, and diligence in managing all my handwritten notes and the printed versions of the manuscript.

I also thank Thomas Abraham, Poulomi Chatterjee, and the book production team at Hachette India for their generous help with the printing and distribution of the book.

During the years I spent writing this work, I was sustained with intellectual nourishment in the form of thoughtful conversations, introductions to great thinkers, and unstinting support from Yoav and Holly Lev. Many of my insights into human nature came from long discussions, over the years, with my sister, Monsoon Bissell, who has the gift of seeing human relations with great clarity. I also thank Samir and Meera Jain for their thoughtfulness in having me over for dinner whenever I was alone and for our wide-ranging philosophical conversations.

I am indebted to Stanley Siegel, Kaushal Kumar, and Dr. Paul Browde for helping me understand the power of introspection and its ability to reveal our true nature. And to Angela De Giacomo for listening patiently and offering her very practical advice.

I am deeply appreciative of many insightful conversations with my father-in-law, Vijai Kapoor, whose thoughts on government, laws, and public administration helped me understand so much about how complex societies ought to be administered; and with Vikas Vig, who can delve into the most intricate financial ratios and operational details with the same rigour and precision as he can discuss esoteric subjects like consciousness.

The chapters on science and medicine have gained immensely from my conversations with Dr. Paul Salins.

This book might not have happened if I hadn't spent so much of my childhood and early adulthood in the company of two extraordinary men whom I was lucky to have as my grandfather and great-uncle: Rai Bahadur Pran Nath Nanda and Lt. Gen. Hare Krishan Sibal (Mahavir Chakra).

I am grateful to my aunt and uncle, Marie and Tim Prentice, and my cousins, Nora and Phoebe Prentice, for their open hearts, love, and support. They provided me with a home and the warmth of family whenever I returned to Connecticut. And to Jane Craig, who has believed in me and in this project for twenty years.

When I reflect on the trajectory of my life and the choices I made, I realise that I was fortunate to meet Saurabh and Varsha Mehta in 1997. They have been good friends and mentors, and I have benefited greatly from their sound advice.

My thanks to all my colleagues at Fabindia, who over the years helped me live my vision and put up with my many organisational experiments, turning several of them into successful models. Among those colleagues, Charu Sharma and Mukesh Chauhan in particular lent their unwavering support to our pioneering work with community-owned companies.

Finally, my gratitude to Anjali Kapoor-Bissell for the journey we have shared during the past twenty years and all that we have learnt.

The helpfulness and commitment of all these people have convinced me that each one of us possesses the ability to evolve to a higher state of consciousness, and therefore, that our species has a chance to overcome the many problems it faces and create a better social order. I have written this book to begin a discussion on what that social order could be and what kind of humanity it could foster.

William N. Bissell
Delhi, October 2019

Contents

List of Tables

List of Figures

Introduction: What This Book Is About

This is a manifesto.

People in the 19th century wrote manifestos when they wanted to influence the course of politics, bring about social change, or ignite a revolution. A manifesto is more than a political treatise. It presents a coherent and innovative ideology, and offers a comprehensive policy programme that addresses every facet of our lives. This manifesto, outlines a new vision for society.

In modern academia, the all-pervasive spirit of political correctness has narrowed debate to either intellectual minutiae or discussions so tactful and padded with euphemisms as to become devoid of meaning. Anything even faintly ideological is deemed unworthy of scholarship. My book is a refutation of this trend. I believe ideology has an important place in discussions on the world's future, and I define it as an intellectual project that offers a logically consistent interpretation of the social phenomena around us. Accordingly, my manifesto is an attempt to construct a new organisational paradigm that can explain and give structure to a new way of being.

What makes this paradigm new? First, the theories and prescriptions presented here strike at the current paradigm – the neo-liberal world view (for want of a better term). *The Next Enlightenment* explores the key constructs of our current model of organisation and where they have come from. It also encourages us to see that this system is the root cause of the seemingly intractable issues we face today, from poverty to terrorism, from chronic disease to environmental degradation, from corrupt political forces to failing educational systems.

Second, the manifesto proposes to replace the current system with a new order undergirded by a fresh vision. It attempts to create a new social and organisational model applicable to all of humanity entire. The model consists of an ideological framework; a historical approach to understanding the forces behind many of our current habits, beliefs, and institutions; and a comprehensive set of policy proposals, many of them original, intended to redirect the course of civilised society.

The Next Enlightenment is the first step in a revolutionary movement. It is not merely a bundle of abstract ideas, but a practical prescription for reforming the vital institutions and concepts that support modern civilisation: liberty, democracy, free markets, the justice system, economic and monetary policies, medical practice, agriculture, and education.

The starting point of this movement may strike the reader as unconventional. The new paradigm I propose requires, first and foremost, an inner, personal transformation in each individual, and the willingness to seek a higher degree of self-awareness. *The Next Enlightenment* offers a method for how to develop this new level of consciousness and how to apply it to our relationships with others.

It is important for the reader to keep in mind that the book's apparently distinct parts – one about spiritual exercise, and the other about the nuts and bolts of social administration – are fundamentally interconnected. One cannot exist without the other. This is the crux of my proposal for the future: no set of policy initiatives, no matter how sensible and creative, can succeed in rescuing us from the morass of the present, unless and until it is accompanied by an equally sustained effort to lift our minds and hearts to a higher level of awareness.

Therefore, I ask those readers who are interested primarily in policy proposals to read carefully the early section on personal development, to understand that such development is the prerequisite for what follows. Conversely, I hope that those who are keen mostly on discussions of meditation and personal fulfilment will read the entire book to discover how a higher consciousness can be applied to yield the practical solutions that the world desperately needs.

Part I

Conceptual Frameworks

1

What It Means to Be Human

I am attending a conference of business leaders in the soothing interiors of one of Delhi's luxury hotels. We are a gathering of the ultra-privileged – the tiny fraction who control the majority of India's wealth – sitting in one of the most lavish settings that a poor country can offer. The discussion moves through topics relating to business and government policy. Then, a woman raises the issue of Rohingya migration out of Myanmar, which has been dominating the news. At this point, one of the most successful leaders admonishes her for her softness. He labels the refugees 'illegal migrants' and wants all of us to understand the geopolitical significance of this event, rather than be softened by wishy-washy humanitarian ideas. According to him, India needs to take a hard line on the Rohingyas to curry favour with the quasi-military regime that runs Myanmar (together with the Nobel Prize winner Aung San Suu Kyi), because favourable relations with Myanmar are crucial for strategic rebalancing of frontline status to counter China's power in the region.

Is migration to escape genocide an illegal act? I ask him what he thinks we should do. He replies that India must push the Rohingyas back to where they came from. I am stunned by the callousness of his answer, and by now, even more dismayingly, I can see that the attention of this group of high achievers has dwindled. Everyone seemingly accepts the geopolitical logic of India's 'interference', and the man who first responded to the question concludes that the Rohingyas should be left to their own fate. He brushes the remnants of a chocolate-chip cookie from his conference pad.

And then I realise that he is right. The inescapable logic of our world and the way it is constructed means that the 250,000 Rohingya refugees, and the one million more who have been left behind, are just an inconvenience that those in charge of the world's affairs would like to see disappear without too much soul-searching in the pages of the *Guardian* or the *New York Times*.

The conversation about the Rohingyas may be new in its particulars, but in substance it has taken place many times in the last century alone. Since 1900, we have had two catastrophic world wars, several hundred smaller conflicts, and many episodes of genocide. Whether the victims were Muslims in Bosnia, Tutsis in Rwanda, Jews during the Holocaust, or Armenians in the Ottoman Empire, the unanswered question is the same: what is it about *Homo sapiens* that predisposes us to such primal, violent behaviour? Amidst an age in which many of us have long since recognised the value of peaceful coexistence, mutually profitable trade, the rule of law, and human and civil rights, our actions continue to raise this question.

The brief exchange at the business leaders' conference was not an exceptional occurrence. At another event that I attended, the speaker lectured eloquently about the practical, no-nonsense, 'transactional' nature of China's political and business interventions. The 'false' idealism of the United States' and the United Kingdom's insistence on human rights, he said, would now be replaced by the simple logic of 'transactionalism', shorn of any bothersome morality. This kind of rhetoric is used repeatedly by powerful people, adept at recognising how the world works and optimising their own success as a result, like the chief executives who sacked thousands of workers in the wake of the financial crisis whilst rewarding themselves with golden parachutes and new ways of structuring their bonuses.

Saying simply that many of the world's rich and powerful are selfish, uncaring people, fails to capture the real problem. These individuals are not especially evil. They are merely successful representatives of a society that rewards self-serving, individualistic values. They have set aside morality and altruism because it is what they must do to get anywhere in this world. This is how our world works: it traps us into thinking that selfishness is the only way to succeed.

We need look no further than our political and economic systems globally to see this playing out. The evidence of corrosion is everywhere: our schools practise learning for the sake of career advancement, our hospitals practise medicine for profit, our banks and stock markets fund those who can make the most money, our politicians are concerned only with remaining in power, our governments busy themselves attracting voters or suppressing opposition, and our natural environment is being plundered and destroyed with only token restraint.

The Culture of Transactionalism

What if all these worrisome trends are not discrete problems that call for piecemeal solutions, but rather symptoms of a far greater malaise – a fundamental limitation in the way modern society is structured and organised? The same limitation perhaps led my interlocutor at the caucus of the wealthy to dismiss the plight of the Rohingyas so blithely. The same malaise perhaps encourages us all to focus on personal gain rather than the welfare of our fellow human beings and the safekeeping of the earth.

In other words, could there be something terribly wrong with the very model of civilisation that defines the global society of the present? Let us call that model – the amalgamation of intellectual and institutional structures that underpin modern civilisation – the First Dimension. And let us posit that, although it may have brought us great advances in technology, health, international cooperation, and impressive wealth and comfort, the First Dimension is profoundly flawed and has reached its sell-by date.

That this is the case should surprise no one: even the most cherished ideals and institutions of the First Dimension seem to be falling apart. In a time that has already seen Brexit and the election of leaders such as Donald Trump (in the United States) and Rodrigo Duterte (in the

Philippines), it is not an exaggeration to say that democracy, as we know it, does not work. In a time when a global economy can be brought to its knees by the shady machinations of a few, as happened in 2008, it seems redundant to say that free markets can lead to disaster. And in a time when racially motivated shootings are the order of the day in the United States, terrorist attacks are ubiquitous in Europe, and violence stemming from ethnic and religious differences is still prevalent in many parts of Asia and Africa, we must concede that our systems of education, justice, and welfare are far from successful.

How did we get to such an intractable state of affairs?

I think our evolutionary heritage, dating back to our past as hunter-gatherers and primitive settlers, endowed us with certain qualities necessary for survival in the harshest of environments: a focus on self-preservation, competitiveness for scarce resources, and aggressive behaviour in the face of threats. Although we are no longer hunter-gatherers, we have been unable to distance ourselves from these mental formations, and they continue to condition much of our behaviour.

Those millennia of deprivation and struggle also conditioned us to yearn for greater comfort, to stockpile resources, and to seek dominance over the natural world. As humans settled in organised societies, this yearning became a persistent quest for knowledge and innovation that could be turned into wealth, security, power, and increased productivity. It ultimately led to Scientific, technological, and Industrial Revolutions that enabled an exponential improvement in the quality of human life for many, and the creation of material prosperity to a degree that our ancestors could not have imagined.

A driving force of our progress in the last few centuries has been the application of a rational, scientific approach to our understanding of the world, by relying on the measurement and mathematical modelling of the phenomena we observe. The ability to greatly simplify the problems before us to single-variable models that provide specific solutions enabled us to tackle the most debilitating obstacles to subsistence, health, and commerce.

Yet in this drive to understand and master the observed universe through its measurement and quantification, we impoverished ourselves and the richness of our world, and lost sight of another principle: that the whole is greater than the sum of its parts. In measurement lies a reductionism profoundly antithetical to the diversity that exists within and around us. The rationalist, reductionist mindset that has dominated our endeavours since the time of Descartes and has shaped today's society ultimately catalysed a soulless, utilitarian culture that favours the selfish desires of individuals rather than the best interests of entire communities. Entrapped in this value system, we have refined political, economic, and social institutions and practices that reinforce our basest impulses: greed, competition, ruthlessness, and a desire for power.

This is what it means to be human in the context of the global culture I have labelled the First Dimension. We are a species made up of self-interested individuals with little awareness of where our self-serving behaviour comes from, and we are surrounded by a world of our own making that prizes utility and profit above all else.

Is there a different way to define what it means to be human and to organise ourselves to bring out the best of human nature? Many of us ask this question. Some of us are working from the inside of the system to change it – in humanitarian efforts to alleviate poverty or suffering, environmental efforts to save rainforests and mitigate climate change, and peacekeeping efforts to bring justice and functional infrastructure to places ravaged by war or civic unrest. But we know, deep down, that such efforts can only bring limited, temporary, and isolated improvements.

An Alternative Definition of Humanity

We stand, without fully realising it, at a fork in the road. By travelling in one direction, we can continue as before, buffeted by evolutionary, psychological, and societal forces that we do not understand, and unconsciously moulded into self-serving, confrontational individuals. But if we head in the other, alternative direction, we have the opportunity to take up a journey of self-discovery, fulfilment, and harmony.

I believe that human beings have an innate desire for peace, harmony, beauty, and spiritual fulfilment. Although all are born with a roughly equivalent set of basic cognitive abilities, many human beings are unaware of the potential that their life holds. Each human being is uniquely endowed with the ability to transcend the limitations and impulses of their own conditioning, be it hereditary, social, or cultural. We are capable of directing our minds and hearts towards ever higher levels of understanding, towards a state that some call 'enlightenment', but which I prefer to call 'higher consciousness'.

Embracing this innate capacity within each of us requires commitment to a journey of personal transformation. This journey begins by acknowledging everything that connects us to (rather than divides us from) our fellow human beings and to life itself. One way to pursue this journey of inner transformation is through a consistent and dedicated practise of meditation (see Chapter 3). There are, of course, other equally effective forms of introspection. With dedication and support, everyone is capable of this journey towards higher consciousness.

This, too, could become a way to define what it means to be human. We seek peacefulness and inner fulfilment. We are a species capable of stillness, introspection, and inspiration. With some practice, this allows us to understand the world and ourselves with clarity and insight. It also allows us to begin transcending the impulses that tend to determine our emotions and behaviour. This liberation allows us to naturally express our latent qualities, such as compassion, unity, creativity, and generosity.

In the pages that follow, I discuss how we might choose this definition of human nature over the other. I offer a method for the development of higher consciousness and a blueprint for an alternative model of social organisation that could result from such heightened consciousness. This book, therefore, advocates a logical system – a set of internally coherent ideas – that helps to create structures, policies, laws, and governance that would bring out the best of humanity whilst quelling the worst.

Implicit in this discussion is that our world as it is organised today – created by a primitive state of consciousness – reinforces our primal tendencies. The objective of *The Next Enlightenment* is to elaborate a new paradigm that could supersede the dominant organisational model of modern society, and to describe how we might implement this new paradigm. The alternative framework it represents requires everyone who cares about the future of humanity to make a commitment to taking this journey and raising their own state of consciousness.

2

The Three Dimensions

Three Models of Civilisation

Before we can hope to create an alternative future for humanity, we must understand the forces that have shaped our present and that determine much of our behaviour. To explore these forces, and the possibilities that exist to transcend them, I have developed a framework of Three Dimensions.

These are not dimensions in the geometric sense (such as height, width, or depth) or in a metaphorical sense (aspects or facets of a situation). Instead, these dimensions are sets of attitudes, behaviours, and belief systems commonly held by social groups. A dimension is thus an organisational paradigm that governs the way individuals and societies interact, so it shapes the way human societies are structured and the way they function.

The First Dimension (Dimension of Cause and Effect) is the dimension of the present: it describes our current model of civilisation, with all the ideas and institutions that define it – things like a free-market economy, inquiry based on the scientific method, impartial and evidence-based justice, a largely democratic system of governance, free and compulsory education, the widespread use of digital communication technologies, and so forth. The Second Dimension (Dimension of Interdependence) and the Third Dimension (Dimension of Transcendence) represent more enlightened, prudent ways to organise ourselves. They are paradigms that will exist in the future, once we have decided to work toward them.

It is important to note that after we transition from one dimension to the next, the previous dimension continues to exist and to remain relevant to particular situations that are appropriate to it. To visualise the relationship among the dimensions, imagine three concentric spheres (Figure 2.1). The First Dimension is encompassed by the Second, which, in turn, is surrounded by the Third. The Second and Third Dimensions denote more evolved and more resilient ways of interacting that are within our reach.

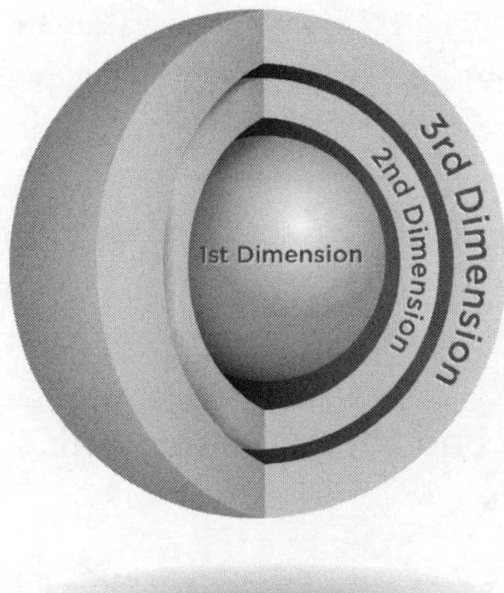

Figure 2.1: Relationship Among the Dimensions

Thus, First Dimension ways of thinking are not necessarily wrong, but they are not necessarily applicable to new circumstances. They are foundations upon which further advances can be built. But they cannot help us to function at our best as we move into more expanded ways of conceiving ourselves and interacting with the world. When we feel the pressure of new insight forcing a change in us, the temptation may be to cling harder to what has worked before or to what we know. But that is just the moment to let go, abandon the older model, and allow something better suited to our current reality to emerge.

Consider the aerodynamic principle of lift. At high speed, the flow of air over and under an aircraft's wings causes an uplift that enables it to fly. The air is necessary for this to happen, and the more of it there is (that is, the greater the air density), the more lift can be generated. Close to the earth, where air density is higher, lift is strong. Higher in the atmosphere, the air is less dense, and lift starts to weaken until, in the uppermost reaches, it ceases to work altogether. Thus, the principle that worked well at lower altitudes is a hindrance when a certain limit is exceeded. If we continue to rely on lift alone, we will stall and plummet out of the sky. To go even higher into space, we need technologies based on more advanced principles, such as rocket propulsion.

Similarly, ways of being, thinking, and interacting that emerge within a historical context become ineffectual and often detrimental when that context changes. In the face of new challenges and needs, we can continue to operate in the same ways and use the same tools that worked in the past, or we can let them go in favour of more suitable and supportive models. At the heart of such an evolutionary process is a shift in our consciousness.

The Dimensions and the Development of Consciousness

Each dimension is the result of a certain level of consciousness – a degree of understanding and awareness about ourselves and the world around us, and an ability to recognise the nature of reality and our place within it.

The nature and origin of consciousness have been debated extensively, both in academic literature (in psychology, philosophy of mind, and religious studies) and in everyday discourse. For me, consciousness, when fully realised, is the ability to recognise an omnipresent reality. It is the ability to see everything, including ourselves, our fellow human beings, our communities and societies, the natural world around us, and life itself, with clarity and detachment.

I believe that we can attain deeper states of awareness, or higher levels of consciousness, through meditation. Developing our consciousness means being increasingly able to recognise and understand the silent forces – the mental baggage that lies within our subconscious mind, including what we experienced in childhood, and what we absorbed from our parents and from social interactions – that condition our behaviour and the behaviour of others, and ultimately to transcend them.

In Chapter 3, I will develop a more exhaustive framework to help us understand and develop our consciousness. For the time being, it is sufficient to accept that the Three Dimensions I have defined above are intimately related to the overall level of consciousness of the societies that they support. In other words, the First Dimension is an expression of the typical level of consciousness held by individuals nowadays. I anticipate that future societies will be capable of spawning more enlightened social paradigms – the Second and Third Dimensions.

The level of consciousness of both an individual and a group is not fixed. It fluctuates constantly; it can leap forward but it can also retreat. Imagine that you come home after a long and stressful day at work. The children want to play with you and your spouse has lots to discuss with you. But your fatigue and frustrations boil over and you end up yelling at the children and quarrelling with your spouse. We can say that you are exhibiting a low level of awareness, because you have allowed certain emotions that have accumulated over the day to sneak up on you and make you behave in a way you had not intended. Later that evening, you are able to calm down and think about what just happened. Why, you ask yourself, did I rage against my family? Had they done anything to deserve it? Was I just bringing home emotions and worries from work? Was it this emotional 'baggage' that caused me to act so irritably? Do I owe my spouse and kids an apology? In the greater scheme of things, is what happened at work so dire that it should ruin my time with the family? Now, after some introspection, you can be said to have regained a higher level of awareness. You may even feel guilty for slipping up earlier, losing control of your emotions, and losing sight of what is important.

This example illustrates that self-awareness (consciousness) can rise and fall temporarily. Just because we are capable of a high level of consciousness does not mean that we can maintain it all the time. Conversely, just because we operate at a low level of consciousness most of the time, it does not mean that we are not capable of moments of great insight or empathy. Indeed, there have been times in the past, even in ancient history, when individuals and, at times, entire societies have experienced great surges in consciousness. In most cases, however, these episodes of heightened consciousness were fleeting and failed to bring about a stable and enduring social paradigm that might amount to a higher dimension as I have defined it. An outstanding example of this are the Edicts of Ashoka in the third century BCE.

Ashoka – an emperor of the Mauryan dynasty who ruled over most of the Indian subcontinent from 268 to 232 BCE – converted to Buddhism, possibly because he felt remorse over the carnage that his wars of conquest had caused. Not long afterwards, he began a systematic programme to share his new beliefs with his subjects via a number of formal inscriptions etched into pillars, rock faces, and cave walls throughout his vast empire. Known as the 'Edicts of Ashoka', these inscriptions were meant to be read by everyone. Although one of their goals was, of course, to propagate and legitimise the Buddhist faith, the Edicts focused on social and moral issues rather than religious rituals or the philosophical underpinnings of Buddhism. They were a genuine attempt to solve some of the problems that a complex society like the Mauryan Empire faced, by introducing Ashoka's extraordinarily enlightened vision of benevolent governance and proper behaviour. Far ahead of their time, the Edicts strike us as progressive even today. They state, for example, that all religions share a common truth, and they encourage tolerance and understanding of other religions. They contain revolutionary ideas like the call for humane and fair treatment of prisoners and criminals, and the need to preserve the natural environment, especially wildlife, to the point that the emperor himself gave up hunting. Ashoka, either as a result of his religious conversion or through other means, was able to see the world around him with the clarity and unity that comes with heightened consciousness. Indeed, his

Edicts represent a tremendous leap in consciousness, one that inspires admiration even millennia later.

Did the Edicts have any lasting effect on the society around Ashoka and long-term repercussions on the history of civilisation in India and elsewhere in the ancient world? After all, they were largely forgotten until the 19th century, when scholars were able to decipher and translate the inscriptions. They may have helped to propagate Buddhist teachings, but did they have any real impact on culture, on ideas of governance and social collaboration, or notions of kingship and good conduct? It seems more likely that only Ashoka himself, and perhaps his immediate courtiers and advisers, experienced a new level of consciousness. The moral, ethical, and organisational principles described in the Edicts were probably neither understood nor welcomed by his subjects – a vast population still very attached to inherited behavioural norms and therefore far from a level of self-awareness that could have occasioned a shift to a higher dimension.

I brought up this historical episode to illustrate two simple observations. First, history is replete with instances of heightened consciousness. These occurrences may have been brief and they may not have had important social outcomes. In some cases, they can be regarded as milestones in the general trajectory of civilisation, while in many others they were probably inconsequential. But they show that both individuals and groups have been capable of expressing a higher level of awareness than what prevailed around or before them.

Second, there is a connection between the paradigms or models that govern complex societies and the level of consciousness that brought about those paradigms. As the example of Ashoka shows, the fact that a ruler or a ruling elite espouses a more enlightened vision of social well-being is insufficient to usher in a new organisational paradigm (that is, a new dimension). Such a shift requires a critical mass of the population to have achieved a higher degree of self-awareness. This is still the case today. In most countries there exists not only the rule of law, but also enlightened ideals about civil rights, environmental protection, neighbourly conduct, humanitarian kindness, health standards, and so forth. Nevertheless, everywhere, even in countries with strong civic institutions, abuses are rife, whether it is police brutality or worker abuse, dumping of toxic waste or unfair legal tactics, tax evasion or corporate malfeasance.

To say that these are instances where either laws or universal principles of cooperation have not been enforced properly is missing the point. The truth is that for the vast majority of today's citizens, the norms that theoretically bind civilised society are merely rules written by an elite and administered by an abstract government entity or a distant institution. They have not been internalised by each and every one of us, because they are not the fruit of a reasoned inner process of understanding, and the logical conclusion of an increased awareness of the reality around us. Until a quorum of humanity has reached a sufficiently high level of consciousness, through meditation or other means of introspection, the unanimity required to fashion a better world will be lacking.

In the First Dimension, our behaviour – individual as well as collective – reflects a relatively low level of consciousness. We perceive ourselves as separate individuals, disconnected from other individuals and often oblivious of our impact on them, or their influence on us. We are governed mostly by our own primal interests and agendas. As our consciousness expands, we can begin to experience ourselves as part of a greater whole, connected with one another and all forms of life. From this more expanded perspective, the impact of our actions upon others and upon the natural world becomes increasingly evident. With this understanding we can attempt to build a better, fairer, more respectful and inclusive society. We can move to a higher dimension.

Figure 2.2 summarises schematically the relationship between consciousness and dimension. The feedback loop shows that the manner in which the organisational rules of any societal paradigm are applied can, in turn, affect the underlying level of consciousness, either by reinforcing it or nudging it to a higher plane.

The First Dimension

Much of the world we live in today operates according to First Dimension principles. These are embodied by a system of ideas that evolved over many

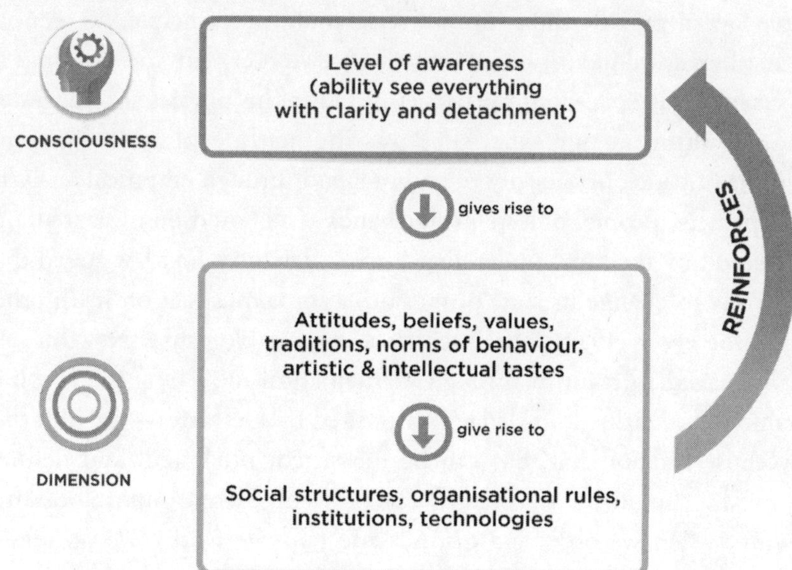

Figure 2.2: Relationship Between Consciousness and Dimension

centuries of civilisation, from our time as nomadic hunters and gatherers through the intellectual and practical innovations brought by the great civilisations of antiquity and the Middle Ages. This model of civilisation is the sum of all we have achieved and learned as human beings. It is largely a Western model of civilisation, which Europeans forced upon the rest of the world during centuries of colonialism and cultural hegemony.

While the development of the First Dimension began long ago and has been shaped by contributions from many periods of history and several different cultures, it owes its identity especially to the intellectual and scientific revolution of the early modern period. This revolution began some 400–500 years ago and radically reshaped our world view, eventually coalescing into the set of beliefs, value systems, and cultural norms that constitute modernity. It is the world ushered in by Descartes and Galileo, by Luther and Machiavelli, by Hobbes and Locke, and above all by the discoveries of Isaac Newton.

It was Newton who brought the heavens down to earth by demonstrating the compatibility of celestial and terrestrial laws of mechanics. Under the simple law of gravity, the entire universe could, in principle, be reduced to a mathematical identity. Not only did Newton explain the workings of objects falling in space, but the persuasiveness of his physics also suggested that everything in our experience was implicitly explicable. Nothing might lie outside our capacity to comprehend through empirical analysis. Suns, planets, people, objects in our hands – all could be measured and understood by the same underlying forces. Newton's first law stated that for a body to change its state of motion, a force must act on it. In other words, for every effect there must be a measurable cause. Newton had thus managed to confirm through mathematical modelling the absolute certainty of scientific knowledge first posited by Descartes – the idea that only those phenomena that can be measured, predicted, and defined empirically should be accepted as real and considered important. After Newton, when we observe a distinct effect in the world, we no longer have space for the existence of mysteries and magic; we search for unique and measurable causes, and certainty. This scientific, reductive approach to the world characterises the First Dimension (the Dimension of Cause and Effect).

Its scope is so vast and its influence so pervasive that it is hard to imagine that there could be other ways of viewing reality. We have, since the rise of Newton and his fellow luminaries, recreated the world in our image. The application of scientific knowledge and skills helped to build sophisticated technologies and problem-solving mechanisms, which, while they were complex in their engineering, were simple in what they sought to achieve. If the variable was profit, the system generated more complex structures to increase profits. If it was the concern over our safety and the desire to subdue others, we developed ever more lethal weaponry. If it was comfort, we built homes and machines and products that would make our daily lives more pleasant, predictable, and manageable. Since the Scientific Revolution, man's endeavour has been defined by the ability to discover the inner workings of nature, and use this knowledge to develop technologies that could exploit nature's forces. In the final analysis, science has allowed us to achieve mastery over our environment and thus to augment our comfort, prosperity, and power.

This momentous intellectual and scientific movement went hand in hand with another change: the emergence of the individual citizen as the primary actor on the social, political and economic stage. The early modern individual was no longer merely a silent part of a greater whole, such as a clan, a tribe, a guild, a social class, or a religious group. He was an independent entity with individual needs, desires, and interests, and he asserted, with increasing conviction, his right to pursue these interests independently of what his family, community, or sovereign wanted. We can see how the intellectual developments of the last few centuries played into this. Luther's translation of the Bible into German and, later, the translation of the Bible into English under King James I, meant that every literate individual could now read the Gospels and access spiritual knowledge for himself. The availability of printed texts in vernacular languages meant that more people than before had access to written knowledge. They could read the works of Copernicus and Kepler and decide for themselves whether their theories made sense, in spite of what the Church might say. Knowledge was no longer in the hands of a few priests and theologians; it belonged to everyone. The advent of experimentation meant that scientific theories could be tested independently, and the results of those tests could be replicated by anyone. The language of mathematics allowed researchers to deconstruct natural phenomena into simple algebraic statements that could convey their ideas succinctly to readers anywhere.

Besides science and technology, there were various other factors, such as urbanisation, that contributed to this sea change in attitudes. (I will describe them in greater detail in Chapter 5.) Our political and social systems changed together with our new understanding of ourselves. They became based on the rights of the individual and the conviction – as Adam Smith formulated it – that individual self-interest can appropriately organise society. This led to the creation of election-based, democratic systems of governance; professionalised, evidence-based systems of justice; free markets; educational and healthcare institutions available to everyone; and much more.

Who can doubt the benefits our recent history has heaped upon us? Order, governance, better relations between the social classes, technological innovation, economic growth, the codification and protection of individual liberties under the rule of law – few realms of learning or experience have been untouched. Furthermore, the application of technologies, coupled with the political and economic rights of individuals, has ushered in an age of unprecedented prosperity, a higher standard of living, and quality of life on a scale never experienced by humanity.

Progress has been uneven, with many falling behind. We have tended to favour the innovators with disproportionate advantages, and sometimes alarming discrepancies between peoples have emerged, but in general the world is a much better place today than it was yesterday. We tell ourselves that, surely, this is how the world is meant to evolve, and that in time, when those at the bottom or hidden in the shadows are brought into the fold, they too will reap the rewards. We are a First Dimension world and intent on becoming more so.

Yet, amidst all this material prosperity many feel that we have lost something precious – a closer connection to each other and to nature. While giving us control over many of nature's secrets and enriching us materially, the First Dimension has impoverished us deeply. Once all of nature's phenomena could be explained away mathematically, its mystery and power were gone. Our natural environment became a thing separate and far removed from us, an entity to be studied, defined, codified and, ultimately, controlled. The technology that this scientific knowledge engendered allowed us to exploit nature's resources with vastly greater purpose and efficacy, so that the natural environment became little more than a reservoir of resources to be extracted and consumed – energy to feed the machines, and raw materials to create more and more products for our use, comfort and entertainment.

Perhaps even more worryingly, the advent of First Dimension technology alienated us from each other. It is no longer necessary to meet with a cobbler to have new shoes made, or with a tailor for a new dress, because these items can be mass-produced in mechanised factories and bought in department stores or online. Farmers need no longer rely on other farmers or their extended families, because a single tractor can do the job of many. And even entertainment, which was once synonymous with spending time with family and friends, can now be enjoyed in solitude through television, video games, live streaming, and many other channels.

Science and personal liberty allow us to pinpoint physical and human nature, respectively, with unprecedented exactness. But the nature of this measurement creates a world of limited variables, separate components, and hence restricted values. Inevitably we measure what is amenable to measurement. The potent but simple-minded First Dimension has given us mastery over whatever can be manipulated mechanically, but that which lies outside the instrumental framework tends to be dismissed as insignificant, discounted as worthless, or ignored altogether as unreal. Surely, the world is more than the sum of what can be itemised.

Concurrent with the alienation and spiritual impoverishment that the First Dimension has brought about are the alarming and increasingly obvious signs that the vast edifice of the First Dimension is crumbling around us. The evidence of failure at a systemic level is overwhelming. Climate change is progressing at an alarming rate, each year now hotter than the last. Economic inequality has reached such staggering proportions that a few wealthy individuals now seem to own more than the poorer half of the world (some 3.8 billion people). Various nation states around the world – Iraq and Afghanistan, Syria and Libya, Somalia and Venezuela, to name a few – seem to have collapsed, or are on the verge of implosion and unable to return to functionality. Mass migrations by desperate populations escaping grinding poverty, persecution, and war are threatening stability on every continent and fuelling ethnic and racial mistrust and violence. The oceans hold vast amounts of plastic, while tropical forest cover is being cut down or burned faster than ever. Corruption and incompetence among politicians and government administrators are common. Cherished democratic systems have shown themselves powerless to avert decisions that are wrong-headed or the election of candidates who are unqualified to lead. Chronic disease, the spiralling costs of healthcare, and increasing microbial resistance to antibiotics are threatening to undo the advances that medicine has made in the last century. Natural resources are being extracted and consumed at unsustainable rates, often with disastrous environmental consequences, while global biodiversity is in steep decline, with over a quarter of all species having been lost in the last thirty-five years.

The First Dimension way of operating has reached its limits. It has given us so much – everything from light bulbs and vaccines to human rights and universal suffrage. But it also remains deeply enmeshed in primitive forms of consciousness that result in a focus on personal advantage over common welfare, hoarding of wealth rather than equitable distribution, corruption and power-seeking rather than good governance, competition over collaboration, and strip-mining rather than preservation of nature's resources.

The 20th-century philosopher of science Thomas Kuhn wrote in *The Structure of Scientific Revolutions*,

> Political revolutions are inaugurated by a growing sense, often restricted to a segment of the political community, that existing institutions have ceased adequately to meet the problems posed by an environment that they have in part created. In much the same way, scientific revolutions are inaugurated by a growing sense, again often restricted to a narrow subdivision of the scientific community, that an existing paradigm has ceased to function adequately in the exploration of an aspect of nature to which that paradigm itself had previously led the way. In both political and scientific development, the sense of malfunction that can lead to crisis is prerequisite to revolution.

The Second Dimension

At the heart of the First Dimension is a loss of connection with ourselves, with each other and with life as a whole. Many of us feel an internal sense of discomfort with 'the way things are', knowing that the values and belief systems that dominate First Dimension ways of operating are no longer serving us well, and are not able to resolve the complex problems we face today. To overcome this internal dissonance, we seek another way – a more subtle, nuanced, and encompassing way of being and relating, with deeper insight. We seek a new societal model demanded by all those who clamour for change or write about reform: the Second Dimension (the Dimension of Interdependence).

On one level, because of our programmed 'separateness', it is difficult for us to connect with this deeper understanding of our world. Yet on another, it is a natural realisation, if we can let go of our thinking mind for a time. What we may observe, when we do so, is that the natural and man-made worlds are deeply interdependent. Our thoughts, physical bodies, forests, biospheres, politics, and cities, for example, are all complex systems that are interacting with one another in every moment. Once we begin to see the complex interplay of thousands of variables, and to recognise the dense network of bonds that connect us to nature and to our fellow human beings (those in our immediate neighbourhoods as well as those on the other side of the world), we will have taken an important step toward raising our consciousness. This, in turn, will prepare us for the new social paradigm that is the Second Dimension.

The Second Dimension, then, is a different way to organise ourselves and relate to each other. It will realign our goals and priorities as a race, and that will make it possible to do away with inequality, violence, poor governance, pollution, and excessive consumption. This new paradigm starts with a higher level of consciousness and a new way of thinking. Attaining it will require great personal engagement from each individual – a personal transformation that begins by acknowledging that we are neither separate nor distinct from our fellow human beings.

One way to attain this inner transformation is through a consistent and dedicated practise of meditation. Meditation allows our mind to develop great subtlety and insight as it uses human faculties which, though they have lain dormant for lack of use, can help us comprehend the nature of interdependence. Insight acquired through meditation enables the observer to cultivate a profound understanding of what is observed; it can bring us to a different vantage point within ourselves. However, meditation is only one form of introspection, and I offer it merely as one example of an avenue to insight.

Whether through meditation or another means, we can arrive at a breakthrough, just like a scientist who finds a new theory to explain something better than the previous theory. As Kuhn noted, when scientists discover better and more holistic explanations, a 'paradigm shift' occurs.

The advent of a higher level of consciousness is such a shift, and it allows us, each and collectively, to usher in the Second Dimension. As we move from a world based on the reductionist notions of simple cause and effect to one based on a profound understanding of the interdependence in which everything is rooted, we naturally develop ways of being and interacting that are more inclusive, holistic, and liberating.

A shift to this organisational paradigm would fundamentally reorganise the way society operates. Creating a fixed or predefined structure for how humanity's alternative future should be is not my intention; the Second Dimension should be imagined through a collaborative creative process. In the second half of this book (especially Part III, A Global Society, and Part IV, The Economy), I offer a possible blueprint for how a Second Dimension reality could manifest here on earth. It includes a set of proposals for how society could be restructured to function in a more harmonious, connected, and egalitarian way, from justice systems to healthcare management, and from corporate governance to education. Some of these proposals are novel, while others are refinements of ideas already in the public sphere. Some are quite detailed, while others are general. All, however, are logically consistent with a vision of reality that I have labelled the Second Dimension, and with the theory of consciousness that I have outlined here. All are invitations for dialogue and exchange, and are intended as departure points for shared exploration, analysis, and coordinated action.

The Third Dimension

Eventually, even the Second Dimension will prove to have its limitations. Beyond it lies something even more sophisticated and powerful: the Third Dimension (the Dimension of Transcendence). While the Second Dimension will have taught us to reject solutions based on a simplistic understanding of causation, and to instead embrace and act upon the interconnectedness of all life, it will still be a dimension in which the phenomena that we observe, as well as those we create, remain separate from the mind of the observer. This duality of thought creates the artificial distinctions upon which the First and Second Dimensions are built. But somewhere beyond this way of perceiving the world, and somewhere in our deepest selves, I believe that there is a dimension defined by the unity of thought and of all observed phenomena.

In the first two dimensions we make sense of the world and organise what we see in ways that attempt to cope with the complexity of our world and our lives. In the Third Dimension we realise that all phenomena are constructs of our minds, and as such they can be remade. As our consciousness evolves to bring the Dimension of Transcendence within our reach, a moment occurs where the duality of thought that creates distinctions, and upon which the First and Second Dimensions are built, ceases to be relevant. This journey of deepening and reconnecting to our truest selves is, for me, the ultimate goal of our existence.

Imagine that you are asked to observe a small group of people intimately and report your findings. If you are doing so in a context of the First Dimension, you will probably note their age, record their professions and achievements, and monitor their life expectancy. In the context of the Second Dimension, you might try to observe the quality of their lives, what they do, their relationships with friends and family, the level of their generosity, and so forth. From a Third Dimension perspective, however, what would really matter is their way of being – how they are, how they are managing the condition of being present, both acting and observing, and how they apply their awareness to every action and thought they undertake.

I do not know what the Third Dimension will look like, or what new forms of life and exchange between individuals, communities, and nature it will bring. Nevertheless, in the chapters of this book, I attempt to sketch what the Third Dimension might bring to some of the fundamental facets of daily life. This vision is blurry, but I trust that you will be able to recognise its general contours: it is a global society inhabited by citizens devoted to each other's well-being, and a civilisation geared for the continual betterment of consciousness.

Part II

TRANSFORMATIONS

3

The Awakening of Consciousness

Our Context in the First Dimension

At the heart of this book are two transformations, one personal and the other global. The two are intimately related: to bring about any fundamental change in the external world as a whole, we must change the way we see and relate to ourselves and one another. In other words, we must transform ourselves. This book, and the movement for an alternative future that it proposes, will not succeed without a commitment to personal transformation.

Most efforts to address the challenges we face today focus on external factors: gross domestic products and current account deficits, international summits and casualty counts, demographics and polling data. These indicators are important for understanding the causes of our predicament, but they do not capture the whole picture.

As we discussed in Chapter 2, the state of the world is a reflection of our own value systems, which result from the way we perceive ourselves and the world around us. Without a shift in this level of seeing and experiencing the world, little radical change in our outer systems will be possible. Conversely, by working to transform ourselves, we can transform the world in ways we cannot yet imagine. By reorienting the mind inward, we can begin to understand the sources of our identity and, as a result, to perceive different ways for us to coexist together in a more harmonious world.

To begin with, we must acknowledge that we are all born into a context. We are the product of myriad forces, circumstances, and events over which we have little control. From my observation, much of our behaviour is an outcome of six elements or influences – pre-birth conditions, evolutionary heritage, biological necessities, familial frameworks, social/cultural conditioning, and life experiences. Each is described below.

Pre-Birth Conditions

This is a fundamental nature that we are born with, whether by genetic heritage, astrological causation, or sheer coincidence. Every parent knows that each child is remarkably different in temperament, and this is apparent even when children are infants. Babies often seem to be born with certain behavioural tendencies (such as crying a lot or a little, being obdurate or accommodating, being gregarious or reticent), such that a part of their personality is already determined. Many cultures have acknowledged and analysed the existence of such predisposition. India's Vedic tradition, for example, has delved into this aspect of human nature quite thoroughly.

Science, too, has addressed the issue of the genetic provenance of psychological traits and personality. Laboratory research aimed at identifying specific genes that may determine or condition behaviour, and how they interact with each other, has thus far made only limited progress. Behavioural genetics has, however – via twin, adoption, and family studies – probed the issue of whether behaviour, personality, and psychopathology are inherited or environmentally acquired. Twin studies, in particular, have yielded convincing evidence that human behaviour is genetically determined to a substantial degree. Twin studies typically compare behavioural and psychological traits between identical twins (monozygotic twins who share almost 100 per cent of their genes) and fraternal twins (dizygotic or non-identical twins who share only 50 per cent of their genes).

Among the more famous examples of twin studies is the Minnesota Twin Family Study, a group of research projects involving twins that began in 1979. A landmark study conducted within the framework of the Minnesota Twin Family Study looked at pairs of twins – both fraternal and identical – who had been separated at an early age (usually because of adoption) and raised apart. The study concluded that there was evidence of 'strong heritability of most psychological traits' because the twins who had been raised apart showed similarity in multiple personality measures (such as occupational interests, social attitudes, and temperament) as twins who had grown up together.[1] A more recent study conducted by the University of Edinburgh on 837 sets of twins also found that genetics was more influential than the home environment in shaping certain important personal traits such as self-control, sense of purpose, and the ability to get along with others.[2]

Evolutionary Heritage

This is a set of traits that we share with all other members of the human species. It is the result of millennia of human evolution, and is heavily shaped by the long periods of existence spent as primitive hunters and gatherers, exposed to the dangers and uncertainties of life in the wild, and organised in small, kinship-based clans. Conditions of extreme scarcity have habituated us to see relationships in binary terms: friend–enemy, individual–group, self–other, us–them. Mutual suspicion – the legacy of a more primitive age – is therefore hardwired in all of us. We may cooperate with our kin, but beyond that, vast swaths of 'others' remain strangers, not to be trusted until they can prove otherwise. Many of our automatic responses to competition, sharing, and collaboration arise from this influence.

The discipline that attempts to reconcile human behaviour with evolutionary history is known as 'evolutionary psychology'. It first came to prominence in 1992 with the publication of a landmark collection of essays by anthropologists Jerome Barkow and John Tooby, and psychologist Leda Cosmides.[3] Evolutionary psychology is essentially defined by a few key principles: (*a*) the cognitive mechanisms that underlie our behaviour are adaptations, that is, they came to be as a result of our ancestors adapting to certain environmental conditions and necessities; (*b*) these cognitive mechanisms cannot be detected directly, but have to be studied by observing behaviour patterns in modern-day humans and hypothesising the cognitive adaptations made by our ancestors to develop such behaviour, usually in response to specific and recurring problems in their hunter-gatherer environment during the Pleistocene (from about two million years ago to ten thousand years ago); (*c*) the human mind consists of a complex array of such cognitive mechanisms, also known as 'modules' or 'mental organs'; and (*d*) these modules evolved through natural selection and now define universal human nature, superseding individual and cultural differences.[4]

One common example of evolutionary psychological inquiry is the observation that most modern-day human beings, in many cultures, seem to have a predilection for foods that are either very salty or very sweet. Why? After all, salty and sweet foods are not good for us, so we would not expect the body to have developed an instinctive predilection for them. Salts and sweeteners were scarce in the Pleistocene, as they occur naturally quite rarely (in rare finds like salt licks and honeycombs, respectively). But they were probably highly prized by our hunter-gatherer ancestors – salt because it could flavour food and helped with moisture retention, and sugar because it offered highly concentrated energy. The hundreds of thousands of years that humans spent as hunter-gatherers conditioned them to crave these rare commodities and to binge on them whenever they became available. Modern humans, on the other hand, have only had modern diets (where salts and sugars are common) for a few centuries, and have only known about the harmful effects of these substances for a few decades. Hence our long-standing evolutionary craving for them prevails, and we continue to eat them in unnecessarily large quantities whenever we have the opportunity. The same could be said of saturated fats, which were also a rare find for our ancestors.

Evolutionary psychology has encountered plenty of criticism along the way, especially that it relies heavily on hypotheses that are difficult or impossible to test. Many of the hypotheses that ostensibly explain the adaptive nature of human behavioural traits are just-so stories, that is, neat explanations for the evolution of given traits that are not corroborated by any empirical evidence. After all, designing experiments to test them is extremely difficult, while finding and studying primitive societies that still lead a hunter-gatherer lifestyle and are entirely cut off from modern influences is equally unlikely. Nevertheless, the basic tenet of evolutionary psychology – that our behaviour, especially many of our unconscious choices and reactions, is at least partly traceable to how our Pleistocene forebears coped with their environment – is firmly entrenched in both academic and popular debates on human nature.

Biological Necessities

Much of our behaviour is dictated by our natural desire for biological essentials – the physical prerequisites for life, such as shelter, food, water, safety, and reproduction. They correspond roughly with the two lowest rungs (physiological needs and safety needs) of Maslow's hierarchy of needs, a five-tier classification of human motivation first developed by American psychologist Abraham Maslow in 1943 and still popular.[5]

If we take the most immediate physiological needs, such as the need for nourishment or rest, as examples, it is fairly straightforward to confirm their effect on behaviour, at least in the short term. We all know that hunger can cause us to become irritable and distracted, and that sleep deprivation can make us moody and unresponsive, and can impair our ability to perform our daily tasks at work or school. Beyond this anecdotal evidence, however, there is also plenty of scientific confirmation for the long-term psychological effects of being deprived of our most basic needs. A famous starvation study conducted at the University of Minnesota during the Second World War showed that prolonged hunger caused not only physiological changes (decreases in stamina, body temperature, heart rate, and sex drive) but also made the study subjects irritable, depressed, apathetic, and constantly obsessed with obtaining food.[6]

More recent studies on malnutrition have documented the lasting effect of food deprivation, even after the shortage of food has ceased. One study published in 2010 showed that adults who had suffered severe starvation as infants were significantly more anxious, less sociable, less interested in new experiences, and more hostile, than those who enjoyed adequate nourishment during childhood.[7] While these scientific studies look primarily at conditions of extreme deprivation, there is also evidence that deprivation of a more everyday sort – poverty – can have debilitating effects on the psyche, forcing poor individuals to live in a constant state of stress over their next meal or their outstanding rent or utility bills, such that their cognitive abilities (including intelligence) are measurably reduced.[8]

Under the category of 'biological necessities' we can also include psychological necessities, such as physical connection, love, recognition, and even gossip, some of which are unique to the human species. These correspond, roughly, to the third rung in Maslow's hierarchy of needs, which he labelled 'love/belonging'. That physical connection to our kin is important, for example, is borne out by studies showing that children who were never held by their parents develop quite differently than those who were.[9]

Familial Frameworks

The influence of family, both nuclear and extended, in the formation of identity and social norms is profound. Familial frameworks shape our choices without us being consciously aware of them. Children, in particular, learn much of their behaviour, values, and attitudes from the role models they encounter in their immediate surroundings – at school, family gatherings, the playground, and especially at home.

Although it may seem obvious that children learn mostly by social learning (observing and imitating their parents and relatives), the relationship between personality development and parental influence has nevertheless been subjected to extensive scientific investigation by psychologists, neurologists, and behavioural scientists. In the 1960s, for example, a series of studies known as the 'Bobo doll experiments' showed that young children who had witnessed aggressive behaviour by an adult model were much more likely to exhibit aggressive behaviour during play than those who had been exposed only to peaceful role models.[10] In a recent study, toddlers' eye movements and brain wave patterns were measured while they were shown cartoons containing either prosocial behaviour (sharing, helping) or antisocial behaviour (pushing, tripping) by the main character. The test results were analysed in conjunction with data on each toddler's parents' values regarding empathy, justice, and fairness, which had been collected previously via questionnaire. The study revealed that even at a very young age, before any formal teaching can be administered, children's morality (the ability to distinguish and evaluate good and bad) was heavily reliant on parental attitudes.[11] 'The most important thing we need to understand as parents is that everything we say and do for the first seven years of our children's lives is being recorded, and will become their beliefs and behaviours,' says Bruce Lipton, a specialist in epigenetics.[12]

Social/Cultural Conditioning

Like the influence of family, the impact of our social environment – from our extended kinship group to our local community to the national identity of the country we live in – plays a large and easily detectable role in the formation of our character and behaviour, particularly during childhood. It is a kind of subconscious programming derived from learning experiences, especially during the first decade of life, that determine many of our subconscious beliefs about the way the world is and the way we are.

Jared Diamond and other anthropologists have shown that humans have an evolutionary need to develop ways to cooperate and form groups, and, at the same time, a need to develop equally strong ways to differentiate between groups. Essentially, this inspires two tendencies in humans. The first is group cooperation, which also involves peer pressure and becoming followers, or what is commonly known as 'herd behaviour'. The second is the ability to see everything in differences, to create our identities by differentiating them from other identities. Identities are sharpened by difference. As the psychoanalyst Jacques Lacan said, 'The I is always in the field of the Other.'

As a result of the first tendency (to cooperate), human beings have been a social species from the very origins, and our collective identity has been instrumental to our survival. But while the need to be part of a group and to cooperate is inherent, it is not automatic. We are naturally inclined to help those with whom we share a close genetic link (our family and immediate kinship group), but our willingness to collaborate rarely extends beyond that. Forming social units that are larger and more stratified than small, kinship-based bands has always been problematic. Larger societies had to develop rules, codes, and a prescribed 'morality' to help maintain social order, often using religion to legitimise rules and hierarchies. Over time, these rules and codes became culture.

Culture is passed on via behavioural templates, also known as 'memes', that exert a huge influence on who we are, what we do, and how we react to the world around us. In *The Selfish Gene*, evolutionary biologist Richard Dawkins defines a meme as 'a unit of cultural transmission', which acts by carrying symbols, ideas, or practices, and transmits them from one person to another. A meme may be a practical skill, such as how to light a fire, but it may also be a custom or concept whose practical purpose and persistence are less obvious, such as the belief in an afterlife. The transmission of multiple memes creates culture, and much like genes, these memes are programmed to replicate and ensure their own continued survival, which is why it is hard sometimes to get the tune of a song out of your head, but also to avoid or even recognise social prejudices and biases. In *Sapiens*, historian Yuval Noah Harari writes, 'Even what people take to be their most personal desires are usually programmed by the imagined order.'

Cultural conditioning becomes a programme humming in the back of our mind, one that most of us are unaware of, though it largely determines the way we process information and the way we react to stimuli and situations. By conforming and becoming part of what writer William Whyte called 'groupthink',[13] we surrender our individuality but get, in return, safety in numbers, economies of scale, and the synergies of collective action.

Of course, the identity of an individual (and his or her resultant behaviour) is not always in line with her culture, which is to say, the codified behavioural template that her social group has inherited. This tension between the individual and the collective lies close to the heart of what it means to be human. Using incentives and disincentives, society attempts to reconcile such tensions before they become too problematic. Social conditioning circumscribes the life of the individual, sanctioning and supporting types of behaviour that are deemed positive while punishing behaviour regarded as negative.

Life Experiences

One of the most evident influences on the way we experience the world is the collection of life experiences, in the form of memories, acquired knowledge, traumas, and likes and dislikes that we gather over the course of our lifetimes. This collection of frameworks and associations continues throughout adulthood and can direct many of the choices we make in life. We are conscious of some of them, such as rejecting a particular job or a relationship with a particular type of person because we had a negative experience in the past. But many remain below the surface of our awareness.

Empirical investigation of the effects of life experiences on patterns of behaviour is understandably difficult to carry out. Shifts in behaviour or personality are easiest to detect in the aftermath of extremely negative experiences, such as trauma. Thus, an extensive body of literature on the behavioural changes shown by victims of trauma and post-traumatic stress disorder has emerged over the last two decades. Researchers have observed behavioural changes in survivors of domestic violence, sexual violence, natural disasters, war, terrorism, and historical episodes like the Holocaust. Studies have shown that trauma is most damaging when suffered in childhood, but its effects are very much detectable in adults as well. It can affect victims of traumatic events as well as those who merely observed such events, and it can even be transmitted across generations, affecting the offspring of trauma victims.[14] Traumatic experiences can alter brain anatomy and function,[15] and can result in permanent changes in personality and attitudes, including shifts in intelligence, the ability to express emotion and to experience happiness, sociability, impulse control, and sexual orientation or desire.

While trauma is only an extreme case of how life experiences, even in adulthood, can shape our behaviour, it clearly evinces that even those behavioural traits that we often consider set and immutable can be changed by our evolving exposure to social and environmental elements. Indeed, recent studies show that it may even be possible for adults to alter their personality traits by sheer volition.[16]

Mental Formations

For most of us, the context shaped by the influences I have described acts like baggage that we are mostly unaware of. This baggage interferes with almost all our activities. Imagine seeing a person already known to you. As soon as your eyes recognise this person, something is triggered in your mind to produce a response: like, dislike, love, or maybe indifference. If you dislike the person, then the mind is provoked into further emotional reactions, such as fear, anger, distrust, envy, and so forth. In short, a complex process has been set in motion based on a personal history combined with the automated, context-driven processes of the unaware mind. The result is one or more mental formations (ideas and feelings) produced by our mind. If we dislike the person, and they provoke fear, we may not want to appear friendly to them. But if the person is in a socially dominant position, and if we have been trained since childhood to recognise social hierarchy, for example, our reaction toward them could be quite friendly and accommodating despite the dislike we feel.

Because we are born into a context produced by these influences, they are part of us; they are part of our subconscious mind. Becoming free of them is difficult, but it should be the ultimate goal of any effort to improve ourselves at a personal level, which, in turn, is the gateway to reshaping our societies. As philosopher J. Krishnamurti said, 'Without freedom from the past, there is no freedom at all, because the mind is never new, fresh, innocent.'[17]

Most of these influences are outside of our control, but that is not to say that we are powerless. There is one resource that empowers us to recognise them and not to be bound by them: our state of consciousness. We have a degree of control over our state of consciousness, and through it we can transform our lives and thus the world. Before we embark on the process of transcending our context, however, we must fully understand it.

Our context is the source of many of our instinctive thoughts, intentions, fears, insecurities, cravings, addictions and longings, which can be collectively referred to as 'mental formations'. Much like a software programme, it works on predefined algorithms to drive our responses. In other words, the design of the programme allows for only a certain number of predetermined outcomes based on the information it receives. For example, I can ask the word processing programme that I am using to write this book to do a number of things based on a menu of options. However, I cannot ask it to do something that is not predefined in the menu provided by the programmers who designed it.

This is how most of humanity functions when acting from an unconscious space within ourselves. What we experience – the ever-changing information we collect through our sense organs – is our received data input. Our unconscious mind analyses these data based on certain pre-programmed rules (our context) and produces an output (our instinctive reactions and feelings). This passive state or, borrowing from Plato, 'our unexamined life', is the life that most of us live. The development of consciousness allows us to break free from the constraints of our contextual software and allows us to write and live our own script.

I once introduced two people who I was sure would get along well because they had similar interests and ideas. But they did not. Each carried deeply held beliefs about the other's religion. During their first meeting, instead of focusing on what they had in common, they interacted solely at the level of their deeper programming, which gave them many reasons to disagree. They were unaware that their respective contexts were manufacturing feelings of mistrust and animosity toward each other – mental formations that led to obstructive patterns of behaviour. These mental formations blocked their capacity for love, caring, and generosity, which naturally flow when we operate from a space of greater awareness. This is another example of how we are conditioned so deeply that we remain unaware of our context's influence over us.

We are prisoners of the subconscious mind and taming it is the hardest yet potentially most valuable task we can assign ourselves. Only when we tame the mind by recognising and understanding the sources of our feelings, and acknowledge that which is not known, can we begin to discover new ways of approaching old problems and arrive at solutions that were previously inconceivable.

Transcendence from automated responses, that is, the patterns of behaviour generated by our context, is a fundamental step toward true freedom. From this more conscious vantage point within ourselves, we can overcome our fears and insecurities, and discover the qualities of true generosity, openness, curiosity, self-esteem, and the ability to love. The question, of course, is *how* we can transcend our mind and open up to higher levels of awareness.

The Role of Meditation in Enhancing Consciousness

Meditation is one of the most ancient techniques for enhancing our awareness. It is a practice that sharpens the mind, allowing it to retool itself so that it is able to progress from one state of consciousness to another. It is an art and needs to be practised, preferably with a teacher in a group, just as ballerinas need ballet lessons and football players need to train under a coach.

To understand this, let us think of a person who lives on the ground floor of a tall building. If he exercises regularly, he will develop the physical capacity to climb the many flights of stairs required to reach the top of the building. Exercising and improving endurance and strength are akin to the focus and concentration that develop in someone who meditates. The resting heart rate, insulin levels, and mental clarity of a person who exercises improve as his muscles and organs become more efficient, using less oxygen to achieve better performance. This is similar to concentration and focus producing awareness and insight.

As this fit person climbs the stairs, he begins to see a different view on each floor. This changed perspective is what I call 'heightened consciousness'. Having seen the view from the higher floors will forever shift the climber's perception of his neighbourhood, even if he looks at it again from a lower vantage point.

From a state of higher consciousness, we become increasingly able to see the mental formations that underlie our thoughts and behaviour. When we are aware, we are present. Being present does not mean that we are calm. It does not mean that we are free from all thoughts, emotions, desires, urges, or fears. It just means we are able to watch ourselves with a degree of detachment. Indeed, our mind is always full of activity. It is never still. Even though we live in the present, the mind keeps spilling into the past and future. It alternates between memory and anticipation, and through these transformations it produces emotions, desires, urges, and fears.

These mental formations appear because our mind has the tendency to conceptualise reality rather than to experience and see it as it is in the present moment. By being present, aware of the mind's wavering, we begin to see that these fears and desires have no basis in reality. Thus, awareness can dissipate mental formations.

I am writing these lines in an aircraft that is experiencing turbulence. I can sense fear arising in me. The fear increases as my plane passes over the South China Sea, triggering the memory of another aircraft that disappeared there a month ago. The association of this turbulence with the disappearance of the aircraft heightens my fear. But as I watch it and do not react, I feel the fear dissolve. Other ideas and other mental formations may interfere. But by being present, I can see them arise, and I simply will them away.

Until a few years ago these mental formations would hold me in their grip. I would feel paralysed by fear, driven by desire, and pushed around by many urges that seemingly had power over me. With time and meditation, I have found them to greatly diminish so that they no longer affect me.

The hardest part of meditating for a beginner is to learn to sit either cross-legged on the floor or on a seat and do nothing for thirty, then forty, then fifty, and eventually sixty minutes, and to learn to do this every day at the same time. Most of us feel an intense restlessness when we attempt it at first. Ideas come to us, to-do lists form, memories invade our mind, and expectations and feelings build up. Even if we are not especially busy in our daily lives, when we start to meditate, our minds typically try everything they can to distract us.

In this early phase you can do two things to support your practice: join a group, because peer energy helps to discipline and support you; and try certain breathing exercises. In the early phases, these breathing techniques (such as alternate-nostril breathing) are very effective in steadying the mind. It took me ten years to learn to be still, and one of the mistakes I made in the early years of my efforts in meditation was not joining a group.

When you watch yourself, you see anxiety emerge in your mind. As your practice of meditation deepens, you begin to see the source of that anxiety, and to understand how it emerged, until it becomes so insubstantial that you see through it. As you recognise the insubstantial nature of the root of your anxiety, it loses its power over you. This is what I mean by 'freedom': a liberation that comes not from suppressing or ending our fears, but from seeing them for what they are. It is not liberation via a struggle or fight. It is liberation that comes from the simple act of seeing. Freedom is the reward for awareness, for being present in the unfolding of one's own life.

Because our mind has a tendency to grasp, it creates patterns. Anxiety, insecurity, fear, hope, desire, envy, anger, aspiration, and expectation are all patterns linked to causes that have their roots in the six elements I discussed at the outset of this chapter – pre-birth conditions, evolutionary heritage, biological necessities, familial frameworks, social/cultural conditioning, and life experiences. The six elements produce an absent mind. An absent mind is a fragmented mind. It sways all the time. By practising meditation, which means being present and seeing all the time, we watch the swaying of the mind. The mind sways either into the past or into the future. It thinks of things that give us pleasure or pain. But these are formations or imaginations, and not reality. Reality exists only in the present, so the meditator's task is to continually bring the mind back to the present. The more we practise meditation, the less our mind wanders. Gradually, with discipline and regular practice, we become freer from the habits and limitations of our minds.

An absent mind is swayed because it allows these patterns to take it over. Think of what happens when you resent someone. The process of resenting is triggered when you see them or hear about them. Why? Is it because of an old memory, an association they have with a difficult event in your life? Is it because they have attacked you? Think this through. Why do they have this hold over you? Why do you give them this power? When you are present, you can see the baggage of the past trying to intrude on your mind. See this baggage for what it is. You will feel a reactive emotion well up in your mind toward the person. Allow yourself to feel it. Seeing these formations take shape and being aware of their existence, be present when you meet the person. Be kind, open, and considerate. You might see elements of what you dislike about the individual surface in the current interaction. Instead of reacting, merely watch them.

There is no task we will ever face in our lives that is as difficult and as rewarding as taming our mind so as to liberate ourselves from the shackles of the six elements. Think of this task as training your ear to hear another frequency that exists but requires a calibration of the mind. One of the most effective ways to achieve this calibration of the mind is a consistent and honest practice of meditation. It is not the only way one can deepen one's conscious awareness. There are other ways, and other forms of introspection that may be equally effective, easier, and more appealing for some. Meditation has been an important part of my own life, so I have chosen to highlight it in this book.

The goal of meditation is to be present. Every moment, encounter, or episode in our lives has its own reality – there is a particular flow of energy around that event, and a unique set of circumstances that have brought it about. When you are present and aware you are able to see the web of interdependent motivations that underlie each moment. For example, imagine that you are in a corporate board meeting. The air is laden with tension because some members of the board are angry over a previous incident, or because there is an important and potentially divisive decision to be taken. In such a situation, heightened awareness allows you to 'see' and understand the dynamics at work in the room with an unfettered mind. You recognise, for example, that anger is a form of historical baggage that comes from bringing a memory of the past into the present. It can, if not recognised, interfere in the present and create resentment. But it can also be defused by someone who is present in the moment.

A consistent practice of meditation works in two broad ways. First, just as regular exercise leads to a lower heart rate, reduces blood pressure, and increases the functioning of many organs, consistent meditation leads to more focus, better concentration, a calming of the mind, and a sense of mental clarity. Second, it helps us live in a state of heightened awareness. This sustained awareness enables us to see our mental formations, habits, and patterns of behaviour, and then to rise above them.

During the initial years of meditation, I experienced a restless mind – distracted, impatient, and wilful. My mind was held in thrall by the constant chatter of mental formations and whatever was going on around me. It was almost like a theatrical performance so riveting that you forget you are watching a play, and begin to think the play is real. It took a decade or more for me to settle down into consistent daily practice.

The practice of meditation gradually began to affect me in subtle ways. As a child, I suffered from a type of attention deficit disorder. I could not concentrate for more than a few minutes, and in school my teachers noticed this. I had trouble sitting still for more than five or ten minutes, and I could never complete a Lego set. When I first attempted to meditate, I noticed that I was always somewhere else in my mind. But even during the first decade of meditating irregularly I noticed a big change in the quality of my concentration.

This deepening of concentration changed every aspect of my life. The ability to focus my mind like a beam of light passing through a convex lens enabled me to quickly complete tasks that had previously appeared daunting. I was able to write a book, execute complex plans, and achieve great success in my work. There was a point where I felt a huge temptation to plateau, to settle down, relax, and become complacent. This happened because the euphoria that comes from this newly acquired power is so great that it gave me the feeling of having arrived at a point of liberation and freedom. It is tempting to abandon the practice at this moment, luxuriating instead in the heady benefits that the power of concentration brings to one's work, personal life, and social interactions. For a while, I stopped persevering. But I could sense that more expansive possibilities remained, and that this was only the first step in a long journey.

Through continuing practice, I found that a more concentrated mind was able to begin understanding my subconscious programming. This is the process wherein the mind turns on itself – it separated itself from the mass of emotions, fears, passions, desires, attitudes, and feelings that resulted from the influences and experiences of all elements of my past. I finally separated myself from the theatrical production I had been attending.

The interactions of the six elements are deeply embedded in what we call habits – ingrained forms of reactive behaviour. These are like the cloud formations that change on an almost hourly basis during the monsoon season in India. For example, I once knew someone who, having lived a large portion of his adult life on a very limited salary, suddenly inherited a fortune. Many of the deeply ingrained patterns that had served him well in leading a parsimonious life continued, preventing him from doing things that he really wanted to do. He was a generous person by nature but could not see his new-found wealth as an opportunity to change. During a conversation, I explained to him that if he spent 80 per cent of his interest and dividend income and reinvested the balance, he would still have more than he needed. With this money, he could support charities and enterprises he believed in, as well as enjoy some travel, about which he was passionate. Even with the facts in front of him, the habits had too strong a hold on him. In the end, he continued to live as before: frugally, without any ambitions or desire to change his own circumstances or those of others. This happens often in our lives: we cannot align our behaviour with our changing circumstances. Habits prevent us from changing.

A mind that has cultivated the quality of self-reflection by being in a state of heightened awareness can easily see patterns. What is very difficult is letting go of the deeply ingrained habitual reactions that are triggered by an event. Even after seeing patterns, it has taken me years to break the cycle of automated reaction. And whenever I am in a weakened state of awareness, the habitual reactions return quickly. Our conditioning runs very deep, so we tend to fall back on our mental habits. The only insurance is awareness.

Another pattern that comes to light through meditation practice is our desire for control – for wanting things to be a particular way. We want people to admire us, and we also want to mould them in a particular way. We cling to certain outcomes and shut our minds to other possibilities. We hold deep anger and grudges against perceived injustices. Once our minds begin to see the patterns produced by our mental formations, we begin to gain a certain distance from these influences, and gain a capacity to see them clearly for the illusions that they are.

All these are mental formations that prevent us from seeing reality more completely. Blindly following a set of concepts rooted in the six elements of our context imprisons us in a web of mental formations. When we do not get our way, we suffer from stress, anger, and bitterness. When we do get our way, we experience elation, excitement, and anticipation. Both are sides of the same coin called control, and both generate fear and worry at the thought of moving either out of one state or into another.

Our minds have two particular qualities. First, editorialising, where an unstable mind is constantly flooded with thoughts and expectations. It seeks affirmation and acknowledgement from the external world, without ever being in a state of peace. Second, being judgmental, where the mind expends precious energy to pontificate or judge the other. Both these qualities have the ability to make us situationally unaware, which is precisely the point where the six elements of our context play their role and cloud our judgment. This inevitably causes pain and stress. The idea, as many spiritual teachers remind us, is to see the world with 'fresh, unknowing eyes'.

With mindfulness, we begin to see the nuances that are necessary to understand a world of interdependencies. Instead of a strictly dualistic world view based on self and the other – what we have inherited from our evolutionary history – we begin to see the individual as part of a complex matrix and influenced by the constellation of elements in that matrix. Indeed, the First Dimension hems us into a dualistic world, defined by binary oppositions: us and them, individual and society, winner and loser, friend and enemy, and observer and observed. But this is a simplistic and divisive way of looking at things. Such binary pairs are reductionist interpretations of the multifaceted reality around us.

We can break free of the dualist delusion not by abandoning self-interest but, rather, by understanding self-interest in a much wider scope, that is, by pursuing goals that benefit us not only as individuals but also as members of communities. As our consciousness develops, our notion of self-interest also grows to encompass the communities of which we are a part. Once we see ourselves not as isolated, independent individuals but rather as nodes in a complex web of relationships that bind us to family, neighbours, fellow citizens, and nature itself, we will understand that what is in the best interest of our community and of humanity entire is also in our personal best interest.

By abandoning the prison of dualism, we begin to move from the Dimension of Cause and Effect to the Dimension of Interdependence. Remember that during this journey of consciousness you do not forget the First Dimension world. Rather, you see it for what it is, but you also see the world in a richer context of interconnections. From here onward, the journey of awareness takes us to transcendence.

Table 3.1 describes the eight stages of self-awareness that we can hope to reach with a sustained practice of meditation. It also represents my own journey, as yet incomplete, in meditation.

Meditation as a Vehicle to Higher Dimensions

The Second Dimension is but a midpoint in the journey toward the Third Dimension, which is the Dimension of Transcendence. Just as moving from the mindsets and tools of the First Dimension to the Second Dimension involves a process of transforming our minds, a similar gradation is required when we move from the Second to the Third Dimension. Once again, this transformation must first happen inside each individual. For this voyage, the practice of meditation can continue to be our means of progress.

To employ an analogy, imagine your mind to be a piece of wood – a flotsam – being tossed around on the surface of a rough sea whose waves are thoughts, emotions, and other mental formations. By developing

Table 3.1: The Eight Stages of Meditation Practice

Step	Goal	What you experience	Result
1	To establish a daily practice of meditation	Whenever you sit by yourself, you feel a sense of restlessness, and the need to be somewhere else. Your mind wanders. After a few sessions of meditation, however, you notice that the number of times your mind wanders and the length of time between each distraction are reduced because you are now 'watching' your mind. You begin to realise that there are two minds within you: an 'automatic' mind that seems to be running its own programme, and an early-stage 'watching' mind that can be directed.	You are able to watch your mind.
2	To be present during meditation	Having established a routine, you have become a consistent practitioner. With more practice, you become aware of the many different directions in which your mind is being pulled. Sometimes you make a list of things to do, you worry about a family member or a friend, or you are distracted by fears, desires, ideas, or plans. By being aware of these conflicting priorities you begin the process of separating the mind of the observer from the observer himself.	You are aware and watchful, and able to analyse what your mind is doing.
3	To develop the ability to direct your mind and sustain it in a state of concentration	Sustained meditational practice allows you to focus your mind with increased precision and for longer periods. In daily life, you can now listen to others with greater concentration, work with a single-mindedness you never experienced before, and be present in all your activities and encounters. Liberated from distractions and forgetfulness, you begin to experience the incredible power of the mind and its capacity for seeing and understanding at a fundamental level. There will be a pull to use this new-found ability in everyday life – to improve performance at work, for example, to earn more money or gain a promotion. You must not succumb to this pull which stems from the lingering presence of First Dimension values.	You achieve mindfulness – a state in which you are able to focus consistently on the present, while acknowledging and accepting your own feelings, thoughts, and sensations.

4	To become aware of the 4th and 5th elements of your context (familial frameworks and social conditioning)	Sustained concentration leads to the development of insight. (Some Buddhist and Hindu teachings refer to insight as the opening of the 'third eye'.) This direct 'seeing' will allow you to see, for the first time, the interplay of familial and social conditioning. In this state, all the needs created by familial and social norms, like the need for praise, security, and conformity, lose their power over you.	Your state of mindfulness allows you to go a step deeper – to understand the programming received from family and society.
5	To become aware of the 2nd and 3rd elements of your context (evolutionary heritage and biological necessities)	From your heightened level of consciousness, you begin to understand the evolutionary and biological roots of deep-seated cravings, desires, and elemental needs (such as the need for power and the herd instinct). Once this happens you cannot go back to your earlier state of ignorance or unawareness. Mindsets that generate feelings of jealousy, greed, craving, illusion, and neediness evaporate like fog vanquished by strong sunshine.	You recognise the programming that results from our evolutionary past and from biological needs.
6	To understand the 1st element of your context (your basic nature)	Every individual is born with certain traits. In Ayurvedic thought, these traits form an individual's constitution, or *prakriti.* The combination of physical and mental dispositions (*dosha*s and *guna*s, respectively) form a blueprint of each individual's nature shaped in the womb and influenced by our parents as well as by unknown forces (fate, astrological causation, or sheer randomness). Thus, each individual possesses an elemental nature, which is later influenced by other elements to yield a programmed state of being. A heightened level of consciousness will allow you to identify this elemental nature.	You perceive your fundamental nature.

Table 3.1: The Eight Stages of Meditation Practice (contd.)

7	To recognise how the elements of your context manifest themselves in your thoughts and determine your behaviour	Your mind has now reached a level of consciousness where it is able to see differently, listen differently, and watch its own leanings and inclinations. At this point, it sees reality as a complex web of interdependencies, in which no action is devoid of consequence, no achievement can be separated from its purpose or the means used to attain it, and no intention can be isolated from its sources. By this stage, you have managed to de-programme yourself by seeing and understanding the six elements. You recognise that the interplay between them and your sense organs is shaping your perception of reality.	You are conscious of the profound interdependence of life's many facets. This level of consciousness is conducive to a new social paradigm – the Second Dimension.
8	To achieve a higher consciousness	Thoughts, actions, and morality are liberated from attachments of all kinds – attachment to outcomes, fears and expectations, desires, control, and ways of thinking and relating to one another.	With full awareness, your mind is capable of seeing reality as it unfolds in the present. You and your fellow practitioners are ready to build the Third Dimension.

consistency and discipline, you are able to put a small rudder on this piece of wood and steer in a particular direction. By developing concentration through meditation you are able to mould the raw piece of wood into the shape of a boat, and over time the boat grows a sail, and with its rudder it can navigate its way through the turbulent seas. With the deepening of awareness, imagine this boat with its sail and rudder becoming lighter and lighter, and at some points skimming the surface of the waves till it is able to rise like a seaplane taking off. The crashing waves with their ceaseless crests and troughs remain, but your boat has risen above the surface and will not be tossed about any more.

As awareness suffuses our lives, it instils within us an understanding that there exists a unifying force in the universe that permeates all beings and all phenomena. An aware mind can see the limitations of the dualistic mode of thinking. Where an unaware mind sees the self and the rest of the world as two different things, the aware mind sees the connection between them.

With honest, disciplined, and persistent meditation, we begin looking more deeply at the nature of things. And in doing so, we begin to develop insights into the nature of systems. As we gain access to the nature of systems, we start walking the path to transcendence. Many great religious thinkers and mystics – St. Augustine, Rumi, Epictetus, and Kabir Das – have walked a similar path and left us accounts of their findings.

Meditation, or the practice of awareness, is a training of the mind to help it connect the part with the whole. If meditation is our teacher, life is our classroom. We can let our lives lead us – our context determining our conduct, our restlessness pulling us in a thousand directions, our fears preventing us from doing what is right – or we can lead our lives. We should lead our lives. To do this we must practise detachment, which is the ability to be present but not engaged in the spectacle that is life.

Meditation is a journey of revelations, beginning with a growing awareness of our mental formations and how they influence us. As we continue our practice, many other shifts begin to take place within us. My experience is that if we stick with this practice long enough, we will begin to experience the following shifts in ourselves:

- From consistency of practice and disciplined commitment arises **concentration**.
- Concentration over time **focuses the mind** in the same way that the sun causes a seed to germinate.
- This concentrated mind with stillness produces **insight**.
- Insight is the ability to **see things as a whole** or to grasp their essence.
- Seeing things as a whole allows us to produce **intention** that is aligned with reality.
- Such intention gives rise to **motivation**.
- The roots of motivation anchor the germinating seed in the earth and allow the shoot to travel toward the light. If motivation is the root, then **action** is the shoot which will always grow toward the sun.

The progression from meditation to action is presented schematically in Figure 3.1.

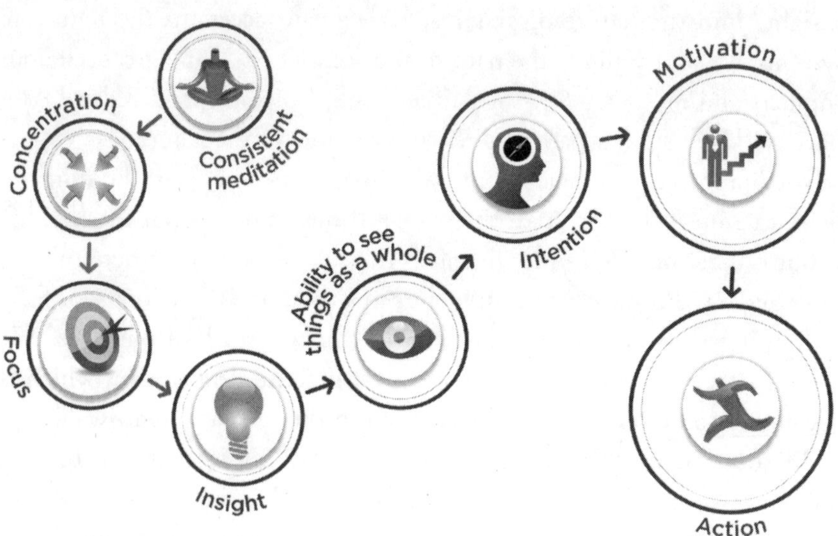

Figure 3.1: The Journey of Meditation

To illustrate this progression of deepening insight and greater awareness, I will return to the analogy used earlier in this chapter, where I compared the development of consciousness to climbing to higher floors of a building to gain a better view of the surroundings. Let us say you are pacing about in your living room, anxious about an urgent parcel that has not yet arrived, when your neighbour comes to complain that you have parked your car so badly on the street that he cannot easily access his driveway. Now, you and your neighbour have never been on particularly good terms. In fact, you think he is selfish, petulant, and litigious, and so you are inclined to ignore what he says. You peek out of the window, and you can see that you have indeed parked badly, but it does not seem like you are blocking anything. It is as you suspected: the neighbour is trying to provoke you again. Just to be sure, but without giving the neighbour any satisfaction, you climb to the upper floor and have a look from there. From the improved vantage point, you realise that you really are blocking his driveway, and that he is forced to manoeuvre at length to get in and out. What is worse, several cars are backed up behind him because entering his driveway takes some time and effort. You decide to climb all the way up to your rooftop to have a proper look, and from up there you can now see that your crooked parking has created a traffic jam that extends down the street and around the block. And there, stuck in the traffic jam, is a delivery truck! No wonder the package you were expecting has not arrived.

Attaining higher levels of consciousness is like climbing higher and higher. From each floor the view is more comprehensive and reveals more information. It reveals, for example, that your inconsiderate behaviour is not merely a dispute between you and the grouchy neighbour, but an issue that affects the entire neighbourhood. In addition, the climb to the top has given you a wholly new perspective. When you climb back down, you can no longer ignore the problem, or set aside the knowledge you have gained. And finally, you realise that being more considerate to the neighbour and the entire community will ultimately benefit you as well.

One important detail that is not in the story is that climbing to the rooftop is ultimately a journey you have to undertake for yourself. If someone else were to say, 'The view from the rooftop explains everything,' it would not do you much good. You must struggle up there by yourself to see things in a different way and completely.

A Transformed Mind

With the deeper awareness that can arise from a meditation practice comes a new mind. How does this new mind emerge? As we undertake the journey of elevating our consciousness through meditation, we begin to see inside our minds. We notice that the components of our mind and the nature of our thoughts change dramatically with changes in the level of our consciousness.

As the quality of our consciousness changes, our thoughts and actions take on a corresponding quality, and begin to shape our reality in new ways. As we examine the contents of our mind, we begin to understand that our thoughts and our reactions hold us at a particular level of consciousness, and the awareness of this motivates us to seek a higher level. As the quality of our consciousness changes with awareness, we begin to see how the outcomes in the external world reflect the mindset of the societies we live in.

No problem can be solved by the level of consciousness that created it.[18] As our consciousness expands and begins to overcome the limitations of the binary, cause-and-effect mind, we start to see the interdependencies of the world. We begin to see that the answers to the problems of the First Dimension cannot be provided by a mind operating at a low level of consciousness. The mind that recognises this is a transformed mind.

The transformed mind sees all the influences upon us – internal and external – with greater clarity and detachment. It sees that our thoughts, feelings and conduct are results of deep conditioning and life experiences. Because this mind is freer, it sees the impoverished nature of the First Dimension world, and how it is rooted in self-serving motivation. It sees that the world, rather than being governed by isolated causes and individual effects, is actually deeply interconnected. In this state, we realise the limitations of the concepts and goals we have held to be true, and we see beyond them.

With a deeper capacity to see ourselves with more clarity and less baggage, the possibilities for different ways of living also become clearer. We begin to see that the value systems we have been living by no longer apply, and instead, new values that are better aligned with our aspirations as a global community become obvious.

4

Bonds and Love: A Path to Transcendence

Our bonds are not simply our relationships with one another. They are fundamental to who we are as a species. Without them, we are not fully human. For most of human history we were defined by our bonds. We belonged to a tribe, or a clan, or a religious group. Our identity was determined not by our individual pursuits, but by our responsibilities to the community to which we belonged. In some parts of the world, this is still largely the case. In this chapter, I look at how human bonds have changed over time and how we can envision their future forms. Love (itself not a bond but a feeling) will play a pivotal role in how bonds are forged in higher dimensions.

Our Bonds in Premodern Times

We have historically tended to form four types of bonds: family, marriage, friendship, and community.

Parents, Children, Family

Our parentage was the most important source of identity. Indeed, being the son or daughter of someone was often sufficient to establish identity.

Family also acted as a sort of biological insurance, in that it ensured that someone (our parents when we are young, our children when we are old) was always available to help us in times of need. Even today, the bond between parents and children is the most enduring; it forms a cornerstone of communal life.

I once had the opportunity to closely observe a family in their business and personal relationships. The father of two children was a rich entrepreneur who was ruthless and unrelenting in his business dealings, and seemed not to have the least concern for his employees, customers, and competitors. When he came home, however, he was an adoring father who worked tirelessly for his children and cared for their welfare with single-minded devotion. He was quite capable of affection, but only to his immediate kin.

The unconditional bond between close family members is the outcome of the strongest biological impulse mammals possess: the need to care for our young, who represent the future of our species. It manifests itself naturally because it is a deeply embedded social convention built upon biological urges reinforced over millennia of evolution. It is the easiest bond for us to form and maintain because we are hardwired for it.

The genetically enforced bond between parents and children automatically spawned a larger kinship group. Parents' blood ties to their own parents and siblings implied a more extensive network of uncles and aunts, nephews, and cousins to whom we were bound by consanguinity. While the bond to relatives was not as powerful and permanent as the bond to nuclear family, it nevertheless defined the extent of social interaction. In traditional societies, the extended kinship group was the social web within which most other meaningful bonds were formed – your brother was also your business partner, your cousin was your best friend, and your uncle (if not your father) became your mentor in a trade or profession.

Marriage

Usually understood to be heterosexual and monogamous, marriage was meant to meet the emotional need for companionship and the biological need for sexual intimacy. More importantly, it was a form of collaboration that was indispensable to raise children and to retain and augment property. Marriage was also a means to establish alliances between families, clans, and later ruling dynasties, thus enlarging the network of bonds that tie communities together. Traditionally, love was not part of the marriage equation. If love and affection grew between the spouses, it was a bonus. The idea that love is a prerequisite for a successful marriage is relatively new.

Friendship

Friendship has been a constant feature of social intercourse throughout the ages and in all cultures. According to some scholars, however, friendship had a different meaning in traditional societies of the past.[19] In many cases it was largely circumscribed by kinship groups or severely limited by the constraints of gender, age, ethnicity, and geography. Often it was a proxy for economic or political alliances and characterised by obligatory reciprocity more than the enjoyment of one another's company. It was instrumental rather than sentimental, arising from the need for mutual support in difficult situations. This was certainly the case with Homeric *xenia* (guest-friendship). Its cornerstone was hospitality offered to a traveller, usually of equal rank, in a foreign land. Once given, and cemented with gift-giving, this bond functioned as an alliance that implied reciprocal protection and non-aggression, and extended to the families of the two individuals involved.

Friendship as we know it today – a relationship between two individuals based on shared interests or experiences, and often involving self-disclosure as the basis of trust – is largely a modern construct. The advent of industrialisation, urbanisation, and free economic exchange allowed individuals to interact more freely and forge new bonds based on congeniality and common, non-occupational pursuits. As British sociologist Ray Pahl noted,

> The replacement of much previous instrumental friendship by the rules of commercial society allowed the free expression of a new, morally superior

friendship based on 'natural sympathy' unconstrained by necessity. These new, freely chosen relationships reflected the new universalism emerging in civil society.[20]

Fellowship and Community

This is the more general bond we share with those who are not in our immediate, nuclear family, but who are nevertheless part of our daily lives, such as relatives, neighbours, co-workers, and members of the community we live in. In modern times, this type of bond encompasses professional associations, recreational clubs, alumni groups, neighbourhood committees, and so forth. In premodern times, this bond was usually defined by kinship: our community – the only community available to us – was the extended family, tribe, or clan. As societies became larger and more complex, however, our bond to a larger community outside the family nucleus was determined by gross identifiers like social stratification (class or caste), ethnicity, and religion. The latter meant adhesion not only to a religious belief, but also to a narrower sect, worship group, or parish within that religion.

Thus, the communities with which premodern individuals interacted and to which they were bound were usually not a matter of choice but a consequence of belonging to a particular group. The bond between an individual and his larger community was not spontaneous; it was conditioned by circumstances. The same is true, for the most part, of all the bonds I have discussed here. The bond between children and parents is conditioned by a genetic link. The bond between spouses was, for much of history, ordained by relatives, elders and chieftains, whereas the couple entering into the marriage usually had little say in it. And even the bond of friendship, which we think of as entirely voluntary in our time, was limited to certain kinship or occupational groups, and often based on the expectation of reciprocity.

In premodern times, individual choices about whom to befriend and whom to avoid were recognised, but only within the context of something larger and more important. The Bhagavad Gita delves into the personal struggle faced by Arjuna as he prepares to battle his own kin, but this dilemma is portrayed within the context of his duty as a Kshatriya, that is, a member of a particular social class. In the Platonic dialogues, Socrates argues that each person must reason for himself, but only within the confines of a greater truth that exists outside the individual, and in service of a *polis* guided by this truth.

To better understand how closely the premodern individual was bound to his family and his immediate community, let us look at personal names from three places: Iceland, England, and North India. Here are two typical Icelandic names: Sigurd Jenssen and Kristina Sigurdottir. In translation, these mean 'Sigurd, son of Jens' and 'Kristina, daughter of Sigurd', respectively. Iceland is a relatively homogenous society where until a century ago everyone lived in small communities in which such names were practical. Today Icelanders are more mobile, and names mean less. It has become difficult to identify who a person is and where they come from, based on their name. There is even a popular dating app, for smartphones, that helps ensure that the person you just met at the pub is not your cousin.

In medieval England, a smith was someone who worked with metal. As was common, many people adopted it as a surname to mark their occupation. Similarly, 'Taylor' meant cloth worker and 'Mason' meant stone worker or builder. The name 'Smith' has gone from being a very specific badge of one's trade and identity to becoming not only the most common surname in the English language, but also the least informative.

Here is a typical name for a Rajput clansman from Rajasthan, in northern India: Yogendra Singh Mertiya. Yogendra is his first name, Singh denotes the larger caste group of warriors and rulers (Kshatriyas) to which he belongs, and Mertiya signifies a particular clan of Kshatriyas known as descending from the moon god Chandra. It is also the name of a place connected to this lineage.

In a world of limited geography, an individual's name placed him in a specific context so that those who interacted with him could easily identify who they were dealing with. A person was simply a small part of a larger group who derived his identity, role and position in society, and lifestyle, from a common ethnic or religious heritage, a profession, or a tradition of residing in the same area. The urbanisation, communications, and travel that have come to embody modern life have opened up a new set of opportunities to interact with others and to form bonds in ways that are no longer limited to one's kin.

Human Bonds in the First Dimension

The Rise of the Individual – A Revolutionary Idea

The key difference between tradition and modernity is that in traditional societies people's allegiances are involuntary, fixed even before they are born, whereas allegiances in modernity – whether to a friend, a company, a university, or even a professional association of, say, accountants – are often voluntary. In the premodern context, you could not overcome the world you were born into. Historically in India, for example, caste was the most important grouping to which you belonged. It dictated the trajectory of your life and almost all choices. Today, most of us are still born into a family, a caste or social class, an ethnicity or a religion, but we can choose our friends, our profession, and sometimes even the country where we live. Modernity offers choice, or, as sociologists call it, mobility.

Modernity transformed the nature of our bonds. Whereas in traditional settings, humans were deeply enmeshed in the context of their family and tribe, modernity created the idea of an individual divorced from this context. This individual owed allegiance to artificial associations and 'imagined communities' (to use a term popularised by political scientist Benedict Anderson), such as the nation to which he belonged and the corporation for which he worked, but was increasingly isolated from the traditional ties of family, kinship, ethnicity, and tribe.

The shift from traditional collectives to modern societies composed of independent individuals has been one of the most dramatic changes in human history. It is the source of much of the conflict in the world as societies at various stages of progress deal with the shift of allegiances that modernity demands from them. At the heart of this upheaval was individuation – the process by which the individual became a separate entity with specific desires, needs, and rights. This idea – an individual distinct from the sources of his identity – is taken for granted today, but in much of the world it was not the case even half a century ago. It is the most disruptive concept introduced by modernity. When I was a university student, I often thought of Karl Marx's *Communist Manifesto* as being a truly revolutionary work, one that rewrote the social order and changed the course of history. But the consequences of ideological developments like communism pale in comparison to the upheaval wrought by the concept of the individual. This individual, imbued with certain inalienable rights and whose purpose was to maximise his well-being, became the idea that legitimised all the structures and institutions that followed. (I will discuss how this came about in Chapter 6.) The traditional identity based on kinship and community had provided a person with a point of reference from the earliest period of humanity, but it would gradually lose its relevance in the modern age.

However, the image of the individual revolting against the oppressive forces of society (embodied by an authoritarian government, a dogmatic religion, or a conservative community), and thus forging a new era of freedom and enlightenment, is a myth that fails to capture the slow, impersonal, inexorable evolution of civilisations. As historian E.H. Carr noted, 'the increased individualization which accompanied the rise of the modern world was a normal process of advancing civilization.'[21] The rise of ever more sophisticated societies demanded an increasing level of professional specialisation in everything from painting to engineering to record-keeping. Thus, the means of creation – not just economic, but especially administrative, technological, artistic, and intellectual – were increasingly in the hands of specially trained individuals. This, in turn, gradually resulted in a social ideology that 'strongly emphasized the role of individual initiative in the social order.'[22]

This ideology is on display in the writings of some of the great European thinkers of the 16th, 17th and 18th centuries who helped to consolidate the primacy of the individual and turned it into a blueprint for modernity. Niccolò Machiavelli was one of the first modern thinkers to write extensively on the free will of the individual as the basis for overcoming chance and fortune through reason. René Descartes famously introduced the dualism of mind and body: the world was made up of the material, which cannot think, and the mental, which has no physical substance. The intersection between these two aspects of the world is the individual, who exercises his reason and operates in the material world.

Thomas Hobbes, John Locke, Jean-Jacques Rousseau, and Immanuel Kant are all famous for their treatises on the state of nature (that is, what the existence of people might have been like before societies came into being) and on the social contract, but they all took for granted that the individual was the fundamental building block of humanity. The economists Jeremy Bentham and Adam Smith formulated their theories on maximising utility with limited resources based on the rational individual as the primary actor. What we see repeated in the great theories of the early modern era is a tendency, a necessity even, to consider the individual as the primary subject of inquiry.

The Invention of Love – Another Revolutionary Idea

In the previous chapter I discussed the elements that create the context for our subconscious programming. Traditional societies were built on three of these elements in particular: biological necessities, familial frameworks, and social conditioning. This has been the nature of our social development. These three elements, along with religion, exerted the strongest influence. Before the medical advances of modernity and the social services provided by developed, modern states, shorter lifespans and the need for cooperation to survive ensured that the individual remained an indivisible part of a social group and acted in the interests of the family or the tribe.

Arranged marriages are a good example of this social mindset. For most of human history, marriage was something decided by family and community, not individuals (and this is still the norm in some countries). Love between two independent, rational, utility-maximising individuals, each acting out of supposed free will to marry, was an uncommon concept. Instead, marriages were alliances in which the spouses were peripheral in the larger scheme of things. This logic held sway as long as people were not seen as individuals with independent and imperative emotional needs, such as love.

The bonds I have written about in this chapter are societal norms – patterns of behaviour by which members of a society have learned to commit to each other. Love, on the other hand, is an emotion or a feeling.[23] In recent times, we have come to believe that all four of our fundamental bond types are underpinned by love. We assume that in all but the most dysfunctional of families, parents love their children and children love their siblings. We do not pause to think whether our biological connection has anything to do with it, or whether we actually like spending time with our parents or siblings. We take it for granted that we are bound by familial love. In marriage or any other form of sexual partnership, too, love is assumed to be the guiding force, at least in progressive societies. Even friendship is a form of love, though we often prefer to use a different label (say, affection) to describe it so as to distinguish it from marital love. If the sexual implications of marital love are ignored, however, love and friendship are quite similar – they both entail liking the company of the other, emotional intimacy, and knowledge acquired through reciprocal self-disclosure. Finally, love is often present in discussions of our bond to society at large. It is not uncommon for patriotic individuals to declare their love for their country, for example, or for religious practitioners to feel personal attachment to a spiritual leader whom they may not have met in person.[24]

As we saw at the beginning of this chapter, human bonds have changed significantly since prehistoric and premodern times. What about love? Today we think of love as a feeling of deep, intimate affection, but what was it like in the past? Did it exist? It is hard to say what our earliest ancestors – hunter-gatherers living tens of thousands of years ago – felt toward each other because they have left little evidence of their feelings. Bands of hunter-gatherers were small, so almost everyone was related. Sexual relationships were probably not monogamous, so children belonged to the entire clan. Members of the band needed each other at all times to face dangers and hardships together. In these conditions, did they love one another? Adult members probably felt the longing to procreate, a duty and an urge to protect their young, and perhaps the desire to play rough-and-tumble games with them during times of leisure. But did these impulses amount to love in our understanding of that emotion?

Later periods of history that have left us written records provide much more information about human feelings, including love, at least about romantic or erotic love. As perhaps the most powerful emotion a human being can experience, sexual love has inspired artistic expressions for millennia, especially in poetry and song. The understanding of love that we gain from studying highly stylised poetic compositions, however, is limited. For one thing, they mostly describe a hopelessly one-sided feeling. Like the twenty-five poems that Catullus addressed to his beloved Lesbia,[25] these works often capture the unrequited passions of the poet, but not a mutual sentiment we might call love today. This one-sidedness was especially pronounced in the lyric poetry of the Middle Ages. The troubadours of the 12th and 13th centuries were inspired by their unfulfilled longing for women they had sometimes never met or even seen. Dante probably met his muse, Beatrice Portinari, only twice, and very briefly. Laura, the object of Petrarch's love, was equally remote and may not have existed at all in flesh and blood. Love, as expressed in such works, is no more than a literary convention. The unfulfilled desire for an unreachable woman (who is too far, or too far above the poet's station, or already married, or who spurns the poet's advances) is a tool to unleash the poet's creativity. It is love for love's sake, not for another.

Yet even amid the stylised, affected courtly literature of the High Middle Ages we sometimes find evidence of a more 'modern' love. Nowhere is this more evident than in the letters exchanged between the scholastic philosopher Peter Abelard and his one-time pupil, lover, and secret wife, Heloïse. Writing almost fifteen years after the end of their tumultuous romance, which had threatened to destroy both their lives, Heloïse, by now an abbess, acknowledges the overwhelming potency of her long-suppressed passion:

> I am, I confess, a sinner, but one who, far from weeping for her sins, weeps only for her lover; far from abhorring her crimes, longs only to add

> to them; and who, with a weakness unbecoming my state, please myself continually with the remembrance of past delights when it is impossible to renew them [...] I know what obligations this veil lays upon me, but I feel more strongly what power an old passion has over my heart.

Smouldering with unabashed feeling and unflinching honesty, Heloïse's letters make compelling reading even nine centuries later. They are testament to love's endurance, to be sure, but they also present a strikingly modern definition of love. True love, she opines, has nothing to do with one's position in society, occupation, wealth, or social provenance: 'True tenderness makes us separate the lover from all that is external to him, and setting aside his position, fortune or employments, consider him merely as himself.' Love is forever, and must include not just carnal desire, but a communion of minds:

> I will still love you with all the tenderness of my soul till the last moment of my life. If, formerly, my affection for you was not so pure, if in those days both mind and body loved you, I often told you even then that I was more pleased with possessing your heart than with any other happiness, and the man was the thing I least valued in you.

Love, then, is 'the union of two persons who love each other with perfect liberty, who are united by a secret inclination, and satisfied with each other's merits'. Such is the explosive, all-or-nothing quality of love that it cuts against the grain of social convention. Indeed, when Abelard had entreated her to marry him in order to cover up their scandalous affair, Heloïse had refused at first: 'I despised the name of wife that I might live happy with that of mistress.' Marriage, in other words, is too confining for love.

What we see in the correspondence between Abelard and Heloïse is a conundrum that would vex lovers more and more in the course of the following centuries: how to reconcile love – an emotion so powerful and irresistible, but also so isolating because it is felt only by individuals – with one's obligations to society? How can love be made to fit in the framework of socially acceptable relationships, such as family and marriage, that have defined human bonds since the beginning? How can love be turned into a constructive social force, rather than a disruptive one?

During the early modern period, with its increasing emphasis on the fulfilment of individual needs and desires, including emotional ones, literature probed this fundamental dilemma frequently. *Romeo and Juliet* is perhaps the best-known story of tragic love – a love that is doomed because it threatened an established social order, yet one so powerful that the lovers choose death rather than give it up. Another example, from the sentimentalist literature of the post-Enlightenment period, is Goethe's semi-autobiographical *The Sorrows of Young Werther*. Its protagonist also chooses suicide once he has accepted the impossibility of his love for Lotte, who is already married. Much like his troubadour predecessors, he wallows in the poetic self-absorption that love can bring, but he never considers breaking the sanctity of the social status quo by transgressing against the bond of marriage.

Only a few decades later, in the romantic novels of Jane Austen, however, we see the marriage–love dichotomy being treated in a new way. The four heroines of *Sense and Sensibility* and *Pride and Prejudice* all search for the assurances that marriage can bring – financial security, safety, and respectability. At the same time, they yearn for the kind of intimacy and fulfilment that only love can bestow. They feel sufficiently independent to turn down advantageous marriage proposals from men they know they cannot love, and they continue to aspire to a union that will bring happiness and stability in equal measure. After a series of vicissitudes, intrigues, and fortuitous developments, they all achieve this goal. Austen shows us a social milieu in which the emotional desire for love – being both loved and allowed to love – has become central to the aspirations of young people, and integrating it in the established social bonds of family and marriage is increasingly important. Narratives that juxtapose love and social obligation have remained extremely popular in literature and film ever since Austen. Today, they are especially ubiquitous in soap operas and Bollywood movies where differences of caste, religion, or social status stand in the way of love.

In more recent times, our understanding of love has been affected profoundly by the freewheeling approach to relationships in the 1960s. The rebellious generation of that decade believed that love was universal and should be freely exchanged, without the need for any formal bonds like marriage. Brotherly love and especially sexual love were held up as transformative experiences that could heal a fractured world; everyone was encouraged to engage in them without worrying about the obligations that society associated with them. While casual sex free of any attachments may have materialised only in a few hippie communities, the 1960s undeniably changed our perception of what love ought to be. Though still frowned upon, extramarital sex is now commonplace in many countries and no longer a crime under the law, while divorce offers an avenue to legally and conclusively end an unhappy marriage. Most importantly, the idea that love is a fundamental human need, and that it should be the primary ingredient in a successful union, is deeply ingrained in our psyche and in our expectations. What was relatively new in Austen's stories is now a universal conviction – that true love leads to marriage and, conversely, a marriage without love is not worth entering into.

While arranged marriages remain common in some countries, such as India, most advanced societies today approach the union of two life partners with the assumption that love is prerequisite for marriage. Love encompasses not only physical attraction, but also spiritual intimacy arising from a deep appreciation of each other's likes and dislikes, fears and joys, secrets, and desires. As a result, when two individuals are married in the 21st century, their expectations of happiness and personal fulfilment are high. They expect to find a soulmate, not just a partner with whom to share the travails of life. In the words of the Swiss-British philosopher Alain de Botton, 'The new ideal set before the world the compelling notion that one might solve one's most pressing needs all at once with the help of just one other person.'[26]

The literature, cinema, and popular culture of our times support this complex mythology. But it is a mythology that leaves us unfulfilled and constantly in search of an elusive perfection. Modern couples are constantly assessing the quality of their marriage: am I happy? Does my lover or spouse make me happy? Would I be better off with someone else? If they are unhappy, modern society allows them to end the marriage and seek happiness elsewhere. Instead of focusing on finding common ground and working through their struggles, partners are encouraged to use one another and discard when done. Love is reduced to an impulse to be satisfied and to a predominantly self-serving activity.

This recurring evaluation tends to remove an individual's responsibility for her happiness and projects it onto the partner. Ideas of devotion, understanding, and improving oneself rarely enter into the picture. We look for faults in the other person; instead of working towards happiness, we keep judging one another. As the 19th-century novelist and playwright Honoré de Balzac put it in *Physiologie du Mariage*, 'The more one judges, the less one loves.'

The Society of 'Me'

Marriage and family are not the only social institutions that have been challenged by the rise of the individual. Ever since the Reformation, human inquiry has moved steadily away from knowledge either handed down by members of one's extended family, or monopolised and dispensed by religious institutions, and toward independent, critical thinking, empirical observation, and conclusions based on experimentation, reasoning, and the free exchange of ideas. This change relied heavily on each individual's ability to think for himself and form opinions and beliefs based on his own interpretation of what he saw around him. Individualism, therefore, gradually spelled the end of religion's control on knowledge. Once the frontiers of learning began to be controlled by new players, such as independent thinkers and secular universities, the clergy lost its monopoly on knowledge and intellectual authority.

Art and our very understanding of beauty have also been affected by the increasing emphasis on individual achievement. Art is no longer understood as an expression of a communal devotion to something (a deity, for example), but rather as the work of creative and independent individuals. French impressionism, for example, consists of the paintings of Monet, Renoir, Manet, Pissarro, and Cézanne. Try finding out which individuals carved the great sculptures of the Ellora caves in Maharashtra or the Mahabalipuram temples in Tamil Nadu. Even if the names of a few artists and artisans do survive, they do not dominate the discourse. Those artistic structures are an expression of a larger community, but less the work of individuals. Increasingly, however, the individual is becoming the only avenue to understanding the world.

The shift from group identity to individual identity as the defining social force of the modern age engendered two far-reaching ideas: free will and the belief in individual rights. Indeed, from the revolutionary idea of individualism arose the inward-facing person who possessed free will – the ability to act independently of the needs and priorities of society at large, at least within the space granted by law. The individual now wielded his free will to take advantage of the rights and freedoms to which he was entitled as a distinct legal entity, and to pursue all his personal needs and desires to achieve the highest possible level of comfort and happiness.

The natural outcome of a society increasingly bent on satisfying the needs of individuals was a polity – which we now call democracy – that derived its legitimacy from individuals, and whose objective, at least in theory, was the preservation of individual rights and the pursuit of individual priorities. As we shall see in a later chapter, the individual exercising his or her free will became the source of constitutional legitimacy, and democratic political systems became the vehicles by which individuals conferred legitimacy in a manner that was accepted by the majority. The idea of the individual owed its attractiveness to the limitless freedom it promised, and it spread rapidly thanks to modern media and communication technologies, starting with the printing press.

Let us tread back into the past for an instant, and imagine the scenario of a man not marrying a woman he likes because it would go against the traditions and interests of his family and community. Imagine a frugal person spending his entire life's savings on religious functions to bring honour and cohesion to his community. Imagine a person willingly supporting a ruler who extracts huge taxes because the ruler is the living embodiment of a divine being. These are very realistic snapshots of the past;

this is how most of humanity lived for much of our settled existence. But such behaviour is increasingly rare, especially in the developed world.

Instead, the First Dimension built a society, a popular culture, a consumption-based economic system, and art and literature, all of which took their sanction and derived their *raison d'être* from how effectively they fulfilled our individual need for happiness. Traditional societies have tried to defend themselves against the onslaught of self-referential Western individualism by emphasising the benefits of collective identity, by harking back to a pre-colonial golden age, and especially by reaffirming a religious identity distinct from the liberal, Western model. This is particularly evident in the resurgence of Islamic cultural expressions, including fundamentalism, in the Middle East, Africa, and Central Asia during the last few decades. In India, the same period has seen a renewal of Hindu nationalism as a means to set cultural values in sharp relief against 'foreign' attitudes (Muslim as well as Western). This tension between Western, individualist modernity and collective, traditional culture is a facet of the 'clash of civilisations' posited by political scientist Samuel Huntington, that is, a geopolitical reality in which cultures defined primarily by religion become the fault lines of conflict.[27]

The modern world is increasingly becoming a society of me. In 2006, *Time* magazine's person of the year was 'You'. Elevating the individual to such prominent levels is fraught with pitfalls. It informs each member of society that his individual desires and needs are paramount. Indeed, the most ubiquitous and consequential question that members of modern societies ask themselves is an entirely self-referential one: am I happy? In a world where the main goal of life is the satiation of one's desires, we can see how the modern consumption-based society arose. Humans have always had selfish tendencies as an aspect of themselves, but to promote and cherish individual selfishness as the primary goal of our existence is what has created most injustice and inequality in the First Dimension.

The problem with a society focused on individual happiness is twofold: it often absolves the individual from playing a role in her own happiness, and it creates an intensely transactional way of looking at everything and everyone. An individuated society inevitably becomes a utility-driven, consumption-based society. It is, in short, a society in which every interaction is appraised for its value toward furthering someone's needs and wishes.

Narcissism is an inevitable by-product of such a transactional society. The valuation of individual needs and priorities above all else creates a mindset incapable of recognising the profound interdependencies that connect members of every social group. We become focused on our own trajectory and fail to see that our successes and failures, the decisions we make, and the projects we undertake are conditioned by circumstances outside our control and heavily influenced by those around us. First Dimension values tend to shut us off from this reality, such that we become self-centred and blinded by our own ego – narcissistic individuals often incapable of expressing genuine concern for our fellow human beings. It is no wonder that in an age that offers so many possibilities to meet and interact with other people, we are plagued by loneliness. How is it possible to live in a city of 20 million people and feel alienation? In the past, our bonds were the glue that held society together. As the idea of the individual gained prominence, this glue weakened and the result has been a highly atomised society in which we have lost the most fulfilling part of being human.

Today's children are taught from a young age that the principal reason for their existence is to fulfil their personal destiny, become whoever they want to be, and pursue whatever career they like best or will bring the most wealth and stability. They are told to be independent individuals, not to conform too much, and to be themselves, as though it were a crime to model oneself on somebody else. Children are encouraged to set themselves apart in order to leave a mark the world. And all the while, we tell them that their freedom to choose will guide them.

Human bonds in the First Dimension (summarised in Table 4.1) are a zero-sum game. We calculate the causes and effects of our happiness and unhappiness, and use one another to achieve the results. In the end, we are never satisfied. The grass will always be greener elsewhere. We rarely consider the possibility that there might exist a higher purpose to our lives, because First Dimension habits and conditioning urge us to appreciate only those bonds and activities whose direct benefits we can easily quantify.

This book tries to show that overcoming this way of being, as a society, will require a shift in the level of consciousness from which we are operating. For this to happen, awareness of our situation is essential. It is only when we are aware that we begin to notice that the modern

Table 4.1: Summary of Human Bonds in Premodern and Modern Times

Type of bond	Premodernity	Modernity
Parents and children, immediate family	Often seen as indivisible from the individual, family bonds were part of a continuum of which the individual was an integral part.	The bond with immediate family remains a fundamental building block of social organisation. Though taken for granted, it is nevertheless assumed to be based on affection and evaluated for its contribution to each member's self-fulfilment.
Marriage	Primarily an alliance between two collective entities, with the goal of procreation, social security, and resource accumulation.	The free expression of a utility-maximising individual based on the fulfilment of his or her needs. Love – a deep spiritual and physical intimacy – is considered indispensable, but it is increasingly used as an avenue to individual happiness rather than communal harmony.
Friendship	Usually founded on the need for mutual support in difficult situations. Friendships within the extended family and kinship group often fulfilled this purpose.	Group identities no longer matter much in the creation of friendships. They are individualistic and voluntary, usually based on common interests, experiences, and points of view.
Bonds of fellowship and community	Based on tribal, ethnic, and kinship ties.	Civic and associational. Built around modern professions, recreational interests, and citizens' duties.

individual, conditioned to reference all activity to individual desires and needs, is set up for an impoverished life. We are more than the sum total of our desires, just as ecosystems are vastly more than the sum total of their individual species. It is only when we begin to see the inherent limitations of our First Dimension approach to our bonds that we will be able to transcend them.

Love in Higher Dimensions

The rise of the individual has been a defining idea of the First Dimension system, and a major revolution in the way we relate to each other. It has brought along with it the belief that love is the most important emotion a human being can express and thus that it should be the cornerstone of our bonds with family, spouses, and friends. But it has also engendered a self-centred, utilitarian understanding of these bonds and a narcissistic vision of the individual's place in society. As a result, many of us feel disconnected from each other. Even though we live in large urban centres, we often feel isolated, distant from our families and neighbours, and alienated from the millions of other citizens with whom we share our cities and towns. We yearn for a closer, more meaningful bond with each other, but we often don't know how to go about it, besides joining a cooking class or a sports club.

Returning to a more primitive form of social organisation so as to recover the kinship and communal bonds that used to tie us together is not the answer. Improving the deteriorated quality of our bonds, however, remains a pressing need – we have always been a social species, and we continue to be defined by our ability and desire to associate with others. Increasingly, we also recognise this need as a physical one because close human bonds tend to make us healthier and happier. There has always been rich anecdotal evidence of this tendency, but recently it has been confirmed by scientific studies as well. In particular, the Harvard Study of Adult Development,[28] which charted the lives of 724 men from 1939 to the present, has shown that the quality of human relationships can have a powerful influence on health. Various analyses of the data collected over eighty years revealed that good relationships – with spouses, family, friends, and community members – help to delay mental and physical decline and are better predictors of long-term health than physical indicators like cholesterol level.

Nurturing human bonds and maintaining close relationships are fundamental to who we are and necessary for our psychological and physical well-being. To restore interpersonal relationships to their rightful place in the make-up of social organisation, I propose taking one of the First Dimension's achievements – the invention of love – and turning it into a universal goal, by making it the template for all our social interactions in the future.

This seems like a radical idea – to use love, the same feeling that we normally associate with our most intimate relations (marital partners, family, close friends), to form a bond with every human being, including complete strangers. It is hardly new, however. In the Western cultural tradition, it is at least as old as the Gospel of Luke, in which Jesus clarified, with the Parable of the Good Samaritan, that when following the Biblical commandment, 'Thou shalt love thy neighbour as thyself' (Leviticus 19:18), every human being should be considered one's neighbour. Eastern philosophies also recognised, long ago, that love (or at least compassion) must be shown to all human beings, irrespective of our relationship with them. The Buddha, for example, taught that reaching enlightenment requires not only wisdom, but also compassion (known as *karuna*). In Buddhism, compassion is not a passive feeling, but rather 'an empathetic altruism that actively strives to free others from suffering',[29] and a deep intimacy (known as loving-kindness) with all other sentient beings, not just humans.

Despite its ancient roots, the notion of extending love to all our fellow human beings remains radical, especially in a social environment in which individualism holds sway and continually encourages us to focus on self-interest. It seems out of reach. I believe, however, that love is the logical outcome of a heightened consciousness. In what follows, I offer a path to developing genuine love – a deep and unconditional commitment to, and involvement in, the well-being of others. In higher dimensions love will form the basis for all human bonds because it is the most powerful way in which a higher consciousness expresses itself.

Love in the Second Dimension: The Three Liberations

Shifting from an outwardly seeking, self-absorbed, narcissistic individual to one who is committed to her fellow human beings requires an inner journey. This journey sets the foundations for Second and Third Dimension society. In the previous chapter, I described one way in which each of us can approach such a journey: meditation. As we deepen our meditation practice (see Table 3.1), and connect with ourselves more deeply, the process will bring with it three liberations.

The **first liberation** consists of knowing yourself fully. It is a liberation because knowing yourself requires you to break free from the distractions created by the six elements of your context. As we saw in Chapter 3, self-knowledge can be achieved through deep reflection on the leanings, yearnings, fears, insecurities, and cravings of the mind – all manifestations of the six elements of our context. By methodically parsing out all the things that influence your mind, you discover who you really are. This is only possible if you are prepared to analyse your own thoughts and actions dispassionately, and willing to have an open, reasoned dialogue with yourself. Once you have grasped your true nature you are, by definition, free of the influence of the six elements. (This achievement corresponds to the sixth progression in the programme of meditation suggested in Table 3.1.)

My father often said that the most meaningful bond we must form is with ourselves. He said this in the context of people who lied, cheated, hurt others or were corrupt, and when we discussed such instances he would always say the same thing: 'You have to live with your conduct in life, because in life you spend far more time with yourself than with anyone else.' When a yarn trader cheated me in a business transaction many years ago, my father said the trader had done an awful thing not only to me, but to himself. At that time, I did not understand what he meant, but years later as my business grew and prospered I noticed that the trader had acquired a reputation for dishonesty, had a terrible quarrel in his family over property, and faced financial difficulties. His deceitful ways, and especially his unwillingness to be truthful to his own conscience, seemed to have caught up with him.

It takes courage and humility to know yourself, to accept and embrace the parts of yourself that you do not like, and to stand up for what you believe in, even in the face of the prevailing social conditions. Knowing yourself means understanding the origin of your thoughts and motivations, and taking responsibility for your actions, rather than blaming them on a particular situation or on others. If you form an honest bond with yourself, characterised by moral courage and a commitment to being more self-aware, you will also be able to form strong, meaningful relationships with others.

Meditation is an effective route to knowing oneself and understanding why we do what we do. With the deepening awareness that comes from meditation, we begin to deprogramme ourselves from the conditioning that pushes us to see everything from the narrow perspective of self-gratification. Such a practice, over time, can help us understand who we are. When I started meditating I realised that I knew nothing about myself – neither who I was nor why I did what I did. Even my simplest reactions to events and encounters were a mystery to me. After many years of meditation, I was able to identify and list the 182 emotions that triggered my reactions. I began to see how the inclinations of my mind were influenced by the elements of my context, and how these in turn fuelled my worries, hopes, anxieties, and dreams. I understood that my greatest fear was of being alone and feeling empty inside if I did not constantly fill my life with social activities, superficial friendships, professional goals, and long to-do lists. I was finally able to see the hollowness of many of the edifices that I carried in my subconscious. Eventually, the fears, desires, and cravings that appeared so real became unsubstantial and lost the hold they had over my mind.

I also noticed that most other people, like me, were in thrall to their mental formations. When you know yourself, you begin to see patterns and interconnections in a way that was invisible before. Some of the comic books I read as a child had advertisements for X-ray glasses that claimed to allow you to see people's skeletons. This is what knowing yourself will do. From seeing patterns in your own mind, you learn to recognise them in others, and become aware of the deep connections that affect our lives.

This is what I call the **second liberation**: breaking free of the illusion that we exist in an isolated, entirely self-referential space, and accepting and embracing our dependence on others. (This liberation corresponds to the seventh progression in Table 3.1.) We are not isolated because we are all connected through bonds of family, marriage, and community. What we do in these relationships reverberates in the complex ecosystem of our bonds, either enriching or impoverishing it. The second liberation stems from the recognition of what Fritjof Capra (in his book *The Web of Life*) and epigeneticist Bruce Lipton describe as the complex web of interdependent relationships that make up our world. It allows us to recognise what the philosopher Nagarjuna describes as the artificial boundaries imposed by the constructions of our minds.

Understanding interdependence enables you to be kind, considerate and thoughtful, curious, a good listener, and concerned for others. The more you connect with these qualities within you, the richer your relationships become. Suppose the opposite were true: if you are selfish, vain, egotistical, manipulative, and narcissistic, you will end up living in a world with nothing more than transactional relationships, user acquaintances, and relationships based on your ability to control others.

With the powers of observation that come from a mind in a higher state of consciousness, you can see this clearly. You also see that intense conditioning, particularly in relation to fears, has made it difficult for people to be generous, loving, and devoted. These qualities are seen as weaknesses or traits that others can take advantage of; generosity toward others is seen as distracting the individual from his ongoing efforts to satisfy his limitless desires.

You will often encounter people whose actions and opinions bewilder you because they appear to be self-defeating. They are unaware of the baggage of the past with which they live – prisoners of a context they do not recognise, unresolved pain from relationships, and roads not taken. If we keep viewing ourselves as the sole reference point in the world, we prevent ourselves from getting closer to our true nature.

Love in the Third Dimension: Love as an Attitude

The first and second liberations are prerequisites for the **third liberation**, which ushers in a Third Dimension concept of love. From understanding ourselves and from the awareness of interdependence we are able to cultivate the capacity for genuine commitment to each other – not just to our own kin and close friends, but to everyone. How does this happen? Our understanding of ourselves and our dependence on others yield a higher level of consciousness in which devotion, forgiveness, and compassion arise. They arise in us not because we have read a self-help book or because someone has ordered us to feel in a particular way. They arise as a natural evolution when we see, with clarity, our place in an interdependent world. **Devotion** to others is the way consciousness teaches you to free yourself from the prison of First Dimension selfishness, ego, and narcissism. **Forgiveness** is the way consciousness teaches you to let go of the baggage of the past – perceived failures, broken marriages, dysfunctional families, pain from different sources, even your addictions and cravings – and to recognise and accept such afflictions in others. **Compassion** is the way your consciousness teaches you to love.

Once we have experienced the three liberations, we are ready to reshape our human bonds. As consciousness deepens, we become aware of the interdependence of all life. Love for our fellow human beings is the natural outcome of this. We see ourselves as bound to others and by extension related to all of humanity. We also see that hurting someone else ultimately hurts us, too. People who have caused others great pain – criminals, invading soldiers, prison guards – are often traumatised by their actions. After the Vietnam War, for example, a whole generation of Americans returned scarred for life. Prison guards often have unhappy home lives, while many criminals are consumed by guilt. Causing pain contributes to how one's reality is shaped and inevitably causes pain in one's own life.

The ability to relate to people with whom we have no biological ties was rare in premodern societies that had to focus on how best to secure help towards survival. It is equally rare in the utility-maximising First Dimension, which grew out of this primordial mindset and focuses on individual achievement and accumulation of benefits. It requires a surrender of self and identity that is contrary to the First Dimension. At a higher level of consciousness, however, you release yourself from a notion of self that is defined by blood ties or tribal relationships, and you are able to recognise and value people outside those frameworks.

In higher dimensions, therefore, love is unconditional and is extended to all persons, not just our close family, our spouse, and our most intimate friends. Expressing unconditional love depends on a capacity for selflessness and concern for others. In *The Art of Loving,* psychoanalyst and philosopher Erich Fromm says,

> The main condition for the achievement of love is the overcoming of one's narcissism. The narcissistic orientation is one in which one experiences as real only that which exists within oneself, while the phenomena in the outside world have no reality in themselves, but are experienced only from the viewpoint of their being useful or dangerous to one. The opposite pole to narcissism is objectivity; it is the faculty to see other people and things as they are, objectively, and to be able to separate this objective picture from a picture which is formed by one's desires and fears.

To be capable of loving means that you know yourself well and have developed the ability to understand others and to be devoted to the goodness in them. The key, as we all know, is loving someone for who they are, not what you want them to be. Accepting people for who they are implies that you appreciate their qualities. This releases the energy you spend in trying to mould them into what you think they ought to be and allows you to focus this energy on knowing yourself. However, if you do not know yourself and you are not on a journey to develop your own higher qualities, altruism will not come naturally. This kind of acceptance will be a struggle. You are going to think, 'If I help a stranger with his problems, and get nothing in return, I am belittling myself in some way.' You take a utilitarian view of measuring contributions to each other's lives, which is a doomed approach because it focuses on what you get from the other person instead of what you can offer. If we focus on the limited perspective that we are at the centre of everything and that fulfilling our individual needs is the sole purpose of our existence, we will never experience real love. Love is impossible in a transactional relationship. Love means being unattached to outcomes and thinking about one another as more than just a means to an end.

For love to work, you need to make a commitment to your own development. In doing so you become a better human being – more curious, thoughtful, caring, and generous. This, in turn, makes you inherently attractive. It evokes similar feelings in the other person. When you are aware and observant of what is happening inside your mind, you become more aware and observant of what is happening in other people, which in turn makes you more considerate, forgiving and, most of all, devoted, without the expectation of reciprocity. When you are devoted and compassionate without expecting anything in return, you encourage people to love you.

At the heart of any loving relationship is the ability to nurture, that is, to stimulate the expression of certain qualities in others. If you nurture a garden it will produce leafy trees, healthy bushes, and colourful flowers. In the same manner, nurturing students in school yields capable, thoughtful, well-adjusted children. Nurturing a personal relationship is much the same. If we think of love as a form of self-development and actively cultivate certain qualities in ourselves, we will naturally encourage similar qualities in others. The first column in Table 4.2 lists a few qualities that a self-aware individual would strive to develop, qualities that constitute nurturing behaviour. In the second column I have tried to imagine what the consequence of this loving attitude might be; it lists qualities that can be expected to arise in our fellow human beings if we approach them with devotion and compassion.

Imagine that you are looking for a life partner or a friend or even a business partner, and you encounter someone whose sustained practice of awareness has yielded the following qualities: humour, kindness, curiosity about the world and the ideas that drive it forward, helpfulness toward strangers as well as friends and family, and freedom from the baggage of past history. If you are present in the unfolding of your own life, you will learn to love this person because you can recognise and appreciate the qualities that he or she has developed. This, to me, is the meaning of love in a higher dimension.

Table 4.2: The Effect of Nurture in Personal Relationships

Personal quality	What it may evoke in another
Affection, intimacy	Desire, passion
Consideration	Respect
Curiosity	Admiration
Empathy, generosity	Gratitude
Hard work	Appreciation
Honesty	Trust
Hospitality	Camaraderie
Humour	Perspective
Kindness	Reciprocity
Loyalty	Commitment
Mindfulness	Devotion
Sincerity	Dedication
Thoughtfulness	Insight

If you have the ability to love, you have the ability to nourish others with your love. From this more expanded perspective, it is a natural progression for your love to reach out and embrace the entire planet. You begin to consider how you use resources, and what impact your life has on non-humans and all the natural systems upon which we depend for survival. The new love of the Third Dimension is all-encompassing and not limited to the pigeonholes in which we tend to categorise it – fraternal or marital, conditional or unconditional, physical or Platonic, religious or intellectual. It becomes a state of mind. As Fromm says in *The Art of Loving*, 'Love is not primarily a relationship to a specific person; it is an attitude, an orientation of character.'

Third Dimension love is characterised by devotion to others, whether family or strangers, because you are willing to give everything. It is forgiving because you accept the other person for what they are. And it is compassionate because you are committed to the other person's well-being with no expectation of reciprocity.

Love cannot be taken for granted. It is a capacity that needs to be developed in each of us. It is a sign that we have abandoned our primal impulses and are engaging our higher faculties. Like meditation, love is a practice that requires commitment. Because of our conditioning, love is not always the default setting for human interaction. We are all born with the ability to love, but unless this capacity is nurtured, it may not express itself. Third Dimension love between unrelated people does not happen spontaneously. Unlike in the First Dimension, you do not fall in love. Love is deliberate and conscious.

5

Community: The Petri Dish of Humanity

Forces of Social Evolution

The majority of our time on earth has been spent living in small groups based on family and tribal affiliations. These small social units defined who we were and how we behaved. In Chapters 3 and 4, I discussed the momentous changes to our social environment that were brought on by the rise of individualism during the early modern period. This process progressively distanced the individual from his social context – his community – such that he came to understand and define himself as an independent entity driven by personal goals and interests rather than by a world view inherited from his community.

Besides the ideological changes that I described in Chapter 4, there were several other forces at work that contributed to this profound change in the way we relate to one another and the way we organise society. Indeed, the make-up of modern social interaction, and the resultant alienation of the individual from his community, have their origins in several important developments that occurred in the last few centuries, as described below.

Agriculture and Urbanisation

Between 10,000–13,000 years ago, people living in the Fertile Crescent began to cultivate food crops and domesticate animals for food and labour. This was a milestone in the emergence of a new type of social organisation based on the production of food in a fixed location. Agriculture provided, for the first time, consistent supplies and surpluses of food, which allowed for the specialisation of labour. Increasing specialisation, in turn, led to larger settlements and eventually cities, so that a variety of specific skills could be easily accessed. Denser populations gave rise to complex social structures, such as institutional religion and governmental organisations. Agriculture also enabled population booms and created new possibilities for leisure time, which led to sophisticated cultures capable of expressing their imagination through architecture, literature, music, and visual art.

So, agriculture and the urbanisation that it fostered have been a part of the human story for a very long time. They are hardly new developments. The great empires of antiquity and the kingdoms of the Middle Ages were made possible by agricultural surpluses and were structured around urban cores that supported the bureaucratic, organisational, and military resources needed to control them. But the pace of agricultural and urban development has accelerated enormously in recent times. The increasing mechanisation and intensification of agriculture in the last two centuries, with concomitant improvements in yields, have enabled farmers to produce ever-larger surpluses. Today, in most industrialised countries, only 2–3 per cent of the population is engaged in agricultural work. One man with a tractor can easily do the work of several dozen farmers of old and their teams of oxen or mules. Modern methods of preserving and transporting food around the globe have mitigated much of the risk associated with weather, bad harvests, political instability, and warfare, such that food shortages are far less common now, especially in the industrialised world.

Consumers, in turn, have become completely separated from the agricultural processes that produce their food. They have little understanding of the work that goes into farming or the complex distribution mechanisms that bring fresh produce to their supermarkets. They have forgotten about the seasonality of agriculture because they can buy peaches imported from the other hemisphere even in the dead of winter. They are, in short, completely severed from the land that feeds them and the agricultural communities that work that land, to a degree that was never possible in former times.

The massive surge in agricultural productivity has resulted in an equally dramatic rate of urbanisation, spurring the development of megacities – metropolitan centres numbering in the tens of millions. The United Nations (UN) estimated that, in 2008, for the first time ever, more than half of the world's population lived in large cities. By the middle of the current century, this figure is expected to increase to 65 per cent. The megacities of today allow for unparalleled commercial and cultural opportunities, highly specialised forms of employment, and extensive infrastructure. But they are also vast, formless agglomerations of population, where it is impossible to know even a fraction of your neighbours, or to engage with the organs of civic administration, and where it is all too easy to conceal antisocial, selfish, and wasteful behaviour. In earlier times, there was always a concept of the 'other', a stranger who lived elsewhere and with whom one never interacted, but in an urban world, the multiple 'others' of the world are living right beside one another because, more than ever before, it has become possible for diverse groups of people to mingle with one another. In such an environment, the natural inclination to look out only for oneself is more pronounced.

The Printing Press and the Dissemination of Knowledge

The systematic representation of language through signs and symbols, which emerged in the 4th millennium BCE, allowed for information and ideas to survive and be transmitted in ways that were unimaginable in earlier periods, when the dissemination of knowledge relied on oral traditions and memory. Written record-keeping and communication made it possible to administer larger social formations such as states and empires. The invention of the printing press in the 15th century was almost as important as the invention of writing itself, in that it allowed for the mass production of written material. This meant that both the production and the consumption of knowledge were democratised.

The wide distribution and democratisation of knowledge made possible by the printing press led to momentous developments in intellectual and social exchange, enabling seminal historical transformations like the Protestant Reformation and the Scientific Revolution. At the same time, however, the increasing importance of knowledge written down by scholars and scientists, and printed in faraway cities, weakened more traditional forms of knowledge transmission. Age-old wisdom that had been passed on orally, especially in smaller, rural communities, and which had been based on centuries of observation of natural rhythms, lost its relevance. More importantly, those seeking knowledge now relied less and less on their neighbours and elders in the community because they could access it directly through printed materials and at the urban educational institutions where the new knowledge was forged. The community, therefore, became less important as a locus of learning.

Technology

Hominid species have been capable of using tools for millions of years,[30] and human beings eventually developed a variety of implements and mechanisms to make survival, competition, transport, and construction more efficient – everything from weapons to agricultural tools to machinery like pulleys and windmills. But whereas the use and improvement of tools has been a constant throughout human history, there was a tremendous acceleration in early modern times, especially beginning in the 18th century. The rapid mechanisation of manufacturing was made possible by the invention of sophisticated new technologies, most notably in the textile industry, where the punch card, the flying shuttle, and the spinning jenny revolutionised manufacturing. With the application of the steam engine (perfected by James Watt from 1765 onwards) to production, power looms and spinning mules completed the mechanisation of the production cycle. Within little over a century, therefore, textile manufacturing morphed from a cottage industry where weavers produced cloth in the home or in small workshops, to a highly centralised mass operation, with factories employing thousands of workers. Labourers moved in large numbers from rural areas to urban centres where the factories were located, abandoning their community-based lives to work in harsh conditions and live in slums, either alone or accompanied only by their immediate family. In such circumstances it became difficult to maintain a connection to the community they had left behind, or to form a new community.

While the squalor of 18th- and 19th-century factories is largely a thing of the past in Western countries, factory workers continue to toil in the developing world, especially in the manufacturing hubs of Asia, in hazardous and underpaid conditions, while forced to live apart from the communities in which they grew up, and often unable to form extended communities in their place of work. One need only think of giant electronics manufacturers like Foxconn, which operates its own 'cities' in China where hundreds of thousands of labourers work long shifts with little time off, all the while sleeping in dormitories and eating in canteens provided by their corporate employers.

In the 20th century, technological advances in transportation (rail, ferries, commercial airlines, the automobile) made long-distance travel an integral part of daily life. The ability to commute to faraway locations, vacation in distant places even for short periods, and migrate overseas, have all worked against the traditional set-up of community life, where work, residence, schooling, and entertainment all happened within a small distance.

More recently still, the sweeping innovations in communication technology of the last few decades have further eroded the value of our immediate communities, replacing them with virtual ones. First telephones, TVs and radios, and then the Internet and mobile phones have brought about a world where we can as easily communicate with people across the globe as with our neighbours, or avoid face-to-face interaction entirely, preferring to rely on technology for entertainment, education, and exchange of information.

The Corporation

Legal entities independent of religious and governmental frameworks, such as guilds, merchants' associations and knightly orders, have existed since ancient times. The mercantilist period (roughly the 17th century) saw the emergence of a new player in this category of social institution: the corporation. By the time of the Industrial Revolution (the late 18th and early 19th centuries), corporations were generating enough independent wealth to command a significant share of power in society. Indeed, by the mid-19th century, one of the world's first great corporations, the East India Company, managed, as an asset, a large portion of India's territory, employing its own army and complex bureaucracy, and collecting taxes even while its ostensible purpose was merely trade. Today, the market capitalisation (the total value of publicly traded stocks) of companies like Apple and Google is larger than the gross national product of many economies in the world.

It is common knowledge today that corporations assert a great deal of control on governments around the world and that their influence is only growing. What is particularly interesting is that, as a result of globalisation, corporations are becoming increasingly delinked from their countries of origin. They are also redefining how populations are distributed in terms of where they live and work. Unfortunately, corporate interests, which are motivated almost entirely by monetary profits, are often at odds with the interests of consumers, employees, and the natural world.

The role of corporations will be discussed in later chapters on capitalism and economics. For the time being, I merely want to stress the innovative nature of the concept of the corporation, and what consequences it had on social structures. The invention of a type of ownership that could encompass thousands of investors – each owning just a few shares of the corporate project – and that limited the liability of each owner, allowed for the deployment of vast amounts of capital toward profitable trade and manufacture. At the same time, however, the corporation enabled individuals to invest in various creative efforts, trade voyages, and manufacturing initiatives without actually participating in those activities.

This separation of ownership of an enterprise from the activity of that enterprise meant that investors were able to look far beyond the confines of their communities for the development of new business opportunities. In other words, some of their investment went toward faraway activities from which they hoped to reap financial gain, rather than into local initiatives that required personal involvement. By the same token, the workers hired by corporations in far-flung locations laboured no longer to supply local customers with the crops and merchandise they needed, but rather for customers with whom they had no connection.

Above all, the capital aggregated and mobilised by corporations fuelled the industrialisation of manufacturing, so that large, mechanised factories took over the role previously played by small, village-based cottage industries. Labourers migrated in large numbers to the urban centres where factory work could be found and left their rural communities behind.

The Bureaucratic State

The idea that a community of people living in a particular territory ought to be governed by an institutional framework that is independent of hereditary lineage may not seem all that special today, but it is a very modern phenomenon. As Francis Fukuyama explains in *The Origins of Political Order,* once the modern state was able to choose a ruling class based on ability instead of bloodlines, it was only a matter of time before this meritocratic system of governance overwhelmed the more primitive competitors, which were merely inflated tribes and clans. Increasingly, the nation state governed by a professional bureaucracy has become the locus of the modern citizen's allegiance, both ideological and practical. This is a phenomenon that we shall investigate in greater detail in Chapter 12 – how the lives of individual citizens came increasingly to be governed not by community traditions and covenants, but by an abstract and entirely ideological construct (the nation state) based on a gross identifier, such as language or ethnicity. In essence, the rise of the centralised nation state as the most common political model has meant an ever-diminishing role for local communities in the construction of culture and identity.

The world is still coming to terms with a revolution in social thought and organisation caused by the relatively recent historical developments I have just described. These developments have resulted in an increasingly atomised society, in which individuals act almost exclusively according to their own volition and priorities, abstracted from their context (their immediate community) while accepting guidelines set by a faraway and highly abstract political entity (the nation state), itself heavily influenced by the economic interests of a few impersonal entities (corporations, unions, and special interest groups).

First Dimension Society

Throughout much of history, communities have been held together by a variety of forces: kinship, ethnicity, ties of faith, fear of the other, a need for defence, child-rearing and security, the ability to optimise resource use by banding together, and so on. Traditional society functioned as one giant insurance policy and was often sanctioned by religious institutions. Modern society, on the other hand, has rendered this obsolete in many ways. The biological imperatives (such as the need for water, nourishment, shelter, and protection) that drove most of social organisation in earlier times have been conquered to a large degree. Improvements in technology and shifts in ideology have enabled us to prioritise our own wants and needs over those of our extended families and communities. The modern individual does not need any social insurance from family and immediate community because he or she is taken care of (at least conceptually) by the larger institutions of the state, allowing the individual to pursue his or her own interests independently of the community. The current period – the last one hundred years or so – is the first time we have managed, thanks to a variety of innovations, to exist without an overriding *need* for a community.

How did this come about? In Chapters 3 and 4, I pointed to the rise of individualism as one of the main factors driving the development of modernity. In upcoming chapters (Chapter 6 on liberty and Chapter 7 on rights and freedoms) I will contextualise this notion to show that individualism itself arose in conjunction with the idea of liberty – the freedom to determine one's own fate, to pursue one's own happiness and goals, and to live without fear of coercion or oppression. This notion, which we can trace back to early modern times, was a fundamental catalyst for the development of our current, First Dimension, paradigm. It led eventually to the formulation of certain basic civil and personal rights that reside in the individual citizen. These individual rights are considered inviolable and today form the basis of social organisation.

As I will show in Chapter 8, the codification and elaboration of these individualistic rights and freedoms resulted in an extensive and increasingly complex corpus of laws – normative behavioural prescriptions written down and agreed upon by everyone, and in a justice system to uphold and enforce these laws. In keeping with individualistic rights and freedoms, and individualistic laws, First Dimension justice (the subject of Chapter 9) recognises the individual as the only possible locus of responsibility. By convincing us all that we are free to pursue our own ends and that to do otherwise would make us less free, modern societies have de-emphasised the six elements of our context (mostly influences from our childhood, upbringing, family, and social networks), allowing modern legal systems to hold the individual solely responsible and accountable for his actions. Thus, the First Dimension rips people from their contexts and leaves everyone under the impression that we are independent rational actors, when, in fact, we are inseparable from our contexts, and our contexts are what drive our behaviour. For example, if a criminal suspect was, say, brought up in a violent household by a substance-abusing single parent, and/or in a dysfunctional society that glorified guns and drugs, then perhaps we ought to take this into consideration when assigning responsibility for his actions. I do not mean merely to show leniency because the suspect had a troubled personal history, but rather to involve his family, his community, his supposed mentors, and his educators, in both his punishment and his rehabilitation. Such a broad and balanced thought process cannot be considered in a social system that is solely based on individual rights and responsibilities and where the concept of free will goes unchallenged.

The individual's increasingly assertive demand for self-determination has meant that most First Dimension societies have gravitated toward democratic systems of governance. But, as I discuss in Chapter 10, large, urbanised societies quickly outgrew the direct and genuinely participatory model of Athenian democracy, and were forced to shift to representative democracy, characterised by the election of legislators and executive officers. Such a system, however, is too easily hijacked by tendentious political groups (parties) and special interests. In fact, most First Dimension democracies deceive individuals into thinking that their voice is heard and that they have made a difference by casting a vote, whereas they have merely participated in a hollow and misleading show of egalitarianism. In reality, indirect democracies give the individual a momentary illusion of control (the election) and then promptly remove all decision-making authority to a faraway capital, into the hands of elected officials who are beholden to the special interests that fund their campaigns and the political parties that propel them to the national stage.

Thus, the process of individual liberty, born of a desire to escape the oppression of the tyrants and potentates of old, has ultimately resulted in the alienation of the individual citizen from his or her community and from an authentic process of democratic governance. Governance (discussed in Chapter 11) in most First Dimension societies is carried out by the state – a vast, impersonal, and imaginary construct that centralises power unto itself and operates through multiple impenetrable layers of bureaucracy. The most common model of statehood in recent times has been the nation state – a state purporting to represent a homogenous group of people who share a common language, heritage, or ethnicity. A nation state thus expects to act as a grand community for all its citizens, guaranteeing each one the same individual rights and freedoms. By the same token, it demands the individual's direct allegiance, unmediated by any local community, religious group, or other affiliation. In First Dimension society, the fiction of the nation state as the only social grouping necessary for each individual's well-being, aided by urbanisation, took over the imagination and overwhelmed the need for community. In Chapter 12, we will see how political centralisation of power in the nation state sucked all power to itself, disenfranchising and emaciating local communities, contributing to the fading of the community from its previously central and valued position in everyday life.

By safeguarding the individual's rights and freedoms, the nation state claimed to be the only social entity that mattered. In return, it demanded little: that the individual abide by the law (and the letter of the law was sufficient) and pay taxes. It did not require or expect the citizen to engage in governance, neither at the community level nor elsewhere. All it asked was that the individual participate in the pageantry of periodic elections, while it entrusted real decision-making to its own bureaucracy. This understanding between the state and the citizen meant that the system could dispense with in-between structures of governance and allegiance. The local community became merely a quaint relic of the past, with minimal authority to decide where street signs ought to be located, and how to fund local festivities. The truly important matters affecting the lives of citizens – taxation, education, infrastructure, health, economic development, welfare – were taken over by the centralised apparatus of the nation state.

The fact that the individual had responsibilities only to an impersonal and faraway construct like the nation state, and not to his or her immediate neighbours, meant that the individual was ever freer to pursue his own needs, aspirations, and wishes by exercising his rights – to a more comfortable life, a materially better future, and a more narcissistic form of self-expression. Nowhere was this more evident than in the commercial sphere, where capitalism (which I discuss in detail in Chapter 14) was the most blatant example of individual advantage trumping the needs of the community. It engendered greed and an assured utilitarianism by assigning a value to all interactions, such that if a thing cannot be measured, and if its benefits cannot be quantified and monetised, it has no value at all.

First Dimension society is thus characterised by a utilitarian approach and a focus on monetisation, so as to ascribe a value to everything. As the philosopher Michael Sandel put it in *What Money Can't Buy*, 'The most fateful change that unfolded [...] was not an increase in greed. It was the expansion of markets, and of market values, into spheres of life where they don't belong.' The result of this is that every interaction is seen in a transactional light, and utilitarianism has now infused personal relationships as well as social formations. This is how individuals were taught to become selfish: the prioritisation of self-interest overwhelms all else, and society is valued by how it satisfies the individual's every need. Vedantic philosophy cautions us about the entrapment of an individual whose goal is the satiation of all his sensory desires, because such individuals are enslaved by an endless cycle of craving. Such a mindset will never overcome the 'chains of illusion' (to borrow a phrase from Erich Fromm) that prevent the growth in consciousness.

Second Dimension Communities

Communities and Personal Transformation

Communities are the Petri dish of humanity. The lessons of cooperation and interdependence are best taught in vibrant, close-knit communities because it is in human-to-human relationships, negotiations, settlements, and disagreements that we begin to recognise ourselves in others. Community teaches us about interdependence because in a community we begin to realise that people have different skill sets, which are best used in different ways to generate the maximum benefit to everyone.[31] Once we recognise the interdependence that binds us to one another, we begin to notice and challenge the First Dimension's restrictive ways of thinking and we can move to change them.

The key change in Second Dimension society as I envisage it, therefore, will be a return to community. The community unit – during most of humanity's history – has been the transmittal structure for the templates, social conditioning, and human relationships that we collectively call 'culture'. If we are to bring about a substantial improvement in the quality of human lives, we need to invest in communities and place them at the centre of our lives.

Communities are the basic political, social, and administrative building blocks of society. They are vital in that they teach us about cooperation and understanding, and give us frameworks and reference points through which to form and negotiate our identities. When we work, live, and socialise in close-knit communities, the idea of individual responsibility – let us call it our 'conscience' – is strengthened, because in intimate communities we can see the consequences of our actions on the lives of others. They allow us to participate in society and cooperate with a directness that is lacking in the larger structures of state, bureaucracy, and corporation. Communities facilitate the development of trust in our fellow citizens and our civic institutions, that is, the 'social capital' that Harvard sociologist Robert Putnam has identified as the key ingredient of prosperous societies with a high degree of civic engagement.[32]

The awakening of our conscience is intrinsically linked to awareness of interdependence. Our conscience begins to glow more brightly when we see the interdependent nature of our world and the value of our social relationships. The close interaction that is possible only at the community level helps us to develop a moral compass upon which to anchor our conscience. Communities are, in short, capable of transforming individuals by overriding the elements of our conditioning that I described in Chapter 3 – elements that otherwise steer us toward more selfish, individualistic pursuits like the accumulation of resources, gain of power over others, and self-fulfilment.

The vision of community that I have given here may seem rose-tinted, and its role in fostering a better society in higher dimensions too optimistic. Unfortunately, history, both ancient and recent, is replete with examples of how small communities have made poor decisions, perpetuated primitive or tribal ideals, or led their citizens to act in wrongful, belligerent, or selfish ways, thus promoting violence and ostracism. Small communities can be closed, inward-looking microcosms rife with petty rivalries and jealousies, long-running family feuds, and partisan politics based entirely on kinship allegiances. As Indian social reformer B.R. Ambedkar (1891–1956) famously put it, 'What is the village but a sink of localism, a den of ignorance, narrow-mindedness and communalism?'[33]

We need look no further than some recent events covered by the media in India to remind ourselves of this. For example, in October 2015, in a village in the state of Uttar Pradesh, a Muslim man was murdered by a mob on the suspicion that he had stored beef in his house. A television journalist visited the village and reported in shock about the absolute absence of discernible conscience in the community. The villagers seemed to have lost the ability to see the commonality of human life; they had lost touch with the idea of a collective conscience, and the result was that they condoned the murder of a minority citizen.[34]

Or we can cite various cases of tribal community councils that instigated atrocities against women or members of other castes as a form of punishment for alleged infractions of tribal rules. In January 2014, for example, a group of tribal elders ordered the gang-rape of a young woman in Subalpur, a remote village in the state of West Bengal in India, ostensibly because she had a romantic relationship with a Muslim man from a neighbouring village and could not pay the fine they had demanded. (This incident is similar to the widely reported case of Mukhtaran Bibi from the village of Meerwala in Pakistan. In June 2002, she was gang-raped on the orders of a tribal council to atone for an alleged infraction by her twelve-year-old brother against a higher-caste tribe.)

Clearly, community micro-cultures can encourage and perpetuate the most primitive and barbaric behaviour. Therefore, it is important to clarify what I mean when I speak of the communities of the Second and Third Dimensions. It is misleading to equate such future communities with the isolated, backward villages that Ambedkar inveighed against, and that still make up the majority of rural settlements in many developing countries today. The communities I envision will be largely urban, reflecting the overall shift of populations to large cities. Thus, a Second Dimension community will, in most cases, be an urban unit, that is, a city district or neighbourhood that constitutes an independent municipality but is nevertheless fully embedded in a larger conurbation. It will enjoy a close connection to other communities around it through modern transit systems and, more importantly, it will take part in all the cultural and political manifestations of a cosmopolitan environment. Even those rural communities that will continue to be remote from the centres of cultural and social exchange will be closely connected to the rest of the world thanks to the mass communication technologies that much of the world already enjoys in the present – television, the Internet, mobile telephony, and so forth. These communication tools will ensure that citizens of rural communities have access to the same education, liberal ideals, and political engagement as their urban counterparts.

Communities, I believe, can have a positive effect on their citizens. Close-knit communities with Second Dimension identities – communities that espouse enlightened ideals and implement forward-thinking policies – can slowly push even the most recalcitrant members toward a higher consciousness by overcoming any prior, inbuilt mental programming that conditions individual behaviour.

That this is not only possible but also achievable in the near future became clear to me when I began to travel on Delhi's new metro system a few years ago. My expectations upon boarding the metro in the early days were not very high. After all, I had used India's regular rail system for decades, and I was accustomed to overcrowded platforms, rickety trains that are perennially late, rubbish and human excrement on the rail tracks and in the stations, smelly latrines, and uncouth behaviour on the part of most passengers, who regularly push and shove to gain access to carriages, spit openly, and mistreat other passengers, especially women. I was surprised, therefore, to find that the metro was quite different. It ran on time, and its platforms and carriages were immaculately clean. Nobody spat, shoved, talked loudly, or behaved aggressively. It helped, of course, that the platforms were continually swept by an army of attendants, and that the loudspeakers on the trains frequently repeated public service messages reminding passengers not to spit, sit on the floor, or molest women. Above all, however, I realised that the environment itself – the cleanliness, the on-time arrivals, the sheer functionality of the system – led to a deep sense of pride and responsibility in this communal asset and conditioned passengers to adapt to certain norms of civilised behaviour. In other words, the quality of the environment itself seemed to condition the behaviour of the passengers for the better. (On one rare occasion I witnessed a passenger spitting in the carriage. He was immediately berated by several other passengers for his bad manners and forced to exit the train at the next stop.)

In the same manner, communities characterised by high civic engagement, diversity and sound local administration will naturally nudge their citizens toward greater collaboration and higher consciousness. For this reason alone, the Second Dimension must be built with an empowered community as its basic building block.

A New Administrative Structure

How do we restore community to its rightful place as a determinant of social identity? How do we make it, once again, the primary locus of human activity and exchange? And, lastly, how do we create communities that are built upon and encourage the highest ideals so that they can help their individual members achieve higher levels of consciousness?

To begin with, we must devolve much of the authority and control that currently resides in national or federal government to the local level. In my first book, *Making India Work*, I stipulated that the hierarchy of governance in India should be restructured into four simple levels, as shown in Table 5.1, such that all citizens reside in a social environment that is appropriately scaled to their needs and in which they have a chance to participate in community activities and local governance. I am suggesting now that the same structure be applied in every country.

Table 5.1: Four-level Hierarchy of Governance

Government level	Composition	Maximum population
Community	A geographical unit (such as a rural district, or a small municipality, or a neighbourhood in a large city) consisting of approximately 25,000 inhabitants	25,000
Area	Up to 100 contiguous communities	2.5 million
Region	Up to 10 contiguous areas	25 million
Nation	All regions within a national boundary	Unlimited

My argument is not simply a call for smaller government, or greater emphasis on local government. The concept I am proposing and justifying is the **correct scaling** of government. In a nutshell, we can say that every issue or problem confronting today's citizens and leaders, and every aspect of governance and oversight, has an appropriate level of effective jurisdiction.[35] There are issues and concerns that ought to be addressed at a community level, and others that rightly belong to higher perspectives. For example, a decision on expanding a local park, or whether or not to make a particular street or neighbourhood pedestrian-only, should be taken at the community level. These are issues that have immediate impact on the citizen and should be adjudged by a jurisdiction as close to him as possible. On the other hand, there are problems that cannot be dealt with at the local level, and must therefore be addressed at higher levels, such as managing a large transport hub like an airport, controlling disease outbreaks, or issuing policies on climate change or multilateral trade.

I believe there are, in total, six levels of governance required to manage human affairs appropriately – the four aforementioned levels (Community, Area, Region, Nation) plus two supranational levels (Continent and Global). Examples of each level's responsibilities are shown in Table 5.2.

Table 5.2: Responsibilities of Each Level of Governance

Government level	Example of responsibility
Community	Parks, schools, taxation, healthcare, citizenship, urban design, local roads, local commerce
Area	Water and sewage, power distribution, cultural programmes, welfare
Region	Agricultural policy, higher education, major road networks, airports
Nation	Defence, national transport systems (railways, air ways, etc.), currency
Continent	Riparian systems, disease control, peacekeeping, development aid
Global	Global commons (high seas, atmosphere), migration, climate change

The rationale for correct scaling is quite simple. The success of decentralisation in some countries (such as Switzerland) has shown that citizens participate actively in governance, both as voters and as elected officials, because (*a*) they believe they can have a significant effect on decision-making; and (*b*) they feel that local government is small enough to give each of them a voice and adequate attention to their needs.

Correct scaling of governance starts with the fundamental recognition that people live in communities. They may nominally belong to a nation state, but they do not live in nation states. A nation state is too vast, both as a territory and as an idea, for an individual to belong to. Most citizens feel much too distant from the national centre of power where decisions are being made that affect every aspect of their lives. Even in democratic countries, casting a vote means sending a representative to a faraway capital, with little or no control over what happens next.

Many of the details of how such a reorganisation of society could take place will be discussed in later chapters, but for now it is sufficient to stress the need for community governments to have far greater powers in important matters that are often controlled by regional and federal governments, such as taxation, creating a concept of community-based citizenship, and healthcare. Restoring such authority to the community will not only reshape governance at all levels, but it will also revitalise every citizen's relationship to the structures of local governance and to his fellow members of the community. When individuals recognise the opportunity to have their views heard and to make a genuine impact on the welfare of their village or town, they will participate in decision-making and community activities much more eagerly and frequently, setting the tone for the essential ingredient of democratic government – participation.

Voluntary participation in the various organs of local governance – executive positions, committees, councils, and advisory groups – however, is not enough to instil the proper commitment to community values that will be required in higher dimensions. Harmonious communities of the future will also need a new awareness, in each community member, of the interdependence of all individuals. Indeed, every individual can contribute to the daily functioning of a community (in terms of labour, skill, time, and interest), and a community thrives on the diversity of talent that resides within it.

First Dimension society is often plagued by the polarity of winning and losing. The modern world is structured such that the whole of society focuses on the so-called winners who, while they generate personal wealth, do not necessarily generate social value: a banker is a winner, but a school teacher is not. This is a dichotomy in which basic respect for different roles, types of work, and forms of value creation does not exist. In future societies, therefore, community members must be able to contribute their skills, energy, and time to the community in multiple ways that will harness their individual talents and interests toward an effective, holistic, and cordial coexistence.

Third Dimension Communities

In the Third Dimension, all communities will strive to be communities of consciousness. They will consist of citizens who live together and cooperate with the primary intention of supporting the growth and development of individual and collective consciousness. They will endeavour to bring mindfulness to every activity and decision, creating an environment in which generosity, thoughtfulness, sharing, devotion, and caring can flourish. The ultimate purpose of a community of consciousness will be to develop higher consciousness in all its members. Accordingly, the community will continually provide opportunities for each citizen, either individually or communally, to practice and enhance their level of consciousness through group meditation sessions, spiritual and natural retreats, and advanced study for those inclined to deepen their knowledge through academic channels. Importantly, the appropriate spaces and venues for such activities will be available to every community member, and the time to engage in them will be built into the regular rhythm of life, that is, scheduled as part of everyone's work commitment.

Second Dimension initiatives are meant to bring renewed focus on community life and identity by restructuring the administrative levels of governance, and by giving individual citizens more immediate access to local governance. Once these goals have been achieved, the next step toward the Third Dimension is to give each community even greater cohesion and functionality by reorganising its very labour structure.

Third Dimension communities will require each member to devote a substantial proportion of their time (say, 30 per cent) to voluntary community support activities, and a smaller fraction of their time (say, 10 per cent) to activities that enhance and develop their capacity for meditation, concentration, and spiritual awareness. This leaves only some of their time (60 per cent) available for income generation through entrepreneurship or private-sector employment. These allocations of time would of course be different for individuals who work for the community, or for area or region government agencies, as their main source of employment.

If 60 per cent employment seems insufficient, from a First Dimension point of view, to allow for a satisfactory income and to support a family, we must consider that much else would be different in the Third Dimension. Heightened levels of consciousness will lead to greater powers of concentration and focus, for example, resulting in greater efficiency and productivity in the majority of skilled jobs, such that work at 60 per cent time in the Third Dimension would likely be equivalent to full-time employment in the First. Moreover, participation by the entire adult population in the administration of the community and in the operation of its various services would imply reduced government spending, and thus a smaller tax burden, leaving more income at each family's disposal. (As I will explain in later chapters on economics and money, in the Third Dimension all taxation will be indirect. Individuals will not be subject to income tax, in part because they are already contributing to public expenses in labour rather than money.)

Recall also that the Third Dimension is the Dimension of Transcendence. At this stage, most adult individuals will be advanced practitioners of meditation, and able to recognise and appreciate the inherent logic of a system based on heightened consciousness and cooperation. The dedication of 40 per cent of one's time to the community and to consciousness-enhancing pursuits will not seem like a burden that needs to be monitored or enforced by others. It will come naturally to most citizens because all Third Dimension citizens will find the greatest fulfilment through community participation and a shared effort to raise consciousness.

Part III

A Global Society

6

Liberty: A New Interpretation

The Invention and Rise of Liberty

Liberty is a relatively recent invention. Modernity – everything that we associate with modern life, including the political, economic, and intellectual structures that we take for granted nowadays – is derived ultimately from this ill-defined expectation of individual freedom that we call liberty. Indeed, in everything we do, we are unwittingly guided by the assumption that each individual, by virtue of being human and being alive, has the right and the ability to live freely, to pursue his or her own needs, desires, interests, and forms of expression, with minimal limitations.

The notion of liberty arose originally in reaction to expressions of power by some individuals or groups over others. In ages past, when the rule of law was either unknown or enforced inconsistently, individuals were often subjected by others to violence, theft, and coercion. Even in structured societies, they suffered under the yokes of tyranny, religious oppression, ostracism, serfdom, and slavery. (Indeed, the oldest and most common meaning of 'liberty' or 'freedom' in classical antiquity was the absence of slavery.)[36] The constraints of either lawlessness or oppression meant that most people could not express themselves freely on the political, religious, or economic stage, that they lived in fear of reprisal and strife, and that they were unable to define and pursue their own destiny.

Liberty arose not as a utopian ideal, but as a stabilising factor between competing power structures, such as the sovereign, the aristocracy, religious institutions and, later, the bourgeoisie. One of its earliest manifestations was the Magna Carta of 1215, in which England's barons sought to curtail King John's power by making him sign a charter that guaranteed certain rights, such as 'no unlawful imprisonment'. The competitive dynamics of the struggle for power between classes gave rise to the modern notion of liberty. It effectively created a demand for rules, so that multiple loci of power could coexist.

What prompted citizens of societies of the past to demand greater political and economic liberty from their sovereigns, and, at times, to risk their lives to do so? As a conceptual novelty, liberty owed its formulation to two seminal ideas that themselves came into being over the course of several centuries of Western civilisation: *(a)* individualism, and *(b)* the assumption that human beings are endowed with free will.

In prehistoric times, individualism – the notion of a selfhood distinct from one's family, clan, caste, or class – was probably unknown. The individual simply didn't exist as an independent entity possessing needs and desires of his own, much less the ability to confer legitimacy to a polity. Instead, the subject was an inalienable part of a socially constructed entity consisting of a powerful hierarchy of kinship, ethnic group, and religious group. In such an environment, the notion of free will was also absent. When it came to explaining the unfolding of events, a simple determinism prevailed, focused on the arbitrary will of invisible gods.

Debate on the twin ideas of individualism and free will began in classical antiquity, like so much else. Socrates' trial and execution at the hands of the Athenians has often been interpreted as an example of individualism defying the conformity of society. Ancient philosophers, including Plato, attempted to reconcile human freedom with the law of cause and effect, to hold man responsible for his actions.[37] But it was Christianity that brought these two concepts into the mainstream of Western intellectual debate.

Jesus' message was intended for all those open to his words, irrespective of tribe or kinship group. Each person was treated as an individual worthy of divine grace and blessing. Every person, as one of God's created, could attain salvation through individual effort and renunciation of worldly concerns. Thus, while Christian worship could be a communal undertaking, and Christian belief could be the basis of social organisation, the ultimate purpose of Jesus' sacrifice – redemption of the soul – was an individualistic affair (mediated, of course, by the increasingly complex machinery of the Church). Only the actions and intentions of the individual on earth could yield a passage to heaven. Only belief, commitment, and repentance expressed by an individual could ensure salvation.

At the same time, Christianity taught its followers that they were endowed with the free will to choose between good and evil, right and wrong, and faith and heresy, and that they were therefore fully in control of their spiritual fate. Theologians were vexed by the seeming incompatibility of this free will with the omniscience of God, but they continually found ways to explain the coexistence of both.

The reformative ideas of Martin Luther greatly reinforced the centrality of the individual by suggesting that a faithful Christian was responsible directly and immediately to God, without the intervention of the Church. And while Luther himself did not believe in free will, the Reformation nevertheless taught, in the long run and perhaps beyond Luther's intention, that individuals are free to pursue whatever spiritual practices they wished without being subject to the whims of traditions or institutions. This eventually crystallised in the work of philosopher John Locke, who proposed a vision of religion as a purely voluntary association that every individual was free to adopt or abandon.

Locke's philosophical predecessor, Thomas Hobbes, ascribed to all individuals a natural liberty which entitled them to undertake whatever actions were necessary to defend themselves from their fellow creatures. Locke, though disagreeing with Hobbes on much else, agreed with the postulation of naturally or divinely granted liberty of all individuals, which he presented as an absolute right to preserve one's life and to acquire any goods one needs for survival. To accomplish this, each individual was endowed with physical and mental faculties, including reason and conscience. For Locke, therefore, the individual constituted the basic unit of social and political analysis.

The 18th and 19th centuries witnessed an increasingly central role for the individual. One aspect of the intensified interest in the individual was the rise of capitalism, an economic system that emphasised the individual both as the holder of self-interest and as the source of all legal and economic rights. Adam Smith famously argued that the welfare of society is best served when every person seeks his own, personal advantage, provided he does not violate any laws.

The intellectual culmination of individualism can be found in the utilitarian doctrine, formulated clearly by Jeremy Bentham, that social policy should promote the greatest good for the greatest number of people. It rested on the notion that all individual estimations of utility deserve equal treatment and respect in comparison with all others. Thus, no person could claim that his pursuit of happiness was more or less important than someone else's. A fair society should treat the needs and wishes of each citizen with the same weight. Bentham thus applied Smith's insight to the full range of social interactions. The belief in individualism, therefore, was well entrenched in the Western intellectual tradition by the early 19th century, and it is today the principal component of legal theory and political organisation.

The concept of free will, on the other hand, has been subjected to insistent criticism since the 17th century. Hobbes noted that human beings are self-centred, their actions set in motion by impulses to satisfy their desires. Consequently, if individuals are behaving according to the dictates of self-gratification, then they have no genuine free will. What we think of as free will is, in this line of reasoning, little more than instinct. David Hume further posited that while human will might well bring about actions, such willed actions are the inevitable consequences of prior causes and circumstances. Thus, human beings are part of a material world where every event has a cause with a determined outcome, and therefore, actions cannot be said to arise from an unencumbered willpower.

Modern science, from Newtonian determinism (in which there are no spontaneous movements) to probabilistic models like thermodynamics and quantum theory, brought repeated blows to the idea of self-willed choice. Even more damaging has been the development of our understanding of the human psyche and the role of the unconscious. Today, most philosophers and cognitive scientists agree that free will is a delusion. Our actions, though seemingly free, rational, and independent, are in fact largely conditioned by our subconscious, which is itself a complex agglomeration of inheritance, childhood experience, and the influence of family and other social groups. Indeed, the subconscious is, in my understanding, entirely the creation of the six elements that I defined and discussed in Chapter 3: pre-birth conditions, evolutionary heritage, biological necessities, familial frameworks, social conditioning, and one's life experiences. Individuals who have not yet recognised the presence and influence of the six elements of our context are usually controlled by them, and ruled by the subconscious patterns engendered by this context rather than by a free will arising from the application of 'rational' thought. Thus free will, which we so often assume to be the backbone of liberty, is merely a mirage.

These, however, are academic debates on the presence or absence of free will. Most ordinary citizens in the First Dimension believe that their choices are their own, and that we are all capable of overcoming crude impulses through reason. The concept of free will is so firmly rooted in our cultural formula that almost everyone today continues to accept it, such that it continues to underpin many fundamental aspects of modern life, such as justice systems and economic markets.

In summary, the twin ideas of individualism and free will have been with us for centuries and have conditioned much of our thinking about our place in society. Liberty grew out of them. It took for granted the beliefs that the individual is the fundamental component of all social constructs, and that this individual, in his drive to maximise benefits to his own person, is acting according to a reasoned, rational, and free sense of volition. Liberty is the ultimate entitlement of the individual acting on free will, and it first found expression in the struggle against coercion of the individual by arbitrary power.

The modern idea of liberty has seeped into all aspects of life, replacing traditional forms of social organisation with a new ideology centred around satisfying individual needs. Love is understood as an event between two rational, utility-maximising individuals exercising their free will; consumption is the means to express an individual's free choice in the acquisition of goods and services; elections are mechanisms that transfer legitimacy from individuals to the state; art is an expression of an individual's feelings or his reactions to the reality that surrounds him. Each of these ideas reinforces the others, creating a powerful justification for liberty.

Immigrants to America spread the idea of liberty to the new continent. Many of America's early immigrants were themselves the greatest advocates of liberty, often escaping economic deprivation and religious persecution to settle in a land that they considered the new home of liberty. As a political idea, it replaced the ruler's subject with the voting citizen. As an economic idea, it replaced social consumption with individual desire. As a social idea, it created a new concept for all forms of art, literature, and music, which were turned from religious representations to acts of individual gratification. It transformed every aspect of our lives and became the ideology of modernity.

Such was the power of liberty (along with its twin expressions of individualism and free will) that it became the defining force in the modern world. It drew its power from an ideology that was highly attractive to individuals living under the yoke of theocratic states, feudal monarchies, or dominant ethnic or religious groups. Its central idea – that pleasure, happiness, and freedom are the prerogatives of each individual, and that each person is an economic actor whose wishes need to be satisfied – tinged every major aspect of modernity, from art to economics to democracy.

The frescoes in the Sistine Chapel and the stone carvings at the Ranakpur temple in India existed to please the divine, and were sanctioned by rulers who believed their authority stemmed from the divine. Andy Warhol's art, on the other hand, even while reflecting the primacy of consumerism in popular culture, was an expression of the individual artist's free will and was created for individual consumers. A ruler drew his legitimacy not from his lineage or his defence of the Church, but by the number of individuals who voted for him. Whether Britain should exit the European Union (EU) was determined not by technical experts carefully weighing the consequences of such a decision, but by the capricious will of private citizens voting in a referendum.

The power of liberty came from its continual emphasis on giving each of us the right to pursue our individual happiness. This simple and profound thought led to benefits that many of us have come to accept as a given in the First Dimension. Yet, in the moment of its greatest triumph, liberty began to reveal its deep flaws.

The Shortcomings of Liberty

The first limitation of liberty, as practised in the First Dimension, is that it is incomplete. If we define liberty as the absence of coercion, is it enough to guarantee the fulfilment of man's needs and desires? John Stuart Mill was perhaps the first thinker to suggest that the absence of coercion – later labelled 'negative' liberty – amounts only to a partial liberty. By itself, negative liberty is not enough. It may mean that an individual enjoys the protection of the law and may avail of certain rights in the political and civic arena, but if that same person is poor, malnourished, uneducated, and unemployed, then does he really have the opportunity to pursue his own goals and ambitions? The absence of coercion is, surely, the first step toward the full realisation of liberty, but to be truly free, an individual must also possess the opportunity and the means to do what he or she wants. In more recent debates on liberty, this has been labelled 'positive' liberty, defined as the absence of deprivation.

Today, citizens of many industrialised societies may be said to possess both negative and positive liberty, in adequate measure. In many developing countries, however, large parts of the population still live in poverty, deprived of basic amenities like nutrition, healthcare, hygiene, and with limited access to education. In such circumstances, the lack of coercion is relatively meaningless, because a citizen weighed down by the daily grind of survival cannot be said to live in liberty.

The second limitation of liberty is that it leads, inevitably, to the fragmentation of society into atomised individuals lacking any sense of community. Social commentators were worried about this in the 18th century already. Edmund Burke, for example, predicted that the spread of democratic ideals would undermine the natural order of societies. He suggested that authoritarian forms of government would exploit this dissolution of societal bonds by providing an artificial identity that could remedy the alienation felt by individuals – something that happened, with disastrous consequences, in the 20th century.

The expectation of liberty (especially positive liberty) in many modern-day societies has meant that citizens are increasingly free to pursue their individualistic ends with little or no regard for the welfare of their neighbours and fellow community members. The individual has become solely responsible for his thoughts, preferences, and actions. Ultimately, liberty has generated a sense of narcissism according to which the desires of the individual reign supreme. Satisfying these individual desires, needs, and aspirations has become the primary endeavour of life in the First Dimension. This culture of self-absorption has seeped into all aspects of daily life, as if individuals existed in isolation from each other. The resultant loss of communal identity in the First Dimension, which I discussed at length in Chapter 5, has socially corrosive side-effects like political and social alienation, and unrestricted consumerism.

Liberty in the Second and Third Dimensions

Liberty in higher dimensions is no longer to be understood merely as freedom from oppression and coercion, or from violence and uncertainty, but rather as liberation from the constraints of our physical and mental contexts. This means, first of all, release from the stultifying everyday worry over nourishment, shelter, safety, and health. A supportive, well-structured, and appropriately sized Community ought to be able to guarantee all the necessities of life to each citizen. (A few advanced countries can claim to have achieved this already.) This can only happen if these necessities become synonymous with essential rights and freedoms, and are enshrined in the proper legal and constitutional framework. In the course of the Second Dimension, the citizen will be freed from these constraints and will be able to participate fully in all the new society's functions, including active engagement in matters of governance. She will also be able to turn increasingly to higher pursuits, especially the development of consciousness. Whilst the journey toward higher consciousness is an individual effort that each person must undertake independently, in higher dimensions it will be supported by educational curricula (see Chapter 19) and by the Community (see Chapter 5), especially through school and work schedules that reserve substantial amounts of time for consciousness-developing activities. The new liberty, therefore, can be interpreted as the commitment of a society to help its citizens to transition to higher levels of consciousness.

Second, living in the Second Dimension implies recognition of a fundamental truth: that we live in, and are conditioned by, a densely interwoven world in which we are unable to function properly as isolated individuals. Thus, the myths and narratives of individualism and free will that have given rise to the First Dimension understanding of liberty must be set aside. Indeed, we must recognise that they are fallacies.

Man is a social animal, not a solitary one. He has sought out the company and cooperation of others since prehistoric times. In all civilisations and ages, he has formed deep social bonds with those around him, ranging from simple kinship groups to complex, stratified societies numbering in the millions. He cannot be separated from his community, in physical, psychological, or legal senses. Therefore, I recommend that the rights and wishes of communities should be at least equal to those of individuals. This does not mean that we must throw out the hallowed concept of liberty to which we adhere currently, or its attendant framework of individual rights and freedoms, or the judicial systems to uphold them, but rather that civil rights and freedoms must be rewritten in a manner that accurately reflects man's role in social groups and in the natural world. The new rights and freedoms will emphasise not individualistic needs and desires, but rather those hopes and future plans that can be expressed by communities.

The objective is to shift away from the transactional and self-referential world of the First Dimension by bringing back the context that naturally belongs to every individual, that is, family (both biological and of choice), community, and nature, and the idea that everyone is an interdependent part of these larger entities. This conscious acceptance of interdependence will transform our ideas of responsibility, freedom, and choice.

Here, and elsewhere in this book, 'interdependence' means multiple things. First, it represents the recognition that human beings, as social beings, are interdependent. It makes no sense, therefore, to separate the needs and aspirations of one individual from those of the community he lives in. Doing so may satisfy his personal cravings in the short run, but eventually alienates him from his fellow citizens, and relegates community – once the fundamental constituent of organised society – to a peripheral role in the lives of most people.

Second, interdependence means that all aspects of our lives – from the way we engage in commerce to the way we think about governance; from personal relationships to health; from how we educate our children to the way we plan our cities – are profoundly interconnected. It is counterproductive, in the long run, to plan and develop these various aspects of civilised coexistence in isolation from each other.

In the next chapter, I shall discuss how our notion of liberty has led to the formulation of a canonical list of human rights and freedoms that underpin our assumptions of what civilised coexistence ought to be. But in the First Dimension these fundamental rights and freedoms have been formulated in such a way that they ignore each other. The right to life, for example – the first and most hallowed right that follows from an acceptance of liberty as the leitmotif of modernity – is quite limited in its significance if it is not accompanied by equally valued rights to all the things that make life itself worth living, like the right to clean environments, the right to adequate nutrition, the right to free and efficacious healthcare, and so forth. Building a new framework of rights and freedoms is necessary to transition to a higher concept of human cooperation, and it starts with the understanding that all our endeavours and needs are linked and must be addressed holistically.

As for free will, most cognitive psychologists and moral philosophers now concur that it does not exist, at least when operating within the

First Dimension paradigm. Various experiments have suggested that our decisions to undertake certain actions are often disconnected from a rational, conscious, and verifiable volition. While the accuracy and reliability of such experiments may be called into question, there has been enough research in neuroscience to show that the origin of intentions and actions is an exceedingly complex subject. Author and philosopher Sam Harris, in his succinct essay *Free Will*, aptly concedes that 'the emergence of choices, efforts, and intentions is a fundamentally mysterious process'. Thoughts and intentions, he writes, 'emerge from background cases of which we are unaware and over which we exert no conscious control'. We are all complex products of a variety of factors – genetic, familial, societal, and environmental. These influences coalesce in our subconscious, which inexorably determines our choices and actions in the First Dimension.

'Consider what it would take to actually have free will,' writes Harris. 'You would need to be aware of all the factors that determine your thoughts and actions, and you would need to have complete control over those factors.' While complete control may be an unattainable target, awareness is not.

Free will is not possible while we are controlled by the six elements of our context, which are working away in our subconscious. Recognising and accepting them is the first step toward overcoming them. Once we are able to see the complex forces that have shaped us, we may work toward transcending our biological and social conditioning. Only by overcoming our conditioned identities can we attain true consciousness, breaking free of the programming of the six elements of our context. And only when we have gained true consciousness will we be able to express a genuinely free will – the ability to look dispassionately at our motivations and subject them to reason and compassion. From this can arise true liberty.

7

Rights and Freedoms: A Detailed Formulation

Rights and Freedoms as Hallmarks of Modernity

In premodern times, specific rights, if they existed at all, were typically bestowed upon subjects by the sovereign or by a religious authority, as a matter of benevolence, not a legally constructed norm. They were, therefore, temporary, revocable, and limited in scope and application. They were valid in a finite jurisdiction, and often restricted to matters of religious worship and trade. Examples included the right to worship in a place or with a rite different from the one practised by the majority, and the right to conduct certain commercial activities, such as moneylending or the import of luxury goods, within the sovereign's jurisdiction. Such covenants were concessions rather than rights, and were neither codified nor managed by dedicated institutions of government. Moreover, they were often granted to groups – religious congregations, guilds, ethnic minorities, family businesses – rather than individuals.

The social and intellectual trends toward greater individualism and free will brought about an increasing desire for liberty. The concept of liberty began as relief from oppression and injustice, primarily political or religious. But in time it evolved into something much greater and more encompassing – the idea that all individuals are free to choose their own destiny. To do so, the individual must possess certain unalienable rights that exist regardless of the political and social order in which he lives. The need to protect and support these rights created a demand for a type of government that, instead of merely guaranteeing and legitimising the rule of a sovereign, could guarantee and protect each individual's rights against the claims of others. This, in turn, led to the revolutionary idea of a government rendered legitimate by the consent of the ruled, and the need for the rule of law to codify the safeguards afforded to each individual.

The long and difficult process of defining and agreeing on what constitutes a human and civil right led, ultimately, to the drafting of various documents by lawmakers, rulers, and governing bodies in many parts of the world. These seminal texts sought to clearly and unanimously define the rights and freedoms that we can all agree are indispensable, that is, the rights and freedoms that constitute liberty. Among these documents are the British Bill of Rights (1689), the United States Bill of Rights (1791), the French Declaration of the Rights of Man (1789), the United Nations Universal Declaration of Human Rights (1948), and, most recently, the International Covenant on Civil and Political Rights (1966), and the International Covenant on Economic, Social and Cultural Rights (1966).

While conceived in different historical moments and in reaction to specific historical circumstances, all these efforts sought to establish a minimum standard of human and civil entitlement. Despite their differences, their cumulative effect is the creation of a basic set of rights and freedoms that anyone living in a progressive, democratic 21st-century society would recognise, and that are now enshrined in most national constitutions. Pared down to their most elemental definition, they comprise the following:

- Right to life, dignity, and security of person
- Right to fair treatment under the law

- Right to participate in government
- Right to own and trade property
- Right to education
- Right to marriage and family
- Right to privacy
- Freedom of peaceful assembly and association
- Freedom of thought, conscience, and religion
- Freedom of opinion and expression
- Freedom to work and choose employment
- Right to equal access to public service
- Freedom of movement
- Right to a nationality/citizenship
- Right to participate in cultural expressions

(The first four rights in this list will be discussed in depth in later chapters. I have given them close attention to illustrate how basic First Dimension rights can be refined and extended in the Second and Third Dimensions. We can similarly look at the upgrade of *all* the rights listed above in the Second and Third Dimensions, but doing so would prove overly lengthy and cannot be accommodated in this book.)

In many societies today, an individual can expect these fundamental rights and freedoms to be protected by the state. Living in an organised society, however, entails certain limitations on the behaviour of the individual. Just as I have a right to life and to property, so does my neighbour. This means that I cannot kill him with impunity, or steal his property, even though, as some may argue, violence and greed are natural instincts. This, in essence, is the social contract that political philosophers have discussed since the 17th century, foremost among them Thomas Hobbes, John Locke, and Jean-Jacques Rousseau. The social contract is a compact that individuals enter into when they agree to live together in an organised society. In a simplified form, it is an individual's agreement to relinquish certain impulses and desires to ensure that others do the same. Thus, for example, I agree to give up the desire to injure my neighbour and seize his property provided that he does the same. Alternatively, we can think of it as relinquishing certain freedoms so that other freedoms can be upheld. For example, I relinquish the ability to enslave another human being in exchange for the right to remain immune myself from all forms of bondage.

A fundamental ingredient of the social contract is that the citizens of a society delegate the authority to pass laws and enforce them (that is, to ensure that everyone's basic rights are respected) to a person, institution, or group. This entity – the government – may be a monarch or a democratically elected group of officers, but regardless of its number or composition, it is understood to wield absolute power (sovereignty) over the society that has delegated it, within the bounds of the laws established by that same society. In modern political thought, the primary purpose of government is to safeguard everyone's rights and freedoms by establishing and maintaining a balance between the rights of one individual and the rights of another. The government, therefore, may only secure the rights and freedoms of an individual to the extent that his actions in the exercise of those rights do not result in harm to another citizen.

Limitations of First Dimension Rights and Freedoms

In the classical rendition, liberty is the freedom to do whatever the individual wishes, provided no harm comes to others as a result of his actions. In a simple example, I may own a sports car with a powerful engine, and enjoy driving it very fast. However, driving too fast on roads that I share with other motorists is likely to lead to accidents, resulting in injury to my fellow motorists and damage to their vehicles. Accordingly, the government steps in and curtails my freedom to use my property (my sports car) as I like, by setting a speed limit. If I exceed it, I am now liable for punishment. Thus, in pursuance of the classical conception of liberty, the government has effectively balanced my personal freedom with everyone else's right to life and safety. This adequately describes a First Dimension trade-off in which the concept of rights and freedoms under a social contract works well.

Let us turn now to a more difficult case that exemplifies the dilemmas faced by complex, highly interconnected 21st-century societies. Let us say that I am a wealthy citizen, and that I own a large home that requires a lot of energy to heat in the winter and for air-conditioning in the summer. I also own several large cars that use a lot of petrol. It can be said, therefore, that I consume a disproportionate amount of energy. However, none of my actions is harming any of my neighbours. I am simply exercising my right to property – by owning multiple vehicles as well as a large home with many appliances – and my right to privacy, in that what I do in my own home is nobody else's business, as long as I am not breaking any laws. In short, I am infringing upon no one else's First Dimension rights. The government or the local power utility may try to discourage my excessive consumption of energy by billing above-average use at a higher rate, but as long as I can afford it, there is nothing to stop me from continuing with my energy-intensive lifestyle.

Now consider the fact that my immoderate consumption is generating a disproportionate amount of air pollution and carbon release, so that I am contributing more than most to atmospheric pollution, global warming, and climate change. Thus, without doing anything wrong according to the laws of my society, I am acting against the greater good of the global community. I am, in fact, infringing upon the unspoken rights to health and safety owed to all other human beings, including people whom I have never met, who may well live thousands of kilometres away, or, indeed, people who may not even be born yet.

This example demonstrates the unavoidable interconnectedness of life in our times. No action taken by an individual – however small, private, and seemingly harmless – can be evaluated in isolation from society and exonerated from responsibility to society. All actions have consequences, sometimes distant and unintended, but nevertheless far-reaching and profound. The First Dimension rights and freedoms that we all understand and agree on are simply not equipped to be applied to the complex, multidimensional reality of today.

Liberty has been a seminal and powerful idea that helped us to transition from primitive, often violent, and unfair forms of social organisation, to the more stable and enlightened forms that we espouse today – democracy, justice, and freedom of expression. But like so many First Dimension ideas, it is no longer sufficient. First Dimension rights and freedoms, therefore, must be expanded in scope and meaning to remain relevant in higher dimensions.

Rights and Freedoms in Higher Dimensions

We can begin to rewrite our entire understanding of human rights and freedoms by analysing in greater detail the first and most fundamental of all First Dimension rights, namely, the right to life, dignity, and security. The right to life is far more extensive than its one-line definition suggests. In the first column of Table 7.1, therefore, I have unpacked its current meaning. The right to life, dignity, and security encompasses the following: the right to be protected from violence and crime, or any form of brute force; the assurance that we will not be killed arbitrarily by those in power; the certainty that we will not be tortured or humiliated; and, in many countries at least, the knowledge that even if guilty of a crime, we will not be subjected to the death penalty. This definition of the right to life corresponds largely to a First Dimension view and to what many societies in Europe and other parts of the world put in place in the second half of the 20th century. Many developing societies, however, continue to struggle to achieve simple First Dimension rights even today.

In the second column, the right to life has been expanded in accordance with a vision of a more enlightened future. Simply put, the First Dimension right to life, by itself, is not enough. It guarantees safety from violence and execution, but it does not address the issue of the *quality* of life. Safety from violence may be sufficient to overcome injustice in a primitive society in which might is right, but it fails to yield the comprehensive, multifaceted well-being that we expect in a more advanced civilisation. After all, how valuable is life, if it is lived in misery? How valuable is life, if the citizen has no access to essential benefits like clean air to breathe, safe drinking water, and free and effective healthcare when ill or injured? How good is a life spent in hunger? How fair is life if it is continually exposed to hidden hazards, like pollutants in the goods we use daily, or toxic chemical additives in the food we consume?

Table 7.1: Right to Life, Security, and Dignity of Person in the Three Dimensions

First Dimension	Second Dimension	Third Dimension
Right to life, dignity, and security of person: • Right to be protected from violence and crime • Freedom from arbitrary detention and execution • Freedom from torture and death penalty	• Right to clean air • Right to clean drinking water • Right to beautiful urban and natural surroundings • Right to access open parklands and wilderness areas near one's residence • Freedom from toxic contaminants in our food, water, and communities • Right to peaceful and violence-free habitat • Right to safe environments for women • Right to free healthcare and palliative care • Right to adequate nutrition • Right to a standard of living adequate for well-being • Access to hygienic and discreet public toilet facilities • Right to respectful treatment in all circumstances	• Right to contemplation, including necessary time, venues, and support • Right to a level of mindfulness in all citizens • Right to a level of compassion in all citizens • Rights of unborn generations • Right to life and dignity extended to all living beings

For the Second Dimension, I argue that certain goods and services are indispensable for a wholesome and fulfilling life – a life that is worth living. By explicitly including, in the definition of the right to life, key benefits like clean air and water, peaceful environments, healthcare, nutrition, and modern living standards, I hope to build a new understanding of that right, and to encourage governments everywhere (not just in the developed world) to guarantee these important benefits with the same commitment as they guarantee the sanctity of life. These modified, expanded human rights will form the basis upon which the quality of Second Dimension governance is evaluated.

Finally, in the last column, rights and freedoms have been expanded even further to encompass benefits that we may well consider overly difficult to achieve, sophisticated and esoteric, and unviable. But they will form the core of human interaction in the Third Dimension, though this may not become apparent until the majority has reached the Second Dimension. Under the right to life, Third Dimension entitlements include access to beauty, manifest in urban design and public art; access to wilderness areas within everyone's reach; and the setting aside of adequate spaces and sufficient time to allow every citizen to engage in contemplative pursuits.

Above all, in the Third Dimension every citizen will expect a heightened level of mindfulness and compassion in his neighbours and fellow citizens, to match his own. In other words, it will be the responsibility of the society as a whole, including individuals, enterprises, voluntary associations, and especially government agencies, to ensure that every adult individual expresses the accepted level of consciousness and patience, such that interactions among all citizens will be exclusively peaceful and cooperative. This will be achieved through the reformation of education, governance, ownership, the free-market economy, and justice – all subjects that will be treated in due course in this book. Reformation of society to such a radical degree may seem like a tall order now, but the gradual implementation of Second Dimension ideas will yield the desired results.

In Table 7.2, I examine three other fundamental rights and freedoms – the right to fair treatment under the law, the right to participate in government, and the right to own property. The table further exemplifies how rights and freedoms must be expanded to be enforced fully in a Second and Third Dimension context. I am especially interested in these particular rights because the specifics of how they will be extended are discussed in this book in the corresponding chapters on justice, governance, and ownership, respectively. (For definitions of terms used in the table, the reader may refer to the relevant chapters.) Eventually, however, governments in the Second Dimension will have to develop similarly detailed and expansive definitions of *all* fundamental rights and freedoms.

Table 7.2: Other Rights in the Three Dimensions

First Dimension	Second Dimension	Third Dimension
Right to fair treatment under the law: • Recognition as a person before the law • Right to equal protection against any discrimination • Freedom from arbitrary arrest, detention, or exile • Right to a fair and public hearing by an independent, impartial tribunal • Right to be presumed innocent until proven guilty • Right to free legal defence	• Access to free legal advice • Ability to file class action lawsuits to protect group rights • Right to speedy resolution and enforcement • Right to simple, transparent processes for contract enforcement • Observance of strict statutes of limitations • Right to reduction in number of laws • Right to simple laws distinct from rules and protocols	• Expectation of crime prevention instead of prosecution • Complete rehabilitation of offenders via repentance • Expectation of a high level of conscience and morality in all citizens

Right to participate in government: • Right to vote in local, regional, and national elections • Right to candidacy in local, regional, and national elections • Right to information regarding government decisions and government officers	• Right to vote in Community leader elections only • Right to high-performing leaders and office holders selected on merit in all other government positions • Right to review tenure of any elected officer every year • Right to a detailed plan on how leaders will reach the higher rights and freedoms as rapidly as possible • Right to a periodic review process to score leaders at all levels of government, based on performance • Freedom from governance tainted by political parties, special interests, and other forms of favouritism • Right to fair, transparent, and continual assessment as a government officer • Equal access to employment in government, based on merit alone	• Right to link the quality of governance with the growth of observable traits in the wider citizenry – amount of volunteerism, amount of giving, and amount of service and participation by local citizens • Right to assess the quality of governance by measuring variables like levels of violence, incarceration, and opioid use, and to develop other measures to gauge the level of happiness, compassion, and love in society • Right to assess the quality of the environment, and to develop and measure detailed quality of life parameters

Table 7.2: Other Rights in the Three Dimensions (contd.)

Right to own and trade property: • Right to own movable and immovable property • Right to enter into contracts regarding property • Right to buy and sell property unhindered • Freedom from unfair taxation • Freedom from trespassing • Right to speculate on property value using approved channels • Right to earn interest from loans and equity investments	• Right to own and trade one's own personal data • Right to enjoy common and public goods • Right of apportionment of natural resources • Right of employees to share in the ownership, profits, and governance of private enterprises • Access to public capital without collateral for the creation of new businesses and expansion of small and medium enterprises • Freedom from monopolies and collusive activities	• Right to fair distribution of wealth among community members • Right to affordable prices for immovable property, subject to valuation caps determined by the Community • Right to public works funded by philanthropy of the wealthy

Ramifications

First Dimension liberty is, for now, the seed of our entire social, political, and economic construct. In particular, we can say that the notion of liberty has led directly to the development of the three pillars of modern life, namely, the free-market economy, democracy, and the institution of an impartial judicial authority. In the next few chapters I will take each of these complex structures of modernity in turn, and analyse their aetiology and effects. By way of a preview, I have summarised the undesirable consequences of each 'offspring' of liberty in Table 7.3. This book finds ways to restructure, expand, and revamp each of these pillars, in order to give them a new lease of life, and a new meaning that will be consonant with the needs of 21st-century societies.

Table 7.3: Liberty's Undesirable Consequences in the First Dimension

<table>
<tr><th>Foundation</th><th>Offspring</th><th>First Dimension consequences</th></tr>
<tr><td rowspan="3">Liberty</td><td>Justice</td><td>Degradation of community rights, over-complexification of laws, litigiousness</td></tr>
<tr><td>Democracy</td><td>Political paralysis, inefficiency, abuse and corruption, and the tendency to polarise and appeal to extreme views in order to garner the votes of undecided voters and fringe groups</td></tr>
<tr><td>Free-market economy</td><td>Capitalism, inequality, poverty, environmental degradation</td></tr>
</table>

The reformulation of human and civic rights and freedoms discussed in this chapter is the lynchpin of our movement's ideology, and thus it forms the leitmotif of this book. In the chapters to come, I shall propose a variety of reforms to the fundamental structures of modern civilisation, everything from capitalism to justice to agriculture. All these reform initiatives share the same backbone in that they are founded on a new interpretation of rights and freedoms; and in that the new structures that will come into being in the Second and Third Dimensions will be designed specifically to support, strengthen, and continually develop human rights and freedoms. All leaders of tomorrow, whether heading private firms or government departments, should be evaluated according to their performance in furthering the expanded rights and freedoms. Civic responsibilities like taxation, elections, and education will also be restructured to align with them.

How we define rights and freedoms in the Second and Third Dimensions is crucial to revitalising democracy, improving the quality of governance and justice, and bringing in a new type of economics. When the rights and freedoms we hope to achieve are clearly articulated and can be measured at the relevant level of government, we will be able to move rapidly toward the society we wish to create.

8

Laws: The Rule of Conscience

The Origins of Law

In formal terms, a law is 'a behavioural prescription that a community recognises as regulating the actions of its members and which it may enforce by the imposition of penalties.'[38] Laws are normative social instruments intended to guide human conduct, but they are not the only source of standardised behaviour in most societies. Social conventions, etiquette, a general concept of propriety, and religion also determine human manners in ways that are similar to laws. What sets laws apart from these other behavioural norms is that (*a*) they are written and codified; and (*b*) a coercive force underlies them, because society, through the government and its agencies, has the determination and the ability to enforce them with the threat of punishment.

The oldest known set of behavioural prescriptions that fulfils these two requirements – written and coercive – is the *Code of Ur-Nammu*, inscribed on two clay tablets around 2100 BCE by order of the Sumerian king Ur-Nammu. While it neither discussed the source of legitimacy for laws, nor the rationale for them, it listed a number of crimes and their corresponding punishment. Three centuries later, the Babylonian king

Hammurabi commissioned a more extensive set of laws, known as the *Codex Hammurabi*, and had it inscribed on several steles in his kingdom. It consisted of 282 laws, which identified offences and their punishments, including the well-known admonishment of 'an eye for an eye'.

These examples from ancient Mesopotamia suggest that laws become necessary to manage increasingly complex, stratified societies. Laws like the ones in the *Codex Hammurabi* codify punishments and rewards that maintain balance within societies. Societies flourish only when there is a degree of order within them. Law is the tool that supports the power and authority of the structures that constitute a civilised society. In other words, laws provide legitimacy to the exercise of power.

Ancient history also shows that the growing complexity of societies translated into correspondingly complex written norms. The most illuminating example of this tendency is the *Arthashastra*, a monumental treatise on statecraft compiled in India during the Mauryan Empire (322–185 BCE) and expanded and redacted in the succeeding four centuries.[39] It covers a variety of important topics, including economic policy, military strategy, the duties of a king, ethics, government administration, and a framework which we would today recognise as foreign policy. It also contains twenty chapters on justice. They form a comprehensive body of laws, so detailed as to account for many eventualities found in daily life, from unpaid taxes to wives running away from home. Table 8.1 offers a few examples from the *Arthashastra*'s extensive list of criminal acts and their respective punishments, collated from different sections of the treatise, to give the reader an idea of its scope and detail.

Despite its unprecedented scope and influence on Hindu theories of statesmanship over the following millennium, the *Arthashastra* was forgotten by about the 12th century CE and was rediscovered only in 1904. The first English translation was published in 1915.

Far more consequential to the modern concept of legislation was Roman law – an intellectual effort that gained momentum at roughly the same time as the *Arthashastra*. The writing of the Twelve Tables was perhaps the earliest attempt on the part of the Romans to create a complete legal corpus. A commission of ten men (*Decemviri*) was appointed in 455 BCE

Table 8.1: Some Criminal Acts and Punishments Listed in the *Arthashastra*

Offence	Punishment
Suicide	No funeral rights; body dragged through the streets
Seller not delivering movable property sold along with immovable property	Fine – 24 panas (silver ingots)
Falsely accusing a bride of not being a virgin	Bride may repudiate her husband, reclaim her dowry, and not reimburse marriage expenses
Husband falsely accusing wife of refusing to sleep with him	Fine – 12 panas
Wife caught in adultery	Mutilation by cutting off the nose and an ear, or 500 panas
Stealing from a corpse	Cutting off both feet, or 600 panas
Throwing vomit, urine, or faeces at someone equal in status	Below the navel – 12 panas Above the navel – 24 panas On the head – 48 panas
Abducting, confining, or disfiguring a prostitute	1,000–2,000 panas depending on status
Killing deer or birds in protected forests	200 panas

to draw up a code of law that would be binding on all parties and which magistrates (initially, the two elected consuls) could enforce impartially. Besides listing criminal behaviour and corresponding punishments, the Twelve Tables described proper procedures for court trials and the settlement of debts, and codified, on the basis of customary norms, such fundamental concepts as family rights, legal guardianship, inheritance, commerce, and land rights.

Roman law was cumulative, so that new laws could be added to the legal corpus or supersede previous ones. As the republic grew in population, extent, diversity, and power, and eventually morphed into an empire, the Twelve Tables were no longer sufficient to address all legal and constitutional matters. They were rapidly overlaid with a multitude of statutes, senatorial decrees, decided cases, and edicts from the emperor, magistrates or other officials. In the later empire, Roman jurists attempted to compile all the sources of law into compendia. The last and most comprehensive was the *Codex Justinianus*, willed by Justinian I, who ruled the Eastern Empire from 527 to 565 CE. In addition to a summary of the laws of the empire, Justinian's work also contained a vast collection of all the classical jurists' writings on law and justice.

Though largely forgotten during the Dark Ages, the compilation of Justinian (and through it, Roman law as a whole) experienced a revival from the 11th century onwards. New editions of the work were given the name *Corpus Iuris Civilis* (Body of Civil Law) and became the foundational source for civil law in the Western tradition. Indeed, when legal scholars instructed by Napoleon to modernise French civil law set about their work in the early 19th century, they based their efforts on the *Corpus Iuris Civilis* in order to override the motley patchwork of feudal laws that had been in use in France since the Middle Ages. Similarly, legal scholars in Germany reached back to Roman law when writing the foundational text of German civil law, the *Bürgerliches Gesetzbuch*. Most systems of law prevailing today have borrowed heavily from one of these two modern codes.

There is, however, a competing concept of law in use in many countries – common law. The term 'common law' dates to 12th-century England, where King Henry II established secular English tribunals in which judges were to dispense justice fairly and evenly by adhering to a 'common' (that is, uniform) understanding of law. This common law superseded all older legal codes and relied for uniformity on the idea that each judge must emulate decisions made by other judges in similar cases. Common law is, in theory, not codified – unlike Roman civil law, it does not rely on a comprehensive compilation of legal rules and statutes from which to derive legal decisions. Instead, it is based largely on the application of customary law and, increasingly as more decisions are handed down, on documented precedents. As a result, individual judgments can become normative and binding on future cases. Judges, instead of legislative assemblies, thus become the primary lawgivers. This system of law spread to all corners of the British Empire and remains in use (though mostly in a form mixed with civil law) in many English-speaking countries, including the United States and India.

In the foregoing paragraphs I have outlined briefly the historical development of written, codified laws. I have, however, skirted around the key issue that has always framed all debates on legal theory: where does the very idea of law originate? Where do we derive the ability to distinguish lawful from unlawful? How do laws, written or unwritten, acquire their legitimacy?

The oldest answer to these questions is the concept of natural law, which has ancient roots in the work of Aristotle, and was the subject of various formulations by St. Thomas Aquinas, Thomas Hobbes, Hugo Grotius, and John Locke, among many others. In a modern, secular interpretation, natural law means that right action is immanent in nature, and can be discovered and identified through the normal process of resolving conflicts by applying reason. In other words, there is such a thing as morality, which is universal by virtue of occurring in nature, and humans are predisposed to it, that is, they are able to distinguish between right and wrong. The desire to live, for example, is a natural instinct found in all living creatures, including man, and therefore the right to protect one's life is a natural law. From this follows the realisation that all men and women must have an equal desire and right to enjoy their lives. The only reasonable conclusion is that killing another person wantonly is unlawful. Similarly, the natural propensity of all humans to make their living conditions more comfortable has given rise to a variety of goods, from umbrellas to iPhones, and possessing such goods is therefore lawful, whereas taking them away from others by force or stealth is not. Secular natural law thus represents a system of norms derived from the physical, biological, and behavioural processes of nature as perceived by the human intellect and elaborated through reason.

In opposition to natural law is the equally widespread concept of positive law, according to which law is entirely a societal phenomenon, not a natural one. Legal positivists argue that laws are man-made behavioural norms that are prescribed by a sovereign or government. Their legitimacy lies in the government's monopolistic ability to enforce them through the threat of punishment. In such a legal order, laws need not necessarily be just or conform to any prevailing sense of morality. They merely need to be enforceable by the sovereign authority. Indeed, throughout human history the law has been a coercive concept, enforcing behavioural norms on the sovereign's subjects by means of threats and violence. Laws are therefore linked to the power structure of the state and of the individuals who control the state, and this often creates a powerful, deeply entrenched elite who use the law to gain authority.

In this view, several forces drove humanity toward adopting a system of positive law, the most powerful of which was the need of a ruler or sovereign to impose his will upon his subjects. This included the desire to maintain control over the terms of commerce in the market economy, to legitimise one's rule through organised religion, and to justify territorial expansion. Ultimately, positive law stems from a small group's desire to gain control over other, larger groups, and to restrict control of resources and their exchange. Laws were written by those in power, and maintained through social conditioning (including religion), peer pressure, and fear of retribution.

The Proliferation of Laws

The advent of modernity brought about a great struggle for supremacy between the laws of ethnicity and community, and those of society, the state, and the sovereign. The winner was the modern state, whose laws became pre-eminent, backed by the various legal and judicial institutions of the modern state. These laws, made by people's representative forums, had a greater legitimacy and were backed by the full authority of the modern state and its various organs. They were built upon the idea of individual liberty and rights and freedoms as enshrined in a constitution. The most important feature of the modern state's sovereignty was its monopolistic authority to impose its law upon the people living within its jurisdiction. This idea of the 'rule of law' became the *raison d'être* of the modern state, which styled itself as the provider and guarantor of law and liberty.

Just as the Twelve Tables became outdated and inadequate to fulfil the needs of a Roman society rapidly growing in number, complexity, and geographical extent, so too the written rules upon which modern societies rely – constitutions, bills of rights, penal and civil codes, rules of trade – have had to be revised and amplified continually, and have been overlaid many times with new regulations. This is an inevitable result of the development of stratified, diverse civilisations in which the complexity of competing interests can no longer be solved through simple legislation that can easily be summarised in a handful of commandments or a pair of clay tablets.

For example, a merchant who falsifies his record books to conceal his revenues and thus avoid taxation is a straightforward case of fraud that would require little or no written law at all. We would all agree that his actions are fraudulent, and any sensible, educated person could be called upon to establish his guilt and recommend a suitable penalty. But what about a more elaborate case of corporate tax evasion, of the kind that happens frequently in the modern global economy? Large multinational corporations can set up regional or global headquarters in countries like Ireland, where they have pre-negotiated tax breaks, and then transfer a huge portion of their revenue to this entity by charging their subsidiaries in other countries hefty fees for centralised corporate services like accounting, human resource management, marketing, and so forth. In doing so, they may not be breaking any one country's laws, but they violate the spirit of what was intended by the tax regimes in all the countries where they sell their products or services. Is this fraud? How can anyone understand, let alone pass judgment on, such a difficult scenario without the help of extensive and detailed written regulations to parse out its complexity, and an army of lawyers, accountants, and inspectors to perform the analysis and debate its finer points?

Indeed, laws in all countries have become so extensive, detailed, and hermetic, that most citizens cannot understand them. In many cases, they have to resort to the expensive services of specialists to be able to enforce their rights in courts of law or in the face of the massive and labyrinthine workings of government bureaucracies. A case in point that has been much debated and derided in the popular media is tax law in the United States. Many commentators and politicians have lamented its monstrous length, pointing out that the official set of federal tax laws (that is, the statutes regarding taxation that have been passed by Congress and are compiled in Title 26 of the *US Code*) is 2,600 pages long. As conservative politicians have mentioned repeatedly, this is twice as long as the Bible.

And yet these pages are merely the tip of the iceberg. To fully comply with tax regulations, individuals and businesses must also peruse the more detailed tax regulations contained in the *Code of Federal Regulations*. These are further rules issued by the competent government agencies (in the case of taxation, the Internal Revenue Service on behalf of the US Department of the Treasury) to explicate and specify what is left unsaid in the *US Code*. On taxation, these regulations are set down in approximately 9,000 to 13,000 pages, depending on whose estimate you believe. And even this is not enough, because a lawyer or accountant involved in tax litigation would probably have to consult the massive corpus of case law pertaining to taxation, which currently consists of over 70,000 pages.[40]

How did laws become so lengthy and complicated? Our cherished sense of individualism requires that all laws must apply with equal precision to every individual, corporation, and instance, no matter how varied human experience may be. Thus, there ought to be as many laws as there are human experiences, to adequately cover every situation in which we might find ourselves. And because we have come to see the state as the guarantor of our liberty, and therefore of all our rights and freedoms, we expect it to insulate us from all conceivable threats to life, security, or well-being. Indeed, we have become entirely dependent on the state to formulate and enforce proper behaviour, and this has absolved individuals and communities from having to make moral decisions on their own.

In mandatory situations, such as the penal code and the tax code, our incessant efforts to shirk our responsibilities mean that government must continually modify and expand laws to account for new behaviours and new tactics of avoidance. In voluntary scenarios, the need for regulation is even greater. When we walk into a restaurant, we expect that the restaurant fully complies with health and safety regulations. When we seek treatment at a hospital, we expect that all safety and biohazard regulations have been adhered to, and that the hospital employs qualified personnel and carries the necessary malpractice insurance. When we send our children to school, we expect the school to comply with all safety rules, to employ teachers and administrators who have the proper certifications and have been subjected to background checks, to follow all guidelines on curriculum and testing, and to offer programmes for children with special needs. When we enter an office, we expect it to have followed all building codes, including fire safety and disability access, to be fully insured against mishaps, and to regulate the behaviour of all employees so that we are not subject to abuse, exploitation, or sexual harassment. When we shop at a supermarket, we expect all products to have been grown, processed, and packaged according to strict safety and hygiene standards, and to be correctly and fully labelled so that we can avoid allergens, contaminants, and expired ingredients. When we buy an electronic product or a pair of jeans, we expect that the manufacturer has obeyed all laws regarding quality assurance, safety testing, fair labour practices, and disposal of waste.

These are our expectations as consumers in the economy and citizens in the society we share. Because these expectations are so extensive, diverse, and detailed, we need laws that are equally sophisticated. Essentially, we want every potential instance of disagreement predicted and legally described, either in statutes and regulations (civil law) or, at the very least, in legal precedents (case law). As a result, we live in an environment where the average citizen is far removed from the impenetrable thicket of laws, neither fully understanding them nor able to comply with or contest them without the help of specialists, often with considerable cost, difficulty, anxiety, and commitment of time and other resources. In the face of such alienation, I must ask: is this the realisation of the dream of a civilised, rational, effective society? Is it the culmination of all our aspirations to liberty, democracy, and fruitful coexistence? Is the law, as we know it, a manifestation of liberty or an impediment to it?

The current state of law is not only a practical handicap in everyday life but also a pressing economic problem. Excessive regulation in business leads to higher costs for the consumer, because companies have to invest heavily in compliance officers and procedures, as well as insure against all potential litigation. Legal obstacles to starting and operating businesses make an economy less competitive, leading to losses in productivity, employment, and especially investment. And large, beneficial infrastructure projects are frequently delayed, or shelved indefinitely, because of the need to comply with myriad national and local laws.

The sheer multiplication of laws and statutes, and the corresponding exponential increase in the complexity of the legal system, means that legal matters can no longer be understood, let alone litigated, by a layman. Legal proceedings are the exclusive preserve of highly specialised, skilled, and sought-after attorneys and legal experts. Only these experts, who have expensive educations and years of experience specialising in a particular type of proceeding and navigating the maze-like environment of legal confrontation, may hope to participate in the process. Their knowledge of the legal system and its various loopholes, hidden traps, extensions, and exceptions allows them to exploit the system in the client's favour, often dragging out proceedings until the opponent has exhausted their patience or financial resources.

Not surprisingly, such skill and specialised knowledge comes at a high price. The Laffey Matrix (a widely used schedule of reasonable hourly rates for attorneys in the United States) reports that in 2015 the average hourly compensation for an entry-level lawyer with less than three years' experience was about $330, while an experienced partner with twenty years of bar experience typically billed close to $800 per hour. At the top corporate law firms, these rates can be even higher. The *National Law Journal* reported in 2014 that senior partners at top law firms in New York often charged in excess of $1,000 per hour. At such firms, even the time of a simple paralegal may be billed at close to $200 per hour. These exorbitant legal fees have translated to high overall legal costs. The US-based non-profit organisation National Center for State Courts reported in 2013 that a simple automobile tort case typically cost $43,000 to litigate, while a malpractice suit had a median legal cost of $122,000.

In the high-stakes corporate arena, these costs can balloon quickly. A survey of Fortune 200 companies undertaken by Duke Law School in

2008 found that these firms paid, on average, $115 million in outside litigation costs each year. Another report issued in 2008 by the litigation outsourcing firm eLawForum (now DryStone Capital) estimated that the combined spending by Fortune 500 corporations on litigation was $210 billion, equivalent to one-third of after-tax corporate profits and dwarfing other much-debated costs, such as chief executives' compensation. The legal system, in other words, has become the domain of the wealthy, because only companies and individuals with deep pockets have the resources to persevere long enough to prevail.

In India, the legal system has become a punishment to anyone who dares to tangle with it. The backlog of cases is legendary. At the end of 2013, there were over 30 million open cases pending in Indian courts, including four million in high courts and 65,000 in the Supreme Court. As a result, most of India's vast prison population are detainees awaiting trial, not convicted felons. Courts in important metropolitan centres are hopelessly clogged by decades-old land and property disputes, hindering commercial and industrial development. This colossal inefficiency in India has more to do with the dearth of judges, endemic corruption, and incompetence, than with anything else. Nevertheless, it shows how easily a First Dimension legal system can be paralysed beyond repair by the existence of too many incomprehensible laws that can be so easily abused in a litigious society.

Finally, the proliferation of laws has given rise to intellectual problems as well. In the dense tangle of rules and protocols that seem to regulate everything from a lemonade stand to a multinational conglomerate, we have lost sight of the moral core of law-making. Today, much of our effort goes into observing the letter of the law rather than the spirit of the law. This has effectively removed any sense of individual responsibility from thinking about or even being aware of one's obligations as members of families, communities, businesses, and nations. As a result, even discussion of the moral basis of laws has been removed from public debate because such a debate cannot take place when society itself is overwhelmed by the sheer number and complexity of rules.

It is easy to see that rules proliferate in the absence of moral responsibility and conscience. I recently signed a 4,200-page shareholder's agreement, and it surprised me to find out that nowhere in the contract was there any mention of any moral obligation to behave humanely. Page after page in dense legalese covered improbable eventualities but failed to capture the essence of so fundamental a thing as 'behaving morally'. If one sets out to cover every eventuality, a contract could stretch to infinity. The tireless efforts of lawyers to cover everything ends up creating an absurd level of convolution.

Clearly, there is a deep and urgent need to redefine our understanding of the law, starting with a drastic simplification in the number, length, and level of detail of laws to which both individuals and businesses are subject. I am neither the first nor the most eloquent commentator to suggest this, but perhaps I tread new ground in proposing that freedom from excessive regulation, and ease of doing business, ought to be guarantees in their own right. Indeed, the right to a simple, accessible legal code that can be exercised by everyone without the help of lawyers is a cornerstone of the Second Dimension.

The Limitations of First Dimension Law

Complexity and Literalness

The most obvious drawback of First Dimension law is that the volume and complexity of legislation have far outstripped the citizen's capacity to comprehend all the legal implications of living in a large society, and to stay abreast of the frequent changes in the legal corpus. The exercise of one's rights via the legal apparatus has become so unmanageable as to require highly paid specialists and extensive funds to be effected. The complexity of modern legal systems has thus alienated the average citizen from the law itself. The notion that a wronged individual could present himself to his chieftain or sovereign to seek justice – a justice he could demand on the basis of moral principles derived from natural law or from tradition – is as improbable today as it is quaint.

This alienation is compounded by the remoteness of modern-day social responsibility. The exercise of conscience on an individual level is no longer necessary because we have entrusted the creation of laws and the administration of justice to the machinery of the state – a vast, bureaucratic, and impersonal entity. Today, it is government, acting through its various branches (the legislature, the judiciary, and law enforcement agencies), that is responsible for ensuring order. Indeed, First Dimension law depends entirely on the state for implementation, and absolves individuals and communities from having to make moral decisions. We can safely ignore the prompting of our consciences because it is not in our hands to ensure that justice is carried out. The First Dimension leaves no room for conscience to develop because we do not have to take ownership of our actions and their consequences. When we conform to the law, we do not do it out of concern or respect for the needs and rights of our neighbours or fellow community members, but only out of fear of being fined or arrested. When we break the law, we often do it with only perfunctory feelings of guilt, because we feel we are acting against the dictates of a distant and oppressive legal entity, not against our neighbours or fellow community members.

This apathy encourages us to flaunt the law whenever we can. We continually under-report our earnings to reduce our tax burden, we drive faster than the speed limit whenever we can get away with it, and we engage in litigation over property whenever there is an opportunity, a loophole, or a technicality, which will allow us to gain something that we know does not properly belong to us. Even when we abide by the law, we do so only to the letter of the law. In the First Dimension, individuals and corporations are not required to exercise moral judgment as long as they follow a literal interpretation of the law. Doing what is morally right is replaced by doing what is legally defensible, though the two are often quite different. Even using loopholes and exploiting so-called grey areas is condoned as long as we (and our lawyers) feel we meet the most literal interpretation of the law. The state absolves us as long as we are 'law-abiding' in the most technical sense and thereby acknowledge its monopoly on the law. This reduction to literalness is the second fundamental limitation of First Dimension law, and it stems ultimately from the fact that the law is no longer rooted in a moral foundation.

Laws Favour Elites

Another limitation of our current concept of the law is that it favours society's elites. First Dimension law is largely a positive law created by the elites in whichever society it exists. Historically, the elites who controlled and benefited most from the establishment of laws were just a monarch and his immediate family and followers. Later, elites were synonymous with landed aristocracies. Today, elites are such primarily on account of wealth. The makers of laws (legislators) require sizeable war chests in order to be elected to office, and no law can be passed without extensive negotiation between political parties, unions, special interests, and corporate representatives, in a process that favours the stakeholders who can devote the most funds to lobbying and publicity campaigns. Meanwhile, users of laws (litigants in the judicial process) are also at an advantage if they are wealthy. As noted earlier, the exercise of laws in the judicial process is expensive and favours litigants who can afford the best lawyers and technical experts. Even in most developed countries, the professed central principle of First Dimension legal systems embodied in the maxim 'all are equal under the law and entitled to a fair trial' rarely applies in practice. Wealthy individuals and corporations can hire the more highly trained lawyers and prolong the legal battle till the opponent's resources and patience are exhausted; they benefit from a huge bias because of their social position, and in many cases from laws that were written with their interests in mind to begin with.

The Legal Person as a Rational Actor

The final limitation of First Dimension law is that it is based on the idea of a rational, utility-maximising individual whose behaviour can be controlled by a series of incentives and deterrents. As we have seen in Chapter 4, this is the most crippling aspect of the First Dimension, because this individualistic understanding of the law ignores everything that makes us human, like the six elements of our conditioning (pre-birth conditions, evolutionary heritage, biological necessity, familial frameworks, social conditioning, and life experiences). It posits that the fundamental locus of behaviour and responsibility is the individual, and offers no alternative concept of lawfulness.

By extension, First Dimension law removes any context from the actions of the individual and makes him solely responsible for his actions. We know well, however, that personal histories inform our behaviour and our modes of thinking. Someone who was raised in an abusive home or who suffered trauma (such as a war) may have a severely impaired ability to assimilate. And yet even the subject himself is unlikely to be able to see the extent of this impairment, because to do so requires a level of consciousness that rarely exists in the First Dimension. The erasure of context prevents us from appreciating the effects of our actions on both ourselves and those around us, and the power that knowledge has to alter behaviour.

Simplified: The Law in the Second Dimension

Our first task, in the Second Dimension, is to radically simplify the corpus of laws. This can be done, first and foremost, by shortening laws and reducing them to their essential civic value. Laws are powerful things, almost mystical things, that ought to be referenced directly to the extended rights and freedoms that the state guarantees to its citizens. Today, too many laws have been trivialised with excessive detail and casuistry, such that they are often confused with rules and protocols. Let us begin, then, by distinguishing the three forms of legal regulation:

- A **law** is a social covenant dealing with a profound, all-encompassing principle related to the creation, extension, and deepening of a right or freedom.
- A **rule** is the adoption of a generally accepted set of parameters to achieve the principal objectives of the law in an operational realm.
- A **protocol** is the transmission of a generally accepted best practice into a template (akin to good housekeeping).

Laws, at the top of the hierarchy, ought to be succinct and lucid, and need only be revised or added to on rare occasions, when a fundamental change in a society's needs or beliefs has occurred. The desegregation of schools, the decriminalisation of homosexuality, the new definition of privacy in the age of electronic data – these are landmark issues that signal a fundamental shift in our understanding of what it is to be human and a member of society, and therefore merit the attention of the highest legislative body. They must be enshrined in new laws because they are at the vanguard of human development. They should be aspirational, pointing the way to an ever more enlightened future, rather than merely reacting to current events or pressure from entrenched interests. Stripped of cumbersome legal language and specific applications, such laws ought to take up no more than a few sentences of text.

Rules and protocols will operationalise laws by filling in the details, describing variances in specific circumstances, and providing practical guidance in their application. They will be composed and maintained by specialised government agencies staffed by experts. In the Second Dimension, they will continue to be enforceable, maintaining the full vigour of law.

By way of example, let us take one of the fundamental Second Dimension rights – the right to clean air (itself an offshoot of the First Dimension right to life). From this indispensable right, one may derive a handful of laws governing access to clean air. These laws would be quite brief and simple, not much more complex than a simple statement requiring that all citizens have free, uninterrupted, and unfettered access to air deemed to be clean enough for human consumption by the appropriate environmental agency. From these laws could be derived rules to make the laws practicable. In this case, the rules would most likely consist of a set of indicators of air quality, and the minimum measured values required to fulfil the law. Finally, a more comprehensive and detailed set of protocols would further elucidate how, where, when, and by whom the rules must be upheld. These protocols are essentially 'best practices' developed and added to, over years of operations. In this case, they would contain technical details such as the equipment to be used, the proper location where the equipment must be installed, how frequently measurements must be made, how daily and annual averages are to be computed, what international standards are to be applied to the measurements, what audit procedures must be observed, and so forth. The protocols would also include mandatory benchmarking so that we can measure ourselves against the most advanced standards, which are constantly evolving.

The multi-tier structure of laws, rules, and technical protocols, you might argue, already exists in many First Dimension areas of law. Referring to the discussion of US tax laws earlier in this chapter, for example, we might very well say that Title 26 of the *US Code* constitutes the laws, while the rules are found in the *Code of Federal Regulations*, and the protocols in other documents, including the many volumes of case law pertaining to taxation. Now imagine that the 2,600 pages of tax law could be stripped down to 26, and the roughly 10,000 pages of Internal Revenue Service (IRS) rules could be condensed and simplified to 100. How could such a radical diminution be achieved?

The answer is to push more and more legal requirements down to the level of technical protocols, and to further rationalise these protocols by making them universal, such that authorities in different jurisdictions, even different countries, can adhere to the same standards. If we live in a world where human rights and freedoms are considered universal and transcend all boundaries, then laws derived from them ought to be equally universal, and so on down to the level of protocols.

Some of the most useful protocols already govern many activities that are indispensable to modern life. For example, national accounting standards like the US Generally Accepted Accounting Principles are gradually being subsumed under the International Financial Reporting Standards (IFRS), which represent a common language for businesses everywhere and will ensure that company accounts are legible and comparable across international boundaries.[41] In a completely different field, the Federal Aviation Administration's safety regulations, which have helped to create the safest, most reliable, and most efficient air transportation system in the world, have become a *de facto* global standard for commercial air travel. The Basel Accords, whose third iteration came into full effect in 2018, form the core of a universal standard of banking regulations and procedures.

Detailed, exhaustive regulations are necessary in highly technical domains, but they can be confined to protocols consulted only by specialist users like aviation engineers and risk managers. They form a blueprint for the day-to-day operation and maintenance of vital systems like banking, transport, electronic communications, and environmental protection. They should not, however, be confused with laws, which must remain foundational interpretations of our endeavours as a civilisation, accessible to all in meaning as well as relevance.

Ultimately, the success of a Second Dimension society will lie in how accessible Second Dimension laws are and how well they create the conditions for the preservation and extension of more sophisticated rights and freedoms.

Conscience: The Law of the Third Dimension

Ultimately, the simplification of laws and their reduction into rules and protocols will not be sufficient to yield a synoptic legal primer, one that is short and clear enough to encapsulate society's entire expectation of behaviour in a few pages. In a Third Dimension setting, therefore, we must turn inward and allow our conscience to determine a far greater proportion of our daily decision-making process. As the lawyer and writer Philip K. Howard remarked recently, the solution to the legal tangle in which we find ourselves is 'to restore human responsibility as the activating force of law and regulation'.[42]

By the end of the Second Dimension, we should have created conditions in which human consciousness begins to reawaken based on a deep, personal inner recognition of the interdependent nature of existence. We will be able to develop a personal code anchored in an inner morality, and laws will be based on the insights of an aware mind and not the external conditioning or coercion on which the laws of premodern and First Dimension societies were based. The emphasis in law-making will shift from the letter to the spirit of the law, and we will focus on bringing that spirit in alignment with our inner morality. This inwardly directed morality or conscience then becomes the basis for law in the Third Dimension.

I believe that conscience, or moral responsibility, is the ability of an individual and a collective to see the wider implications and consequences of their actions and to infuse their actions with this understanding. I remember how horrified I was when I was introduced to a group of young, smart, aggressive, and arrogant fund managers who worked for a private equity fund that a friend had recommended I invest in. I could see immediately that although they were technically skilled in statistics and finance, they were self-serving and egotistical, and lacking integrity and decency as they made risky trades with the funds entrusted to them – primarily pension funds. It struck me then that these young men had no notion of what they were doing (essentially, playing recklessly with retirees' savings) because they failed to see their activity in the greater context around them. When their equity fund collapsed because of their irresponsible investment behaviour, they simply started afresh by organising a new fund and seeking new clients. Throughout, they seemed unable to sense how their flippant approach to investment had profound repercussions on the lives of others. They were not, strictly speaking, breaking any laws, but they nevertheless acted without conscience.

Many people today go about their business blithely ignoring that every action, decision, or choice they make is connected to the lives of others. No action or choice made by one individual, therefore, is exempt from moral responsibility. And the only way to acknowledge this is to look around ourselves and understand the myriad ways in which we are bound to other individuals, common interests and histories, and the social environment within which we move. This is the only way to develop genuine conscience and apply it consistently to every activity and intention.

The awakening of conscience as we approach the Third Dimension will be the natural outcome of a society that is moving toward a recognition of the interdependence of all things. In a Third Dimension society, laws will be aligned with the imperatives of conscience. More importantly, the fact that individuals are driven to act according to their conscience will reduce our reliance on written, codified laws, such that most legal codes can be slimmed down, in most areas, to essential guidelines.

My understanding of conscience and moral responsibility is informed by the concept of dharma. Dharma is a complex and elusive principle that has vexed generations of scholars because it has no exact definition or translation. In English, it has been variously translated as duty, custom, law, destiny, morality, virtue, justice, character or nature, righteousness, and so forth. But each of these definitions invariably reduces its meaning. The problem is compounded by the fact that dharma is a central tenet in several Eastern religions (Hinduism, Buddhism, Jainism, and Sikhism), but has a different meaning and interpretation in each.

From my readings and conversations with Hindu, Buddhist, and Jain teachers, I believe that one can distil the basic concept of dharma to this simple statement: *Dharma is the recognition of the interconnectedness of all life, and the resultant duty to live in harmony with all life.*

Dharma relies on the observance of some essential practices, especially self-control, patience, forgiveness, compassion, truthfulness, reason, learning, and the avoidance of anger. Some of these practices may have been defined originally in ancient Vedic texts, but even a cursory review shows that they are common to several of the world's great religions. More importantly, they are universally accepted norms that constitute civilised behaviour in any progressive, enlightened society.

In the Third Dimension, everyone will abide by their dharma or duty to harmonious living. Dharma is the only morality necessary. Peaceful coexistence becomes the only law. By applying dharma to all decisions and actions, individuals, groups, and organisations will be able to identify the proper course of action. At a personal level, individuals will be guided by the ancient but simple idea of doing unto others as we would like them to do unto us. In other words, to treat people in every situation in the way that you would have liked to be treated, had roles been reversed. By doing so, society will develop positive karma, that is, it will resonate with the quality which is generated when large groups of individuals act not out of a fear of retribution, religious dogma, or social ostracism, but from a highly developed conscience based on a deep understanding of the interdependent nature of our existence (dharma). The widespread existence of moral conscience in people will signal our arrival as a Third Dimension society and this, in turn, will lead to an upsurge in well-being and happiness, and a large-scale reduction in violence and unnecessary suffering.

Trusting our fellow citizens to follow their conscience and conform to their dharma sounds rather risky, of course, especially from our sceptical, cynical First Dimension vantage point. That is because, to quote Philip K. Howard once again, 'We have tried to create a hands-free legal code, without any risk of human frailty.' The preponderance of detailed laws and courts of law has lulled us into believing that all we have to do to be considered civilised is to follow the letter of the law. We have abdicated moral responsibility to an impersonal written document and the attendant machinery of justice, relying entirely on the state to implement and enforce laws. In the process, we have lost the ability and the willingness to make decisions based on our own inner moral code.

If, however, we place moral responsibility squarely on the shoulders of each person, we restore accountability to the level of individual behaviour. The absence of detailed laws, rather than their proliferation, will encourage individuals to act according to their conscience. And the widespread application of conscience will greatly reduce the need for oversight by judges, courts, and juries, because conscientious behaviour will be audited by the entire community: by our families, neighbours, and co-workers.

9

Justice: From Retribution to Restoration

Elements of First Dimension Justice

Justice, like many other social structures, is an elusive and complicated concept. Where does it come from? Do humans possess an innate sense of justice (call it conscience, morality, or a desire for order) that naturally allows us to distinguish between what is fair and what is unfair? Or, as some social theorists have argued over the centuries, is justice, like the law it enforces, merely a social construct, an artificial mechanism that ensures peaceful coexistence, and thus becomes the very hinge on which the social contract pivots?

While theories of justice may be difficult to understand, we are all familiar with the practical manifestation of justice – the judiciary. The judiciary is an apparatus of procedures, judges, courts, juries, lawyers, and clerks that manages the application of laws. When there is an infraction of a law, or a dispute between two parties, the perpetrator, who is presumed innocent until proven guilty, is prosecuted by a state authority tasked with finding out the 'truth', assigning guilt, and meting out punishment to the offender, proportionate to the gravity of the offence.

Regardless of how much or how little we know about the judicial process, we all assume that it conforms to certain fundamental criteria. First, it is impartial, meaning that all defendants and plaintiffs will be treated and evaluated equally, without regard to their wealth, position in society, ethnicity, occupation, or religion. To remain impartial, justice must be evidence-based, so that only factual, verifiable evidence (as opposed to opinion, bias, assumption, like, or dislike) can be used to prove or disprove guilt. In addition, the judicial system is presided over by professionals, that is, experienced judges who have studied the law in depth and whose sole occupation is to apply it. These three attributes of First Dimension justice – impartial, evidence-based, and professionally administered – are inherently sound and ought to remain the foundation of future justice systems.

There are three more attributes of First Dimension justice that we usually accept without putting much thought into them: deterrence based on reason, individual responsibility, and retribution.

The threat of punishment is assumed to **deter** crime. The fear of retribution administered by the judicial authority will, in theory, force individuals to consider carefully whether or not to commit an infraction. As the gravity of the crime increases, so does the punishment and, correspondingly, our desire to avoid it. The notion of deterrence assumes that each individual is the unique locus of behaviour, and that he is rational. In other words, every would-be criminal is expected to be capable of rationally evaluating the costs and benefits of each action he undertakes, of calculating the probability of being caught, and endowed with the free will to act or not act according to this evaluation.

First Dimension justice is **individualistic**. The judicial system is based on the understanding that the individual is solely responsible for his conduct. Thus, the individual acting of his own free will is the unique source of behaviour, both good and bad. Accordingly, when crimes occur, the justice system imputes them to the individual. It can never put entire communities, groups, or classes on trial. Even when there are multiple defendants in a criminal case, their role in the crime must be established on an individual basis, and the punishment is also applied individually.[43]

Justice is **retributive**. When an individual violates the social contract by breaking the law and committing a crime, he must be punished. Punishment is meted out not merely to discourage the criminal from committing the same crime again, but also, and especially, because the rest of society requires it. Retributive action is the only way to confirm the sanctity of the social order and restore faith in the legitimacy of the social contract. At another level, it feeds the voyeuristic urge of humans, as evinced by the large crowds that used to attend public executions in the past, or the media circus that accompanies high-profile trials nowadays. Justice, rather than a tool to discourage crime, becomes a spectacle.

Contradictions of First Dimension Justice

Just like impartiality and evidence, we take deterrence, individualism, and retribution for granted when we think about justice. These three concepts, however, lead to deep flaws in the administration of justice and need to be revisited if a more effective, humane, and lasting notion of justice is to emerge in the Second Dimension. Indeed, these three elements limit the efficacy of our judicial system because each contradicts a fundamental trait of human nature.

Deterrence Based on Reason

The element of deterrence, perhaps more than any other, is a shortcoming of First Dimension justice. It presupposes that every human being behaves like a rational, utility-maximising individual in every moment of his life, that is, a potential criminal will decide whether or not to commit a crime by dispassionately calculating the potential benefit of the crime, the likelihood of being caught, the likelihood of being convicted, and the opportunity cost of being incarcerated. In fact, most crimes, especially violent ones, are extremely irrational and impulsive. Criminals are rarely able to foresee the consequences of their actions or appreciate the pain and suffering that these actions might cause, to themselves as well as their victims.

Take the case of Rajat Gupta, who from 1994 to 2003 was managing director of McKinsey & Co., the most prestigious management consultancy in the world. In 2012 he was convicted of securities fraud in the biggest insider trading case in US history and sentenced to two years imprisonment. Gupta had fashioned a fruitful career out of the consistent application of reason – from an engineering degree at an Indian Institute of Technology, to an MBA at Harvard, to a long, successful career at McKinsey, rising steadily through the ranks of a firm that many associate with the most systematic and consistent application of rational thinking to business decisions at the highest level. He was a living example of rational thinking refined to the utmost.

Why, then, many commentators wondered, would a person so committed to reason allow himself to be drawn into a case of blatant financial fraud? He certainly was not in need of money – he was reportedly worth more than $100 million when he was arrested. Was it some latent sense of insecurity, or peer pressure to succeed in the sphere of billionaires and world movers? Or was it a moment of sheer vanity as he sought to end his career with a bang? This, perhaps more than a violent deed committed in a fit of rage or passion, illustrates that most crimes cannot be evaluated or understood in terms of reasoned, calculated volition.

Most crimes are irrational, and arise out of various factors, some of them deep-seated and beyond our conscious control. I believe that most crimes, especially violent crimes, are rooted in one or more of six conditions, which are mostly social in nature:

- **Tribal mentality:** A tribal mindset is, broadly speaking, conformity to a set of beliefs and cultural norms specific to a community, religious group, or ethnic group. Typically, such beliefs are ingrained in the individual since childhood through continual reiteration and example-setting. Tribalist attitudes are traditional behavioural norms that often run counter to the laws of the country in which the group finds itself, but are nevertheless tolerated out of fear of communal strife. The perpetrators of crimes predicated on tribalist attitudes are often unaware that they are committing a crime, and act in the belief that they are upholding hallowed, community-sanctioned ideals. An example of such a crime would be the killing of men and women accused of adultery, disobedience against family's wishes, or religious non-conformity – an all-too-frequent occurrence in some developing countries. One such case occurred in Balochistan (in Pakistan) in February 2014, when a man and a woman believed to have committed adultery were stoned to death by a mob of neighbours that included the woman's husband, in an action that was allegedly approved by a local cleric.

- **Peer pressure and herd mentality:** Crimes in this category arise from perceived peer pressure, the need to belong to a particular group or alliance, or the herd mentality that often supersedes reasonable decision-making when mobs assemble. Examples include gangs in the United States and Latin America, football hooliganism in Europe, and communal riots in India.
- **Dysfunctional family and/or childhood abuse:** It is well documented that children growing up in dysfunctional, fractured, or litigious families are much more likely to engage in criminal activities when they grow up. Likewise, children who have suffered physical, emotional, or sexual abuse are more likely to become abusive and violent themselves.
- **Mental illness:** Crimes arising from mental disorders ought to be judged according to parameters different from other crimes. Examples of mass murderers who acted out of insanity abound, unfortunately. Two recent cases are Anders Breivik, the Norwegian right-wing extremist who shot and killed seventy-seven people at a summer camp in 2011, and Adam Lanza, who shot twenty children and six teachers at Sandy Hook Elementary School in Newton, Connecticut, in December 2012. Such crimes are the result of unbalanced minds. A reasonable response to them is confinement and treatment in mental institutions.

- **Poverty:** Poverty can be a strong motivation for crime, especially property crimes such as theft, robbery, and graft. It can also be a driver of money-seeking activities that are often classified as illegal, such as prostitution, the selling of drugs, gambling, and smuggling, when the person perpetrating the crime perceives no other way to survive.
- **Political beliefs:** Finally, there are crimes that owe their motivation, in theory at least, to political convictions, and the desire to force political change by violent means. Examples include the European terrorist organisations of the 1970s, such as the Red Army Faction in Germany, the Irish Republican Army in the United Kingdom, and the Red Brigades in Italy; the recent assassinations of various journalists and activists in Russia; and, indeed, most of the acts of terror perpetrated by Islamic fundamentalists in the last two decades. In *Violence as Communication*, scholars Alex Schmid and Janny de Graaf lay out a compelling case for violence as a political act, especially because, in our hyper-connected world, violent acts tend to receive disproportionately extensive coverage in the media, which are addicted to the sensational.

In outlining the factors that contribute to criminal behaviour, I am suggesting that crime is a highly complex phenomenon with multiple causes that are often difficult to detect. Some of these causes (like tribalism, childhood abuse, and peer pressure) are deeply psychological and have much to do with the elements of our context, which I discussed in Chapter 3. Others are biological (mental illness) or ideological (political beliefs). With the possible exception of poverty and political conviction, these motivations for crime are not rational, that is, the result of a reasoned decision. Therefore, deterrence based on the expectation that a would-be criminal will apply reasoned judgment is simply a fallacy.

Focus on Individual Responsibility

The individual focus of First Dimension justice also makes little sense. Throughout history, and until very recently, individuals have been situated within the context of their families, economic conditions, kinship bonds, religious and ethnic structures, and the community in which they grew up. This contextual heritage has the largest influence on shaping an individual's personality and actions, but usually the First Dimension justice system does not take it into account.

By ignoring the source and development of human behaviour (criminal as well as law-abiding), modern justice effectively denies that there exists any collective responsibility, and thus absolves all social groups and institutions of any blame in the occurrence of criminal behaviour. Most crimes are the end point of a long process in which the criminal typically has been exposed to a variety of influences, including abuse, deprivation, injustice, or illness. Justice systems in most countries have just begun to understand this and sometimes accept exposure to such conditions as a mitigating factor. The truth, however, is that the abuses or deprivations to which criminals may have been exposed previously are themselves the result of societal dysfunctions that allowed them to occur. Criminals come not only from broken families, but also from indifferent communities.

The effect of physical and sexual abuse on children is now well documented as a progenitor of criminal behaviour. The same can be said of poverty, unemployment, neglect, trauma, mental illness, and alcohol and drug abuse. The role of physiological and hereditary causes is also increasingly being studied as a source of criminal tendencies: genetic make up, excess testosterone, and even an especially slow heartbeat have been linked to aggressive behaviour. But what few are willing to admit is that crime is the end point of a lifelong corruption of social skills, which was engendered in a community dysfunctional and neglectful enough to allow it to happen. Thus, while crime may be a phenomenon that manifests in individuals, responsibility for it must be communal.

There is no dearth of examples to elucidate this point. I will choose, deliberately, one that is as blatant as it is famous: the brutal assault, gang rape, and murder in 2012 of a young physiotherapy student (affectionately nicknamed Nirbhaya, or 'fearless', by the media) in a bus in Delhi. It was a criminal case that shocked the nation and the world, and prompted much soul-searching, protest, and amendment of legislation in India. Anger over the case resurfaced two years later, when one of the rapists, while awaiting his sentence, released an interview in which he showed no remorse whatsoever, and implied that the victim had somehow deserved the bestial crime. Justice was served, apparently, when the perpetrators were sentenced to death by hanging.

But even a cursory look at the background and life histories of the rapists showed that sentencing them to death could neither bring emotional closure to the case, nor assure anyone that such crimes would not occur again. Several of the rapists lived in squalid conditions in a Delhi slum – they had migrated to the city from the poor, hopeless heartland of India; they were uneducated and capable only of intermittent employment in menial jobs; they came from fatherless, fragmented families that were unable to give them anything resembling a caring upbringing; they had themselves suffered abuse, disenfranchisement, poverty, and callousness throughout their lives. In Nirbhaya, perhaps, they recognised someone from a social background almost as poor and hopeless as their own, who nevertheless had managed to escape the limitations of poverty and was well on her way to a stable, successful career.[44] Their alienation brewed seething resentment and unspoken anger, which found outlet in an unspeakable act of violence that they themselves probably did not understand. While none could possibly excuse their conduct or imagine a way in which such inhuman criminals could be reformed or reintegrated in society, it is also not difficult to see what gave rise to their behaviour. It is reasonable to expect many more cases of similar brutality, given the vast population of poor, abandoned, uneducated, uncared-for young migrants living in abject conditions in slums all over India.

An entire society – including district-level, state-level, and federal-level governments; social welfare institutions, educational institutions, urban and rural development institutions; neighbours, co-workers and relatives – must accept the blame for allowing and perpetuating the conditions that engendered this crime. A society in which the very fabric of social interaction – family life, community involvement, and gainful employment – has become so shredded that it is able to ignore the development of such violence is thoroughly dysfunctional and must be rebuilt from the foundations up.

Retribution

The retributive aspect of modern justice satisfies society's need to reiterate a commitment to the social contract, but it rarely brings closure to criminal cases, either for the victims of the crime or for the perpetrators. The inability to understand the motivations of the crime, and to accept the series of societal and institutional errors that allowed it to occur, typically rankles in the victims well beyond the conclusion of the trial. Convicted felons, on the other hand, face punishment, incarceration being the most common. And this, too, very rarely brings closure to their criminality.

We justify imprisonment as necessary to keep the rest of society safe from the criminal, and as an opportunity for the criminal to understand his mistakes and learn from them. However, incarceration rarely achieves either of these ends. More often than not, it results in a hardening of antisocial attitudes and a recurrence of criminal behaviour, rather than in rehabilitation. This is confirmed by a quick look at recidivism rates (the rate of reincarceration of inmates released from prison) across the world. Crime statistics from different countries are extremely difficult to compare because they are compiled according to different criteria, but we can say, very roughly, that national recidivism rates during the last twenty years typically have been in the range of 40–50 per cent.[45] This means that almost one in two inmates will return to prison within a few years of his release. It shows clearly that retribution is not effective as a means to rehabilitate criminals. In fact, many analysts believe that prisons often harden criminals instead of reforming them. Moreover, high recidivism suggests that the fear of incarceration is not an especially strong deterrent, most likely because the idea of deterrence itself is deeply flawed.

The truth, then, is that societies like to confine criminals in prisons not because they truly expect them to repent or learn positive social behaviour and thus become rehabilitated and ready to take on a productive role in society. We incarcerate criminals merely out of a need for retribution – the vengeful feeling that all is well in society as long as evil people get their comeuppance. Genuine rehabilitation, such that the former criminal can engage fully and collaboratively with his fellow citizens, is a rare thing indeed.

Principles of Second Dimension Justice

Modern justice systems rely heavily on deterrence, individualism, and retribution. All three elements are quite improbable as conceptual foundations for an effective and sensible justice system. They are derived from the fallacies we have inherited from our application of the concept of liberty. They take for granted the individual's control of his actions through free will, which is increasingly seen as a misconception by modern researchers. And they disregard the heavy baggage of prejudices, inclinations, inherited attitudes, ingrained social norms, and forgotten feelings that form the personal and societal 'context' that defines each person. We may be aware of some of them, but the bulk of these psychological factors are stowed away in our subconscious, and only come to the fore at unpredictable moments, when crime is most likely to occur.

It is necessary to develop an entirely new philosophy that will pervade the Second Dimension's approach to justice. This new conceptual framework for justice (Table 9.1) entails a correction of the three misplaced assumptions of First Dimension justice: deterrence based on rational decision-making, individualism, and the need for retribution. Instead of the threat of incarceration, I offer various social stimuli (censure and reward) as a means of deterrence; in lieu of individual responsibility, I propose communal responsibility; and in place of retributive justice, I suggest restorative justice.

Social Stimulus

I am reminded of an event I witnessed in person. My wife and I were invited to a lavish wedding ceremony – the kind where flowers are imported

Table 9.1: Conceptual Frameworks of Justice in the First and Second Dimensions

	First Dimension justice		Second Dimension justice
Deterrence	Reasoned fear of punishment	→	Social stimulus
Responsibility	Individual	→	Communal
Goal	Retribution	→	Restoration

from overseas, where only single malt whisky is served, where a rich and elaborate buffet of delicacies is served, where the groom receives a sports car as a gift from his father-in-law, and where the bride is wearing a large amount of gold and diamonds. The host of this extravagant affair, the father of the bride, was a tax inspector. There was an obvious contradiction between his official income as a government servant and the wealth on display at the party. Everyone, in other words, was well aware that he had been collecting hefty bribes for many years, and thus had an illicit income that dwarfed his government salary. Nevertheless, when I raised this subject, in hushed tones, during the wedding party, I found that no one was willing to speak about it. Instead, most guests were full of praise – and, occasionally, envy – for the lavishness of the celebration, and too busy enjoying the expensive wine and food, or listening to the musicians flown in especially for the occasion.

Now imagine a society that will not tolerate such ostentation and blatant corruption. Imagine a party such as the one I have described, but devoid entirely of guests. The waiters are milling about aimlessly, not knowing what to do with themselves, the band is tuning their instruments for hours, the food is going cold. All because no one has accepted the invitation. Everyone has shunned the event out of disgust and disapproval of the inspector's corrupt ways. The message – that an advanced society cannot tolerate graft and bribery in any form – would be so powerful and immediate, that the inspector and others like him would quickly understand the reason, and either mend their ways or move to a different city.

The same could be said of violent behaviour. If everyone, acting individually but thinking collectively, were to avoid the company of persons known to be abusive or violent, selfish or greedy, then such patterns of behaviour could be reduced to a minimum. The hallmark of a society that has achieved a high degree of consciousness is its ability to regulate itself without much input from judicial authorities and law enforcement agencies. A Second Dimension Community would therefore employ social censure to curb undesirable behaviour.

It is not only censure, however, that I am advocating here. Just as communities can quietly discourage illegal or antisocial behaviour, they can also stimulate positive behaviour by publicly celebrating collaboration and generosity. To illustrate how social stimulus can yield positive outcomes, I will discuss briefly the development of philanthropy in different countries. My native country, India, has a relatively weak tradition of charitable giving. A seminal study published by Bain & Company in 2010 showed that charitable giving in India in 2006 amounted to just 0.6 per cent of the GDP. While this was more than in many other developing countries, such as Brazil and China, it fell well short of the 2.2 per cent given in the United States. Moreover, a large proportion of that 0.6 per cent came from central and state governments, while only a small fraction (about 10 per cent) came from individuals and corporations.[46]

In 2010, the World Giving Index published by the Charities Aid Foundation ranked India a dismal 134th in the world in giving, based on the proportion of the population that had made charitable donations. Australia and New Zealand topped the list, with the US coming in 5th.[47]

India's low rate of charity evinced by these reports gave rise to much soul-searching, and to attempts at explaining this trend. Rich countries obviously have more money to donate than poor countries, some argued. But even if we restrict the analysis to charitable contributions made by high net worth individuals (HNWIs), of which there are now many in India, we are lagging far behind Western countries: Indian HNWIs donated only 1.6 per cent of their household income in 2010. This pales in comparison to the United States, where even low-income Americans were found to be giving 4.5 per cent of their income to charity.[48] Nowadays the richest

Americans, the likes of Warren Buffett and Bill Gates, are better known for their philanthropic efforts than for their corporate exploits – something that cannot be said of their Indian counterparts, even though some of them (like Mukesh Ambani and Lakshmi Mittal) are among the world's ten richest individuals.

Others argue that much of Indian-style charity simply does not find its way into statistical analyses and global reports. For example, Indians tend to make substantial (but largely undocumented) donations and loans to their extended families, kinship and ethnic associations, and religious groups. But this merely highlights the cultural problem with giving in India – donors are willing to contribute to specific causes that favour their own religious organisation or their extended kinship group, but reluctant to extend that generosity to the population at large. Charity, in other words, tends to follow the country's fractured identity politics rather than the needs of the poor.

Charitable giving has improved a lot in India since 2010. Subsequent studies have shown progress on all fronts: HNWIs are giving more, and the 2013 Companies Act now requires all corporations of a certain size to devote at least 2 per cent of their profits to corporate social responsibility (CSR) programmes. In the 2017 edition of the World Giving Index, India's rank had improved to 81st.[49] Bain & Company's *India Philanthropy Report 2017* noted that private donations made up 32 per cent of total contributions to the development sector in 2016, up from a mere 15 per cent in 2011; and that philanthropic funding from private individuals had recorded a sixfold increase in the same span of time. However, the report also noted that in terms of visible philanthropic outcomes, 'India still has a long way to go.'[50]

The relatively low rate of philanthropic giving by wealthy Indians is a cultural phenomenon. We do not enjoy a cultural or community environment that praises and encourages philanthropy enough. The accumulation of wealth, and the ability to show off such wealth, still tops the wish list and the efforts of most households in India. Admiration and social clout are bestowed upon those who succeed in these twin aims. Some Western countries, on the other hand, have developed a culture that rewards philanthropy more than the simple hoarding of riches. In the United States, this may have historical roots in a Protestant work ethic, or it may have something to do with the weight of public opinion in the social and political arena, or it may be the consequence of a tax regime that encourages charity. Regardless, it has spawned a culture of generosity unparalleled in any other country. This, in short, is the power of what I have called 'social stimulus': the ability of communities and societies to steer behaviour (in this case, financial benevolence) toward positive outcomes for the entire population by creating appropriate social incentives.

Communal Responsibility

As a young man, I used to live in a small village in rural Rajasthan. The village, Rampur, was inhabited primarily by farmers and artisans, so its daily life was dictated largely by the rhythms of agriculture and rural existence. There were very few distractions or outlets for entertainment, but it was also a close-knit and peaceful community. Everyone knew each other, and no one put locks on their doors. Nevertheless, there were occasional incidents of strife and violence. There was one villager named Ram Singh[51] who was known to be a troublemaker. He often absconded from his work to drink cheap liquor and then roamed the dirt lanes of the village shouting abuse at anyone he came across, vaguely accusing others of ill-defined wrongs to provoke them. He would often brandish an old, rusted sword to intimidate others and call attention to himself.

His behaviour was not only a nuisance to the other villagers, but was also prone to exploitation. Anyone who had a dispute with another villager over property, or with a relative over family matters, could easily co-opt Ram Singh's allegiance by plying him with liquor. He could then be deployed to intimidate the other party with his abusive antics.

Once, when Ram Singh roughed up another villager who had not paid his rent, and then peed on his door for good measure, a group of villagers decided they had had enough; they went together and complained to the village headman. The chief – a wise and well-respected elder with much experience in handling such matters – summoned Ram Singh and berated him in front of all those assembled there. He ordered him to curb his drinking, attend to his work more consistently, and stop his aggressive behaviour against fellow villagers. Then he turned to the villagers who had witnessed his pronouncement – a group that included both Ram Singh's relatives and those who had lodged the complaint against him – and charged *them* with supervising Ram Singh's rehabilitation. It was their responsibility, he said, to watch over him, to ensure he did not drink excessively and worked harder, to counsel him if he strayed from the path of diligence, and to admonish and restrain him every time he was on the verge of misbehaving. If Ram Singh should resume his loutish conduct, or commit any violence, the headman added, then he would hold all those assembled there that day equally responsible for Ram Singh's actions.

In a small, rural community like Rampur, where there was neither police nor judiciary, the responsibility for identifying and reforming unpleasant behaviour that might lead to crime fell on the shoulders of the entire community. Indeed, most crime does not spring up suddenly and out of nowhere. With a modicum of observation, it can be seen coming from a mile away. Instead of abdicating responsibility for crime to institutions of government, every Community must take it upon itself to watch out for signs of distress or imbalance among its members. Most antisocial behaviour manifests itself clearly and can be nipped in the bud well before it becomes crime. Every neighbour, co-worker, relative, and passer-by ought to be responsible for recognising the signs of incipient crime, report them, and become part of well-intentioned interventions to find the cause of aberrant behaviour and address it.

I am not advocating vigilantism and witch-hunts. A Community's right to intervene in such matters would be limited to the provision of counselling, recommendation of therapy, and signalling the potential for crime to the proper authorities. It could never include the right to take punitive action. We must think of the Community as an extended family, observant and caring enough to apply social pressure when required.

Many years ago, I witnessed the turning point in a man's life brought on by an intervention organised by his extended family. The man in question was a friend of my father who had a severe problem with alcoholism. It was so dire that his immediate family was disintegrating around him –

his wife alienated and angry, his children neglected and afraid. His work suffered, as did his standing in the neighbourhood and among his peers. It was heart-wrenching to watch his life spiralling out of control because of his addiction, dragging his family down with it, even though he was an intelligent and successful businessman with much to look forward to. Finally, his entire extended family and friends – no fewer than fifty – decided to come together and confront the problem. They organised a surprise party for him, and at this event, each spoke to him directly, in front of the assembled group, and told him in clear terms how his alcoholism had spoiled their relationship with him, and the extent to which his continual drunkenness was destroying all the bonds with his family and friends. The man was moved to tears that evening by the realisation that his actions had caused so much harm and negativity around him, and by the determined show of concern from all present. A few days later he entered a ninety-day detoxification programme in a medical facility. He completed the programme successfully and managed to avoid alcohol for the rest of his life. He was able to mend much of the damage he had caused previously, though of course some scars remained, especially in the emotional development of his children.

Although the examples of communal responsibility that I have offered here may seem too small and insignificant to address criminality and other aberrant behaviour on a greater scale, the strategy of relying on community intervention to avert crime is readily applicable everywhere, if we accept Community as a basic building block of organised society.

In March 2016, in the city of Brussels, terrorists associated with Islamic State (IS) detonated several suicide bombs in the airport and metro, killing thirty-one people and wounding many more. Terrorism, especially Islamic militancy, relies on a never-ending supply of unemployed, angry, disaffected, often delinquent young men who can easily be turned into tools of terror by any group with an extremist ideology, be it IS or al-Qaida or the Taliban. But these young men – these same individuals who are so willing to throw away their own lives in support of a futile, nihilist ideology – must at some point have been members of a family, community, or greater kinship group. If their community had looked out for them more carefully, if they had been offered better education and job opportunities, and especially if their tendency to disgruntlement and violence had been identified early on and addressed with determination and compassion, then they would not have reached a point where they were willing to don a suicide vest. Their communities failed to care for and integrate them, and to give them instruction and affection; the result was that they fell into violence and callousness. They retreated into semi-segregated areas like Molenbeek, the so-called jihadist ghetto of Greater Brussels, from which there was no escape but through violence.

Restorative Justice

In the Second Dimension, the goal of the justice system will be to awaken in the dysfunctional and damaged individual his conscience, his morality, his inherent humanity, and a feeling of genuine repentance for his actions. Reawakening these qualities can be accomplished through rehabilitation programmes where criminals are exposed to the pain and suffering that their actions have caused or, indeed, to human pain and suffering in general. Witnessing first-hand the harm caused is likely to lead to genuine repentance and, in turn, to cessation of the impulses responsible for the crime. At the end of this exercise, the convicted criminal and society will both have been healed.

How might such carefully directed restorative programmes be set up? Instead of being sent to detention facilities, where their propensity to crime will be enhanced rather than curbed, violent offenders could, for example, be assigned to work in supervised settings in places where they are exposed to aspects of life that would awaken a sense of repentance while interrupting the cycles of anger, pain, and hatred that might have led to the original crime. With proper design and monitoring, places such as hospitals, hospices, old age homes, and other specialised facilities can become settings for long-term healing. There, offenders would come into direct contact with the abject suffering of the terminally ill, the destitute, the handicapped, paraplegics and amputees, and other patients who cannot take care of themselves. The daily routine of washing withered bodies, comforting the old, cleaning out bed pans, removing human remains, and watching and listening to the harrowing sights and sounds of human suffering would ultimately force even the most hardened offender to acknowledge the frailty of the human condition, appreciate the value of health, safety, and life, and confront his own ruthless disregard for them.

Juveniles who have demonstrated violent behaviour or destructive tendencies like vandalism, drug abuse, assault, and hooliganism could be made to work in more traditional community service roles that emphasise the creation and maintenance of healthy, useful spaces. (Such programmes are already in place in many First Dimension justice systems.) This could include clean-up of littered alleys and parks, removal of graffiti, rebuilding of crumbling fences, gardening and landscaping in community parks and public areas, forestry tasks in national and regional parks, and agricultural labour. The goal would be to rectify deviant behaviour by coaxing into prominence the creative, constructive, and collaborative nature latent in every human being.

Non-violent crimes would call for different types of restoration. A white-collar criminal (like Rajat Gupta) could be assigned several years of full-time community service commensurate with his considerable skills. He could be made to dispense financial and legal advice, provide tax services, compile loan and benefit applications, and file insurance claims on behalf of the poor. In the sentencing regime, every convict could even be given a choice of various forms of redressal. Ultimately, however, incarceration would never be an option, except for the criminally insane interned in secure mental facilities.

During rehabilitation, the authority responsible for dispensing justice must also be able to judge the genuineness of the repentance and determine whether the convict has been rehabilitated to the satisfaction of the Community and the victims. The goal of restorative justice is not to exact a punishment that is quantitatively commensurate with the crime, but rather to reintegrate the offender in the Community by finding ways to awaken his or her humanity.

Second Dimension Justice in Action

The new judicial concept I have discussed above relies on social stimuli, communal responsibility, and restorative programmes, and is intended to render justice much more ubiquitous and accessible – a pervasive and constant aspect of everyday life that is played out in the community rather than in a court of law. If the notions of social censure and communal responsibility are allowed to take hold in the civic imagination of the Second Dimension, they will result in a vast reduction in crime. And if restorative programmes become the norm in the resolution of criminal behaviour, then before long we will be able to dispense with much of the First Dimension's correctional apparatus.

However, it is unrealistic to expect that crime will ever be fully eradicated or controlled. Human behaviour, even in the most peaceful and enlightened social circumstances, is unpredictable and prone to mutability; so, a zero-crime environment is difficult to imagine. Therefore, a judicial process will continue to be necessary. How will it be different from what exists in the First Dimension?

Before the Judicial Process

In the Second Dimension, every case, be it a civil suit, a criminal offence, financial misconduct, or violation of a contract, will be reviewed by a specialised entity (the Causality Committee). This will happen before the offence can proceed to trial or arbitration.

Civil cases

When making an initial determination on civil lawsuits, the Causality Committee may decide that a trial is indeed required, but it also has the authority to divert proceedings to a community arbitrator, and to dismiss charges outright. First Dimension civil suits are notoriously lengthy, fraught with delays and delaying tactics, and the playground of unscrupulous lawyers bent on dragging out the proceedings. As delays (procedural as well as deliberate) mount, stretching from months into years, most civil cases become a war of attrition: the party with the most patience and the most money to spend on legal representation usually prevails. This serves the interests of neither the plaintiff nor the defendant, and least of all the justice system as a whole, which is clogged with cases that could be resolved with minimal fuss in a single hearing. The only ones who profit from such cases are the lawyers themselves, who not only continue to charge their high representation fees for years, but also cement their reputation as indispensable resources in the attainment of a favourable result.

The vast majority of civil cases are relatively straightforward – they involve firms arguing over cost sharing or broken contracts, relatives squabbling over property or inheritance, litigants hoping to extract settlements from insurance firms or wealthier defendants, corporations unwilling to contribute their fair share to consumer protection or, conversely, consumers unwilling to accept reasonable risks of using a product or service. In most such cases, a solution and a compromise could be arrived at quickly and easily if the parties were forced to sit face-to-face before an arbitrator and were willing to negotiate in good faith without the interference of legal representatives or third parties. But the vested interest of lawyers – to prolong proceedings – and especially the formal and highly bureaucratic nature of legal proceedings combine to prevent simple solutions. Once parties enter the judicial process, they are enslaved by its complex and rigid structure, which necessarily involves pleadings (a series of claims and counterclaims); motions and counter-motions; a lengthy and often acrimonious discovery phase, where delays and deceit are most likely to occur; and various pretrial conferences and hearings. This intricate system lends itself to deliberate delays and obfuscation by wily barristers. But even when two sides are willing to proceed in good faith and as speedily as possible, the nature of the process itself – which requires each party to respond and react to the other party according to an established ritual – locks all participants in a slow, inefficient, and ultimately demoralising crawl toward resolution.

The Second Dimension's Causality Committee would require a preliminary hearing for all civil suits. Importantly, no legal representatives would be allowed, and the hearing would be presided by highly qualified professional judges – keen legal minds with the experience, expertise, and precision to recognise quickly the legal merits of a complaint. In an informal setting, the Committee would hear both sides of the complaint and, in the majority of cases, the Committee would be able to dismiss the case outright because it is frivolous, unfounded, or has little hope of being resolved within a reasonable amount of time and reasonable evidentiary proceedings. Or, while recognising that proceedings are in order, it would redirect the case to a community arbitrator where it deems that a simple, face-to-face discussion between plaintiff and defendant will most likely bring about a satisfactory resolution.

Criminal Cases

In criminal cases, the primary job of the Causality Committee will be to ascertain what *type* of crime was committed. The Committee must establish the following:

- Was the alleged crime the result of an accident or negligence? For example, if someone reversed a car without paying attention and injured a passer-by.
- Was the crime the result of gross irresponsibility? A car accident caused by a drunk driver, for instance. Or a fire that ignited due to substandard electrical wiring or disregard of fire regulations.
- Was the crime premeditated and intentional?
- Was the crime systemic? For instance, when the crime was perpetrated by an entire institution, or was part of the culture of a company, community, or group? The Enron scandal – one of the best-known cases of corporate fraud on an institutional level – comes to mind.
- Was mental illness a factor?

In addressing these questions, the Causality Committee must be guided by the principle that crime is rarely a rational act imputable to a lone individual. Rather, it is usually the symptom of a deeper social malaise that needs to be analysed and corrected. Thus, the Causality Committee's work must be underpinned by a thorough understanding of the psychology of criminal behaviour and the social interactions that can lead to it. The Committee must, therefore, be well versed in distinguishing between the various causes of antisocial behaviour (tribalism, dysfunctional family background, peer pressure, mental illness, poverty, political motivation) and able to recognise the wider social interconnections that led to the criminal act.

When confronted with a criminal act, the Causality Committee must first analyse it. From which of the six sources of criminal behaviour outlined above did it arise? Did it come from a combination of them? This is critical because any remedial measures that can be taken must be based on the conditions that provoked the problem. In the case of Nirbhaya in Delhi, once the context of the perpetrators is considered, it becomes clear that tribal mentality, dysfunctional family, and poverty were all strong contributing factors.

Crimes cannot be understood, judged, or punished in isolation. When a crime is committed, it represents the end of a complex chain of causality that began months or years before the crime itself, and it is rooted in one of the causal conditions I have outlined. Second Dimension justice recognises that almost all crime arises from one of these causes. Besides passing judgment and punishment on individual criminals, it seeks to address these root causes and recommend the necessary societal reforms to ensure that crimes do not occur at all.

The Causality Committee's analysis of the crime can be forwarded to the court or to arbitration processes handling the case, so that it can become an integral part of the resolution of the case, whether by trial, plea bargaining, out-of-court settlement, or other process.

The Causality Committee's intervention *before* any judicial proceedings can take place adds an extra step to the process of administering justice. One may argue, therefore, that it complicates things rather than simplifying them. However, its role, in both civil and criminal cases, would be instrumental in both reducing the load on justice systems and in expediting those cases that do end up in the courts.

The Judicial Process

In the First Dimension, the formal judicial procedure from arrest to judgment is a complicated process, which after arraignment and pleading, assignment of prosecutors and defence litigators, depositions and extensive fact finding, and culmination in a trial, is a labyrinthine ecosystem populated by lawyers and judges, and rendered impenetrable by a complex web of procedural norms. How must it be reformed in the Second Dimension?

In the Second Dimension, justice systems must focus on improving the fairness, efficiency, and transparency of proceedings, and the speed with which cases are disposed of. Judicial processes must be subjected to a comprehensive quality assurance system.

In the last few decades, court systems in several advanced countries have been working on initiatives for self-assessment and improvement. In 1983 and 1987, respectively, the Conference of State Court Administrators of the United States and the American Bar Association published case processing time standards for their courts. Both institutions were reacting to growing public demand for greater accountability in case management. Also in 1987, a group of trial judges, court managers, and legal scholars developed a measurement mechanism intended to help US courts dispose of cases more fairly and efficiently. This resulted in the Trial Court Performance Standards (TCPS), which articulated the fundamental purposes of courts and provided a rudimentary tool to evaluate the quality of the services delivered by the court.[52] The key elements of the TCPS are summarised in Box 9.1.

Though the TCPS were not successful immediately, the quality approach on which they were based was revived in 2005, when the so-called Courtools were published. These practical measures were intended to bring the performance areas identified in the TCPS in line with mainstream quality models such as the balanced scorecard. Indicators included clearance rates, age of pending caseload, reliability and integrity of case files, effective use of jurors, court employee satisfaction, cost per case, and others.

Box 9.1: Key Areas of Trial Court Performance Standards (TCPS)

- Access to justice: courts should be open and accessible.
- Timeliness: decisions should be delivered in a timely manner.
- Equality, fairness, and integrity: courts should provide due process and equal protection.
- Independence and accountability: trial courts must establish legal and organisational boundaries, monitor and control their operations, and account publicly for their performance.
- Public trust and confidence: courts should work in an accessible, fair and accountable way such that they enjoy a high level of public trust.

The 1990s saw the beginning of initiatives in several European countries (including the United Kingdom, the Netherlands, and Finland) to improve the quality of public services delivered by government institutions. Acting on the stimuli provided by these initiatives, in 2007 the European Commission for the Efficiency of Justice (CEPEJ) created a working group on quality, whose first contribution was the publication of a checklist for quality in the judiciary.

Elsewhere, the Singapore government and judiciary began to reform the courts in 1990, aiming to reduce the backlog of cases and develop a framework for timely proceedings. By the end of the 1990s, Singapore's Subordinate Courts had introduced a Justice Scorecard as a tool for performance measurement. In 2007, the positive results of applying the Justice Scorecard led a senior district judge to propose a global charter for court quality. Soon thereafter the International Consortium for Court Excellence[53] was created to develop the International Framework for Court Excellence (IFCE), a quality management system designed to help courts anywhere in the world better their performance. In 2012 it issued a revised primer, *Global Measures of Court Performance*, describing eleven core performance measures for courts, including court user satisfaction, case clearance rate, on-time case processing, court file integrity, and cost per case.[54] The primer's measures represent universally accepted judicial values and areas of excellence defined by the IFCE.

Thus, much bureaucratic work has already gone, and continues to go, into efforts that properly reflect what is already a Second Dimension attitude. The universal standards of courtroom quality that have taken shape over the last two decades, and are now formally documented in the IFCE, can be applied in their entirety to all courts and in all countries.

Court proceedings may be made leaner and faster by following the tripartite hierarchy of legislation (laws, rules, protocols) introduced in Chapter 8. For every type of law that is broken there ought to be a separate judicial process performed and judged by specialists in that level of the legal pyramid. If a law is at stake, then the case must land in a court not unlike what exists now. But if the case involves a rule or a protocol that has not been met, then there ought to be a different process, more streamlined and rapid, presided over by a specialist who is familiar with the industry or issue in question. Infringement of complex banking regulations, for example, will be dealt with by a financial court; non-compliance with safety regulations will be addressed by a court specialising in public safety and industrial hazards.

After the Judicial Process

Crucially, the Second Dimension judicial process does not end with the passing of a sentence. In fact, as much effort must go in the post-trial analysis of the crime as went into the trial process. I envision that a case that has been concluded in the courts or through an arbitration process should return to the Causality Committee. After noting the evidence uncovered in the trial proceedings and the final determination by the judge or jury, the Causality Committee will conduct a post-trial analysis of the case. This analysis will give the Committee the chance to revise its initial assessment of the crime's root causes. The findings of the case, as laid bare by the judicial process, will allow the Committee to determine not only the immediate causes of the crime (based on the six-term classification of criminal behaviour outlined previously), but also to conduct a thorough review of the chain of responsibility for the crime. This analysis relies on the understanding that most crimes are the result of a long chain of causation, and that they occur within a dense web of highly interdependent social circumstances. Here, Second Dimension justice differs significantly from its First Dimension version in that it does not look at the offender in isolation but acknowledges the many factors acting on the perpetrator, directly or indirectly.

In the 2016 terrorist attacks in Brussels, the First Dimension response was to address the immediate symptom, that is, to hunt down any bombers or conspirators who survived the suicide mission. The reach of the judicial intervention might stretch to encompass networks of people who might have sheltered, aided, funded, or otherwise helped the terrorists carry out the attacks. A Second Dimension response, as articulated by a Causality Committee, on the other hand, would be to delve into the root factors of the crime as far as possible, to reveal the full chain of causality. In the case of Islamic terrorism, the chain of causality might be summarised in the schematic shown in Figure 9.1.

The terrorist, as shown in the diagram, is merely a bit performer in a complex play. The Committee's report on a terror-related crime might condemn not only the terrorist himself, but also the various other influences on his life and thinking that led to the act of violence: the Belgian state, which failed to successfully integrate immigrants from diverse cultural backgrounds; the local preacher, who may have radicalised wayward youths under his influence; and, all the way at the top of the chain of causality, the malicious effect of foreign policy decisions made by the United States and other world powers, including support, for reasons of strategic self-interest, of countries that directly or indirectly foster the rise of terrorist ideologies.

In the case of, say, Afghanistan, such support is direct, as extremism like the Taliban was the long-term result of the US's decision to arm and train mujahideen fighters and help them develop a lucrative financing plan through the drug trade in the 1980s. In the case of Saudi Arabia, it is indirect. The US's unwavering support of the Saudi Arabian kingdom

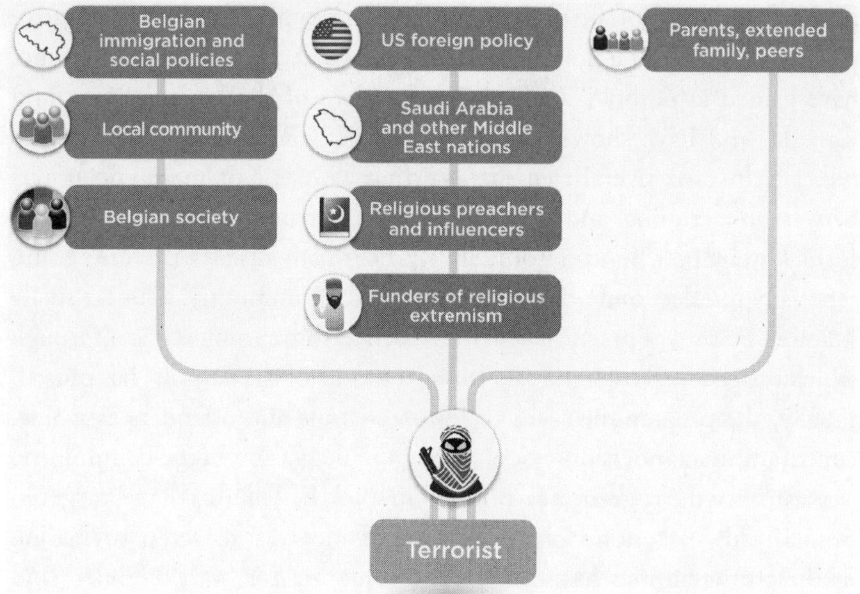

Figure 9.1: Root Cause Analysis of Crime in the Second Dimension

– despite its regime's fundamental incompatibility with all the values of freedom, progressive liberalism, civil rights, equality, and democratic rule that are synonymous with America's ideological stance – means indirect support of the Wahhabite principles around which the Saudi Arabian state is organised and, therefore, the continued existence of extremism.

In such a case, the Causality Committee's findings would reveal that arresting and punishing the terrorist and his accomplices, though necessary and appropriate, would not by itself resolve anything. The complex hierarchy of causality in play would lead to a variety of interventions at each level in order to fix the societal malfunctions that engendered the crime and to prevent such occurrences in the future. Ultimately, the terrorist himself may be viewed as a victim of various societal and institutional lapses.

Once all causal links have been established by the Causality Committee, the Restorative Programme Office (RPO) comes into action. The Office's mandate is to create, manage and continually evaluate various restorative programmes appropriate to different levels and types of crime. Restorative programmes are not a novelty – in the last two decades, such programmes have gained a foothold in the judicial system of the United States and Canada, and have shown promising results.[55] Restorative programmes typically involve several elements, starting with one or more encounters between the criminal and either the victims or community members who form a neighbourhood accountability board, to discuss the crime and especially its effect on both the victims and the community. This is usually followed by a set of practical activities (such as community service) through which the criminal can take steps to repair some of the harm he has caused. Finally, the programme seeks to restore victims and offenders as whole, contributing members of society through reintegration in the community.

Restorative programmes piloted in North America have targeted primarily low-risk, non-violent, juvenile offenders. Moreover, participation in these programmes has always been voluntary for both offenders and victims. These two factors have led to a certain selection bias, such that the efficacy of restorative programmes and especially their applicability to the full gamut of criminal offences remains difficult to evaluate. But I believe that these programmes do indeed point the way to a better, more humane, and more productive application of justice. Their hallmarks – direct encounter, restitution, community participation, and a principal goal of rehabilitation rather than imprisonment – are in line with the ideals of Second Dimension society.

In the Second Dimension justice system, therefore, restorative programmes will be the norm for *all* crimes, except those in which mental illness was a factor. RPOs, which will function initially at the Area level, will have discretion over applying restorative justice principles to each crime in their jurisdiction. Unlike restorative programmes currently in effect, however, Second Dimension restorative processes will extend farther than the victim, the perpetrator, and their relatives. Acting on the findings of the Causality Committee, the competent RPO will not only mandate encounters between offenders and victims, restitution commensurate with the crime, and reintegration of the criminal in the Community, but will also make binding requests for amendments to any complicit policies or operations that have been identified in the Causality Committee's analysis. In the previously discussed case of a terrorist act by Islamic radicals, the RPO could require parents of minority children and schoolteachers in the Area to enrol in a programme that helps them recognise and monitor budding extremism and violence in youths, both at home and in the classroom. It could require banks and other financial institutions to block channels that have been used to fund extremist activity. It could recommend indictments for radical preachers or other individuals who have been shown to have had influence on the terrorists. The Office's mandate, in other words, would extend along the entire chain of causality.

While RPOs will operate at the Area level, it is vital to understand that the concept of restoration must extend across all levels of governance. As we have seen above, an Area-level RPO may be confronted with findings from the Causality Committee that ascribe responsibility to individuals, institutions, and entities that are above the Office's jurisdiction. Therefore, there must be equivalent restorative programmes at the Regional, National, and even Global levels that can take over the responsibility of implementing changes made necessary by the Area-level RPO's recommendations. In such cases, the Area-level RPO will have the option to escalate a case to Regional or National restorative bodies, or indeed to Continental or Global authorities, which have the means to complete the restorative process.

In the terrorism example, part of the restorative process would involve restitution and policy changes on the part of National government agencies as well as foreign governments. For instance, by analysing the causality flowchart we can see that some reparation, fundamental policy adjustments, and possibly punishment would be required of several countries: from Belgium for its failure to properly integrate immigrant groups; from some governments in the Middle East for allowing radical interpretations of Islam to persist and be funded; and from Western powers for supporting such regimes.

In the First Dimension, demanding restitution and change from international entities seems like a purely rhetorical step that cannot have any effect on the decisions and actions of sovereign governments.

In Chapter 13, I outline a new system of international cooperation that will support the governance structure of the Second Dimension. The authority of nations in world affairs, and their ability to affect the outcome of international negotiations and agreements, will depend not on their economic or military might, but primarily on their track record in delivering higher-dimensional rights and freedoms to their own citizens, as well as to any other populations in their sphere of influence. This record will be quantified in a score that will determine each country's voting power in international assemblies. Ignoring a request from an RPO might negatively impact this score, compelling each country to consider seriously all recommendations issued by RPOs from both its own Areas and Areas in foreign countries.[56]

A Self-Reinforcing Structure

I have introduced two agencies into the Second Dimension justice system – the Causality Committee and the RPO (Table 9.2). The former is an analytical working group that will investigate the genesis of crime and ascertain its causes, both immediate and distant. The latter is an operational organisation that will turn the Committee's findings into corrective actions that will hopefully bring about reconciliation between victims and offenders, rehabilitation of offenders into the Community, and larger-scale adjustments in social policy to avoid the recurrence of crime.

These two agencies operate in close collaboration and reinforce each other's work. The Causality Committee informs the RPO's activities,

Table 9.2: Judicial System in the Second Dimension

	Required mechanism	**Supported by**
Prevention of crime	Social stimulus	Community
Responsibility for criminal behaviour	Society/Community	Causality Committee
Goal of justice	Rehabilitation of the offender	Restorative Programme Office

while the RPO can demand changes at all levels of society – from how individuals interact in the Community, to how national governments formulate social policies and the Global Forum regulates international diplomacy. The continual inputs from many RPOs, spread across countries and levels of governance, will act as a constant force to help communities evolve toward more enlightened values. In the long run, the influence of the Causality Committee's recommendations and the RPO's application of those recommendations will result in a continuous refinement of attitudes and relationships among community members until they are ready for a self-directed, conscience-based justice in the Third Dimension.

Karma and Justice in the Third Dimension

In Chapter 8, I concluded that laws will be much simplified in the Third Dimension, their application to particular situations relying increasingly on a new-found trust in our conscience, rather than on complex legal language and overly detailed specification. Conscience, I argued, will be the law of the Third Dimension.

In the Western philosophical tradition, the definition of conscience has at least two principal parts. The first is this: conscience is the innate human ability to distinguish right from wrong, or good conduct from bad behaviour. From this ability naturally arises morality – the duty to do right and avoid wrong. In Chapter 8 I tweaked this definition of conscience to move away from a strict right–wrong dichotomy, suggesting that conscience is the ability to see the wider implications and consequences of one's actions and to infuse them with this understanding. This allowed me to tie the Western idea of conscience to the Eastern concept of dharma, which I defined as the recognition of the interconnectedness of all life, and the resultant duty to live in harmony with all life.

But there is also another important component of conscience as defined in the Western tradition, especially in psychology: conscience is a *feeling* that results from having made a choice either in accordance with, or in contradiction to, our innate morality. Thus, a feeling of either inner peace and rectitude (good conscience) or of guilt and remorse (bad conscience).

With this aspect of conscience in mind, it is time to introduce the Eastern concept of karma.

Despite its important role in Eastern philosophies and religions, especially Hinduism and Buddhism, karma is often misunderstood. If we avoid facile definitions like 'what goes around comes around', or leave aside its role in the transmigration of souls, we can define karma as, simply, a theory of causation. Karma is the universal causal principle by which the actions, words, and intentions (both good and bad, moral and amoral) of an individual affect the future quality of that individual's existence. In some interpretations, this causation extends across the cycle of rebirth and thus into future lives, but I prefer to focus on the fact that intentional deeds have a profound effect on the person undertaking them, in this life, either in the immediate or long-term future. Good deeds tend to bring about happiness and goodwill in a person, whereas evil ones typically corrode a person's self-esteem, peace of mind, and ability to function in society. This is a fundamental observation that need not be couched in the language of Eastern philosophy, but that nevertheless forms the core of this principle.

In Chapter 8 we defined dharma as the recognition of the interconnectedness of all things, and the resultant duty to live in harmony with all things. This means that when you harm one part of life's whole, the harm is passed on and reverberates through the universe. Every action taken is either aligned or misaligned with dharma and thus generates a reverberation. That reverberation – the effect that an action can have as a result of the unseen connections between the actor and the rest of the world, in the present as well as the future – is karma. The existence of karma implies that one's present actions can and will resonate in one's future life. Karma is self-reflective because it throws back at you what you send out.

Third Dimension justice will be karmic in nature: it will recognise the unavoidable influence of amoral deeds on one's self-conception. Simply put, we must all be able to live with ourselves, and with the knowledge of what we have willed and intended in the past. Karma is thus a pervasive and powerful corrective element that forces us to come to terms with the motivations and repercussions of our actions. Criminal behaviour engenders bad karma, which, in turn, haunts our future and renders us ever more anxious, guilt-ridden, and unable to move forward. The task of Third Dimension justice will be to help all individuals recognise the karmic structure of action and reaction, cause and effect, and its consequences on the self, so that criminals can swiftly acknowledge their misdeeds and embrace repentance.

The goal of justice in the Third Dimension is a universal spirit of compassion – a compassion born of understanding, not charity. A higher level of consciousness will enable all members of the Community to understand and appreciate the pre-existing conditions that gave rise to criminal behaviour. Compassion for individuals involuntarily burdened by their subconscious will fuel our ability to forgive criminal actions and to participate in the offender's rehabilitation. Such rehabilitation will not require prisons or other forms of punishment; it will be achieved through collaborative analysis, exposure to plight and, ultimately, a self-guided repentance.

While living in Jodhpur in 1990, I witnessed communal rioting that had been incited by a speech delivered there by a well-known religious firebrand. On the second day of rioting, I decided to leave the city. By then, military troops had been deployed to restore order. A friendly army officer offered me a ride to the railway station in his jeep, suggesting that it would be difficult for me to get there due to the presence of various mobs marauding in the area. While riding in the jeep, I saw a gang of rioters, armed with rods and other blunt weapons, at the nearest intersection. Among them I recognised, much to my dismay, a fruit vendor whom I knew, having purchased his produce many times in my neighbourhood. He had a bandana around his forehead, was armed with a rusty piece of rebar, and was shouting slogans, along with his fellow rioters. I found out later that there was much violence that night. Many members of religious minorities were being attacked and beaten, and twenty people were killed.

Weeks later, after the riots had died down and order had been restored in the city, I met the vendor at his fruit stall. His eyes were vacant. He seemed distracted and visibly distressed. I approached him with the pretext of buying some fruit. When he recognised me, I asked him what had happened the night of the riots. What had impelled him – an otherwise peaceful and accommodating fellow – to take part in the violence? It took some time to get him to open up, but eventually he admitted that he had been part of the mob, and that he had participated in the killings that night. But he could not understand or explain why. He had been only peripherally aware of what he was doing, he said. He did not even know why he was participating, or why minority groups should be hunted down and beaten in the streets, or what all the fuss was about. He only knew that he had been caught up in the violent frenzy of the rioting, almost against his will and better judgment. And that remorse about the event had been gnawing at his conscience ever since. He was distressed and at a loss for an explanation, or a way to redress the wrong he had done that night.

I could see in his demeanour, and hear in his voice, that he suffered as a result of the terrible karma he had created. If this man had a channel to address his guilt, a forum to express his repentance, a way to atone for his misdeeds, and a counsellor to help him understand what had happened, he might be able to return to his normal self, purged of the bad karma and able to resume his productive role in society. This, I realise, should be the goal of an enlightened justice system: to provide the appropriate mechanisms for understanding, repentance, and atonement.

In most schools of Eastern thought, karma is entirely self-reflective – one's karma can only affect one's own quality of life. Only a few interpretations, particularly in Buddhism, accept that karma is transferable from one person to another. I believe that the quality of our intentions and actions *can* have wide-ranging repercussions on those around us, and on their own actions and intentions. This, in practice, is tantamount to saying that good deeds and bad deeds can create energies of corresponding goodness and badness (the good or bad 'vibes' we refer to colloquially) which, in turn, cause others to act accordingly. Karma, in other words, can subtly influence the law of interconnectedness.

Ultimately, our movement seeks to create a society so self-aware and capable of high levels of consciousness that it will consistently implement policies that are beneficial to entire communities by virtue of vast reserves of positive karma generated by the continuous application of conscience to decision-making. In rare cases where criminal behaviour still occurs, the role of Third Dimension justice will not be punitive, but conciliatory. It will seek to counter the bad karma generated by the criminal action through a process of understanding, reconciliation, reform, and repentance, until the criminal is ready to resume his place in society, having been purged of the ill effects of his own negative karma.

Heightened consciousness and increased reliance on conscience in the Third Dimension will translate to a drastic reduction in the number of crimes and disputes, and thus also in the number of court cases. Civil suits, especially, will decrease in number because many disagreements will be settled directly by citizens able to reason their own way to an equitable solution. Nevertheless, even in the Third Dimension there will be need for a formal judicial procedure. But not, I hope, for a professional judiciary, at least for civil cases. Whenever a dispute arises in the Third Dimension, a community mediator will be assigned[57] – someone with good standing in the local Community (or Area or Region, if the dispute involves parties in multiple jurisdictions) who, however, need not have any professional legal training. In lieu of having to serve jury duty, as citizens do in many of today's common law systems, community members in the Third Dimension will be called upon to arbitrate civil disputes as needed. (This is part of the 30 per cent time they have to contribute to the Community, described in Chapter 5.) The assigned arbitrator will have templates to follow when reviewing the evidence and issuing a verdict, and strict guidelines, especially with regard to timing (that is, there will be terminal deadlines for both discovery and argument).[58] If one of the parties (plaintiff or defendant) is not satisfied with either the arbitrator or his finding, they may appeal and request a second arbitration proceeding, but if the results of both arbitrations are the same, then the matter must be considered closed. If the results are different, then the case must proceed to trial in a traditional court of law.

This will hopefully expedite civil cases (typically the slowest and most cumbersome type of legal proceedings) and reduce the load on courts. This community-level arbitration system can be applied to some criminal cases as well, at least where the potential penalty does not exceed a certain limit.[59] To some extent, this system is modelled on the small claims courts that operate in the United States, expanded to cover a much greater range of situations, and using community arbitrators instead of professional judges. In theory, every Third Dimension adult should be able to evaluate evidence objectively and reach a reasoned conclusion in the majority of non-technical cases, especially if laws have been simplified to the point that non-professionals can use them. Indeed, this is the very litmus test for my proposal to simplify laws: can they be understood and applied by regular citizens, without reliance on legal specialists?

Justice is the foundation of civilised coexistence. For the individual citizen, no social construct embodies an advanced, peaceful, and enlightened social environment as much as a well-functioning and fair justice system. The certainty that one's rights will be recognised and that one's actions (both legal and illegal) will be treated fairly and equally according to an impartial law administered by an unbiased, efficient, and humane justice system – that is the most basic assurance a person needs to be able to engage fully and industriously in society and to accept the restrictions that society necessarily imposes on her. Today, even in countries where the justice system functions with an acceptable degree of certainty in outcomes, it is fraught with such slowness, inefficiency, and inconsistency, and it demands such unreasonable levels of financial input and technical expertise, that the average citizen is alienated from it. The philosophical overhaul and the practical modifications that I have proposed for the Second Dimension are intended to transform justice into a process that is far more accessible and compassionate, and which will yield far more desirable results – genuine closure of crimes, rehabilitation of criminals, and prevention of crime through the joint efforts of entire communities. Eventually, in the Third Dimension, justice will become internalised in every citizen's exercise of his or her conscience, engendering high levels of positive karma and thus requiring less and less of the judicial apparatus that we regard as indispensable today.

10

Democracy: A Farewell to Politics

Democracy in the First Dimension

As we have seen in our discussion of liberty (Chapter 6), individual freedom is the starting point of almost everything that we associate with modernity, including human and civil rights, the free-market economy, and egalitarian society. But in any group that consists of more than a handful of members, the individual can never be truly free to do whatever he likes, because his desires and pursuits will inevitably infringe upon the freedoms of others. Hence a communal body (a government) will always be necessary to regulate human activity to a certain extent, such that peace and order are maintained. This government, therefore, acts as a coercive force because it can only guarantee certain freedoms by curtailing others. In the simple example I offered previously, a city may wish to safeguard its denizens' right to circulate freely and safely on city streets, but it can only do so by limiting the freedom of motorists to drive as fast as they like. Any form of government authority, in other words, tends to limit individual freedom.

For liberty and government (that is, the freedom of the individual and the needs of society) to remain in a workable balance, a consensus is necessary that the government's laws express the wishes of all (or at least the majority of) its citizens. This balance can be achieved if the ruled are contemporaneously the rulers. In other words, you must be a member of a free, self-governing civil association if you hope to enjoy the maximum possible individual liberty. And that is most likely to happen where the ruled and the rulers are the same group of people.

Today, most people think of democracy as 'the rule of the people' and as having been 'invented' by the ancient Greeks, as a polity in which every individual has an equal say on how the state is run. In fact, the democracy of classical antiquity, as practised in the city states of ancient Greece, was rather different from what it is now. In Athens in the 5th century BCE, the rights to hold office, participate in legislative assemblies, and vote were restricted to a select group of people. To be a 'citizen' one typically had to be male, adult, free (that is, not a slave or a freed slave), and born of Athenian parents. This made the citizenry (though not necessarily the inhabitants) of the state a homogenous group. The welfare of the state was usually aligned with the wishes and aspirations of its elite citizens, since a group of adult, free men, who also shared the same provenance, ethnicity, and religion, were also likely to agree on most important matters. This homogeneity was perhaps the very premise for democracy in antiquity, but, in spite of it, Athenian democracy (and later Roman democracy) was fraught with problems, dissension, and inefficiencies, and was the subject of strong criticism by contemporary thinkers, including Plato and Aristotle. Indeed, all ancient democratic forms of government were eventually superseded by monarchic ones.

Also, Athenian democracy, for the most part, was a direct democracy. Any citizen over the age of twenty could participate and vote in the legislative assembly, or *Ecclesia*, which elected some officials, passed decrees and legislation, and tried political crimes.[60] In any society larger than a small city state,[61] however, direct participation is impractical. Already in the time of Republican Rome (509–27 BCE), the important innovation of democratic rule by representation had been introduced. Today, democracy[62] is always understood to be representative or indirect, such that citizens elect a small number of representatives to a legislative body and/or executive offices, and delegate authority to them. Direct democracy, in which decisions are made personally by all adult citizens in assembly (that is, almost everything is decided by referendum) has survived only in subnational or local governments, such as two Swiss cantons and some New England towns in the United States.

Modern democratic systems can be distinguished further as either parliamentary or presidential. In the former, in operation in many European countries as well as in India, the electorate votes representatives into a legislative group (such as a parliament), which in turn appoints the head of government. In the latter, used in the United States, voters not only elect representatives to the legislature, but also choose the head of government directly.

Thus, when we sing the praises of democracy, as well as when we decry its limitations, we must remember two important details about its origins. First, while we tend to associate democracy with the modern nation state, the idea of democracy was forged in a social environment that was quite different, that is, in a small city state with a homogenous citizenry. Second, democracy was conceived as a form of communal government, and as such it was intended to be direct. When it began to be applied to ever larger social groupings where direct decision-making was not feasible, the concept of representation had to be introduced.

When the two foundational elements of democracy (homogeneity and directness) are set aside so that democracy can be applied to large, highly diverse societies through the mechanism of representation, democracy begins to fail.

The Limitations of Representative Democracy

In the 21st century, there are pockets of the world where democracy can be said to function fairly well – places like Finland and Norway. Not surprisingly, these fortunate countries are similar to ancient Greek city states in two fundamental ways: they are small nations (by modern standards), and they are inhabited by relatively homogenous populations.[63] Their citizens adhere predominantly to the same race, religion, level of education, and, especially, social stratification. The disparity in wealth between the richest and poorest members of these societies is not as great as it might be in a developing country, because they offer more extensive educational and employment opportunities to their citizens, and because they have more effective taxation and welfare systems.[64]

The largest democracies in the world, on the other hand – countries like the United States, Brazil, and India – have enormous populations numbering in the hundreds of millions, and are characterised by tremendous diversity in race, ethnicity, tribe, caste, religion, education, and income level. In such complex, polarised, multifaceted societies, it is unreasonable to expect that everyone would want the same thing, accept the same policies, and envision the same future. In such societies, citizens are often unable to agree on anything but the most basic elements of social organisation. They can just about agree that all children should be educated, but not on the kind of schools they should attend, what they should learn, how they should be tested, and how education should be funded. They can agree that everyone ought to be healthy, but not on how patients should be treated, or who should pay for treatment. They can (barely) concede that taxation is necessary, but not how extensive it should be, how much everyone should pay, or how those tax revenues ought to be spent. They can agree that living in peace and safety is a desirable thing, but not on what the police can and cannot do, whether citizens ought to carry weapons, or how criminals ought to be punished.

What happens in such a fragmented social landscape? Individuals will associate with others who they believe will hold the same views, most often because they find commonality in a shared ethnicity or religion or economic class. They band together in groups that are intended to support and further the views and desires of the group, in opposition to the views and desires of other members of society.

And so, politics is born – the attempt by one group to control the decision-making of an entire community, through either persuasion or weight of numbers. In this fashion, democracy has been taken hostage, almost everywhere, by special interest groups, such as large businesses in the United States, unions in Europe, and associations organised around caste, tribe, and religion in India and other developing countries. Indeed, political parties themselves can be thought of as organisations bent on furthering the interests and dominance of one segment of society over the rest. This is obvious in Europe, where there are green parties to support the concerns of environmentalists, labour parties to prosecute the interests of workers' unions, pensioners' parties to represent the priorities of retirees, and so forth. Political parties, in such cases, are larger versions of special interest groups, functioning like 'pressure groups' more than interest-aggregating political parties.

The representative nature of today's democracy makes it especially vulnerable to special interests and party politics. When campaigning for election, candidates cannot persuade voters on the basis of their position on a long list of specific governance issues; so, instead, they take advantage of general affinities with certain sections of the electorate. The questions they invite voters to ask themselves are not 'Does this candidate have the right skills and experience to govern effectively? Will he make the right decisions that can benefit society as a whole?' but rather, 'Is this candidate as similar to me as possible? Will he make decisions that can benefit me directly, or at least my ethnic minority or religious group or social class?' In essence, today's democracies have become sites of identity politics, that is, political bodies and structures of power motivated not by a desire and duty to pursue the common good, but almost exclusively by a gross common identifier shared by their members, be it religion, tribe, ethnicity, class, language, or geographical location.

Once representatives are in office, it is relatively simple for special interests or identity politics to affect their decisions. Let us say that I wanted to encourage the passage of a new law that favours me and my associates directly (for example, a generous new subsidy for garment manufacturers). If this were to be decided by popular referendum, I would have to convince thousands of voters to support my motion. In a representative set-up, on the other hand, I have to convince only a handful of elected lawmakers, through campaign contributions, lobbying, horse trading, or outright bribery. Thus, a representative system plays into the hands of a self-interested few, irrespective of whether their proposal is well-meaning or malicious.

Another major flaw of democratic systems, especially those that are made up of just two parties, is the simple but inescapable arithmetic of elections. If two parties are certain of receiving, say, 40 per cent of votes each, then to win the election they know that they must appeal to the 20 per cent of voters who are as yet undecided. Often parties will pander to the views, interests, or leanings of this minority to secure their allegiance, that is, to add a vote bank to their tally. Thus, the long post-war period of European stability characterised by centrist parties in France, Germany and other Western European nations is now being overturned by parties espousing extreme views in an attempt to attract the attention of all those disillusioned by the perceived failings of centrist politics – economic stagnation, overly liberal social reforms, bloated bureaucracies, complicity in corporate corruption, and so forth. The predictable results of such vote bank politics are xenophobia and anti-immigration policies, harsh and unreasonable crime legislation, and economic protectionism. Parties that aim to rule are forced to support extreme positions merely to appeal to larger numbers of voters. The power of fringe vote banks is especially evident in the US's Republican Party and India's Bharatiya Janata Party (BJP), both of which have pandered to extremist social and religious views held by some of their supporters.

Democracy, therefore, has become little more than a circus of parties, identity groups, and special interest associations jockeying for power. Whenever new legislation is drafted, every party and group seeks to influence it this way and that, in an attempt to secure some advantage or concession favourable to the group they represent. In order to be passed, laws must be whittled down and diluted to the lowest common denominator, and the simplest and least assertive level. Consider, for example, how insurmountably difficult it has been, for the last several decades, for the United States to pass effective legislation to provide healthcare to all its citizens, or to reduce the level of gun violence on its streets. These seem like the simplest issues imaginable – everyone agrees that health is good and gun violence is bad. But legislation to address these issues has made very little progress, as special interest groups have managed to stymie almost every effort. This, more than any other, is the ultimate outcome of democracy applied to large societies and, indeed, to the world as a whole – paralysis in the face of perpetually conflicting special interests and needs, such that we cannot move forward except by the smallest and most trivial of steps.

Modern societies are extremely complex organisms. As I have argued thus far, this complexity stems primarily from their diversity. But there are other contributing factors as well, such as the vastness of the population, the role of technology in our lives, and advances in everything from medicine to financial engineering to scientific inquiry – all activities that throw up as many new complications as they solve. Think of the financial crisis of 2008, which cast the world into a turmoil from which it has yet to recover fully. The seed of that crisis was the unfathomable complexity of modern finance, a system so evolved, automated, interdependent, and utterly complicated that even those who were supposed to regulate it – central banks, insurers, and rating agencies – were unable to understand it.

In a different example, think of the complexity of decisions on urban design, a discipline that requires an understanding of demographics, infrastructure, mass transit, sewage systems, air quality, building codes, taxation, commerce, security, health systems, crime, crisis response, heritage preservation, the dynamics of public spaces, and the ability to forecast how any new development might affect these aspects of urban living. It is unreasonable to expect that most elected leaders (individuals skilled primarily at public speaking, campaigning, fundraising, being liked, wheeling and dealing, and beholden to special interests) can be equipped with the right skills and experience to address issues of such complexity. Ultimately, representative democracy is no longer suitable for the needs of modern societies because it fails to deliver the appropriate leaders. Democracy increasingly seems to discourage great leadership, focusing instead on an artificial political process that has overwhelmed the original purpose of democracy, that is, enacting the wishes of its citizens.

Indeed, in much of the world, democracy has been reduced to the formality of election – the favoured mechanism for securing representation.

We often celebrate the electoral process, especially if voter turnout is high, because we see it as the embodiment and expression of the democratic ethos. India, for example, is often touted as the world's largest democracy, and its national election in 2014 was covered with much fanfare as over 800 million voters exercised their electoral rights in a vast and unprecedented process that took two months to complete. Such grand displays, however, can lead to the erroneous notion that representation via election is the soul of the democratic process. Representation has proved to be the scourge of democracy rather than its soul. It ensures that politicians, rather than professional managers accustomed to guiding complex organisations or systems, continue to be elected.

This is a predicament not unlike testing in educational systems. We introduce standardised tests to objectively and efficiently measure the efficacy of education, but invariably this leads to teaching methods that ensure success on the tests rather than comprehensive, useful intellectual development. Standardised testing delivers students with high test scores, but not necessarily the skills required for university or the workforce, or, for that matter, more elusive qualities like emotional intelligence, empathy, and tolerance. Representative democracy fails in the same manner – it successfully delivers leaders who are good at winning elections but not necessarily good at managing highly complex organisations like cities, provinces, and nations.

Moreover, the nature of electioneering is such that most elected officials are always campaigning. Even after winning one election, they must continue to raise funds for the next one; they must help their party or clients to compete in by-elections, regional elections, midterm elections, and so forth. As a result, they are always in campaign mode, and their principal concern is to remain in power and raise funds, which leaves them at the mercy of lobbies and special interests. Focusing on issues of governance – on long-term plans, on the hard decisions of whether to sign a new free trade agreement, how to reform education, or how to stimulate job growth – often takes a back seat. Most importantly, the power that politicians are so desperate to hold on to is immensely corrupting. Thus, democracy creates situations where elected leaders will not make decisions or pass legislation that may be necessary or in the best long-term interest of the community because they fear they might alienate or disappoint certain groups and thus lose the next election. They therefore default to emotionally charged social issues (such as gay marriage or abortion in the United States, or religious conformity in India) to distract voters from the need for substantive reforms and sensible, forward-thinking policies.

Today's representative democracy is a trap. It is a system that tends to empower the wrong leaders – the ones who are self-serving, manipulative, and hungry for power, rather than those genuinely committed to the betterment of society. Even on those rare occasions when a visionary, thoughtful, well-meaning, and reasonably untainted leader is elected, he finds that the odds of implementing meaningful long-term policies are stacked squarely against him by the very make-up of the system that elected him: continual electioneering dominated by identity politics and special interests, and, as I will discuss shortly, a misplaced trust in outdated constitutional safeguards like checks and balances.

Representative democracy may have been a useful and productive polity in the past, especially as an improvement over the repressive regimes of the pre-Enlightenment era, where power was concentrated in very small groups. But, like all First Dimension instruments, it seems to have outlived its usefulness.

Democracy's current limitations can be summarised as five interconnected flaws. The first is that power is highly corrupting, especially for individuals at a lower level of consciousness (see Chapter 3), who continually strive to accumulate more power when they are in office. This in turn leads to the second flaw, which is that elections tend to become a matter of arithmetic instead of issues. Every time I talk to someone with experience in Indian elections, they pull out pen and paper and start adding up numbers by various divisions – X people from this religion, Y from that caste, and Z from this class – and with this simplistic arithmetic they figure out a candidate's chances of success. There is little focus on the quality of governance or on improving lives; the focus is on identity politics and on encouraging antipathy to those not in one's ethnic, religious, tribal, or other subnational group.

The third problem is that we do not have anyone to defend the public good. In *Saving Capitalism from the Capitalists,* economists Raghuram Rajan and Luigi Zingales remark:

> The behavior of government is determined, in part, by public mood. But to a greater extent, it is also determined by the special interests being regulated. This is why the free market system is fragile. Not economically (as Marx theorized), but politically. While everyone benefits from competitive markets, no one in particular makes huge profits from keeping the system competitive and the playing field level. Thus, nobody has a strong vested interest in promoting and defending free markets.

The same can be said of the public good: when it works, everybody benefits, but it is in nobody's interest to champion the cause.

The fourth flaw of modern democracy is that, because of the four–five-year election cycle, it tends to inculcate a short-term view when it comes to policymaking. Politicians pay more attention to immediate, emotive threats, and ignore ones with far worse consequences in the long term because they are not flashpoints in the present. They do not affect re-election, and they may not even affect our lifetime. Thus, governments will readily respond to an act of terrorism by quickly passing new legislation, increasing defence and intelligence budgets, and deploying countermeasures. The very real and potentially devastating threat of climate change, on the other hand, is sufficiently far in the future that we can continue to debate its causes and dilly-dally on confronting it with any real commitment or unity. In the same manner we jump on outbreaks of contagious disease but are sluggish in acknowledging the destructive effects of smoking, alcohol and drug consumption, and poor diets high in saturated fats and refined sugars. We will fight a bush fire with all means available, but we cannot see or understand the likely impact of our deteriorating natural environment.

Finally, even when politicians see the long-term problems or espouse the public good, it is virtually impossible to fight the power of entrenched interests that arise from identity politics. As Jean-Claude Juncker, president of the European Commission, put it, 'We all know what to do, we just don't know how to get re-elected after we've done it.'

The answer to all these flaws, however, is not to regress to a simpler form of democracy, like direct democracy. After all, just as it was unreasonable to expect an elected official to be able to cope with the complex demands of modern decision-making, it would be unreasonable to assume that the average citizen could understand issues of great complexity and deliberate on them in a referendum. What is needed is a new, revised democratic edifice that can not only cope with the diversity and complexity of modern experience, but also help us transition to a higher level of consciousness.

The New Democracy

The goal of the Second Dimension is to build a system that strengthens and extends the rights and freedoms outlined in Chapter 7. The role of the elected leadership is to secure for their people access to better quality of rights and freedoms. The new democracy recognises that power is highly corrupting and ensures that the individuals who govern are chosen from a group of people who (*a*) have demonstrated, by managing complex organisations, that they have the skills necessary to run a country; and (*b*) they have done so with a high degree of success, where this success is measured according to transparent, quantifiable metrics. The rights and freedoms of citizens will be built into scorecards and the leaders will be judged on the basis of an annual assessment of those scorecards.

The new democracy will also be a system that addresses the flaws of First Dimension democracy, because it will remove the need for identity politics and derive its value from merit. My aim is to create a new form of political practice that combines the ideal of democracy with the necessity of meritocracy, along with the ability to manage complexity at scale. In the Second Dimension, democracy will have a new, enhanced meaning. The key ingredient of democracy – the enfranchisement of people and their right to vote in free and fair elections – will be retained, at least at a local level, but elections will no longer be an empty ritual to be rehearsed periodically. The new democracy will be a synthesis of quality (meritocracy) and equality (democracy), built around a clear mandate to deliver meaningfully on rights and freedoms.

In the Second Dimension, governance will be carried out by individuals with proven capabilities in running complex organisations, elected from a pool of qualified candidates. Within the bounds of their jurisdiction, these new leaders will be empowered to govern almost unilaterally, such that decisions – even bold ones – can be made efficiently and productively. The complexity of modern societies and the systems upon which they rely require administrators who have a high degree of technical know-how and managerial skill. This is a fundamental tenet that ought to require no explanation – just as the most skilled and experienced candidate should be chosen to fill a vacancy in a private enterprise, so too in governance. A movie star may be photogenic and likeable, and she may have played the part of the good mother convincingly on the silver screen, but is she therefore someone to whom you would, in real life, entrust your children? By the same token, a politician tends to win an election on the strength of his ability to campaign, to generate enthusiasm, to solicit funds from donors, to deliver moving speeches, and to manipulate media coverage in his favour. But is he qualified to govern effectively? Does he have a thorough command of finance and macroeconomics, of communication technology and international politics, of developments in education and energy policy? Above all, does he have the managerial and organisational skills to harness the vast human and financial resources that he is likely to have at his disposal?

In essence, I am suggesting that government administrators in the Second Dimension will be selected from among the best managers. I pause here to define what constitutes good management. In my view, good management is simply the ability to understand a vision, and to deliver on it. That vision may be a vision of the future of society, or, more modestly, an idea for a new product or service. Delivering it requires sufficient technical knowledge to intuit all its aspects and consequences, and a high degree of organisational skill. Good leadership, as I shall discuss in Chapter 11, is more than good management. It requires the leader to not only understand and deliver on a vision, but also to formulate that vision and convince everyone of its goodness. Good leadership in governance involves the ability to articulate a vision of the near future that is enlightened, progressive, and feasible. The overriding goal of any vision must be to improve the lives of all those who follow, whether they be citizens, employees, or customers.

In the Second Dimension, leaders will continue to be elected directly by their constituents only at the lowest level of governance, namely, the Community. In Chapter 5, I proposed a four-tier hierarchy of government administration for the Second Dimension, of which the Community would be the lowest. This governance structure is reproduced in Table 10.1.

Table 10.1: Proposed Four Levels of Governance

Government level	Composition	Maximum population
Community	A geographical unit (such as a rural district, a small municipality, or a neighbourhood in a large city) consisting of approximately 25,000 inhabitants	25,000
Area	Up to 100 contiguous Communities	2.5 million
Region	Up to 10 contiguous Areas	25 million
Nation	All Regions within a national boundary	Unlimited

(This sizing model works well, I believe, for most modern nation states, which have populations numbering in the tens of millions, or, as in the case of very large countries like Brazil and Indonesia, in the hundreds of millions. For very small countries, however, the model would have to be adjusted. A country of, say, 10 million people, would not even be able to form any Regions, because Regions, in this model, must comprise at least 25 million inhabitants. In very small countries like Iceland, which has a population of just 330,000, even Areas would be impossible to form. In such cases, the size of a Community could be lowered to 10,000 inhabitants and the number of Communities in an Area could be reduced to five, while Regions may have to be dispensed with altogether.)

At the local level, a leader will be elected directly by the adult citizens of that Community. The prerequisite for candidacy will be that the candidate must have occupied a position of leadership in an institution of lower impact for at least two years. To explain what I mean by 'institution' and 'impact', see Table 10.2. The table illustrates how each organ of

Table 10.2: Levels of Institutions Based on Impact (Government Sector)

Level	Example of government institution or public service	Head officer
20	Local library	Chief Librarian
19	Local fire station	Fire Chief
18	Local school	Principal
17	Community arbitration court	Chief Arbitrator
16	Community registry	Registrar
15	**Community**	**Community Leader**
14	Area-level police force	Police Chief
13	Area-level hospital	Hospital Director
12	Area-level dept of public works	Chief of Public Works
11	Area-level judicial court	Judge
10	**Area**	**Area Manager**
9	Regional transportation board	Transport Commissioner
8	Regional dept of agriculture	Agriculture Commissioner
7	Regional tax authority	Revenue Chief
6	Appellate court	Judge
5	**Region**	**Regional Governor**
4	National parks, forests, and agriculture	Minister for the Environment
3	National defence	Commander-in-Chief
2	**National government**	**Head of State**
1	**Continental/Global government**	–

government, from the smallest, community-level organisation (the example given is a local public library) to the highest executive institution in the land (the head of government) can be categorised into a clear, twenty-tier system depending on its impact. This impact score, for government agencies at least, depends on the number of citizens served by that organisation.[65] Thus each government agency, department, or institution can be assigned a score from 20 (lowest) to 1 (highest) according to the impact it has on society.

According to this categorisation, the executive office of a Community is a Level 15 organisation, that of an Area government is Level 10, and that of a Region is Level 5. The entire nation state, represented and managed by a Head of State, is rated at Level 2. (The highest level, Level 1, is reserved for supranational organs of governance, such as Continental and Global assemblies. They will be the focus of Chapter 13.)

How are positions of leadership in this twenty-tier system assigned? For leadership positions at the lowest levels (Levels 16–20), candidates are selected by the Community Leader and his staff. When a vacancy for Community Leader (Level 15) arises, any officer who currently has responsibility for an organisation one or two levels below it (either Level 16 or Level 17) may apply, provided his performance score in his two prior years of service is sufficiently high. The candidate may then campaign for the vacancy in the same manner as politicians campaign today, with an election carried out across the Community. An outright majority awards the seat directly, with the option of a runoff between the top two candidates if no one has achieved that mark.

Once elected, the Community Leader will have overall authority, much like a chief executive officer of a private firm, over the Community, with the ability to select members of his managerial team and appoint specialists to various positions in local government, such as for public works and internal revenue. The Community Leader's tenure will be indefinite, but it must be reviewed on an annual basis. At the end of each year, his performance will be evaluated according to a balanced scorecard that considers a variety of factors, and directly references his success in guaranteeing to each and every member of his Community the expanded rights and freedoms (Chapter 7). The exact composition of the Community Leader's scorecard will vary depending on his performance in prior years, and the needs of his particular Community. (For the structure of governance scorecards, see Chapter 11.)

A Leader scoring 90 per cent or more will have his tenure renewed automatically, but lower scores will result in other scenarios, as shown in Table 10.3. This is merely an indicative proposal and could be adjusted to suit different situations. For example, a Leader's target score should be 90 per cent or higher once he is established in his position, but a concession might be made in his first year in the job, by temporarily lowering the target score to 80 per cent.

Table 10.3: Performance Scores and Leaders' Tenures

Score range	**Consequence**
90% and above	Tenure renewed.
80%–89%	A new election may be called, but only if there is a motion, backed by majority vote in a Community-wide referendum, to hold a new election. If an election is called, the incumbent may run.
70%–79%	A new election is mandatory. The incumbent may run.
Below 70%	A new election is mandatory. The incumbent shall not run.

In such a system, the performance of the Community Leader would be evaluated regularly and transparently, and he would be directly accountable for the welfare of his flock. The only parameter is performance toward the goals of the Community, not popularity, adhesion to a particular ideological programme, or membership in a minority group. This system cuts politics and political parties out of democratic governance.

The same system of evaluation and election would apply in higher spheres of government. The important difference, however, is that there would be no direct voting at higher levels, but an indirect election by one's peers. For example, if a vacancy for Area Manager (Level 10) should arise, only administrators who currently occupy positions no lower than two rungs below Level 10 (that is, at least Level 11 or Level 12) would be eligible to stand for elections for this post, provided their average performance score over the previous two years is 90 per cent or better. This means, of course, that a Community Leader could not make the leap directly to Area Manager without having first transitioned through one or two Area-level administrative posts (Levels 11–14), enabling him to become acquainted with the needs and operations of the Area as a whole. The candidates who stand for election to the post of Area Manager will therefore be drawn from a pool of administrators who possess the skills and competencies required to fill that role. The winner will be chosen in an indirect election where all one hundred Community Leaders in that Area may vote. Again, an absolute majority would determine the winner, with a runoff if the election yields a lesser mandate.

Thus, while the Community-level election retains the spirit of direct democracy, the Area-level election echoes the spirit of representational, parliamentary democracy. In both cases, candidacy is predicated exclusively on merit, as demonstrated in previous governance experience and measured objectively by a scorecard. Politics and electioneering are absent; only the most skilled administrators and those leaders capable of delivering results would rise to the highest echelons of government and, once elected, their tenure in that role would be determined exclusively by their competency and leadership skills.

At even higher levels of government (Region and Nation), the same rules would apply. In the case of a vacancy for Regional Governor (Level 5), only candidates with experience in Level 6 or Level 7 would qualify, assuming their performance scores over the previous two years are good. Voters in such an election would comprise all Community Leaders and Area Managers in that Region. In these situations, the voters would be choosing from a group with proven capabilities, that is, whoever they elect would have the necessary competencies, skills, and abilities required of that position. However, each Community Leader would cast only one vote (for a total of 1,000 votes), whereas each Area Manager's vote would have one hundred times the weight (for a total of 100 votes per Area Manager × 10 Area Managers = 1,000 votes), such that the Managers, as a group, would have as much influence in the election as the cohort of Community Leaders.

This mechanism is replicated again for selection of the country's Head of State. Only candidates with experience in Level 3 or Level 4 administration would qualify, provided their performance scores are adequate. And the election would be carried out by all Community Leaders, Area Managers, and Regional Governors, with one vote for each Leader, 100 votes for each Manager, and 1,000 votes for each Governor.

The overall electoral mechanism is summarised in Table 10.4. The numbers given in the table assume, by way of example, that the country has approximately 150 million inhabitants. It should be noted that the

Table 10.4: Proposed Electoral Mechanism of the Executive

Position	Who votes?	Number of voters	Voting rights	Available votes
Community Leader	All adult citizens in the Community	Up to 25,000	1 vote each	Up to 25,000
Area Manager	All Community Leaders in the Area	100	1 vote each	100
Regional Governor	All Community Leaders and Area Managers in the Region	10 Area Managers + 1,000Community Leaders = 1,010	100 votes each 1 vote each	(10 × 100) + (1,000 × 1) = 2,000
Head of State	All Community Leaders, Area Managers and Regional Governors	6 Regional Governors + 60 Area Managers + 6,000Community Leaders = 6,066	1,000 votes each 100 votes each 1 vote each	(6 × 1,000) + (60 × 100) + (6,000 × 1) = 18,000

system is intended to select leaders in Levels 15, 10, 5, and 2. Officers at all other levels are appointed by the relevant leader. For example, a Community Leader may appoint section heads in levels below him (Levels 16–20) when a vacancy occurs; Area Managers may appoint heads in Levels 11–14; and so forth.

Why, you might wonder, are more senior administrators given a disproportionately large vote share when it comes to electing their superiors? When electing a Regional Governor, for example, just 10 Area Managers wield as much control over the outcome as all 1,000 Community Leaders put together. Is this not undemocratic? Has the will of the people (who elected the Community Leaders directly) not been diluted to the point that it is insignificant?

The answer to these objections has two parts. First, this model helps to distribute electoral influence more evenly, such that every level of the administrative hierarchy contributes the same voting weight to the overall outcome. This ensures that a high-level candidate is elected with broad-based support. For example, a candidate for Regional Governor would not be able to rely on the support of just the 10 Area Managers to be elected, nor would the support of the Community Leaders be sufficient without the agreement of at least a few of the Area Managers. This ensures that once elected, the Governor would have a positive, collaborative relationship with the Area Managers under him, with whom he works more closely than with the Community Leaders. As I shall show in Chapter 11, this closeness is also reflected in the way in which governance scorecards are computed. The Regional Governor's scorecard is to a large extent an aggregate of the scores attained by the Area Managers under him. The Area Managers, in turn, rely on the Governor's support to improve and maintain their own scores. Because the Governor's impact on their scorecards is so considerable and so immediate, it stands to reason that the Area Managers should have a significant say in his election. In other words, they should be heavily involved in selecting their boss. The key to building a successful hierarchy of governance is the perfect alignment of the interests and goals of each executive level. This system will also prevent the cronyism that plagues so many political and administrative appointments today: voting for someone who is not qualified for the post, just because you owe him a favour, or because he is your cousin or a member of your minority group, will probably result in your own performance score falling in the long run.

Second, it is important for the reader to let go of certain quaint but misleading aspects of First Dimension democracy. In theory at least, everyone and anyone can stand for election and occupy a leadership position in First Dimension democratic states. This notion is appealing because it is very egalitarian, but it is an unwieldy relic of the class struggles of yesteryear and irrational. Would you be 'democratic' when selecting a surgeon to perform an operation on your child, by accepting any doctor listed in the phonebook? Of course not – you would seek out the most qualified surgeon–the one with the most impressive medical degree, the longest experience, the best track record in performing life-saving surgeries, and the most considerate bedside manner. Is the governance of society any less important a responsibility than performing a surgery? Is it any less critical, given that the lives and livelihoods of so many people depend on it? Should it be left in the hands of any candidate who is popular enough to win an election, who can debate well on television, or who has the financial support of a few large donors? Or should it be entrusted to a person who has a documented track record of efficient and productive management of complex organisations?

The system I propose here uses clearly defined standards and scorecards to determine eligibility, and leaves election to the highest offices in the hands of a candidate's peers. In higher dimensions the key goals of representative forums will be to define the rights and freedoms, and to appoint the bodies that monitor and review each leader's achievement of goals aligned with those rights and freedoms. The goal of executive leadership will be to deliver those enhanced rights and freedoms. Democracy, therefore, must be a system that helps us identify candidates capable of delivering higher-order rights and freedoms, and appoint them to administrative roles with a clear mandate.

This is a fundamental shift from the way representative democracy functions (or is supposed to function) in a First Dimension context. In the Second Dimension, adhering to a process in which elected officials will have to both meet applicability criteria and be scored on an annual basis will radically change the incentives of those in power.

My first book opened with the line, 'India is not a poor country. It is a poorly managed country.' Not much has changed since its publication in 2009. Monumental mismanagement continues to plague India, which continues to languish near the bottom of every human rights indicator, even though by all rights it should have become a prosperous, middle-income country by now. This means that 600–700 million human beings in India are still denied the basic benefits of healthy nutrition, clean water, uncontaminated food, a roof over their heads, a decent education for their children, and reliable healthcare. Accepting this in the 21st century, when we have at our disposal the means to address these issues, is a human tragedy unparalleled in scale. It is happening because the nature of First Dimension democracy creates a critical misalignment between the performance of elected leaders and the practical outcomes that the average citizen desires.

Representative Forums

The proposal for today's societies to be managed by capable, professional leaders – their selection and tenure almost entirely merit based – will ensure both the best possible management of communities and the elimination of political distractions like parties, special interests, and electoral campaigning. From addressing the executive needs of government, let us turn to the legislative function of the new democracy. My proposal is for the same executive officers, assembled in a parliamentary style, to make up the necessary legislative bodies. The duty to pass laws, in other words, will fall to gatherings formed by leaders of Communities, Areas, and Regions.

Checks and Balances Revisited

One of the most hallowed pillars of First Dimension democracy, as we all learned in civics class, is the division of the executive, legislative, and judicial functions of the state. The separation of these three branches of government ensures both independence and balance in the democratic state, in theory at least. In reality, however, the separation of power has resulted in rigid, cumbersome, and often immovable states, incapable of making reasonable, progressive decisions. This is especially obvious in presidential systems like the United States, where often the legislature and the executive try to pull the country in different directions. In recent years this has often been the case, with Congress dominated by one party and the White House occupied by another. The selection of Supreme Court judges, meanwhile, can degenerate into a partisan standoff between the majority and minority in Congress. The result has been continual bickering and pettiness, political stasis, and the paralysing inability to pass any meaningful and reformative legislation. Even passing a federal budget has become deeply contentious, such that government operations have had to be shut down repeatedly when the president and the legislature cannot agree on a budget. Even a highly intelligent, visionary, and dedicated president like Barack Obama failed miserably to push through any lasting, substantive reforms. He often publicly regretted his inability to introduce effective gun control legislation, for example; and his attempt to pass a comprehensive cap-and-trade bill to combat climate change was also stopped in its tracks. Even his landmark achievements, such as the Affordable Care Act and the agreement with Iran to reduce its nuclear capabilities, were quickly dismantled by his successor, Donald Trump. As the United States remains hopelessly polarised, future presidents will be similarly limited to the smallest of achievements. Public frustration over this kind of cultural and administrative stasis continues to grow; we are likely to see the deterioration of even the most basic First Dimension rights and freedoms as a result of the election of more extremist and divisive politicians.

In parliamentary systems, the division between legislative and executive functions is less pronounced, but there too its legacy is dismal. In most nations that use a parliamentary system, no party can secure an absolute majority. As a result, most large democracies, such as Germany, Italy, and France, must rely on executive governments that are coalitions. Coalitions are frail and prone to crisis. In some countries, this means frequent elections when governments fall; in others, it means extremely slow, inefficient, and lumbering progress toward reform as the competing interests of coalition members must be balanced.

To move into the Second Dimension, we need much better alignment and communication between the executive and legislative elements of government. To move more quickly toward a sophisticated and purposeful definition of human rights and freedoms (see Chapter 7), we must achieve better cohesion of interests among all the members of governance structures. One way to achieve this is to do away with the separation between the executive and the legislature. Centralising authority, both executive and legislative, in the hands of leaders elected exclusively on merit will result in a far leaner and more efficient state. Abuses of power by these individuals will be checked by the scorecard system itself. As I have already explained, each officer's tenure will be subject to evaluation and review every year, in a system rendered transparent and fair by the use of goal-based scorecards (to be detailed in the next chapter) that can quantify every leader's success in delivering what her constituents need.

Composition of Representative Forums

I now turn to the structure of the representative forums composed of elected executive officers. The legislative body closest to the people, known as 'Area Caucus', would comprise all the Community Leaders within an Area, that is, 100 members, plus the Area Manager, for a total of 101 members. There would exist as many such Caucuses as there are Areas in a country. A higher assembly, known as Regional Assembly, would consist of all Community Leaders and Area Managers in a Region, plus the Regional Governor himself, for a total of 1,011 members. Finally, the highest legislative body in the land, the National Council, would comprise all Area Managers and Regional Governors in the country, plus the Head of State. This proposal is represented in Figure 10.1.[66]

Membership in the National Council would vary with the size of the country. For example, in a country that has approximately 150 million

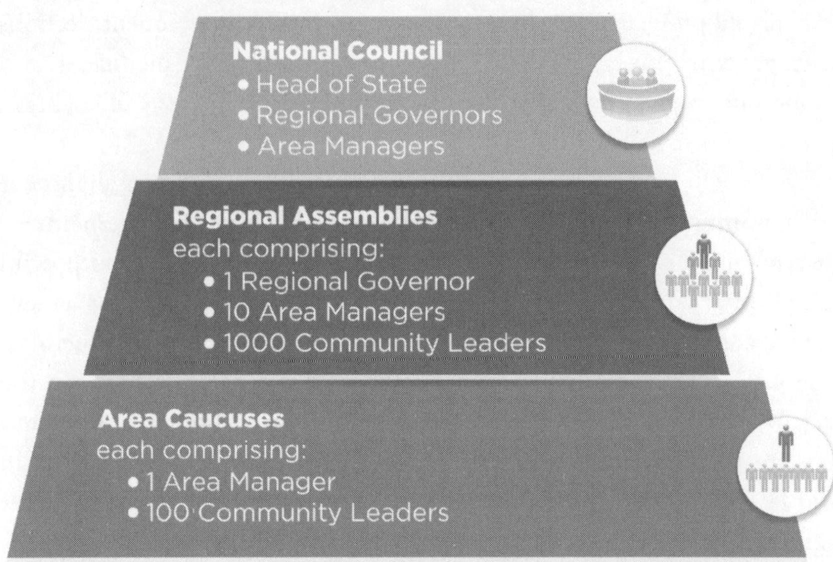

Figure 10.1: Proposed Pyramidal Model of Legislatures

inhabitants, there would be six Regions. The National Council would, therefore, consist of sixty-seven members: the six Regional Governors, sixty Area Managers (ten Area Managers for each Region), plus one Head of State. The National Council would, of course, have to be sized carefully in smaller countries. In a country of, say, 20 million people, there might be only a dozen members in the National Council, which would be an insufficient number to provide the right scale of decision-making by vote. In such a case, the composition of the National Council could be altered to include additional representatives chosen, on a rotating basis, from the Area Caucuses. Alternatively, the way in which the country is divided into smaller units could be altered, for example by creating Regions that consist of just five Areas instead of ten. Adjustments might also have to be made for extremely large nation states. China, for example, with a population of almost 1.4 billion, would have a National Council consisting of 617 legislators, which might be too large for the highest forum in the land.

Voting on new or amended legislation in the representative forums would proceed as outlined in Table 10.5.

Table 10.5: Proposed Electoral Mechanism in the Legislatures

Forum	Members	Voting rights	Available votes
Area Caucus	1 Area Manager + 100 Community Leaders = 101	100 votes 1 vote each	(1 × 100) + (100 × 1) = 200
Regional Assembly	1 Regional Governor + 10 Area Managers + 1,000 Community Leaders = 1,011	1,000 votes 100 votes each 1 vote each	(1 × 1,000) + (10 × 100) + (1,000 × 1) = 3,000
National Council	1 Head of State + 6 Regional Governors + 60 Area Managers = 67	60 votes 10 votes each 1 vote each	(1 × 60) + (6 × 10) + (60 × 1) = 180

This system leverages the same assemblies that were introduced previously in connection with the election of Community Leaders, Area Managers, Regional Governors, and the Head of State. Indeed, the idea is to focus authority in the same bodies. The Area Caucus, for example, will make legislative decisions that apply to the Area it represents, and thus to all the Communities in it. When the Area Manager position for this Area is vacant, the same Area Caucus (minus, of course, the Area Manager, who is outgoing and therefore not involved in the election) will elect a new Area Manager from the pool of qualified candidates. Thus, there will be a certain cohesion between the executive and legislative functions in the Area, not unlike the parliamentary democracies of today. The voting system for legislative decisions echoes this same principle. At the Area Caucus level, differential voting rights ensure that the opinion of the Area Manager has the same weight as that of all the Community Leaders put together. Thus, no legislative decision can be made without the Area Manager's approval. Conversely, if a 75 per cent quorum were required to pass new legislation or amend existing legislation, no such legislation could be pushed through by the Area Manager alone without securing the support of at least half of the Community Leaders under him. Similarly, in the Regional Assembly it would be very difficult to push through any changes without the cooperation of the Regional Governor, who wields one-third of the votes. At the same time, however, it would be impossible for the Governor to force any legislation without the support of the majority of Managers and Leaders.

It is important to clarify that the Area Caucuses, Regional Assemblies, and National Council are not intended to be permanent or standing legislative bodies. They would meet only occasionally, as needed, to accomplish three tasks:

- Pass new laws (or amend existing laws) that are appropriate to their jurisdiction. (Any rules and protocols that are developed from these laws would also require the forum's approval.)
- Periodically review benchmarks for standards of rights and freedoms. (These benchmarks would be developed and analysed by an independent authority.)
- Appoint members of four technical groups (described below) responsible for the creation and implementation of a scorecard system applicable to all leadership positions (Community Leader, Area Manager, Regional Governor, Head of State).

Thus, while the personnel engaged in legislative and executive roles would be the same, the legislative function would be only intermittent, and would not be an excessive burden on leaders. As explained in Chapter 8, the increasing reliance, in higher dimensions, on each individual's conscience will result in fewer laws, distilled down to minimalist renditions. Therefore, assemblies of executive leaders (the Area Caucuses, Regional Assemblies, and the National Council) will have to convene only rarely to discuss and write new laws, as needed.

Moderators of Power: Four Technical Authorities

The representative forums will be responsible for appointing the members of four independent institutions:

Jurisdictional Authority. This body will assign responsibility for every decision or action undertaken by government to the appropriate level of administration. For example, if a city park needs maintenance or new landscaping, the task falls to the Community. However, if an inland canal that flows through multiple communities requires refurbishment, the Jurisdictional Authority would analyse its course and impact on various segments of the population, and assign the task to the Area government–unless, of course, the canal crosses multiple Areas, in which case the competent authority might be the Region. (These examples relating to infrastructure are relatively simple and clear-cut, but in matters relating to judicial proceedings, for example, or to education or health, the determination could be much more difficult. Hence the need for a specialised committee to make such decisions.) The Jurisdictional Authority functions at a National level and would therefore be classified as a Level 3 or 4 entity. While it may have multiple branches dedicated to specific Regions and Areas, it is necessarily a single, monolithic body to avoid contradictions and split opinions over jurisdiction. Members of its executive committee are appointed to this office (for terms of, say, five or ten years) by the National Council, using some of the same criteria used for the election of Area Managers and Regional Governors, that is, successful completion of two consecutive years in office in a position not more than two levels lower than the Jurisdictional Authority's level.

Scorecard Development Authority (SDA). This body will be responsible for researching, developing, reviewing, and updating the scorecards applicable to all chief officers (Community Leaders, Area Managers, Regional Governors, and Head of State). A detailed discussion of its mandate and operations follows in Chapter 11. There are multiple SDAs operating in a country. One SDA would be required for each Area to develop and continually update scorecards for all the 100 Communities in that Area. The executive boards of these SDAs are appointed directly by the Area Caucus and are Level 10 institutions, that is, at the same level as the Area Manager. These measures ensure that each SDA retains a high degree of autonomy and has the authority to counter attempts to influence its work from the Area Manager and from Community Leaders. There must also be Regional SDAs (Level 5) to compose scorecards for Area Managers and, finally, a National SDA at Level 3 or 4 to oversee the development of scorecards for Regional Governors and the Head of State.

Scorecard Evaluation Authority (SEA). This authority, which must at all times remain independent of the SDA, will be responsible for auditing compliance with the scorecard system, and especially for calculating each officer's score at the end of the year. An SEA exists to match each SDA. Therefore, SEAs operate at the Area, Regional and National levels. Like the SDAs, each SEA is headed by an executive committee appointed for a fixed term by the corresponding representative forum.

Election Committee. Election Committees are responsible for publicising, organising, and conducting elections at various levels of government. Election Committees will operate at the Area level (to supervise Community Leader elections in the Area), at the Region level (to supervise elections of Area Managers in the Region), and at the National level (to supervise elections of Head of State and Regional Governors). The heads of these Election Committees are appointed directly by the corresponding representative forums. Direct, popular elections will be retained only when electing Community Leaders. The Election Committee for the Area where a Community Leader election is taking place will be responsible for monitoring its progress and certifying its results. If the Election Committee is notified by the competent SEA that a Community Leader has failed to achieve his annual scorecard target, the Election Committee must initiate a new election. Higher executive positions, such as Area Manager, Regional Governor, and Head of State, are elected not by popular vote but rather by the members of the relevant representative forum, as discussed above. In such cases the Election Committee must verify each candidate's qualifications to determine whether he or she may stand for election, and will audit the results.

The political architecture and evolution that led to the democracy we know, with the bicameral legislature and the division of powers, was a phenomenal leap for humanity and one of the great achievements of First Dimension thought. However, for humanity to progress further, we need a new political system that is designed for, and capable of, a more evolved and sophisticated understanding of social cooperation. The system as it exists is proving to be a liability in the creation, extension, and development of more subtle rights and freedoms. The creation of these rights and freedoms is urgent for a planet badly in need of a system that is able to encompass the complexity and variability of our world. Human relations – relations between nations and within nations – are becoming more complex as technology, urbanisation, and diversity conjure up both fantastic new ways of doing things and new threats. We need a political system that is better designed to guide us through the 21st century. That is what I have attempted to define in this chapter, while bringing the political system in alignment with some of the other ideas that inform interdependence and put us on the path to the Third Dimension.

Is the proposal here too revolutionary? The ideas that form the basis of what I have called 'the next enlightenment' are far less drastic than what was proposed in seminal documents like the Magna Carta (1215) or the Federalist Papers (a little over two centuries ago). In their day, these landmark texts contained radical blueprints for a more enlightened future. That is what our times demand of us today.

Addendum, April 2019

As this book went to press, Brexit, seemingly in its death throes, dominated the international news. The utter failure of democracy seen in the Brexit episode is simply too valuable an example to pass up, so I will comment on it here, however briefly.

As I have argued in this chapter, modern democracies suffer from various problems that tend to cripple their effectiveness, such as the influence of special interests, corruption among politicians, and constant electioneering. In discussions on the state of democracy, we often tell ourselves that democracy could be an ideal polity if only we could eliminate, or at least reduce, the impact of these debilitating features. The case of Brexit, however, clearly shows that there are serious *systemic* faults in democracy as it is set up in the First Dimension. The Brexit stalemate came about not because its political protagonists are corrupt or because special interest groups lobbied one way or the other (though these factors may have played a role as well). In fact, Brexit is simply First Dimension democracy stretched to its inevitable conclusion.

First, Brexit has shown that *direct* democracy (in the form of a referendum) has severe limitations. While referendums can be used to decide simple matters, such as whether shops in Switzerland ought to be open on Sundays or not, they are counterproductive when deliberating on complex issues, such as whether a country should or should not leave a trade alliance. The economic, administrative, and societal ramifications of Brexit are so profound and impenetrably complicated that it is unreasonable and unfair to assume that the average citizen could have anticipated them when she was asked to vote.

Second, the Brexit debacle shows that *representative* democracy, too, is systemically flawed. At the time of writing, British MPs had already voted down Prime Minister Theresa May's proposed exit agreement (which she had painstakingly negotiated with the European Union over the previous two years) three times, plus they had voted 'no' to eight alternative proposals, and 'no' to everything, once again, when those proposals were whittled down to a smaller number. Cross-party talks had also failed to yield a way forward, so May was twice forced to request deadline extensions from the European Union, hoping the extra time would be enough to resolve the impasse in parliament. To the average observer, it is unclear why the United Kingdom's elected representatives are so hopelessly unable to come to a sensible agreement over what to do next. Are they held back by genuine ideological differences, or are they simply playing political games in an effort to secure some advantage for themselves or their party? The question is irrelevant; either way, their conflicting priorities have resulted in a complete gridlock – the logical terminus of First Dimension democracy.

11

Governance: A Template for the 21st Century

The Role of Organisations

Broadly speaking, organisations are groups of people who come together for a specific purpose, to fulfil a particular societal need, or to systematically perform a task that is either necessary or desirable to substantial numbers of people. These organisations – whether they are government agencies and departments, religious associations, professional guilds, profit-seeking private enterprises, or advisory councils – are as old as civilisation itself. In premodern times, when hunting and gathering and subsistence agriculture were the only economic models available, there was little or no need for coordinated action, domain knowledge, and structured governance. But as soon as societies began to produce agricultural surpluses, and thus developed division of labour and trade, it became necessary to systematise many aspects of community life, such as enforcing civic order, taking care of the poor and the sick, managing community assets, streamlining the exchange of goods and services, and so forth. Organisations helped to bring about more structured social environments by pooling the resources and skills of many people; through collective effort, they were able to achieve far more than individuals ever could. Eventually, the advent of organised religion, empires, and long-distance trade created the need for large, impersonal bureaucracies that could manage all the needs and responsibilities of organised society.

As these organisations grew in size and influence, they created a managerial class of technocrats with specialised skills in running the complex systems required by large governments, big businesses, and vast religious organisations. Most First Dimension organisations were built around the ideals of power, control, order and, in the case of private businesses, profit. These priorities were in line with the concomitant ideas of liberty, economic rights, and democracy, and in many ways complemented the existing power structure of First Dimension societies.

The vision and purpose of many organisations, however, were neither coordinated with those of others, nor aligned with the welfare of the citizenry as a whole. Business organisations, for example, were created with the solitary goal of increasing sales and profits, irrespective of how these goals were achieved, or whether they were in line with the goals of society in general. Religious organisations aimed to perpetuate their faith and expand their membership, and, in some cases, to influence civic behaviour and legal norms toward their vision. Again, this was done with the interest of the organisation and its members in mind, but not necessarily with a view of bettering society as a whole, or respecting the desires of other religious groups.

Unlike businesses, guilds, and religious associations, which had clearly defined and narrowly focused goals, the role of governance systems was never very clear, especially because 'good governance' is an ill-defined concept that can be interpreted in various ways and is subject to continual change. It may shift due to changes in the population, in technology, in environmental conditions, and especially in the nature and inclination of the sovereign authority.

The result was that many First Dimension organisations operated, and still operate, in relative isolation, and at cross-purposes, with often disastrous consequences for the general populace. Religious wars and religious discrimination, which have plagued many complex societies in the past, and continue to work against equality and prosperity in many developing countries, are the most egregious example of this lack of synchrony. But private enterprises focused solely on profit are equally damaging to general welfare. Their disregard for the wider consequences of their activities has led to widespread income inequality, environmental degradation, depletion of natural resources, and many other problems. Finally, guilds, industry associations, and political bodies have worked consistently to further the interests of their members, and have more often than not misled, abused, or taken advantage of political systems vulnerable to special interest. In Chapter 10, I described how democracy, the very polity that we currently accept as the best possible model of governance, suffers especially from the corrosive influence of special interest groups.

Indistinguishable: Organisations in the Second Dimension

In the Second Dimension, all organisations, irrespective of their purpose (governance, business, social, or scientific), will be treated equally in terms of taxation and status before the law. This is an important deviation from current practice, according to which organisations exist under very different regulations, depending on whether they are for profit or non-profit, trusts or corporations, public or private. The fundamental idea driving this 'normalisation' of social enterprises is that all organisations, irrespective of their composition, size, or funding structure, must share the same goal, namely, the betterment of *all* of life's constituents, including all strata of society, all communities and individuals, and the environment. Though ambitious, this inclusivity must be enshrined in the mission and vision statements of all organisations, and carried out in their daily operations. It must also be measurable according to transparent, objective, and quantitative criteria, such that all organisations will be evaluated primarily on the *impact* they have on society and nature.

For government organisations, impact must be defined as the number of citizens they serve, while performance must be a measure of their ability to uphold and extend rights and freedoms (Chapter 7). Guaranteeing and managing the (enhanced) rights and freedoms of its citizens will remain the overriding responsibility of government at every level.

For all other types of organisations (such as private businesses, social enterprises, and scientific or academic institutions), the determination of impact will be based on a combination of size (revenues or budget) and staffing level. In Chapter 16 (on ownership), I will discuss a different scoring mechanism (the Stewardship Index) that can be used to assess the performance of these non-governmental organisations. Table 11.1, showing the impact levels seen in Chapter 10, is expanded to include enterprises from all spheres of professional activity, including business, social, and scientific. In the impact level table, governance institutions are shown on par with institutions from other spheres. Their level can be equated by realising, for example, that a large private company with thousands of employees can have the same impact on economic and social welfare as an Area government, or, for that matter, a well-respected news network with high visibility.[67]

Table 11.1: Levels of Institutions Based on Impact (All Sectors)

Level	Example from governance	Leader	Example from other sectors	Leader
20	Local library	Chief Librarian	Company, branch, or franchise with <10 employees	CEO/MD
19	Local fire station	Fire Chief	Policy think tank	Director
18	Local school	Principal	Department/Faculty of a university	Head of Department
17	Community arbitration court	Chief Arbitrator	Company with about 100 employees	CEO/MD
16	Community registry	Registrar	Large museum	Director
15	Community	Community Leader	Company with >1,000 employees	CEO/MD

Table 11.1: Levels of Institutions Based on Impact (All sectors) (contd.)

14	Area-level police force	Police Chief	Daily newspaper	Chief Editor
13	Area-level hospital	Hospital Director	Large Non-governmental Organisation	CEO/MD
12	Area-level dept of Public Works	Chief of Public Works	Finance dept of a mid-sized company	CFO
11	Area-level judicial court	Judge	University	Chancellor
10	Area	Area Manager	Enterprise with at least $10 billion in revenues, and/or 10,000 employees	CEO/MD
9	Regional transportation board	Transport Commissioner	International sporting federation (FIFA, International Olympic Committee, etc.)	President
8	Regional dept of agriculture	Agriculture Commissioner	Technology dept of a large company	CTO
7	Regional tax authority	Revenue Chief	Enterprise with at least $25 billion in revenues, and/or 25,000 employees	CEO/MD
6	Appellate court	Judge	Enterprise with at least $50 billion in revenues, and/or 50,000 employees	CEO/MD
5	Region	Regional Governor	Enterprise with at least $100 billion in revenues, and/or 100,000 employees	CEO/MD
4	National parks, forests, and agriculture	Minister for the Environment	–	–

3	National defence	Commander-in-Chief	–	–
2	National government	Head of State	–	–
1	Continental/ Global government	–	–	–

CEO: Chief Executive Officer
CFO: Chief Financial Officer
CTO: Chief Technology Officer
MD: Managing Director

The table shows the new, meritocratic democracy described in the previous chapter. The scorecard mechanism allocates responsibilities to each level of governance and assigns to leaders of each level specific, quantifiable goals and deliverables to ensure that the needs of the citizenry are met. This system extends down the line to all those responsible for fulfilment of those deliverables.

A way to ensure that complex organisations (governmental or otherwise) will deliver on their goals is for their leaders to be selected on the basis of demonstrated skills and experience, and held accountable by way of measurable results. They should not be chosen for their likeability or because they are good at tweeting or giving divisive speeches, or for their ability to crush dissent within their own party, but by their ability to improve the lives of those they govern. Similarly, the meritocratic nature of the new democracy will be guaranteed through the use of a sophisticated, transparent, quantitative tool to evaluate the year-on-year performance of leaders and, by extension, their suitability for even higher positions of authority to which they may aspire. As we shall see shortly, this tool is a balanced scorecard whose basic building blocks are the rights and freedoms that each level of government is expected to deliver to its citizens. It is the critical component in the machinery of the new democracy because it ensures that leaders at every level are perfectly qualified to fulfil their managerial responsibilities, and that their qualifications are documented in their track record of successful governance.

You may object that countries cannot be run like private companies, and even the best business leaders often do not make good prime ministers. Private companies are driven by a clear goal (profitability), whereas the goal of a government is the welfare of its citizens – an outcome much more elusive and difficult to quantify, and one that almost always involves undertaking projects and instituting policies that are *not* profitable. This objection, however, is mired in a First Dimension model that prizes profitability above all other outcomes. The Utility Index that will be used in the Second Dimension (see Chapter 16) to evaluate all enterprises (public or private) does *not* include profitability among its criteria. Rather, the index represents a novel way of rating enterprises according to their social utility, their overall impact on the economy, and their ability to innovate and create efficiencies. The incentive to nudge enterprises in this direction is taxation: a high score on the index invites a contribution from the tax authority (that is, negative tax), whereas a low one incurs a heavy fiscal burden. Now, if the focus of firms can be shifted away from 'maximising shareholder value' and redirected toward greater social utility through mechanisms like the Utility Index, then can we not say that we have made them more similar to governments? If profit is no longer the primary motivation for private enterprise, then do we still hold that governments cannot be run like private firms?

A convenient outcome of this system is that leadership would be fungible. In other words, the system allows for, and encourages, leaders to be engaged in both public governance and what we currently call private enterprise. The underlying assumption here is that good leaders and good managers can flourish in both types of organisations, and can bring their advanced managerial skills to bear on both. (As the reader may recall, in Chapter 10 I defined good management as the ability to understand a vision and to deliver it to its stakeholders. A good leader, while possessing all the attributes of a good manager, must also be able to *formulate* a vision that improves the lives of all stakeholders.) And the best leaders are usually men and women capable of a vision greater than narrowly defined economic profit. Given the right level of autonomy, a clear mandate, control over their own tenure, and the recognition and respect of the public, most experienced, successful leaders would probably opt in favour of positions that have a significant impact on society and a wider social and ecological utility over ones that are merely economically profitable.

Governance Evaluated: The Scorecard

Recently, while travelling in the US state of Connecticut, I was held up at a car rental agency office because the employee processing my reservation was having trouble spelling my name. Of course, 'William' is a common name in English and not especially difficult to spell, so I was surprised and annoyed that it should cause so much confusion and delay. I resisted the urge to complain and tried to be helpful and conciliatory. When she heard that I was a 'real American' even though I did not look like one, she commented on how foreigners were taking away American jobs and thus keeping wages low, including her own.

This sounded like the standard political narrative accepted by many voters who supported Donald Trump on his way to the presidency. The truth, I realised, was that this young woman, despite living in one of the richest and most progressive countries in the world, was the victim of poor governance on many levels. She had probably suffered from a poor education, which in turn had led to a poorly paid, uninspiring, dead-end job, which rather than being taken away by immigrants or outsourced overseas would likely become automated in the near future, making her redundant (indeed, several car rental companies have now begun to use automated kiosks to manage the issuance and return of vehicles). Millions of Americans probably suffer from the same predicament as this young woman because successive US governments – federal as well as local, Democratic as well as Republican – have failed a large portion of their citizens. They have failed to deliver quality education, meaningful employment opportunities, equitable social conditions, and an adequate safety net of services to support disadvantaged communities. They failed in these goals because they are trapped in a system that does not incentivise good governance, hold leaders accountable for delivering the desired results, and provide an objective way to measure progress toward such results.

What if the leaders of all enterprises, including and especially institutions of governance, were subject to annual performance evaluation by way of balanced scorecards? What if they were given clearly defined targets in every sector under their direction (for example, transport, education, health, and welfare), and failure to meet those targets could result in dismissal, whereas only success could open the door to advancement? This simple idea is in keeping with what I proposed in Chapter 10, namely, that governance of the future should be entrusted to highly skilled managers with proven track records, rather than politicians whose primary skill is the ability to be elected. And the capability of administrators, and their adequacy as managers of society, must be continually ascertained through a fair, transparent, and quantifiable system. The balanced scorecard, therefore, is a template that can define good governance in the future.

Government requires an extensive and specific set of performance criteria because, in most cases, it affects a far greater number of people than, say, a university or a car manufacturer. More importantly, if we accept that the government's primary role is to guarantee the fundamental rights and freedoms of its citizens, then those very rights must become the measuring stick by which it is evaluated. In other words, rights and freedoms, in their Second Dimension guise, must determine the line items in every public administrator's scorecard. The ability to deliver Second Dimension rights and freedoms to the citizens in his Community, Area, Region or Nation, becomes the measure of a leader. This radical overhaul of how leaders who run large organisations, companies, and governments are selected will affect every aspect of society. It is designed to move humanity toward the Second Dimension.

How Scorecards Are Created

Before we turn our attention to a concrete example of a Community Leader's scorecard, we must understand how, and by whom, scorecards are compiled. As mentioned in Chapter 10, it is the responsibility of the competent Scorecard Development Authority (SDA) to create scorecards for governance leaders in its jurisdiction. The SDA is a technical working group tasked primarily with the research, selection, and quantification of the specific criteria or key performance indicators (KPIs) that make up a scorecard. The overall vision for the progress of a Community, on the other hand, must come from the Community Leader herself. Hers is the prerogative to offer her constituents a progressive, enlightened vision of the future, and then to deliver on that promise. Indeed, this vision of her Community's near future is, in fact, a compendium of the campaign promises she is likely to have made when vying for election to her post.[68]

At the beginning of each five-year planning cycle, therefore, Community Leaders will be required to provide a Vision Statement to the Area-level SDA. In the Vision Statement, the Community Leader must explain her plans to improve the Community's welfare in ten domains:

1. Citizen services (including employment and welfare)
2. Education
3. Environment
4. Finance and economic development
5. Health
6. Housing and property development
7. Leisure, culture, and tourism
8. Public works
9. Safety and justice
10. Transport

The Vision Statement is not a technical document. It requires the Community Leader merely to describe the overall trajectory of her tenure. She may put forward a reduction in crime as a key priority, or the improvement in economic welfare through upgrades in education, business opportunity, employment, and social services. She may pledge to reduce traffic congestion significantly, or refurbish dated public infrastructure. Her vision, at this stage, needs only broad strokes.

Once it has received the Community Leader's Vision Statement, the SDA will begin work to turn it into a workable scorecard with which to measure the Community Leader's fulfilment of her own vision. The SDA will take the following steps:

1. **Alignment with appropriate rights and freedoms:** The priorities and goals set forth in the Vision Statement must align closely with recognised rights and freedoms, such that each individual KPI, once elaborated, can be referenced to a specific right or freedom.
2. **Formulation of KPIs:** For each goal of the Vision Statement that can be aligned with a specific right or freedom, the SDA formulates one or more KPIs that accurately represent progress toward those goals.
3. **Determination of potential:** The SDA determines the degree to which improvement is possible for every KPI in the draft list of KPIs. By comparing the Community with other communities that have a similar socio-economic profile (in the Area, in the Region, and in other countries), the SDA must estimate the extent to which improvement is possible.
4. **Identification of benchmarks:** The SDA must now define the appropriate benchmarks upon which the target values of each KPI will be based. It will draw on its previous comparative analysis to single out the most successful example available in an administrative unit of similar profile.
5. **Quantification of KPI target values:** Armed with the results of its analyses of potential and benchmarking, the SDA can now set quantitative targets for each KPI. These are the five-year target values that feature in the Leader's scorecard, with interim targets for each year.

Let us see how the SDA's work might unfold by way of a simple example – juvenile crime in an imaginary Community called 'Middleville'. In recent years, Middleville has seen an alarming rise in criminal activity, especially violent crimes such as assaults and armed robberies, many of which occur in connection with drug trafficking. Of special concern to its citizens is the fact that many of these crimes are being committed by juveniles. Reacting to public pressure to address youth crime, Middleville's Community Leader has pledged, in her Vision Statement, to significantly reduce juvenile delinquency.

In **Step 1** of its working procedure, the SDA must reference the Community Leader's stated goal to a human right or freedom. In this case, it is a simple task, as crime reduction in any form is easily aligned with the right to life, dignity, and security of person, which is universally accepted in the First Dimension and will enjoy a more detailed formulation in higher dimensions. The reference would be articulated as follows:

Right to life, dignity, and security of person

→ Right to be protected from violence and crime (First Dimension)

→ Right to peaceful and violence-free habitat (Second Dimension)

→ Right to a level of compassion in all citizens (Third Dimension)

The SDA also notes that reducing crime in Middleville is well within the purview of the Community Leader. In this case, therefore, it does not need to consult the Jurisdictional Authority.

In **Step 2**, the SDA proceeds to define one or more KPIs that accurately capture the goal in question, namely, a reduction in juvenile delinquency. This is the most technically demanding part of the process; it requires extensive research on crime statistics and trends, analysis of crime prevention strategies, and review of best practices. Simply mandating an overall reduction of crime is not enough. While reducing crime in general may be one of the Community Leader's goals, it will be addressed by a different set of KPIs. The issue at hand is to reduce *juvenile* crime. Nor is it adequate to measure such a reduction in absolute terms. For example, imagine if the SDA were to put the following mandate in the Community Leader's scorecard: 'reduce the number of juveniles arrested for violent crimes by X per cent'. An unscrupulous Community Leader could easily meet this goal by inviting Middleville's police force to 'go easy' on juvenile suspects when investigating crimes. Conversely, a mandate to 'increase the conviction rate for juvenile crime by X per cent' might lead the police to focus excessively on juvenile suspects, and to treat them with prejudice. So, neither of these KPIs would yield the desired result, namely, a genuine, long-term improvement in the quality of life of the Community's youth, which, in turn, would result in lower levels of juvenile delinquency.

After much study and deliberation, therefore, the SDA decides that the following KPI best encapsulates the goal of curbing juvenile crime: 'reduce violent crimes committed by juveniles *as a proportion of all violent crimes* by X per cent'. Note that this KPI does not address violent crime overall, but rather the participation of underage youths in criminal activity. Also, it is unlikely to lead to knee-jerk reactions like profiling of juveniles or flooding the streets with more police officers. Rather, it will encourage the Community Leader to implement thoughtful measures that are known to reduce juvenile crime in the long term: monitoring and early intervention in families at risk; reduction in truancy, bullying, and antisocial behaviour in schools; mandatory mentoring of youths at risk of violent behaviour; development of recreational and after-school programmes; rehabilitation of juveniles released from detention; vocational training opportunities for school dropouts; and so forth.

In **Step 3**, the SDA investigates the potential for improvement, that is, the degree to which an improvement in juvenile delinquency is realistically possible in Middleville. By analysing local crime data, the SDA discovers that the proportion of violent crimes perpetrated by juveniles in Middleville is 34 per cent. This compares unfavourably with the corresponding rates in the Area, Region and Nation, all of which hover around 20 per cent.[69] The SDA concludes that the potential for improvement in this KPI is high. Therefore, the SDA can set an aggressive target for this KPI.

In **Step 4**, the SDA searches for a precedent on which to base its recommended target value. It finds another Community – Youngtown – which, despite being in a different country, has a demographic and socio-economic profile similar to Middleville's. It, too, has had to confront high rates of juvenile crime. By implementing a comprehensive and balanced set of preventive measures, Youngtown managed to reduce the percentage of violent crimes perpetrated by juveniles by half over the course of a few years. The SDA concludes that Youngtown's success in combating juvenile crime is the best available model anywhere, so it must be adopted as the benchmark for Middleville's own youth crime prevention efforts.

In **Step 5**, finally, the SDA can quantify the targeted improvement in Middleville's juvenile crime levels. The relevant line items in the Community Leader's scorecard are shown in Table 11.2.

Table 11.2: Juvenile Crime Reduction Targets

Category	**Subcategory**	**KPI**	**Current value**	**5-year target**	**Interim annual targets**
Safety and justice	Crime prevention	Percentage of violent crimes perpetrated by juveniles	34%	17%	32%, 30%, 25%, 20%

The overall goal is similar to Youngtown's: to reduce the percentage of violent crime perpetrated by juveniles by half within five years. Such a reduction will bring Middleville's youth crime rate to 17 per cent, which would beat the Area and Region averages and thus become a new national benchmark. Recognising the fact that measures to curb delinquency among youths may take time to take effect, however, the SDA has set very accessible targets for the first two years. Thereafter, it expects the rate of improvement to accelerate significantly.

Upon receiving her scorecard, the Community Leader may query specific provisions in it, or negotiate lower performance targets directly with the SDA should she feel that they are unreasonable. Any changes resulting from these negotiations must be approved by the Area Manager's office. Ultimately, however, the SDA will have the final say. To achieve the scorecard's targets, the Community Leader is free to implement whatever programmes she and her advisers deem appropriate. In the case of Middleville's high rate of juvenile crime, she may opt for expanding the police department's resources and the scope of its activities, or to increase community outreach activities, or start various youth development programmes, or encourage the formation of neighbourhood watch associations. (Ideally, she will set up a task force from various municipal departments and tackle the problem through a combination of these measures.) Whatever her decision, she will have unfettered control of, and responsibility for, the operations aimed at achieving the desired targets.

Example of a Community Leader's Scorecard

Table 11.3 shows a detailed example of what a Community Leader's scorecard might look like. At first glance you may find it daunting because it is long and contains many indicators and values. Governance is a complex undertaking, especially in the sophisticated and highly structured societies of our time, so it requires an equally elaborate measuring mechanism. This is why scorecard development (including appropriate benchmarking) and scoring will be the key responsibilities of all supervisory institutions in the new, meritocratic model of governance.

Under each of the ten headings outlined in the Leader's Vision Statement there are several indicators chosen by the SDA of the Area where the Community is located. In the scorecard, the SDA has selected various improvement indicators and has set a five-year target for each one. For example, in the very first line item, it has recommended that the Community should reduce the proportion of indigent population (those receiving welfare support) from 18 per cent to 3 per cent within five years, which is equivalent to an improvement of 3 percentage points per year. This is an ambitious target and judging from the high number of points at stake for achieving this goal (shown in the last column), it is a high priority. The Community Leader will earn 10 points for every percentage point reduction she achieves in a given year. This KPI, therefore, is progressive in that a partial attainment of the annual target will result in a partial award of the allocated points. Other KPIs may award points only for full completion of the target value. Some target values are dependent on partially subjective criteria, such as the results of satisfaction surveys, whereas others may be actual physical measurements (for example, the required fuel efficiency of public transport vehicles) or monetary quantities (for example, per capita expenditure on public works).

The KPIs and target values shown in Table 11.3 are only examples. Each scorecard would be different. While the health of every Community and the success of every Community Leader would be measured in the same ten general areas of concern, the individual line items and target values could differ greatly because different Communities may have significantly different needs at different times. For example, in a scorecard intended for a Community in an advanced, developed country, no points would be awarded for adequate delivery of basic services like water, sewage removal, electricity, gas, and telephony, presumably because the entire population already enjoys those services. For a Community in rural Niger, on the other hand, this might be quite different. Only a minority of its citizens might have piped water and electricity supply, so the Vision Statement of that Community's Leader would probably have prioritised the delivery of basic services and the development of infrastructure over other needs. Accordingly, the scorecard might award points for the extension of sewage, water, communications and electrical systems to an increasing proportion of the population while delaying the introduction of more sophisticated indicators until these fundamental services are well established.

Each scorecard is also a dynamic tool in that it changes from year to year in at least two ways. First, targets for each indicator may be revised every year, depending on the needs of the Community and the availability of new information or new technology. For example, if the Community is making progress toward its five-year target much faster or much slower than expected, the SDA may decide to adjust it.

Second, if a Leader has achieved a target ahead of schedule, the SDA will either set a new target value or replace that line item altogether with a new indicator that reflects the Community's more advanced status. In the previous example of a poor Community in Niger that still provides running water to only a few citizens, the priority would be to extend the provision of piped water to all households. Once that is achieved, the corresponding indicator (percentage improvement in the number of households served by the water supply system) would be changed to something more advanced, such as the quality of the water supply measured by how much water is wasted in leakage, or by the microbial purity of the water itself.

The idea behind these moving targets is to constantly raise the bar for the leadership, pushing them toward deeper, more meaningful and accessible rights and freedoms. This relentless striving for excellence will bring forth a meritocratic leadership whose goals will be aligned in a way to maximise collaboration with all functions that report to them. The changing nature of the scorecard means that, over the course of several years, a Community Leader, and therefore the Community he represents, will transition through several increasingly sophisticated scorecards that include more and more Third Dimension ideals.

The continuing refinement of each scorecard would also help to maintain the Leader's focus on the ultimate goal of governance, namely, the achievement of a healthy, prosperous society. You may recall from the previous chapters that the continuance of each Leader's tenure would depend exclusively on his scorecard performance, as only a score of 90 per cent or higher would guarantee his position. The scorecard would thus also render political parties and special interest groups meaningless, and remove them from the landscape of democracy, because only a Leader's own managerial skills, and not any political affiliation or cronyism, would help him achieve his target score. (As we shall see shortly, however, a Community Leader would need the help of his Area Manager to perform well in his role. The Area Manager, in turn, would need all the Community Leaders under him to perform well to achieve his own scorecard target.) Even so, the changing nature of the scorecard instrument itself would ensure that there is no complacency even in the work of a previously successful manager, because goals are being revised continually.

The transaction cost of such a system would be high. It would require an SDA and a Scorecard Auditing and Evaluation Authority at each higher level of governance (Area, Region, Nation), a veritable army of analysts, statisticians, auditors and assessors, and an elaborate machinery to manage these complex and detailed evaluation efforts. This cost, however, pales in comparison to the cost of poor governance.

Finally, before we turn our attention to the scorecard system applied to higher levels of government (Area, Region, and so forth), there is one item in the Community Leader's scorecard that needs explanation. There are eleven domains of public service, not ten. At the very end of the scorecard is an item labelled 'Constituency' that carries a heavy point value, amounting to about 15 per cent of the overall score. This line item reflects the Community's overall satisfaction or appreciation of the Community Leader's work as expressed in an annual survey administered to a sizeable sample of the population. This generalised indicator is essentially a corrective measure. It ensures that whatever measures a Leader takes to achieve the required goals do not cause undue hardship to the Community. This is the ultimate check and balance: each Leader must balance the achievement of the enhanced rights and freedoms with ensuring that his constituents understand and support the measures he puts in place.

Imagine for a moment that a Community Leader must work hard to reduce traffic congestion in his city. It is a pressing problem, and therefore the weight of that line item on his scorecard is substantial. He could, in theory, achieve the required target quickly by enforcing draconian measures, like banning vehicles from most roads, imposing extremely high vehicle registration fees, introducing exorbitant road tolls, and so forth. Such measures would help him to quickly reach the required target, but doing so would cause considerable hardship to many of the Community's residents. This, in turn, would probably result in a low appreciation or 'Constituency' score (item 11.1 in the scorecard), which would bring the Leader's overall score down. This built-in check forces the Leader to opt for innovative, long-term solutions to the traffic problem that not only achieve the desired objective (traffic mitigation) but also prove popular with residents. In this case it might mean improvements in public transport facilities, construction of pedestrian and bike lanes, launch of vehicle sharing programmes, design and implementation of alternative routing, and so forth.

The Constituency score also acts as a corrective measure in a different way: it prevents the Community Leader from setting overly timid goals for her Community. Indeed, critics may argue that the scorecard development mechanism I have described here is flawed because a Community Leader, no matter how well intentioned, will often tend to setting limited, conservative goals for the Community. After, all, her score and continued tenure depend on the achievement of the goals spelled out in the scorecard, so it is in her best interest to keep those goals simple and easily achievable. It will be the task of the SDA to turn her limited ambitions into a more robust commitment to bettering the Community's welfare. Even if the SDA fails in this duty, however, the Constituency score will act as a safety net. It is an overall satisfaction score from community members that is independent of the Leader's performance on the scorecard's other KPIs. Therefore, if a Leader is too conservative in her vision for the Community, and the citizens see that there has been too little improvement in their lives, they will most likely give her low marks in the annual survey that determines the Constituency score. So, by setting herself low targets, the Leader risks being punished with a low Constituency score, which means she may not achieve the 90 per cent score required to renew her tenure.

Scorecards at Area and Regional Levels

What about administrators operating at higher levels, such as Area Managers, Regional Governors, and the Head of State? They would be held accountable for their effort in delivering the full spectrum of rights and freedoms to their entire areas of jurisdiction. Some responsibilities necessarily fall outside the purview of a Community Leader and are assigned to the Area Manager above him, or even higher in the hierarchy of governance.

We can illustrate this with a simple example. Let us imagine that the Community Leader of Middleville – the same municipality that faced high rates of youth crime – stipulated not only crime reduction in her Vision Statement, but also significant improvements in the Community's solid waste management system. In the past, large piles of smelly refuse on the

Table 11.3: Community Leader's Scorecard

	Indicator	Measurement	Current value (example)	5-year target (example)	Expected annual progress (example)	Scoring criteria	Available points
1. CITIZEN SERVICES/EMPLOYMENT/WELFARE							
1.1	Poverty	Percentage of households eligible for vouchers and TCs	18%	3%	–3 percentage points	10 points for every 1% improvement	30
1.2	Employment	Number of citizens employed at 40% time or more	14,500	19,500	1,000	5 points if target met, 0 otherwise	5
1.3	Community engagement	Average attendance at neighbourhood meetings	69	200	26	5 points if target met, 0 otherwise	5
1.4	Community participation	Average number of hours per week volunteered by citizens toward Community administration and events (under the 30% time scheme)	96,000	140,000	9,000	1 point for every 1,500 improvement	6
1.5	Community staffing	Number of full-time Community employees per 1,000 residents	–	–	Within 5% variance from Area average	5 points within range, 0 points otherwise	5
1.6	Citizenship	Number of new citizens welcomed into the Community	–	–	Within 5% variance from Area average	5 points within range, 0 points otherwise	5

Table 11.3: Community Leader's Scorecard (contd.)

1.7	Diversity	Score on ethnic, religious and linguistic diversity index	–	–	Within 5% variance from Area average	5 points within range, 0 points otherwise	5
2. EDUCATION							
2.1	Overall quality of primary education	Average score in annual parent survey	65%	90%	5 percentage points	2 points for every 1% improvement	10
2.2	Performance of primary school students	Percentage of students completing elementary school with grade average in top quartile nationally	70%	90%	4 percentage points	1 point for every 1% improvement	4
2.3	Overall quality of secondary education	Average score of teacher evaluations filled out by (a) high-school students and (b) headmaster	81%	95%	3 percentage points	3 points for every 1% improvement	9
2.4	Performance of secondary students	Percentage of students graduating high school with grade average in top quartile nationally	58%	80%	4 percentage points	2 points for every 1% improvement	8
2.5	Improvement and upkeep of school facilities	Capital expenditure as a proportion of overall education budget	–	–	Within 5% variance from Area average	5 points within range, 0 points otherwise	5

2.6	Teacher development	Percentage of full-time teachers who undertook at least 30 hours of professional development in approved programmes	36%	50%	3 percentage points	2 points for every 1% improvement	6
2.7	Discipline	Score on annual composite disciplinary index (measures truancy, tardiness, petty delinquency, academic dishonesty, bullying, etc.)	421	300	–40 points	2 points for every 10-point reduction	8
2.8	Extra-curricular engagement	Percentage of students enrolled in after-school programmes, athletic teams, afternoon study halls, volunteer initiatives	42%	60%	4 percentage points	1 point for every 1% improvement	4
3. ENVIRONMENT							
3.1	Energy efficiency 1	Percentage of Community facilities with energy-efficient upgrades	41%	100%	12 percentage points	1 point for every 2% improvement	6
3.2	Energy efficiency 2	Percentage of homes that meet recommended standards of energy efficiency	14%	30%	3 percentage points	2 points for every 1% improvement	6
3.3	Natural landscape and biodiversity	Extent of Community land certified for apportionment use	1.2 sq km	2.5 sq km	0.25 sq km	5 points if target met, 0 otherwise	5

Table 11.3: Community Leader's Scorecard (contd.)

3.4	Landfill diversion rate	Proportion of total Community waste diverted to alternatives (recycling, waste-to-energy, composting, etc.)	20%	45%	5 percentage points	2 points for every 1% improvement	10
3.5	Water and sewage usage	Per capita water usage	380 litres/ day	250 litres/ day	–30 litres/day	1 point for every 6 litre reduction	5
3.6	Businesses	Proportion of businesses operating in the Community with green certification	11%	50%	8 percentage points	1 point for every 1% improvement	8
4. FINANCE AND ECONOMIC DEVELOPMENT							
4.1	Community income	Total income to the Community from property taxes, financial transaction fees, etc.	$23 million	$31 million	$1.75 million	1 point for every $250,000 improvement	7
4.2	Budget ratio	Operating expenditure as a proportion of revenues	–	–	Within 5% variance from Area average	5 points within range, 0 points otherwise	5
4.3	Continuous improvement	Per capita expenditure on public works and service delivery	$742	$1,000	$50	1 point for every $10 improvement	5

4.4	Job creation	Number of full-time jobs located in the Community (incl. by non-members)	4,701	6,000	300	1 point for every 50 jobs created	6
4.5	Job quality	Score on annual job satisfaction survey	64%	90%	5 percentage points	1 point for every 1% improvement	5
4.6	Business development	Commercial/Corporate/ Business vacancy rate	29%	19%	–2 percentage points	3 points for every 1% reduction	6
4.7	Business friendliness	Number of business licences issued or renewed	78	100	4 percentage points	1 point for every 1% improvement	4
4.8	Business value	Weighted average Utility Index score of all businesses headquartered in the Community	11/20	15/20	1 point	5 points if target met, 0 otherwise	5
5. HEALTH							
5.1	Emergency health service delivery 1	Number of non-emergency cases treated at Community health facility	6,522	5,000	–300	1 point for every 50-unit reduction	6
5.2	Emergency health service delivery 2	Emergency medical service response time within goal	61%	90%	6 percentage points	1 point for every 1% improvement	6
5.3	Quality of health services 1	Score on patient satisfaction survey	73%	90%	4 percentage points	2 points for every 1% improvement	8

Table 11.3: Community Leader's Scorecard (contd.)

5.4	Quality of health services 2	Medical professionals per 1,000 inhabitants	–	–	Within 5% variance from National average	5 points within range, 0 points otherwise	5
5.5	Preventive medicine 1	Number of routine Ayurvedic/holistic/ preventative consultations at Community health facility	592	1,000	80	1 point for every 20-unit improvement	4
5.6	Preventive medicine 2	Score on preventive medical programmes (scored by Area)	47%	75%	5 percentage points	1 point for every 1% improvement	5
5.7	Population health 1	Rate of chronic disease per 1,000 inhabitants	418	350	–15	3 points for every 5-unit reduction	9
5.8	Population health 2	Rate of participation in Community-sponsored fitness and mental health programmes	5%	25%	4 percentage points	2 points for every 1% improvement	8
6. HOUSING AND PROPERTY							
6.1	Availability of affordable housing	Number of affordable housing units available to, and occupied by, Community members	329	500	40	2 points for every 10-unit improvement	8

6.2	Quality of affordable housing	Score in annual satisfaction survey for Community-sponsored affordable housing	58%	75%	5 percentage points	1 point for every 1% improvement	5
6.3	Housing cost	Percentage of Community households that pay more than 33% of household income on housing	43%	25%	–4 percentage points	2 points for every 1% reduction	8
6.4	Property value residential	Average cost, per square metre, of residential property	\$2,875	\$2,300	–\$100	1 point for every \$20 reduction	5
6.5	Property value commercial	Average cost, per square metre, of commercial, office and industrial property	\$1,900	\$1,650	–\$50	1 point for every \$10 reduction	5
6.6	Aesthetic value	Percentage of buildings (in excess of 100 sq m surface area) that meet aesthetic standards set by the Area	23%	35%	3 percentage points	2 points for every 1% improvement	6
6.7	Urban development	Land ratio of new building development to new recreational or environmental acreage	2:1	1:3	1-point swing	5 points if target met, 0 otherwise	5

Table 11.3: Community Leader's Scorecard (contd.)

6.8	Housing density	Average floor space index	–	–	Within 5% variance from National average	5 points within range, 0 points otherwise	5
7. LEISURE / CULTURE / TOURISM							
7.1	Land set aside	Per capita acreage devoted to parks, playgrounds, green areas, recreational zones, sporting fields, etc.	41 sq m	80 sq m	8 sq m	1 point for every 1 sq m improvement	8
7.2	Density of recreational facilities	Percentage of population living within 500 m of a park	37%	75%	8 percentage points	1 point for every 1% improvement	8
7.3	Events	Number of festivals, fairs, Community events, cultural events, exhibitions, meditation activities, etc. staged	17	30	3	4 points if target met, 0 otherwise	4
7.4	Tourism	Revenue of local hospitality and tourism businesses (restaurants, cafes, hotels, tourist attractions, museums)	$14 million	$25 million	$2 million	1 point for every $250,000 improvement	8

7.5	Cultural development	Community funds spent on activities of cultural significance (art film screenings, art commissions, public lectures, theatre, concerts, free museum exhibits, etc.)	$0.9 million	$2 million	$0.25 million	5 points if target met, 0 otherwise	5
7.6	Consciousness development	Number of free mindfulness, silent retreat, contemplation, yoga and meditation activities staged by the Community	8	20	3	5 points if target met, 0 otherwise	5
8. PUBLIC WORKS AND TECHNOLOGY							
8.1	Capital development 1	Funds allocated to capital projects	$37 million	$50 million	$3 million	5 points if target met, 0 otherwise	5
8.2	Capital development 2	Percentage of capital projects completed within budget and on time	34%	90%	10 percentage points	1 point for every 2% improvement	5
8.3	Overall quality of public infrastructure	Score on annual third-party assessment	64%	90%	5 percentage points	1 point for every 1% improvement	5
8.4	Overall quality of public services (excluding transport)	Score on annual citizen satisfaction survey	82%	92%	2 percentage points	1 point for every 0.5% improvement	4

Table 11.3: Community Leader's Scorecard (contd.)

8.5	Road upkeep	Total km of road/bike lanes/pedestrian walkways upgraded or extended	35	60	5	5 points if target met, 0 otherwise	5
8.6	Basic service delivery	Number of breakdowns of Community-operated water/sewage/refuse/power/ Internet services	24	5	–4	5 points if target met, 0 otherwise	5
8.7	Technology development	Number of technology upgrades to municipal systems, communication facilities, or services	6	20	3	5 points if target met, 0 otherwise	5
9. SAFETY AND JUSTICE							
9.1	Road safety	Number of transport-related accidents resulting in death or serious injury	21	0	–4	5 points if target met, 0 otherwise	5
9.2	Non-road safety	Number of non-transport-related accidents (fire, construction, chemical hazard, factory, utilities, school, etc.)	129	50	–15	3 points for every 5-unit reduction	9
9.3	Crime prevention 1	Number of Community relation initiatives by police	8	20	3	3 points if target met, 0 otherwise	3

9.4	Crime prevention 2	Number of violent crimes considered by Causality Committee	33	10	–5	2 points for every unit reduction	10
9.5	Crime prevention 3	Number of non-violent crimes considered by Causality Committee	78	40	–8	1 point for every unit reduction	8
9.6	Crime prevention 4	Percentage of crimes (both violent and non-violent) perpetrated by juveniles	19%	5%	–3 percentage points	2 points for every 1% reduction	6
9.7	Justice restoration	Number of restorative actions administered by Restorative Programme Office	46	25	–4	5 points if target met, 0 otherwise	5
9.8	Justice efficiency	Case resolution rate by local arbitration court	59%	85%	5 percentage points	1 point for every 1% improvement	5
10. TRANSPORT							
10.1	Public transportation quality	Score on annual transport satisfaction survey	61%	90%	6 percentage points	1 point for every 1% improvement	6
10.2	Public transport usage	Percentage of commuters using public transport at least three times a week	55%	90%	7 percentage points	1 point for every 1% improvement	7
10.3	Public transport efficiency	Average fuel efficiency of public transport	39 L/100 km	29 L/100 km	–2 L/100 km	5 points if target met, 0 otherwise	5

Table 11.3: Community Leader's Scorecard (contd.)

10.4	Private vehicle usage	Number of private passenger cars per capita registered in the Community	1.4	0.9	–0.1	5 points if target met, 0 otherwise	5
10.5	Pedestrian and bicycle-friendliness	Percentage of roads matched by dedicated pedestrian and bicycle paths	46%	80%	7 percentage points	1 point for every 1% improvement	7
10.6	Traffic mitigation	Average daily vehicle throughput at 10 busiest intersections/junctions	2,730	2,000	–150	1 point for every 30-unit reduction	5
10.7	Access to Area/Region/ National transport networks	Average time required to reach main transport hub (inter-Area train station, airport, or ferry terminal) between 6 a.m. and 10 p.m.	34 minutes	19 minutes	–3 minutes	2 points for every 1-minute reduction	6
11. CONSTITUENCY							
11.1	Overall satisfaction of constituency	Score on satisfaction survey (sample of 1,000 constituents)	–	–	–	Full points for score above 80%; half point for score from 60% to 89%; no points below 60%	80
					Total points available		**540**

pavement have been a source of much frustration for Middleville's citizens and embarrassment for city officials. The Community Leader would like her Community to be able to achieve near-zero solid waste as soon as possible. Waste management is not in the purview of the Community, however. Efficient waste management systems require costly assets like state-of-the-art recycling plants, incinerators and/or landfill sites, and collection and sorting systems operating on a cost-effective scale. The Community alone cannot bring about the desired change. The Area SDA, therefore, would refer this item up to the Regional SDA for inclusion in the Area Manager's scorecard. Indicators for which an Area Manager is directly accountable would have five-year targets as well, as shown in the sample scorecard (Table 11.4).

What is apparent immediately is that the Area Manager's scorecard is shorter and simpler than the Community Leader's. Indeed, under each of the ten headings there are only a handful of indicators or line items. This is because many of the citizens' needs have been addressed at the level of governance closest to them – the Community. Only Area-level services make an appearance in the Area Manager's scorecard. For example, the quality of primary and secondary education is already evaluated in the Community-level scorecard, but tertiary education (universities, technical institutes, vocational schools) is an Area-level responsibility for which the Area Manager is accountable.

In addition to KPIs for which she is directly responsible, however, the Area Manager's scorecard also takes into consideration the scores from the Community Leaders under her. Indeed, this line item (11.1 Community Scores) makes up the bulk of her overall score – 300 points out of 470. This score is simply the average score (expressed as a percentage) of all the individual scores that Community Leaders in her Area have achieved for that year. Rather than delivering certain rights and freedoms to citizens herself, then, the Area Manager becomes an organisational head whose responsibility is to supervise and support her 100 Community Leaders in a manner that allows them to achieve the highest possible score in the assurance of all rights and freedoms. The Regional Governor would similarly derive a large part of his performance score from the performance

Table 11.4: Area Manager's Scorecard

	Indicator	Measurement	Current value (example)	5-year target (example)	Expected annual progress (example)	Scoring criteria	Available points
1. CITIZEN SERVICES/EMPLOYMENT/WELFARE							
1.1	Employment	Area-level unemployment rate	11%	5%	–1%	5 points if target met, 0 otherwise	5
1.2	Poverty	Percentage of households eligible for vouchers and TCs	20%	3%	–3 percentage points	5 points for every 1% reduction	15
1.3	Social services	Percent of Area budget allocated	10%	20%	2 percentage points	5 points if target met, 0 otherwise	5
2. EDUCATION							
2.1	Access to tertiary education	Percentage of high school graduates attending an Area university or vocational institute within two years of graduation (survey sample)	74%	90%	3 percentage points	2 points for every 1% increase	6
2.2	Quality of tertiary education	Percentage of university graduates in full employment within one year of graduation (survey sample)	63%	80%	3 percentage points	2 points for every 1% increase	6
2.3	Quality of vocational training	Average score on national vocational graduation exam	–	–	In top 20% nationally	5 points if target met, 0 otherwise	5

3. ENVIRONMENT							
3.1	Air quality	Average percentage of good air quality days (when air quality meets or exceeds the required value on the Air Quality Index) as measured in 10 Communities chosen at random	61%	90%	6 percentage points	1 point for every 1% improvement	6
3.2	CO_2 emissions	Million tonnes of carbon dioxide released	3,569	3,000	–100	5 points if target met, 0 otherwise	5
3.3	Area parks and protected areas	Total acreage of natural landscapes graded A	74 sq km	100 sq km	5 sq km	5 points if target met, 0 otherwise	5
4. FINANCE AND ECONOMIC DEVELOPMENT							
4.1	Corporate taxation	Corporate tax levied	$4.2 billion	$5.2 billion	$0.2 billion	5 points if target met, 0 otherwise	5
4.2	Businesses headquartered in Area	Number of businesses with sales in excess of $25 million	17	30	3	5 points if target met, 0 otherwise	5
4.3	Area budget	Total budget for Area infrastructure and services	$6.3 billion	$7.5 billion	$0.3 billion	5 points if target met, 0 otherwise	5
5. HEALTH							
5.1	Specialised Area hospitals	Average score in all Area hospitals for excellence in provision of medical services (third-party evaluation)	66%	86%	4 percentage points	2 points for every 1% improvement	8

Table 11.4: Area Manager's Scorecard (contd.)

5.2	Health expenditure	Percentage of Area budget allocated to Area hospitals and other Area health services	–	–	Within 5% variance from national average	5 points if target met, 0 otherwise	5
5.3	Overall population health	Health index score (survey sample)	171/250	197/250	5 points	1 point for every 1-point improvement	5
6. HOUSING AND PROPERTY							
6.1	Corporate and industrial zones	Number of businesses operating in Area-sponsored corporate and industrial estates	122	150	5	5 points if target met, 0 otherwise	5
6.2	Urban development financing	Total loans to Communities for urban development projects	$145 million	$200 million	$10 million	5 points if target met, 0 otherwise	5
6.3	City:country ratio	Ratio of agricultural land to urban/suburban zones	–	–	Within 5% variance from national average	5 points if target met, 0 otherwise	5
7. LEISURE/CULTURE/TOURISM							
7.1	Museums	Total attendance at all Area-funded museums and exhibitions	850,000	1.1 million	50,000	1 point for every additional 10,000	5

7.2	Cultural events	Number of large-scale cultural events (music festivals, theatre/ film festivals, sporting events, etc. with attendance in excess of 5,000) hosted by Area	8	15	2	5 points if target met, 0 otherwise	5
7.3	Tourism	Number of tourist-days spent in Area	0.9 million	1.2 million	60,000	1 point for every additional 15,000	4
8. PUBLIC WORKS AND TECHNOLOGY							
8.1	Power generation 1	Average cost per MWh generated (inclusive environmental costs)	\$122	\$100	–\$5	1 point for every \$1 reduction	5
8.2	Power generation 2	Percentage of power generated from renewable sources	11%	25%	3%	5 points if target met, 0 otherwise	5
8.3	Capital development	Percentage of Area-level capital projects completed within budget and on time	53%	78%	5%	1 point for every 1% improvement	5
9. SAFETY AND JUSTICE							
9.1	Area-level courts 1	Number of violent crime cases brought to trial	2,600	2,100	–100	5 points if target met, 0 otherwise	5
9.2	Area-level courts 2	Number of non-violent crime cases brought to trial	4,950	4,000	–200	5 points if target met, 0 otherwise	5
9.3	Justice efficiency	Case resolution rate by local Area-level courts	73%	90%	3 percentage points	5 points if target met, 0 otherwise	5

Table 11.4: Area Manager's Scorecard (contd.)

10. TRANSPORT							
10.1	Mass urban transit	Number of passenger-km travelled	143 million	193 million	10 million	1 point for every additional million	10
10.2	Area roads	Score on third-party road audit (measuring quality of infrastructure, traffic throughput, network reach, etc.)	17/30	25/30	2 points	5 points if target met, 0 otherwise	5
10.3	Area airports	Weighted average score on airline and passenger satisfaction surveys	69%	89%	4 percentage points	5 points if target met, 0 otherwise	5
11. COMMUNITY SCORES							
11.1	Community Leader performance	Average Community Leader score in all Communities in the Area	84%	–	–	Average score in percentage × 300	300
					Total points available		**470**

of his Area Managers, and so on up to Head of State. This accumulation of scores is shown in Figure 11.1.

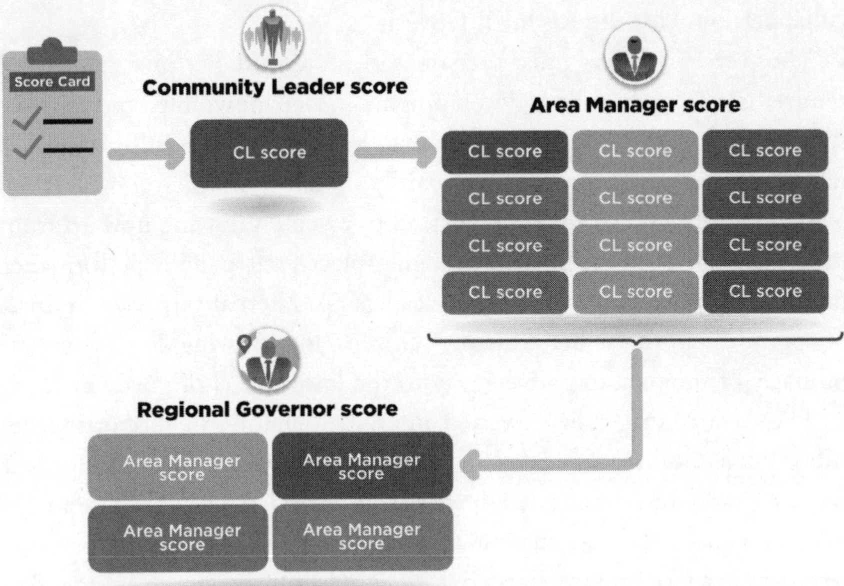

Figure 11.1: Aggregated Scorecards for Area Managers and Regional Governors

Outwardly, this scheme resembles the structure of multilevel marketing (MLM).[70] Unlike MLM, however, the multilevel scoring mechanism that I have outlined here is not intended to augment anyone's profit. Rather, its aim is to encourage high performance at all levels of leadership by mirroring the pyramidal structure of governance. In other words, each officer's performance is tied directly to outcomes below him, not above. After all, the Head of State's primary concern, and the only admissible measure of success, should be the overall health, safety, prosperity, and happiness of the citizens of the Nation. But each citizen is also a constituent of a Community. The most immediate responsibility to deliver and safeguard his rights and freedoms lies with his Community Leader, whose performance score is directly related to this mandate. Above him, the Area Manager's score is for the most part an aggregate of his Community

Leaders' scores. Similarly, Regional Governors must closely follow the work of the Area Managers below them, because their own score is so heavily dependent on theirs. And the Head of State, finally, must work in close collaboration with the Regional Governors.

Thus, every officer's most pressing task, to ensure her own continued tenure, is to closely follow developments in her 'downline' and actively support any leader below her who may be struggling to fulfil scorecard targets. Such a system, though outwardly similar to multilevel marketing, is in fact its exact reverse. Here, instead of revenues flowing upward from lower ranks to swell the pockets of higher-placed salespeople, performance metrics flow upward to reward good leadership. Alternatively, we can think of commitment to the betterment of citizens' lives flowing down from the pinnacle of the pyramid all the way to the lowest level of governance.

The Area Manager has a vested interest, therefore, in supporting her subordinate Community Leaders in every way she can, monitoring their activities and intervening when she feels help is needed toward achievements of certain goals. She may channel technical, human, or financial Area-level resources to a Community in need, for example. Or she may recommend to the SDA a temporary adjustment to scorecard items that the Community Leader cannot meet due to unforeseen circumstances. Or she may push a Community in need to adopt measures that have been successful in other Communities.

The objective of this exercise is to carefully align interests along the entire governance hierarchy, so that the lowest organisations at the grass roots have the same goals as the highest level of leadership. And it should be the overriding goal of the high-level leadership to ensure that they support the lower tier of leadership to accomplish their goals. This kind of bottom-up approach will create an organisational environment that current political structures do not have and will resolve most of the paralytic inertia of governments throughout the world.

Complex systems with many interdependent variables that need optimisation are in themselves very difficult to run. When you add a multiplicity of goals and the desire to achieve a high level of organisational performance, the job requires exceptional leadership. The balanced scorecard captures the multiplicity of goals and assigns a weightage, measurement criteria, and a scoring methodology to each goal so that the scorecard as a whole can yield a reliable and fair overall assessment of each leader's performance.

Bottom-Up Accountability

I will now illustrate in greater detail the mechanism by which governance objectives will be synchronised and aligned along the entire chain of responsibility. By way of example, we will consider the role of the Regional Governor of the city of Delhi.[71] As discussed, the Regional Governor's scorecard tally is, in part, an aggregate of the scores achieved by the Area Managers below him in the fulfilment of their duties, as outlined in their own scorecards. However, there are a few targets in his scorecard for which he is personally responsible. Among these is clean air, a key deliverable because it is an essential component of the right to life. Why is clean air a deliverable for the Regional Governor and not for Area Managers and Community Leaders? Air quality cannot be managed effectively over small zones. Airborne pollutants drift easily from one place to another, and therefore air pollution must be tackled on a regional scale. There are only a few things that communities can do to limit air pollution, such as banning open fires, controlling emissions from local workshops, and regulating local traffic. To that extent, therefore, a score for air quality, with relatively small weight, may find its way into a Community Leader's scorecard. The bulk of the responsibility for delivering clean air to the citizenry, however, rests with the Regional Governor.

Air pollution has been a grave problem in Delhi for many years, and very little progress has been made to date toward resolving it. (The extent of Delhi's air pollution crisis is explained in Box 11.1 at the end of this chapter.) In our hypothetical Second Dimension scenario, Delhi's Regional Governor has pledged, in his Vision Statement, to reduce air pollution substantially. The competent SDA has translated this pledge into an actionable KPI: the Regional Governor must increase the number of days per year when Delhi's air is deemed at least 'satisfactory' by 30 per cent within five years. (See Box 11.1 for a detailed explanation.) Let us assume, for the sake of arithmetic simplicity, that the weight given to this item on his scorecard is 10 per cent. In other words, if he achieves or exceeds his air quality target, he may gain the full 10 per cent score allocated to this line item. But the Regional Governor shares the responsibility for this line item with all his direct subordinates, that is, the executive officers that he has directly or indirectly appointed to positions of authority at regional levels of administration (Levels 6, 7, 8, and 9). His ability to achieve the target rests entirely on the skill, commitment, and hard work of the technical and managerial staff below him.

In the organisational chart (Figure 11.2), we can follow just one thread (on the extreme right of the diagram) of the devolution of responsibility

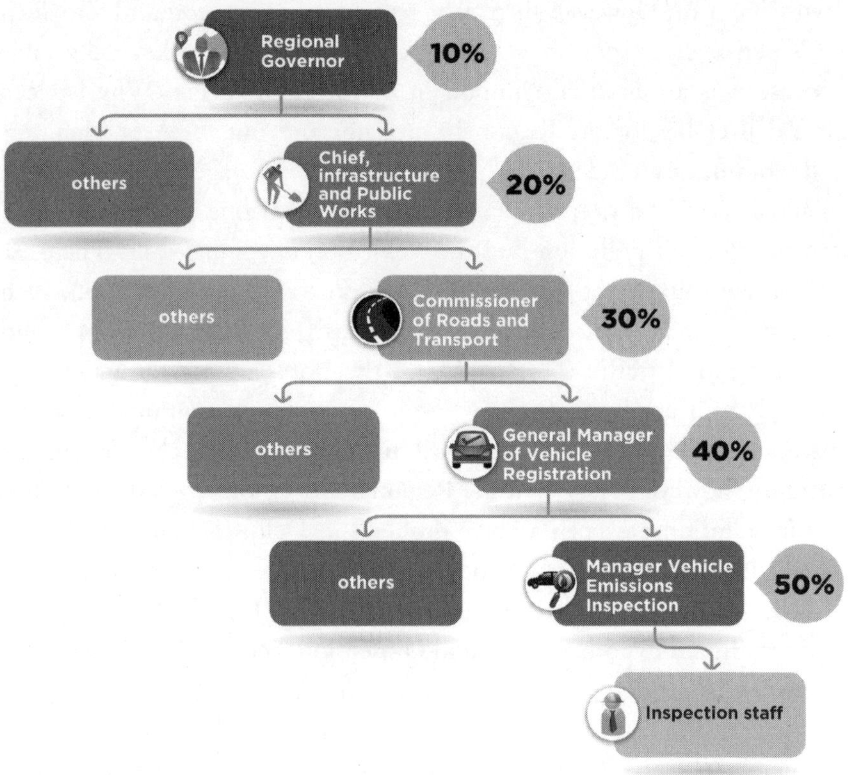

Figure 11.2: Devolution of Responsibility for Clean Air in a Region

for clean air in a Region. Starting at the top, we can see that several department chiefs report directly to the Regional Governor. Here I have included only the few whose responsibilities touch on the issue of air quality. Among these chiefs is the regional Chief for Infrastructure and Public Works. Because his department's activities have a significant impact on air quality, this item on his scorecard takes up an equally significant weight of 20 per cent in the composition of his performance score. Below him, his reports include the regional Commissioner of Roads and Transport, whose area of responsibility has a more direct impact on air quality. Hence the weight given to air quality in his scorecard is a hefty 30 per cent. Further below, one of the Commissioner's reports is the regional General Manager (GM) of Vehicle Registration. An important part of the latter's responsibilities is to ensure that all registered vehicles comply with emission standards and to keep pushing for more stringent standards. Accordingly, air quality makes up 40 per cent of his performance score. Finally, one of the managers reporting to the GM of Vehicle Registration is the regional Manager of Vehicle Emissions Inspections. He is directly involved in measuring emissions from registered vehicles, and thus air quality makes up no less than 50 per cent of his personal overall score. (The remainder will come from other items on his scorecard, such as the efficiency and cost-effectiveness with which he runs the network of approved emissions testing centres, and the extent to which he has been able to innovate procedures and equipment used for testing.)

This, I believe, amounts to a new paradigm in collaboration. It ensures that all levels of governance are aligned with the same goal (in the example, air quality) and that all officers are incentivised through the scorecard mechanism to accomplish the same goal in full collaboration with officers above and below them. The goal of making the air cleaner cascades from the top. As it gets closer and closer to the operational level, the weight given to it increases until it reaches a very large proportion of the lowest-level scorecard. I call this approach a 'bottom-up' accountability system because if the lowest levels achieve their goals and obtain full marks, the score keeps getting aggregated upwards until it reaches the Governor's scorecard. Thus, the success of the leadership is inextricably tied to the success of the lowest level of management. So, while at lower levels a much larger proportion of the score is made up of a single item, a Governor's scorecard may involve dozens, even hundreds of such individual items.

It should be noted, of course, that for this system to work properly, the leader (the Regional Governor in this example) must have unfettered power to make decisions, especially in appointing the right technical and managerial personnel upon whom he relies for achieving the targets set out in his scorecard. If he will be judged in part by their performance, after all, it is appropriate for him to have the right to appoint administrators he trusts, as well as to dismiss those who are unable to meet their targets. The reader may recall that in our system of governance, only senior leaders at each level of governance (Community Leader, Area Manager, Regional Governor, and Head of State) are chosen by election. Staff who report to them are appointed directly by these leaders. Since these leaders' scores and tenure renewal depend on scorecards, and their scores rely in part on personnel appointed by them,[72] each leader has a vested interest in appointing the best people available. They will be chosen not because they are friends or dependants of the leader, or because he owes them favours, or because their appointment is a political compromise, but because they are skilled professionals who can deliver the scores the leader requires to retain his tenure the following year. However, the Regional Governor may only appoint administrative personnel in keeping with the usual rules. For example, let us say that he wishes to appoint a new regional Chief for Infrastructure and Public Works, which is a Level 7 post. He may only appoint to this post a professional who has previously served in a position that was rated Level 8 or Level 9, and who has served with distinction in that previous assignment, achieving a score of at least 90 per cent in the previous two years as measured by an internal, post-specific scorecard.

The assertiveness to make unilateral decisions and the willingness to accept responsibility for them are fundamental ingredients for good leadership. First Dimension democratic systems are often bogged down by the absence of such executive authority. Current systems, as a seasoned politician once explained to me, always give everyone the right to object, but they hardly ever give leaders the freedom to build and create. Giving the leaders full authority over their mandate allows them to flourish in their jobs and to strive for excellence knowing that they will be judged exclusively on their performance using a sensible, quantitative, and transparent scorecard system that is constantly evolving towards rights and freedoms of the Second and Third Dimensions.

A Scorecard for the Nation

At the very highest layer of authority, the level occupied by the Head of State, the criteria and methodology of evaluation would be no different. The Head of State in the new nation state is not a politician who attained that position on the strength of a protracted, expensive, and often divisive electoral process. Rather, he is a seasoned leader who is capable of consistently delivering outstanding results as a public administrator and who has risen through the hierarchy of governance (or, for that matter, the hierarchy of private enterprise). At each stage of his career, this exemplary administrator must have demonstrated exceptional skill by consistently achieving high scores. Only those performance-related achievements allowed him to rise through the ranks of government. In the beginning, when he first became Leader of his Community, he must have won a popular election on the basis of his skill as a campaigner and his ability to address his Community's concerns – much like a First Dimension politician. Thereafter, however, he must have risen through the ranks of the Second Dimension's governance hierarchy by excelling as an administrator at each level. The reader may recall from Chapter 10 that candidates for positions like Area Manager, Regional Governor, and Head of State are elected by their peers, rather than by the general population, on the basis of strict selection criteria. Only administrators with consistently high scores (greater than 90 per cent for two consecutive years) are eligible for candidacy, and only after having occupied administrative positions that are no more than one or two rungs below the one they hope to be nominated for.

The Head of State's tenure will continue for as long as he can maintain a high score for the Nation. Like all administrators below him, the Head of State is required to achieve a 90 per cent score every year to extend his tenure automatically. (Lower scores may bring about a new election, in which he may or may not participate.) His scorecard will contain a few indicators for which he is directly accountable, relating to responsibilities of national concern, such as national defence, monetary policy, foreign policy, and trade alliances. For the most part, however, it consists of the aggregated scores of all the Regional Governors, which in turn consist largely of the aggregated scores of all the Area Managers below them, and so on down the line. To ensure his continued tenure, his first and foremost duty will be to counsel, encourage, support, and monitor the performance of his Governors and Managers, and intervene quickly and effectively in situations where a subordinate's score is under threat – in other words, in situations where the rights and freedoms of the Nation's citizens are not being upheld.

The Head of State's personal score, therefore, becomes an overall assessment of the health of the Nation, as measured by the degree to which Second Dimension and Third Dimension rights and freedoms are being developed and maintained. The Head of State's score is thus also the Nation's score. As we shall see in Chapter 13 on international relations, a country's score will determine the degree to which it may participate in global governance.

Today there are numerous indicators that can be used to evaluate the health of a nation, and some of them feature frequently in national and international news. In Chapter 15 I will discuss a few that are more advanced and useful than Gross Domestic Product, such as the Human Development Index and Bhutan's innovative Gross National Happiness (GNH) index. To these we could add many others, such as the Gini coefficient, which measures wealth disparity in a country; the Economic Intelligence Unit's quality of life index; Freedom House's *Freedom in the World* publication, which offers a comparative assessment of global political rights and civil liberties; or even more domain-specific indices like the World Bank's ease of doing business ranking.

Most of these indicators, though enlightening, afford only a partial assessment of a country's performance in securing the well-being and happiness of its citizens. Moreover, these indicators are not especially useful because they have no repercussions on an international scale. Typically, new releases of these rankings and indices garner attention and spur national leaders to new resolutions because they highlight areas where a government is especially guilty of negligence. Often, however, such efforts are aimed at a specific issue alone, and their resolve is limited to the tenure of the party in power. Poor performance on these indicators and indices is not tied to any responsibility and has no political consequences for the government. The universally accepted concept of national sovereignty ensures that these indicators and indices remain nothing more than suggestions. High scores bring no rewards, low scores bring no punishment, and whether to act on them or not, and how, is entirely up to the national government.

The scoring system I have outlined here, on the other hand, is intended to have wide-ranging ramifications. As I shall suggest in Chapter 13, a Nation's score can be the cornerstone of global governance. Each Nation will be able to participate fully in decisions of Continental and Global importance, and each Nation's input at such transnational bodies will be dependent entirely on its national performance score.

The purpose of the exercise of governance at every level of society, whether head of a university, a research institute, an Area, or a Nation, is to ensure that the goals are clearly understood, aligned with the wider public interest, and codified in a transparent scoring methodology and built-in measurement criteria. The result of this will be a meritocratic system, and people with proven capabilities and competencies will end up in places where they can make the greatest difference. One of the great tragedies of contemporary India, for instance, is that there are people of great competence who are denied positions of authority because of differing viewpoints or an unwillingness to behave in a certain way. Delhi, for example, has been transformed by one technocratic administrator who built the Delhi metro, E. Sreedharan. In the beginning he faced tremendous hostility and a bureaucratic system that only created obstructions, but he persevered and bequeathed to the city in ten years one of the most modern and efficient transport systems in the world – something nobody believed possible in India. If we did this – give competent people the remit to execute change – more frequently, we would be able to transform every aspect of our civic, political, and social lives.

Box 11.1: Targeting Delhi's Air Pollution Crisis

Delhi – India's National Capital Territory (NCT) – has suffered from alarming levels of air pollution for at least two decades. In recent years, the hazardous quality of Delhi's air has finally begun to make international headlines, drawing increasing attention to the catastrophic ambient air conditions prevailing in much of northern India. Delhi's air is clogged by pollutants originating from a variety of sources, especially diesel-powered vehicles, and it suffers especially from high levels of very fine particulate matter known as $PM_{2.5}$. This pollutant is particularly dangerous because it can penetrate deeply in human lungs, with serious health repercussions. The massive impact of Delhi's pollution on health and on the economy has been analysed and documented in various studies.

Not surprisingly, Delhi often appears at the top of pollution rankings. In 2016, a World Health Organization (WHO) report[73] labelled Delhi as the most polluted megacity in the world (megacities are those with over 14 million inhabitants). Another report released in 2018[74] showed that 12 of the 15 most polluted cities in the world (in terms of $PM_{2.5}$ concentration) are in northern India. They include Delhi and several of its satellite cities (Gurugram, Faridabad, and Noida).

What if Delhi's pollution were to be subjected to the scorecard-based system of continuous improvement that I have outlined in this chapter? Here is how a SDA would assess the situation using the methodology outlined earlier in this chapter:

Step 1: Improving air quality falls squarely within the most fundamental human right, the right to life. In its Second Dimension incarnation, the right to life includes the right to healthy air (see Chapter 7). Therefore, air quality improvements can be included in a leadership scorecard. After consulting the Jurisdictional Authority, the SDA confirms that air quality is a matter of regional concern. An air quality KPI should therefore be included in the Regional Governor's scorecard.

Step 2: The SDA determines that the most intuitive and widely reported measurement tool for air quality is the Air Quality Index (AQI), which combines the levels of five major air pollutants (particulate matter, ozone, sulphur dioxide, nitrogen dioxide, and carbon monoxide) into a simple number on a scale of 0 to 500. An AQI of 0-50 is considered good, 50–100 is moderate or satisfactory, and all levels above 100 are harmful. The value of the AQI can vary drastically based on the location of the measurement, the time of day, and the time of year, but a daily average that is representative of the entire NCT can be calculated. The SDA identifies the following as a suitable KPI: 'the number of days per year when Delhi's AQI is below 100'.

Step 3: Delhi's mean daily AQI in 2018 was well over 200. In comparison, Los Angeles, which routinely ranks as the most polluted large city in the United States, had a median daily AQI of just 70. In the same year, Delhi enjoyed only 52 days when its AQI was below 100, while Los Angeles had 265 such days.[75] Therefore, the SDA concludes that the potential for improvement is very high.

Step 4: The SDA quickly identifies a suitable comparable – Beijing. The Chinese capital is similar to Delhi in two important ways: both are megacities, and both are located in countries experiencing rapid economic development. Like Delhi, Beijing has been battling high levels of ambient pollution for years. In early 2013 matters came to a head when much of northern China experienced its worst levels of air pollution of the last half-century, in a winter period dubbed 'airpocalypse' by the media. Later that year, the Chinese government declared an all-out war on air pollution and unveiled a comprehensive action plan to control it. Among other targets, it sought to reduce the level of PM_{10} in large cities by 10 per cent compared to 2012, the level of $PM_{2.5}$ in the Beijing–Tianjin–Hebei cluster by at least 25 per cent and in Beijing itself by 33 per cent.[76] These targets had been achieved and exceeded by 2018, albeit by resorting to heavy-handed methods like an outright prohibition on burning coal in winter, arbitrary traffic restrictions, and forced closure or relocation of heavy industry works. Overall $PM_{2.5}$ levels in Beijing have fallen by about 40 per cent from their 2013 peak, though they remain five times higher than WHO guidelines. This improvement was reflected in the number of 'blue sky days' (days when the AQI was below 100), which increased from 176 in 2013 to 226 in 2017,[77] that is, by 28 per cent over four years.

Step 5: The SDA notes that Beijing and Delhi are quite different in one important respect: their political profile. China's one-party system enables it to undertake radical action quickly and without much opposition, whereas in India, which is a rights-based democracy, change must run the slow, tortuous gauntlet of consensus-building. It also notes that the Chinese AQI is computed differently from the Indian one, suggesting that the high number of 'blue sky days' reported by Chinese authorities is misleading. Despite these misgivings, the SDA concludes that Beijing's efforts to combat air pollution do indeed constitute a suitable benchmark for Delhi's, and a better one than other available precedents, such as Mexico City's *ProAire* programme. It decides to set a five-year target intended to replicate Beijing's recent achievements, formulated as follows: 'To increase by 30 per cent (from 2018 levels) the number of days per year when Delhi's AQI is below 100'.

12

Nations to Communities: The Devolution of Authority

The Importance of Correct Scaling

John Stuart Mill (1806–1873), writing in *On Liberty*, raised three objections to state interference:

> The first is, when the thing to be done is likely to be better done by individuals than by the government. Speaking generally, there is no one so fit to conduct any business, or to determine how or by whom it shall be conducted, as those who are personally interested in it. This principle condemns the interferences, once so common, of the legislature, or the officers of government, with the ordinary processes of industry [. . .]
>
> The second objection is more nearly allied to our subject. In many cases, though individuals may not do the particular thing so well, on the average, as the officers of government, it is nevertheless desirable that it should be done by them, rather than by the government, as a means to their own mental education – a mode of strengthening their active faculties, exercising their judgment, and giving them a familiar knowledge of the subjects with which they are thus left to deal [...]

> The third, and most cogent reason for restricting the interference of government, is the great evil of adding unnecessarily to its power.

When we look at the modern nation state, it is plain to see that Mill spoke true. Since the 16th century, when the modern nation state began to take shape, it has been a great concentrator of power and, consequently, a remover of power from the hands of individuals and local governments. This concentration of power was partly because the state began to be seen as the only actor that could effectively unite the people. The nation state concentrated power, taking it from communities, cities, and countries, which, if left in control, could have been threats or competing centres of authority. In most cases, usurping that power made administration less efficient, because what could be done effectively by local institutions was often done poorly by a highly centralised and far-removed bureaucracy. At the same time, the nation state also crippled any global and continental forums that emerged, preventing them from being effective, because it saw such effectiveness as a violation of its sovereignty.

In many contemporary societies, too much authority has been concentrated in the nation state. Throughout the world, the modern nation state has been a ruthless usurper of people's ability to be a part of the decisions that most affect their lives. Issues that directly impact individual citizens – like citizenship, taxation, public expenditure, security, and especially the enforcement of rights and freedoms – are the purview of national government agencies. This helps, at times, to create a national identity shared by every citizen in the land, but it also leaves individuals with less attachment and allegiance to the community in which they live. It renders the individual helpless and entirely in the control of a remote, impersonal, and insensitive national monolith. Above all, it reduces the individual's ability to control his own destiny through participation in government at the local level, because local institutions are left with minimal power to effect change.

In *Democracy in America*, the French diplomat and political scientist Alexis de Tocqueville (1805–1859) wrote the following of democracy:

> By this system the people shake off their state of dependence just long enough to select their master, and then relapse into it again. A great many persons at the present day are quite contented with this sort of compromise between administrative despotism and the sovereignty of the people; and they think they have done enough for the protection of individual freedom when they have surrendered it to the power of the nation at large. (Book Four, Chapter VI)

This is the other side of the problem with the nation state: it reduces its citizens to helpless children, who only have power in the brief and transient act of voting, after which they are subjected to the whims of the lobbies in power.

In the First Dimension, the nation state is bloated with power. This makes it less effective in delivering what it promises to the people. Only by scaling that power correctly can balance be restored to the relationship between people and their government, because correct scaling will ensure that authority returns to the hands of those most effectively positioned to wield it. As we move into the Second and Third Dimensions, our goal is to achieve this transfer of power and alter the meaning of both government and citizen.

In Chapter 10 we identified four levels of governance: Community, Area, Region and Nation. I now add two more (Continent and World) to complete the continuum of potential governance, that is, a complete hierarchy of all the levels of governance that may impact the life of a citizen, wherever he may reside.

Figure 12.1 represents the distribution of power among the six levels of governance as experienced by a typical First Dimension citizen. The graph suggests that authority over most of society's functions, and therefore over the welfare of its citizens, is highly concentrated in the central or national government. Local and regional governance, on the left of the graph, have a smaller impact on the daily lives of citizens. Continental and global governance, on the right side of the graph, has an even more negligible impact, because the defence of sovereignty at the expense of international cooperation has been a fundamental ingredient of each nation state's international policy for so long.

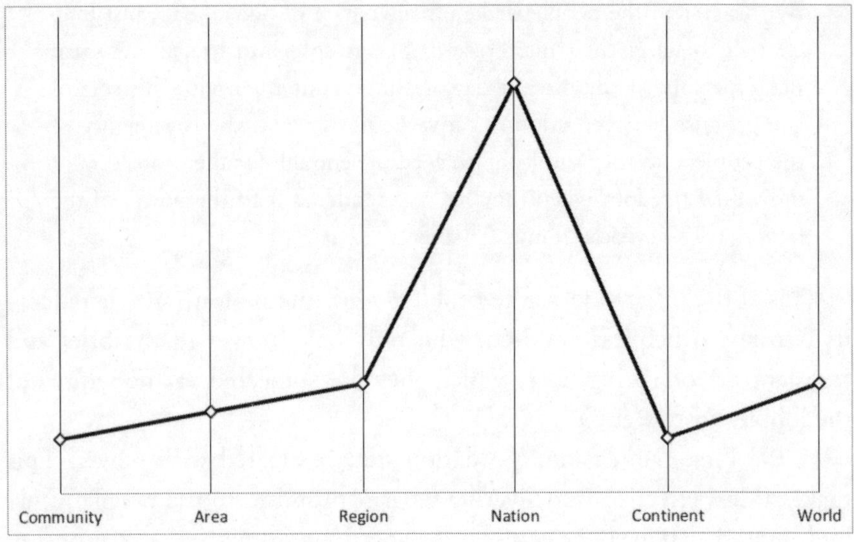

Figure 12.1: Distribution of Power in the First Dimension

The Rise of the Nation State

How did the nation state come to occupy such a prominent role in the governance of peoples around the world? What historical development led to its almost unchallenged hegemony over human affairs?

In casual parlance, we refer to countries as 'nation', 'state', 'nation state', and 'sovereign state', as if they were synonymous, but they represent different concepts. A nation denotes a group of people who regard themselves, and are seen by others, as belonging together on account of a shared heritage, usually composed of a combination of language, ethnicity, religion, and a history of residence in a particular territory. Strictly speaking, however, a nation is not a territorial entity. The Kurdish nation is an example of this. Kurdish nationals are spread out across Turkey, Iraq, Syria, and other countries. But they do not have a country of their own.

A state, on the other hand, is an institution of governance (a political entity) that has complete control over a clearly defined geographical area and its inhabitants. The combined term 'nation state' therefore implies that the two concepts, nation and state, coincide. In other words, that the state in question is inhabited exclusively or primarily by one particular nation. Yet most of today's larger countries, like India, China, the United States, Russia, and Brazil, are inhabited by diverse populations that can hardly be said to constitute a single nation. Even formerly homogenous European countries like England and France now contain significant ethnic and religious minorities as a result of postcolonial policies, immigration, and expansion. For the most part, these modern states are held together by the assumption that their citizens approve a constitution, and that they live within defined territorial boundaries. They do not necessarily belong to a dominant nation within those boundaries.

If we glance briefly into the past, we can see that the tribal idea of belonging to a group or a community has always been a necessity (social as well as biological) for human beings, from early hunter-gatherer clans to agrarian communities to more settled, urbanised civilisations. This drive toward belonging to ever larger and more structured groups culminated in the creation of what historian Benedict Anderson has called 'imagined communities'. These communities were defined territorially and ethnically, but ultimately required the group member to pledge allegiance to a notional idea of belonging, divorced from his everyday experience in his immediate community. In *Imagined Communities*, Anderson argues:

> [The nation] is imagined because the members of even the smallest nation will never know most of their fellow-members, meet them, or even hear of them, yet in the minds of each lives the image of their communion [...] [It] is imagined as a community, because, regardless of the actual inequality and exploitation that may prevail in each, the nation is conceived as a deep, horizontal comradeship. Ultimately, it is this fraternity that makes it possible, over the past two centuries, for so many millions of people, not so much to kill, as willingly to die for such limited imaginings.

Some European countries were constituted as nation states as early as the 16th century. England, France, and Russia already had the geographical shape and cultural traits that we associate with them today. The rulers of these countries had by then managed to consolidate their territories (mostly by force of arms) and to centralise authority over them in a single person (the king) or, more broadly, in a single institution of governance: the sovereign. Spain, too, by virtue of its prolonged struggle against Muslim invaders, had managed to unite under one sovereign and consolidate its territory in the Iberian peninsula. In these countries, the political control of a centralised state entity essentially created nations. While the populations under them may have been diverse before, centuries of living together under one central authority, speaking a common language mandated by the central authority, and mostly practising a religion supported by the central authority, ensured that these states became nation states.

Other European countries had to wait till the 19th century to become nation states. Italy and Germany were fragmented into many small principalities. In their case, a popular feeling (nationalism) that the inhabitants of all these mini-states really belonged together on account of a common culture, led to unification of their territories and establishment of corresponding nation states. In other words, the nation came first, the state later (unlike countries like England and France, where the opposite was true). We might put the United States as well in this category, because a common desire (independence from Britain) and a common history of residence in North America united the colonists into a nation before they could establish their own state. But regardless of whether nation or state came first, we can say that by the 19th century the predominant model of statehood in much of the Western world was the nation state.

By that time, however, several of these nation states had also made progress toward democratic forms of government. The ultimate authority over their territories was no longer wielded exclusively by an individual sovereign, but rather by a multi-layered bureaucratic state designated by its people for the purpose of governance. Thus sovereignty – supreme authority within a territory – had passed into the hands of the people and was enshrined increasingly in one or more documents that defined how the state should be constituted.

The democratisation of governance only reinforced the importance of the nation state. For example, a modern concept of justice – where justice is the same for everyone and where it is not reliant on the whim of a feudal lord or a prelate, but is administered professionally on the basis of a legal corpus – requires a highly codified and structured justice system managed by an extensive bureaucratic apparatus. Similarly, a free market that affords equal opportunity to all competitors requires clearly defined rules of participation, adequate safeguards for corporations and banks, a currency available to all economic agents, a central monetary authority to supply and regulate it, oversight bodies to monitor commerce and taxation, and so forth. When governments became acutely aware of the need for social welfare in the 19th century, a centralised system to provide common minimum services was needed, operated by the social services arm of the state rather than being left to religious charities. In short, as societies became more sophisticated and more equal, they needed a single, powerful central authority, a pervasive bureaucratic machine with many specialised agencies and huge numbers of employees that could ensure that modern, rules-based economic and social systems would function properly. The nation state filled this need.

Thus, by the late 19th century, the great powers of the world were constituted as nation states, and they were secure in their claim to sovereignty. This mix, however, proved highly toxic. A state organised around a single cultural identity – a nationalist principle – fosters a conviction that one's nationality is preferable to others, and that it is superior. This leads to jingoism, arrogance, racism, and colonial ambitions to expand the territory under its control. And the notion of sovereignty suggests that the nation state may act with impunity within these extended boundaries, beyond the reproach or intervention of other nation states. It can be said, therefore, that the primacy of the sovereign nation state led ultimately to imperialism and the nationalist excesses of fascism.

The nation state is a structure that relies on identity – articulated as difference from those who do not belong to the nation – and, to maintain this identity, on a state of enmity toward other nation states. Indeed, the nation state has a tendency to make war continually. The British army officer Rupert Smith, one of the greatest generals of our times, noted, 'Armed conflict is a human condition, and I do not doubt we will continue to reinvent it from generation to generation.' In the modern-day democratic state, the imperative to have an external focus toward which to channel discontent is all the more pronounced, since a homogenous national identity does not exist. War provides the best way to do this while keeping alive the fiction of the nation state's own value and intrinsic goodness.

The US diplomat and historian George Kennan wrote in *Russia and the West under Lenin*,

> There is [...] nothing in nature more egocentrical than the embattled democracy. It soon becomes the victim of its own war propaganda. It then tends to attach to its own cause an absolute value which distorts everything else. *Its* enemy becomes the embodiment of all evil. *Its* own side, on the other hand, is the center of all virtue. The contest comes to be viewed as having a final, apocalyptic quality. If we lose, all is lost; life will no longer be worth living; there will be nothing to be salvaged. If we win, then everything will be possible; all our problems will become soluble; the one great source of evil – our enemy – will have been crushed; the forces of good will then sweep forward unimpeded; all worthy aspirations will be satisfied.

The conflagrations of the first half of the 20th century were the direct result of an idea – the nation state – that had taken root in the 19th century and had become the dominant form of social organisation. After two world wars, European civilisation lay in a shambles, and the authority of the nation state was finally on the wane. Not only had history shown that the nationalist core of the nation state would lead to disaster, but the new superpowers of the post-nationalist period (the United States and the Soviet Union), as well as emerging global players like India and China, were countries organised around political ideology rather than nationhood.

Since the end of the Second World War, the nation state's claim to absolute sovereignty within its own borders has also come under increasing pressure. The post-war era was characterised by a global political system based on international agreements and supranational blocs, such as the North Atlantic Treaty Organization and the Soviet alliance. The devastation on a global scale also brought the realisation that the excessive assertion of sovereignty must be curbed by consensus, that is, by an association of states acting in concert. The UN was created especially to moderate dissent among sovereign nations. Over the next several decades, its role as an arbiter in international conflict progressed to the point that it has, on a few occasions, infringed directly upon the sovereignty of nations, most clearly in Iraq in 1991.[78] The International Criminal Court is another recently developed global institution that cuts across sovereign boundaries.

In Europe, the creation of a trading alliance led gradually to the development of the European Union, to which its member states have ceded various powers that were formerly part of their sovereign right, such as determining economic policy and issuing currency. It is an example of a 'continental grouping'. Other non-state actors, such as multinational corporations and non-governmental organisations, and the global flow of capital have also contributed to the erosion of the economic and political power of nation states.

In post-colonial countries, meanwhile, the notions of nationhood and sovereignty inherited from European colonial masters were embedded in the constitutions of many new republics. There, however, they have come into continual conflict with deeply entrenched, premodern allegiances to kinship group, caste, religious group, ethnicity, or tribe. In the absence of a strong constitution backed by a strong judiciary, and checks and balances which are difficult for developing nations to achieve, a ruling elite belonging to the same tribe, clan, or religious sect begins to dominate the governance of the nation, leading to all manner of institutionalised discrimination. In many countries in Africa and Asia, these tensions erupt periodically in dissent and violence, especially when individuals must adhere to Western-style judicial and political systems, but are also expected to abide by traditional cultural and religious mores. Honour killings are an example of such a clash of understanding, but there are also less blatant and violent cases, such as special concessions made to tribal communities in the exercise of ancestral hunting and fishing rights, political appointments made because of tribal or caste affiliations, and the limitation of women's and minority rights on the basis of religious traditions.

Most of all, however, it is the widespread recognition of the human rights of individuals that has dented the legitimacy of sovereign nation states. The Universal Declaration of Human Rights, adopted by the UN General Assembly in 1948, set forth 'a common standard of achievement for all peoples and all nations' and explicitly denied, in Article 30, the authority of any state, group, or person to curtail the rights and freedoms outlined in the Declaration. This gave the community of nations represented by the UN the right (though rarely exercised) to act in contravention of national sovereignty when it deems that human rights are under threat. The recognition that human rights like life, freedom from oppression, and justice are universal means that they transcend national boundaries. Their very universality implies a reduction in the warrant of the sovereign state.

The Nation State as an Obsolete Concept

In the foregoing discussion we have seen that the formation of the modern state (nation state, sovereign state, or country) was predicated on consolidation of a particular territory and centralisation of authority. Despite many recent developments, like the creation of the UN and the global recognition of human rights, most modern states still operate under the assumption that they are sovereign (i.e., that their governments should enjoy unfettered control over affairs within their territorial limits). These two characteristics of the contemporary nation state – centralisation and sovereignty – have contributed to ineffective systems of national and international governance.

What has not changed in the last two hundred years, however, is the conflation of identity with nationality, even though the modern nation state rarely has a homogenous identity as a nation. While we no longer necessarily have the ethnic identity of a nation to hold on to, we have transferred that attachment to the nation state. Citizens of nation states 'carry strong attitudes and beliefs about their own people and about others, who feel their attachment to their nation passionately, and who even, at times, act with great cruelty against their enemies', according to psychology professor Joshua Searle-White in *The Psychology of Nationalism*.[79] It is a basic human need to seek out group identities and loyalty. This need is essentially primal in nature as it helped our ancestors to survive in an uncertain environment. As political scientist Daniel Druckman points out, '[at] the level of the nation, the group fulfils economic, sociocultural, and political needs, giving individuals a sense of security, a feeling of belonging, and prestige'.[80]

The United States took nationalism to another level. The idea of 'manifest destiny' was deeply imbued with a sense of identity and belonging, and an understanding of what it meant to be American. The dominant myth and national narrative of America is its exceptionalism – the idea that America is entrusted with a mission because it is unique. This notion is expressed everywhere, from cinema, literature, and television to political speeches and state policy. As shown by the American example, the success of the nation as an idea lies in its ability to subsume other identities and demand primary allegiance to itself.

The idea of the nation state is deeply rooted in the human psyche, buttressed by the human need to fix our identity in something outside ourselves and by our addiction to power. The nation state has become the repository of our identity, and we imbue it with all the characteristics we wish to possess. It feeds our innate need for identity and belonging. As the history of the 20th century shows, identity formation on the basis of nationalism leads to the conviction that we are different, separate, and in most cases arrogantly superior, to other nations. This artificial mental construct pits the lower-consciousness individual against all national, ethnic, or religious groups perceived as 'other' than ourselves, such that we find ourselves thinking continually in binary terms – us versus them, the chosen ones facing the apostates, the true nation against the intruders. This dualistic mode of thinking leaves no room for real dialogue to occur between states.

Our natural addiction to power and control is in evidence in the nation state's vast bureaucracy, which is meant to regulate almost every aspect of a citizen's existence. The lower the level of consciousness of an individual, the more deeply embedded these cravings are. As consciousness changes, it becomes easier to escape the hold these primal needs have on human behaviour and thought. As we begin to shift our collective imagination to look at Community and the other levels of governance, the whole edifice of 'nation' crumbles. But first we must develop our consciousness so that we may overcome the primitive impulses (the need to belong, the desire to control) that are closely associated with the concept of the nation state and its supremacy. Without a shift in consciousness we won't be able to move beyond the binary way of thought – and the concomitant addiction to control – that characterises the modern nation state.

Disempowering the Nation State in the Second Dimension

Figure 12.2 reproduces the power distribution discussed earlier in this chapter, and presents two alternatives. The grey line shows a more equitable distribution of governance that may be found in a few contemporary societies and that, in the terminology used here, may be said to be functioning in a Second Dimension context already.

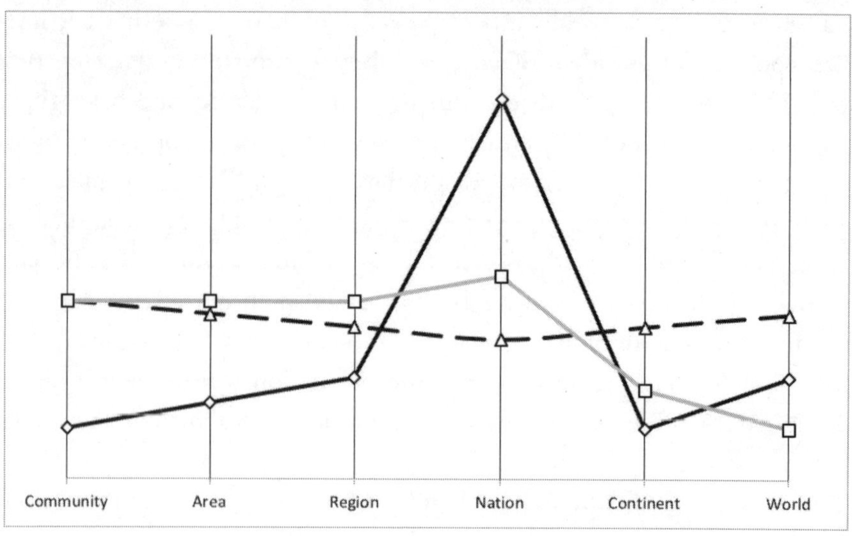

Figure 12.2: Distribution of Power in the Second Dimension

A good example is Switzerland. Despite its small size, Switzerland has a fully decentralised government following a strong tradition of fiercely independent local and regional governance. Switzerland is divided into twenty-six cantons which, in turn, comprise of some three thousand communes. A federal government joins the cantons into one nation state, but this central authority controls only matters that are relevant to all cantons, such as foreign policy, national defence, and the federal railways. All other issues (education, labour, welfare, domestic security, and even immigration) are determined by cantonal and communal governments. In order to be able to manage all these programmes, each commune and canton has a great degree of authority over taxation, such that most Swiss citizens pay an equal amount of tax to each tier of government. Each canton has its own parliament and constitution, and the communes, which vary in population from a few hundred inhabitants to a few hundred thousand, also have their own legislative and executive councils. Cantonal and communal governments are elected by their denizens.

Such extensive decentralisation of power works well in a multicultural state like Switzerland, which is made up of several different language groups – German, French, Italian, and Rhaeto-Romansh. In the past, when conflicts arose between linguistically or religiously defined groups, the Swiss resolved them by allowing each of the competing groups to govern itself. Thus, some cantons have divided into half-cantons, while new cantons have been created, and some communes lying along borders have opted to secede from one canton to join another. In this manner, the Swiss have developed a structure that permits people of different languages, religions, and traditions to live together in relative harmony.

Because many decisions are made at the local level, Swiss citizens are typically quite engaged in the laws and regulations that affect their lives. Each canton may enact substantially different policies, and this allows citizens to see for themselves which policies work best. For example, one canton might have high taxes and expensive welfare programmes, while another might prefer lower taxes and incentives for private charity. Each citizen can decide which policy suits her best and 'vote with her feet' by moving to a canton whose policies she supports. As a result, good policies tend to succeed and be adopted elsewhere, whereas bad ones are usually short-lived.

Swiss voters can also take matters in their own hands when they wish to bring about legal or constitutional change by relying on the frequent use of referendums. These instances of direct democracy are very common in Switzerland, at the federal as well as cantonal and community levels. They have been used to make decisions relevant to everyday life, such as whether shops should be allowed to open on Sundays, and whether power from renewable sources should be subsidised. Anyone eligible to vote has the right to propose a referendum and can follow through by collecting the requisite number of signatures. At the cantonal level, a few thousand signatures are sufficient.[81]

For a society like Switzerland, therefore, the power line (shown in grey in Figure 12.2) is almost flat on the left, as power is equally spread out among the three tiers of governance (commune, canton, nation). Nevertheless, on the right, the line plunges downward because Switzerland is powerless to affect policies in other nation states; also, it is not subject to many external interventions in its own policies.

The third line (dotted) shows an almost ideal distribution of authority. It is nearly flat, such that power is shared equally among all levels of governance, from the local Community to the global, world level. My argument here, much like in my book *Making India Work*, is not simply a call for smaller government or greater emphasis on local government, but for the **correct scaling** of government.

In a nutshell, we can say that every issue or problem confronting today's citizens and leaders, every aspect of governance and oversight, has an appropriate jurisdiction. There are issues and concerns that ought to be addressed at a community level, and others that rightly belong to higher perspectives. For example, a decision on where to locate a new city park, or whether or not to raise property taxes, should be taken at the community level. These are issues that have immediate impact on the citizen, and should therefore be addressed by a jurisdiction as close to him as possible. Accordingly, at the community level the citizen should have the right to elect his executive representative (the Community Leader) directly. As you may recall from Chapter 10, the election of community leadership is direct, with all adult members of the Community able to vote. (At higher levels of governance, leaders are voted into office *in*directly, that is, they are elected by their peers from a pool of candidates who are qualified on the basis of strict experience and performance criteria.)

On the other hand, there are many problems that cannot be solved at the local or even national level, and must therefore be addressed in higher forums. For example, issues that concern multiple nations, or indeed the world as a whole, such as climate change, mass migration, and international trade policy, must be addressed by continental or global bodies, even if this means acting against national sovereignty. The ideal distribution of administrative responsibilities is shown in Table 12.1.

The rationale for correct scaling is quite simple. The success of decentralisation in Switzerland suggests that citizens participate actively in governance, both as voters and as elected officials, because they believe that they can have a significant effect on decision-making and are empowered by their self-determination.

The correct scaling of governance starts with the fundamental recognition that people live in communities. They may nominally belong to a nation state, but they do not live in nation states. A nation state is too vast, both as a territory and as an idea, for an individual to belong to. Most citizens feel much too distant from the national centre of power where decisions that affect every aspect of their lives are being made. In democratic countries, casting a vote merely means sending a representative to a faraway capital, with little or no control over what happens next.

Citizens live in communities, and in this level of governance lies the true meaning of democracy. Therefore, the first step toward righting the imbalances created by the reliance on nation states as forms of organisation is to shift the authority to grant citizenship from the nation state to the Community.[82] While all those born in a Community would automatically be citizens, the Community would also be able to grant citizenship to newcomers, that is, migrants. Immigration would be different from what exists today; it would be motivated by careful selection of one Community over another, rather than by economic hardship or persecution.

Table 12.1: Scaling of Government

Government level	Representative body	Examples of responsibility
Community	Community Leader's advisory group	Parks, primary and secondary education, taxation, healthcare, urban design, local roads
Area	Area Caucus	Water and sewage, power distribution, cultural programmes, welfare
Region	Regional Assembly	Agricultural policy, tertiary education, major road networks
Nation	National Council	Defence, national transport systems (railways, airways, etc.), national currency
Continent	Continental Congress	Tutelage of environmental landscapes (mountain ranges, riparian systems, inland seas), disease control, peacekeeping, accretion/depletions to Gross National Reserve (GNR)/Gross Global Reserve (GGR)
World	Global Forum	Global commons (high seas, atmosphere), mass migration, climate change, rights and freedoms multiplier for the Global Forum, global settlement currency, rogue nations, trade policy

A newcomer would start his induction by requesting permission to reside in the Community temporarily and would confirm this through his physical presence, that is, by purchasing or renting a property in the Community's territory. After a suitable amount of time, he would be able to apply formally for citizenship. The Community would decide whether to grant him citizenship based on a transparent process that does not allow for discrimination based on race, religion, or nationality. A point system could be instituted, by which his suitability is determined based on the fundamentals of community involvement: has he contributed to the Community in a meaningful way, and was the contribution mutually beneficial? Does he have gainful employment in this or a neighbouring Community? Has he paid his taxes[83] in full and on time? Has he shown interest in community administration through involvement in local councils, committees, and boards? Has he avoided fines, citations, or unreasonable litigation?

This is, in effect, a point system, not unlike systems used nowadays by some countries (such as Australia and New Zealand) to objectively evaluate immigration applications. These First Dimension point systems, however, tend to reward the professional qualifications of applicants, with some consideration given to age, level of education, and financial assets. Thus, an engineer is much more likely to be granted citizenship than an unskilled labourer. The system I propose here, on the other hand, would put much more emphasis on the human qualities of applicants, such as the willingness and desire to cooperate, dedication to civic values, moral integrity, openness to dialogue, and so forth.

Such a system would ensure that any individual can earn the right to be a member of any Community. The prerequisites for this right would be responsibility, recognition by one's fellow citizens, and participation in the governance of the Community. (If the citizen is no longer satisfied with the policies of the Community, he can easily transfer his residence to a different Community, and seek a new citizenship there.) This would result in more diverse communities, not in the 'multicultural' sense currently championed by liberal thinkers, where 'tolerance' is the buzzword, but where, instead of merely being tolerated, citizens would earn genuine respect for each other because everyone has realised that concepts like nation, country, race, and caste are artificial.

The economist and philosopher Amartya Sen captures this idea succinctly in *The Idea of Justice*:

> I believe the warning against seeing someone merely as a member of a group to which he or she belongs [...] is particularly important in the present intellectual climate in which individuals tend to be identified as belonging to one social category to the exclusion of all others, such as

> being a Muslim or a Christian or a Hindu, an Arab or a Jew, a Hutu or a Tutsi, or a member of Western civilization. Individual human beings with their various plural identities, multiple affiliations and diverse associations are quintessentially social creatures with different types of societal interactions. Proposals to see a person merely as a member of one social group tend to be based on an inadequate understanding of the breadth and complexity of any society in the world.

This Second Dimension plan for a Community-based immigration policy would benefit both the immigrant and the Community. Knowing that permission to immigrate would depend on demonstrating the civic values espoused by the Community, the immigrant would be encouraged to make a contribution to the public life of the Community, abide by its rules, and become involved in its operation and governance. In doing so, he too would gain the acceptance and respect of his fellow citizens quickly because implicit in his contribution is that he has embraced the values of that Community. The Community, meanwhile, would be almost certain to gain a productive, engaged member who would bring new skills, energy, and diversity. It would look forward to assimilating the new member, much as a sports team is boosted by the arrival of a star player who increases their chance to win a championship.

Contrast this with how immigration unfolds in the First Dimension, where it is almost always set in motion by hardship faced in the country of origin, such as economic deprivation, persecution, violence, discrimination, and injustice. Migrants migrate, in other words, because they feel they have no alternatives. The rich nations where they hope to resettle typically grant citizenship (via an asylum process, or through amnesty or guest worker programmes) only grudgingly because they do not see much value in migrants. In fact, they fear loss of jobs, loss of social stability, and dilution of their cherished culture and values. Local populations therefore do not help much with the integration of new migrants, often allowing them to become segregated, forced into a peripheral existence, often living in ghettos with little hope of betterment, and resentful of the more prosperous majority.

The key change in social identity in the Second Dimension is to shift the right to grant citizenship from nations to communities. This move would ensure that migrants can earn the right to be members of a Community of their choice through merit alone.

Ultimately, the evolution of consciousness in more people will help them to recognise the hollowness of imagined constructs like nationality and sovereignty, and accept the fundamental idea that our humanity is shared. The evidence of everyday living, as reflected in both international news and personal experience, overwhelmingly shows us that humans of all countries, races, and convictions share the same fundamental aspirations, desires, and needs. What is needed is a rejection of the shackles of jingoism, patriotism, pride, superiority, and indifference that the idea of nationhood promotes. Nations are imaginary constructs that keep us apart.

The way forward is to devolve power from an imagined entity (the nation) and award more of it to those administrative structures that are closer to the individual human being: his Community first and foremost, as well as his Area and Region. At the same time, supranational entities must also siphon away some of the authority currently vested in the nation and enshrined in the seemingly impregnable concept of sovereignty. As I will explain in Chapter 13, Continental and Global forums should play a much more significant and pervasive role in the everyday lives of citizens, at the expense of national sovereignty. Embedded in the idea of sovereignty is the right to monopolise the use of power and coercion. The concept of sovereignty is outdated because it does not consider the wider imperatives of humanity, which demand a more balanced approach to governance, both at the Community and Global levels. It sees both local and global governance as a threat to its existence and has thus become a hurdle to human development. It can only be overcome by creating a global movement for change that will challenge the status quo.

13

The New International Order: Beyond Sovereignty

International Relations in the First Dimension

Conquest and religion were two of the driving forces of premodern history, and their currency was power. Power meant military power – in a world where rulers were despots who could wipe out the villages they conquered, economic power played a smaller role than it does today. The players of the power game were city states, empires, and kingdoms, all of which formed loose and shifting alliances to fight wars, promote trade, and occasionally to keep the peace. Eventually, this led to the need for policies that could codify relations between cooperating and competing entities. Such preoccupation with managing one's neighbours appears repeatedly in history. Kautilya's *Arthashastra*, Sun-Tzu's *The Art of War*, and Niccolò Machiavelli's *Prince* are three texts written in different places and at different times, but they all advise a ruler on how to deal with other states. The most effective way to do so was by exhibiting superior force or threat of force, not only by having a strong military presence but also by signing treaties and forming coalitions that held the promise of power should the need arise. Over time, this rule of force was replaced by the rule of law.

International relations as we know them today are played out primarily among sovereign nation states. After the Reformation, Europe was wracked by religious wars between Catholic and Protestant powers. Religious strife culminated in the devastating Thirty Years' War (1618–1648), a conflict that embroiled much of the continent and resulted in a stalemate. At the ensuing Peace of Westphalia in 1648, the warring parties agreed that henceforth each territorial state would be free to determine and manage religious affairs within its own borders without interference from others.

While the Treaty of Westphalia was intended to guarantee autonomy for each nation state to determine its religious affiliation, it also established the notion of territorial sovereignty as a norm of non-interference in the affairs of other nations (so-called Westphalian sovereignty). The budding nation states of Europe now had a legal and ideological framework for asserting themselves on both the domestic stage and the international stage. Within its territorial borders, the nation state had the authority to manage its own affairs without interference from other nation states, or from the supranational remnants of an earlier age, such as the Catholic Church and the Holy Roman Empire. The authority of the nation state over its territory was supreme, indivisible, centralised, and recognised by all. Thus the Peace of Westphalia enshrined the nation state as the pre-eminent territorial and political entity of the day and signalled the beginning of modern diplomacy and international relations.

By the time of the Treaty of Utrecht in 1713, the military impasse of the Thirty Years' War had resulted in a return to the notion of balance of power, an important idea in international relations, whose guiding principle is the maintenance of peace. The concept had been around in the time of Thucydides and resurfaced in 15th-century Italy, when five powerful city states warred continually for control of the peninsula with no resolution in sight. In 18th-century Europe, it meant that states came together to guarantee the preservation of geopolitical balance, such that no one state could dominate another or prescribe laws to the rest. And, because it was mutually beneficial for this balance to be maintained, states were given the right to intervene forcefully if the conditions were infringed. The notion of the balance of power continued to dominate diplomacy in 19th-century Europe. The Austrian statesman Metternich (1773–1859) and the Prussian statesman Bismarck (1815–1898) worked toward this goal. The idea of balance of power enforced by the threat of violence highlights the central role that war plays in First Dimension international policy.

The high noon of statesmanship based on rationality came in the 20th century, with the concept of deterrence and the consequent theory of Mutually Assured Destruction (MAD). The MAD doctrine holds that whenever a country or alliance that has the nuclear capability to completely destroy its adversary should attack, the other side must respond with the same or greater force, thus ensuring the total annihilation of both sides. A key aspect of this is the possession of second-strike capability, such that if hit by nuclear force, the state is still able to respond with equal force. The very ideas of deterrence and balance of power are based on the assumption that the central player in international relations is a rational, utility-maximising nation state capable of deploying deadly force if forced to do so.

At the height of the Cold War, the *Bulletin of the Atomic Scientists* used to publish the 'Doomsday Clock', which told us how close we were to a nuclear catastrophe. Many theorists of the nuclear age, including Herman Kahn and Kosta Tsipis, prophesied the coming of a nuclear winter. Today, we live in an age where everyone feels that such concerns are over. Though hardly anyone looks at the Doomsday Clock any more, it still exists.[84] But I would argue that because of the nation state's pre-eminence in world affairs, we are at a more dangerous point than we have ever been before. The sovereign nation of Pakistan, for example, today owns approximately four hundred nuclear weapons. By developing a nuclear arsenal, Pakistan is merely exercising its sovereign First Dimension right to protect itself against its traditional adversary and neighbour, India, which enjoys a 3:1 superiority in conventional forces. Pakistan, however, is a highly unstable nation state that has been through several military dictatorships. Its weak institutions are unable to deliver on the needs of its burgeoning population; religious radicalism is rampant; and it is widely recognised that the Pakistani army is infiltrated by radical elements. Violence, perpetuated by religious terrorism as well as tribal backwardness, is pervasive among its restive population.

Thus, a failed state on the verge of disintegration and all-out strife nevertheless possesses nuclear weapons that could very easily fall into the hands of rogue elements and be deployed against Western and Indian targets. This is the legacy of the First Dimension's over-reliance on the concept of the nation state as the unrivalled heavyweight in the modern balance of power. In a world governed by a Second Dimension social paradigm, the global community should be empowered to disregard Pakistan's sovereignty and intervene to both disarm it and rebuild its broken institutions.

As an idea, the nation state is nearing its sell-by date; its structure is becoming a massive obstacle to the future development of humanity. Like many First Dimension ideas, it played an important role in the bridge to modernity but, because most nation states spread myths about ethnicity, religion, and complexes of superiority, and because they are now locked in a tangled strategic game that seeks to balance power, they have ultimately led to a world that, while it is globalised, is made stagnant and unable to progress further. That is why we need to move beyond the nation state and strip it of the central role it plays in human affairs.

From Treaties to Global Governance

In Chapter 12 we saw how redefining the role of the nation state and scaling it correctly can lead to a better interpretation of citizenship, as well as more effective governance and enhanced citizen participation. The fundamental change proposed there was to siphon authority away from the national level and restore it to the community level. Here, I suggest that the correct scaling of power must also come into play on the international stage. By de-emphasising the nation state as the central actor in international affairs we open society to a paradigm shift that allows continental and global forums to be empowered and play a more incisive role. Without a drastic reduction of the nation's power over the fate of individuals and communities, we will not be able to create continental and global institutions that can address the most pressing issues of our times.

The idea of global governance – an assembly of nations in a permanent, parliamentary-style session – is less than a century old. Its first incarnation was the League of Nations, which was founded in 1920 as a result of the Paris Peace Conference that concluded the First World War. Until then, international agreements had taken the form of treaties between individual nation states or alliances of nation states, and usually covered issues of territorial control, royal succession, and trade. They were changeable, revocable, and sometimes limited in temporal scope, depending on the inclinations of each country's sovereign. More importantly, treaties were invariably the outcome of violent actions (wars, invasions, occupations) or at least the threat of violent action (gunboat diplomacy, blockades, massing of forces on borders). In other words, the most important factor in international negotiations was always the military force of each country, and the willingness to deploy it. Legitimacy and power were the result of force of arms. Might was right, and those without military means had to endure the hegemony of the strong. This state of affairs was as old as civilisation and was echoed in Thucydides' Melian dialogue: 'The strong do what they can and the weak suffer what they must.'

In the wake of the unprecedented devastation caused by the First World War, the League of Nations was created with the specific purpose of preventing such disastrous confrontations in the future. Its stated mission was to ensure peace among its member countries, which, in the beginning, numbered forty-two. Despite some early successes, in which the League was able to negotiate peaceful settlements to territorial disputes, it failed miserably to prevent aggressive expansion by a number of nation states, especially the Axis powers (Germany, Japan, and Italy), and to prevent another worldwide conflagration.

Its failure was caused by various factors. In a practical sense, the League had no military resources of its own to enforce its mandate. From a political point of view, the world, especially Europe, was still too attached to the ambitions and delusions of imperialism to give the League a fair chance. The First World War had been fought ostensibly to make the world safe for democracy, and to avert all future wars, but essentially it was an imperialist war for the division and redivision of European territory and colonies. The League was willed and founded by the victors of the war, and thus it reflected the political and imperialist desires of those victors. In the absence of the United States and Russia,[85] the League was dominated by England and France and became an instrument of their policy in Europe and elsewhere. These powers were not interested in peace so much as in the maintenance of their imperial dominions, and they were not prepared to cede control over global affairs to this fledgling supranational organisation. Finally, the League idealistically assumed and expected unanimity in its decisions, with the result that any member, including the smallest, had the right to veto any resolution and could thus hamstring the League in its actions.

In the aftermath of the Second World War – a conflict the League had been powerless to avert – the League was disbanded and replaced by the United Nations. Today the UN is truly a global assembly of nations numbering 193 members. Although peacekeeping is an important part of its mission (managed primarily by the UN Security Council), its activities and interventions span the entire gamut of cooperation between states, with various agencies engaged in economic development, health, international banking, cultural exchange, food and agriculture, labour relations, and in defence of the needs of vulnerable groups, such as children, women, indigenous peoples, migrants, and refugees.

In its role as global arbiter, however, the UN still suffers from some of the same limitations that plagued the League of Nations. Without a standing army of its own, the UN relies on military contributions from its member states to deploy peacekeeping forces in areas affected by violence and strife. Moreover, the five permanent members of the fifteen-member Security Council have the ability to veto any resolution. These five nations (United States, United Kingdom, France, Russia, and China) are, once again, the victors of the last worldwide conflict. Their control of security matters rests, as it always did, on the outcome of a war, as well as their continued maintenance of vast military capabilities, which include nuclear weapons. The right of each of these nations to veto resolutions to intervene in conflicts, as well as the cumbersome and slow machinery of UN negotiations, have often stopped the UN from intervening urgently in matters of large-scale violence.

Indeed, though UN peacekeeping missions have met with success on some occasions, the UN has failed utterly to stop the most brutal events of the last few decades, including the Somali civil war (1991–1992), the Rwandan genocide (1994), and the Srebrenica massacre (1995). At the time of writing, the UN is showing no resolve to intervene in countries desperately in need of international intervention and external arbitration, like Libya and Syria. It also has been unable to prevent the brazen aggression against Ukraine by Russia, one of the members of its very own Security Council. In essence, it is able to act (through military action or economic and political sanctions) only when all five permanent members of the Security Council are in agreement, when military resources are made available, when there is widespread popular pressure to act against an injustice, and when the intervention is in the economic and strategic interests of a good number of its more powerful members. Not surprisingly, these conditions rarely coincide.

Besides the global assembly represented by the UN, the last half-century has seen a proliferation of other transnational organisations. In the sphere of continental affairs, the Organization of American States represents all thirty-five nations in the Americas, while the African Union comprises almost all countries in Africa. While both work mainly through diplomatic channels to strengthen regional ties and promote continental trade, the latter has also deployed peacekeeping forces on a few occasions. More influential than these continental organisations are subcontinental groups focused on improving trade between neighbouring blocks of nations. These include the South Asian Association for Regional Cooperation and the Association of South-East Asian Nations in Asia, and the MERCOSUR in South America. The European Union, too, began life as an economic organisation, but has since morphed into a closer group of nations that share not only economic policy but many other aspects of governance as well, including agricultural and welfare policies, foreign relations outside of the Union, development goals, and fundamental assumptions about human and civil rights. Global economic alliances like the G20 also play a prominent role in modern-day foreign relations. Finally, there are military alliances, such as the North Atlantic Treaty Organization (NATO) and the now defunct Warsaw Pact, which are intended to set out common security policies and pool military resources.

The proliferation of transnational bodies in the last century clearly evinces the need for ever greater international cooperation in all areas of governance. What still holds back such bodies from fulfilling their duty of international governance, and from undertaking tangible, consequential steps to ensure international peace and prosperity, is the lingering and slavish adhesion of most nations to the obsolete principle of national sovereignty.

Figure 13.1 graphically represents the distribution of power among all layers of governance. The solid line represents the typical distribution of governance in the First Dimension, whereas the flatter, dashed line shows the ideal distribution in the Second and Third Dimensions. The reason why global assemblies like the UN fail to properly influence matters of global importance in the First Dimension is shown in the

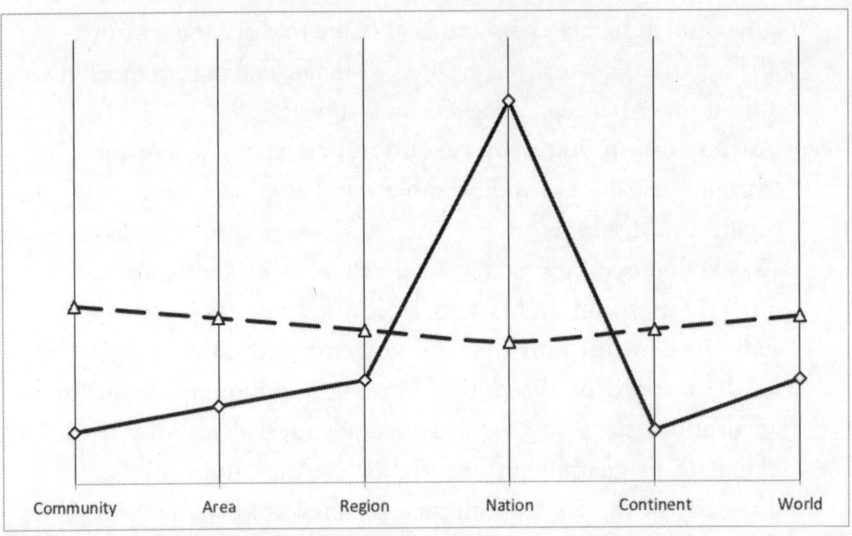

Figure 13.1: Comparing the Distribution of Power in Different Dimensions

solid line: nations are loath to relinquish the power they wield over their own citizens, and their ability to pursue their own goals with little regard for the needs of other nations. The First Dimension understanding of sovereignty is a zero-sum game: giving up a degree of sovereignty to strengthen continental and global institutions is considered a loss of power and authority rather than a sensible extension of good governance that accurately addresses the needs of humanity as a whole.

The Second Dimension: Empowering Continental and Global Forums

The State of the World's Nation States

We live in an era where only a small percentage of the world's 7.6 billion humans[86] have access to anything approaching higher-quality rights and freedoms. Current systems of government could be broadly classified as in Table 13.1 and characterised as follows:

- **Failed and collapsed states**: regions of the world where a government barely exists and is not able to discharge any of the functions normally associated with national governance. Often these states are plagued by civil war.
- **Authoritarian states of various types**: states where the citizen is usually a powerless subject and enjoys very limited rights and freedoms.
- **Weak democracies**: states where there is a semblance of First Dimension rights and freedoms, but they largely exist in constitutions that are not enforced consistently, as the respect for the rule of law, the functioning of the institutions necessary for a democracy, and the ability of the state to guarantee those rights, are all compromised. In many of these states, internal regional conflicts prevent a proportion of citizens from enjoying any rights. Often, they are characterised by low-intensity internecine wars.

- **Functional democracies**: states where there is a much higher degree of individual freedom guaranteed and largely available to the majority of the population because of the existence and efficiency of institutions to protect and enforce the law. This ensures that basic rights and freedoms are available to all citizens.
- **Early Second Dimension states**: exceptional states where the majority of the population already operates at a higher level of consciousness. Their policies and programmes, and the quality and widespread availability of rights and freedoms enjoyed by the population make them unusual examples.

Table 13.1: Current Types of Government

Type of government	Examples of states	Approx. aggregate population	Percentage of humanity
Failed and collapsed states	Afghanistan, Syria, Yemen, Somalia, Libya, Sudan, Venezuela	1.94 billion	25.5%
Authoritarian or pseudo-democratic states	China, Saudi Arabia, Bangladesh, Philippines	2.54 billion	33.4%
Weak democracies	India, Indonesia, South Africa, Malaysia, Brazil, Argentina, Nigeria	2.26 billion	29.8%
Functional democracies	United States, United Kingdom, Japan, Germany, France, Italy, Belgium, Poland, Australia	820 million	10.8%
Early Second Dimension states	Norway, Sweden, Denmark, Finland, Iceland, Switzerland	35 million	0.5%

It is clear that except for a few Scandinavian countries, the rest of the world falls into low First Dimension categories. The fact that only 11 per cent of today's citizens enjoy any meaningful set of rights and freedoms is a shocking indictment of the First Dimension world. The table is a reminder of the work that needs to be done: almost 90 per cent of humanity lives in nations that do not even provide basic First Dimension rights and freedoms.

The ideas developed several centuries ago, such as human rights and liberties, and the popular legitimacy of government, were revolutionary then. Today, we stand at a cusp in human evolution, where we have the means and technology to overcome many of the problems that our world faces. There is no reason why billions of people must continue to live with few or no human rights. Our goal is to work toward this new period for humanity, even though it may well take fifty years to manifest itself. The march of human evolution must turn in this direction because if we do not focus on human consciousness and reawaken our humanity, the alternative is to continue with a logical system built upon our basest instincts. Each one of us has a choice. Our political movement is about making that choice. We should remember the words attributed to the cultural anthropologist Margaret Mead: 'Never doubt that a small group of thoughtful, committed citizens can change the world; indeed, it's the only thing that ever has.'

Voting in Continental and Global Assemblies

In Figure 13.2, the top two legislative groups have been added, showing how the highest domestic assembly (the National Council) will be superseded by transnational assemblies at the Continental and World levels. In structure and purpose, these bodies would be similar to the continental and global assemblies that already exist. However, decision-making at these levels would proceed in a radically different manner – a manner that ignores the availability of brute force and relies instead on each country's record in assuring and developing its citizens' rights and freedoms.

The Continental Congress and the Global Forum exercise their jurisdiction in six areas:

- They operate Continental and Global arbitration councils.
- They work closely with national governments to monitor the rights and freedoms indices by which the voting weight of each country is calculated.
- When a nation state's rights and freedoms score is declining rapidly, and there is threat to human life and the complete abrogation of liberties, they may invoke a suspension of the sovereignty provision that requires all members to impose punitive sanctions and, in extreme cases, to intervene militarily and place that nation under the trusteeship of the Global Forum.

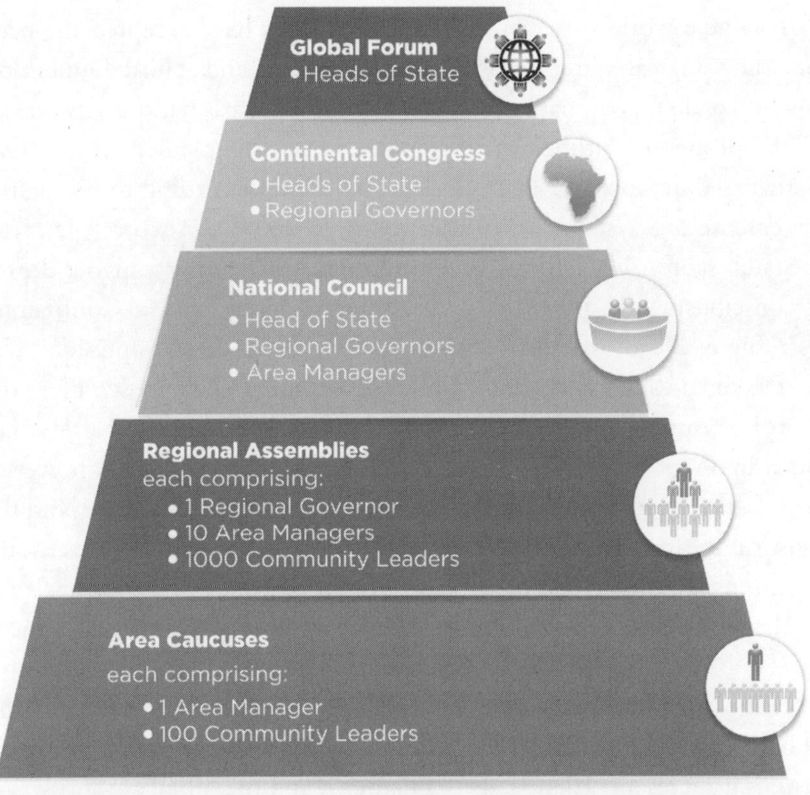

Figure 13.2: Full Pyramidal Model of Legislatures

- They appoint expert groups to calculate the new economic indicators (Gross National Reserves, Gross Continental Reserves, and Gross Global Reserve, discussed in Chapter 15) that will replace Gross Domestic Product as the primary means of measuring the well-being of nations and of the global community.
- They ensure free trade and support the use of the Global Unit of Settlement (GUS), the sole global currency for international trade and capital settlements (see Chapter 18).
- They supervise the issuance and exchange of two new financial instruments (or meta-currencies) that will be needed to trade intangible assets in higher dimensions (see Chapter 17).

Imagine a world order in which most nations have accepted the need for a new logical system that aspires to Second and Third Dimension values. To align governance with this aspiration, most nations have taken up the proposals outlined in this book and have implemented the new, merit-based democracy. Their leaders are judged according to the rights-based scorecard system. Every country, therefore, has a score (the Head of State's score) that reflects its commitment to fostering a higher degree of consciousness in its citizens. At a supranational level, a Continental assembly of Heads of State[87] – the Continental Congress – presides over matters of continental concern, while above that, a Global assembly – the Global Forum – not dissimilar from the UN, oversees all matters that touch upon global concerns. Unlike the UN Security Council, however, the Global Forum has the moral authority, the political mandate, and the logistical means to intervene in any matter where the rights and freedoms of citizens are threatened or inadequately supplied.

All nation states (not just a few, like in the UN Security Council) may sit at the table where decisions are made whether to intervene across sovereign lines or not. However, each nation's ability to influence the global gathering of nations is dependent on two things: the number of citizens it represents (that is, its population), and the moral authority that it wields as a result of its own enforcement of rights and freedoms (that is, its national scorecard). No one has the ability to veto, and a two-thirds majority is necessary to make any resolution operational.

Table 13.2 shows how the vote share of a few sample countries, chosen at random, would be computed based on their population (according to 2016–2017 estimates) and national score. The national score values given here are merely guesses of where each of the selected countries would perform if they were subjected to the scorecards developed in Chapter 11. As the table shows, the score is mapped to a multiplier (Table 13.3), which can either reduce or enhance the country's voting 'weight', otherwise dependent only on the size of its population.

Table 13.2: Hypothetical Vote Shares of Some Countries in the Global Forum

Country	**Population (million)**	**Estimated national score (%)**	**Rights and freedoms multiplier (Table 13.3)**	**Vote share (million)**
Canada	35	88	10	35 × 10 = 350
China	1,400	29	0.3	1,400 × 0.3 = 420
India	1,300	26	0.3	1,300 × 0.3 = 390
Saudi Arabia	33	34	0.5	33 × 0.5 = 17
Singapore	5.5	72	5	5.5 × 5 = 28
Sweden	10	93	20	10 × 20 = 200
Thailand	69	48	0.7	69 × 0.7 = 48
United States	325	69	2	325 × 2 = 650

Table 13.3: Calculation of Vote Share Multiplier

Rights and freedoms score (%)	**0–10**	**11–20**	**21–30**	**31–40**	**41–50**	**51–60**	**61–70**	**71–80**	**81–90**	**91–100**
Vote share multiplier	0.1	0.2	0.3	0.5	0.7	1	2	5	10	20

Sweden, for example, is home to about ten million inhabitants. Despite its small population, it is an advanced democracy that has not only developed the infrastructure to consistently deliver a high degree of material well-being to its citizens, but has also put in place extensive human, civil, and intellectual rights and freedoms. It is one of the most enlightened societies in the world and can be said to be functioning in the Second Dimension already. As a result, its score on the scorecard would be quite high, leading to a twentyfold increase in its vote share. Sweden, in other words, would be able to cast 200 million votes in any international or continental forum, despite having a small population.

In contrast, Saudi Arabia is able to punch at only half its weight. Massive oil wealth ensures that Saudi Arabia can deliver good infrastructure and a comfortable quality of life to many of its citizens, but it would score very low on most other rights, due to its notoriously dismal record in issues like humane justice, women's empowerment, religious freedom, democratic political engagement, and the negative ecological impact of its main economic activity (oil and gas extraction). Its overall score, therefore, would likely be low, leading to a vote share multiplier that reduces the number of votes the country can cast.

The Asian behemoths India and China too would fall in a low vote share category, though for different reasons. India is often touted as the largest democratic state on earth, and it has done much to grant its citizens extensive political freedoms, ensuring participation in government from all strata of society, as well as protection (at least in theory) of religious, ethnic, and tribal minorities. However, the enforcement of these guarantees of equality and fairness is lax in most parts of the country. Moreover, India has done a poor job of delivering the essentials of modern living (such as clean water, nutrition, sanitation, and healthcare), so that a large proportion of its citizens still live in miserable conditions. China has achieved more than India in this regard but, conversely, its authoritarian, single-party regime has a poor record on many other fronts, such as the treatment of ethnic and regional minorities, freedom of speech, privacy, and political participation. Both India and China would therefore obtain a low overall score for their efforts toward guaranteeing Second Dimension rights and freedoms, such that their vote share would be roughly only a third of their population.

This system for international cooperation assigns the power to make decisions of international consequence to those nations that have done the most to secure their citizens' rights and liberties. It also empowers the international community of nations to intervene in the defence of human rights everywhere, because the very foundation of international collaboration is no longer the recognition and respect of each other's national sovereignty, but rather the betterment of the human condition based on a universal set of values.

Case Studies

Let us now look at a few case studies that illustrate how an international assembly might be called upon to settle disputes of Continental or Global significance. A pressing matter of Continental concern is China's plan to build a series of large hydroelectric power dams on major rivers in Tibet, as well as to divert vast amounts of water from these rivers to feed the thirsty mines, factories, and cities of eastern China. Though China would be undertaking these projects within its national borders, they are a matter of Continental concern because the Slaween, the Brahmaputra, and the Mekong rivers, which have headwaters in Tibet, all cross international boundaries. Including China itself, over one billion people downstream from Tibet depend on these rivers. Damming and diverting them may have a damaging impact on their lives and on the environment. The ability of downstream communities to grow water-intensive crops like rice and wheat will be severely curtailed, fish stocks will plummet, and ecosystems will be destroyed. Within Tibet itself, millions will have to be relocated and will have to find a new livelihood to make way for dams and reservoirs. The UN has done little to prevent any of this. The Watercourses Convention, which sets out guidelines for sharing water across national boundaries, came into effect in 2014, but it is not binding and China is not a signatory.

The Brahmaputra–Mekong riparian system is a precious resource shared by many countries in Asia so it has many stakeholders. Therefore, it is the type of situation that a Continental Congress should address. A balanced discussion of the issue in such a forum would quickly reveal the folly of China's plans. If the matter came to a vote, China's vote share, diminished by its poor record in implementing rights and freedoms, would be insufficient to hold sway. After negotiations, the Chinese government would be forced to reconsider its plans, and either scale them back substantially, or cancel them altogether. Even if it did proceed with a reduced plan to dam and divert Tibetan rivers, it would have to pay compensation to downstream communities (under the new monetary order discussed in Chapter 18), who could then use those funds to mitigate the impact of China's riparian projects. Such compensatory schemes would be transacted using a specialised currency (Chapter 17).

Recent and current examples of problems that require a global solution, and therefore a global assembly, include Somali piracy in the Indian Ocean, and the increasingly frequent and dangerous migration of impoverished Africans and Asians from the north coast of Africa and Turkey to Europe. Piracy affects all nations because it threatens international shipping lanes, and ships, crews, and financial interests from various countries. The migration issue, too, is global: migrants attempting to cross the Mediterranean include people from sub-Saharan Africa, the Middle East, and Central Asia; their destination is Europe; and the smugglers involved are from Libya, Egypt, and Niger. Such cases are clearly the purview of a global assembly empowered to pass resolutions on these matters swiftly and to deploy resources to address them. A transparent voting system that favours Second Dimension democracies would enable the Global Forum to make the correct decisions without being held up by the particular interests or lack of resolve of individual countries.

The Third Dimension: Trusteeship and the Triumph of Human Rights

Piracy and migration across the Mediterranean both make an excellent case for an effective Global Forum driven exclusively by the need to bring peaceful resolution and enhanced freedoms to citizens of every nation. Moreover, they highlight an issue of special concern to the international community: the failure of sovereign states. Piracy off the coast of Somalia is, simply put, a glaring indication that Somalia has failed as a state. It is not functional as a government because it cannot ensure even the most basic rights of its people, such as law and order. Similarly, mass migrations under perilous conditions from North Africa and the Middle East to Europe are only possible because several countries along the African and Asian coast of the Mediterranean have fallen into complete disarray.

Libya has become a wasteland where several different factions, including terrorist groups loyal to al-Qaida and the former Islamic State, vie for control of territory and oil resources. Violence and lawlessness are rife, with no hope of any near-term improvement. In this decayed state, there is ample opportunity for unscrupulous human traffickers to conduct their business with impunity. Syria, meanwhile, is only now emerging from a distressing civil war that has been waged for eight years. As a result of the continued warfare between the Assad government (supported militarily by Russia) and several rebel groups (some of which were at one time supported by Western powers, including the United States), the country is in tatters, and, until recently, the playground of terrorist organisations like Islamic State. Millions of its inhabitants have been displaced internally or have found refuge in neighbouring countries. Many more continue to flee in hopes of reaching Europe.

Both Somali piracy and mass migration across the Mediterranean are not only problems of global scale and concern, but also problems that must be dealt with by addressing their root causes. The most important cause of mass migration is the failure of transit nations such as Libya, as well as the inadequacy of governance in the countries from which the bulk of migrants are attempting to flee.

In the Third Dimension, the Global Forum will have the authority and the means to place failing nations in trusteeship. Trusteeship is not unlike the so-called 'mandates' of the League of Nations, or the UN's Trusteeship Council (no longer operational). It means that the community of nations represented in the Global Forum may decree that a Nation has failed consistently and alarmingly to deliver basic rights and freedoms to its citizens, and that intervention is therefore warranted.

The first step in this process would be for the Global Forum to suspend the sovereignty of the country in question. This would provide the legal basis for intervention by a multinational military force tasked with enforcing peace and rebuilding the country. This is not unlike certain efforts undertaken by the UN and by US-led coalitions in recent years, in places like Iraq and Afghanistan. However, there would be important differences. To begin with, the multinational force in charge of trusteeship would, as its very first task, pursue a comprehensive and forcible disarmament of the local population. All weapons, with no exception whatsoever, would have to be turned in, or seized, by whatever means necessary. This is a fundamental requirement before any peace or rebuilding process can take place. Once the populace has been completely disarmed, the multinational trusteeship force can set about rebuilding not only infrastructure, but also institutions like the police, the judiciary, educational and health systems, and welfare agencies.

Importantly, however, this must be done under the supervision of administrators who are foreign, highly experienced, and externally recruited. While the ultimate goal of any such intervention is always to develop strong local leadership and capable, judicious local administrators, this can only be a long-term goal. In the near term, it is paramount to bring infrastructural systems back online and to instil in the citizenry the faith that the rebuilding effort will be conducted efficiently, without preference or corruption. This can only happen when all senior administrators are brought in from the outside. (These administrators would of course be required to consult the local population to determine what forms of governance would work best for them in the absence of the old regime, and what administrative reforms are needed most urgently.)

This may smack of colonialism. But if a country has shown itself incapable of self-governance, the international community acting as one has the right and the duty to impose order from the outside, even if that means forcing the local population to live under foreign administration. The trusteeship would be clearly limited in time, so that the local population can keep in sight a target date to return to self-governance. In most cases, this interval would be fifteen years – the minimum time needed to retrain public servants and rebuild trust in government institutions.

Rebuilding nations from the ground up in this manner would ensure that their inhabitants have a fair chance at securing the rights and freedoms that other countries take for granted. It would also enable the Global Forum to address many continental and global problems at their roots, in places where civilisation has faltered and given way to chaos.

To begin to move toward a new world order, we have to create the conditions for people to become aware of the deep psychological roots and conditioning that hold the concept of a nation state in place. As the world becomes more interdependent, the concept of identity must begin to dissolve as we see more of what we have in common as humans, and less of what separates us as individuals. In *Sapiens*, historian Yuval Noah Harari says,

> As the twenty-first century unfolds, nationalism is fast losing ground. More and more people believe that all of humankind is the legitimate source of political authority, rather than the members of a particular nationality, and that safeguarding human rights and protecting the interests of the entire human species should be the guiding light of politics.

And the ideas of cultural, racial, religious, and military hegemony must begin to move to the dustbin of history, where they belong.

Part IV

THE ECONOMY

14

Capitalism: Making the Hand Visible

Capitalism and its Discontents

Capitalism is the most successful application of First Dimension thought. Since the demise of the Soviet Union, it has emerged as the pre-eminent global economic system in the world. The theoretical foundation of capitalism is the market economy – an exchange system in which decisions regarding investment, production, and distribution of goods and services are based on supply and demand. In such a system, the prices and quantities of goods and services can be determined by the interaction of buyers and sellers, with little interference from external players, such as government.

Capitalism and the market economy are not the same, however, even though these terms are used interchangeably in common parlance. In capitalism, the means of production are largely or entirely privately owned. The surplus capital accumulated as a result of for-profit operation is used primarily to augment the private wealth of business owners, as well as to fund the expansion of capitalist activity. A market economy, on the other hand, does not necessarily presuppose the existence of private property in the means of production. We can envision a market economy consisting of various types of cooperatives, collectives, and autonomous government agencies that exchange goods and services with each other in an unfettered pricing environment. Even profit can find a place in such a system, shared among workers, reinvested into the business activity, or spent on public works.

Other key characteristics of capitalism, besides supply and demand and private ownership, are the use of wage labour and the competitive nature of the market, where many producers vie to fulfil customers' demands.

The allure of capitalism lies in its immediacy: it ties all economic activities to individual human desire – the desire to acquire objects and hire services that will make life more comfortable and pleasurable. Thus, the principal actor in the capitalist world view is the rational, utility-maximising consumer, who is expected to estimate the utility or value of any product or service, and use this understanding to make decisions that will maximise his own benefit. This individual's right to acquire products and resources to satisfy his needs and desires is accepted as a fundamental right of every citizen, and is as sacred as the rights to life, freedom, justice, and expression. Modern capitalism is thus rooted in the democratic ideals that we hold so dear: each individual has the right to own things and the freedom to dispose of them as he wishes.

Pure capitalism has never existed because a perfect market economy cannot exist; it is impossible to organise a society in such a way that government does not interfere at all in economic activity. As the philosopher Adam Smith stipulated, there are essential services that a market economy, especially capitalism, can never spontaneously provide, such as a fair, unbiased system of law and order, and a comprehensive structure of public works that serves the needs of every citizen. Therefore, a modicum of government involvement will always be necessary. Most modern societies that we define as capitalist are, in fact, mixed or social market economies, that is, market economies with varying degrees of regulatory oversight and governmental provision of public services, as well as, in many cases, a variety of state-run enterprises. In such economies, the government wields indirect macroeconomic influence through fiscal and monetary policies designed to counteract economic fluctuations and capitalism's tendency toward financial crises and unemployment. The government also plays a prominent role in the promotion of social welfare for the entire population.

Despite the continuing intervention of governments in capitalist economies, capitalism has led to serious problems. First and foremost, its underlying focus on profit has led to social and economic inequality of staggering proportions. The degree of this inequality has been documented again and again, and continues to make headlines on a regular basis, with the figures only becoming more worrisome. For example, according to the *2017 Global Wealth Report* compiled by Credit Suisse, the richest 1 per cent of the world's population own more than 50 per cent of global wealth, while the bottom half of the global population own less than 1 per cent of that wealth. A 2014 report by Oxfam suggested a more extreme level of inequality: the 85 richest individuals in the world, taken together, own as much wealth as the poorer half (3.6 billion people at the time) of the global population.[88] A more recent investigation by Oxfam, published in January 2017, indicates that the situation may be even more dire than previously thought: just *eight* individuals account for as much wealth as the poorest half of the world's population.[89]

The inequality figures published by Oxfam are notoriously sensationalist, often released to coincide with the World Economic Forum's annual summit of global business leaders in Davos. A more scrupulous inequality metric frequently invoked by economists is the Gini coefficient, a statistical measure of income distribution in a country that can range from a value of 0 (perfect equality, that is, all adult citizens enjoy the same income) to 1 (complete inequality, where, theoretically, only one individual earns all the income, while all others earn nothing). Recent studies have shown that the Gini coefficients of most countries have been on the rise (that is, inequality has worsened). A 2011 report by the Organisation for Economic Co-operation and Development (OECD)[90] found that the Gini coefficient had increased significantly in most of its member countries during the previous thirty years. Worryingly, the increase was evident in northern European countries normally known for their stable democracies, generous welfare regimes, and traditionally low levels of inequality.

Another report, published in 2013 by the EU-funded GINI Project,[91] also revealed a consistent upward trend in the Gini coefficients of the EU and OECD countries over three decades. (A few OECD countries, such as Mexico and Turkey, as well as several Latin American nations, have lowered their Gini scores considerably since 2000, but usually this has been an improvement from previously very high values.)[92] Overall, the evidence of a widening gap between rich and poor is quite compelling.[93]

It is naive to think that the super-rich individuals identified by the Oxfam reports – whether there are 8 or 85 or 85 million of them – are evil. Many private fortunes may have originated with forceful appropriation of land or other natural resources, and unfair acquisition of rights and licences that led to monopolies. But an equal number of modern fortunes were built on innovation, entrepreneurship, and hard work. The individuals, families, and groups who managed to accumulate such extraordinary fortunes were simply fulfilling the mandate of capitalism by responding to demand – offering products and services to fulfil that demand, competing in the market, accumulating profits, and using those profits to acquire more resources that could then be used as a means of more production. Capitalism leads, almost by definition, to inequality.

Another consequence of capitalism, in the First Dimension, is unbridled consumption. The accumulation of profits that defines success in capitalism requires a constant, and always increasing, production and purchase of goods and services. On the supply side, firms must continue to produce and sell better products, and more of them, to reward their investors, especially through higher equity valuations fuelled by growth forecasts. On the demand side, consumers must always work harder to earn more income with which to purchase more of the products and services that they desire. This incessant urge to consume has led to a massive and unsustainable depletion of natural resources, from petroleum and forests to fresh water. It has also brought about undesirable externalities in such proportions that they can no longer be ignored – everything from accumulation of refuse and defilement of waterways to climate-changing air pollution. Above all, capitalism's continuous consumption has greatly impoverished humanity by defining the economic actor as a consumer with unlimited desire, whose excesses of greed are, perversely, good for the economy. Capitalism, in short, has turned us into the sum of what we consume. We are what we consume, and our consumption affects every aspect of our society and our environment.

The fundamental shortcoming of capitalism is that, in its purest form, it can only address the needs and desires of individuals. In other words, it caters only to the demand of the individual consumer. If enough individuals desire something – whether this is a direct, naturally occurring need (for food and shelter, for example) or a more indirect, contrived desire (for chewing gum, telecommunication devices, or weight loss therapies) – capitalism will deploy science to investigate it, technology to engineer a product that will satisfy it, private capital to fund it, wage labour to produce it, and the market economy to price and distribute it to the right customer.

Steeped in the notion of individual liberty, and functioning in an environment where only demand and supply can determine what is produced and sold, in what quantity, and at what price, the capitalist economy is able to value only benefits (arising from the use of either goods or services) that can be easily priced because their ownership, before and after sale, can be established. Capitalism has difficulty in pricing goods that do not belong to individuals or companies, and that often yield intangible benefits, such as street lighting, health, biodiversity, knowledge, fresh air, and peaceful coexistence.

To make this limitation clearer, it is useful to repeat here a diagram (Table 14.1) often invoked by economists to distinguish between four fundamental types of goods. Private goods, in the top left-hand corner, are the easiest to price, and therefore the only ones that are traded efficiently in capitalist economies. They include all goods and services that are intended to satisfy individual demand, such as an apple, a pair of trousers, an iPhone, a car, and an airplane ticket. In academic parlance, they are 'excludable' (only those who paid have access) and 'rivalrous' (one

Table 14.1: Four Fundamental Types of Goods

	Excludable	**Non-excludable**
Rivalrous	PRIVATE (e.g., iPhone)	COMMON (e.g., public parks)
Non-rivalrous	CLUB (e.g., satellite TV)	PUBLIC (e.g., sunshine)

person's use or enjoyment of that good precludes anyone else's consumption of it).

Club goods, in the bottom left-hand cell, are also excludable, but they are non-rivalrous. A common example of a club good is satellite television – some consumers can be excluded from the service (if they do not pay), but those who pay and watch have no effect on each other (how much television they watch has no effect on someone else's enjoyment of the same benefit).

The goods of special interest to our discussion are in the right-hand column. Common goods and public goods, though often confused, are not the same. Both are non-excludable because they are accessible, without payment, to all citizens: there is no way to preclude anyone from enjoying sunshine (a public good), and there usually is also no way to discriminate over who can access a public park (a common good). But common goods are rivalrous (competitive), whereas public goods are not. My enjoyment of sunshine has no effect on anyone else because I cannot deplete the sunshine, or change its quality, or carve out a piece for myself. The city park, however, is different. If thousands of people enter the park at the same time, my enjoyment is diminished. I may not find a bench to sit on, or an empty lawn to eat my picnic lunch; I may be struck by an errant Frisbee, or I may trip over someone's poodle. In short, my benefit is reduced by the presence (the consumption) of other users, to the point that I may opt to leave.

Public and common goods are an indispensable component of human welfare. But the absence of well-defined property rights in these categories makes it difficult for a capitalist economy to deliver them fairly and efficiently. As these goods are not owned privately, it is difficult for us to express demand for them in a manner that the capitalist economy can understand. As a community, for example, we might desire to live in a city that is less congested by traffic and clogged by pollution and car exhaust; we want efficient, cheap public transport, bike lanes, pedestrian areas, and elevated walkways to cross roads. But as individuals, we also want the benefit of going from point A to point B in the most comfortable, exclusive, and effortless way, which is by private car. Clearly, it is much easier for an economic system to satisfy the latter demand (build a car and sell it to me) than to mobilise the vast resources and consensus required for the former. In most countries, therefore, most common goods, and some public goods, are made available by governments, local as well as national, with varying degrees of inefficiency.

The fact that common and public goods lie outside the purview of capitalism often leads to gross inequality, unsustainable consumption, and negative externalities.[94] Nowhere is this more evident than in the consumption of natural resources and pollution of the environment. Natural resources like coal, timber, fresh water, natural gas, metals, and minerals do not really belong to anyone. They are nature's gift to us, and as such they ought to be considered common goods. But their 'commonness' typically means that the right to extract them is assigned by a central government to private companies, in an often opaque and corrupt system of bidding. The bulk of the proceeds from extraction activities like mining, logging, and pumping are shared between the private company and the central government. Local communities in whose vicinity the extraction happens rarely benefit from these resources, yet they often bear the pollution and environmental degradation that the commercial activity brings. This is a case of massive inequality, but also and especially an example of how negative by-products are not factored into the financial calculus of resource exploitation. Mining, petroleum, and logging companies deplete natural resources and create harmful by-products, but often are not required to dispose of them properly, or to rehabilitate the land. If the rights of local communities were asserted, and the true cost of these activities deducted from profits, the viability of such endeavours would be called into question.

A more transparent example is traffic congestion and transport-related emissions in large cities. The excessive number of cars on the road degrades a public good (the air), and several common goods, such as urban beauty, greenness, pedestrian access, and road infrastructure. Because common goods do not enter a capitalist computation, however, this collateral damage is not included in the price of a new car. Some local governments (such as London) have tried to intervene with automated road pricing to discourage driving in congested areas, especially at peak times, but this type of taxation tends to reduce car use, not car ownership. Singapore has perhaps gone the farthest in this regard. In addition to its well-known Electronic Road Pricing scheme, it also imposes a hefty one-time fee on the right to register a vehicle within its national boundaries, with the result that car ownership is relatively low, and traffic cannot exceed the capacity of the road infrastructure. While we might be tempted to think of this as an arbitrary form of taxation, it is representative of correct pricing of a private good to reflect its impact on community and natural resources.

A Better Capitalism in the Second Dimension

The Spectrum of Demand (Figure 14.1) shows all the types of demand that may manifest themselves in a market economy. There are individual forms of demand on the left, but also other, non-individual forms on the right.

As the diagram shows, capitalism functions relatively well in the 'utility' and 'desire' portions of the Spectrum because these types of demand express themselves naturally as extensions of human impulses. Our first, innate priority as human beings is to secure comfort and pleasure for ourselves, and this results directly in a consumer's wish to acquire products and services that are either utilitarian (everything from laundry detergent to cutlery to a tablet computer) or gratifying (an airplane ticket to go on vacation, a designer handbag, or a bottle of

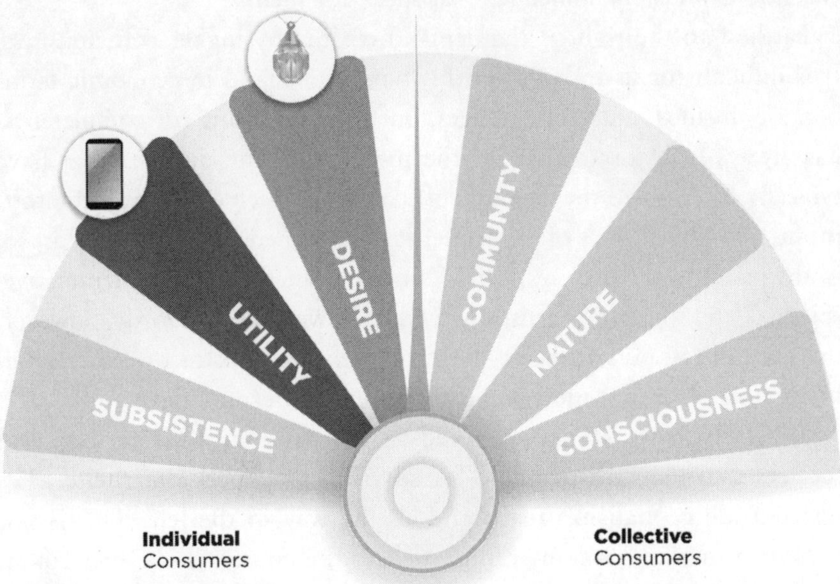

Figure 14.1: Capitalism and the First Dimension's Spectrum of Demand

wine). In these parts of the Spectrum of Demand, capitalism works well by responding to individual, impulse-driven demand arising out of need or desire.

Capitalism, however, starts to fail in the other segments of the Spectrum, both on the right (community, nature, consciousness) and on the left (subsistence). In its current form, capitalism cannot respond to the latent demands of communities and nature. The demands of communities and nature can be equated broadly with the demand for common and public goods. After all, nature itself, in all its bounty, variety, and beauty, is the ultimate public good. The benefits derived from it should always be both non-excludable and non-rivalrous. But nature cannot speak for itself. Communities can, but as they become more populous and complex, they struggle to express their communal needs clearly and unanimously, especially when these needs seem to conflict with those of individuals or of other communities. For these portions of the Spectrum to come alive and find expression, someone must speak for them.

Farthest to the right is the demand created by higher consciousness. It is difficult for us to envision this type of demand in economic terms because, in most cultures and ages, our inner yearning for completeness has always been juxtaposed to the more mundane pursuits that have typically determined the structure of economies, such as survival, comfort, profit, and power. It is often diametrically opposed to material needs, so, in the past and the present, it has found utterance only in contemplative, spiritual, and sometimes artistic activities. As we shall see shortly, however, this categorisation is artificial. Even this seemingly abstract need can find its rightful place in a more sophisticated market economy.

Similarly, subsistence, defined as demand for those goods and services that are indispensable for survival, like food and shelter, lies just outside capitalism's reach and all the way to the left. This is not because a market economy cannot deliver these essentials to consumers, but because capitalism typically does a terrible job of addressing the needs of the poor, for whom these goods are especially important. The poor, by definition, lack money, which is the signalling mechanism in the capitalist system and forms the basis for the allocation of goods and services. Because the poor do not have money they cannot signal their needs and thus lie on the 'unattended' left side of the Spectrum of Demand. Products and services vital to the poor, like low-income housing and affordable healthcare, exist in capitalist economies only if they are provided for free, or heavily subsidised, by governments or charitable organisations.

The Peruvian economist Hernando de Soto, in *The Mystery of Capital*, captures the conundrum well when talking about poverty in developing nations:

> Most of the poor already possess the assets they need to make a success of capitalism [...] but they hold these resources in defective forms [...] houses built on land whose ownership rights are not adequately recorded,

> unincorporated businesses with undefined liability, industries located where financiers and investors cannot see them. Because the rights to these possessions are not adequately documented, these assets cannot readily be turned into capital, cannot be traded outside of narrow circles where people know and trust each other, cannot be used as collateral for a loan, and cannot be used as a share against an investment [...] The poor inhabitants of these nations do have things, but they lack the process to represent their property and create capital. They have houses but not titles; crops but not deeds; businesses but not statutes of incorporation. It is the unavailability of these essential representations that explains why people who have adapted every other Western invention, from the paper clip to the nuclear reactor, have not been able to produce sufficient capital to make their domestic capitalism work.

Creating a better economy, consonant with Second Dimension thinking, does not require the dismantling of the entire capitalist construct. It is not necessary to invent a new economic system, like communism, to address the ills of capitalism. Thus far capitalism has failed to address the demand of some segments of the Spectrum, but this does not mean that a market economy cannot succeed. I am advocating *more* free-market initiatives, not less. We must render the free-market economy more inclusive and diverse, and less reliant on ownership; we must bring all facets of economic life into the free market; we must expand the market economy so that it can encompass those parts of the Spectrum that are currently left out, as shown in the modified Spectrum diagram (Figure 14.2).

How do we put this abstract notion into practice? It entails various legislative, fiscal, and commercial initiatives, and a radical rethinking of several key economic concepts that we usually assume to be immovable. Here is a summary of how we can bring the entire Spectrum of Demand to life:

- Simple, efficient legislation to create various market-like mechanisms that allow for the pricing and trade of intangible goods to satisfy unspoken demand on both sides of the Spectrum (details later in this chapter).

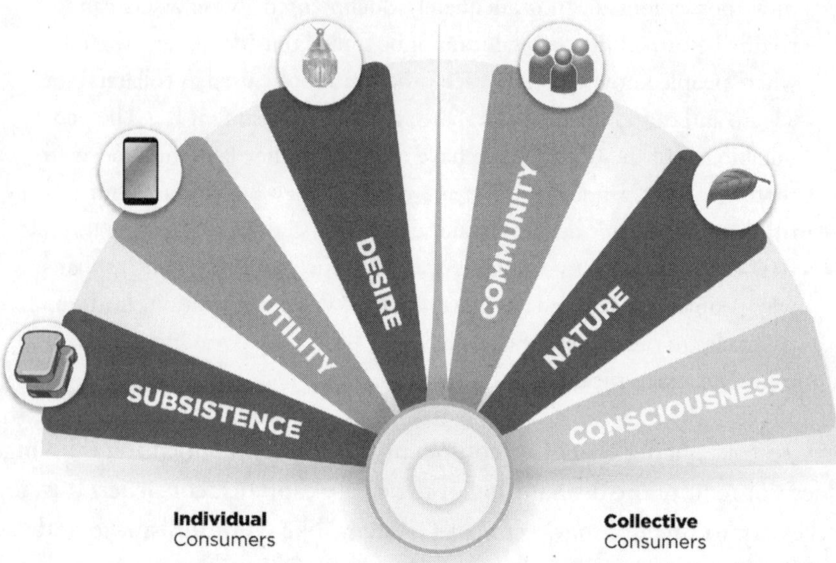

Figure 14.2: Capitalism and the Second Dimension's Spectrum of Demand

- A new way to measure economic activity, by moving away from Gross Domestic Product (GDP) as the fundamental measure of economic progress and adopting instead the concept of a Gross National Reserve (GNR), to ensure that economies operate not only to satisfy individual demand, but also to address the sustainability of the natural environment (details in Chapter 15).
- A new model for ownership of organisations (companies, partnerships, trusts, government agencies, and so forth), whereby all organisations are evaluated according to the utility they bring to society, and taxed or incentivised accordingly. This will ensure that the interests of communities and society as a whole are put ahead of individual needs and desires (details in Chapter 16).

- New financial tools (meta-currencies) in addition to cash. The use of a separate, dedicated currency for each segment of the Spectrum will guarantee that the pursuit of individual needs and wants (which will continue to be transacted in cash) will not interfere with, or be detrimental to, the demand from other segments of the Spectrum (details in Chapter 17).
- A system for the global regulation of the supply and exchange of these new meta-currencies, such that they can be distributed fairly among consumers in all nations and used everywhere (details in Chapter 18).

A More Inclusive Market Economy

In this chapter I will focus on how to tweak the market economy to encourage it to function more efficiently and sustainably in the under-represented segments of the Spectrum. The goal here is to *create* individuated demand for those goods and services that are currently not being produced by the capitalist economy, such as common goods, social goods, and goods needed by the poor. Creation of demand can be accomplished by passing simple, effective legislation that will engender, wherever possible, market-like mechanisms that allow for the pricing and trade of intangible goods. Rather than establish moral imperatives and enforce them by fiat, it is more practical to set up market-like exchanges and corresponding currencies.

Exchanges and currencies are purely notional concepts – artificial constructs that allow societies to carry out certain trading functions efficiently and transparently. Demand for an intangible commodity, as well as the exchanges and currencies needed to trade it, can be created and extinguished at will, by either consensus or legislation. This realisation was brought home to me quite clearly in the early years of my work at Fabindia. When I began to focus on Fabindia's operations in the early 1990s, I had to learn all the intricacies of the quota system imposed by governments on garment exports. Those were the days of the Multi Fibre Arrangement (MFA), a complex international agreement that governed the world trade in textiles and garments from 1974 until 2004. Under the MFA, the United States and the EU imposed quotas on the volume of garments that developing countries like India could export to them, to protect their own domestic textile industries from the considerably lower labour costs that countries like India, China, and Bangladesh enjoyed.

The Indian quota was administered by the Government of India, who set up a complex system of bidding and trading to apportion shares of the quota to Indian companies producing yarn and garments. The system was outrageously complex, plagued by manipulation, and opaque. Companies could obtain a share of the quota on account of their past performance, but there were also shares of the quota dedicated to new entrants in the market, to the production of high-value items, and to small- and medium-sized enterprises. There was also a portion of the quota that was doled out on a first come, first served basis. And it was also possible to transfer some of the quota shares from one producer or distributor to another, giving rise to a veritable market in which shares were traded freely. The system spawned an extensive service economy of quota experts, quota brokers, and accountants specialising in ways to game the system (apart from shady fixers and many others).

This is an example of how trading mechanisms can be created out of nothing, to trade in assets that are entirely intangible. Here, one piece of international legislation (the MFA) created a new market (the quota system) and a corresponding currency (quota shares) to trade in it. But when the MFA came to an end on 1 January 2005, the quota system vanished overnight.

Today, discussion of alternative or virtual currencies is dominated by the newest arrivals – cryptocurrencies. A cryptocurrency is a digital medium of exchange that is decentralised, that is, it does not rely on a central authority (such as a government-controlled reserve bank) to guarantee its validity and to regulate the quantity of currency in circulation. Instead, cryptocurrencies are validated using blockchain technology, a continuously growing list of digital records, called blocks, which are secured using cryptography and are linked through a peer-to-peer computing network collectively adhering to a protocol for confirming new entries. The blockchain acts as a common ledger distributed (replicated) over many computing systems, such that transaction data, once recorded, is extremely difficult to alter.

Only a few merchants and institutions accept cryptocurrencies as a mode of payment for goods and services. Therefore, cryptocurrencies like bitcoin and Ethereum are exchanged primarily as derivative assets with the expectation that they will grow in value over time. They are viewed by many analysts as financial assets rather than genuine currencies. (Because most cryptocurrencies impose a finite limit on the quantity of their coins in circulation, they have been likened to commodities like precious metals.) The relative novelty of cryptocurrencies has also meant that their value is subject to high volatility, and that many financial regulators are as yet uncertain how to treat them. Several countries, such as China, have restricted the issuance and use of cryptocurrencies.

Another recent and pertinent example of an artificially created exchange economy is the Clean Development Mechanism (CDM) stipulated under the Kyoto Protocol. It generated demand for an intangible benefit (reduction in carbon emissions) by creating exchanges to trade this good (primarily the European Union's Emission Trading System, or EU ETS), and a currency with which to transact the exchange (Certified Emission Reductions, or CERs, also known as 'carbon credits'). As in the MFA example, here a legislated commitment gave rise to demand for a new commodity, which, in turn, created the necessary tools to enable investors to trade. (The most important of these tools is a specialised currency used exclusively in one type of exchange. I will discuss currency in greater detail in Chapter 16.)

The market for CERs is also a good example of how externalities like carbon emissions, waste water, solid waste, and industrial and agricultural by-products, can be traded on a national or international scale. Such measures enable consumers and producers to price the externality, and thus to include it in cost-benefit analyses, macroeconomic calculations, and feasibility studies. Intangible benefits arising from natural resources can also be handled similarly. In *Making India Work*, I suggested the creation of an Environmental Per Capita Quota (EPCQ) by which every community would be required to maintain a certain surface area of natural environment (forest, wetland, prairie, and so forth) per inhabitant. The system would operate at the community level. Every citizen would be registered for the EPCQ at birth. Every Community would be obliged to have sufficient EPCQ credits for all its members. Communities with surplus forestry or biodiversity credits would sell them to those that lack them. A dedicated standards authority would determine the price per unit and maintain a ratings system. For example, a rural Community that includes forested land or a rich local biosphere would have sufficient per capita credits for its members and would be able to sell surplus units. An urban Community, on the other hand, might not have any EPCQ credits and so would have to buy these from others that do.

As the price for forest cover increases due to deforestation, communities would recognise this as a business opportunity, with substantial profits to be made. This would inevitably result in communities and businesses making investments by upgrading and extending their forest cover or natural zones so that they qualify as biospheres. Such a system would incentivise reforestation and biodiversity conservation, both in urban and rural areas. It would also change the balance of wealth, with rural communities able to profit from their abundant natural resources without depleting them. Today, because communities rarely benefit from protected biospheres, protecting the environment is often at odds with supporting the local economy.

Again, a simple legislative prompt would create the exchange mechanism and the currency with which to price and trade units of ecological common goods. The trading mechanism can be refined to account for varying quality of the ecological commodity. Thus, for example, one acre of virgin, old-growth forest might be enough to fulfil one EPCQ, whereas 1.5 acres of secondary or partially degraded forest might be required to do the same. Similar trading constructs could be devised for other ecological resources, like fresh water, biodiversity, fish, and wildlife.

As I have argued thus far, it is possible, with a bit of political will and ingenuity, to implement mechanisms that would allow us to bring both externalities and ecological resources – goods that were previously peripheral, at best – into the fold of the market economy, so that they can be accounted for fairly. This might help to correct some of capitalism's imbalances. But what about social goods? These, surely, would be much more difficult to include in any kind of free-market mechanism, because they are almost always intangible, not to mention contentious.

Here are a few socially desirable goods that are rarely delivered by capitalism:

- thought-provoking art film;
- kinetic sculpture;
- high-quality investigative journalism;
- sensibly planned low-income housing; and
- immunisation against deadly Third World diseases like Ebola.

Why does the capitalist economy typically fail to deliver these goods? Because there isn't sufficient demand for them, one might reply. But, demand for some of them can be quite significant. Every person in Africa would want vaccination against Ebola, and every poor person in the United States would love to have access to low-income housing. But demand is not the same as desire or need. It is merely a concept invented by economists to answer the following question: 'How many units of this product would you buy at this price?' Unless the price covers, at least, the average cost of producing those units, the product is not manufactured at all, irrespective of whether some people want it. That is the case with the items on our list. The only reason these products exist at all is that someone is subsidising them – either a local or national government, an international agency, a non-governmental organisation, a philanthropic organisation, or individuals.

So, another way of answering 'Why does capitalism fail to deliver these goods?' is to say that there is not enough *individuated* demand. Those who desire these goods are unable to express their demand individually because they do not have enough money to support the production of these goods. And money is the only viable signalling mechanism in the capitalist construct. The very notion of demand, in capitalism, is predicated on the availability of cash to express it. If you do not own capital, you cannot express your needs in a way that the capitalist economy can understand and react to.

What if we enacted simple legislation to mandate a certain supply for these goods? Imagine that every cinema, to maintain its licence, had to devote 20 per cent of its prime-time screen time to films by independent production companies. Or, what if a magazine was compelled to devote a certain number of pages in each issue to thoughtful, high-quality articles? Or, if Big Pharma companies had to earmark a part of their research and development budget for contagious diseases that affect primarily developing countries? Or, if cities were required to commission a number of new low-income housing units corresponding to the number of high-income units built by private developers within their city limits? (Such regulations already exist, in limited forms, in some advanced countries.)

In the case of journalism, magazines and think tanks would begin to specialise in intelligent investigative journalism, creating a surplus of articles that could be traded, with or without exclusivity, to other, more mass-market print media, in exchange for advertising income. In the housing development example, sensible, thoughtful legislation could also bring about the desired outcome without physical intervention by government. I am reminded of the urban development history of Cornwall, an affluent rural community in Connecticut. Gifted with natural beauty, a progressive and enlightened populace, and convenient location (driving distance from New York City), Cornwall real estate was the natural target for many wealthy New Yorkers seeking to build second homes or holiday homes. Real estate prices rose continuously, and low-income inhabitants were priced out or prevented from moving there. The community addressed this imbalance by changing the zoning rules for certain tracts of land: they divided large plots (one, three, and five acres) into much smaller plots. Wealthy buyers were not interested in such small units, so demand for them was lowered. This, in conjunction with a state-sponsored programme to extend low-interest, low-down-payment home loans, ensured that lower-income inhabitants could acquire homes in an otherwise affluent place like Cornwall. The top-down intervention was minimal (changing a zoning regulation) and the market economy took over to generate the required result.

Market dynamics can be brought into play to fund many types of common goods. Another good example is a metropolitan rail transport system like Delhi's metro. The metro is the source of much pride in India, and rightly so. Still under development, it carries well over two million passengers every day. It has been operating profitably, for the most part, since it opened in 2002, with no government subsidies to its operational income. Early phases of construction were delivered within budget and ahead of schedule, thanks in no small part to the exemplary leadership of its managing director, E. Sreedharan. Owned jointly by the governments of India and Delhi, the metro was funded through equity from these partners, and soft loans from the Japan International Cooperation Agency (JICA). Its operational revenue comes primarily from passenger fares and property development (rental of retail space in the stations and of advertising space in stations and trains). Other sources of revenue include consultancy on metro development projects in other Indian cities, rental of trains and stations for film shoots, and, at one time, even carbon credits.

While impressive, the metro has not gone far enough in recognising the extent of its influence on city life. A common good like an efficient urban rail system contributes in many other ways to the welfare of the city – ways that the metro's current revenue model fails to capture and monetise. For example, urban public transport systems are known to have a significant effect on the value of real estate along their routes. Both commercial and residential property rises significantly in value near mass transit lines. Simple zoning legislation to raise the maximum allowable floor space index[95] for property within one kilometre of every station would have increased the value of such property, making it more viable for commercial development. A small percentage of this increase in value could have been chargeable by the metro, leading to significant revenues every time a property within one kilometre of a metro station is sold or developed. From another angle, it is also undeniable that the development of a mass transit system reduces traffic in the city – another benefit that is not captured in the economic valuation of this common good. This could be done easily by imposing a metro fee on each car registration within the city, or by levying an additional tax on petrol sold within the city. These ideas, among others, were discussed and considered in the planning of the Delhi metro, but ultimately not adopted.

Thus, simple, thoughtful legislation can effectively bring market dynamics to bear on the deployment of common goods, such that the benefits derived from such goods can be priced and traded. The simple legislation to jump-start these initiatives comes from outside the market. It is imposed, mandated, or coerced. The market-like mechanisms I have spoken of may replace the more old-fashioned interventions of government (taxes, price controls, and subsidies), but do they not ultimately amount to the same? Yes, for the most part, except that, crucially, they use some of the same mechanisms as the market economy to deliver the desired results, absolving government from the considerable burden of executing them. In other words, they require smaller government, not bigger government.

The purpose of EPCQs and other per capita apportionments (see Chapter 17) will be to enlarge the field of operation of the market economy. Once legislated and linked to rights and freedoms, they will hugely reduce the economic role of governmental administration, which often leads to static, unresponsive mechanisms. My objective here is to move government out of all aspects of the Spectrum of Demand both on the left and right sides by expanding and creating alternative ways to value, trade, and allocate environmental and public goods, and share externalities transparently and fairly.

In the end, the legislation needed to create such a shift derives from moral judgment. A government decides that certain goods, though not expressed through individual demand, are desirable for the welfare, edification, and happiness of its citizens, and orchestrates for them to be delivered through a market-mimicking process. There will always be a moral imperative to supersede the amoral functioning of a free market. What is important, however, is the very definition of that morality. When I say 'moral' here, I do not refer to the morality of old, based on ethical or religious notions of good and evil, but rather a new, Second Dimension morality based on the recognition of interdependence. Simply put, each individual's right to trade a private good must not interfere with another's right to enjoy a public good or derive benefit from a common good.

Higher Consciousness and the Marketplace

There is still one class of demand that is not addressed in the Second Dimension: the demand created by elevated consciousness. Here we are treading on esoteric terrain. Why am I treating consciousness – an abstract concept – as a stakeholder in the marketplace, as shown in Figure 14.3? What are the economic repercussions of heightened consciousness? What

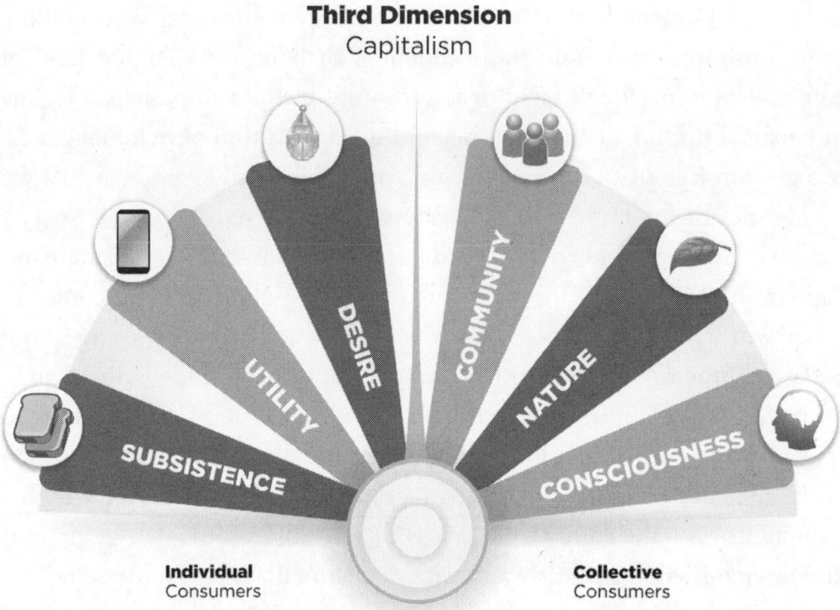

Figure 14.3: The Third Dimension's Spectrum of Demand

would a capitalist economy look like if the majority of its actors – individuals as well as enterprises – behaved in a manner that is not predicated on the maximisation of utility or on the prevalence of self-interest?

Perhaps the best way to approach these questions is to imagine a society that has achieved most or all goals of the Second Dimension. With regard to the market economy, this society has overcome the First Dimension's narrow focus on fulfilling individual needs and wants. By tweaking market dynamics, it has addressed the needs of the poor, of communities, and of nature. As a result, the society enjoys a high degree of peacefulness, equanimity, clean and sustainable natural environments, and an everyday existence filled with rich cultural and social interactions.

You will say that this is a highly idealistic scenario. Nevertheless, let us assume, for the sake of discussion, that such a transition has occurred, partially if not completely. When the needs represented by the first five segments of the Spectrum have been adequately and sustainably met, what is left? Ultimately, every individual, when his needs – First as well as Second Dimensional – have been satisfied, will aspire to something more profound and more transcendental. Striving for a higher level of consciousness may be thought of as a spiritual exercise, or perhaps a feeling of personal fulfilment that goes beyond the acquisition of material goods, recognition by our peers, and the enjoyment of family.

The desire for higher consciousness will arise naturally in a society that has addressed all other needs. There is no market mechanism, legislation, or financial incentive that can bring about this outcome. In other words, initiatives that may have been introduced to bring about Second Dimension capitalism no longer apply here. This is in keeping with the overall argument of this book: ideas, systems, and initiatives spawned by lower-dimensional thinking eventually reach the limit of their usefulness and must be superseded by new ones. The desire for a higher consciousness – the ability to see the reality around us, in all its gradations and interconnections, clearly and with detachment, and to understand our place in it – will arise naturally in higher dimensions, just as the demand for food and shelter arose naturally in the First Dimension. Citizens will demand consciousness because they will understand that it is the only avenue to a life of contentment, and the only solution to create societies that are peaceful and compassionate.

In economic terms, the Third Dimension will see a shift from the policy inputs that were needed in the Second Dimension. Many of my policy recommendations for the Second Dimension market economy entail, fundamentally, interventions by various tiers of government. Most of the policy elements suggested – such as the introduction of EPCQs or of certain quality or affordability requirements on private enterprises – rely as much as possible on market-like mechanisms and economic incentives to elicit outcomes that are beneficial to all stakeholders (including communities, nature, and the poor). But they are, nevertheless, top-down impositions on private enterprise and private citizens. While such interventions may be necessary to jump-start the shift to a more efficient and inclusive capitalist economy in the Second Dimension, they will no longer be necessary in the Third.

In the Third Dimension, economic exchange will be guided primarily by love and respect of our neighbours. As you may recall from our discussion of emotional bonds in Chapter 4, the Third Dimension will be characterised by the development and continual application of the qualities of devotion, forgiveness, and compassion. These qualities are the foreseeable outcomes of a heightened consciousness and will enable us to express a new level of empathy toward our fellow human beings. If such qualities are the very definition of the Third Dimension, then by extension it can be expected that they will also redefine our system of economic exchange.

In particular, much government expenditure aimed at achieving positive public outcomes and at building healthy communities and natural environments – things like infrastructure and public services – will most likely have been taken over by philanthropy. I briefly touched upon the evolution of philanthropy in Chapter 9 in our discussion of social stimuli. There, I suggested that certain cultural values can stimulate positive, altruistic behaviour, of which philanthropy is an example. Now, however, I propose philanthropy (exercised primarily at community level) as the centrepiece of the Third Dimension economy, in which most community facilities and services are funded by private donations rather than government expenditure.

Today's mega-rich individuals have already shown us the way. The richest individuals on earth, whose personal fortunes amount to billions of dollars, have already begun to disburse their wealth, systematically and consistently. They do not wait for the end of their lives to do so, or for the companies they have founded to be sold or inherited by their progeny. Individuals like Bill Gates and Warren Buffett, having amassed fortunes well beyond anyone's imagination, have dedicated much of the rest of their lives to giving them away. Why should we expect the majority of wealthy people to follow their example in higher dimensions? Simply because the higher level of consciousness which they will have achieved will dictate that they do so. In a social environment that welcomes and fosters philanthropy, most wealthy individuals will recognise, before long, that the only sensible thing to do with a large fortune is to apply it to the betterment of society, especially the immediate social environment we live in.

In the Third Dimension, however, the vertiginous income inequality that afflicts the world today will no longer exist. As we shall see in Chapters 16 and 17, a variety of Second Dimension economic initiatives will have evened the economic playing field, such that the crassest excesses of wealth accumulation will no longer be possible. In other words, there will be no ultra-rich individuals any more. Nevertheless, a degree of income diversity will always exist. Moreover, many more earners will have been pulled out of poverty and will enjoy middle-class incomes large enough to support donations, albeit in more modest amounts.

Imagine, therefore, a Third Dimension society where many community needs are met by philanthropy. Some will donate their time (recall the suggestion, made in Chapter 5, that all adult citizens devote 30 per cent of their time to working for the Community); others, especially businesses, may donate in kind, but most will donate in the simplest way of all, namely, in cash. Most needs requiring capital expenditure will be funded almost entirely by such donations, from the new municipal sporting facility to the upgrade in communications infrastructure to the provision of free career counselling or life coaching at the local community centre. Businesses, especially corporations, will participate in this effort as well. As we shall see in Chapter 16, their primary goal in higher dimensions will no longer be financial profitability, and this will allow businesses to engage in social and environmental betterment on a scale much greater than modern-day corporate social responsibility programmes allow for.

Much of the economic exchange in the Third Dimension will have shifted away from today's purely transactional forms, where goods and services are purchased anonymously, without any obligations or considerations, using an impersonal financial instrument like money. As author Charles Eisenstein has suggested,[96] much of the economy of a society that has reconciled its spiritual and practical needs will have reverted to a gift economy. Many goods, and professional and personal services, will be exchanged freely (that is, without the burden of an accurate valuation or the mediation of currency) by economic agents at community level. They will be gifted to one's neighbours and fellow citizens out of compassion for their needs, or devotion to their well-being, without much expectation of reciprocity. I do not mean merely trading a few hours of babysitting in exchange for an invitation to dinner, but rather a complete gamut of economic activity that proceeds unfettered by regulation and encompasses most everyday needs. From remodelling the kitchen to receiving psychological counselling, from borrowing a holiday home to sharing agricultural crops, from financial advisory to driving lessons, from used cars to new clothing – many of our needs will be met by a continuing exchange of gifts and favours.

Reverting to a gift or barter economy may seem like a quaint but impractical idea. And it may smack of a commonplace escapism by which we tend to assume, wishfully, that primitive societies and their habits were somehow better and more genuine than our own. In fact, the notion of a gift or barter economy is not obsolete – it is rapidly regaining its place in the economic landscape of the present. What makes it modern and more viable than ever is the advent of new technologies that enable it to function in larger, more stratified social settings: the Internet, primarily, as well as location-based services reliant on the global positioning system and sophisticated data analytics. Think, for example, of how innovators like Uber and Airbnb have disrupted and redefined the ground transport and hospitality sectors, respectively. Now, these services are not part of a genuine gift or barter economy because someone (the driver in Uber's case, the homeowner in Airbnb's) is still earning money. But imagine that instead of earning money they were able to earn points or credits, which could be applied only toward their own transport or housing needs in the future – would that not bring them much closer to a genuine barter economy?

Indeed, such platforms already exist. BlaBlaCar, for example, is a ride-sharing platform that connects drivers and passengers willing to travel together between cities in several European countries. The only money that changes hands is a contribution from the rider toward travel costs, and a small commission to the technology operator who enables the exchange. In the hospitality sector, there are already several home exchange services (for example, www.guesttoguest.com) that allow homeowners to swap homes for a period, without paying anything. These sharing services leverage modern technology to achieve what was possible only on a local scale in the gift economies of the past. The Internet allows users to find exact matches to their needs across vast distances, while location-based data allows systems to be optimised so that each user can find the supplier who is available soonest or in the desired location. Most importantly, these sharing platforms have managed to solve the problem of trust, which, in the past, rendered barter almost impossible beyond one's immediate community. They do so by providing reciprocal rating and review mechanisms, guaranteeing payments and security deposits as an interested third party, and mediating disputes. What we now call the sharing economy, therefore, is merely a new, technologically enabled incarnation of an ancient custom of reciprocal gift-giving. And it will play an increasingly important role in the future.

I began this section by wondering why 'consciousness' is shown as a stakeholder in the Spectrum of Demand, but I still do not know the answer in its entirety. I struggle to fathom the future and to see clearly what evolved Third Dimension individuals – who will operate at a much higher level of consciousness than most of us enjoy today – will really want from their everyday lives, what they will hope to achieve, and what they will expect from their economic system. I assume that they will demand more of the goods and services that we associate with an improved state of mind nowadays: meditation and yoga classes, silent retreats, natural recreation areas, organic fruit shakes, art exhibitions, and maybe even interfaith religious services. But I am certain that their heightened consciousness will result in a pressing demand for participation and engagement: participation in the administration of their communities; engagement in shaping the present and especially the future; and a deep involvement in how humanity progresses, both at the microscopic level of community and in the wider field of global affairs. This desire for involvement will frequently be channelled through various forms of philanthropy. In other words, a Third Dimension individual will demand to participate directly in giving direction to society, and he will actualise this civic engagement with philanthropy.

15

Economics: Measuring What Makes Life Worthwhile

The Role of Gross Domestic Product

Economics is the study of the processes governing the production, distribution, and consumption of goods and services. It analyses the material well-being of human societies, and its primary avenue of inquiry is how human beings use limited resources to satisfy needs and desires. Therefore, we can say that economics is fundamentally a study of human behaviour – how individuals, families, companies, associations, and governments deploy resources to maximise the well-being of their stakeholders.

The demise of socialism toward the end of the 20th century has meant that, today, most national economies adhere, to varying degrees, to free-market versions of economic exchange. Thus, economics has become, increasingly, the study of free-market models of production, consumption, and wealth distribution. As discussed in the previous chapter, this implies an overall acceptance that human beings are guided in their economic choices by individual goals and ambitions, and, indeed, by greed for material possessions. Ever since Adam Smith's analysis, we have come to recognise, at least on some level, the notion that individual consumption, whether to satisfy need or greed, leads to the production of goods and services, in adequate quantity and variety, to satisfy all demand. This impetus creates not only the products and services themselves, but also employment, public goods like infrastructure, and the accumulation of wealth, which, in turn, spurs further economic activity.

Economists attempt to quantify economic activity using a variety of metrics and indicators, but the most widely used tool in their arsenal is GDP and its spin-offs, including GDP growth and GDP per capita. In formal terms, GDP is the value of all the finished goods and services produced within a country's borders in a specific period. Notice the word 'finished'. This means that GDP is a measure of value added rather than just sales: it counts the value added by each firm in the process of manufacturing a product or delivering a service. In other words, GDP is an accretive measure. It posits that, once upon a time, there was such a thing as zero GDP, and over time, economic activity has continually added to its value.

GDP can be computed in several different ways. The most intuitive method is to add up the gross value (the market price) of all products and services produced in a country, and subtract the value of intermediate consumption (the cost of raw materials or parts used to create those products and services).[97] The most common model, however, is the expenditure approach, whereby three types of consumption are summed, namely, consumption by individuals, consumption by firms (investment), and consumption by governments (government expenditure).[98] As long as these parties continue to consume, GDP continues to grow. The more we spend, irrespective of the utility of our spending, or the collateral consequences of our spending, the better off we are, at least according to GDP.

Therefore, GDP is not a measure of welfare, just as its early proponent, economist Simon Kuznets, had warned. It measures economic activity in isolation, without measuring its effect on other spheres of life. This is easy enough to demonstrate with a few banal examples. Let us say, for argument's sake, that all our kidneys suddenly stopped working due to an epidemic of renal disease. We would then need millions of new dialysis machines, so the manufacture of such machines would have to be ramped up immediately. When coupled with dialysis performed at hospitals three times a week for a large portion of the population, the GDP would skyrocket. (Note that the value of properly functioning kidneys, and of correspondingly healthy people, does not enter into the calculation in any way.) But, surely, we cannot argue that a country afflicted by renal disease on a massive scale is now better off as a result of an enhanced GDP.

Let us take a simpler, more realistic example in which individual choice plays a role. You step out of your home one day and must decide how to get to work. You do not own a car, so your options are to walk, take public transport, or hire a taxi. Let us also assume that there are no extraneous factors affecting your choice, such as disability, the weather, or the need to keep an urgent appointment. If you walk, you add nothing to GDP. If you pay for a bus ticket, you consume a service, so you add a little to GDP; if you pay for a taxi ride, you add more. In an absurd extension of this thought experiment, you could hire a luxury stretch limousine, and *really* contribute to GDP. Unquestionably, however, the best option in non-GDP terms would be to walk: it is better for your health, and it reduces traffic congestion and pollution. Indeed, you would be contributing to the preservation of several common and public goods, like road infrastructure and clean air. Thus, in this case, the GDP approach to economic measurement assigns the highest value to the choice (hiring a taxi) that is the least beneficial to society as a whole.[99]

GDP may be a useful measure of economic activity, but clearly it is a terrible measure of the health of an economy, the welfare of a society, or, indeed, the happiness of its citizens – those very individuals whose consumption fuels GDP. In 1968, US presidential candidate Robert Kennedy eloquently remarked that GDP, while including cigarette advertising and new jails and the logging of redwoods, failed to celebrate the health of the nation's children, the quality of education, the beauty of poetry, or the integrity of public officials. He famously concluded that GDP 'measures everything [...] except that which makes life worthwhile'.

Dissatisfaction with GDP as a measure of well-being has spawned various attempts at constructing different, more intelligent and comprehensive estimates of well-being, personal as well as economic.[100] One of them is the concept of Gross National Happiness (GNH), introduced by the king of the tiny Himalayan kingdom of Bhutan, Jigme Singye Wangchuck, in 1972. The king applied the four pillars of the GNH (equitable economic development, environmental preservation, cultural resilience, and good governance) in the implementation of various policies and programmes. The GNH came to global attention in 1986 when the king announced, in an interview, that 'Gross National Happiness is more important than Gross National Product.' Since then, the Centre for Bhutan Studies (CBS), based in Thimphu, has formalised the concept of GNH by developing the GNH Index, a measurement compiled by analysing and aggregating the results of a questionnaire administered to a representative sampling of citizens. The latest GNH questionnaire, which was used in the 2015 GNH survey of over 7,000 citizens, consisted of 148 questions that measured 33 indicators in 9 domains (psychological well-being, community, culture, governance, knowledge, health, living conditions, time use, and harmony with the environment). A 2009 report, *Gross National Happiness in Bhutan: A Living Example of an Alternative Approach to Progress,* by the University of Pennsylvania's Wharton School, ended thus:

> All these global movements that seek to promote more sustainable, equitable, and prosperous societies are reasons for optimism in the collective effort to improve measures of progress. Societies around the world should observe and learn from these movements, especially from GNH in Bhutan, in order to ask the right questions, develop the right indicators, and construct institutions and policies that foster genuine well-being and progress in society.

Another effort to quantify national well-being is the United Nations Development Programme's Human Development Index (HDI), developed by economist Mahbub ul-Haq in the 1990s. Although useful and widely cited, the HDI is as reductionist as the GNH is expansive, because it takes into consideration only three measures: life expectancy, education, and income per capita. Recently, the New Economics Foundation

(NEF), the United Kingdom's leading think tank on social, economic, and environmental justice, already known for the development of the Happy Planet Index (HPI), introduced the concept of National Accounts of Well-being. This is a proposal to directly measure people's subjective well-being, including experiences, feelings, and perceptions of how their lives are going. It calls for these measures to be collected on a regular, systematic basis via surveys, and published in reports.[101] Like the GNH, the NEF's National Accounts of Well-being, though comprehensive and thoughtful, is difficult to compute, and even more difficult and costly to compile on a regular basis.

A New Indicator: Gross National Reserve

A Second Dimension approach to economics must consider many more factors, processes, and assets than what GDP can identify. In the previous chapter I suggested that the primary model of economic organisation – capitalism – should not be abandoned merely because it has outlived its usefulness, but rather that it must be expanded so that it can encompass portions of the Spectrum of Demand hitherto ignored. My proposal for a new economic science is similar: we must devise a method to measure economic progress that, unlike GDP, is capable of accounting for the many facets of life that are not immediately quantifiable when economic activity is tallied, but are nevertheless fundamental to human welfare. My leitmotif is to make economics more inclusive, so that it tallies the exchange of goods (or, more broadly, economic benefits) not only between consumers and producers, but also between individuals and communities, and between communities and nature.

The central tenet of my proposal is the creation of an alternative to GDP inspired by the idea of a national balance sheet suggested by Umair Haque, the author of *Betterness: Economics for Humans*. I will label this measure the 'Gross National Reserve' (GNR). Unlike GDP, the notional starting point for this quantity is not zero. In fact, it is a very high number – trillions of dollars for some countries. When we aggregate the GNR of all countries, we obtain a Gross Global Reserve (GGR), which is an even more useful measure in this context because, as we shall see, GNR contains some assets that are transnational. The starting point of the GGR is the value of everything that we have inherited from our planet, including clean air, fresh water, arable land, virgin forests, mineral deposits, ocean fish stocks, wild fauna as well as domesticated livestock, recoverable gas and petroleum reserves, landscapes of tourist interest, and historical monuments. If we calculate the value of all these assets by using traditional methods,[102] we will arrive at a starting GGR value of several hundred trillion dollars. What I suggest here is to take into consideration the vast reserve of nature's capital that, more often than not, most economists ignore.

Like a double-entry bookkeeping system, every economic activity is recorded twice, to account for both its accretive and depletive effects on GNR. An accretive effect is not unlike an increase in GDP, whereas a depletive effect is a reduction in the GNR due to consumption of a natural resource, or reduction in the value of a natural resource or a public good. In the case of a factory, for example, the economic output it generates can be measured under First Dimension economics: the added value of the goods produced and sold to consumers. But using Second Dimension economics we would also measure the millions of cubic metres of clean air it has polluted in the process, and the amount of waste water generated. We would then compute dollar equivalents for these by-products, and debit them against the GNR. If in a given period the factory has produced and sold, say, $100 worth of goods, but has also caused environmental degradation valued at $60, then its net impact on the GNR is only +$40.

The aim is to create a framework that encourages activities that have a positive net contribution versus activities that may give a positive GDP contribution but in fact yield a negative adjustment to GNR. In the case mentioned, the factory would be encouraged to adjust its production to reduce its polluting emissions or trade them using a mechanism like Certified Emission Reductions.

The case of a firm harvesting and using a natural resource is even more clear-cut. A logging company, for example, may have already accounted for the cost of cutting down the trees, and the licence paid for the concession to do so. This is part of their cost of goods sold and is reflected in their profit. It is also reflected in GDP because the timber is sold on to other firms for further processing. What it has failed to compute, however, is the loss incurred by the earth, and the loss of the services provided by the trees to nature and to human communities at large, such as carbon capture, water retention, prevention of soil erosion, and preservation of animal habitats and biodiversity. Under the proposed GNR system, these lost services would be valued in dollar amounts and debited from GNR. This would reveal the true cost of logging and allow governments to evaluate sensibly whether such activities are worthwhile.

Table 15.1 offers another example, this time on a scale that would force an Area or Regional government to weigh the pros and cons of economic activity carefully.

Table 15.1: Partial Estimation of the Impact of an Economic Activity on GNR

Activity	Accretive impact	Depletive impact	Overall annual change to GNR
Building an industrial development zone in a wetland	Added value of goods produced annually in the industrial zone: \$100 million	Annual loss of water and biodiversity services due to wetland destruction: \$30 million	\$100 – \$30 = \$70 million

Let us look at this example more closely, because its simplicity is deceptive. Let us assume that the wetland straddles multiple Areas, so whether or not to develop an industrial park at that location is a decision that must be made by the Region. Using the simple arithmetic in the table, the Jurisdictional Authority[103] might decide to undertake the project despite the environmental damage it may cause, because the net impact on GNR is positive. But is this situation really so simple? I have left out the all-important element of time. The useful life of an industrial zone might be thirty to fifty years. The destruction of the wetland, on the other hand, is forever. In other words, it would deprive the earth and future societies of the biodiversity services it currently provides, in perpetuity. As mentioned earlier (in Chapter 7, 'Rights and Freedoms'), one of the fundamental aspects of the right to life, seen from a Second or Third Dimension point of view, is the safeguarding of the rights of future, unborn generations. These human beings of the future have no voice to represent them in the present but must be included in any decision process that may permanently alter the environment. The Region's government, therefore, must consider the cost of wetland loss carefully, and amortise it over at least one hundred years. Doing so will yield a very different annual debit from the GNR, and the project may well fail to be approved.

In this manner, the GNR approach forces decision-makers to think in the very long term. First Dimension economics is, for the most part, near-sighted. Private businesses usually base their calculations and forecasts on a five- to ten-year horizon. Because of the vagaries of the global economy, they find it almost impossible to forecast market conditions beyond this short time span. A manufacturer of sporting equipment, for example, cannot foresee whether jogging will be as popular and widespread in twenty years as it is now. When deciding whether or not to go ahead with a new product, such as a new type of running shoe, the firm must ensure that it can recover its costs and make a satisfactory profit within a few years. Some products and public projects (like pharmaceuticals and infrastructure, respectively) may be evaluated on a longer timescale, perhaps up to twenty or thirty years, but rarely beyond. In this manner, capitalism's focus on near-term profitability forces all economic players to plan for the relatively short term. The GNR, on the other hand, forces decision-makers to consider a much lengthier period.

Now, it is easy enough to argue in favour of an indicator like GNR when talking about trees, forests, and wetlands – assets that everyone with an even peripheral concern for the environment respects already. But the situation is no different for natural resources like groundwater, natural gas, petroleum, coal, rare earth minerals, quarried marble, or sand for construction. Extraction of these commodities has various side effects, ranging from pollution to adverse health outcomes to degradation of landscapes (with opportunity costs relative to tourism potential, real estate value, and so on). By assigning a value to these effects and debiting it from GNR, a more accurate picture of the economy will emerge.

Enabling Mechanisms for GNR Economics

The GDP-based First Dimension accounting methodology makes an unfair assumption that all accounts begin at zero. In the GNR model, we attempt to remedy this shortcoming. We start with 'Global Accounting of Assets' – a mammoth, one-time undertaking to compute the value of all the existing natural resources on earth.[104] This quantity is the GGR, which is an aggregate of separate values compiled at lower levels of governance. Each Area would therefore be required to compute its own 'Gross Area Reserve' (GAR), which is then aggregated with the GARs of other Areas in the Region to obtain a 'Gross Regional Reserve' (GRR) and ultimately a country-level figure, the GNR. The GGR is the sum of the GNRs from every country in the world.

Our duty will be to act as custodians of nature's bounty. Indeed, once computed, the GGR should never diminish. From year to year, it would either remain stable or increase slightly. This may seem odd on first inspection. After all, natural resources like petroleum and natural gas are consumed and not replenished. And despite our efforts to conserve the natural environment, the sheer pressure of population growth is depleting natural landscapes and habitats continuously, and releasing vast amounts of carbon into the atmosphere. It is also true, however, that economic activity itself, in a growth phase, can increase the GNR, just as it does the GDP in the First Dimension. Moreover, private enterprises as well as governments (at any level) will be able to increase both their local reserves and the GGR by undertaking activities like reforestation of denuded hillsides, cleaning up of polluted waterways, restoration of natural habitats, and seeding them with endemic flora and fauna. If enough such projects are undertaken on a regular basis, it will be possible to maintain each GNR (and thus the overall GGR) in balance, such that depletive and accretive activities offset each other. A private enterprise, for example, could first reduce its environmental footprint as much as possible by adopting state-of-the-art technologies that minimise waste, emissions, and effluents. It can offset any remaining depletive impact by restoring a degraded forest or waterway, or simply purchasing credits for such projects from companies or Communities that specialise in them. Municipalities (that is, Communities) could do the same. To some extent such plans have been enacted already by forward-thinking companies in developed countries, usually under the aegis of CSR programmes. Such balancing efforts should be mandatory for all entities (private enterprises as well as levels of government), not by fiat but by enabling mechanisms that would naturally nudge institutions in the right direction.

The first such enabling mechanism is the Utility Index, a scorecard-like tool that would allow for the evaluation of every enterprise (private or public) according to the impact it has on society. If GNR and GGR are merely macroeconomic indicators, private enterprises may not feel especially incentivised to change their ways. They might see in GNR a useful tool for calculating the impact of their operations on the environment and on local communities, but, aside from adjusting their CSR programmes, they would not be affected. As we shall see in the next chapter, however, each firm's balance with respect to GNR will affect its Utility Index, which, in turn, will be the basis of a new system of economic incentives, rewards, and taxation.

Another enabling mechanism specifically developed to ensure compliance with the principles of the Second Dimension is the novel method for participation in the Global and Continental assemblies that I discussed in Chapter 13. Each country's right to vote on important resolutions at such assemblies would hinge on its score in the national scorecard (effectively the score achieved by each country's Head of State in his or her scorecard). Countries that allow their GNR to diminish would achieve low scores and thus suffer a reduction in their voting rights.

The third enabling mechanism is the creation of a new financial instrument or meta-currency dedicated exclusively to accretive and depletive transactions in the GNR/GGR. To illustrate how such a meta-currency would work, and why it is necessary, let me return to an example we discussed a few paragraphs ago: the development of an industrial zone in a natural wetland area. In Table 15.2, the numbers have changed, reflecting a revised computation that accounts correctly for the longevity of the impact on GNR. Namely, the industrial park generates economic value in the form of an accretion to GNR for only a few decades, whereas the depletion caused by the destruction of the wetland is forever.

Table 15.2: Full Estimation of the Impact of an Economic Activity on GNR

Activity	Accretive impact (30-year horizon)	Depletive impact (indefinite annuity)	Overall annual change to GNR
Building an industrial development zone in a wetland	Added value of goods produced annually in the industrial zone: \$100 million	Annual loss of water and biodiversity services due to wetland destruction: \$55 million	\$100 – \$55 = \$45 million

As the numbers suggest, the Regional government has decided to go ahead with the project because it generates a net accretion to GNR despite its environmental side effects. This computation is not merely an arithmetic exercise. It would generate real cash flows, as follows. Every year, the companies that own the manufacturing plants operating in the new industrial park would have to collectively pay \$55 million to account for the depletive impact of the industrial park. (Ultimately, these funds would come from consumers. The companies operating in the industrial park would have to increase their product prices to recover the depletion charge.) For simplicity, let us call this payout a 'debit'. This debit would flow into a collective account held by the interested level of government (in this case, the Region). Though levied in the cash currency (here, dollars), this sum, once deposited in the collective account, would be denominated as a different currency, which may be used only for GNR-accretive projects or transactions. What was a debit for the companies that had to pay the equivalent dollar sum now becomes a credit to the authority in charge of maintaining the account and dispensing the funds deposited there.

The Regional government can now employ these credits to fund accretive activities in its jurisdiction, such as designation of new wildlife preserves, improvements to recycling and waste reduction programmes, retrofitting of government buildings with energy-saving design and equipment, development of solar-powered public transportation, and landscaping of new urban public parks. The most important aspect of this scheme is that once converted into the new debit/credit meta-currency, these funds could be used only for activities that are designed specifically to increase the GNR. By dedicating a special currency to GNR accounting, the Second Dimension economic system ensures that the funds in question are used responsibly and transparently. As I will show in Chapter 17, debits/credits make up just one of several new financial tools that will be needed in the Second Dimension and beyond.

GNR and the Spectrum of Demand

In the foregoing discussion we have seen, albeit in broad strokes only, how a balance sheet approach like GNR could lead to a fairer accounting of our use of natural resources. It is sensible and intuitive; the only complex task would be the accurate computation of the intangible benefits of many of the natural resources that capitalist enterprises either consume or degrade.

We can also connect the GNR principle with the Spectrum of Demand model (Chapter 14). Like the capitalist system, GDP metrics describe only one portion of the Spectrum of Demand, as shown in Figure 15.1. Like capitalism, GDP only values goods and services that are provided by a market economy in response to individual needs and desires. It falters when interrogated about the well-being of communities, and when called upon to evaluate the benefits provided by nature.

Does GNR address the same demand segments as GDP, with the important addition of only nature (as in Figure 15.2)? How can GNR be the fulcrum of Second Dimension economics?

In fact, the concept of a global reserve is not limited to natural resources. It is far more ambitious and comprehensive. To accurately reflect the

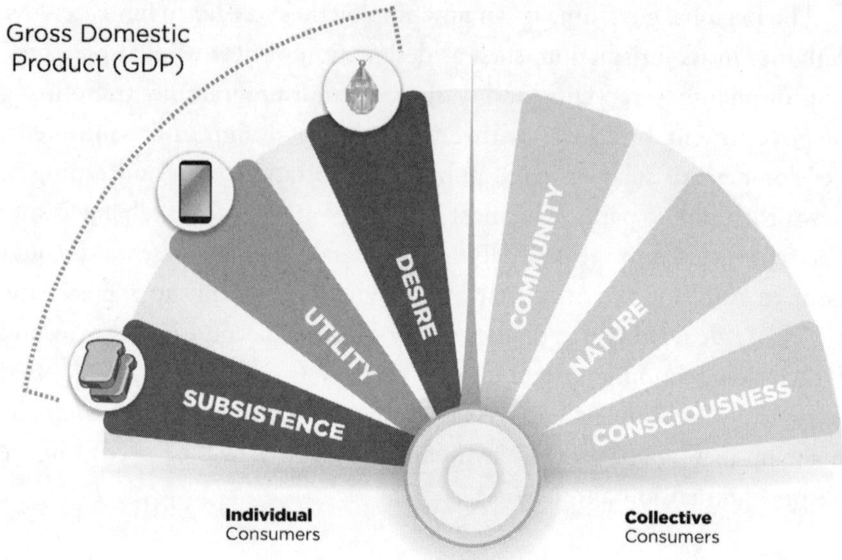

Figure 15.1: GDP in the First Dimension's Spectrum of Demand

health of an economy, it must include *social* goods and services as well – a vastly more challenging collection of previously uncalculated benefits. The inclusion of social benefits and, ultimately, of benefits derived from a higher level of consciousness, would propel GNR economics into the Third Dimension.

As Robert Kennedy pointed out, GDP fails to calculate the value of good education, good health, and good governance, to name a few social benefits that we take for granted but to which we cannot assign a monetary value. Only when these benefits fail do we calculate their impact on GDP. Only when education is poor do we quantify the value of this absence in terms of remedial measures and loss of skilled labour. Only when a person is sick do we calculate the value of her health by summing the cost of treatment and lost wages. Only when public officials are accused of corruption or incompetence do we remember the value of good public administration by estimating losses due to bribery, inefficiency, abandoned infrastructure projects, or poorly executed social programmes.

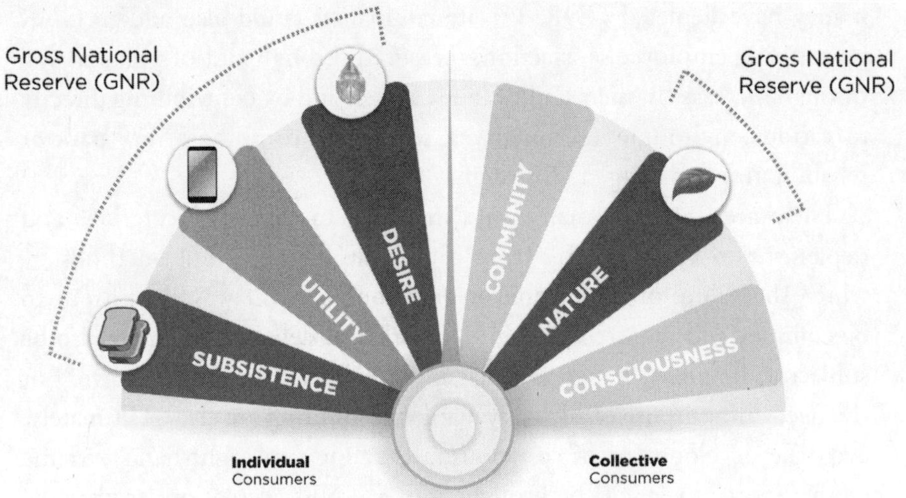

Figure 15.2: GNR in the Second Dimension's Spectrum of Demand

The GNR approach would address this oddity by assigning a value to each social benefit, public good, and common good, and adding them to GNR. We would assess the output of every government agency, trust, non-profit organisation (and, theoretically at least, of every individual), and determine whether it has added to GNR or depleted it.

In the realm of education, for example, each school could be rated according to comprehensive criteria. For each student who graduates and either enters university or a vocational institute within one year, the school would be able to claim a certain credit to GNR. Universities would do the same, adding to GNR by virtue of how many graduates continue their studies or enter the workforce. In public administration, each unit of government (Community, Area, Region, and Nation), will be set annual goals, financial as well as operational, which are captured in the scorecards of its leader, as seen in Chapter 11. If those goals are met and certified by the relevant Scorecard Evaluation Authority, the administrative unit would have added value to GNR, whereas if they are not met, leading to unnecessary expenditure, delay, and inefficiency, then it may have depleted GNR. Private companies could also add to GNR by ensuring employee satisfaction, measured through end-of-year surveys; through increases in their Utility Index scores; and by contributing directly to various environmental initiatives, such as landscaping a new park or rehabilitating a damaged ecosystem.

There are, in short, many ways in which to calculate accretions and depletions to GNR arising from intangible benefits. The methods by which the values of these additions are computed may well turn out to be complex and require much initial work and debate. They may also be subject to frequent change as social and economic conditions evolve. But the need and purpose of such a system of accounting are clear. Ultimately, even the development of consciousness, at the very right-hand extreme of the Spectrum, could be brought into a GNR calculation, so that the now-familiar Spectrum diagram would look like Figure 15.3.

It is difficult, from our First Dimension perspective, to imagine how higher consciousness might translate into a quantifiable accretion to GNR.

Figure 15.3: GNR in the Third Dimension's Spectrum of Demand

How could this be done? How would it be measured? The starting point for such an exercise is, once again, understanding the ultimate goal of a heightened consciousness – to create a harmonious society of contented citizens whose behaviour exhibits the fundamental Third Dimension qualities of devotion, forgiveness and compassion toward each other (Chapter 4). Toward the end of Chapter 14, I discussed how these goals can replace profit-seeking and self-interest as the pillars of a new free-market economic system. In a Third Dimension economy, much government expenditure would have been replaced by philanthropy and volunteerism, and a substantial portion of goods and services would be exchanged freely (that is, without precise valuation and the use of currency) among individuals and businesses, in a gift economy motivated by altruism rather than selfishness.

These efforts – philanthropy, volunteer work, and even gift-giving – can be measured. We can measure the amount of philanthropic giving in absolute terms, as a percentage of an overall community budget, or in terms of the number of households making contributions. We can measure volunteerism in the number of man-hours donated, or in corresponding wages saved, or, better yet, in the level of happiness and goodwill generated through them via a survey mechanism. And we can, if we wish, measure gifted goods and services by summing up the theoretical value of those goods and services. These measurements would be proxies for what we really want to gauge: the level of devotion and compassion in the general population, and its effect on social interaction, including economic exchange. These indirect measurements, however, would allow us to make relatively accurate adjustments to GNR, which ultimately measures the well-being of a nation rather than the amount of material goods it produces.

In the First Dimension, we like to divide and categorise – economics, rights and freedoms, democracy – and keep things separate. What we learn in the Second Dimension, however, is that these are parts of a continuum that I have attempted to capture in the value spectrum of higher-dimension economics. The goal is to create an ecosystem-like structure supported by a logical system that recognises that there is much outside the First

Dimension field of vision that cannot be addressed effectively by First Dimension banking, economics, and money. I have tried to link these to the essential rights and freedoms of the First, Second, and Third Dimensions, and link those in turn to the nature of democracy in the higher dimensions, and through these interlocking ideas – on liberty, governance, organisations, democracy, and economics – present a cohesive alternative framework to lead us to the Second and eventually the Third Dimension.

16

The Enterprise: From Ownership to Stewardship

Ownership and Control: A Failing Marriage

A market economy is an economic system where, ideally, trade is guided only by the independent forces of supply and demand, with little state intervention. Though capitalism is based on the idea of the free market, it also includes elements that are not necessarily part of a market economy, for example, private ownership and the persistent focus on financial profitability. Indeed, capitalism is an economic system where industry and trade are controlled primarily by private owners (instead of the state), and conducted for profit. Private enterprise is the fundamental building block of the capitalist edifice. How will it be affected if, as I suggested two chapters ago, we expand the concept of the market economy to cover the entire Spectrum of Demand?

A seminal contribution made by the First Dimension to the development of the economy was the idea of moving ownership from physical assets (such as land, cattle, and gold) to non-material assets (printed money, intellectual property, and shares). The invention of the limited liability corporation (LLC) with divisible, tradable stocks allowed for a whole new area of ownership based on the control of intangibles called shares, which were backed by the authority of the state. This created new, dematerialised asset classes that had nothing to do with direct ownership of physical assets. Today the wealthiest individuals in the world are those who own large amounts of stock in multinational corporations.

The LLC is a fictional legal entity, that is, one that does not physically exist but whose existence is created in our collective imaginations by laws and covenants. The most important aspect of an LLC is that it allows risk to be spread between large numbers of shareholders while limiting their personal financial liability. An LLC lets people who want to invest in, say, drug discovery, do so without fear of being personally liable (beyond the equity capital they invested) if the drug has negative effects in trials. The LLC allowed the modern economy to use capital, take risks on converting scientific discoveries to everyday technologies, and harness the power of entrepreneurship to fuel the rise of the modern world's enormous wealth. By bringing together physical assets, working capital, intellectual capital, and labour in varying degrees and harnessing them to entrepreneurship, the LLC paved the way for everything we have invented in the past century, from the iPhone and the passenger jet to Facebook and polar fleece.

Corporations whose shares are traded in stock markets are characteristic of capitalism, because their scalability enables companies to mobilise large financial resources, and thus achieve the equally large revenues and profits that move the capitalist economy forward. A corporation can access vast amounts of funding by issuing equity to millions of investors, that is, by devolving ownership to a large number of shareholders, and drawing on their combined reserves of wealth.

The capitalist corporation is a brilliant First Dimension construct that has enabled tremendous achievements in product innovation, research and development (R&D), and the expansion of markets. However, it also suffers from great and seemingly insurmountable limitations. The corporate structure effectively separates ownership, or at least a substantial part of ownership, from those who manage the firm and may have founded the firm in the past. Through the acquisition and trade of shares, ownership of the corporation transitions to various individuals – often represented by pension funds, mutual funds, or hedge funds – who do not take part in running it. These owners invest in the corporation for one goal only, namely, profit. They are generally uninterested in other aspects of the business, such as product quality, employee satisfaction, environmental compliance, or social responsibility, until these concerns have a direct bearing on profitability and stock price. This is not to say that most equity investors are callous or insensitive; some of them may well be inclined to philanthropy as well. If they wish to better society, they may do it through other initiatives, such as charity. But the main reason why they purchase company stock is to earn a return. In essence, the corporate financial structure enables investors to become owners of enterprises without sharing any of the responsibilities associated with operations.

Because the majority of a corporation's owners are thus concerned only with profit, we can say that they wield most of the control. By 'control' I refer to the ability to define the company's overall objective and to direct its operations toward that goal. It is a company's *raison d'être* – its mission in society and its purpose in the economy. All too often nowadays, a corporation's mission is summed up in that ubiquitous adage: 'to maximise shareholder value'. This is a euphemism for profit, whether that profit be understood as dividend distributions or capital gains, or a combination of both. Again, there is no value judgment here – the stock exchange, like the market economy, is perfectly amoral. It is simply a financial mechanism for aggregating and deploying large amounts of money. The result, however, is that control rests in the hands of owners who are only, and can only be, interested in profit. After all, think of most people's equity holdings: they are likely to be bundled in a portfolio managed professionally, containing shares from dozens of different companies. In most cases, an average investor cannot realistically understand in detail, and attempt to affect, the operations of each company in the portfolio.

In this scenario, increasing shareholder value becomes the primary goal of the corporation.[105] Diluted ownership effectively forces the corporation to prioritise profit maximisation. Other goals that the company's founders or managers may have – such as contributing to social needs, ensuring the welfare of employees, or designing products that are environmentally friendly – must be subordinated to this imperative. Owners, therefore, all too often control the overall trajectory of the firm. They dictate that its overriding purpose be maximisation of share price and dividends. These owners, via large pension and mutual funds, control the firm's ultimate role in society.

From Ownership to Custodianship

The most debilitating aspect of the capitalist LLC is that its ownership structure forces it to focus almost exclusively on profit. As a result, First Dimension capitalism measures the success of enterprises on the basis of profits alone. It never takes into account an organisation's utility, that is, its usefulness to society, or its impact on that society, which are far more important for our well-being and that of our planet than the sole attention to profits.

In the Second Dimension, on the other hand, we will focus on these major concepts – utility and impact – by changing the ownership structure of enterprises. Indeed, to prioritise goals other than revenue growth and profitability, a forward-thinking private enterprise must first make adjustments to its ownership structure. The fundamental principle at work here is that there must be separation of ownership of profits from control of the enterprise. Specifically, a company must either separate ownership from control entirely, or at least ensure that the owners understand and actively support the company's non-financial goals. And there are indeed companies that have tried to disentangle themselves from the yoke of profit by pursuing one of these two solutions. Let us look at an example of each strategy.

At one end of the spectrum is Google. Its founders and leaders, Sergey Brin and Larry Page, secured control of the firm's activities by reserving class B shares, with ten times the voting weight of class A shares.[106] But even this was insufficient as acquisitions, employee stock options, and other financial transactions continued to dilute their ownership (and the associated voting power) in the company. In 2012, therefore, they announced the issuance of a new class of shares (class C shares, eventually issued in 2014), which had no voting rights at all. After this stock split, Page and Brin controlled 58.4 per cent of the voting shares, while owning only 13.9 per cent of the company. In this manner, the founders, while still able to attract extensive equity funding via the stock market, continued to maintain unfettered control over the direction of the company. In October 2015, Google was restructured again with the creation of a new parent company, Alphabet, Inc., which now holds Google as well as several former Google subsidiaries in its portfolio of companies. This strategic reorganisation led to more adjustments in ownership and voting rights, but the overall picture remains unchanged, as Page and Brin, who now serve as Alphabet's CEO and president, respectively, retain roughly 51 per cent of the votes while owning only 11 per cent of the total equity.

Google's stated goal is to codify and systematise all information useful to mankind, and deliver it, mostly for free, to digital users, in the most efficient way possible. Google can now continue in this quest without being encumbered by shareholder demands for certain profit targets, even though some of the company's pursuits are thoroughly unprofitable (such as mapping, with street-view capability, every corner of the world, including remote, mostly uninhabited locales, where the likelihood of a return on investment is nil). A simple change in ownership structure (the invention of class C shares) has enabled the founders to completely wrest control of the corporation from other shareholders, effectively redefining the very nature of the corporate concept.

The John Lewis Partnership (JLP) has achieved much the same result by an entirely different route. The Partnership is an employee-owned UK company that operates the John Lewis chain of department stores and the Waitrose chain of supermarkets. In accordance with the vision of its founder, John Spedan Lewis, the company is owned by a trust on behalf of all its employees, who receive a share of annual profits. Every employee is a Partner and has a say in the running of the business through branch forums, which discuss local issues at every store, and Divisional Councils. Above these lies a Partnership Council, to which the Partners elect at least 80 per cent of the representatives, while the chairman appoints the remainder. The councils may discuss 'any matter whatsoever' and are also responsible for the non-commercial aspects of the business. The chairman's performance is measured against five criteria, only one of which is profitability, and the Council has the right to vote his removal should he underperform. By democratising the Partnership to include everyone who works there, the company has fused ownership with labour, and purpose with employee engagement. Thus, it has effectively achieved a balance between the needs of ownership (profit) and the stated managerial goal of the firm, which is employee happiness.

Despite travelling along different paths, both Google and JLP exhibit traits of the Second Dimension enterprise. They have renounced the dated and restrictive capitalist concept of ownership, which reduces all endeavours to a pursuit of financial gain. Those who control these enterprises have abandoned conventional structures of ownership and have recast themselves as custodians, rather than owners. A sound return on investment is a desirable by-product, but not the main goal, of either of these firms. Despite this, Google stock has always maintained a high valuation, and JLP has consistently delivered solid profits, routinely outperforming similar retail chains; each year, it provides sizeable returns in the form of bonuses to its employees.[107] This is another way of saying that companies that have clear goals and are run by capable, efficient managers will almost always deliver above-average returns, even though profitability is not their primary motivation. This is an example of what economist John Kay has called *obliquity*: the attainment of a goal through indirect means.

The fact that Google's and JLP's new breed of owners (founders and employees, respectively) are not really owners any more, but rather custodians of each firm's vision, can also be expressed in a different way. We can say that rather than addressing primarily the needs of the equity shareholders, these companies have prioritised the needs of other groups who are affected by the company's operations. In Google's case, the beneficiaries of the company's vision are the end-users of its many useful technologies, that is, its customers. For JLP, the main beneficiaries are the employees.

In Table 16.1, I summarise the ownership adjustments discussed here.

Table 16.1: Owners to Custodians

	Typical corporation	**Google**	**JLP**
Ownership	Shareholders via pension funds, mutual funds, hedge funds	Shareholders via pension funds, mutual funds, hedge funds	All employees
Control	Shareholders via pension funds, mutual funds, hedge funds	Sergey Brin and Larry Page	All employees
Management	Board of directors and senior management team	CEO Sundar Pichai and senior management team	Chairman Charlie Mayfield and senior management team

Figure 16.1 categorises all the different groups or entities affected by a private firm's operations, what we might call its stakeholders. Second Dimension thinking revolves around the recognition of the interconnectedness of all human activity, and commercial activity is no exception. Every firm must understand its operations and purpose in the context of all the different parties it affects or may affect. Owners, directors, employees, and customers are stakeholders in any enterprise, but to these we must also add silent stakeholders – communities and the environment – on whom the firm may have profound effects as well.

As the diagram illustrates, custodianship of the kind shown by Google and JLP ensures that the needs of employees and customers are not only met, but prioritised. The next step in this evolution – to the Third Dimension – is for every enterprise to target the greater needs of communities and of nature. That entails a graduation from an individual-centred, profit-seeking notion of ownership to a higher goal, which is stewardship.

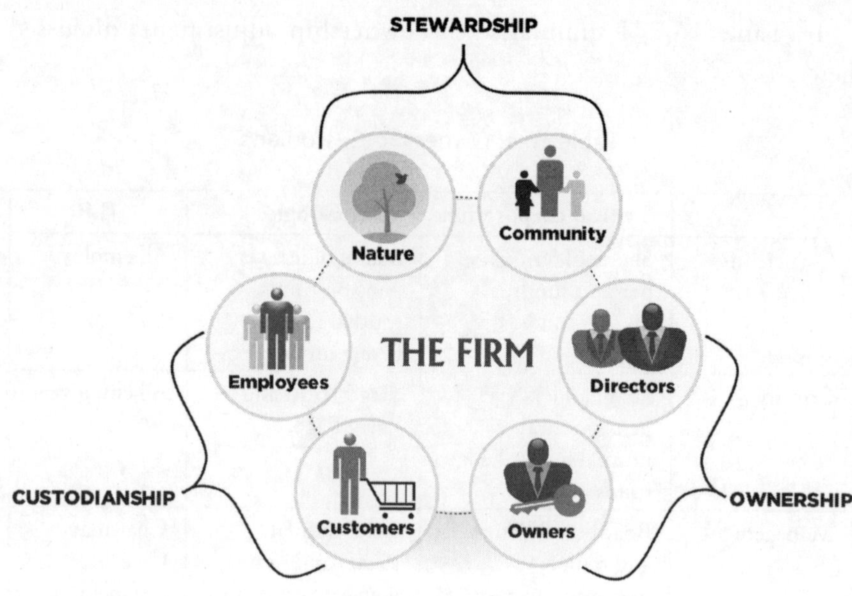

Figure 16.1: An Enterprise's Stakeholders

Stewardship

Simply put, stewardship is the alignment of the company's goals with the overall goals of bettering both humanity and the natural environment, such that its impact is always accretive to GNR, and significantly so. This can be achieved by shifting the measurement of success of companies away from profit and toward a balanced scorecard that reflects Third Dimension values. A rudimentary proposal for such a scorecard, which I call the Utility Index, is shown in Table 16.2. Each company's score derived from this Index would have a direct repercussion on the level of corporate tax it pays. Because taxation will depend entirely on the Utility Index, tax authorities will be in charge of computing the relevant scores for all companies in their jurisdiction. For local enterprises, the Area-level tax authority would be responsible for assessing the score and collecting taxes or disbursing grants (more on this below), whereas for larger businesses that have operations in multiple Areas or nationwide, the Regional or National tax authority would take charge.

The Utility Index comprises five criteria by which a company's activity can be rated – and profitability is not one of them. The first is utility, that is, the usefulness of the product or service the company offers to the individual consumer and the general community. A score for this criterion, on a scale of 0 to 10, would be assigned by the tax authority itself.

The first company under consideration is Mars. While a successful enterprise with good financials (boasting $35 billion in sales in 2016) and a strong brand, Mars nevertheless scores poorly in this category because its marquee product, the candy bar, cannot be said to have high utility.[108] Though it may have some nutritional and recreational value, overall it is neither particularly good for one's health nor essential in daily life.

Google, on the other hand, receives a high score for this line item, because its products (web search, digital maps, etc.) are highly valuable to all consumers and, indeed, have become almost indispensable in modern life. JLP scores well too, because its department stores and grocery chain are useful contributors, but lower than Google because they are less indispensable, since there are other retail chains that deliver similar utility. Finally, Médecins Sans Frontières (MSF), a humanitarian aid non-governmental organisation and Nobel Peace Prize laureate, scores maximum points because they deliver a life-saving service in places and conditions where nobody else is willing to do so. Note here that I am evaluating MSF – a non-profit organisation – with the same measuring stick as three for-profit enterprises. This is not a mistake.

Ownership structure is the second criterion. As discussed, when the demands of ownership (profit) in capitalist organisations dictate the direction of the firm's undertakings, inequality, degradation, and over-consumption follow. Therefore, the Index rewards firms where the ownership structure does not interfere with a firm's mission and goals. Community-owned groups and large partnerships score much higher than companies owned exclusively or in large part by individuals and families (for example, Mars, which is owned entirely by the Mars family), and run primarily for profit.

Innovation and eco-efficiency are rewarded in the third criterion to stimulate all companies, including those that are engaged in activities with

Table 16.2: Utility Index

Criterion		Score range	Company			
			Mars	*Google*	*JLP*	*MSF*
Utility		0–10	3	9	7	10
Ownership structure • Majority of profits and voting control with one individual or family • Majority of profits shared between unrelated shareholders, but voting control with one individual or family • Corporation, profits and voting control with widely dispersed unrelated shareholders • Community owned	 0 2 3 5	0–5	0	3	5	5
Innovation and eco-efficiency		0–5	2	4	3	4
Monopoly		–3–0	–1	–3	–1	0
Transparency		–3–0	–1	–3	0	0
Total			**3/20**	**10/20**	**14/20**	**19/20**

high utility and high GNR accretion, to continue to develop cutting-edge technology and new ways to conserve resources. The degree of innovation expressed by a company's products and/or internal processes is difficult to measure objectively, but several methods already exist, including 'Return on Product Development Expense' (RoPDE), as elaborated by the Balanced Scorecard Institute.[109] Eco-efficiency measures a firm's ability to produce goods and services while minimising the amount of resources used in the production process and the volume of waste products emitted. While various specific indicators can be computed to represent this quality, it is often expressed as a ratio of the environmental impact of a product (for example, tonnes of carbon released into the atmosphere or of waste that cannot be recycled) to the value added by that product to GDP.[110]

Google scores higher in this respect because of its relentless betterment of all the technologies it has developed, while JLP, whose offerings cannot be said to be on the cutting edge of product innovation, gets relatively high marks on account of the efficiency of its operations.

The final two criteria, monopoly and transparency,[111] award only negative points. If a company is a monopoly in its industry, or actively deters competition in its industry, then it may receive negative marks. Here, Google is penalised heavily because it is a monopoly in almost every product category it offers. Its near-monopoly in certain areas, such as search and digital mapping, can be regarded as a positive thing because it creates global standards that make the exchange of information much simpler for everyone. However, its monopoly in other areas (such as search-based advertising) means it can charge exorbitant prices with impunity, much to the detriment of smaller businesses. Google's power of monopoly has been challenged repeatedly in various antitrust cases against the firm in Europe and other countries.

Transparency addresses how honest companies are in their dealings with customers, employees, and fiscal authorities. For example, many multinationals today manage to reduce their corporate income taxes, or avoid paying them altogether, by shifting corporate profits to low-tax or zero-tax countries. This complex exercise involves transfer pricing, shell companies in tax havens, and the exploitation of legal loopholes in countries that offer incentives to companies for setting up operations there. It is all legal, more or less, but clearly intended to avoid paying taxes. A raft of recent revelations (in incidents such as the Panama Papers and the Paradise Papers) have shown the extent to which many individuals and corporations thus avoid taxation. In the transparency category, Google is penalised again on account of the manner in which it manages its corporate tax liabilities, as well as the unethical use of personal data through several of its applications.

The overall scores (out of a possible total of 20) are shown in the bottom row of Table 16.3. Clearly, an organisation dedicated exclusively to a social cause like MSF scores the highest – a near perfect 19/20. The score each company receives would be directly reflected in the level of tax levied, according to Table 16.3.

Table 16.3: Utility Index Scores and Tax Rates of Companies – An Example

Index score	Tax rate	Company
0–2	80%	
3–4	70%	Mars
5–6	60%	
7–8	50%	
9–10	40%	Google
11–12	30%	
13–14	20%	John Lewis Partnership
15–16	10%	
17–18	5%	
19	–10%	Médecins Sans Frontières
20	–20%	

In the above example, companies like Mars, Google, and JLP are taxed a percentage of their profits, just as they are in the First Dimension. Enterprises that score extremely high on the Utility Index, like MSF, on the other hand, experience negative taxation, which means they *receive* a contribution from the tax authority rather than having to pay income tax. Tax revenues collected from companies subject to taxation would flow into a fund known as Budgetary Assistance Grant (BAG), which would be created at various levels of governance, including Area, Region, Nation, and World. Funds from the BAG will be used to allocate contributions to high-performing organisations such as MSF. For enterprises that do not make a profit, like MSF, the amount allocated would be calculated based on the company's budget. For example, if MSF's operating budget (excluding overheads from its global headquarter) in the previous fiscal year was $100 million, it would qualify for a grant of $10 million from the BAG on account of its score in the Utility Index.

For a monopoly like Google it would make sense to either sell off business units where its monopoly is too great, or to encourage its own competitors in those industries to develop and expand their services. As other companies gain market share, Google would reduce its penalty in the monopoly line item of the Utility Index. This will eventually translate into a lower levy rate.

In the scoring and taxation mechanism, organisations would pay levies or receive funds from the BAG in the jurisdictional level in which they operate. For instance, as Google operates globally, it would pay levies to, or receive contributions from, the global BAG. MSF's contribution would also come from a global BAG fund, as MSF has operations all over the world. John Lewis, on the other hand, operates primarily in the UK, and would therefore be taxed or granted funds from a national BAG pool. This would help prevent one of the biggest problems of the First Dimension economy, tax inversion, by which companies try to pay minimum tax by shifting their legal domicile to countries where they have minimal or no operations, but where corporate taxes are lower.

Firms with a very low score (below 9) in the Utility Index would incur very high rates of tax, and the hope is that they would progressively improve their operations to lessen their levy burden, and, in some cases, abandon certain lines of business altogether and focus on activities with both high utility and high addition to GNR.

The Enterprise of the Future

In our examples, MSF scored high enough to warrant a contribution from the tax authority. But I have included MSF not only as an instance of a firm rewarded by the Utility Index, but also and especially to suggest that this system of evaluation should be applied to *all* enterprises. The distinctions we make currently – between for-profit and non-profit organisations, between corporations and trusts, between associations and partnerships, between sole proprietorships and cooperatives, between private firms and government agencies – are conditioned entirely by differences in the ownership structure of these entities, and by the way they dispose of revenue. But if we de-emphasise ownership and accumulation of funds

– both holdovers from First Dimension capitalism – then all enterprises can be evaluated according to the same criteria, that is, by objectively measuring their relevance, efficiency, and contribution to the GNR. In higher dimensions, the distinctions used to characterise different forms of organisation and different distributions of operational funds will become increasingly irrelevant.

Provisionally, in the Second Dimension, all organisations will be sorted broadly into four sectors (governance, business, social, scientific). Eventually, however, all organisations will be assessed according to an Impact Scale, which will consider the following criteria:

- Overall budget or sales revenues
- Number of employees
- Utility (as measured in the Utility Index)

Once an impact score is computed, all organisations, from neighbourhood libraries to multinational corporations, will be assigned a ranking, or impact level, ranging from 20 for the simplest to 1 for the most complex and influential. Table 16.4 illustrates this stratification of all organised human activity, starting from the simplest organisations, such as local schools and libraries, all the way up to the pinnacle of national government.

For each impact level, I have given representative examples from governance as well as from other spheres of activity. The hierarchy of governance follows principles first outlined in *Making India Work* and covered in detail in Chapter 10 of this book. The reader will recall that there are four levels of national governance: Community (Level 15), Area (Level 10), Region (Level 5), and Nation (Level 2). This hierarchy of governance already exists in many countries, albeit with different labels (municipality, county, state, etc.), but in Chapter 10 it was defined precisely and used as a universal model of governance.

An important consequence of the Impact Scale is that governance institutions are shown on par with institutions from other spheres, including businesses, scientific organisations, and social enterprises. Their level can be equated by realising, for example, that a large private company with thousands of employees can have the same impact on the general population as an Area government, or a well-respected daily newspaper with high circulation.

Table 16.4: The Impact Scale

Level	Example from governance	Leader	Example from other sectors (business/ social/scientific)	Leader
20	Local library	Chief Librarian	Company, branch, or franchise with <10 employees	CEO/MD
19	Local fire station	Fire Chief	Policy think tank	Director
18	Local school	Principal	Dept/Faculty of a university	Head of Department
17	Community arbitration court	Chief Arbitrator	Company with about 100 employees	CEO/MD
16	Community registry	Registrar	Large museum	Director
15	**Community**	**Community Leader**	Company with 101–1,000 employees	CEO/MD
14	Area-level tax authority	Chief Auditor	Daily newspaper	Editor-in-Chief
13	Area-level hospital	Hospital Director	Large NGO	CEO/MD
12	Area-level dept of public works	Chief of Public Works	Finance dept of a mid-sized company	CFO
11	Area-level judicial court	Judge	University	Chancellor
10	**Area**	**Area Manager**	Enterprise with at least $10 billion in revenues, and/or at least 10,000 employees	CEO/MD

9	Regional transportation board	Transport Commissioner	International sporting federation (FIFA, IOC, etc.)	President
8	Regional department of agriculture	Agriculture Commissioner	Technology department of a large enterprise	CTO
7	Regional tax authority	Revenue Chief	Enterprise with at least $25 billion in revenues, and/or at least 25,000 employees	CEO/MD
6	Appellate court	Judge	Enterprise with at least $50 billion in revenues, and/or at least 50,000 employees	CEO/MD
5	**Region**	**Regional Governor**	Enterprise with at least $100 billion in revenues, and/ or at least 100,000 employees	CEO/MD
4	National parks, forests, and agriculture	Minister for the Environment	–	–
3	National defence	Commander-in-Chief	–	–
2	**National government**	**Head of State**	–	–
1	Continental/ Global government	–	–	–

CEO: Chief Executive Officer
CFO: Chief Financial Officer
CTO: Chief Technology Officer
MD: Managing Director

Earlier in this chapter I suggested that the focus of private companies could be steered away from profit and market share by making structural adjustments to the relationship between ownership and control of each firm. I offered the UK's JLP as an example of a Second Dimension enterprise whose stated goal is not maximisation of shareholder value, but rather the happiness of its employees. Since the employees own the partnership, JLP has effectively fused the needs of ownership (profit) with the managerial purpose of the firm (employee happiness). Here is a successful, profitable organisation, then, which is owned by its 'people', administered by its 'people' via a fair, democratic system, and whose primary aim is to ensure the welfare of its 'people'.

Now consider also that JPL has revenues (let us call it a 'budget') of about £10 billion, and a staff ('population') of 90,000, and you will begin to recognise that in scale as well as structure it is operating as a small government, roughly equivalent to an Area government. Who is to say that JPL's chairman could not use the skills and expertise he has gained running JLP to become an Area Manager and, eventually, a Regional Governor or a Head of State? In this manner, the leaders of 'private' organisations must be held to the same standards of accountability as those in 'public' office. Moreover, leaders should be able to transition between the four spheres almost seamlessly.

There is no equivalence between governance and other spheres of activity at levels above 5, as no business, scientific, or social enterprise can be said to have the same impact as a governance institution of national scale. (Exceptions, however, may be made in countries that are the headquarters of very large enterprises with high utility scores.)

Finally, let me illustrate how the Utility Index can be applied to organisations that we currently think of as belonging exclusively to government, by taking an indispensable agency like the police. (This is not a random choice: as you may recall, Adam Smith posited that certain public services, like law enforcement, could never be delivered by a pure market economy.) A local police department would naturally score well on the Index owing to its high utility and the fact that it is a Community-owned agency, resulting in the receipt of contributions from the Area BAG. This would be a significant source of its operating revenue, in addition to its contractually agreed payments from the Community. (The police force would also earn cash income from fines levied for minor infractions, such as traffic and parking violations, and possibly some targeted catalyst income for special services performed for disadvantaged members of the Community. Targeted catalysts and other meta-currencies will be discussed in Chapter 17.)

An underperforming police department, however, might score lower on the Utility Index and, as a result, be liable for taxation rather than receive contributions. With its overall income curtailed, the police department might have to wind down operations and relinquish its mandate. The Community would then have the option of removing the police operator altogether and replacing it with a competitor. A Community that is not satisfied with the performance of its police force could invite the police department from a neighbouring Community to extend its services to cover both communities; or, it could contract a firm that has hitherto been providing only independent security services to local businesses.

Though this may sound odd at first, it is not at all unreasonable. Think of the great extent to which security, defence, and public safety have been privatised in many countries. Private police forces have existed for a long time, at least as far back as the mid-19th century, when the Pinkerton National Detective Agency was established in the United States. Many private police forces exist today, including railway police, airport police, and campus police at many universities. And, of course, there are security personnel protecting individuals and private property everywhere in the world, in what is a burgeoning industry. In the United States alone, there are well in excess of 1 million security guards, easily outnumbering the number of public police officers.

Some of these private policing firms have wide-ranging powers. The University of Chicago Police Department (UCPD), for example, has jurisdiction over some 15 square kilometres of the city. Within this zone, its officers are responsible for the safety of 65,000 residents, most of whom are not students, and wield full policing powers, including the right to search, arrest, and detain. However, in most cases of police privatisation – where local municipalities have turned to private companies to take over tasks normally performed by public police – private contractors are usually given only non-front line responsibilities like parking enforcement, forensics, and neighbourhood patrolling. The wholesale replacement of a public police force with a private firm, with full authority to investigate crime, pursue suspects, use deadly force, and make arrests, has been attempted only in very small municipalities, and with mixed results. In most cases these experiments were short-lived because they met with resistance from the citizenry, who felt that private police officers were insufficiently trained and prone to abuse of authority because, as private contractors, they were often not bound by the same rules of accountability as regular police.

Imagine, however, that in a Second Dimension scenario, the enterprise responsible for policing is held to account using a clearly defined set of indicators that are assessed externally. First, the chief of police is subject to a scorecard similar to the examples we saw in Chapter 11. His scorecard is, by extension, a performance evaluation for the entire police force, and it contains five-year targets for the reduction of crime, the success rate in the resolution of investigations, the recruitment and training of officers, and so forth. Crucially, just like the scorecard of the Community Leader to whom he is answerable, his scorecard also contains a substantial subjective element – a satisfaction score from the inhabitants of the Community. This balancing factor ensures that the police force does not overstep its bounds in pursuit of performance targets and keeps the desires of the general population in mind, who are likely to want effective but respectful and self-restrained officers patrolling their streets and answering their calls for help. Because the police chief is not an elected official, but rather is appointed directly by the Community Leader, it is up to the latter to decide whether or not to retain the services of his security firm at the end of each year. In all likelihood, however, the Leader would apply the same performance criteria to the police chief's tenure that he is subject to himself. In other words, he may take action if the police chief's overall score falls below the expected value.

In addition, the police force's financial health is affected by its score in the Utility Index. Its utility, as assessed by the tax authority, would vary depending on its success at improving various crime statistics in the Community it services. Clearly, the Index would have to be modified slightly for a sensitive industry like public protection. For a police force to do its job effectively and without interference, it must enjoy exclusivity (monopoly) within its jurisdiction, with competition coming into play only on contract renewal. Therefore, monopoly could not be a line item in the Index. The transparency indicator, on the other hand, would award a larger proportion of points. A poor Utility Index score would lead to the police force being taxed rather than receiving contributions from the BAG, thus jeopardising its ability to fulfil its mandate properly. A good score, on the other hand, would translate to increased earnings through the BAG system, allowing the police to improve or extend its services, or pay bonuses to its officers, or invest in new equipment or advanced training. The need to achieve a high Utility Index score at the end of each fiscal year would force the police to perform at or above the standard expected.

The key to this model of ownership in higher dimensions is to introduce a fair, transparent system of evaluation that is the same for all organisations, irrespective of their purpose. And, of course, to add the quintessential free-market element of competition to what used to be a government monopoly. This would create an intelligent system of incentives and disincentives with the goal of maximising each organisation's Utility Index score. The idea of treating all organisations the same, where no boundaries remain between for-profit, non-profit, NGO, charities, and other organisations, would bring in a paradigm shift, as each organisation, no matter what the type, would be evaluated holistically, ensuring a net positive impact on humanity.

The Valuation of Enterprises

Some of the changes proposed – separating ownership and control of enterprises, and evaluating the contribution of companies using the Utility Index – require a substantial overhaul of the capitalist economic model. Are these extensive changes really necessary?

It is not only the desire to mitigate income inequality and make everyone happier that motivates my recommendations. It is also obvious to me, from my many years of observing and participating in the daily churn of industrial production, that the last few years have brought such momentous and rapid changes in the way we make and sell goods and services that the current model of the free-market economy is simply not adequate any more. It cannot accommodate the new realities of 21st-century global commerce, capital flows, monetary imbalances, technological novelties, and inequalities in labour skills.

Let me illustrate with an example that concerns productivity. In recent years, there has been a tremendous and unprecedented rise in productivity thanks to the advent of new technology – production technology that involves automation, robotics, and artificial intelligence, as well as communication technology (smartphones, the Internet, etc.) that allows us to stay abreast of, and react to, every new development, with astounding speed and ease. At Organic India (which is partly owned by Fabindia), we recently acquired several new machines for packaging our organic tea. These machines take a herbal mixture (the production of which is also largely mechanised), fill and seal it into individual tea bags, attach a tag and string to each tea bag, place 25 bags in a box, check and seal the box, and then assemble 50 boxes in a carton – all without requiring any human labour. They use an artificial intelligence algorithm to analyse every step of the production process and respond automatically to any anomalies or malfunctions, and to recalibrate themselves once the error has been addressed. The older machines that we used for the same tea-bagging process used to require two technicians per machine to maintain and troubleshoot them. They were capable of producing about 60 bags per minute or 3,600 bags per hour, whereas the new machines can roll out 300 bags per minute or 18,000 bags per hour while requiring only one highly trained technician for every four machines.

If you do the maths to compare how many man-hours were required to produce 1,000 tea bags then and now, you will find that there has been a staggering fortyfold increase in productivity. This enormous rise in efficiency is greater than anything that the Industrial Revolution gave us. And it has happened with remarkable rapidity. Indeed, the older machines that we replaced were manufactured only fifteen years ago, though their operational design was essentially inherited from the

Industrial Revolution. The new machines, on the other hand, are not direct descendants of the Industrial Revolution; they rely on new technologies and represent an entirely new way of producing. This is happening in many manufacturing industries and will soon be happening in service sectors as well, as increasingly sophisticated software algorithms become capable of performing intelligent tasks such as design, analysis, evaluation, research, and training, by interpreting nearly unlimited amounts of data and applying a vast selection of templates to fulfil service needs.

My contention is that the current economic system is not equipped to deal with this sea change in productivity. The most dramatic repercussion of this development is that it will make millions of people redundant, especially at the lower end of the skills scale. It will lead to mass unemployment at a time when the world's population is still growing, and will result in much unhappiness and, ultimately, civil unrest. And it can only exacerbate income inequality, as those who own the new, highly mechanised means of production, as well as those who can invent and build them, will benefit from the new level of productivity far more than everyone else. My vision of a future defined by higher dimensions of thinking, though still unpolished, already addresses some of these problems. As I mentioned in Chapter 5, in the Third Dimension most citizens will devote at least 40 per cent of their time to non-lucrative occupations, including volunteering in their Community (30 per cent) and engaging in contemplative activities (10 per cent). Thus, much of the time freed up by improvements in productivity will find a useful outlet. (We must assume that wealth will be more evenly distributed by then, such that a reduction in work time will not translate into enforced poverty.)

Another significant change that has occurred in the last two or three decades is the amount of capital available for investment, and how it is allocated. Until the late 1980s, capital was scarce and was typically allocated only after scrutiny of the earning potential of an investment. Companies were valued based on the profits that they could be expected to generate, that is, on the potential returns on the capital they employed. Valuation could be done by forecasting cash flows resulting from profits and computing their net present value. Investors thus bought equity in firms with the expectation to partake in future profits by way of dividend distributions and, to a lesser extent, through the gradual increase in the value of the shares themselves.

This is no longer the case. Capital available for investment has grown rapidly in the last three decades and is no longer a scarce commodity. Consulting firm Bain & Company estimated that the value of global financial assets grew from $220 trillion in 1990 to about $600 trillion in 2010 – a threefold increase in twenty years. Today, total financial assets amount to nearly ten times the value of the global output of all goods and services. Moreover, Bain & Company estimated that total global capital would expand by half again, to an estimated $900 trillion, by 2020.[112]

The abundance of capital has led to new investment strategies, to changed attitudes on risk and valuation, and to new expectations about growth. The old model – betting on companies that are most likely to generate profits in the relatively near future – no longer holds sway. Some of the largest players in the new economy – Internet giants like Google, Amazon, and Facebook – have been able to obtain abundant funding without promising any substantial returns. Amazon is perhaps the best example of this trend. It made heavy losses for several years after going public, just as it said it would. It eventually began to earn a profit in 2001 and has done so consistently since then. But its annual profits are minuscule compared to its revenues, with net income usually in the order of 1 per cent. And Amazon has never paid a dividend to its investors, preferring to plough these small profits back into the business to fuel expansion into new markets and new product categories, and to gain an ever greater share of the retail market. And yet, Amazon's share price has continued to soar, reaching $1,900 per share in September 2018, up from just $250 in January 2015.

What has happened? Investors in new companies, especially technology companies, no longer care about annual dividends. They purchase stocks in companies or projects that they believe in. In Amazon's case, investors believe that its retail model works, that it will play an increasingly important and permanent role in the economy of the future, and that its vision and goal – making every product on earth available via a few clicks and deliverable to your door – are worthwhile. In other words, they believe in an idea, and they believe in the ability of its founder, Jeff Bezos, to turn that idea into reality. This is no more than the fulfilment of the prediction made by Bain & Company in their seminal report on global capital: 'In today's capital-abundant times, the ability to identify owners of good ideas and help them achieve their full potential will be the hallmarks of investing success.'[113]

If financial markets are already adopting this strategy today – invest in an idea that has merit and in people who can make it happen, without any expectation of returns – a similar attitude to company valuation and financing can prevail in the Second Dimension and beyond. In the capital markets that I envision for higher dimensions, valuation will depend largely on the Utility Index. Just as investors of the present have put their faith in the ultimate utility of Amazon and in the vision of its founder, investors of the future will also pour their money into ventures that provide high utility according to the enlightened values of their society. A company with a high score in the Utility Index will face a low level of taxation, and therefore will offer better returns than companies with a low score. It will also have the potential to add to its asset base by garnering credits through its activities. The Utility Index, rather than profits, will be the signalling mechanism to attract capital. Investors will gravitate toward equity shares of companies that are well managed and innovative, and that contribute meaningful products and services to society – all qualities evaluated by the Index. They will prioritise the idea embodied by each enterprise and its managers over the prospect of gaining from short-term returns.

Second and Third Dimension stock markets, therefore, will function much like current-day exchanges, except that many more entities that have no access to capital markets nowadays because of regulatory and structural reasons will enjoy the benefit of being able to obtain funding through the issuance of shares. Imagine, then, being able to purchase stock in an enterprise like MSF, which will not only be attractive to investors because of a high valuation and resale potential, but will also appeal to them because of the high utility it brings to society.

17

Money:
New Tools for a New Economy

Money and its Limitations

In Chapter 14, I discussed ways in which capitalism can be made more versatile and inclusive, to address the 'silent' demand of the poor, entire communities, and nature. Market-like mechanisms can be created by legislation, whereupon the natural dynamics of the market economy would ensure a fair trade in public and common goods. New financial tools, besides cash, can be created to facilitate the trade in goods that are intangible. For example, demand for biodiversity and natural landscapes can be generated by requiring that a certain square footage of forest be apportioned to each citizen, and allowing for the trade in a new unit (a meta-currency, the EPCQ) that results from this legislation. In Chapter 15, I discussed briefly other meta-currencies that might be used in the Second Dimension. This chapter revisits the concept of currency.

Currency, money, cash – these are various names for the same idea. Money is indeed just an idea, not a real thing. It is primarily a way to measure value, a generalised unit of measurement against which the value of different goods and services can be pegged and compared with a common reference point. As the variety of goods and services available in a society increases, bartering becomes too difficult, and a common unit of measurement is needed. At first, this unit was made of precious metal, giving it an intrinsic value of its own. But eventually (and especially after the Gold Standard was abandoned formally in 1971) money became just a piece of paper, worthless in its own right, or, in recent times, merely an electronic record in a computerised bank account.[114]

Money is thus just a token. It represents a promise made by the government that issued it via its central bank. A promise of what? A promise of value, of course, but also and especially a pledge that its citizens are empowered to use that money in any way they wish, that is, to exchange it in the market economy for any goods and services available there, with the approval and protection of the government. Money, ultimately, is a tool to enable and facilitate the market economy, provided it is issued in the requisite amount. In turn, a government's monopoly over the creation of money confirms its legitimacy in a nation state.

Because it had no intrinsic value, paper money needed two things to gain acceptance. First, it needed laws and a strong central authority to guarantee its value. Second, to create value, the government had to ensure that paper currency was accepted as the only legal way to trade; so, the state became the only body with the authority to create money, and the power to mint money became a defining aspect of sovereignty. The arrival of paper money created the banking system, which used interest rates to establish the value of money. Governments created many ways to leverage, from credit ratios to various types of financing that allowed businesses to raise capital, and they also created the culture of savings that allowed the surplus to be lent to those who needed it. In the 21st century, technology has made it possible for us to replace physical money with 'dematerialised cash' – credit cards and digital wallets in bank accounts that have dispensed with physical notes and coins.

Money works well in the section of the Spectrum of Demand where First Dimension capitalism operates. It works well because it allows individuals who have money to acquire goods and services that satisfy their needs and desires. Accordingly, I have relabelled the familiar diagram in Figure 17.1.

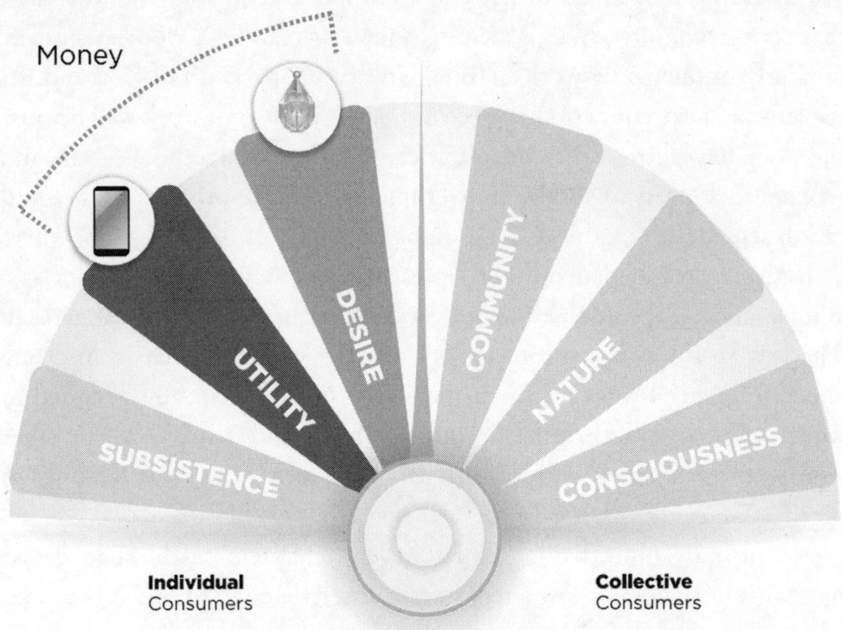

Figure 17.1: Role of Money in the Spectrum of Demand in the First Dimension

Begotten by the free-market economy, money suffers from the same limitations. The market economy functions efficiently only if it can measure goods and services based on what individuals, organisations, and governments are willing to pay for them. As soon as we enter a multivariate universe where it is harder to value public and common goods, collective services, common agendas, common security, and a shared environment, money ceases to work well. In capitalism, anything that cannot be allocated a monetary value ceases to have any value at all. Like the market economy, money is amoral. In a completely free-market economy, it can be used to purchase anything the consumer may desire, in whatever quantity he can afford. The effect of such purchases on other consumers, communities, and nature has no bearing on the use of money.

Money in its current form is like a hammer – a very useful and effective tool for a particular task, namely, putting nails in place. But we cannot use the same tool to do other, equally important jobs in the tool shed that is our economy, like tightening screws or planing a wooden surface. Similarly, money only works in one part of the Spectrum of Demand. At the left-hand extremity of the Spectrum, money does not work well because the poor have little of it and often cannot buy the essential goods and services they need to survive. Governments often resort to subsidies and ration schemes to fix this. On the right-hand side of the Spectrum, where collective forms of demand are represented, money, like capitalism as a whole, fails to capture the value of goods that cannot be easily monetised. The way to solve these problems is to diversify money, that is, to create and use financial tools (meta-currencies) that are specifically designed to work in the segments of the Spectrum where money is useless. In other words, to use a variety of tools instead of expecting the same hammer to be effective everywhere.

My primary objective in the last several chapters has been to devise mechanisms that will allow latent, unexpressed demand to find expression. This change is vital for the evolution of the human race and it is necessary for the transition to higher dimensions. Such mechanisms encompass a variety of initiatives that I have described in recent chapters, including the following:

- Legislative prompts to create market-like exchanges for common and public goods (see Chapter 14);
- The GNR, a new way to measure economic progress that assigns a monetary value to nature's bounty and, potentially, to intangible social qualities (see Chapter 15);
- A Utility Index, with tax implications, that encourages enterprises to be more efficient, innovative, fair in competition, and balanced in ownership, while delivering products and services that have high utility for society (see Chapter 16).

These initiatives and concepts are intended to bring to life every segment of the Spectrum of Demand, not just the part that addresses our innate need for comfort and pleasure. To formalise these initiatives and ensure that they can succeed, all that is left to do is to develop a specialised financial instrument or meta-currency[115] for each segment of the Spectrum.

Currencies and Meta-Currencies

In Table 17.1, I envision a set of five distinct financial tokens, all of which will still be issued and guaranteed by government, albeit by different levels of government.

Table 17.1: Types and Uses of Financial Tokens

Currency	Activity	Issuing authority	Use
Money/Cash	Purchase tangible goods and services	Nation	Individual fulfilment of utility and desire
Vouchers	Acquire essential goods	Community	Fulfilment of basic human needs (goods)
Targeted catalysts	Acquire essential services while creating incentives for the improvement of services	• Community Area	Fulfilment of basic human needs (services)
Apportionments	Create and trade units of public and common goods	• Region • Nation • Continent	Public and common goods
Debits/Credits	Compute the value of activities that are depletive or accretive to GNR and GGR, and allow them to be traded between governments	• Continent • World	Public and common goods

Schematically, the application of different currencies for different segments of the Spectrum of Demand looks like Figure 17.2.

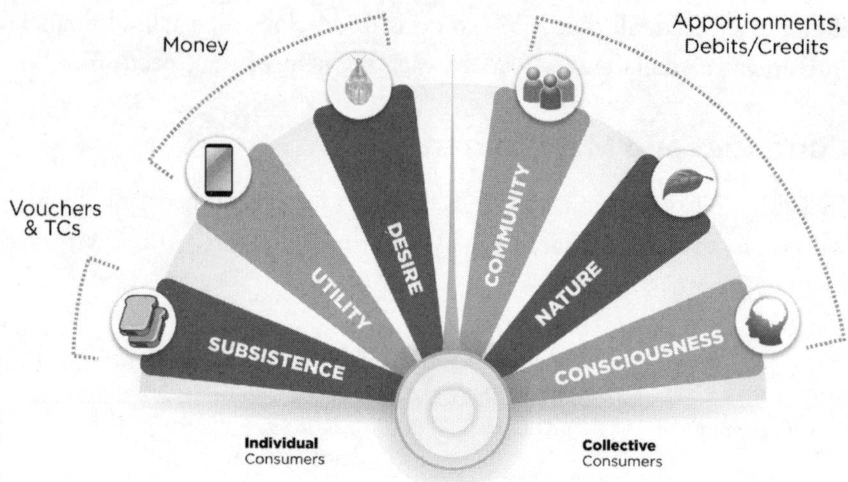

Figure 17.2: Currencies in the Spectrum of Demand in the Second Dimension

Vouchers and Targeted Catalysts (TCs)

Let us start on the left-hand side of the Spectrum. Table 17.2 shows a short list of goods and services that are essential to the subsistence of individuals and their integration in large, diversified societies. Without these needs being fulfilled it is impossible for any society to achieve its First Dimension rights and freedoms (see Chapter 7), let alone Second and Third Dimension rights and freedoms. Products and services like low-income housing and affordable healthcare exist in capitalist economies only if they are provided for free, or heavily subsidised, by government or charitable organisations. In the table, I have suggested that to modify the capitalist economy in such a way that these services are delivered effectively to everyone, we must rethink the very notion of money.

Vouchers and TCs are essentially alternative currencies that are restricted in use.[116] Vouchers may be redeemed only for certain essential goods, like food staples, toiletries, clothing, drinking water, cylinders of cooking

Table 17.2: The Uses of Meta-Currencies

Fundamental need	Meta-currency to address it
Nutrition	Voucher
Clean water	Voucher
Sewage and waste removal	Voucher
Household furnishings and wares	Voucher
Affordable housing rental	Targeted catalyst
Structured healthcare	Targeted catalyst
Basic education	Targeted catalyst
Legal aid	Targeted catalyst

gas, household wares like crockery and linen, and simple furniture. Stand-alone shops as well as supermarkets, retail chains, second-hand stores, and factory outlets would be able to register with a local voucher agency and accept vouchers as payment from their customers, and later exchange them for the national cash currency (money) through the same government agency.

TCs are used to acquire services, such as housing, healthcare, education, and legal aid. Like vouchers, TCs are issued automatically by the Community to families in need. However, TCs differ from vouchers because they are used to purchase services, not goods, and are designed to incentivise the service provider to give better service. This is because they have variable value: when redeemed, the value of a TC depends on the overall rating of the service provider. The rating, which depends on a set of criteria that include customer preferences, is directly linked to the multiplier applied to the voucher. This form of currency is called a targeted catalyst and not a voucher because a voucher has a fixed value associated with specific goods, while a TC can change in value depending on the performance of the service provider who redeems it.

Take a local school. If a school provides excellent education, it will receive a high rating. How exactly this score is computed and certified can be discussed elsewhere and could, in any case, vary from one country or one municipality to another. For a public (that is, government-run) school,[117] the rating could be the same as its principal's scorecard achievement for a given year, because the principal, as an appointed official in a Level 18 institution, is probably subject to scorecard evaluation (Chapter 11). Alternatively, we can envision a standardised system of evaluating school performance based on objective performance indicators, such as university enrolment rates and standardised test scores, but also on subjective elements, like periodic alumni and parent satisfaction surveys.[118] This could be certified by a Regional or National certification authority. Poor families would receive, from their community administration, TCs that allow them to enrol their children in the school of their choice. Depending on the family's income level, these TCs might cover the entire cost of attendance, or only part of it. A school with a high quality rating would be able to redeem the TCs it has earned from parents for a revenue higher than the face value of the TCs, whereas an underperforming school might receive less than the face value. This creates a win–win situation that gives the poor (who normally receive suboptimal public services) the opportunity to get much better services.

Table 17.3 shows a potential way to set up the system. It gives service providers (such as the local school in our example) a strong incentive to perform above expectation. A provider – whether he is an educator or a plumber or a landlord or a dentist – who has a low average rating due to consistently poor evaluations will receive only $60 when he redeems a $100 TC received in payment from his customer. A very good service provider, on the other hand, might receive as much as $200 when redeeming the same TC.

Table 17.3: Valuation of Targeted Catalysts

Redemption value of a TC with face value of $100					
Level of service provided (certified by a Standards Authority)	Very poor	Below average	Acceptable	Good	Outstanding
Value of TC ($)	60	80	100	150	200

Families can use TCs received from their Community to rent affordable housing (from registered landlords), send children to a school of their choice, purchase health insurance cover from a provider of their choice, and seek the assistance of a registered member of the bar to help enforce their rights.

The system of vouchers and TCs rests on two fundamental prerequisites. First, the economy must be entirely electronic. All transactions are captured electronically, so that there is no need for physical currencies, such as cash or food stamps. Every citizen must be equipped with an electronic smart card that records all income and expenditure. Many developed countries are already well on their way to a cashless economy, as most commercial and financial transactions are captured by credit and debit cards, electronic transfers, electronic bank accounts and wallets, and solutions like PayPal. But in developing countries, cash continues to be the primary form of exchange, with significant repercussions. In some countries, like India, the unreported cash economy is estimated to be as large as the formal one. Black markets, bribery, money laundering, tax evasion, theft, and many other problems result from the use of cash. By eliminating it and turning exclusively to electronic transactions, the entire economy would be brought to light, and much wrongdoing would be avoided. This 'dematerialisation' of currency can be achieved at minimal cost almost everywhere.

Second, every citizen's economic existence must be captured in its entirety (income as well as expenditures) and tracked over time in a unique electronic account known as the 'Aggregate Economic Activity' (AEA) record. This information will remain anonymous and confidential. It would be held in a decentralised citizens' database that will be replicated at each level of government and is secured by encryption using blockchain technology. Thanks to the full digitisation of currency, each citizen's AEA would be able to track all financial transactions and holdings that concern that citizen – income, expenditures, bank and credit accounts, investments, property value, and so on. This AEA would be compared periodically (say, every quarter) to a poverty line threshold. If the AEA falls below the threshold for, say, two consecutive measurements, then the system would automatically trigger the issuance of an appropriate number of vouchers and TCs from the Community to the individual or family in need. The AEA would be a transparent process, as opposed to the current blind distribution of subsidies. Its accuracy would be ensured by the fact that vouchers and TCs would be issued automatically once the AEA falls below the threshold.

Table 17.4 illustrates the AEA mechanism, using the annual income and expenditure statement for a household of five people in a poor country, such as India. The household is supported by just one working adult, an unskilled labourer who earns no more than Rs 12,000 per month (roughly $2,000 a year at the 2019 exchange rate). This is the family's only source of income, and it is shown in the column labelled 'Inflow'. The 'Outflow' column shows the AEA threshold (the amount needed to lead a life of basic human dignity in conformance with Second Dimension rights and freedoms) for a given year, as assessed for the particular city or district in which the family resides by the competent Area-level authority, and broken down into the specific goods and services required.

Table 17.4: Sample Aggregate Economic Activity of a Household

	Inflow	**Outflow**	**Currency**
Income as an unskilled labourer (tracked via the AEA)	$2,000		Cash
Family nutritional requirement		$3,800	Voucher
Family clean water requirement		$500	Voucher
Sewage and waste disposal requirement		$500	Voucher
Housing rent/mortgage		$2,000	Targeted Catalyst
Healthcare insurance		$400	Targeted Catalyst
Education expenses		$3,600	Targeted Catalyst
Legal aid contingency		$200	Targeted Catalyst
Total	**$2,000**	**$11,000**	

In this case, the table shows that the threshold is $11,000. The shortfall, therefore, is $9,000. In such a situation, the Community would automatically issue welfare payments totalling $9,000 to the impoverished family. Crucially, these payments would not be made in cash, but rather in vouchers and TCs, as shown in the right-hand column. The great advantage of offering vouchers and TCs, and dematerialising cash, is that local and regional governments would have access to data to measure the impact of the meta-currencies on their goal of eliminating poverty in the shortest possible time. The use of separate meta-currencies would also ensure that the funds can be spent only on essential goods and services, instead of on discretionary items like alcohol or potentially problematic investments like dowries.

Once the destitute begin to receive vouchers and TCs they will rapidly move out of poverty, thereby reducing the need for such subsidies to become long-term forms of welfare. Indeed, the aim of the programme is to gradually reduce voucher and TC payments to each indigent family over time, until the family can sustain itself without assistance. The electronic nature of all transactions and the focal role of the AEA would ensure that each family's progress toward self-sufficiency is measured and monitored.

From the point of view of the Community government, the goal would be to reduce the number of families receiving welfare payments as quickly as possible. As we saw in Chapter 11, this goal would feature prominently in the Community Leader's scorecard. The Community Leader and his team would be strongly incentivised, via the scorecard system, to implement policies and reforms to address fundamental issues like poor education, poor infrastructure, shortage of work opportunities, and ease of doing business, which have a direct impact on poverty.

Moving out of poverty with the aid of welfare payments seems like an optimistic goal, but it is not an unreasonable one. The purpose of welfare payments in the form of vouchers and TCs is to provide basic subsistence and services not only to address each family's day-to-day needs, but also to allow members of the family to take more risks that can pave the way to a better life. In *The Moral Economy of the Peasant*, anthropologist James Scott argued that in subsistence-level societies the exaggerated fear of possible failure prevents people from innovation and risk-taking. Thus, in our example, the head of the family would be reluctant to seek a better-paying job, or attempt to improve his skill set through formal training, because the risk of losing his meagre income and thus falling deeper into poverty is too great. Therefore, even though his job is menial and the income it provides is insufficient, he would nevertheless hold on to it out of fear of making his lot even worse. Similarly, poverty-stricken parents might not invest in education for their children out of fear of worsening their situation by giving up whatever small income each child can contribute through labour or begging.

The goal of voucher and TC payments, then, is to remove the constant worry of being evicted, losing access to electricity and sanitation, and having nothing to eat the next day. Liberated from such fear, poor family members will be more willing to take risks by seeking alternative employment, starting their own business, pursuing higher education, or investing in skills that will help increase future income.

Apportionments

The fourth currency-like financial tool (after vouchers, TCs, and cash) consists of apportionments. This meta-currency is intended to enable the trade in public and common goods by apportioning, or assigning, fixed units of each good to individuals or institutions. We have discussed apportionments in Chapter 14 in all but name when I introduced the notion of EPCQs for assets like forest cover and biodiversity. EPCQs are a type of apportionment, and the easiest to understand as they represent tangible natural assets. Let us see, in greater detail, how such an EPCQ could be calculated and traded. Assume, for simplicity, that every Community in the Second Dimension is required to support just one square metre of forest for every inhabitant. For a typical Community of 25,000 citizens, this means maintaining 25,000 sq m (2.5 hectares) of forested land within its municipal boundaries. That amounts to just under four football fields' worth of land, which is not a lot, especially for a rural Community, which may already encompass plenty of forest and have some fallow land that can be reforested.

Let us assume that the rural Community – let us name it 'Bucolica' – has 60 hectares of forest in excess of what it needs to meet its own apportionment requirement. It can use this surplus forest to sell its unused EPCQ on an exchange where apportionments are traded. Let us say that forest is trading at $2.50/sq m on the exchange.[119] Bucolica can thus sell its excess EPCQ of forest for 600,000 sq m × $2.50/sq m = $1.5 million per year. Who will buy Bucolica's excess apportionments? For every rural Community with excess forest, there is at least one urban Community – let us call it 'Urbania' – that is densely populated and heavily built up, and that may therefore struggle to reserve 2.5 hectares of land to satisfy the mandated EPCQ. To meet the requirement, Urbania would turn to the exchange and purchase the EPCQ units it needs.[120]

This way of distributing responsibility for environmental assets ensures, first of all, that such assets are valued, preserved, and maintained. In our example, Bucolica would have a vested interest, with a very real bottom line, to maintain its forest rather than logging it and turning the corresponding land into agricultural fields or suburban housing units. Indeed, with the help of environmental consultants, Bucolica could well invest in forest restoration to improve the quality or quantity of its forest acreage, so that it may one day fetch a higher price on the apportionments exchange. In addition, the apportionments system would help right many of the imbalances that plague First Dimension economies, starting with the divide between urban wealth and rural poverty that afflicts developing countries especially. Some of the wealth generated by urban communities would flow directly to rural ones, providing much-needed economic development in rural areas, and hopefully encouraging workers to remain there rather than migrating to overcrowded cities in search of better job opportunities. Apportionments will thus lead to more balanced economic growth, greater equality, and a much higher standard of social and environmental health.

An apportionment system could work properly only in the presence of clearly defined standards for the valuation of natural resources. Standards ensure uniformity in quality assessment, which is a prerequisite for the tradability of a commodity. Standards Authorities would be charged with developing classification systems for all those assets that may be traded, and creating a transparent way for pricing them. In the forestry example, the Standards Authority for natural assets would have created a formal rating system to value forest cover, which would take into consideration indicators like tree density, diversity of tree species, acreage of contiguous forest, and the number and type of fauna supported by the forest. Using the universal standard (universal because the Standards Authority operates at World level) issued by the Authority, auditors everywhere, whether employed by local governments or by private firms specialising in certification of natural assets, would be able to survey and grade forest assets, and certify them for trade in apportionment exchanges. A separate Standards Authority will be necessary for each major class of assets being traded in the exchanges.

In the foregoing example, we have seen how apportionments can be used to value and trade natural goods like forests, wetlands, coral reefs, beautiful landscapes, and watersheds. But they can equally well be used to trade undesirable externalities like pollution and waste in the same manner as CERs were used to trade carbon emissions. Imagine, therefore, that landfill acreage, sewage, and industrial waste could all be traded in apportionments exchanges. Moreover, apportionments can also be made to work in favour of social goods otherwise spurned by First Dimension, money-based, capitalist economies, such as high-quality investigative journalism, art film, and vaccines for diseases endemic in the developing world. The introduction of apportionments could provide the means to stimulate demand for these important social goods and render them tradable in the market economy by turning them into discrete units.

In Chapter 14, I imagined a scenario in which every cinema, in order to maintain its licence, had to devote 20 per cent of its prime-time screen time to films by independent production companies, and every magazine was compelled to devote a certain number of pages in each issue to high-quality journalism. These requirements could be grouped under one classification, namely, 'cultural apportionments'. And they, too, could be traded between enterprises that have too many and those that have too little.

Other legislative prompts imagined in Chapter 14 included the requirement that cities commission a number of new low-income housing units corresponding to the number of high-income units built by private developers within city limits; and that Big Pharma companies earmark a portion of their research budget to contagious diseases found primarily in developing countries. These proposals, too, could fit well in an apportionments system, perhaps grouped as 'infrastructure apportionments' or 'technology apportionments'. But whereas natural resources can be apportioned on a per capita basis, here social goods are being apportioned to institutions, including private companies and local governments.

In the Second Dimension, apportionments will work by creating a 'mandated demand' for certain things. The utility and desire parts of the Spectrum are powered by natural demand, which is essentially an individual's desire for something, and satisfied by the market. Mandated demand, however, is created by the government, which can encourage institutions to channel funds in certain directions, and so it mandates demand for certain goods and services with legislation. For example, an Area government could mandate that 1 per cent of the funds spent on any public building must go toward visual art in the building. Or it could require that for every person living in a housing development there must be at least 3 sq m of green space in the plan, thus encouraging developers to plan for parks and natural spaces in urban areas.

In the Third Dimension, however, there will no longer be any need for government intervention or legally binding rules. By then the effect of the Utility Index will be pervasive and ingrained in the mentality and operations of every enterprise, just like profitability is nowadays. The ever-present aspiration to achieve a better score in the Utility Index will naturally spur enterprises toward the creation and maintenance of desirable public and common goods valued by the Third Dimension, everything from pristine mountain lakes to kinetic art.

In summary, there are at least four types of mandated demand that can be covered by apportionments:

- urban and infrastructural development;
- fundamental research;
- natural resource protection linked to GNR and GGR; and
- aesthetics, natural harmony, beauty, and contemplative spaces and activities.

You might question why I place so much emphasis on artistic creation as part of the apportionment meta-currency. Art has great value in the Second and Third Dimensions, because it aids the awakening of consciousness. Kinetic sculpture, inspiring art film, high-quality paintings – all of these generate in the consumer a spirit of mindfulness, which is crucial to the development of consciousness. Seeing a Tim Prentice sculpture makes you think about wind and air and natural movement; it makes you recognise the presence of nature even in the most urban of settings. Hearing Vikram Seth recite poetry elevates the mind to a level where it notices patterns in sound and rhythm and begins to see how they are reflected everywhere, and thus perceives the interconnectedness of the world. Such realisations are vital to building a Third Dimension world, and therefore art must be built into the economic fabric of the new society.

Debits and Credits

Finally, there are debits and credits. This is the last meta-currency that must be introduced in the Second Dimension, and perhaps the most complex conceptually. Debits and credits, introduced briefly in Chapter 14, can be thought of as units needed to correct an imbalance. They are automatically generated with each activity or adjustment that is significantly depletive or accretive to the GNR or GGR. Once generated, debits and credits may be traded among government agencies and between different Communities, Areas, and Regions. They may also be traded among countries, especially if the accretion or depletion affects ecosystems across national boundaries.

As an example, let us take up once again the case of an Area government that has decided to fill in a wetland to create an industrial zone. This decision may have some beneficial effects, such as creating new jobs, but it will also have a depletive effect on GNR. Assume the depletion is valued at $55 million, caused by the loss of biodiversity and by damage to water catchment.[121] The depletion of the GNR triggers a debit of $55 million that the Area government responsible for this land use change must pay into a regional GNR fund. The Area may, in turn, opt to recover the debit value from firms that purchase or rent space in the new industrial zone.

A different Area government, on the other hand, may rehabilitate thousands of acres of previously unusable wasteland to create an ecological buffer zone filled with forest, waterbodies, or prairie. This would amount to an accretive adjustment to GNR of, say, $300 million, which, in turn, will trigger the issuance of a $300 million credit to the Area from the GNR fund. (At each level of governance, there would exist a special fund that can issue, receive, and allocate debits and credits generated by activities in its jurisdiction.) In this manner, accretions and depletions to the GNR are not only elements in the calculus of economics, but also a veritable financial instrument that can be traded.

We can also extend this concept to issues of continental importance, such as the development and water management of riparian systems. An upstream country that alters the course, or the water volume, or the rate of flow of a river – not unlike what China has done with the Mekong and, increasingly, with the Brahmaputra – can cause profound changes in the economy and livelihoods of communities that rely on the river downstream. In such cases, the credit/debit system would ensure that any changes, such as hydroelectric power stations or diversion canals, are undertaken only after extensive consultation of all nations affected. Rather than block all development projects planned by one country, the debit/credit currency would offer a mechanism to compensate affected countries for losses they might suffer, as well as reward countries that safeguard and improve natural resources and landscapes.

Making the Spectrum of Demand meaningful and effective will require that we create a complete set of Second and Third Dimension financial instruments to address adequately the full gamut of human needs. It is clear that the capitalist economy is good at addressing individual utility and desire, but weakens and fails to address subsistence, the needs of communities and natural habitats, and ultimately consciousness. To redress this imbalance, we must alter our approach to money, and, in doing so, we will progress on the journey to the Third Dimension.

Local Government Accounts in Higher Dimensions

To illustrate how the new meta-currencies (apportionments and debits/credits in particular) function in higher dimensions, and what effect they have on financial operations, I will use the example of Sewari, a small poor community in rural Rajasthan (northern India) that I know well. While staying there, I observed first-hand how the current economic system fails its citizens. As I spent more time in Sewari, I realised that it was not a poor community at all. It possesses valuable assets that are essential to the survival of humanity, but they are invisible to the First Dimension economy.

Assume that, in the future, Sewari has been constituted as a Community in a Second Dimension sense. Currently, Sewari has approximately 8,000 inhabitants. To become a Second Dimension Community, its geographic boundaries would have been redrawn to incorporate one or more nearby villages as well as all the land within, say, a day's walk from each village. I will call this newly defined and expanded Community 'Greater Sewari'.

Here are some basic facts and assumptions that apply to Greater Sewari:

- Population: 25,000
- AEA poverty line threshold (as in previous example): $11,000
- If we assume that 50 per cent of the population (approximately 3,000 families) falls below the threshold, then the *maximum* total subsidy[122] that could be paid out in vouchers and TCs is computed as follows:

  Subsistence liability = (AEA threshold) × (number of families in need)

  = $11,000 × 3,000

  = $33 million

How will the Community of Greater Sewari – apparently so poor – generate the large sum needed to fund its voucher and TC programmes? In fact, Greater Sewari is not a poor Community at all; it is poor only in the context of the First Dimension. Falling within its municipal boundaries, for example, is a large reservoir that collects rainwater and run-off from a wide catchment area of partly forested hills. In a semi-arid and perennially thirsty state like Rajasthan, this is a very valuable resource. In addition, the Greater Sewari communal land encompasses some unused and partly denuded forest land around Har Har Gange mountain, as well as a portion of the Jawai Bandh Leopard Conservation Reserve, a unique biodiversity area home to a significant population of wild leopard. In other words, Greater Sewari is blessed with three valuable natural assets that could generate significant income for the Community in the Second Dimension.

The citizens of Greater Sewari can decide to make a sizeable investment in these three natural assets to increase their quality and sustainability.[123] The Community could secure a loan of $100 million for various improvement and rehabilitation projects, distributed as follows:

- Watershed development : $35 million
- Forest regeneration, plantation, and fencing in Har Har Gange : $40 million
- Biodiversity enhancement bordering Leopard Conservation Reserve : $25 million

Servicing this debt would cost the Community $5 million per year in interest (assuming a low interest rate of 5 per cent on a loan provided by banks eager to fund development of a productive asset with stable, long-term returns).

Carrying out these asset development projects would also generate a great deal of local employment and provide new opportunities for local businesses, which would be prioritised in the assignment of refurbishment contracts. Once these projects have been completed, the Community would be able to claim credits for each one of them, because each project amounts to an accretion to GNR and therefore triggers issuance of credits from the global currency regulator. Such credits are a one-time inflow of assets and would thus appear in the Community's capital account (balance sheet). The Community could continually improve the quality of the regenerated forest, or expand its surface area, thus earning more credits at a later date.

Once forest areas and watersheds have been upgraded, the Community would also be able to benefit from them financially through other currencies. It might sell surplus water collected in the reservoir to other communities in Rajasthan that have need of it (building a pipeline having been part of its refurbishment project), thus earning cash income. Furthermore, once tracts of reforested land have been certified, and once the biodiversity improvements to land adjacent to the Leopard Conservation Reserve have been verified, the Community would be able to claim income for these resources through the apportionments mechanism, that is, by selling EPCQs to an urban Community (such as Rajasthan's capital, Jaipur) that owns insufficient natural assets to fill its own quota. Here are some figures for these transactions:

Income generated from forestation of Har Har Gange

- Area developed for reforestation = 22 sq km
- Forest EPCQ required for every individual = 1 sq m
- Revenue generated at $1.1/sq m = $24 million

Income generated from biodiversity near Leopard Conservation Reserve

- Area developed for biodiversity = 30 sq km
- Biodiversity EPCQ required for every individual = 1 sq m
- Revenue generated at $1.2/sq m = $36 million

Income generated from watershed management

- Area developed for watershed = 15 sq km
- Excess water not needed by Greater Sewari = 4 million kL
- Revenue generated at $2/kL = $8 million

We can now compile a simple income statement for Greater Sewari, as shown in Table 17.5.

Table 17.5: Sample Income Statement for Greater Sewari Community

Expenditure	**USD in million**	**Income**	**USD in million**
Cost of vouchers and TCs	$33	Sale of water from the reservoir (4 million kL at $2 per kL)	$8
Salaries of Community Leader and administrative staff	$5	Property tax income (assuming 5,000 homes at $200/home)	$1
Management of watersheds, biodiversity, and forests	$14	Forest apportionments	$24
Interest on capital expenditure at 5 per cent per annum	$5	Biodiversity apportionments	$36
Miscellaneous services (police, fire, public health, etc.)	$10	One-third of national cash transaction fees of 3 per cent	$1
		Miscellaneous contributions from higher levels of government	$1
Total expenditure	$67	Total income	$71
Surplus = $4 million			

As the table shows, the Community would not only be able to meet all its financial obligations, including voucher and TC payments to its poorer members, but in most years it would also enjoy a surplus that could be used for further enhancements to its natural asset base, or for other improvements (infrastructural or social) to the Community.

As noted earlier, Greater Sewari's asset-development projects will have had repercussions on its balance sheet. Reforestation and creation of a biodiversity area adjacent to the Leopard Conservation Reserve amount to accretions to the GNR, so the Community would be able to claim credits for them. What can the Community do with this considerable quantity of newly acquired credits? It would have two options to take advantage of its accretion assets:

- Use the credits to partly offset a depletive activity of its own – an environmentally harmful but necessary project like, say, building a new road or developing a new landfill.
- Sell the credits for cash on a global exchange. (The cash value of the credits would be determined by the demand and supply of credits around the world.) Ultimately, the credits would be purchased from the exchange by another Community that needs to offset a depletive activity. This transaction might require approval from the Area or Regional government, which would sanction it only under certain conditions. For example, the Area or Regional government might require that the proceeds of the sale be reinvested only in other asset-creating projects, such as foresting more land, setting up community gardens, stocking the reservoir with fish, or acquiring solar panels to generate the Community's electricity.

Sources of Government Income

The example using apportionments derived from natural resources shows that a Community can make ends meet and pull itself out of poverty in a relatively short time if the following measures are implemented:

- Use of multiple financial tokens (rather than just one cash currency) to address all aspects of the Spectrum of Demand;
- Local control of basic services (such as welfare) and revenues (such as property tax and natural assets);
- Automatic issuance of subsidies to the poor (vouchers, TCs);

- Valorisation of GNR assets within the Community's purview (debit/credit mechanism);
- Maintenance and development of such assets to generate a sustainable income stream (apportionments system); and
- Engagement of the entire Community in self-governance.

Furthermore, the example of Greater Sewari is a template upon which to build income statements and balance sheets for all levels of governance in higher dimensions. It relies on tried-and-tested First Dimension methods of accounting and finance, such as double-entry bookkeeping, the ability to secure loans against assets that can generate future revenues, and taxation of property. Table 17.6 summarises the sources of revenue that would be available, in the Second Dimension and beyond, to tiers of government above the Community. Individual items in the list are explained below. Tabulating similar examples for all other levels of national government (Area, Region, and Nation), as well as supranational ones (Continent and World) is beyond the scope of this book, as it might well test the reader's patience for accounting details.

Levies are a new form of corporate tax (introduced in Chapter 16). The performance of all enterprises will be evaluated on the basis of the Utility Index, and the score assigned by this Index will determine whether the enterprise pays a levy or receives a grant from the government under whose jurisdiction it falls. For example, a small business whose operations are limited to a few communities will either receive its grant or pay its levy to its Area government. A larger enterprise may have to pay its levy to the regional or national government if its operations are more widespread. A multinational corporation like Apple, finally, will either receive its grant or pay its levy at the global level. This system completely eradicates First Dimension problems like tax evasion and unscrupulous transfer pricing.

User service fees will be generated from the use of public or common services, such as highway tolls; disposal and recycling of garbage; rail lines, airports, or waterways; telecommunications frequencies and infrastructure; power lines; and tourism services.

Table 17.6: Level-Wise Revenue Sources in the Second Dimension

Government level	**Sources of revenue**
Area	• EPCQs (apportionments) on Area GNR assets • User service fees • One-third of national cash transaction fees of 3 per cent • Levies on enterprises with Area-only operations
Region	• EPCQs (apportionments) on Regional GNR assets • User service fees • One-third of national cash transaction fees of 3 per cent • Levies on enterprises with regional presence
Nation	• One-third of international cash transaction fees of 3 per cent • Levies on enterprises with nationwide presence
Continent	• National contributions (like the model currently used to fund the United Nations) • One-third of international cash transaction fees of 3 per cent • Levies on multinational enterprises (shared with World)
World	• User fees on international public services such as airlines, Internet, worldwide telecom, and shipping • One-third of international cash transaction fees of 3 per cent • Levies on multinational enterprises (shared with Continent)

The **3 per cent transaction fee** is an idea I introduced in *Making India Work*. This fee is collected whenever there is a transfer of 'dematerialised' cash, from paying for a cup of coffee, to buying a car, to purchasing securities in an overseas stock market. It is a flat 3 per cent fee that takes place any time there is a *cash* transfer (it does not apply to meta-currencies like vouchers, TCs, apportionments, and debits/credits). Receipts from this 3 per cent fee are split equally among three levels of government. If the cash transaction took place within a Nation, then one-third of the fee (that is, 1 per cent of the transaction value) is distributed to all Communities, one-third to Areas, and one-third to Regions. If the cash moves between countries, then 1 per cent of the transaction value goes to the Nation where the transaction originated, while the rest is split equally between the World and Continent levels (that is, they each receive 1 per cent of the transaction value).

The universal fee on transactions is not a novel idea. It is inspired primarily by the automated payment transaction (APT) tax, first suggested by Edgar Feige of the University of Wisconsin.[124] My proposal differs from Feige's in the size of the tax: the APT tax would amount to less than 1 per cent, whereas my transaction fee is 3 per cent. Moreover, whereas the APT tax hopes to replace all other forms of taxation, my proposal leaves in place property taxes (as discussed in *Making India Work*) and levies (a form of corporate tax, as discussed in Chapter 16, that is collected on the sale of products and services based on the manufacturer's or service provider's Utility Index score).

Neither in the Community-level income statement nor in Table 17.6, is there any mention of taxes on individuals. In particular, two forms of taxation used by all First Dimension governments are conspicuously absent: Value-Added Tax (VAT) and personal income tax. The former will be replaced by user fees and cash transaction fees, which are more transparent and efficient forms of indirect taxation. The abolition of income tax is in keeping with notions of personal and community responsibility that I have introduced elsewhere in this book. As you may recall from Chapter 5, in higher dimensions each citizen will be required to contribute a substantial portion of her working time and energy (30 per cent in the Third Dimension) to performing services on behalf of the Community. This amounts to a form of taxation, in labour rather than cash, thus both fulfilling an individual's fiscal obligation to society as well as keeping government human resource expenses low.

I advocate the abolition of both income tax and indirect taxes like VAT and excise for two reasons. First, such taxes are complicated to assess and collect, and necessitate vast national government bureaucracies. These bureaucracies are slow, inefficient, prone to corruption, and generally mistrusted by citizens. Moreover, they are yet another means of concentrating power at the national level while subduing local and regional authorities, as well as continental and global ones.

Second, I feel that the less governments (of any level) interfere directly in the lives and choices of citizens, the better off we all will be. I believe that in the absence of compulsory taxes wealthy individuals in the Second and

Third Dimensions will spontaneously exhibit high levels of philanthropy. To some extent this is already happening: I know several very wealthy individuals who have carefully structured their assets and income in order to reduce their tax burden, only to then give away a large portion of that wealth to charitable or public causes. How can we explain this odd phenomenon? Simply put, these fortunate individuals have already reached a higher level of consciousness.

Indeed, one of the defining measures of a successful Third Dimension society (as explained in Chapter 14) will be the amount of wealth donated by successful business leaders to public causes. Whereas such large-scale philanthropy, in the First Dimension, may be limited to a few ultra-rich and progressive individuals, in the Third Dimension it will be much more common, and it will be practised by all entrepreneurs who have met with success. Donations from such individuals will be channelled directly to social programmes and infrastructural projects. This, too, will reduce the government's need for tax revenue, such that personal income tax can be dispensed with altogether. The burden of supporting society will fall in substantial part on those who earn the most.[125] But unlike progressive taxation in the First Dimension, which is imposed by fiscal authorities, the impulse to contribute will come naturally to the wealthy.

How can I be certain of this? Generosity of spirit, concern for our neighbours, compassion toward the needy, and unwavering commitment to one's Community – these are the natural outcomes of a mind that has graduated to the Third Dimension, as I discussed in Chapter 3. On laws (Chapter 8), I posited that in their decisions Third Dimension citizens will be guided by conscience rather than self-interest. In Chapter 16, I showed how enterprises, too, can be guided toward responsible behaviour by modifying their ownership structure and by applying the Utility Index as the primary tool of evaluation.

These initiatives, once realised in the Second and Third Dimensions, will yield citizens who sport an entirely different disposition toward each other and toward the institutions of government than what exists now. Acting on conscience and dedication, the wealthy will willingly provide support, financial as well as personal, to all those activities and projects that the

Community requires to adequately fulfil all the needs and aspirations of its inhabitants. That the wealthy will eagerly disburse most of their wealth in favour of their Community's well-being is inevitable.

In the mid-1990s I met a local businessman who wanted to take advantage of a special tax exemption on charitable donations that I had managed to obtain for the Fabindia School in Bali (in Rajasthan). He wanted to make a large donation to the school with the proviso that we would return 95 per cent of it to him. He would thus avoid taxation on a big chunk of his money, while the 5 per cent that the school would retain for this transaction would still amount to a very significant contribution toward its operating costs. I was appalled at this suggestion of money laundering and refused his offer immediately. But over the following years I got to know the district where the school is located, and I realised that many of the institutions that helped the local population – a hospital and a vocational college, for example – had been built with donations from this same businessman.

Years later, shortly before he died, I met him again to pay my respects. On that occasion I asked him why he had wanted to avoid paying taxes by fraudulent means when in fact he was giving away most of his wealth to charitable causes in the district. He replied that he had arrived in the world without any clothes on and would leave it in the same way, but he considered it to be a 'moral crime' to give any of his hard-earned money to a state government, where most of it would be wasted because of poor management, corruption, and political wrangling. Here, then, was a wealthy man who was committed to improving the lives of his fellow citizens and willing to give away most of his wealth to do so. What prevented him from doing it through regular fiscal channels was his distrust of leaky, inefficient government bureaucracies. When allowed to contribute to society on his own terms, he was much more giving than anyone could have expected, and his overall financial contribution to the communities in his district was far greater than what his mandatory tax payments would have amounted to.

18

International Commerce: Creating a Global Unit of Settlement

A Brief History of Trade

Trade is as old as mankind, and it needed only a small surplus to come into being. The very first time that a nomadic hunter exchanged part of his game for, say, a sharper spearhead made by someone else, the concept of commerce was born. The gains in efficiency inherent in the division of labour – let the better hunter supply the food, while the more skilled stonecutter will manufacture the tools – must have been evident immediately. As humans settled into agricultural communities capable of generating surpluses consistently, the pace of specialisation accelerated until there were carpenters and smiths, farmers and cobblers, and weavers and bakers, all able to exchange their goods and services among each other. Settlements grew larger to take advantage of the proximity of diversified labour, regular markets were held, and guilds, industry associations, and cooperatives were formed to facilitate production and exchange. Sovereign authorities, from local chieftains to imperial rulers, sought to regulate, encourage, and profit from trade. To do so, they had to ensure a degree of security as well as basic travel infrastructure (roads and ports), so that goods could move easily. And they had to mint currency.

Currency is the lifeblood of trade. It was difficult for a weaver who needed new shoes to find a cobbler who happened to need a new cloak. So, a medium of exchange was developed to replace barter – an item recognised as representative of value. Obsidian, cowrie shells, and beads were used in some places, but eventually precious metals, like silver and gold, became the most common form of currency almost everywhere. The sparkle of precious metals appealed to everyone; so, their value was universally accepted. Moreover, their rarity gave them value even in small quantities, and gold or silver currency was compact and relatively easy to carry. These metals were not degradable, so they proved to be durable tokens that could change hands or be stored almost indefinitely. Precious metals were scarce, of course, so their supply could not always meet the demands of trade, so that baser metals like copper and bronze had to be employed as well. Minting coinage using such metals allowed the sovereign to broaden the scope of commerce, as well as to signal his authority over it.

The oversight of trade undertaken by kingdoms and empires enabled commerce to flourish on a much greater scale. Long-distance trade routes extended around the Mediterranean and across the Sahara, into the Middle East and toward the spice lands of India and Southeast Asia, and as far away as China with the increasing use of the Silk Route. The Silk Route brought the Roman empire in indirect contact with the Chinese Empire, especially because wealthy Romans developed a voracious appetite for silk garments. The Han rulers of China were able to keep the method of silk production secret and demanded payment in gold exclusively. Such was the volume of trade in silk that the Roman emperor Tiberius attempted to proscribe the wearing of silk to protect the empire's reserves of gold.

This early episode in the history of global trade encapsulates all the dilemmas that would vex monetary authorities subsequently. How can governments control the flow of capital and the quantity of currency in circulation? Is it wise to use items with intrinsic value (like gold) or alternative uses (like grain) as currency? How should global trade be regulated so that all players are satisfied and able to participate? When one country has an absolute advantage over another in the production of certain goods (for example, China's manufacture of silk), is trade nevertheless beneficial to both parties?

Improved seafaring technology, the establishment of overseas colonies, and formal support by nation states from the 15th century onwards brought new impetus to long-distance trade. The invention of the corporation as a means to deploy vast amounts of capital via the sale of shares ushered in an age of unprecedented global trade. First the Dutch East India Company managed to monopolise trade with the East by assuming government-like powers, including the ability to declare war, negotiate treaties, mint its own coinage, and set up colonies. Eventually its hegemony was superseded by the British East India Company, which in its heyday came to rule large areas of the Indian subcontinent, deploying private armies and exercising civilian administrative functions.

As a nation or empire or, indeed, a corporation achieved dominance in the trading world, its currency became the primary medium of trade. Various currencies enjoyed pre-eminence – the Spanish dollar, the Dutch guilder, and the pound sterling, to name a few. Trade was transacted primarily in these dominant coinages, which also served as reference currencies when money had to be exchanged. But as the volume of trade increased, it became increasingly difficult to carry large sums of money in metal specie, so traders and money changers turned increasingly to various forms of paper money, such as promissory notes (a promise to pay someone in precious metal upon presentation) and drafts (receipts for value held on account) issued by commercial banks, corporations, and moneylenders. Though used by the Chinese as early as the 7th century, these forms of paper money began to be used in Europe in the 14th century and became commonplace as a means of payment (that is, in general circulation and payable to the bearer as opposed to a particular individual) by the later 17th century. Eventually the responsibility to issue banknotes was taken over by government banks set up especially for this purpose. The Bank of England, founded in 1694, was the first to initiate the permanent issue of banknotes, and the first to issue printed notes in standardised denominations by the mid-18th century.

Originally, the banknote was simply a promise to the bearer that he could redeem it for gold or silver specie, but in 1833 it was ruled that banknotes would be considered legal tender. Such notes could be issued by many commercial and provincial banks, but in 1844 the Bank Charter Act restricted authority to issue new banknotes to the Bank of England, thus establishing it as a modern central bank with exclusive control of the money supply. At the same time, the Bank of England was allowed to issue new banknotes only if they were fully backed by gold reserves. This provision came to be known as the 'Gold Standard'.

The Gold Standard had become increasingly necessary because prior to it, commercial bankers had begun issuing a greater value of notes than the total value of their physical reserves, because they realised that it was unlikely that all their issued banknotes would be redeemed at the same time. This development was useful in that it morphed the simple promissory note into an opportunity to alter the monetary supply independently of the availability of gold specie or bullion. It led to problems of confidence, however, as creditors began to doubt whether the notes they held could indeed be traded in for gold or silver. Therefore, the acceptance of paper currency relied more and more on confidence in the bank or the government issuing it, and its ability and willingness to stand by its financial obligations. International traders looked increasingly to currencies that inspired trust and that could be counted upon to be a repository of value. In the 19th century, only a few currencies enjoyed the trust, intermittently, of the global trading community, especially when they committed to the Gold Standard. They included the pound sterling, the French franc, and the German mark.

First Dimension Financial Woes

Though firmly established by the end of the 19th century, the Gold Standard failed during the First World War, when many countries suspended it and resorted to inflationary finance. In the turbulent economic climate of the 1920s and 1930s, the Gold Standard was applied only briefly and unsuccessfully, but it was revived in a new incarnation in the aftermath of the Second World War. In the 1940s, Britain, the United States, and other allied powers began to plan for a post-war international monetary system that allowed nations the freedom to promote domestic policies that generated employment and well-being, while also maintaining an integrated but relatively liberal international system. The United Nations Monetary and Financial Conference, held at Bretton Woods (in the United States) in 1944, led to the formalisation of the Bretton Woods system, where forty-two nations agreed to a system of fixed but adjustable exchange rates where their currencies were pegged to the US dollar, which was itself convertible into gold. Under this modification of the Gold Standard, most countries settled their international balances in US currency, and the US government promised to redeem dollars held by other central banks for gold at a fixed rate of $35 per ounce.

After Bretton Woods, international exchange rates stabilised, and international trade flourished. This was also aided by a shift in US policy toward free trade. By lowering or abolishing many tariff barriers, the US sought to provide a vast market for the goods produced by foreign nations. The aim was twofold: (*a*) to boost the economic recovery of countries devastated by the Second World War, such as Japan and Germany; and (*b*) to foster rapid development and a commitment to the capitalist model in poor countries that might otherwise be drawn into the Soviet sphere of influence. The policy was successful, such that by the 1960s, Japanese and German industries experienced a miraculous rebirth and began exporting large volumes of goods to the United States. Before long, the United States was importing much more than it was exporting, leading to trade deficits that it could support only by issuing more currency. Supplies of dollars exceeded the gold that the dollar was linked to and began to undermine confidence in the dollar.

Thus, a flaw had appeared in the Bretton Woods system: there was no mechanism by which the total international reserves could be increased to keep up with continuously growing trade. There was no provision for increasing gold reserves or revising its price relative to the dollar. Market pressures became intense, with further strain on the US currency due to the Vietnam War. Eventually, US President Richard Nixon cancelled the convertibility of the dollar into gold in August 1971, signalling the demise of the Bretton Woods system. Soon after that, the monetary system turned to free-floating exchange rates determined by market forces.

One lasting consequence of the Bretton Woods experiment was the rise of the dollar as the world's pre-eminent currency and the preferred currency of international transactions – a clear reflection of the post-war military, political, and economic hegemony of the United States. Commodities like petrol and precious metals became permanently denominated in dollars, and foreign banks began to hold substantial sums of dollars in reserve. Indeed, though the Nixon Shock was followed by a decade of 'stagflation', with soaring prices, limited economic growth, and high unemployment, when world economies recovered they looked increasingly to the dollar as the reserve currency of choice. Thanks again to the political leadership of the United States during and after the Cold War, the dollar was seen as the safest repository of value of any liquid asset. Thus, foreign central banks began hoarding dollars, forcing the United States, once again, to create increasing volumes of currency.

In the absence of the Gold Standard, the dollar has become the world's favoured reserve currency.[126] Banks and investors everywhere have been storing dollars, thus sustaining the value of the dollar despite the continued creation of currency by the US government and uncertain economic fundamentals in the United States itself.

What happens to these massive dollar reserves held by foreign central banks? Much of these funds eventually find their way back to the United States in the form of investments by sovereign entities that regard US assets, especially government bonds, as safe investment havens. Japan and China currently own in excess of $1 trillion each in US treasury securities – the result of decades of exporting manufactured goods to the West. In October 2018, foreign investors owned $6.2 trillion of US debt,[127] or almost 40 per cent of the debt ($15.8 trillion)[128] held by the public. Such over-reliance on foreign investment has significant strategic implications. Were these creditors to suddenly sell off their treasury holdings, financial chaos would ensue. Moreover, the continuous influx of dollar investments in the US – to purchase not only government debt, but also private equity, insurance bonds, derivatives, and real estate – has often created investment bubbles during which financial markets were awash with cheap credit. The contribution of such conditions to the financial crisis of 2008 cannot be overstated.

The continued issuance of treasury securities to the public, including foreign investors, has allowed the US federal government to sustain a budget deficit since the early 1970s (except for a four-year period from 1998 to 2001, when it enjoyed a budget surplus). In the last few years, the budget deficit has been in the order of $400–800 billion, having peaked at a mind-boggling $1.4 trillion in 2009. This is the amount by which the US government overspends – the difference between government expenditures and tax revenues in a given year. In April 2018, the Congressional Budget Office estimated that if US laws remained generally unchanged in the future, federal debt held by the public would exceed 100 per cent of the GDP by 2028.[129] This would almost certainly lead the United States to default on its massive debt, likely leading to a global financial crisis of unprecedented proportions.

A mountain of debt, recurring financial crises, the near certainty of an economic collapse in the future, a widening gap between rich and poor, and the absence of consensus to make fundamental changes in the way we trade – these are the legacies of the First Dimension. It is the First Dimension's continued misuse of money that has tied the world economy in knots. As discussed in previous chapters, the pursuit of personal needs and desires by the majority of consumers in the majority of economies has created a skewed set of economic priorities and circumstances, misaligned with the goals of human well-being. First Dimension money, exemplified by the dominant currency of today (the US dollar), is one of the root causes of this predicament. In Chapter 17 I discussed how one currency is no longer sufficient to address the real needs of human exchange; nor is a currency so closely and uniquely aligned with the warped trajectory of capitalism adequate in a multifaceted world. The first step toward fashioning a Second Dimension economy, therefore, must be the creation of a new, independent global reference currency against which national currencies can be valued, exchanged, and managed.

A New Reserve Currency in the Second Dimension

The fundamental problem with the continued use of the dollar as a global reference currency lies in its dual use. On the one hand it is the national currency of one country, and on the other it is a universal currency used for international trade settlements and as a reserve. Indeed, in times of crisis and economic instability, the dollar, like gold, tends to be hoarded by investors everywhere. Thus the dollar is not just a currency, but also an asset class. These two purposes create different demands, such that a monetary policy beneficial to one is rarely suitable for the other. This impasse is known as the 'Triffin Dilemma' after the Belgian-American economist Robert Triffin who, in the 1960s, pointed out that a country whose currency is also the global reserve currency must perforce supply the world continually with excess amounts of currency in order to fulfil world demand, thus leading to an ever-growing trade deficit. Triffin warned that the use of the dollar as a global reserve currency created fundamental conflicts of interest between US domestic and international monetary objectives, and would lead to the collapse of the Bretton Woods system – which indeed happened.

The US domestic political preference would undoubtedly be for a weaker dollar to stimulate exports and employment. But the needs of the international market are more pressing. Continued international demand for dollars, especially in times of crisis, has propped up the value of the dollar, keeping interest rates low and perpetuating the imbalance of trade even when the underlying fundamentals of the US economy have been weak. In the past, the US response to this currency strength would have been to lower interest rates, which would force foreign investors to seek better returns elsewhere and thus lower the demand for, and the value of, the dollar. But as the Federal Reserve has laboured to stimulate the US and worldwide economy in the aftermath of the Great Recession of 2008, the so-called zero bound (interest rates close to zero) has already been reached, forcing regulators to look for increasingly esoteric methods to move the economy.

A viable answer would be to relieve the US dollar of its global role by creating a wholly new currency designed especially for international trade settlements. This idea is hardly novel. Already at the Bretton Woods conference, economist John Maynard Keynes had argued against the dollar having a central role in the monetary system, and proposed the creation of a new, supranational currency called 'bancor'. The bancor would be used as a unit of account to track international flows of assets and liabilities within a multilateral clearing system (to be named International Clearing Union). All international trade would be valued and cleared in bancor. Keynes, however, was overruled by the US delegation.

In the wake of the 2008 financial crisis, several political leaders, including British prime minister Gordon Brown and French president Nicolas Sarkozy, called for an overhaul of the global financial system, suggesting that a 'new Bretton Woods' was needed to stave off future financial debacles. In a speech in March 2009, Zhou Xiaochuan, governor of the People's Bank of China, revived Keynes's idea of an independent reserve currency, arguing that national currencies were unfit for use as global reserve currencies because of the Triffin Dilemma. He proposed an increased use of the International Monetary Fund's (IMF) Special Drawing Rights (SDRs)[130] as a centrally managed global reserve currency. His proposal attracted much international attention and discussion among economists.

My suggestion is to create a Global Unit of Settlement (GUS) with some of the attributes of the bancor and SDRs. In the Second Dimension, GUS will be used only as a unit of account, much like the SDR. All international trade would be valued and transacted in GUS through a number of licensed, automated clearing houses. Traders, multinational corporations, and other importers and exporters would thus exchange their national cash currency into GUS to participate in international trade deals, much as they do today with dollars and euros. GUS would also circulate directly among central banks to settle international transactions between sovereign governments.

Initial allocation of GUS to each participating country would be determined by the GUS's regulator (an institution akin to the IMF) on the basis of two factors: GNR and population. Let us take, as an example, an imaginary country called Futura that has a GNR valued at $5 trillion[131] and a population of 60 million. At the inception of the new global currency, Futura would be allocated GUS as follows:

GNR allocation:	$5 trillion × 1 GUS/$ =	GUS 5 trillion
Population allocation:	60 million × 1,000 GUS/$ =	GUS 60 billion
Total:		**GUS 5.06 trillion**

In this example, the allocation derived from population is small compared to the GNR allocation because Futura is modelled on an advanced economy with relatively high GNR (resulting both from extensive economic activity and careful tutelage of its natural assets) and a medium-sized population. The population element, however, would become more relevant when computing the total allocation to a poorer country that has a lower economic output but a much larger population. Thus, in the beginning at least, the allocation system would aid countries that are still struggling with burgeoning populations and low income levels.

Population and GNR change continually, and therefore the international agency issuing GUS would periodically (say, every two years) make adjustments to each country's allocation, either with a top-up allocation to account for increases in GNR and/or population, or redeeming part of the original allocation in response to net reductions in GNR and/or population. This biennial adjustment would also help resolve gross trade imbalances by curtailing the amounts of GUS that have accumulated in central banks as a result of excessive trade surpluses.

Fundamentally, the allocation system means that the quantity of GUS available in the world is determined by things – GNR and population – that change relatively slowly. Unlike the supply of dollars nowadays, which changes rapidly as the United States mints more money to fund its trade and budget deficits, the supply of GUS is not affected by demand. This makes for a more rigid international monetary system, but also a much more stable one. It means that the world economy would be able to grow at a pace no faster than the growth in the value of the assets that underlie productivity – natural and social assets that enable economic activity in the first place. Thus, GUS would insulate the world economy from excessive booms and busts: growth would be fairly modest, but sudden economic downturns would be unlikely.

GUS would not be interest-bearing, nor could it be used, at least initially, to purchase financial assets. These two provisions are important to prevent the imbalances that are plaguing the current monetary system from repeating themselves. Through the normal conduct of international trade, some countries (those that export more than they import) would begin to accumulate a surplus of GUS, that is, reserves of GUS in excess of their allocation. But the excess of GUS would not earn any interest from the global monetary authority (unlike SDRs, which do accrue interest). Moreover, central banks would not be able to invest these reserves overseas to purchase treasury bonds or other financial instruments, thus funding further trade imbalances. These simple measures are intended to keep GUS circulating; it is a nominal currency intended to facilitate trade, and as such it may not be hoarded. Moreover, the biennial adjustment to each country's GUS allocation would take into consideration not only changes in its GNR and population, but also the volume of GUS held by its central bank. Therefore, central banks found to have accumulated as trade surplus, say, 10 per cent more GUS than their previous allocation would risk losing the excess currency.

So, what could the government of a country that has accumulated excess GUS as a result of extensive export activity do to reduce its GUS holdings to normal levels? One solution, naturally, would be to stimulate more domestic demand so that its economy is less dependent on exports, and, indeed, to find ways to encourage imports by the domestic population in order to return the balance of trade to more manageable levels. As levels of consciousness increase in higher dimensions, however, consumerism is likely to wane. Moreover, such policies could require several years to yield the desired results. In the shorter term, the government could use the surplus GUS to encourage its country's businesses to invest (in the form of foreign direct investment [FDI]) in the economies of other countries, especially poorer countries with limited industry. Investment overseas – to build manufacturing facilities or service centres, train workers, and fund operations for the first few quarters until they become profitable – would necessarily mean selling GUS in order to acquire the poorer country's currency, with which to pay for local property, material, and labour.

This, then, would be the new reality of international aid. GUS surpluses would motivate extensive government-funded investments in developing economies, with the proviso that only a fraction of profits derived from those investments may be repatriated. This stipulation would ensure that companies benefiting from their government's handouts to invest in poorer nations would not be tempted to take advantage of those economies to make quick profits and then repatriate them to boost their income statements at home. Rather, it would incentivise multinational businesses to make lasting, long-term investments in poorer countries, complete with extensive educational and skills development programmes, expansion of local markets, and buildout of advanced local manufacturing and technological capabilities. This type of investment would quickly even the playing field between countries with different economic capabilities and accelerate the pace of development in poorer countries, such that citizens of poorer countries would soon be able to both produce export-worthy goods and afford imported goods, thus righting the trade imbalances that had led to the accumulation of GUS in the vaults of central banks.

What about countries that experience trade deficits and thus find that their GUS reserves are falling below their allocation? This, initially at least, would be the case of the United States, which has a large trade deficit with China and other Asian manufacturing hubs. Such countries would have to work hard to boost their own exports through a variety of both micro- and macroeconomic measures. In addition, they could develop programmes to augment their GNR (reforestation of degraded landscapes, for example) and thus receive an additional allocation from the global GUS regulator at the next biennial evaluation date.

Finally, how would exchange rates between domestic currencies and GUS be managed? By accepting GUS as a universal reserve currency, all countries would have to adopt a reserve currency standard, in which the reserve currency performs essentially the same role as gold did in the old Gold Standard. Each country's central bank would fix the value of its own currency to GUS;[132] and each monetary authority would be able to issue only as much currency as is backed by its reserves of GUS, which are, in turn, largely determined by its GNR and population, and subject to change only after periodic evaluations.[133] The role of the central bank in each country's monetary policy would be similar to that of a currency board and therefore quite limited, because the money supply would be determined by GUS reserves. Domestic interest and inflation would also be controlled almost automatically by the system, because the currency board may not alter the money supply and therefore also not be able to manipulate interest rates through open market operations or by raising or lowering discount rates. The peg to GUS would thus keep interest rates and inflation aligned with those prevailing everywhere else.

The advantages of a fixed exchange rate mechanism are well understood. It stabilises economies by preventing high inflation and reducing exchange rate risk, while forcing the country to pursue disciplined economic, fiscal, and trade policies. In particular, it prevents the national currency from appreciating or depreciating steeply, thus regulating capital flows and avoiding currency speculation. Its drawbacks, in First Dimension macroeconomics at least, are equally well known. Foremost among them is its inability to allow for adjustments in the balance of trade, compared to a floating exchange rate mechanism. I have discussed, however, how large trade deficits and surpluses would be addressed by a global monetary system where GUS earned in excess of a country's allocation are forced to circulate rather than being hoarded.

It is also important to remember that in the Second Dimension and beyond, the new universal reserve currency would be functioning in the geopolitical environment described in Chapter 13. In such an environment, the behaviour of nations – financial and monetary, as well as humanitarian, judicial, and political – is subject to continual monitoring and correction by Global and Continental assemblies (to an extent that is inconceivable today, when the concept of sovereignty is still the guiding principle of international interaction). The ability of international forums to intervene in domestic governance in support of universal human rights would impact domestic monetary policy as well, quickly bringing in line countries with dysfunctional economies or unsustainable monetary regimes. In such a future, where the economic goals of all nations are aligned and gross imbalances in trade, per capita income, and access to financial markets have been righted, there is no reason why a fixed exchange rate mechanism that is based on a reserve currency standard and allows for periodic adjustments could not be successful.

Changing the Terms of Trade

Using GUS as an international trade currency would help right the imbalance in the terms of trade that has kept many developing countries in poverty in recent times. (Terms of trade is the ratio of a country's export prices to import prices, or, the amount of imported goods that an economy can purchase per unit of goods it exports.) According to the Singer-Prebisch thesis, the terms of trade for underdeveloped countries relative to richer countries deteriorate over time as poorer countries can purchase fewer and fewer high-end manufactured goods from developed countries in exchange for a given quantity of their own exports. Such exports typically consist of raw materials, agricultural commodities, and simple manufactured goods like clothing and furniture, which can be made by cheap, relatively unskilled labour. For example, a poor economy like Bangladesh must export an ever greater volume of clothing in order to continue to purchase, say, the latest models in commercial aviation technology (such as an Airbus A380 or Boeing's Dreamliner) from Western countries.

The Singer-Prebisch thesis is a cornerstone of dependency theory, which suggests that resources flow from poor, underdeveloped states to wealthier ones (or from countries in the 'periphery' to those in the 'core' of the world system, to use Immanuel Wallerstein's terminology), enriching the latter at the expense of the former. The theory implies that the very structure of the global market leads to persistent inequality. According to a traditional understanding of dependency theory, the main cause of the dependency relationship between core and periphery is the inability of the periphery to develop an autonomous and sustainable process of technological innovation. The core countries control technology and the intellectual and organisational systems required to generate it. FDI in underdeveloped economies can lead to a limited transmission of technology, enough required to conduct some manufacturing activities, but not the culture of innovation itself.

Neo-Marxist interpretations of dependency theory,[134] however, have argued that the fundamental disparity that causes dependency is not technological, but financial. The core countries control not only the consumer markets and therefore the prices of goods, but also and especially vast financial markets that are more sophisticated than any in the developing world. They also control the reserve currencies (dollar and euro) that govern transactions in these markets. As a result, peripheral countries are mostly dependent on dollar-denominated debt to fund large-scale economic development. But they cannot access foreign debt markets because, crucially, they cannot borrow overseas funds in their own currency. For any long-term investment, the risk that the local currency will be devalued against hard currencies is too high. This means that local firms rarely have enough capital to engage in significant development of high-end manufacturing or in the education and research necessary to create a knowledge economy. They are condemned, therefore, to ever-worsening terms of trade, and to dependency.

In the global monetary system proposed here, the imbalance in terms of trade would be rectified by two instruments. First, as discussed, the introduction and use of an independent, neutral currency (GUS) to denominate international trade and act as a reserve currency would reduce the hegemony of rich countries over financial markets, and thus allow poorer countries to borrow with a reduced risk of currency devaluation. In practice, a company in a poor country would be able to fund expansion, or development of a new product, by borrowing overseas debt denominated in GUS. With exchange rates pegged to GUS, the loan would not represent an excessive risk for the borrower. The ability to borrow with no risk of currency devaluation would allow nascent economies to access the funding that Western financial markets have hitherto denied them, and they would be able to grow organically as the playing field is evened.

Second, as discussed in previous chapters, poor countries with limited manufacturing know-how and nothing in the way of a knowledge economy could nevertheless increase their participation in global trade by safeguarding and valorising their natural assets. The value of these assets – such as forest and coastline, wetland and prairie, glacier and riparian landscape – would be traded with industrialised countries through the mechanism of apportionments that I have already described. In addition, the use of debits/credits to account for changes in GNR would mean that poor countries could gain significant credit flows by simply turning more of their surface area into national parks, by rehabilitating blighted landscapes, reforesting and maintaining denuded hillsides, or restocking degraded forests with wildlife. These conservation and regeneration activities can be accomplished with relatively small capital investment while employing substantial numbers of workers. Once accomplished, they repay local communities twofold: (*a*) they create a credit, which a Community can use to offset debits it may have created through development activity, or it can sell it to a debit-laden Community elsewhere through an exchange; and (*b*) each regenerated natural asset, if maintained well, can become a long-lasting source of income through the apportionments system.

Apportionments and debits/credits are two meta-currencies intended to create a sustainable trade in natural assets. Once fully established and functional in the Second and Third Dimensions, they would radically change the profile of international capital flows. Excluding flows of funds related to trade, international capital flows received by poor countries typically include the following:

- FDI – investment in local industry by foreign corporations, such as building a new manufacturing plant;

- Portfolio investment – purchase of local financial assets (equities, bonds, etc.) by overseas investors;
- Official development aid – funds donated by foreign governments and international agencies to stimulate economic development or to improve standards of living;
- Remittances – money earned overseas by migrant workers and sent back to their families.

Let us look at the size of these capital inflows for a poor country, using Nepal as an example.[135] Table 18.1 shows recent estimates of capital flows into Nepal, in order of magnitude.

Table 18.1: Estimates of Recent Capital Flows into Nepal (2016)

Capital inflow	Amount (USD million)	Source
Remittances	6,612	World Bank
Official development aid	1,066	World Bank
FDI	106	World Bank
Portfolio investment	Negligible	–

The list of capital inflows provides a telling snapshot of Nepal's weak economy. Its GDP was just $21 billion in 2016, and remittances from abroad represented a whopping 31 per cent of that because a significant proportion of Nepalese workers have migrated abroad in search of a better livelihood. FDI was small because of continuing political instability in the country, and because of the severe dearth of skilled labour. And due to poorly developed financial markets, there was virtually no portfolio investment.

Indeed, Nepal is one of the poorest and least developed countries in the world, with about one-quarter of its population living in poverty. Agriculture is the most important economic activity, providing a livelihood for about 70 per cent of the population and making up one-third of GDP. Industrial activity is limited to processing of agricultural products and some textile and carpet manufacture. The only service sector that is somewhat developed is tourism connected to trekking and mountaineering. There is considerable potential for hydropower generation, but it is unlikely to be realised in the near future due to political uncertainty and a difficult business climate.

Nepal does not have any significant deposits of natural resources – not, at least, in the First Dimension understanding of that term. However, it does have abundant forests, covering 25 per cent of its land surface (though it is threatened by rapid deforestation, such that only one-tenth of this forest is considered relatively intact primary cover). Nepal also has extensive riparian systems and spectacular high-altitude landscapes in the Himalayas. Now imagine that these areas could be assigned a monetary value in the Second Dimension. After being given a value as part of Nepal's GNR, the worldwide demand for natural assets engendered by the creation of apportionments would encourage local communities to protect their forests, rivers, and mountain landscapes to earn apportionment income. Part of this income, in turn, could be reinvested in environmental rehabilitation of degraded forest and waterways, thus increasing the potential income in apportionments and generating a net inflow of credits for accretions to GNR. Though the volume of these capital inflows is difficult to estimate, it is easy to see that they could rapidly rise to a level that would dwarf current capital inflows. At the same time, such economic opportunity would encourage more of Nepal's working population to remain at home and work in the new environmental industry (if we can call the tutelage and enhancement of the environment an industry) rather than to seek their livelihood abroad, often in the most menial jobs.

First Dimension economists will say, no doubt, that a rapid development of environmental assets would turn Nepal into a pastoral economy afflicted by Dutch Disease. (Dutch Disease is the harmful effect on an economy of anything that causes a sudden inflow of foreign currency, such as the discovery of significant oil reserves. Large currency inflows lead to appreciation of the local currency, making the country's other products less competitive on the export market, thus weakening the country's industries.) But in higher dimensions the occurrence of Dutch Disease would be mitigated by several factors. As I have argued above, Nepal's national cash currency would be insulated from sudden appreciation by the new monetary order. Moreover, the pace of cash inflows would be slow because of the very nature of the assets attracting foreign investment. Imagine how long it takes to grow a forest from scratch, or to restore a certain level of biodiversity to a natural landscape – considerably more time than it takes to extract petroleum, for example. Finally, foreign investment would be limited to manageable levels by the fact that the world supply of GUS – the very fuel that makes international investment and commerce possible – is limited.

Currency Union in the Third Dimension

The ultimate purpose of GUS is to serve not only as a global trading and accounting unit, but also as the local currency everywhere. In other words, eventually to replace national currencies with a single currency that is legal tender in every corner of the globe. This the logical extension of a currency board system in which all national currencies are pegged to the reserve currency.

The concept of a reserve currency used as legal tender in multiple countries is not far-fetched. Since 1999 we have been able to observe a multinational currency in operation: the euro. By some accounts the euro has been a success, yielding great benefits to consumers and businesses throughout Europe. By eliminating exchange rate fluctuations and transaction costs, the euro brought increased cross-border trade, facilitated travel and tourism, and ensured greater transparency. It also fostered solidity in financial markets and macroeconomic stability; and as a result of decreased exchange-rate risk, it lowered interest rates. Above all, the euro has been a powerful motor of cultural integration.

However, in its short lifespan the euro has also been plagued by uncertainty and fluctuations in value. It has also exposed the political and economic incompatibility of the countries in the eurozone. Though at first glance these countries – all advanced economies with relatively stable, democratic governments – seemed like good candidates for a joint monetary undertaking, the pressure of currency union exposed all their fundamental differences in working culture, fiscal policy, economic fundamentals, and political profile. Yet, to maintain a successful single currency, economic decisions had to be taken in cooperation with all members. This led to deep and acrimonious rifts between various members, laid bare especially by the Greek debt crisis of 2010–2015.

The euro experiment continues to stumble along, simply because a return to an independent national currency by one of the eurozone members might be too catastrophic to both financial markets and the dream of a politically unified Europe. But its travails have shown clearly that monetary union should be attempted only by countries that share a very similar economic programme and an identical commitment to values of stability, transparency, equality, fiscal responsibility, and continuous improvement. This state of affairs may come about only when a critical number of countries have transitioned to the Third Dimension. Adopting GUS as a universal currency, therefore, must wait for a Third Dimension future.

Part V

METHODS

19

Education: Schooling for Mindfulness and Insight

In the preceding sections I have elaborated a comprehensive set of policy proposals to reform all the administrative and economic systems that are necessary for the effective operation of an enlightened, fair, and compassionate society in the near future. Armed with these intellectual and institutional building blocks, the reader may now begin to recognise the main contours of life and social exchange in the Second Dimension and beyond.

In this section, I will address four aspects of modern life that are not directly connected to governance but are nevertheless indispensable to sustain an advanced society: education, agriculture, health, and scientific inquiry. I have grouped them under the title 'Methods' because I believe that the very way in which we practise learning, nutrition, medicine, and science can help us attain higher levels of consciousness. I begin here with what may well be the most direct means to do so, namely, education.

Education in a First Dimension World

Premodern education was a form of social and cultural indoctrination, transmitting certain cultural values through religious training and apprenticeship in guilds. In many premodern societies, social class or caste determined one's occupation and trajectory in life, so that most individuals ended up in the same craft or profession as their fathers. Literacy was limited to a tiny fraction of the population: the ruling elite, the scribes and clerks who managed the affairs of state on their behalf, and the keepers of religious authority.

Formal education as we know it did not exist for the majority until the advent of the industrialised schooling system in the 19th century. The educational systems in place throughout much of the world today reflect the great strides – secularism, the Enlightenment, the Scientific and Industrial Revolutions – made by Western societies during the last few centuries. But these advances have also brought with them their own limitations.

From observation, I believe that First Dimension schooling systems are broadly based on four principles.

Functional Literacy

Functional literacy teaches students to read, write, do maths, and, ideally, to think logically. Unfortunately, in many countries, most students end up receiving only minimal functional literacy. In India, for example, literacy and enrolment rates have climbed steadily over the last few decades, but the country still has several million children who do not attend school. Among those who do attend, dropout rates are high, and functional literacy is inadequate. UNICEF reports that less than half of India's Class 5 students are able to read Class 2 texts.[136]

Conceptual Frameworks

In most societies, 'packages', or prescribed lists of things that everyone must learn, are delivered to learners. Conceptual packages are especially prominent in societies that seek to educate populations in the shortest possible time, such as India. Such packages are organised around fundamental theories, that is, they are based on received, rather than observed, wisdom. These frameworks encourage instructors to teach students as a collective, ignoring students' individual strengths, weaknesses, and interests. Exercises for developing writing skills, for example, emphasise set patterns of organising thought (the introduction–body–conclusion structure, for example), instead of any creative, critical, or innovative thinking.

Quantitative Frameworks

This principle, which I call 'positivist-utilitarian', assumes that something that cannot be quantified is less valuable or less relevant. There is a distinct focus on skills that are fit for quantitative domains, such as mathematics and science. Even in qualitative subjects, there is a tendency to teach and measure progress in quantitative ways – think of point deductions for specific grammatical errors, such as split infinitives or incorrect verb–subject agreement; or having to learn a certain number of new words per week; or teaching writing by subdividing every written assignment into standard parts or numbered lists. As a result, quantitative frameworks shape the way we think, and we tend to value things that can be seen and measured materially; we disregard the subtler aspects that arise from the intuitive mind. Most of us, for example, think of development or progress in terms of physical infrastructure like roads and hospitals, while the most important aspect of development, as the economist and philosopher Amartya Sen has pointed out, is the enhancement of certain abstract capabilities, like the freedom and autonomy to make one's own choices.

Increasing Specialisation

The nation states where modern education took shape were characterised by a sophisticated division of labour, which required the development of specialised skills. Specialised study in subjects such as physical science, engineering, law, medicine, philosophy, and language led to a vast compilation of knowledge that quickly became impossible for any one individual to absorb. The real and practical need for specific expertise eventually led to the superspecialisation we see in scholars, engineers, and managers today – specialisations within specialisations. An unfortunate side effect of this trend has been tunnel vision and a lack of balance in learning: schools administer learning in discrete, independent subject areas, with little or no effort to provide an overarching context for all learning.

In many of the educational systems in use today, students begin the process of specialisation in secondary school, by choosing certain subjects, or indeed entire curricula, over others. When they enter universities, they must select a specific field of knowledge (a major or faculty), either immediately or within the first two years. Postgraduate education further narrows the focus of their efforts. This is often true of vocational education as well. At first, an apprentice in an auto mechanic's shop will learn generic skills, such as how to change the engine oil or balance a new tyre, but he will gradually concentrate on a particular brand of car or a specific part of the engine. Maintenance of today's sophisticated automobiles, which have complex fuel injection systems, numerous sensors to enable everything from automatic transmission to airbag deployment, and a variety of electronic control units, requires highly specialised skills. This is increasingly true of most hands-on professions.

Limitations of the First Dimension Education Model

In many ways, education in the First Dimension is a great leap from the way children were taught earlier. Like most First Dimension ideas, however, it has drawbacks. In most schools, education in the First Dimension has become a procedural and dispassionate process. Children are mass-taught in institutions that pay no heed to a child's inner workings or unique needs. As renowned educationalist Sir Ken Robinson has argued, an industrial, 'one size fits all' method is used to train children and young adults by administering pre-formatted educational packages, resulting in a society largely devoid of inquisitiveness, intuition, and insight.[137]

Moreover, the whole system is an alienating one. To quote the philosopher Ivan Illich,

> Schools are designed on the assumption that there is a secret to everything in life; that the quality of life depends on knowing that secret; that secrets can be known only in orderly successions; and that only teachers can properly reveal these secrets. An individual with a schooled mind conceives of the world as a pyramid of classified packages accessible only to those who carry the proper tags.[138]

In its current formulation, education encourages students to approach fundamental components of learning in isolation and focuses their attention on explaining how individual causes bring about individual outcomes. This forces the mind into a mental straitjacket, limiting the development of higher-order mental capacities. The world is not a collection of separate cause-and-effect pairs but, rather, a web of interdependent phenomena (natural, social, and psychological).

The First Dimension educational system prepares the student for a First Dimension world in which what cannot be measured does not matter and the narrower your focus the better you will fit into the job market. The system is also largely responsible for the increasing contemporary tendency towards 'complexification' that leads to students being pushed towards useless specialisations. While a certain amount of specialisation is necessary, the amount of knowledge in each discipline has increased exponentially, and as the range of specialisations has increased, their breadth has decreased to an extent that precludes leaving the field of specialisation without great difficulty.

Anyone familiar with early childhood, however, will know that this compartmentalised, reductionist format for the acquisition of knowledge is not at all innate. In fact, young children are often capable of original, intuitive, and unfettered understanding based on observation, simple reasoning, and direct insight. But in most societies throughout the world, the immense potential of a child's mind is quickly stymied by the institutionalised nature of education. In their book *Breakpoint and Beyond: Mastering the Future Today*, educators George Land and Beth Jarman showed that our innate capacity for divergent thinking (the capacity to be creative) diminishes as we grow older and is hampered rather than encouraged by traditional educational systems. When tested as kindergarteners, 98 per cent of the study's subjects scored at a high level ('genius level') in a test that sought to quantify their divergent thinking, but when retested at age ten, only 32 per cent of the same children scored at that level. That proportion had sunk to 10 per cent by age fifteen. When the same test was administered to adults, only 2 per cent scored at genius level.

The First Dimension education system tends to limit every child's potential for creativity by perpetuating three outcomes, namely, *alienation, grinding,* and *disciplining*, which, in combination, result in the curbing of a child's innate intuition and open-mindedness.

Alienation results from the separation of a child from the environments to which he naturally belongs, and in which interdependencies are at work, that is, family, nature, and society. Students instead inhabit artificial and controlled spaces for the most productive parts of the day during the most impressionable period of their lives, with access denied to the contexts in which they are best equipped to grow and thrive.

Much of this alienation arises from the very spaces – the school buildings – in which education is administered. Most traditional school structures are similar: a series of quadrangular rooms opening on to long, amorphous hallways, with the addition of a few uninspiring common areas (gym, library, cafeteria) at each end. I once visited a school in Phnom Penh, Cambodia, and I noticed that it looked almost exactly like the many Indian schools I had visited in the past. I could immediately guess where the principal's office was and where each classroom would be located. How can different schools in different countries, built decades apart, look identical? How can they be so similar that I automatically knew the layout? There is something much too rigid and fabricated about schools in the First Dimension: they stay consistent across time and space, without any changes being made to reflect the environment or the unique needs of the students. Underprivileged schools also tend to lack outdoor areas, as well as open spaces to carry out activities and experiments conducive to practical, hands-on, interdisciplinary learning.

Alienation also arises from the reliance on conceptual and quantitative frameworks that appear divorced from everyday reality. It is not uncommon for children to wonder how learning seemingly abstract subjects like trigonometry or Sanskrit grammar, without practical contextualisation, can possibly improve their lives or make them better citizens. The kinship between narrowly defined academic subjects and their potential usefulness in private or professional pursuits is often too tenuous for the average learner to recognise. It leads to apathy or even active dislike of entire subjects.

By separating knowledge into distinct domains and reducing it to readily identifiable academic 'skills', this system prevents learners from recognising interdependencies and appreciating the value of unquantifiable attributes like compassion and generosity. By teaching ethics as a subject, for example, the current system of education turns a disposition into an academic pursuit. We cannot teach science and ethics separately, but the two are usually taught in this manner.

Studying subjects in isolation contributes to increasing specialisation as the student progresses in the educational system. This tends to alienate him from other knowledge domains and the very consequential interconnections between them, and from the role played in greater society by the very subject in which he is specialising.

Grinding is the result of students spending years in regimented First Dimension educational environments. We often forget how physically, mentally, and emotionally tiring the process of learning can be under the prevailing system of education. The more students are saddled with tasks, homework, tests, assignments, and deadlines, the more they are worn down. This continual tiredness has a disabling and dulling effect on the student, with their minds and bodies losing the ability to mend themselves. Much of this grinding effect is due to the manner in which functional literacy is achieved in many educational systems: the inculcation of information in discrete, unrelated packages; frequent repetition; homework exercises; and continual testing to measure learning levels.

Even in some Western societies, where education has made significant strides toward a more holistic vision of learning, the risk of regressing to a grinding process is ever present. As educationalist Tony Wagner has shown,[139] for example, the No Child Left Behind initiative in the US, well meaning though it was, relied almost exclusively on standardised testing to measure its effectiveness. This resulted in many subjects being taught entirely with a view to improving test scores rather than improving understanding of the underlying concepts.

Disciplining has become almost synonymous with education. Many aspects of the First Dimension education system can function only by disciplining the behaviour of students. The numerous ways in which students are expected to be and behave – the ingraining of the necessity of order, success, and patriotism – are important values, but they are often wrongly articulated. Disciplining results in a proclivity to convention over innovation, following instead of leading, and copying rather than creating.

These three aspects of First Dimension education result in a gradual curbing of each child's innate desire to learn, leading to the death of certain faculties that are critical to the development of consciousness, namely, curiosity, creativity, interdisciplinary insight, and self-reflection.

Educating Children in the Second Dimension

If the ultimate goal of existence is to raise and develop consciousness, then the biggest impact we can have on people's lives is when they are children, and the best way to achieve it is through the channels of family, community, and education. If we can, in each of these critical areas, create the basis for a logical system that encourages and supports the development of consciousness from an early age, we may be able to transform the human condition in just a few generations. Indeed, without changing the system of education in our societies, we cannot hope to move from the First to the Second and Third Dimensions. This is where those working for change can have the greatest impact in shifting the emphasis in our societies. The goal of education in the Second Dimension is to foster in students the love of learning, curiosity, openness, and the desire to seek wisdom. Literacy is merely the functional aspect of education, which is a love of learning.

To overcome the curbing effect of most First Dimension education, schooling must become more holistic. Schools can no longer be factories that churn out standardised products in varying degrees of quality. They should become environments that encourage intellectual growth and the development of a higher level of consciousness. The purpose of education should be to give children the tools and practices needed to embark on their own inner journeys of liberation.

School should reveal the interdependence of the universe, starting with the natural world and extending to all aspects of life. This will move children out of the reductionist way in which they have been programmed to view life in the First Dimension, where every phenomenon is usually attributed to a single cause. School should also help develop each child's ability to concentrate, which requires a degree of awareness and mindfulness.

In school, beyond learning maths, science, and language (all parts of functional literacy), students should be given the space needed to reflect on the nature of their own inner motivations and to develop consciousness, while learning to observe from a place of mindfulness. As we have seen in earlier chapters, mindful observation leads to awareness, which will lead to a recognition of interdependence and then change the basis of thoughts and actions. It leads ultimately to the development of insight and the awakening of consciousness.

To achieve this, the school day must be lengthened and divided into three distinct parts. The basis of early education is, and should remain, the necessity of functional literacy. Even as we move towards education of a higher order, functional literacy remains the foundation upon which insight, consciousness, and liberation can be built. The **first part of the day** would therefore be dedicated to the development of functional literacy. Advanced educators in the First Dimension already have developed many exceptional methods to teach functional literacy. Therefore, this part of education will not need to be changed as we move into the Second and Third Dimensions, at least as far as elementary education is concerned.

What must be abandoned, however, is the reliance on conceptual frameworks that target all children in the same manner. We know from observation that every child is born with certain inclinations that seem to be part of their inherent nature (the first element of their context). Often, we are struck by how unique each child is even before family and social and environmental conditioning (the other elements of one's context) begin to take effect. Siblings, even twins, can exhibit striking differences in their early interests, capabilities, and reactions to educational inputs. It is vital to recognise that these differences exist and that they are deeply rooted in each child's personality. Educational practice must be built around this recognition.

In a Second Dimension school, teachers must study every child's individual talents and customise the learning plan accordingly. Every child has a natural liking for certain subject areas and activities, and it is essential that teachers and parents try to figure out what they are. In keeping with Howard Gardner's theory of multiple intelligences,[140] I believe that every child possesses different intellectual traits that can be developed into different skills. If we do not follow our natural abilities, we will never be completely fulfilled or successful. Whereas traditional First Dimension curricula focus primarily on the development of the verbal-linguistic and logical-mathematical intellectual modalities, a more advanced and productive curriculum would place equal emphasis on other forms of intellectual ability, such a visual-spatial, interpersonal, and naturalistic intelligences. Thus, a well-designed Second Dimension curriculum would offer an interdisciplinary programme of instruction in which several intelligences are developed and exercised depending on the child's own talents, even from an early age.

Once a child's natural learning inclinations have been identified, he must be steered gently toward activities that are suited to both his interests and his pace of learning. Stimulating interest can be achieved by involving students in interdisciplinary activities, while the acquisition of functional literacy can be achieved by encouraging individual instruction at one's own pace. In Montessori programmes, for example, students teach themselves certain skills through reading and interaction with their peers; the teacher is no longer the provider of information, but rather a resource who can be consulted for further explanation or to help with assignments. In such an individualised set-up, one student may be working on fractions, while his desk mate is already tackling algebra.

During the **second part of the day**, students will study and learn to become aware of the interdependencies inherent in the world around them. For adults who studied in First Dimension schools, recognising interdependencies does not come naturally – it is something we have to work at constantly. One objective of learning in the Second Dimension is to make the recognition of interdependency ingrained in children from a very young age, so that it becomes second nature to them. The principal method to achieve this is cooperation with their peers (group work) in interdisciplinary projects that yield practical results.

I have been running a school in rural Rajasthan for the last twenty-five years (at one point we had over 800 children enrolled, from kindergarten to Class 12), and we have developed a learning matrix of things that students of each age must know. We begin by listing all the specific bits of knowledge that students must learn that year, a necessity in First Dimension education. We then create exercises that are interdisciplinary, so that students engaging in them are learning at least four or five separate things per exercise. In these projects, they study many subjects simultaneously, allowing them to independently realise the interconnections present in every aspect of our existence.

In the early days of the school, which was located on a barren wasteland, we embarked on a project to turn the central portion of the plot into a large rainwater collector. We made small improvements to the natural contours of the land and dug a large rectangular pit measuring 30 m × 75 m. During the first rainy season, the students were amazed to see the rainwater splatter on the hard soil, collect in rivulets, and drain into our new water reservoir. After a few days of rain, the tank was full, and for the next four months the water from it seeped into the surrounding soil, on which we had planted a number of trees that grew rapidly with access to this water. Today, the area around the collector has become a veritable jungle, hosting all kinds of birdlife. This was our first 'open classroom', and the students from those years still talk about their experience of 'greening' the campus. From this successful hands-on project, we derived the idea that the curriculum should include, and indeed be built around, practical interdisciplinary projects.

A great example of this is when the children are asked to set up a vegetable garden on the school grounds. In this project, they have to use drip irrigation (hydraulics); utilise mulching, compost, and fertiliser (soil science, chemistry); make calculations about the garden layout (arithmetic, geometry); analyse the quality of the soil and the vegetables (horticulture, botany); manage the impact of rodents and insects (zoology); study weather and climate patterns (geography); consider the movement of the sun and moon (astronomy); and so forth. Another such project involved the installation of solar panels in our school. The children had to engage in interdisciplinary approaches to weigh the pros and cons of the installation, calculate energy demand and savings, and express their findings in a written report. Even history and mythology were included by considering man's changed understanding of the role of the sun in our lives.

The hallmarks of such projects are (*a*) their thematic nature, which draws on a wide variety of disciplines, (*b*) the very practical outcome of the project, and (*c*) the necessity of collaboration to achieve the desired outcome. In such a system, everything becomes learning, and students are not misled into believing that learning is abstract and compartmentalised. It also makes the students enjoy the process of learning, which will likely stay with them always. In addition, students take on differing roles and perform different types of jobs, which leads to a greater level of respect for all professions and a better understanding of what goes into various kinds of work.

Of course, each school would need to develop a full curriculum that includes a variety of interdisciplinary projects to capture the individual interests and passions of all students. Projects should be centred around the following areas of learning:

- Growing something, preferably vegetables. This would cover botany, zoology, physics, astronomy, and other scientific disciplines.
- Building a mechanical system that helps their school, such as a solar system or a water management system, or a system to collect, reuse, and recycle materials in the school itself.
- A literary endeavour that entails the composition, casting, performance, and review of a play, for example; or creation of artistic objects (sculptures, tapestries, murals, installations) to decorate school buildings and grounds.
- Working as a team to create areas of beauty and contemplation on the campus, such as a tiny Zen garden or a rooftop garden.

- Investigating and researching aspects of the local Community, using diverse methods such as empirical observation and measurement, collection of oral/traditional knowledge, data collection via questionnaire surveys as well as interviews, demographic analysis, etc.

In this manner, the school would be turned into a laboratory for learning rather than an educational institution in the old-fashioned sense. One of the most important outcomes of this educational system is to teach children to value working with their hands, and to be comfortable with physical labour.

These projects will also help students see deeper and less quantifiable connections: relationships between nature and humans, between individuals and social groups, between actions and their consequences. This will manifest itself in the natural emphasis individuals begin to place on beauty, art, science, natural harmony, depth of personal relationships, and the realisation that we are parts of a larger universe and a transient manifestation of it. It will also foster an ability to view problems from multiple angles and to find solutions that address them organically.

Interdisciplinarity has its limitations, of course. In the educational system proposed here, it can be said that the young child is educated to be a generalist trained to perceive the interconnectedness of all aspects of learning, rather than acquiring in-depth subject matter knowledge. As I have argued elsewhere in this book, however, the modern world is one characterised by complexity, where complex problems with interdependent causes require equally complex solutions. Solutions to the vexing problems of modernity – from chronic disease to income disparity to global warming – cannot be found without the deep knowledge that comes from specialisation in a particular technical field. My contention is that once children have grown to love learning itself during their primary and middle years, they will continue to be committed, enthusiastic, proficient learners throughout their lives. Thus, they will be able to catch up rapidly with whatever specialist knowledge is required in their academic careers. As they progress through the educational system – especially during tertiary education – they will be able to focus on increasingly specialised material and apply the intuitiveness and divergent thinking that they acquired in their earlier schooling.

In the new model of education, it is vital for children to develop the ability to concentrate. This is a foundation for all other intellectual advancement. Without concentration, the mind will not develop beyond a certain point. Therefore, during the **third and final part of the school day**, all students must engage in age-appropriate but increasingly rigorous meditation exercises to stimulate focus. By the time they graduate from secondary school, each student would have accumulated at least 1,000 hours of meditation. This process could start with short intervals of meditation for young children – perhaps just five minutes in the morning before lessons start, followed by ten or fifteen minutes toward the end of the school day. These periods could then be increased by a few minutes each year, until students develop enough concentration and focus to be able to engage in longer stretches of meditation in secondary school. In the third part of the school day, formal meditation could also be augmented by less focused and interactive activities that nevertheless stimulate contemplation, such as nature walks and sessions on appreciation of art and music.

Mental rigour and discipline are skills that, sadly, have suffered dwindling relevance in the modern classroom. In an effort to banish rote learning from educational systems, repetition and memorisation have been discarded as useless, stultifying methods, and the mere suggestion of them may draw criticism from education experts, in the West especially. However, memorisation and recitation are powerful tools to train and flex the mind. One only has to think of the fundamental role of mantras in many Eastern disciplines to understand this. It is imperative, therefore, to valorise them once again and encourage their practice. Accordingly, a revised educational framework that strives toward Second Dimension consciousness would make ample use of such techniques to help achieve focus, while eschewing the smothering use of rote learning that so often blighted traditional educational methods. Memorisation is only valuable if it is practised in the context of a richer, interdisciplinary programme and referenced to other learning outcomes.

We all know our parents' and grandparents' ability to recite accurately poems they learned in school many decades ago. Memorisation and repetition were a fundamental part of the learning process back then. When my father-in-law was growing up, he attended a very poorly equipped school, where students could not afford notebooks or pens. Each student had only a small slate or blackboard to write on, and a piece of chalk. At the end of each exercise, however, students had to erase the slate to make room for the next assignment, so they had no written record of the day's lesson that they might refer to when they were at home. As they were still responsible for retaining all the information, he and his friends developed memory games that they would play on the long walk back to their homes, so that they would remember the information from school that day. Not surprisingly, the constant mental exercise during childhood ensured that my father-in-law still has a remarkable memory at the age of eighty. The mind is like a muscle: it must be exercised continually to make sure it does not atrophy. Meditation, stillness, concentration, and memorisation are exercises that should be viewed in this light.

Supporting all three learning components – functional literacy, interdisciplinary projects, and meditation – would require schools to adapt their architecture and landscaping. To offer all these curricular elements, a school would have to feature (*a*) a layout that breaks up the cell-like monotony of standard school architecture and encourages the pupil to be aware of, appreciate, and question his physical surroundings; (*b*) adequate outdoor and indoor space to conduct interdisciplinary projects; and (*c*) a special space dedicated to meditation – a peaceful environment, devoid of noise and distraction, that is conducive to the development of stillness and focus. Such basic modifications are not necessarily limited to schools attended by affluent students. For a meditation space, for example, a clean, empty, well-ventilated room with floor mats will do, or, ideally, a courtyard with a raised dais under a tree.

It should be noted that some of the elements of the educational programme sketched out here already exist, albeit mostly in private,

Western schools. Interdisciplinary approaches to learning, for example, have been discussed and trialled in educational circles since the early 20th century and are becoming more common as their importance is understood by educators everywhere. Though notoriously difficult to implement, such methods have gained a firm foothold in many curricula. The International Baccalaureate's emphasis on thematic 'units of inquiry' in the primary and middle years is a pertinent example. The frequent application, in several countries, of the STEAM pedagogical framework, which integrates science, technology, engineering, arts, and mathematics elements in individual learning activities, is another.[141] Hands-on, collaborative project work is also a mainstay of several modern educational models, including the Montessori method.

As for meditation, training in secular mindfulness – the cultivation of focused attention and awareness to aid mental well-being – has gained widespread acceptance following the pioneering work of University of Massachusetts professor Jon Kabat-Zinn, who first developed a mindfulness-based stress reduction (MBSR) programme in the 1970s to assist patients with a range of conditions. In the last decade, MBSR courses and workshops have found their way into various industries and settings, including corporate offices and school classrooms. Indeed, mindfulness exercises are now practised in many Western schools. In the United States, for example, the effort to bring mindfulness training into school curricula was spearheaded by Mindful Schools, a non-profit organisation founded in 2007. Since its humble beginnings in an elementary school in Oakland, California, Mindful Schools has brought mindfulness training to over 300,000 students across the country, though primarily in California and New York. In the United Kingdom, the Mindfulness in Schools Project (MiSP), a national charity established in 2009, delivers mindfulness training to both schoolchildren and teachers, and works in close collaboration with the Oxford Mindfulness Centre, a leader in mindfulness research.

Studies on the outcomes of mindfulness meditation in schools have shown that it can improve students' attention and focus.[142] It also helps to regulate emotions, allowing students to engage more productively in cognitive tasks.[143] At least one study also found that mindfulness meditation could directly improve performance on standardised exams.[144]

Despite the availability of these innovative ideas on learning, many teachers in today's First Dimension schools feel that they may not deviate from traditional curricula, especially in countries like India and China. Most parents are unlikely to send their children to 'alternative' schools, because any deviation from the standard curriculum is seen as risky and potentially damaging to a child's future. It seems, therefore, that curriculum reform must be a top-down effort by government, at least in the beginning, because in many countries it is unlikely that parents will spontaneously support a new educational programme. But top-down reforms often fail because of poor implementation and lack of favourable attitudes among teachers, parents, and a general public still unconvinced that fashionable new educational models actually promote upward social mobility.

Moreover, it is clear from First Dimension experience that forward-thinking schools cannot succeed in isolation. Rishi Valley School in the southern Indian state of Andhra Pradesh is an excellent example of a school already advanced in Second Dimension methods. Founded by the philosopher Jiddu Krishnamurti, the school is guided by a holistic approach to education that shares many elements with the programme suggested here. It strives to create students who are not only accomplished academically, but also well on their way to becoming whole human beings capable of a heightened aesthetic sense, a global outlook, love of nature, and genuine concern for mankind. Such a school, however, remains an island in the sea of First Dimension society. I have heard from several graduates of the Rishi Valley School who felt alienated and maladjusted to society after they left the school, because the reality they found (in university, work, family, and society at large) was so different from what they had been trained to expect.

How, then, can we ensure that all Second Dimension schools implement the extensive curricular changes that I have described above? The answer lies in the comprehensive restructuring of governance discussed in previous chapters. My various proposals to reform all of society's fundamental systems and institutions – especially public administration, management of enterprises and public agencies, and economic measurement – form a comprehensive structure of mutually supportive elements that will hopefully yield the desired outcomes in all facets of social organisation, including education.

In Chapter 12, I designated primary and secondary education as the purview of each Community, the core unit of governance in the Second Dimension. By definition, a Community will number roughly 25,000 inhabitants. This number is not coincidental. It is a carefully calculated critical-mass value that will enable municipalities to manage many of their own societal needs independently. In the case of education, a Community of that size will have sufficient students and resources to operate its own school district, probably consisting of three–four primary schools and one secondary school. As detailed in Chapter 11, the welfare of the Community will be reflected in the Community Leader's annual scorecard evaluation, with the five-year scorecard having been compiled by the competent SDA. The Community Leader's scorecard will contain several line items relating to education, that is, to the performance of the Community's schools.[145] In the scorecard example given in Chapter 11, the required performance indicators for education included graduation rates, teacher development, and parent satisfaction. It should be remembered, however, that a scorecard in the Second Dimension will be a dynamic tool that is continually modified to reflect the Community's priorities. Once any gross failings of a school have been addressed (such as graduation or university placement rates that are below the norm for the Area), the SDA will begin to include more sophisticated indicators in the scorecard. For example, in the next five-year cycle it could prioritise the development of creativity and innovation by including performance indicators that target those outcomes. One indicator could well be the very divergent thinking test devised by Land and Jarman in *Breakpoint and Beyond.* Other advanced quality indicators might include measurements of the level of compassion and helpfulness exhibited by schoolchildren, or their degree of happiness (measured through a GNH-type survey) ten years after graduation.[146]

Reaching the Third Dimension

The purpose of the new approach to education outlined here is to ensure that the search for truth, meaning, and deeper insight becomes part of each student's lifelong quest. By continuing to apply the central tenets of this educational programme (collaboration, interdisciplinary approaches, mental discipline, concentration, insightful thinking) to all subsequent aspects of their lives, such as tertiary education, work, and interaction with neighbours, students will be able to build sustained awareness – the hallmark of the Second Dimension. This sustained perception will, in turn, lead to the ability to intuitively recognise the nature of the varied problems that life throws at us and, hopefully, to breakthroughs on how to solve them – the transcendence that defines Third Dimension thinking.

The goal in the Second Dimension is to awaken the intuitive mind. In the Third Dimension this educational trajectory will culminate in a state of mind where we experience reality unhindered by the six elements of our context. This state of mind is not devoid of context, because we will always have a context, even in higher dimensions – a context formed by our upbringing, our social environment, our evolutionary heritage, and so forth. But in a more advanced state of consciousness we will be able to recognise that context clearly and with detachment, and we will be able to overcome the strictures it forces upon us. We will be free from its bondage, that is, able to set it aside when making decisions.

Third Dimension education is a moral education, but not in the way the term is used in the First Dimension. It involves inspiring a commitment to one's own development, and to reaching a level where one is aware of one's thoughts at the most profound level: where they are coming from, what is the consciousness from which they arise, how they manifest themselves, and how they become actions. To paraphrase an old saying, your thoughts become your actions; your actions, your character; and, as the Greek philosopher Heraclitus (c. 535–475 BCE) said, 'character is destiny'. So, it is from your thoughts that your character grows, making it vital to be aware of the roots of your character for it to develop holistically.

A moral education is one that helps you make this connection by cultivating a deep awareness of thought alongside the ability to examine intentions closely, and then link your thoughts and intentions to your actions and their consequences. It helps you realise that you are responsible for the energy that you release into the world. It also makes you see that when you act for truth and for justice, or when you act to save another human being, out of a sense of devotion or love, you are acting from your deepest convictions. This is an important goal of the Third Dimension: to help people act from a place of conviction.

We have seen in Chapter 4 how the first bond we form is with ourselves. We have also seen the importance of love and devotion to the development of a higher consciousness, since devotion is the way your consciousness teaches you to break free from First Dimension selfishness, ego, and narcissism. The way of life in the Third Dimension is to stay on the path toward higher consciousness, 'to strive, to seek, to find, and not to yield', as the poet Alfred Tennyson said in his *Ulysses*. This commitment to nurturing love and devotion must start early in life, and it must be a part of education. The purpose of education in the Third Dimension is to show, guide, and support us on the path to a higher consciousness.

Much of the practical execution of schooling in the Third Dimension would be the same as in the Second Dimension. In the Second Dimension, education moves away from the quantitative, marks-based system common in many countries. It is organised around a child's orientation of mind, and in the early years covers functional literacy, which is the fuel that propels the child on its journey. It then moves to a project-based system, of which one key part is to be in communion with nature – the ultimate teacher of interdependence. The third area is doing something that stimulates the creative, imaginative part of your brain, such as visual art, design, music, and literature.

What changes in the Third Dimension is the ultimate focus, which is to strive for higher consciousness. There remains the need for functional literacy, and the main method of learning will be project-based and interactive, to reveal the interdependencies of the world. Parts one and two of the school day continue unchanged. In the third part of the day, there is stronger emphasis on learning to understand oneself and develop inner faculties of morality, conscience, devotion to our fellow human beings, and self-reflection. Meditation focuses on conscious self-awareness: discovering what makes one's thoughts arise, how to recognise intent and action, and how to change one's ways of thinking and acting. As in the Second Dimension, all schoolwork is done in teams in the Third Dimension, to inculcate cooperation and co-creation.

The purpose of education in higher dimensions is to instil in us a lifelong desire for awareness, mindfulness, and consciousness. This process will help us lead lives of contentment and fulfilment. It will create societies at peace with themselves, where most individuals are engaged in developing their consciousness, and the world will be transformed.

The journey to complete awareness can be initiated, supported, and guided by an appropriate educational programme in the school years, but the final step to attain Third Dimension consciousness will remain a personal challenge that must be undertaken by every individual in his or her own time and pace. The foundations for the journey are laid in school; once this type of schooling begins to be supported by the educational system and valued by society, teachers and students will form the vanguard in moving us towards the Third Dimension.

20

Agriculture and Nutrition: Food for a Healthier Society

The Development of Agriculture

Our prehistoric ancestors were hunter-gatherers, living in small groups and foraging for whatever food was available in nature. The closest thing they had to agriculture were forest gardens, where the more useful species of plants that grew near dwellings were identified and nurtured. With the Neolithic period came the domestication of animals and the gradual change from harvesting to deliberate cultivation and higher yields. This eventually led to settlements and larger populations, while the production of food surpluses through farming allowed some to engage in different tasks, leading to the diversification of labour. As humans evolved further, and newer implements and technologies came into being, agriculture slowly began to take the shape we know today.

In the Middle Ages, several important developments altered agricultural production. The rise of monasteries meant that knowledge about agriculture was collected and could be accessed in places different from its origins. Improvements in ironmongering meant the creation of new tools that yielded better results. Crop rotation moved from a two-field system to a three-field system, leaving one field in three fallow for a year and dramatically increasing output. The new rotation meant that different crops could be planted, and this variety improved nutrition. The growth of mills led to more processing and the growing of more grains that could be milled. After Columbus landed in America, there was a global exchange of plants – potato and maize came to Europe, and barley, wheat, and turnips went to the Americas. Potato farming brought the intensive use of fertilisers and artificial pesticides to Europe, which transformed agriculture forever.

Agriculture is not just about growing food, though. It is also about eating it. In premodern times, there was a limit to how much food a natural landscape could produce, and there was minimal processing and preservation of foods. Diets tended to be low in calories, and the scarcity of sugar,[147] which was the most concentrated source of energy, meant that both cravings and digestion evolved to demand and store it. Food was eaten by availability and in combinations that ensured adequate nutrition. Because access to food was limited in prehistoric times, when you found sugar, you ate as much as you could to boost your energy. Whatever was left in your bloodstream would be stored as fat, which you could burn in lean times. In the modern world, this process does not serve us well any more.

As time went by and crops changed, so did diets. During the last two and a half centuries (roughly since the potato became an important staple in Europe) in particular, changes in our diets accelerated. Food began to be prized for appearance, shape, and size; storage improved, and processing increased. We began to eat milled, refined grains instead of whole grains; our vegetables and fruit were grown far away and transported over great distances. Many of these developments have had a negative impact on health, which we are only now beginning to understand. To change this trend, we must first understand the state of agriculture and nutrition today.

Agriculture in the First Dimension

Agricultural crops in production today may be classified in a variety of ways. For the purposes of this chapter, I suggest a threefold classification that takes into account each crop's nutritional usefulness to mankind and its impact on the environment:

- **Primary** crops are crops used exclusively for human consumption. They reach our table without needing to be refined, or with only minimal processing, and they have high nutritional value. Fresh fruits and vegetables are good examples, but this category also contains some of the world's food staples, or 'survival crops', such as lentils, potatoes, and cereals typically consumed as whole grains (whole wheat, oats, rye, millet, quinoa, brown rice).
- **Secondary** crops, too, are intended primarily for human consumption, but they require more extensive processing before they are ingested. This category includes all seeds produced to manufacture cooking oils, and staple crops like wheat and rice.
- **Tertiary** crops are crops used for non-food purposes like livestock feed, textile manufacture, and biofuel production, or that are intended for human consumption but require extensive processing or refining and do not meet any substantial nutritional needs. Many tertiary crops have traditionally been known as 'cash crops', including tobacco, cotton, flax, tea, coffee, and cocoa. All livestock, from poultry to cattle to farmed fish, are also tertiary agricultural products because, in most cases, primary or secondary crops are used to feed them.

There are several crops that straddle two or even three of these categories, depending on their end use. Corn (maize), for example, is the most versatile crop on earth, and, as a result, difficult to classify. When we eat corn on the cob or mix corn kernels in a vegetable dish or a salad, corn is effectively a primary crop. When used to produce corn oil, or cornmeal to make a tortilla, corn becomes a secondary crop. The majority of corn produced in the United States (by far the world's largest producer), however, qualifies as a tertiary crop because it is used for non-food purposes. According to the US National Corn Growers Association, about 80 per cent of all corn grown in the United States is consumed in domestic and overseas livestock, poultry, and fish production. Much of the remainder is used to produce ethanol (a biofuel blended into gasoline), and high-fructose corn syrup (HFCS), an artificial chemical sweetener that finds its way into innumerable processed foods with adverse, and now well-publicised, consequences on health. Because of these tertiary uses, which are enabled by extensive subsidies that support its production, corn is an extremely controversial crop.

This classification of crops allows us to evaluate both the nutritional value and the impact on the environment of each crop type. Primary crops are indispensable. They provide a high degree of nutritional content and result in an acceptable environmental impact, that is, they can be grown without excessive irrigation or contentious by-products. Secondary and tertiary crops, on the other hand, offer a diminishing nutritional contribution to human dietary needs, and their growth causes increasing harm to the earth, because (*a*) they are grown in monocultures that require unreasonable quantities of water, pesticides, and fertilisers; (*b*) their production requires unacceptable consumption of other natural resources, such as arable land, primary crops, forest, and wetland; or (*c*) their growth and processing creates by-products that can pollute the earth and cause global warming. Raising cattle is one of the most damaging agricultural processes in this regard. It is common knowledge that some 15,000 litres of water is needed to produce a single kilo of beef, whereas 1,250 litres would suffice to produce a kilo of maize or wheat. And if a cow were entirely grain-fed, it would take about 7–10 kg of grain to produce 1 kg of beef.[148] The large contribution of cattle farming to global warming, through the release of methane from the cow's digestive tract, is also well documented.

Our classification does, of course, entail certain value judgments about what constitutes a proper diet for humans. It is already biased, if you will, toward the dietary recommendations that will be discussed later in this chapter. Many cash crops, like coffee and sugar cane, and most livestock, are grown to satisfy entirely optional, and often unhealthy, eating habits. And crops that require extensive refinement have also been shown to be of considerably lesser nutritional value than foods eaten raw or minimally processed.

The problems besetting First Dimension agriculture are manifold and have been discussed at length in the popular media and scientific literature. Modern agriculture has evolved into a machinery designed to provide ample quantities of cheap food to feed the world's ballooning population. To achieve these goals – abundance and low cost – it has turned increasingly to highly mechanised, industrial-scale monocultures. A monoculture is the agricultural practice of growing a specific variety of a single species over a wide area for several consecutive years. It is used extensively in modern industrial agriculture and has allowed for large harvests while minimising labour input. The genetic modification of plants is also used to enhance crop production and resistance to pests and drought.

Monocultures bring with them a host of problems, such as loss of biodiversity and a greater susceptibility to disease and pests, which, in turn, necessitates an increased use of pesticides. In addition, input costs for monoculture farming are extremely high because such crops typically require extensive irrigation, artificial fertilisation, and widespread use of chemical pesticides. Over-reliance on monocultures has also impoverished the variety of foods that reach our dining tables, leading to limited food complementarity and, at times, to misguided use of dietary supplements.

The prevalence of monoculture cropping has also dictated the way in which the success of agricultural production is measured. The metric overwhelmingly used in contemporary discourse on agriculture is yield. How many tonnes or bushels of soy, wheat, or rice can a farmer obtain from an acre or hectare of land? Much of the world's effort, attention, and research has gone into the improvement of yields, before as well as after the Green Revolution. But yield, by definition, measures the productivity of land dedicated to just one crop. It places little value on planting several different crops together. Growing several crops in close proximity reduces the usefulness of mechanised harvesting, and therefore is of no interest to large, industrialised agribusinesses with vested interests in monocultures.

But techniques like intercropping (growing multiple crops in close proximity) can produce high yields by making use of resources and synergies that would otherwise not be utilised by a single crop. Intercropping also improves biodiversity by providing a habitat for a variety of insects and soil organisms that would not survive in a single-crop environment. This variety can encourage the presence of predator species which, in turn, helps to limit outbreaks of crop pests, and thus allows the farmer to use fewer harmful pesticides. Biodiversity can also prevent plant diseases and soil erosion. Yield cannot adequately measure the benefits of something like intercropping.

Another factor that is ignored when it comes to the choice of crops is the nutritional contribution of the crop. Is it better for consumers to eat cabbage or wheat, and how much of a role should that play in the choice of which crop to grow? Nutritional value is usually not a factor when consuming or pricing crops.

To secure adequate supplies of food, most countries have further damaged the system by introducing direct subsidies to farmers, as well as price controls and tariffs. While the purpose of these measures – to incentivise farmers to continue to farm the land, for example, or to ensure affordable staples – may have been sensible at some stage, they have since grown into a complex system of market-distorting policies that often damage consumers, in terms of both cost and health repercussions, while benefiting the entrenched interests of a few players, usually large agribusinesses. The most often cited such distortions are US farm subsidies, especially for corn, wheat, and soybean, and the European Union's Common Agricultural Policy. Several Asian countries, including India, also have extensive and multifaceted subsidy programmes for their farmers.

Subsidies and tariffs hinder the development of sensible agricultural practices because they hide the true cost of producing crops. The agricultural belt of northern India, for example, receives very little rainfall outside of the monsoon months, and often irregular rainfall during the monsoon. Despite this relative shortage of water, irrigation-intensive crops like rice and sugar cane are grown throughout this region. Farmers have to rely increasingly on groundwater to irrigate their fields, with the result that the water table is dropping at an alarming rate. But the groundwater itself does not cost the farmers anything (aside for the initial costs associated with sinking a tube well), because, as in much of the world, in India there is no mechanism to regulate and price the use of groundwater. In addition, the electricity needed to operate the well pumps is heavily subsidised in many Indian states.

Therefore, farmers in northern India can continue to grow water-intensive crops, for some of which the government also provides price guarantees. In this example, if farmers were required to pay for the natural resource they are depleting (groundwater) and for the electricity required to access it, and were not shielded from fluctuations in demand, the cost of producing crops like rice and sugar cane would increase dramatically, making them less viable in low-rainfall areas. Farmers would, in all likelihood, turn to crops more suitable to the natural resources and soil quality of their immediate environment. (Soil quality, as it happens, is key to a healthy ecosystem and to sustaining long-term agriculture, but it almost never gets measured.)

We can summarise the many ailments of industrialised First Dimension agriculture as follows:

- Almost exclusive focus on monocultures to increase short-term yields;
- Overdependence on artificial fertilisers;
- Overdependence on pesticides and other chemicals;
- Overuse of water;
- Contamination of water supplies and lack of awareness of the damage to local ecosystems from chemical run-offs;
- Growing of crops not suited to an area because of the distorted economics of food;
- Insufficient emphasis on the importance of soil quality;
- Production of crops with low nutritional content; and
- Excessive reliance on processed foods, which have a longer shelf life and are therefore preferred by supermarket chains.

Agriculture, therefore, appears to be very much in need of reform, especially in (*a*) the manner in which it measures efficiency, by moving away from yield as the primary measure and shifting toward a more comprehensive understanding of agricultural productivity; and (*b*) correct pricing of crops that takes into account input costs as well as environmental consequences.

Challenges of Eating in the First Dimension

While over-reliance on monocultures and incorrect pricing of agricultural crops are examples of the problems created by First Dimension agricultural production, there are also serious complications on the consumption side, that is, nutrition. The biggest change in agriculture in the First Dimension was the rise, in the 20th century, of a globalised food industry dominated by large agribusiness corporations. This highly sophisticated food production and delivery system rewarded us with many blessings. Global logistics and supply chains, for example, made foods available year-round, helped by containerisation and bulk freighters that could move food around easily and inexpensively. It also helped rid us of the scourge of famines caused by the shortage of food in a particular region. Today, famines still occur as a result of extreme poverty coupled with war or political instability, not because food cannot be transported to the affected areas. The widespread use of pesticides, modern storage facilities, and the refrigerated cold chain made it easy to store and protect food from infestations. This ushered in a revolution in how we grew crops, how we processed food, and how we consumed it.

The modern food production system, however, also spawned a host of new problems. Governments began to subsidise farmers and incentivise the growth of certain types of crops over others, like sugar cane in India and corn in the United States, which led to surpluses that the food processing industry then turned into food – food that fed the cravings and addictions to sugar that originated in the evolutionary hardwiring of ancestral humans. This focus on quantity over quality in food production has reduced the discussion of adequate nutrition to the measurement of caloric content. Whenever we discuss malnutrition in poor countries, we do so in terms of calories: an intake of at least 2,000 calories per person per day is considered necessary. When discussing problems such as obesity, we once again do so in terms of calories: most diets recommend reduction and control of caloric intake. But the calorie is only a raw measure of the amount of energy in food, and it fails to account for the nutritional value of the food itself. It is now universally recognised that a diet heavy on processed food, trans fats and sugars can have disastrous consequences on health, though it may satisfy a caloric requirement.

Eating processed food in the First Dimension leads to a high level of fructose and trans fats in the bloodstream, which the body is wired to convert to fat, leading to the contemporary obesity epidemic. The presence of excess fructose in processed food is a risk factor for many other chronic diseases, such as diabetes, high blood pressure, and heart disease. Coping with these conditions results in high healthcare costs, breaking the budgets of welfare states and individual households and bloating the health insurance industry. Ill people cannot work or produce well, which in turn impoverishes the economy.

The industrial agriculture of the First Dimension takes something as natural as food production and consumption and skews it out of proportion to create unnatural growing and unnatural eating. As journalist Michael Pollan wrote,

> […] chemical fertilizers (made from natural gas), pesticides (made from petroleum), farm machinery, modern food processing and packaging and transportation have together transformed a system that in 1940 produced 2.3 calories of food energy for every calorie of fossil-fuel energy it used into one that now takes 10 calories of fossil-fuel energy to produce a single calorie of modern supermarket food. Put another way, when we eat from the industrial-food system, we are eating oil and spewing greenhouse gases.[149]

Increasingly, the focus must shift away from counting calories and move toward assessing the nutritional quality of what we eat. This is already happening throughout the world as consumers are becoming more aware of the complications brought on by the industrialisation of agriculture. This, however, has spawned a dizzying galaxy of confusing and often conflicting prescriptions. Today, most educated consumers are at least peripherally aware that certain foods and classes of ingredients found especially in processed foods are bad for them. We know, for example, to avoid saturated fats as much as possible, but also that some packaged foods contain sinister trans fats, which are equally dangerous.[150] We also know that sugar makes us fat, and that HFCS is even worse.[151] Red meat causes all kinds of problems,[152] but various trendy diets suggest that a meat-centred regimen in the hunter-gatherer mould can help us lose weight. A vegetarian diet is undoubtedly healthier, but if you are not careful you may be missing out on important proteins and vitamins. And a Mediterranean diet is supposed to be ideal, but besides the fact that it includes the use of olive oil, few people understand what it really means.

What is required, therefore, is a simple, intuitive measure of the nutritional quality of the food we consume, which is tailored to our own body types, rather than simply a measurement of the quantity of calories we imbibe.

Agriculture and Nutrition in the Second Dimension

Initiatives for Better Agriculture

Second Dimension agriculture begins, once again, with the recognition of the interconnectedness of all facets of food production and consumption. A subsidy given to producers of corn in the North American Midwest may seem like a good idea because it appears to help farmers and ensures plentiful supplies of a useful crop. But such a programme also has wide-ranging and unexpected consequences, from increased use of HFCS in packaged foods (with adverse health consequences like fatty liver and diabetes), to increased use of corn as livestock feed, to the displacement of other crops to increase acreage for corn, to instability in the price of other agricultural commodities, and so forth. In other words, a decision to subsidise, or impose tariffs on, a particular food crop cannot be made in isolation. The food chain must be real, focusing on real nutrients and the real impact of growing and consuming food, because everything about food production and consumption is connected.

In the First Dimension, righting the wrongs of modern agriculture by a willing and determined government could begin with the removal of price distortions. This would entail gradually eliminating all subsidies, tariffs, and price controls on agricultural products, while at the same time introducing fair pricing mechanisms for natural resources used in the agricultural production process (notably water), as well as taxation to account for the environmental impact of each crop. Thus, for example, cattle ranchers ought to pay a pollution tax on every head of cattle they raise to account for the release of methane into the atmosphere over the lifespan of the animal. Monoculture farmers could be made to pay a pollution tax based on the amount of artificial fertilisers and pesticides used per tonne of crop yield, and so forth. These initiatives would reveal the true cost of each crop, resulting in changes in the kind of crop that is grown, the location where it can be grown, and the manner in which it is cultivated.

In the Second Dimension, the goals of agricultural reform would be the same, but the methods different. Some of the forceful interventions, by regulatory authorities, that I have just suggested would, in fact, be unnecessary, because the economic, fiscal, and administrative structures of the Second Dimension, as outlined in previous chapters, would lead systemically to the same results. For example, all agricultural subsidies and price controls will have been abolished, their counteractive function in the economy replaced by the Utility Index (see Chapter 16), which comes with a built-in system of incentives and disincentives. Moreover, agribusinesses that continue to conduct agriculture as before would receive low scores in the Utility Index, penalised especially by the eco-efficiency indicator because of their excessive use of water, abuse of land quality, overuse of harmful artificial fertilisers and pesticides, and high release of greenhouse gases. Those who maintain extensive monocultures might also fall foul of the Index's anti-monopoly indicator. The consequence would be a high rate of tax, which would encourage such firms to adjust the way they do business. Meanwhile, the resource-intensive, depletive and environmentally damaging characteristics of modern agriculture would generate large reductions to each country's GNR (see Chapter 15), forcing regional and national governments to consider thorough changes in land use.

Indeed, by far the most consequential initiative needed to improve agriculture is the reallocation of arable land almost exclusively to primary crops. Currently, vast tracts of arable land are devoted to secondary and tertiary crops. This has led to one of the most common and most misguided myths about the state of the world's food production, namely, that there isn't enough land to grow sufficient crops to feed the world's ballooning population. It is reported frequently in the media that worldwide demand for crops is increasing rapidly due to growth of the global population, which will reach between 9 billion and 10 billion people by mid-century,[153] and also due to increased biofuel production and changing dietary preferences (especially formerly poor countries like China consuming increasing quantities of beef and pork). The common understanding is that meeting these growing demands will be an insurmountable challenge that will strain the capability of our food system to the point of collapse. In fact, we could very easily feed 9 billion people, if not more, with existing croplands, just by shifting land use from secondary and tertiary crops to primary ones.[154]

A study conducted by the University of Minnesota found that, currently, 36 per cent of the world's crops (measured, not surprisingly, in terms of the calories they can provide) are being used for animal feed, that is, they are tertiary crops by the definition used in this chapter. Furthermore, only 12 per cent of those feed calories ultimately contribute to the human diet (as meat and other animal products consumed by humans). Such inefficiency has, unfortunately, become a hallmark of modern agriculture. The study also found that human-edible calories used for biofuel production increased fourfold between 2000 and 2010, from 1 per cent to 4 per cent of overall crop-derived calories, representing a net reduction of available food globally.[155]

The University of Minnesota study proposed changing the fundamental measure of agricultural productivity from the traditional definition of yield (usually measured in tonnes per hectare or similar units) to the number of people who can be fed per hectare of cropland. Using such metrics, the study found that growing food exclusively for direct human consumption (that is, growing only primary crops) could, in principle, increase available food calories by as much as 70 per cent. This could feed an additional 4 billion people, which is more than the projected 2–3 billion who will be added by 2070 through population growth.[156]

Permaculture

Once the majority of arable land has been diverted to cultivation of primary crops, farming practice must also be weaned off monoculture in favour of sustainable methods modelled on nature. While alternative farming practices, especially organic farming, meet some sustainability criteria, ultimately agricultural production can be made fully sustainable only 'if farms are designed in the image of natural ecosystems, combining the knowledge of science with the wisdom of the wilderness.'[157] Natural ecosystems have, for millennia, maintained high productivity and demonstrated extraordinary adaptiveness to natural disturbances.

An agricultural model that follows nature's example is permaculture. According to biologist Bill Mollison and environmental designer David Holmgren, who coined the term in the 1970s, permaculture is 'the conscious design and maintenance of agriculturally productive systems which have the diversity, stability, and resilience of natural ecosystems.'[158] Permaculture extends the concept of organic farming by applying natural principles to design a self-sustaining ecosystem capable of producing food, fibre, and energy. By weaving together the diverse but profoundly interconnected elements of microclimate, annual and perennial plants, water and soil management, and human needs, the permaculturist can create an energy-efficient, low-maintenance, and high-yielding system. The approach is one 'of working with, rather than against nature; of protracted and thoughtful observation, rather than protracted and thoughtless labour; of looking at systems in all their functions, rather than asking only one yield of them'.[159]

Central to permaculture is the idea of growing food by creating entire ecosystems that mimic nature's own way of growing things.[160] Permaculture, therefore, positions different crops near one another, especially if synergies can be found in the nutrients they require or the insects they attract or repel. A good example of this is the ancient Native American tradition of growing three fundamental crops (maize, squash, and beans, also known as 'the three sisters') together, in small patches. The three crops benefit from each other's proximity. The maize provides a climbing structure for the beans, eliminating the need for artificial trellises. The beans add nitrogen to the soil, which the other two plants utilise. The squash acts as ground cover; it blocks the sunlight, thus inhibiting the growth of weeds and keeping the soil moist. This principle can be applied on a larger scale to replicate nature's ultimate growth environment – the forest. A well-planned permaculture farm might feature a canopy of tall fruit trees, such as coconut palms, which partly shield a middle layer (the shrub layer) of crops, such as bananas, from solar saturation.[161] Farther below, the undergrowth layer could be used to grow vegetables.

Such farm environments may sound wishful – the domain of enlightened gentlemen farmers who produce only a tiny yield of expensive organic crops. There is evidence that organic, or agro-ecological farming, when carried out properly, can deliver yields similar to those from conventional methods. Whether organic agriculture can contribute significantly to world agriculture and, ideally, produce sufficient food to feed the world has been debated extensively over the last two decades. Many scientific studies have been conducted to compare organic and conventional yields for a variety of crops in different parts of the world. Recently, two authoritative meta-analyses[162] of these studies concluded that, overall, organic yields still lag behind conventional ones by about 20 per cent. However, this 'organic yield gap' varies greatly with crop type, soil and precipitation conditions, and land management methods. One study, for example, found that organic farming can outperform conventional agriculture in developing countries.[163] A farming systems comparison trial in Madhya Pradesh, India, observed a significant yield gap for cotton and wheat, but a negligible one for soybeans.[164] Organic methods that include agricultural diversification practices, such as multi-cropping and crop rotation, can also substantially reduce the yield gap.

Permaculture can sometimes produce impressive yields, as demonstrated by the oft-cited case of permaculture entrepreneur David Blume who, in a nine-year experiment on a permaculture farm in northern California, achieved yields eight times what the US Department of Agriculture considered possible, while also dramatically increasing the fertility of the soil he was tilling. His two-acre farm, cultivated with a wide variety of crops (forty-five different crops were planted over the nine-year period), was able to feed 300 people routinely, and at times as many as 450, while also turning a profit.[165]

Permaculture also teaches us the importance of reusing agricultural waste. In most cases, agricultural by-products can be recycled into the system and turned into fertiliser. Or they can be used as animal feed. Provided, that is, that the livestock is nearby. It is against permaculture's principles, and against common sense, to ship waste products over great distances so that they may be used as fodder. If animal husbandry and agriculture are constructed on a small scale, they can be co-located to generate the requisite synergies. Thus, much agricultural waste could be used to feed goats and pigs, while manure from such animals can be used to fertilise adjacent fields.

In general, permaculture thrives on small scale and especially the proximity of crops, livestock, and consumers so as to take advantage of synergies and to avoid expensive and environmentally questionable transport. The ideal permaculture farm, therefore, is one that is only a few miles away from the urban centre where its products are consumed. By extension, we ought to eat only what is produced locally, and we should produce only what can reasonably be raised on the type of soil and climate in our immediate vicinity. The ultimate consequence of a world where this is true is that fantastical desert metropolises like Dubai and Doha cannot exist, any more than subarctic ones like Edmonton.

An Apple a Day

Permaculture is just one instance of many methods to farm differently. The important thing to keep in mind is that the Second Dimension ecosystem is an interdependent ecosystem. Such a system starts with soil. Soil in the First Dimension system of cultivation is depleted by monoculture and poisoned by artificial fertilisers and pesticides. If you deplete the soil, you deplete the food. Next, you need to ensure seed diversity, because different plants grow at different times. In nature, the presence of different kinds of plants replenishes soil nutrients and allows for a variety of animal and insect life, which then all keep each other in check, providing effective pest control. Masanobu Fukuoka, a Japanese farmer and philosopher, came up with the concept of natural farming, also called do-nothing farming, because it involved leaving nature to build an ecosystem that would then sustain itself without weeding, fertilisers, or pesticides.[166]

The produce that results from this kind of agriculture is not pretty, at least not by the standards of First Dimension farming. Imagine a tale of two carrots, if you will. One is perfect, conical, orange, unblemished, plump, and smooth. The other is small and gnarled, covered with ridges and bumps, and of a shape that cannot be named. The former is the 'better' carrot we all choose when shopping at the supermarket; the latter would be tossed out by a produce grower before it even reached a distribution centre, let alone a grocery store. But if we analyse our two divergent carrots more closely, we realise that the second carrot is bursting with micronutrients[167] that are missing from the first. This is where First Dimension agriculture fails – the carrot grown to be plump, pretty, and regular in shape, is full of water and grown with lots more fertiliser than it needs. The obsessive focus on calories and macronutrients means that we ignore the importance of maintaining balanced micronutrients in our food, and forget to check whether the food has them. We do not know the impact of these things on our health, and it is in the interests of the agribusiness industry to keep it that way. As Fukuoka said in *The One-Straw Revolution*, 'Food and medicine are not two different things: they are the front and back of one body.'

Nutrition science is an offshoot of First Dimension science, and as Michael Pollan has discussed,[168] it has always gone about its business in a reductionist fashion. It attempts to isolate components ('nutrients') that are contained in certain foods to determine what effect they have on health, and then tries to synthesise them and artificially incorporate them in foods where they do not belong in the first place.

To say that an apple a day is good for you because it contains vitamins A, B, and C is overly simplistic, because you might be misled into thinking that you can achieve the same result by swallowing a few vitamin pills every day. Things are vastly more complicated than science has been able to explain. The health benefit of eating the apple may very well lie not just in the vitamins it contains, but in how they interact with other, less well-understood substances in the apple; or in the way that your body processes the flesh, skin, and juice of an apple; or in the fact that eating an apple means you probably will not eat a candy bar. Moreover, an apple plucked and eaten from an orchard is different from one that was transported internationally, different again from one baked in a pie, and from an apple pressed and pasteurised to make juice. In other words, the benefit of the vitamins in the apple cannot be understood in isolation because it is the result of a very complex web of chemical interactions, as well as dependent on human eating behaviour in its endless variations. We are only just beginning to learn how differently the gut can absorb nutrients depending on the consumer's state of mind, for example.

Food Labelling in the Second Dimension

There have been attempts to correct the absence of understanding on nutrition in the First Dimension, by the introduction of mandatory nutrition labelling. This has not succeeded well because it springs from the First Dimension focus on calories and macronutrients and ignores the nutritional value of micronutrients in food. Also, it is complicated and often difficult to quickly assess or compare the nutritional values of different foods. The science behind it is inexact, almost primitive.

Second Dimension nutrition must therefore offer consumers a viable, efficient way to make appropriate decisions about what to eat and how much. It could rely primarily on a simple labelling mechanism applied to all foodstuffs, raw as well as processed. Every edible product for sale, from oranges to fresh fish to canned peas to packaged chocolate chip cookies, could be required to include a three-digit code. The first digit in the code is a number between 1 and 9 and reflects that product's impact on the health of the person eating it. Thus, a bunch of raw spinach would probably be labelled 1, whereas a fizzy soft drink laden with HFCS as a sweetener would score an 8 or thereabouts.

The second digit in the code would apply the same rating system (from 1 to 9) to the impact that bringing the food product to the consumer has had on the earth. An organically grown watermelon, grown and sold locally, would probably score a 1 on this scale, whereas a cut of beef sold in Europe but raised in Argentina would score a 9.

The third and final digit in the code would be a letter, between A and F, representing the nutritional category within which that food item falls – a simplified food pyramid. Thus A, for example, might represent foods rich in bulk, like grains and starches, while B could represent foods with high protein content, and C foods rich in vitamins and minerals. Later letters (D through F) might point to high levels of other micronutrients or immune boosters and antioxidants.

The beauty of such a labelling scheme (assuming it is applied correctly and irrespective of the channel through which the food is sold, that is, by both the fruit vendor on the street corner and the hypermarket) would be the extreme ease with which every consumer would be able to make informed choices about their daily diet. Every buyer, however educated or attuned to recent findings in nutritional science, would be able to recognise that a product labelled 1-1-C (the label for organically grown broccoli, for example) is better than one labelled 8-9-B (the code for, say, commercially produced liver pâté). The consumer would thus be gently but continually encouraged to gravitate toward options with low number combinations. The final letter would alert them to overdependence on, or insufficient consumption of, a particular food group in their diet. Simply put, a conscientious parent would have to worry only about ensuring that foods from all letter groups are regularly included in their shopping, without worrying about the complex science that might underlie the labelling itself.

The first two numbers in this labelling mechanism would rely on the latest evidence offered by nutrition science and environmental science, respectively. The numbers associated with each crop or product, therefore, would be changeable, provided this process is monitored by an independently funded and managed oversight institution that cannot be lobbied by special-interest groups.

Labelling requirements exist in many countries around the world. However, they are often difficult to understand, and they are usually available only for packaged foodstuffs. In most countries, labelling requirements are misleading because they encourage the consumer to 'miss the forest for the trees' by focusing excessively on the individual components of the food item, with no reference to its nutritional value or its interaction with other components.

The mechanism proposed here would be applied universally and would be comprehensible to almost everyone. It amounts to a radical simplification of nutritional science to help consumers make sound decisions about their diets. The simplified three-letter coding methodology would 'nudge' the consumer into making good choices based on the nutritional and absorptive value of each food item, the way it was grown and processed, and the complementarity of the foods to each other.

Other Second Dimension characteristics would mirror nutritional initiatives that have already become familiar in many economies, especially in the West. In a nutshell, these recommendations tell us to eat food that is as close to the earth as possible. This gives preference to locally produced over globally sourced, organic over mass-produced, fresh and seasonal over preserved, raw over cooked, whole grains over refined grains, primary crops over secondary and tertiary crops, and (perhaps most controversially) vegetarian diets over meat-centric diets.

Eating in the Third Dimension

In the Third Dimension, the way we grow, trade, and consume agricultural products would be quite different than it is now. After an initial period of adjustment, during which the cost of various staples would have spiked, the world would have to come to terms with different prices for various agricultural products. The removal of subsidies, price controls, tariffs, and other distorting measures, as well as the introduction of indirect taxation on pollution and emissions via the Utility Index and the GNR-based accounting of debits and credits will have meant that previously cheap products are now more expensive, whereas more expensive products have dropped in price, leading to significant adjustments in our selection of food. Diversification of crop cultures will have occurred, ensuring an environmentally more desirable type of agriculture, also less prone to adverse weather, pest infestations, and plant diseases, and more in tune with the natural environment of their surroundings. And it will have yielded a greater variety of vegetables, seeds, and other previously 'rare' items, which would now be available in markets. Significantly, in the Third Dimension, most of the world's arable land will be devoted to primary crops, and acreage under secondary and tertiary crops will have shrunk dramatically. These will be the logical consequences of adopting the measures outlined in this chapter.

Another likely outcome of Second Dimension practices is that much of the world's population will have become vegetarian, or even vegan. While this is not necessarily a prescription to which our movement aspires, it is inevitable that its tenets will lead to an increase in vegetarianism by choice. The world cannot afford any more to devote large tracts of arable land to growing feed for cattle, and the earth cannot cope any more with the environmental impact of huge livestock populations, so most farmland must be diverted to growing primary crops instead. The scarcity of meat, and its consequent increased price, will prompt consumers to buy less of it.

Because a vegetarian diet lacks the protein density supplied by meat and other animal products, an increased rate of vegetarianism will also mean that consumers, using the aforementioned labelling system, will pay closer attention to food complementarity, that is, the practice of combining protein sources in such a way as to aid their absorption by the body. Most vegetarian foods are incomplete protein sources that contain only low amounts of isolated essential amino acids, but this deficiency can be solved by combining two or more vegetarian foods (each with only incomplete proteins) to form complementary proteins, so as to provide adequate amounts of all the essential amino acids. Many cultures have already figured out this complex dietary mechanism. The heavy reliance on the combination of rice and dal (pulses) in the Indian diet is a case in point, like the pairing of corn tortillas and beans in Mexican food. Even American classics like peanut butter sandwiches or macaroni and cheese qualify as adequate complementary pairings.[169]

In the Third Dimension, we will understand the relationship between holistic agriculture (as opposed to organic agriculture, which can be very industrial), complementary eating, and mindfulness. We will achieve an ability to cleanse and maintain the body, and an ability to digest, absorb, and utilise the nutrition in food. We will need regular focus on the quality of digestion, and regular detoxes and cleanses to rejuvenate the digestive system. Yogic knowledge has many such practices: *panchakarma*s and *neeti*s, for example. In the Third Dimension, we must invest in research into these.

The advantage of the mindfulness and frequent meditation of the Third Dimension is that we will receive far more valuable personal bio-feedback. Our bodies will begin to speak to us in a profound way about what we put into them and how we treat them. But we first have to tune our listening through mindfulness and meditation. Indeed, mindfulness must be brought to bear on how we prepare food and how we eat it. Mindful food preparation involves paying close attention to our food and how it combines with other elements in the preparation. Mindful eating involves a focus on the food while we eat it, stopping to notice and savour every aspect of it, from subtle flavouring to texture and temperature. A famous Ayurvedic doctor once told me that it is not what you eat that is important as much as what your body absorbs. You can absorb nutrition well from poor food and poorly from good food. The key elements are the state of mind of the consumer and the quality of his gut bacteria.

Prana

By far the most significant addition, in the Third Dimension, to our dietary practices would be to centre our eating habits on the age-old concept of prana. In simple terms, we can posit that all living things contain, in varying degrees, energy that is ultimately derived from the sun. This energy, which scientists sometimes call bioplasma or bioelectricity, is difficult to quantify because it cannot be reduced to a simple measure of calories or joules. But clearly prana, or 'life force', is present in crops and livestock when they are living, and decays quickly once they are harvested or slaughtered.

Prana means that the living universe is seen as an unbroken thread. If we contaminate the soil, use industrial seed, and grow a monoculture, then the output is a fruit, vegetable, or grain that is weak in all the essential micronutrients. So intricate is this interdependence that it is virtually impossible to separate one strand from another and find out what the absence of micronutrients in a carrot can do to one's health. The concept of prana is one that requires a very high level of consciousness to perceive, but you can see that if the soil is healthy and the seed is healthy, the plant and its fruit will be healthier as well. Research shows that 60 per cent of fungicides and pesticides are used to make food look unblemished and perfect, but they weaken the nutritional value of the food and what our bodies receive.

Prana means that living things contain more energy than dead ones, so it prescribes eating fresh fruits and vegetables rather than meat, which is dead tissue. It recommends eating plant-based foods, especially whole grains, with little or no oil and limited spice, to feel refreshed and charged. It tells us, essentially, something we have forgotten but are gradually learning again: to eat foods that are close to the earth in order to capture as much energy and nutritional value as possible. The concept of prana may sound like an esoteric piece of ancient Eastern wisdom, but it is, in fact, common sense. You do not have to be a licensed dietician or an expert in yoga to realise that a tomato eaten right after you have picked it from the vine is healthier and tastes better than a tomato that you bought at the supermarket and then stored in the refrigerator for a week.

Over the last two decades, scientific inquiry has been able to corroborate much of our instinctive knowledge regarding the nutritional value of fresh foods. Using chromatography techniques (gas chromatography, high-pressure liquid chromatography, paper chromatography, etc.), food scientists have demonstrated that the nutritional value of food – that is, the concentration of micronutrients like vitamins and flavonoids – is depleted after harvest due to storage and transport, preservation (like canning and drying), processing, and cooking. For example, one study found that leafy greens like spinach and rockets contain abundant vitamin C, but the vitamin deteriorates quickly after harvesting and is virtually gone after 10 days of storage. The same study found that the concentration of other nutrients, such as vitamin E and provitamin A (beta-carotene), also decreased, but to a much lesser degree. Another study found that vitamin C losses in vegetables stored at 4°C for seven days range from 15 per cent for green peas to 77 per cent for green beans. Vitamin C was also found to decrease during the canning of various vegetables by between 10 per cent and 90 per cent. Processing and storage of fresh fruits and vegetables also causes losses of B vitamins. Thiamine (B1) and pyridoxine (B6), in particular, are sensitive to heat and light, and reportedly lose anywhere between 7 per cent and 70 per cent of their concentration in vegetables as a result of canning.[170]

Prana, however, is not merely another collective term for micronutrients found in food, because it also posits that energy can radiate from fresh foods in a purer form. This notion has received increasing attention from the scientific community. As early as the 1930s, experiments were conducted to understand and measure the energy value of living things. Studies revealed that all living things emit electromagnetic waves of specific frequencies, and that such radiation varies significantly between plant matter and animal matter, between living and dead tissue, and between raw and cooked food.[171]

Vegetables, for example, are most radiant when freshly harvested, losing about one-third of their potency by the time they reach the supermarket shelf and another third when cooked. (Tubers are an exception; they are fortified by cooking.) The effects of food processing are disastrous: milk has a moderate amount of prana when fresh but loses most of it after pasteurisation. The same is true of pasteurised fruit juices and canned fruits. White, granulated sugar has no prana at all. Other processed foods like margarine, alcohol, and bleached white flour also offer as little prana as meat and other dead things. Dehydration, on the other hand, causes little loss of vigour: sun-dried fruit and spices retain sufficient vitality and, if soaked in water, can radiate almost as strongly as when freshly picked.

While such studies are not universally accepted by the scientific community and are often consigned to the realm of 'fringe science', they nevertheless hint at a scientific basis for prana, but one that we have not yet proved conclusively. The pranic food concept tells us to eat primarily vegetables, whole grains, fruit, nuts, and other foods that emit a radiance higher than the human body's natural radiance. It also suggests that such foods should be eaten very soon after harvesting because their pranic energy dissipates quickly.

Growing crops with high prana value falls in line with all the Second Dimension principles already discussed – local and organic farming, permacultures that create complete agricultural ecosystems, proximity of markets in order to reduce transportation and storage as much as possible, and growing crops that are appropriate for each region's climate and resources. In the Third Dimension, these practices are only reinforced, with special attention devoted to the fundamental role of soil quality.

The Importance of Soil

All plants must grow out of the soil, so it is not difficult to see the importance of soil quality in determining the quality, purity, and vitality of the plants we eat. Soil health has been defined by the Food and Agriculture Organization (FAO) as 'the capacity of soil to function as a living system'. Healthy soils, according to FAO, 'maintain a diverse community of soil organisms that help to control plant disease, insect and weed pests, form beneficial symbiotic associations with plant roots, recycle essential plant nutrients, improve soil structure with positive repercussions for soil water and nutrient holding capacity, and ultimately improve crop production.'[172] In addition, a healthy soil must not pollute the environment; rather, it should contribute to mitigating climate change by maintaining or increasing its own carbon content.

Soil contains an extremely diverse combination of living organisms. Depending on how it is managed, it can be either healthy or depleted. Healthy soil is characterised by the diversity of its biota and the high content of non-living organic matter; it is also resilient to outbreaks of soil-borne pests. A healthy soil can be achieved by using natural fertilisers (such as manure or compost) rather than relying on chemical fertilisers, through crop rotation and the cultivation of cover crops, and by including nitrogen-fixing legumes and trees into cropping systems.

The health of the soil can be monitored using a variety of physical, chemical, and biological indicators, including the following:[173]

- Aggregate stability – how well water can infiltrate the soil during rainfall or irrigation, and how easily soil is washed off or blown away;
- Soil respiration – the amount of carbon dioxide released from the soil, which is an indication of biological activity;
- Bulk density – the weight of the soil per volume, which suggests how well plant seedlings can emerge and how well air can circulate in the soil;
- Conductivity – how well an electrical current travels through soil moisture, which is related to the amount of salt present in the soil;
- pH – the activity of hydrogen ions in soil water;
- Nitrates – the availability of the most important plant nutrient, nitrogen; and
- Earthworm count – earthworms generally enhance microbial activity and soil fertility.

Using these indicators, it is possible to construct a composite index that assigns a single value to soil quality. This value, weighted according to the cultivable surface area that corresponds to it, could be used to assess the overall soil quality of a country, so that soil quality may become a recognised natural asset that can be included in GNR computations (see Chapter 15).

The Future of Nutrition

Renewed attention to soil quality and adherence to pranic principles of food consumption would require a rethinking of the entire food processing industry, including long-distance transport, distribution, preservation methods, and, possibly, the transformation of entire sales channels (such as the supermarket) that rely on these structures and methods. This may sound like a daunting prospect, given the very complex and evolved state of our current food procurement system. But, as we have seen elsewhere in this book, reaching the Third Dimension cannot be achieved through targeted programmes and initiatives alone. While a variety of programmes will be required to sensitise us to the needs of the future, and to nudge us toward the Second Dimension, the final step into the Third Dimension will necessitate a personal effort on the part of everyone, until there is a quorum of enlightened individuals to propel it forward.

Figure 20.1 summarises the desired trajectory of nutrition as we transition to higher dimensions. The First Dimension's focus on caloric value will give way to nutritional indicators that capture primarily the quality of what we eat rather than its quantity or energy content, as well its interaction (complementarity) with other substances. The purity and pranic profile of our food will eventually form the basis for all discussions on nutrition in the future.

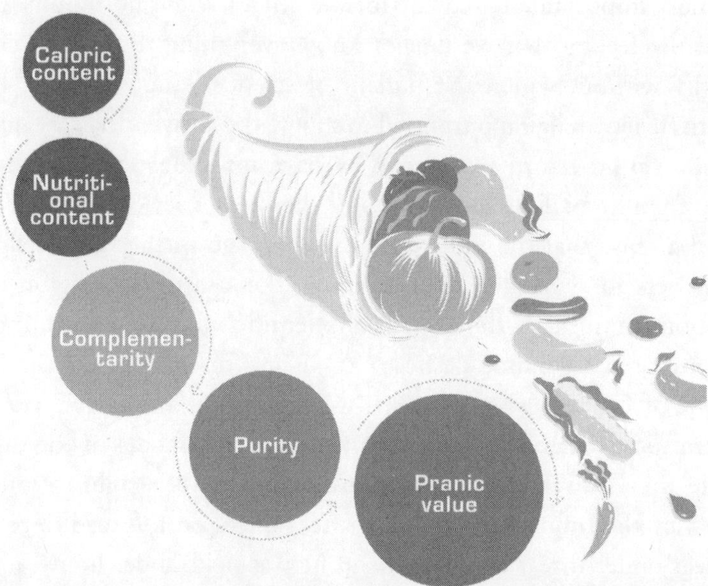

Figure 20.1: Development of Nutritional Indicators

21

Scientific Inquiry: Intuition as Method

The Rise of Science: Modernity's Defining Quest

The most important ingredient for a spirit of scientific inquiry to take root is the feeling that we do not know everything. From this comes a curiosity without which the pursuit of science is not possible. In pre-modern society, religion purported to supply the answers to every question: Why do thunderstorms occur? Why have my crops failed? Why can't we have children? Religious texts and the life stories of religious leaders created a sense that the individual had to go no further than religion to get answers for what he did not know. For centuries, religion created conditions inimical to the growth of scientific inquiry, persecuting those who possessed a genuine desire to know and discover. Take the famous example of Galileo, whose seminal work in mathematics and astronomy led him to advocate the Copernican heliocentric model of the universe, despite the Church's staunch opposition to it. His publications were banned by the Inquisition in 1633, after he had been forced to renounce his ideas under threat of torture, and he was held under house arrest for the last nine years of his life.

This was not limited to any particular religion. As historian Yuval Noah Harari writes, in *Sapiens*, 'Premodern traditions of knowledge such as Islam, Christianity, Buddhism and Confucianism asserted that everything that is important to know about the world was already known.' Hence, he concludes, 'The Scientific Revolution has not been a revolution of knowledge. It has been above all a revolution of ignorance.'

The first people who understood this and began to elaborate upon what we did not know – Avicenna, Al-Biruni, Copernicus, Galileo, Newton, Darwin, and many others – brought about a transformation in scientific thinking. When we began to understand that we did not know things, and how many such things there were, curiosity came to life. Once it was shown that religious orthodoxy did not have all the answers, and that there were things humans could learn about through observation, the period of scientific inquiry began in earnest.

The Power and Limits of Reductionism

The roots of the First Dimension approach to science can be traced to the experiments performed by the great scientists of the modern age starting in the 16th century. The early modern period saw a renewed interest in the systematic observation of natural phenomena. Out of this interest gradually grew a scientific method for explaining them. The first task was to observe a phenomenon carefully and catalogue its effects quantitatively, such as recording the position of a stellar body over the course of a whole year, or measuring the height of a growing plant over several weeks. After tabulating these observations and recognising a pattern, one could hypothesise its causes using inductive reasoning. Then one or more experiments could be devised and conducted to verify whether the hypothesis was plausible. While many early experiments were virtual (that is, thought experiments), real experiments became more common as the quality of instruments improved. A controlled environment like that of a laboratory facilitated systematic experiments where one could isolate a certain variable and perform the experiment by altering that variable while all other variables remained constant. Results could then be tabulated and if they were consistent, one could infer that the hypothesis was either correct or incorrect. Once a hypothesis was tested in one experiment, the next step was for the results to be replicated. Finally, when results were successfully replicated, the hypothesis would become a theorem.

Armed with this powerful First Dimension methodology, science initially made rapid strides because there was plenty of low-hanging fruit. Many theories of simple causality involving simple relationships between a limited number of variables emerged, and thus many of the phenomena around us were explained adequately. Applications of the many theorems and laws that were discovered in this manner gave rise to extensive technological benefits in medicine, transport, construction, communications, hygiene, and agriculture, leading to a rapid and dramatic improvement in the quality of human life.

The growth of capitalism and the limited liability company meant that the inherent risks in funding scientific discoveries could be divided between shareholders, making it much easier to fund research – and the process of experimentation and invention – as the funders knew, increasingly, that there were markets and buyers for the new technologies. The pushback against religious orthodoxy freed scientists from persecution by the dominant religious classes. I remember asking my grandfather why an Indian had not discovered America. He said the crushing orthodoxy that prevailed in India at the time meant that if anyone crossed the sea, they would lose their caste, and their family would have to bankrupt themselves to regain their status. It was the opposite of a spirit of inquiry. The decline in the power of orthodoxy in Europe gave the spirit of scientific inquiry room to breathe. People began to see that there were practical benefits and profits to be made from scientific advances, whether geographical ones like America and Australia, or technological ones like steam engines and spinning jennies.

It was at that point that the connection between science and capitalism was forged. In *Sapiens*, Harari explains how this happened:

> Most scientific studies are funded because somebody believes they can help attain some political, economic or religious goal. For example, in

> the sixteenth century, kings and bankers channelled enormous resources to finance geographical expeditions around the world but not a penny for studying child psychology. This is because kings and bankers surmised that the discovery of new geographical knowledge would enable them to conquer new lands and set up trade empires, whereas they couldn't see any profit in understanding child psychology.

This is the first predicament of First Dimension science: its spirit of inquiry is often directed by the search for utility. Almost every investigative effort must demonstrate that the results will have potential practical applications that will eventually bring about significant and quantifiable benefits to end users of the technology developed with them. Utility, in turn, is frequently driven by the expectation of profit.

The second problem of First Dimension science is that many of the easy gains have already been made. To be sure, in every field, from cosmology to subatomic particles, from genetic sequencing to invertebrate zoology, there are vast domains of knowledge that remain unexplored, and an endless list of research questions to be answered. But many of the mechanisms of nature that impact directly the daily lives of most people have been discovered and exploited already to a sufficient degree that little more needs to be done. Electricity and the light bulb have been invented and refined enough to give us all the lighting solutions we need. While researchers continue to study more efficient methods of delivering these essentials to our homes, the great leaps forward are a thing of the past, and only small incremental gains can be expected. Making new discoveries seems to require exponentially more investment – of time, money, and labour. In the beginning there were a number of things that could be established with simple causality. It was like exploring a mine: it is easy to extract minerals close to the surface, but as time goes by, you have to dig deeper, spend more money and labour, and go off the beaten track to find progressively smaller residues of the precious metal you seek.

The third constraint of First Dimension science is that the experimental methods upon which it is founded typically force us to reduce the number of variables under investigation to make the results discrete and easy to understand. This reductionist approach yielded great returns in the beginning, but, after a while, it hampered our ability to understand the interaction of multiple variables and thus the true nature of the world around us. The tunnel vision of this method – one hypothesis and a handful of variables to be tested in search of a yes-or-no answer – meant that entire realms of nature and spectra of results were ignored.

As the phenomena under investigation have become more complex, however, the power of mathematical modelling has come to the rescue. Most systems in nature are complex, from the fluid mechanics of a flowing river to the molecular interactions in the human body, but they can be tackled using multivariate analytical techniques. Imagine, for example, an epidemiologist trying to determine what is causing an unusually high incidence of cardiovascular disease in a particular population. In her analysis, she must consider a large number of causative variables (risk factors), such as gender, age, the presence of other medical conditions (obesity, diabetes, hypertension, and so forth), each subject's lifestyle (diet, exercise regimen, alcohol use, and smoking habit), environmental factors (air quality, for example), and several others. Yet many of these variables are correlated. Obesity, though it has a genetic component, is closely associated with lifestyle habits, especially diet and exercise. Diabetes, in turn, is closely correlated with obesity. Hypertension is affected by smoking and alcohol consumption. And the incidence of many medical conditions increases with age. Trying to sort through this tangle of correlations necessitates a sophisticated multivariate analysis. Multivariable methods are used to assess and adjust for confounding (when a risk factor is correlated to another risk factor and also to the outcome, but does not actually cause that outcome), to determine whether there is effect modification (when a risk factor has a different effect on different subgroups), and to assess the simultaneous contribution of several risk factors on an outcome. This work is computationally difficult and relies on the use of powerful statistical software made possible by advances in computing over the last few decades.

The study of complex systems such as the weather, climate change, fundamental particle dynamics, and the behaviour of financial markets also relies heavily on the powerful hardware and increasingly refined software that make computational modelling possible. Using computers capable of churning through immense amounts of data, and software that can accommodate the influence of a vast number of variables, computational modelling has become the norm in many modern-day scientific efforts. Simulations based on mathematical models typically yield probabilistic results rather than confirmations of a hypothesis, that is, they predict a range of outcomes and assign a likelihood to each outcome. They acknowledge that many natural as well as man-made systems are far too complex to accommodate simple cause-and-effect interpretations.

The Role of Tangentialism in Second Dimension Science

By adopting methodologies – multivariate analysis and computational modelling – that specifically address the complexity of the natural and artificial systems that surround us, First Dimension science has already come very far. To fulfil its mandate at the cutting edge of human endeavour, however, it must do more. I propose three avenues by which it can achieve new discoveries to supply our need for continual innovation.

Obliquity

Second Dimension science must embrace the notion that knowledge, in the past as well as now, is often arrived at indirectly. The effect of multiple variables cannot be tracked directly. When we track it obliquely, on the other hand, we enter a realm where insight becomes important. Insight is the ability to process information from the 'non-rational mind' or from a different level of consciousness in a way that is very different from the way you process information in the linear, measured context of a scientific experiment. If we come across any information that stretches our hypothesis or demeans our theory, then we must test the efficacy of our tools, or seek better ones. The Second Dimension provides such tools, and science here relies on the abilities of people who have developed great powers of insight.

At present, the pace of scientific research is set by controlled experiments and trials, but increasingly the nature of what we observe will become more oblique. We need to develop a more nuanced mindset to understand the various degrees of influence that each variable exerts in a complex multivariable situation, and how that affects the data we collect. Our methods of gathering and analysing data will need to become more oblique because, as economist John Kay explains in *Obliquity*,

> Obliquity is relevant whenever complex systems evolve in an uncertain environment, and whenever the effect of our actions depends on the ways in which others respond to them [...] Obliquity is inevitable when the environment is complex and changing, purposes are multiple and conflicting, and when we cannot tell, even with hindsight, whether they have been fulfilled.[174]

Philosopher Thomas Kuhn says in *The Structure of Scientific Revolutions*,

> The man who is striving to solve a problem defined by existing knowledge and technique is not, however, just looking around. He knows what he wants to achieve, and he designs his instruments and directs his thoughts accordingly. Unanticipated novelty, the new discovery, can emerge only to the extent that his anticipations about nature and his instruments prove wrong [...] There is no other effective way in which discoveries might be generated.

As Kuhn implies, too often nowadays the scientist shuts off the possibility of a new, unexpected discovery because he is too narrowly focused on achieving a particular result – the confirmation or rejection of a hypothesis. But in the early years of scientific inquiry, when so much less was known, there was a much greater scope for accidental discovery than there is today. If inquiry could recover that original flexibility and rely more on observation of entire systems within nature, rather than narrowly focusing on highly specialised scenarios, the likelihood of discovering new interactions would be greatly increased.

Consider the entomologist Peter Smetacek's brilliant work on butterflies. His theories on butterflies and their habitats are illuminating because he is able to give great insight into natural environments and degradation across species and habitats, simply by extrapolating from his observations of butterfly behaviour. And his insights have been borne out by other scientific research. This is an example of how continuous and careful observation of one aspect of nature – the seemingly insignificant lives of innocuous insects – can yield insightful revelations about entire ecosystems and their evolution. The same can be said of other bellwether species, of course, like frogs and birds of prey; the principle is the same. By observing and recording with increasing frequency and accuracy one phenomenon, without being constrained by the need to obtain the answer to a specific question, we can make significant conclusions and indeed discoveries about other aspects of nature. This amounts to discovery by oblique means – an indirect and tangential approach to scientific inquiry.

Open-Minded Funding

For Smetacek, who runs the Butterfly Research Centre in Bhimtal (in Uttarakhand, India), lack of funding is a constant source of anxiety. Researching butterflies is of no obvious commercial or strategic interest, after all, so First Dimension principles dictate that it should be ignored largely, or treated as a trivial sideshow. Butterflies are not vectors of human disease; they do not produce anything of potential commercial value, like honey or spider webs; they are not indispensable pollinators like bees. This attitude, however, fails to grasp the potential for tangential knowledge that exists in every scientific endeavour, no matter how obscure. Science moves forward as a whole. You cannot expect to advance only selected aspects of scientific inquiry while relegating others to irrelevance. Imagine saying that you need a car to pick you up as soon as possible, and in order to expedite its arrival you are willing to make do with the wheels only. Similarly, the advancement of science occurs along many different fronts simultaneously, and there is no way to judge what the relative value of revelations will be unless all avenues are explored with the same dedication to discovery.

In the Second Dimension, therefore, funding of scientific research must be spread out more evenly and supported more consistently. Today there is some fundamental research happening because of support from government agencies and philanthropic organisations. Much of the most advanced research, however, is currently funded by private entities – corporations driven by the expectation of profit.[175] Private or corporate funding of scientific research invariably affects *what* is researched, with the bulk of funds being spent on projects that have relatively short gestation and that can be monetised easily. Fundamental research is often too risky for corporations to fund. Indeed, research into pure science without any discernible purpose is usually impossible for private companies to support. As discussed in Chapter 14, in the Second Dimension all private firms engaging in R&D of any kind will be required to set aside a percentage of their budget for scientific activities not directly related to any product they manufacture or service they deliver. The funds made available in this manner will be pooled by an independent agency that will oversee the disbursement of such monies to various research activities not already supported by private enterprise or large government grants. Furthermore, in Chapter 16 I showed how we can change the incentives for funding and shift the focus from short-term investments to fundamental research by adopting an innovative system of corporate taxation based on the Utility Index.

Investigation of Alternative Paradigms

The third characteristic of Second Dimension science will be a greater willingness, indeed a stated mission, to embrace and foster alternative forms of inquiry – what we pejoratively call 'fringe science' in the present. In Chapter 22, I will discuss several therapeutic traditions – including Ayurveda, meditation, and yoga – that are still very much on the periphery of what is considered canonical medical understanding, at least in the West. But there is increasing clinical evidence that such therapies do indeed deliver measurable health benefits. They can no longer be dismissed as Eastern fads or pseudo-medical quackery. In other domains of science, too, there needs to be a more concerted effort to valorise and properly investigate all phenomena, however odd they might seem at first, to bring them into the fold of systematic scientific investigation.

I remember an interesting conversation with the epigeneticist Bruce Lipton. He had begun work on a hypothesis that what DNA and RNA themselves contained was not as important as the signals that genes were receiving from their environment, including thoughts and emotions. Like many new hypotheses, it was received with scepticism at first. In effect Lipton was saying: yes, your genes exist, and they are your molecular blueprint, but they do not always manifest the same outcome. They have within them a multitude of pathways that can be activated or deactivated depending on the conditions around them. For example, the body of a person who was always stressed would have more cortisone and adrenaline than the average. The presence of elevated levels of these two hormones, along with a number of other known and unknown reactions in the body, can alter the local cellular environment. Genes can react to this and activate alternative behaviour, which can sometimes lead to cancer or other types of cellular damage. Epigenetics still elicits scepticism from the scientific establishment, but it nevertheless represents a promising area of research that ought not to be dismissed out of hand, and which would be accepted as a legitimate pursuit in the Second Dimension. The same could be said of many other, poorly documented phenomena that are still considered dubious by most, from telepathy to hypnosis to cold fusion.

It is important to remember that there is more to the world than the strictly measurable universe. As Einstein remarked, 'it would be possible [to describe everything scientifically], but it would make no sense. It would be description without meaning – as if you described a Beethoven symphony as a variation of wave pressure.'[176] There is a whole universe beyond the boundaries of First Dimension science, and scientific inquiry should move past them to explore this other world. Just because First Dimension science works well within its boundaries does not mean we should not seek to go beyond them. If we abandon the assumption that only what has been proved experimentally is real, and accept instead that nature still holds a vast reservoir of secrets which we have neither the instruments to analyse nor the intellectual capacity to comprehend yet, then our rate of discovery will accelerate rather than be held back.

The Third Dimension: Scientific Discovery Powered by Consciousness

The application of reason – upon which all inquiry since the Enlightenment has been based, including the scientific method – is helpful only up to a certain limit. In the beginning, science used a reductionist technique to rationalise nature's behaviour. Reliance on simple, single-variable causality yielded tremendous results at first, allowing scientists to explain much of nature's gross behaviour. Under closer scrutiny, however, this method revealed its limitations. In complex situations, in microscopic environments, in structures influenced by too many variables, the reliance on simple causation failed to explain phenomena. When trying to predict the motion of subatomic particles or anticipating gene mutations, the reductionist principle ran into a roadblock. Increasingly divergent theories – such as quantum mechanics, relativity, and string theory – were developed to correct the approximations of First Dimension science. This eventually resulted in a probabilistic interpretation of phenomena aided by computation models. But even that avenue seems to have reached the limits of its usefulness, as manifold increases in computation power have not ushered equivalent leaps in understanding.

In the Third Dimension, therefore, science must turn to a more intuitive approach that will allow us to break the barriers imposed by our primitive understanding of causality. It is the very assumption of causality that distorts our view of reality. In order to go beyond it we must embrace non-linear thought processes and alternative phenomenological explanations – a supra-logical capacity for intuition that all thinkers of the past, from rationalists to shamans, have sought in everything from intoxication to spiritual transcendence. The route to further discoveries lies in our innate, but underdeveloped, capacity for intuition, insight, and clairvoyance – what psychologists call 'thin-slicing'.

Let us assume for a moment that the world we see around us – from what happens at the subatomic level, to the cellular level, to our bodies, our minds, nature, our environment, the solar system, the galaxies around us – is like watching children playing a game. As observers, however, we are forced to watch from a distance, without interfering, as if we were watching the game through a visual telecommunication medium. How we perceive and understand the game played by the children depends heavily on the medium. In the beginning the medium was early black-and-white film with no sound; by watching closely we could surmise certain things, like lip movement and gestures, but we could not hear any sound, so at best we could guess the rules of the game and who the winner was. Then came a new version with sound, and then another version with both sound and colour. In the near future we will be able to watch through an even newer medium that will be able to display the children's brainwaves in real time. It will also maintain a database of their game-playing histories and be able to offer probabilistic predictions about each player's next move based on analysis of this stored information.

With each new stage, with each new medium or tool, the observer is able to reach a closer understanding of the game. But each stage is exponentially more difficult to achieve, because it requires increasingly more sophisticated equipment and computational power. What if there were a faster way to leapfrog all the stages and reach the point of understanding directly? I believe that such a leap forward is possible. It can be achieved by developing our powers of concentration and observation. That is what a rise in our level of consciousness will do. When genuine commitment, mindfulness, and the capacity for deep concentration exist in the mind of the scientist, this mind becomes capable of innovation at a rate and to a depth hitherto unprecedented. The ability to make progress in leaps rather than small steps will result from a heightened level of consciousness.

How will this happen? In his seminal book *The Tao of Physics*, Fritjof Capra suggests the following:

> In our everyday life, direct intuitive insights into the nature of things are normally limited to extremely brief moments. Not so in Eastern

> mysticism where they are extended to long periods and, ultimately, become a constant awareness. The preparation of the mind for this awareness – for the immediate, nonconceptual awareness of reality – is the main purpose of all schools of Eastern mysticism. During the long cultural history of India, China and Japan, an enormous variety of techniques, rituals and art forms have been developed to achieve this purpose, all of which may be called meditation in the widest sense of the word. The basic aim of these techniques seems to be to silence the thinking mind and to shift the awareness from the rational to the intuitive mode of consciousness.

Insight and intuition, in other words, are fundamental ingredients for meaningful scientific advance, and the consistent practice of meditation in the Third Dimension will prime the scientist's mind for frequent and sustained moments of insightful deduction. Now, the definitions of 'insight' and 'intuition' can be ambiguous: insight can mean either a deep understanding that arises slowly from prior knowledge, or it can mean an instant breakthrough that comes like a thunderbolt. Intuition, although often equated with insight, can be more precisely defined as an inner knowledge gained without the use of rational thought. Intuition, I believe, will guide Third Dimension scientists to probe in areas where important discoveries can be made, while insight will reveal such discoveries to them. Insight will indeed take the form of sudden revelation, but such a revelation will be the fruit of extensive previous application. The new acuity gained through consistent meditation will prepare the mind for such insight, such that 'eureka moments' will be much more frequent.

The history of science is replete with instances where a ground-breaking advance was made entirely through either intuition or insight, or both. I will not repeat the most common anecdotes – Archimedes' discovery of buoyancy, or Newton and his apple, or Einstein's first glimpse of relativity during his dull days at the patent office – because they have been retold, embellished, and exaggerated too often. But there are many others worth noting, such as Rene Descartes' invention of the Cartesian coordinate system because he followed the movement of a fly flitting across his ceiling and realised that he could describe its exact position by measuring its distance from each of two perpendicular walls. Or Friedrich von Stradonitz's discovery of the ring-like structure of the benzene molecule as a result of a dream.

In technology, too, insight has yielded many of the useful products that we use today. The lowly Post-It note – an indispensable item on everyone's desk – was invented by 3M employee Art Fry when he realised that a mild glue that had been created years before but was as yet unused because of its weakness could be useful in solving a problem he himself had experienced – how to permanently bookmark a page in his hymnal without damaging it. Swiss mountaineer George de Mestral came home one day after walking his dog and realised that they were both covered in tiny burrs. Intuition told him that this was not a trivial occurrence at all, so instead of brushing off the burrs he looked at them under a microscope, and saw that they clung to his clothes with tiny hooks. His insight was that this mechanism could be reproduced artificially and find useful applications, so he designed a two-sided fabric fastener – Velcro – that mimicked nature. I can imagine that the process must have been much the same for the primordial inventor of the wheel: while walking down a hill he was overtaken by a rolling stone and intuited that this rotating motion could be faster and more efficient than walking. Then the insight struck him: it was the shape that made all the difference.

While we are ready to acknowledge the role of intuition and insight in many important discoveries and inventions of the past, we typically associate such instances with lucky guesswork, or serendipity, or a momentary flash of genius – unexplainable and usually unrepeatable. My contention here, however, is that such consequential moments of insight are neither mysterious nor unique. In most anecdotes that describe such 'eureka experiences', we notice a similar pattern. The scientist, researcher or designer – an experienced thinker or practitioner in his field – thought long and hard about a problem or issue, without being able to solve it. Later, in a moment when he was distracted and thus was able to relax his mind, the insight came to him unexpectedly. This happened because for a brief moment the thinking mind switched off and the experienced practitioner was able to make the connection to the essence of what was being observed through direct, intuitive insight.

Thus it was for Einstein, who famously hit upon the fundamental insight that time is not constant (time can flow at different rates, depending on how fast you move) while riding a streetcar home, after having been vexed by the relationship between space and time for years. After struggling to find a way to create a rotating magnetic field, Nikola Tesla made the breakthrough that resulted in the invention of the AC induction motor while walking through a park in Budapest and reciting poetry. Roger Penrose's understanding of black holes also came to him while he was out for a stroll. Biochemist Kary Mullis developed the idea for polymerase chain reaction (PCR) – a technique that allows a strand of DNA to be copied and amplified – while driving to his cabin on the north coast of California. And German pharmacologist Otto Loewi, thanks to a dream, famously discovered that nerve impulses were transmitted chemically, not electronically.

Original insight and invention are unlikely to occur without hard work and perseverance, of course. Einstein's insight that time is not absolute was the result of years of hard work; the theme of Mahler's 7th symphony came to him when he heard the sound made by the oars of a rowboat, but only after many hours of struggle to find the right tune. As Louis Pasteur put it, 'chance favours the prepared mind'. But even when trying to solve a problem consciously, great mathematicians and scientists employ a process of trial and error that also requires moments of creative, irrational insight for their work to progress. Karl Popper wrote in *The Logic of Scientific Discovery*, 'There is no such thing as a logical method of having new ideas, or a logical reconstruction of this process [...] [E]very discovery contains "an irrational element," or "a creative intuition."'

Unconventional, irrational, inspired ways to access knowledge have been sought by many over the ages – researchers, priests, soothsayers, oracles, Sybils, and psychics – especially with the help of hallucinogenic substances. The collected evidence of such attempts to reach a state of mind that favours brief periods of sharpened intuition was exclusively anecdotal until 1965, when a group of US researchers led by psychologist

James Fadiman conducted an experiment designed to evaluate whether the use of a psychedelic substance like lysergic acid diethylamide (LSD) could enhance creativity in solving scientific and technical problems of a high professional order.[177]

The study subjects were twenty-seven men engaged in a variety of technical professions: engineers, mathematicians, architects, and designers. Each participant brought along a professional problem he had been working on for at least three months, but had been unable to solve. After having taken a combination of drugs, including mescaline,[178] the subjects were encouraged to work on the problems they had brought with them. After completion of the experiment, most subjects reported various changes in their approach to work, including the ability to see the problem in broader terms; enhanced fluency of ideation and heightened capacity to visualise potential solutions; increased ability to concentrate; and an enhanced sense of 'knowing' when the right solution appeared. In many cases, the subject was able to find a new and viable solution to the creative problem he faced. Moreover, in structured creativity tests administered by the study designers both before and after the experiment, the majority of participants showed a significant improvement in fluency of ideas, visualisation acuity, and speed, when under the influence of the psychedelic drug. (Further experimentation was prevented by the Food and Drug Administration's subsequent ban on the use of psychedelics in clinical research involving human subjects.)

Whether induced by a chemical substance or occurring naturally, the potential of heightened states of insightfulness is undeniable. Brief periods of irrational genius have played a clear role in the development of science and technology. To a certain extent, the existence of, and indeed the necessity for, an intuitive and irrational element in scientific inquiry was posited in very scientific terms by one of the greatest minds of our time. In 1931, Czech mathematician Kurt Gödel demonstrated that in any branch of mathematics there would always be propositions that could not be proved or disproved using the rules and axioms of that mathematical branch itself. In essence, Gödel showed that there can exist propositions that we know by insight to be true but that cannot necessarily be proven mathematically.

Although this idea can be stated in a rigorously mathematical way, as Gödel did, what it seems to say is that rational thought alone cannot achieve any ultimate and complete truth. What came to be known as the Gödel Incompleteness Theorem has thus had profound implications for our understanding of the limitations of reason, making, as he put it, 'continued appeals to mathematical intuition' necessary.

If intuition and insight are indispensable ingredients of scientific progress, then the goal of a higher-dimensional methodology for the advancement of science must be to increase the frequency and profoundness of such insightful breakthroughs. In the Third Dimension, the greater elasticity of mind attained through the consistent practice of meditation will foster the qualities of intuition and insight in a greater number of scientists and engineers. As I explained in Chapter 3, meditation increases the mind's ability to focus and concentrate, and this, in turn, opens it to insight. The first step in this process is the ability to still the mind, emptying it of distracting and confounding thoughts. In other words, the starting point is the ability to relax the mind. As we have seen, the alternation of these two mental states – intense concentration and relaxation – has produced some of the greatest scientific and technical breakthroughs in the past. It is reasonable to expect, therefore, that minds trained through years of meditation to achieve both great focus and complete relaxation will be able to intuit with greater agility the many secrets that still lie hidden in nature.

Stated differently, my expectation is that scientists in the Third Dimension will develop a new avenue to acquire knowledge, an avenue that is neither rational nor sensory. That such an avenue exists has long been posited by various traditions of Eastern mysticism, especially with regard to the esoteric concept of the Third Eye. This speculative, invisible eye – often depicted in statues of the Buddha and of Hindu deities as occupying the middle of the forehead – is said to provide perception of a reality that lies beyond ordinary vision. It is a window that allows some to introspect upon the inner reality of higher consciousness, but also to examine the world with special acuity, amounting to an almost supernatural perception that brings out our ability to observe vibes, energies, connections and implications. Stripped of its religious connotations, the idea of a Third Eye simply suggests that a deeper truth can be grasped directly by accessing the mind's extrasensory capacity. The Third Eye – which can be opened and trained through meditative techniques – is merely another term for the intuitive capacity that I have tried to describe and predict in Third Dimension scientists.[179]

Today there are many individuals, in science as well as in other disciplines, who already possess the intuitive ability to see what others cannot, and can at times glimpse solutions and connections that can prove revolutionary. They are the most successful investors, the most productive researchers, the most perspicacious writers, the most inspirational teachers. But whatever heightened level of intuitive understanding they have been able to develop, it is a miraculous quality that sets them apart from the vast majority of their colleagues, who may be equally hard-working and dedicated. It is my belief that the powers of concentration fostered by increased meditational practice in the Third Dimension will result in such levels of natural insight in many more intellectuals, scientists, and thinkers, such that we will enjoy an era of unprecedented discovery and breakthrough in all realms of knowledge.

22

Health and Medicine: Achieving Wellness

Health and Medicine in the First Dimension

Over the last century or so, modern medicine, which by and large means Western medicine, has achieved awe-inspiring results. Through vaccination, antibiotics, and other measures, it has either eradicated or controlled many of the deadly infectious diseases that have plagued mankind for centuries. In surgery, it has developed safe, successful techniques to repair and even replace organs, while making such operations possible through great strides in anaesthesiology and post-operative care. It has managed to correct many chemical imbalances through drugs, to disinfect and suture wounds, to reset broken bones and, when necessary, to replace them with prosthetic devices. Even limb transplants are now possible. Through exploratory surgery, X-rays, MRI, sonograms, pathology tests, biopsies, and various other methods, modern medicine has learned to probe and analyse every corner and recess of the human body. With genetic and microcellular research, it has discovered the genesis and pathology of many non-infectious conditions. Through all these advances, it has greatly reduced the burden of disease everywhere, it has saved countless lives and eased suffering, and it has enhanced both the duration and the quality of human life.

Modern medicine has achieved all this by applying a scientific methodology to occurrences of disease, especially health crises. The first instance of this, as physicist Simon Singh and physician Edzard Ernst describe eloquently in their book *Trick or Treatment*,[180] was the discovery that scurvy – a debilitating and often deadly condition that affected sailors – was attributable to a dietary deficiency (of vitamin C, as it turned out later) and could be resolved by administering citrus fruits or juices, such as lemons, limes, and oranges, to the sailors. Out of this early success grew a methodology for identifying the root causes of health problems and testing various ways to address them, a methodology that eventually gave shape to the randomised, double-blinded clinical trial that remains the gold standard of medical research today. Much of modern medicine functions in the same linear pattern: a disease condition is observed, research is conducted on its symptoms, and a therapeutic solution (usually pharmaceutical or surgical) is developed, tested, and eventually administered to the patient until his condition improves.

Examples of this method abound. For an infectious disease, the key is to identify the microbe or virus that is causing the illness, and to develop an antibiotic to kill it, and perhaps a vaccine to prevent it from emerging in the future. In surgery, doctors identify the affected organ and repair it, from removing a spleen or appendix to performing a liver transplant. For gross injuries, such as a broken bone, a diagnosis by X-ray is followed by setting with a cast. For poisoning or deficiency, such as the case of scurvy, the source of the disturbance is identified, and it is addressed by addition or removal of the correct substance.

In all these examples, we see the overall trajectory of modern medicine: it attempts to reduce a health problem to a single, preponderant variable, to identify a single cause, and to address it with a single solution. In other words, it relies heavily on a unitary cause-and-effect principle: one cause, one effect, one solution. This ability to subject health problems to a reductionist, systematic analysis has been the great strength of modern medicine, but also its greatest limitation. Such a methodology has narrowed the focus of medicine substantially, but has given it powerful focus within that narrowness.

Not all health problems, unfortunately, can be causally attributed to a single variable, because not all health problems have a single cause, or a single solution, like lime juice for scurvy. The vast and perplexing domain of chronic illnesses, also known as non-communicable diseases (NCDs), poses a much greater challenge to modern medicine because these conditions often have multiple contributing factors. The reason for their occurrence cannot be attributed to a single cause, but rather must be viewed in the light of a variety of risk factors. And these chronic diseases, which have much to do with modern diets, work and personal habits, mental and emotional states, and heredity, already constitute a huge and growing portion of the global burden of disease.

According to the US federal public health agency, the Centers for Disease Control and Prevention, 75 per cent of current healthcare expenditure in the United States goes toward treating chronic diseases. A landmark report published by the Milken Institute in 2007[181] looked at seven of the most common chronic diseases (cancer, diabetes, hypertension, stroke, heart disease, pulmonary conditions, and mental disorders), and found that 109 million Americans (over one-third of the population) suffered from at least one chronic disease. Contrary to popular belief, these chronic illnesses do not afflict only high-income populations. A 2010 report on the global status of NCDs by the WHO indicated that 80 per cent of cases occur in low- and middle-income countries.[182]

This trend has led to the rapidly escalating cost of treating chronic diseases. The Milken Institute report estimated the annual cost of treating chronic diseases in the United States at $277 billion (with a further $1.1 trillion in productivity losses). The WHO report suggested that NCDs can cost developing countries up to 6.8 per cent of their GDP. For example, in the period 2005–2015, India is estimated to have lost 1.5 per cent of its GDP as a result of heart disease, stroke, and diabetes. In China, the total direct and indirect costs of obesity alone, among adults, were projected to be 9 per cent of GDP by 2025.

Second, Western medicine has been, to a large extent, a victim of its own success. Its enormous contributions to human health, achieved mostly in the 20th century, have generated a heightened expectation that it can solve any and every health problem. But, like so many other systems, it is subject to the law of diminishing marginal returns. In its halcyon days, it tackled the lowest-hanging fruit, comprised of the infectious killers of old, the likes of cholera, polio, smallpox, diphtheria, and typhus. And it did so with spectacular success, especially when seen against the backdrop of the misguided ideas of medieval and early modern medicine, which relied on unproven, hazardous interventions like bloodletting.

If we take longevity, that is, life expectancy, as a proxy for wellness (a poor proxy, but one that can be quantified easily), we can see that a quantum leap was achieved in the first half of the 20th century. In most Western countries, life expectancy rose, roughly, from the high forties to the high sixties – a whopping twenty years of added life.

Much of the improvement in life expectancy and general health in the 20th century was due to fundamental improvements in hygiene and nutrition. While we now take these things for granted, the development of modern sanitation and sewage systems, the widespread use of soap, and the availability of better, fresher, and more varied foods contributed as much as, if not more than, modern medicine to the establishment of health standards. Simple parasitic illnesses like amoebiasis – which can stunt growth because it has a debilitating effect on a child's ability to absorb nutrition – can be effectively prevented with basic hygiene. Let us take a moment to appreciate this – the dramatic difference to longevity that the simple act of washing our hands can make.

Within medical practice itself, the most significant improvements to life expectancy came through basic changes in prenatal and neonatal care, which drastically reduced infant mortality. In *Sapiens*, historian Yuval Noah Harari writes,

> Until the twentieth century, between a quarter and a third of the children of agricultural societies never reached adulthood. [...] In seventeenth-century England, 150 out of every 1,000 newborns died during their first year, and a third of all children were dead before they reached fifteen. Today, only five out of 1,000 English babies die during their first year, and only seven out of 1,000 die before age fifteen.

Our expectations were raised by these remarkable improvements in health, to the point where we assumed all occurrences of disease could be similarly dealt with. But, as medicine turns increasingly to curing chronic illnesses, the success rate has been much more modest. In the second half of the 20th century, despite further, impressive advances (such as organ transplants and other life-saving techniques), life expectancy climbed by less than ten years. This is still a tremendous improvement, but far less remarkable than what was achieved previously. Now, in the 21st century, life expectancy is stagnating in the mid- or high seventies in most industrialised nations, with little likelihood of rising any higher.

Diminishing returns are also palpably affecting the profits of large pharmaceutical companies. The cost of bringing new remedies to market has skyrocketed over the last few decades, as clinical trial procedures – the very foundation of modern medicine, as we have seen – have become increasingly rigorous and laborious, while the chances of litigation and recalls after the release of a drug have become higher. There has been much debate over what, exactly, is the typical cost of researching and testing a new drug, ranging from as high as $2.6 billion estimated by the pharmaceutical industry itself, to less than $50 million as calculated by its detractors.[183] Whatever the true number, it constitutes a vast investment. Despite the effort required, however, pharmaceutical companies have seen a steady decrease in their return on investment for these R&D expenditures. Indeed, an oft-cited 2012 article noted that the number of drugs invented per billion dollars of R&D invested has been diminishing rapidly over the last half-century.[184]

An analysis by Forbes found that much of the R&D effort made by pharmaceutical companies goes to waste because the majority of the compounds tested for medicinal use in humans fail to be both effective and safe.[185] When taking into account the cost of these failed drugs, the Forbes study concluded that pharmaceutical companies – at least the large ones that are working on dozens of drug projects simultaneously – spend as much as $5 billion in R&D for every new medicine that actually reaches the market. Today, therefore, the development of pharmaceuticals has become a high-stakes game in which only a few large companies with large cash reserves can participate.

Diminishing returns are also very much the story when we consider the impact of treatment on patients with chronic illnesses. To curb the risk of heart attack, for example, a patient is likely to be prescribed several powerful, synthetic drugs to address various risk factors. He may be taking, concurrently, a drug to lower his blood pressure, another to reduce his cholesterol level, and yet another to control his diabetes. As studies have shown, the incremental effect of each additional drug in reducing the risk of infarction diminishes rapidly. Moreover, side effects increase linearly with each additional medication, and the number of potential drug–drug, drug–food, drug–disease, and drug–organ interactions increases exponentially. As a rule of thumb, once the number of medications reaches five, the probability of adverse events is so high as to counterbalance any benefit from additional medications.[186]

In general, current treatment regimens for most chronic illnesses consist of a battery of different medications, therapies, and interventions, with a high incidence of side effects. Treatment for mental conditions such as depression and bipolar disorder, for example, involves combinations of powerful drugs (mood stabilisers, antidepressants, and antipsychotics) tailored to each patient and reformulated frequently, plus regular counselling sessions.

Treatment for cancer can consist of surgery, radiation therapy, plus multiple courses of various chemicals taken together (chemotherapy). Chemotherapy is inherently toxic because it targets cells that grow and divide rapidly – cancer cells and healthy cells that may be fast-growing – including those found in the skin, hair, intestines, and bone marrow. Therefore, chemotherapy is always accompanied by various side effects, ranging from mild, short-term ones, such as fatigue, hair loss, anaemia, nausea, and constipation, to more permanent and debilitating ones, such as osteoporosis, digestive problems, infertility, hypothyroidism, and nervous system changes. Some chemotherapy drugs help cure certain types of cancer only to induce others. For example, patients who have taken prolonged courses of tamoxifen (a drug frequently used to treat breast cancer) appear to have a significantly increased risk of developing endometrial cancer (cancer of the lining of the uterus),[187] while chemicals known as alkylating agents, used to treat a variety of cancers, are known to cause leukaemia themselves.[188]

In the area of infectious diseases, widespread and often uncontrolled use of antibiotic, antifungal, and antiviral medicines has led to increasingly drug-resistant strains of bacteria and viruses, which, in turn, require the development of ever more toxic medicines. Multiple drug resistance and extensive drug resistance are now common for many types of bacteria, including *Mycobacterium tuberculosis*; for many viruses, particularly the influenza virus; and for some parasitic infections, including malaria.

Health and Medicine in the Second Dimension

Western medicine – a scientific discipline based on single-variable crisis management – seems to have reached the limits of its usefulness. To tackle the new reality of 21st-century disease, which is predominantly chronic disease, a new paradigm is necessary.

The first task of Second Dimension healthcare is to step away from the single-cause–single-remedy methodology of First Dimension medicine and redefine itself in two ways: by recognising the deep and complex interconnections of the body's many biochemical and physiological functions, and by practising an *interceptive* approach to disease rather than a responsive one. In order to understand what these fundamental changes mean, we must first consider the predicament of chronic diseases in some detail. We can take diabetes as an example.

Diabetes: A Case Study in Chronic Diseases

Diabetes mellitus is a metabolic disorder characterised by higher-than-normal levels of blood sugar (glucose) for prolonged periods. This condition, if left untreated, can result in long-term complications, including cardiovascular disease, stroke, chronic kidney disease, foot ulcers, and damage to the eyes. According to the WHO's latest *Global Report on Diabetes*, an estimated 422 million adults (8.5 per cent of the world's adult population) suffered from diabetes in 2014.[189] This represented a steep rise in the disease's morbidity from 108 million adults (4.7 per cent of the world's adult population) who had suffered from diabetes in 1980.

Our current understanding of diabetes is relatively simple: it is an excess of circulating blood sugar. The key player in the body's management of sugar levels is insulin, a hormone produced in the pancreas. In a healthy body, the intake of food (such as a meal) triggers the release of insulin. During digestion, the gut (which includes the stomach and the small intestine) breaks down carbohydrates and turns them into a type of sugar (glucose), then transfers it to the bloodstream. Specialised glands in the pancreas, known as beta cells, detect a rise in blood sugar and promptly release insulin. Insulin instructs muscle cells to absorb sugar from the bloodstream and use it as energy. It also signals liver cells and fat cells to absorb excess glucose and store it for later use. Once the glucose has been absorbed by these cells, blood glucose levels return to normal and the release of insulin stops.

There are two types of diabetes. In type 1 diabetes, the insulin-producing beta cells have been destroyed by the body's own immune system for reasons we do not yet understand. The body is thus unable to produce any insulin naturally, so glucose cannot be absorbed by tissue cells and remains in the bloodstream. In type 2 diabetes, the beta cells are functional, but they either produce insufficient insulin, or the insulin they secrete is ineffectual because the sensors on the surface of cells (known as insulin receptors), which are supposed to detect the presence of insulin in the bloodstream, do not function properly (a condition known as insulin resistance). As a consequence, the pancreas has to produce more and more insulin to compensate for this reduction in insulin function.

Type 2 diabetes is the more common form of diabetes. It is strongly linked to obesity, as well as to high cholesterol and high blood pressure. Stress is also known to induce diabetes. (Stress releases adrenaline into the bloodstream, which inhibits the release of insulin.) These risk factors result mostly from modern-day lifestyles and diets, making type 2 diabetes the prototypical chronic disease of our time – it has no permanent cure, it is difficult to manage, and its prevalence is increasing rapidly everywhere, in poor countries as well as wealthy ones, among adults as well as children.[190]

Current methods of treatment aim to reduce circulating glucose to as normal a level as possible; to avoid the acute symptoms of diabetes, such as thirst and frequent urination; and to prevent long-term complications like eye, nerve, and kidney damage. Based on current understanding, insulin is pivotal in managing diabetes. In type 1 diabetes, synthetic insulin must be injected in the patient several times a day for the rest of his life or administered via an insulin pump. In type 2 diabetes, glucose levels are lowered by diet control, increased exercise, and stress reduction. If these measures cannot achieve the desired blood sugar target (as derived from population studies), then oral medications are administered. These medications mostly target the glucose–insulin mechanism alone. They either increase the production of insulin by beta cells, increase the sensitivity of insulin receptors, or decrease the amount of glucose absorbed from food or released by the liver. They include the following:

- metformin and pioglitazone, which reduce blood sugar released by the liver;
- sulphonylureas, which stimulate insulin production;
- DPP4 inhibitors and GLP-1 agonists, which stimulate insulin secretion and reduce appetite; and
- SGLT2 inhibitors, which cause more sugar to pass out of the body in the urine.

In some cases, particularly after multiple years of treatment, insulin production may be so limited that type 2 diabetes patients, like type 1 patients, have to be treated with insulin injections. All these medications are highly targeted and have significant side effects, including diarrhoea (in the case of metformin), nausea (GLP-1 agonists), and weight gain (sulphonylureas). Therefore, their overall benefit is questionable, especially since there is no uniformity in the choice of medications after a diagnosis.

Our brief discussion of diabetes exemplifies the limitations of First

Dimension medicine when faced with chronic disease. First, the First Dimension approach tends to be reductionist, focusing almost exclusively on one functional unit or mechanism in the body (in the case of diabetes, the interaction between blood sugar and insulin). Second, the remedy typically applied by First Dimension medicine is the urgent targeting of the perceived cause of disease through powerful synthetic chemicals. This type of intervention is preferred over other therapeutic options, such as a slow recovery achieved by promoting natural healing processes. This reductionist and interventionist approach is rooted in the scientific methodology that allowed us to combat many of the most devastating infectious diseases in the past. With chronic diseases, however, there are usually no clearly identifiable causal factors that can be eliminated or controlled, so a reductionist approach is likely to fail. Targeted pharmacological interventions in the body's highly interdependent systems tend to provoke a cascade of reactions that keep multiple systems in stress. Even when a degree of control is achieved, a fragile balance must be maintained by continually adjusting drug dosages and lifestyle choices. In this manner, chronic disease can be brought under control, but not cured.

Modelling and Intercepting Chronic Diseases

The first task of an advanced, Second Dimension approach to managing, or indeed reversing, a chronic disease like type 2 diabetes is to focus not only on the control of glucose and insulin levels, but also on the delicate interplay of the body's many systems that impact the disorder. It requires a multifaceted understanding of all the bodily mechanisms that impact insulin production and efficacy. Indeed, it implies a new understanding of disease – what might be labelled a 'systems' approach to diabetes therapy. A systems approach recognises that diabetes is a progressive metabolic condition that exists in a continuum; it is not merely an elevation of blood glucose that can be fixed by achieving certain glycaemic targets. Understanding that continuum requires a comprehensive study of the body's highly interconnected metabolic, endocrine, and circulatory mechanisms.

Modern understanding of disease processes is increasingly making us aware of the gradual progression of a disease well before the threshold for diagnosis is reached. Sometimes, the progression travels along unexpected pathways that involve organs or systems that are not necessarily touched by the disease's symptoms. For example, Parkinson's disease – a degenerative disorder of the central nervous system – is now believed to begin in the gastrointestinal tract well before its extension to the brain.[191] Such interplay of multiple and distantly linked systems in a disease makes a therapeutic strategy based on a single-cause approach inadequate. Therefore, a systems approach to chronic diseases must create a detailed, comprehensive model of all the body's processes, however peripheral, that are relevant to the disease. In the case of diabetes, this would include the role of increased blood supply to the digestive tract immediately after eating a full meal, the effect of excess insulin on the liver, and the relationship of beta cells to other pancreatic cells, such as alpha cells.[192]

Once the disease's relationship to all the body's functional systems is understood, Second Dimension medicine can be mobilised to intercept the development of that disease. Even someone who enjoys good general health may be susceptible to the roots of disease that establish themselves well before the disease manifests itself in detectable symptoms. Interceptive medicine aims to intervene at a stage of disease development *before* manifestation. Interceptive medicine is not merely another term for preventive health. Preventive health involves measures aimed at averting the onset of disease: promotion of a healthy lifestyle through changes in diet, exercise regimen, and behaviour; screening for well-known diseases in order to detect symptoms and begin therapy as early as possible; and removal of environmental and economic barriers to care. Interceptive medicine, on the other hand, is not aimed at preventing disease. It takes for granted the onset of disease, at least of many chronic and genetically influenced conditions. It seeks to intercept such disease at a very early, pre-symptomatic stage by analysing and tracking indicators at individual level, and intervening with composite, natural (non-synthetic) pharmacological products to restore balance to the body's chemistry, so that the body's own healing mechanisms may do much of the restorative work.

An important task of Second Dimension medicine, therefore, is to develop a composite pharmacology. Rather than administer drugs that are highly targeted (that is, their active ingredient is a powerful synthetic compound, delivered at a high dosage to combat a particular infectious agent, imbalance, or dysfunction), a composite pharmacological solution aims to hit multiple targets at a lower level of effectiveness in order to act on multiple pathways that contribute to the disease, and to optimise the patient's chances of overcoming it. An example of such a composite drug for type 2 diabetes might be a substance that helps to reduce stress levels while also stimulating beta cells *and* inhibiting absorption of sugars by the digestive tract. Low dosage of active ingredients and the use of natural preparations (from traditional and Ayurvedic pharmacopoeia, for example) help to reduce the side effects that are typical of more targeted, synthetic compounds.

The Body as a Unique Mechanism

Our detailed discussion of diabetes management (and, potentially, cure) has shown that the future of medicine lies in an improved and well-rounded understanding of the complex interactions that occur in the human body, that is, in a systems approach to therapy. Equally important, however, is the realisation that each human body is slightly different, from the anatomical level all the way to the molecular. It may be the locus of diverse genetic mutations, known or unknown; it may behave differently in response to internal as well as environmental prompts; it may react unpredictably when confronted with infectious organisms; and it may respond differently to pharmaceutical therapies.

The seemingly endless mutability of the human body points to one conclusion: all therapies, including drugs, should be tailored to each individual. This is already the case for certain life-saving interventions, such as cancer chemotherapy. But increasingly, most diseases, and especially chronic disorders, must rely on bespoke therapies and drug combinations that are formulated anew for each individual patient. This may sound prohibitively difficult and expensive, but here, again, the momentous pace of medical discovery can make it a reality in the near future. In diagnostics, artificial intelligence algorithms are being applied to diagnostic tools with rapidly increasing frequency and precision. In a remarkable example of the diagnostic power of artificial intelligence, researchers at DeepMind (the artificial intelligence company owned by Google's parent company, Alphabet) collaborated with London's Moorfields Eye Hospital to develop a 'deep learning' software that analyses 3D scans of patients' eyes, made using a technique known as Optical Coherence Tomography (OCT). After 'training' the software to identify common patterns in the data from nearly 15,000 OCT scans of about 7,600 patients, the deep learning technique was able to recommend clinical intervention based on signs of potential eye disease identified in the OCT scans. When its referral recommendations were compared with diagnoses made by eye doctors using the same scan data, it was found that the software had the same rate of successful diagnosis (about 94.5 per cent) as the best retina specialists.[193]

Another study undertaken by Google and its sister company Verily used the combination of retinal scans and artificial intelligence technology as a new method to assess a patient's risk of heart disease. By analysing scans of the retinal fundus (the back of the eye), the software was able to accurately deduce basic patient data, such as age, gender, blood pressure, and whether or not they smoked. When applied to historical data, the software was able to use this method to forecast a patient's risk of suffering a major cardiovascular event, such as a heart attack, with roughly the same accuracy as current leading methods.[194] Such advances suggest that, in the near future, artificial intelligence will be able to use data obtained from routine and relatively inexpensive tests, such as blood work and retinal scans, and provide accurate forecasts of each patient's risk profile for various disease conditions.

Genetic analysis is another tool that is increasingly being used to manage diseases and chronic ailments. In particular, identifying specific genetic mutations can greatly help to anticipate the onset of disease. Well-known examples of this are the BRCA1 and BRCA2 genes. These genes produce tumour-suppressor proteins, which help repair damaged DNA. When one of these genes mutates, its corresponding protein may not be produced or may not function properly, resulting in an inability to repair DNA damage. Cells whose DNA is not repaired regularly are more likely to develop genetic alterations that can lead to cancer. Specific mutations of the BRCA1 and BRCA2 genes are associated with increased risk of several types of cancer, especially female breast and ovarian cancers. Roughly 70 per cent of women who inherit a harmful BRCA1 or BRCA2 mutation will develop breast cancer at some point in their lives, compared with 12 per cent in the general population; about 44 per cent of women who inherit a harmful BRCA1 mutation will develop ovarian cancer, compared with 1.3 per cent of women in the general population.[195] Information gleaned from genetic testing can help patients manage their risk of contracting cancer. For example, women who test positive for a BRCA1 or BRCA2 mutation may opt to start breast cancer screening at a younger age, so as to increase the likelihood of detecting breast cancer at an early stage, when it can be treated more successfully.

Advances in our understanding of the body's genetic complexity point the way to more effective health management in the future. In the Second Dimension we must continue to invest in the medical and pharmaceutical research that gives us the breakthroughs in early detection and interception, and improve the treatment and standard of care protocols. Indeed, a hallmark of Second Dimension healthcare should be a genetic screening and early detection programme covering the entire population. It will be considered a human right rather than an optional benefit of a healthcare insurance plan.

In the Second Dimension, every Community – which, as we saw in Chapter 10, will be a geographical unit of governance with up to 25,000 citizens – will be served by a community health centre. The health centre will, among other services, offer annual health check-ups at nominal cost for each member of the Community. Data collected during routine exams (such as body mass index, cholesterol, blood pressure, glucose level, and insulin function) would be recorded in regional and national databases and be accessible to epidemiologists and to analytical software powered by artificial intelligence to further study and increase our understanding of the onset of disease. Once processed, these data will allow local triage staff to identify potential problems early on and use everything in the interceptive toolkit to avert the development of disease. This system would go a long way toward reducing the burden of chronic diseases in the population. Currently, many forms of treatable diseases are detected too late because much of the population, especially in developing countries, does not have access to regular primary checks. In the Second Dimension, however, regular wellness exams will be the norm, and citizens will be incentivised to comply because their attendance at such check-ups will affect health insurance premiums. (Health insurance provided by private firms will be mandatory, with financially disadvantaged individuals and families receiving subsidies in the form of TCs, as discussed in Chapter 17.)

From Health to Wellness in the Third Dimension

Ayurveda as a Template for Health Management

Simply identifying a number of risk factors through genetic screening and advanced diagnostic techniques, and mitigating them, is not enough to create a holistic healthcare system suitable for the Third Dimension. What is required is a new approach to medicine that offers highly individualised prescriptions for diet and exercise, mental well-being, social intercourse, recreation, and many other lifestyle aspects that impact our health. A recommended diet, for example, must address not only each individual's specific nutritional needs, but also the equally unique ability of each body to absorb different nutrients in different quantities. A drug prescription must take into account the patient's known allergies, history of medication, hereditary conditions, side effects experienced in previous courses of medication, and interactions with other medications or supplements taken concurrently. In addition, a patient's daily routine and diet – as well as her natural predisposition to certain types of remedy – should be considered when prescribing medication.

Developing a system of health management that is capable of individualised remedies and can also bring into play many disparate components of mental and physical health is not as daunting as it seems. An example of such a system – already time-tested and comprehensive – is Ayurveda, perhaps the oldest coherent body of healing knowledge known to us. Despite its ancient roots (in Vedic Hinduism), Ayurveda, the 'science of life', resonates with much of our contemporary understanding of holistic medicine. It focuses on prevention and promotes the maintenance of health through close attention to diet, meditation, right thinking, and lifestyle. Its fundamental tenet is the idea of balance, especially the balance of body, mind, and consciousness according to one's own individual constitution.[196]

Just as everyone has a unique fingerprint, each person has a particular pattern of energy – an individual combination of physical, mental, and emotional characteristics – that defines his constitution. This constitution is innate and remains the same throughout his life. Many factors, both internal and external, can act upon him to disturb this balance. Examples of these stresses include the weather, food choices, emotional state, work and family relationships, physical trauma, and contaminants or infectious agents. Once the causes of imbalance are identified, one can take appropriate actions to cancel or reduce their effects, thus re-establishing the original constitution. Balance is the natural order, while imbalance is disorder. Similarly, health is order, while disease is disorder.

Ayurveda defines three basic types of energy, or functional principles, that are related to the biology of the body: *vata*, *pitta*, and *kapha*. These principles are collectively known as *dosha*s. *Vata* is the energy of movement, *pitta* the energy of metabolism or digestion, and *kapha*, the energy of structure. All people possess the qualities of *vata*, *pitta*, and *kapha* in varying degrees, but one usually predominates. This defines their overall constitution (*prakriti*). Ayurveda interprets the cause of disease as a lack of proper cellular function due to an excess or deficiency of *vata*, *pitta*, or *kapha*, which, combined with a particular lifestyle, can lead to the accumulation of toxins. Balancing body, mind, and consciousness requires an understanding of how *vata*, *pitta*, and *kapha* work together.

Just as the three *dosha*s combine in varying quantities to define the bodily constitution of each person, Ayurveda also recognises three elements that combine to give form and character to each individual's mental constitution. These three constituents, known as *guna*s, are the three primal qualities that are present in all of nature's manifestations. A person's prevailing state of mind, or disposition, thus consists of a mix of *rajas* (the quality of change, action, and restlessness), *tamas* (the quality of dullness, inertia, and decay), and *sattva* (the quality of intelligence, harmony, and stability). A person in whom *rajas* predominates is usually energetic, wilful, industrious, and keen on acquiring possessions, whereas one predisposed to tamas tends to be slow-moving or downright lazy, self-indulgent, and potentially self-destructive. *Sattva*, the balanced synthesis of the two other dispositions, brings clarity, peacefulness, kindness, and order. The sattvic personality is thus the ideal that Ayurveda aims to perpetuate. Many Ayurvedic prescriptions for mental health are intended to guide the mind toward a preponderance of sattvic qualities.

Whereas modern Western medicine tends to focus on disease and its symptoms, and primarily employs drugs and surgery to remove pathogens or diseased tissue from the body, Ayurveda believes that all life must be supported by energy in balance. When there is little stress and the flow of energy within a person is balanced, the body's natural defence systems are strong and can more easily defend against disease. Maintaining the right balance supports the body's own ability to repair itself. Thus, Ayurveda is primarily a system of preventive health that strengthens the body's regenerative capacity.

Ayurvedic health management begins with consultation with an Ayurvedic practitioner, who will, in the first instance, establish the patient's prakriti through direct questioning, observation, inference, and a physical exam. During an assessment, the practitioner uses basic techniques, such as taking the pulse, examining the tongue, eyes, and physique, and listening to the tone of voice. Direct questioning, however, remains the primary channel of inquiry. Indeed, during an initial consultation, a survey containing as many as 600 questions may be administered. Having established a normative baseline for the patient, the Ayurvedic practitioner can proceed to identify imbalances and prescribe remedies to rectify them, before they can become entrenched and give rise to disease.

Palliative and cleansing measures, when appropriate, can be used periodically to help reduce an imbalance, along with suggestions for removing or managing the causes of the imbalance. Recommendations may include implementing lifestyle changes, starting and maintaining a suggested diet, practising meditation, and using herbs. In some cases, participating in a structured cleansing programme, called *panchakarma*, is suggested to help the body rid itself of toxins accumulated due to poor digestion, poor diet, and environmental contamination. A typical course of *panchakarma* includes emesis, purgation, enema, and detoxification of the blood.

The awareness of subtlety is central to Ayurveda. It constructs a highly customised and individualised portrait of a person. It looks at the individual as a system complete in itself. It recognises that each of us is unique, responds differently to the pressures of life, and possesses different strengths and weaknesses. Therefore, when prescribing meditation, physical exercise, and especially diet, Ayurveda will always yield a highly customised programme. In diet, for example, there may be some general guidelines that are universal: favouring vegetarian foods; avoiding old, preserved, or highly processed foods; eating raw vegetables and whole grains; and so forth. Overall, however, Ayurvedic dietary prescriptions are heavily dependent on one's constitution. Foods that are appropriate for an individual in whom kapha predominates, for example, may be entirely inadequate for a pitta individual. Similarly, prescriptions on meditation and behaviour are dictated by the analysis of the patient's gunas. Thus, a particular behavioural adjustment may be appropriate for a tamasic individual, but not for a rajasic one.

Moreover, diets may have to change depending on the season or on physiological and psychic factors. Let us take a simple example: coffee. We would all like to know, definitively, whether it is good or bad for us, and, if bad, just how bad. But an Ayurvedic practitioner would never provide such a simplistic answer. An intake of coffee could be suitable for one constitution and not another. Furthermore, one would have to take into consideration the following: the time of day when coffee is taken, whether it is drunk alone or in conjunction with other foods, whether it serves a particular purpose or not, what the drinker's frame of mind or mental condition is, whether it is an isolated instance or a habit, how the coffee was prepared, whether the drinker had exercised previously or not, whether there had been any change in his bodily functions, and so forth.

Ayurvedic dietary prescriptions often concentrate on how the body absorbs nutrients rather than on the nutrients themselves. This, again, depends on the bacterial and floral composition of our gut, our state of mind, our own internal constitution, and the way we chew our food. If we are highly stressed, for example, our body might become more acidic and therefore what we eat might be digested in a different way than it would if our state of mind were more relaxed.

The Health Benefits of Meditation

Ayurveda also places much emphasis on meditation as an indispensable method to maintain balance and achieve wellness. Ayurvedic psychology aims to shift the mind from tamas to rajas and eventually to *sattva.* This means transitioning from an ignorant and physically oriented life (*tamas*), to one of vitality and self-expression (*rajas*), and finally to one characterised by peace and enlightenment (*sattva*). Meditation plays a large part in this transition. It ought to be a daily exercise, aided, if needed, by techniques such as mantras, prayer, *pranayama* (breath control), and visualisations. Meditation must be commensurate with the practitioner's capabilities and his current mental constitution (his combination of gunas).

The psychic benefits of meditation, whether practised in conjunction with other Ayurvedic principles or not, are extensive and well documented.[197] They range from lowering stress to aiding concentration to mitigating depression. There is also evidence that meditation can alter the very structure of the brain: one study showed that an eight-week programme of mindfulness-based stress reduction had brought about increases in grey matter concentration in brain regions like the hippocampus and the cerebellum.[198] Increasingly, however, neuroscientists have turned their attention to establishing a biological link between meditation practices and measurable improvements in *physical* health. As a result of various studies on the health effects of meditation, there is promising evidence that meditation influences immune and cardiovascular functions, and pain perception – all markers of physical health. For example, a study conducted by psychiatrists at the Benson-Henry Institute for Mind Body Medicine of the Massachusetts General Hospital in Boston showed that even one session of relaxation-response practice was enough to enhance the expression of genes involved in energy metabolism and insulin secretion, and reduce the expression of genes linked to inflammatory response and stress.[199]

Another study investigated the effects of intensive mindfulness practice in a group of experienced meditators, alongside a group of untrained control subjects who engaged in non-meditative activities. After eight hours of mindfulness practice, several genetic and molecular differences were observed in the meditators, including altered levels of gene-regulating machinery and reduced levels of pro-inflammatory genes, which in turn correlated with faster physical recovery from a stressful situation.[200]

Perhaps the most exciting results in meditation research concern the effect of meditation on telomerase levels. Telomerase is an enzyme that maintains telomeres, the sequences of DNA at the end of chromosomes that tend to get shorter every time a cell divides. When these 'end caps' drop below a critical length, the cell can no longer divide properly, and it eventually dies. So, telomeres shorten with age, and telomere length is an indicator of cell longevity. The rate of telomere shortening is affected by specific lifestyle factors, such as diet, physical activity, and the presence of stress, depression, or trauma. Telomerase can rebuild and lengthen the telomeres so that they can continue to function and subdivide properly. Therefore, the quantity of telomerase in the body is an indicator of how well our cells repair themselves.

During a seminal experiment known as the Shamatha Project,[201] conducted in 2007 at a mountain retreat in Colorado, researchers found that telomerase levels at the end of a three-month meditation course were 30 per cent higher, on average, in the group of intensive meditators compared to the control group.[202] The meditators who achieved the greatest improvement in some of the psychological tests also had the highest levels of telomerase. Following from that investigation, a study published in 2013 by scientists at UCLA and Nobel Prize winner Elizabeth Blackburn found that just twelve minutes of daily yoga meditation for eight weeks increased telomerase activity by 43 per cent in subjects who experienced depression because of their work, suggesting that meditation can slow down stress-induced ageing.[203] While such results are often taken out of context and blown out of proportion by the media (leading to hyperbolic declarations that the gene to immortality has been discovered), they do confirm what Eastern disciplines, such as Ayurveda and yoga, have always known: meditation can offer not only psychological benefits, but physical ones as well.

Ayurveda, in short, is a highly complex body of medical knowledge that provides specific, individualised prescriptions for each person and for each disease. Describing it in depth is beyond the scope of this book, but we can summarise here the aspects of Ayurveda that are relevant to a Third Dimension concept of health. Ayurveda recommends the following:

- A diet customised to each patient, dependent on his constitution or *prakriti*. Special emphasis is placed on the efficient absorption of nutrients, complementarity of foods, and especially to maintaining the balance of doshas that is innate in the patient.
- A state of mind conducive to well-being, free of stress, anger, fear, depression, anxiety, greed, violence, and dependency. The chief method to achieve this is daily meditation. The goal is to guide the patient to an increasingly sattvic disposition.
- Regular exercise appropriate to one's constitution and age.
- Occasional courses of purification therapy known as *panchakarma*.
- Use of herbal remedies to restore balance or counter contaminants.
- Recourse to Western medicine where a single, dominant causative variable can be identified.

Toward Comprehensive Wellness

First Dimension medicine is, fundamentally, the art of crisis response. When disease manifests itself, medicine springs into action and attempts to defeat it by identifying and addressing its root cause. In the First Dimension, therefore, the disease is the starting point of a process that results, we hope, in healing. Its goal is the removal or control of disease, not necessarily the attainment of comprehensive well-being. In the framework of the Third Dimension, our thinking increasingly shifts to an understanding of health as an indispensable good, and the efforts of medicine – Ayurvedic as well as Western – are aimed at maintaining health in the face of all the imbalances that daily life may introduce. In such a system, health is the starting point, its perpetuation is the goal, and intercepting imbalance before it becomes disease is the method.

In a Third Dimension interpretation of medicine, we strive toward a wellness that goes beyond physical health. It encompasses everything from physiological needs to peace of mind, from daily routines to physical exercise, from digestion to spiritual exercise. Wellness becomes a state of mind. It must also include especially mental well-being, since we have come to understand that very often our state of mind can be the most significant determinant of bodily health. The well-known role of the placebo effect shows that the mere belief in the curative potential of a particular drug or treatment can steer the body toward genuine physical improvement.[204] Hence, mental relaxation, and a positive attitude toward one's health, can do wonders for our bodily health. Whereas the ancient maxim, 'mens sana in corpore sano', often translated as 'healthy mind in a healthy body', suggested that a healthy body was necessary to support a state of mental well-being, we are now coming to understand that the opposite is also true: only a healthy mind can beget a healthy body.

There is abundant anecdotal evidence that a mind unbalanced by stress, fatigue, anger, violence, and depression can lead to poor physical health. Increasingly, however, science has also been able to uncover the chemical processes that link mental state with bodily responses. For example, it has been shown that fear and stress can trigger the release of various hormones by the adrenal glands, especially cortisol, which, in turn, raises blood pressure and stimulates the body's ability to absorb and store fat. These were once desirable effects because they enabled primitive humans to react to danger, such as the approach of a predator, by preparing the body for a burst of action (either fight or flight). However, the prolonged release of cortisol as a result of continual stress (induced by work or by family problems), especially if it is not followed by the expected burst of action, becomes a significant risk factor for various chronic diseases.

In the 2015 book *It's All in Your Head*, neurologist Suzanne O'Sullivan draws on her twenty years of experience in the field of psychosomatic illnesses and describes many patients who have symptoms such as chronic fatigue, seizures, and intense pain, with no identifiable physical cause. She argues convincingly that these physical symptoms can be brought about by changes in emotional state. Such evidence confirms the anecdotal observation that mental imbalances lead to physical ones.

A Third Dimension approach to medicine, then, must strive for an integrative understanding of health, by taking into consideration the individual's state of mind and psychological make-up, habits and addictions, diet and exercise regimen, emotions and fears, physical as well as human environment (both at home and at work), physiological routines, and personality traits. Above all, it must be a model that focuses proactively on wellness rather than reactively on sickness.

Wellness primarily involves understanding and supporting the innate intelligence of our bodies and the strong healing and regenerative capacities of our cells. Wellness will not be measured externally, or determined by doctors, dieticians, and trainers. Rather, it will come from our very own bodies via the natural mechanism of bio-feedback. This mechanism is the body's subtle but very real ability to communicate with us. Let us take, by way of example, a food item that we crave because it tastes rich and intense, such as a deep-fried delicacy or a very sweet dessert. Though we desire it, after years of experience we may begin to associate it with undesirable after-effects, such as bloating, indigestion, acidity or heartburn, or diarrhoea. Over time, the association with such unpleasant consequences begins to prevail over our desire for that particular food. Every time we think about it, or see it on offer, we cannot help thinking of the aftermath as well. Eventually, revulsion overcomes desire, and we no longer crave it. This, in essence, is the body's way of communicating to our decision-making faculty that the food item in question is neither necessary nor beneficial. If we listen, we can pick up many such messages.

In the Third Dimension, our advanced state of consciousness will permeate our choices of diet, exercise, and medication. Our bodies will tell us whether we should be eating something or not, how much of it we should eat, when to eat it, when to rest, when and how much to exercise, and when and how long to meditate. This 'innate intelligence' will communicate itself to the individual who lives in awareness and who has developed the subtlety of mind to be tuned to 'hear' his body and read its signals. In other words, we will be able to intuit (rather than infer or measure) the right habits and behaviours that ensure wellness. The connection with our innate intelligence will be the bedrock of a life lived in wellness and contentment.

Objectively measuring such wellness will be a challenge. Wellness indicators in the First Dimension are simple and gross: the absence of disease, first of all, and whether standard measures, such as body mass index, blood pressure, heart rate, blood glucose, and cholesterol, fall within the observed norm. In the Second Dimension, we might look at more sophisticated measures that can be either measured directly or detected through causal inference, such as how quickly the heart rate returns to normal after exercise, the efficiency in the function of certain organs, the ability of the immune system to fight off infections, and the efficiency with which the digestive system is able to absorb nutrients. In the Third Dimension, these indicators continue to be used, but the most significant measure of health in an individual becomes her own unquantifiable ability to intuit and respond to her body's needs without resorting to pathological tests or consultations with a clinician.

The ability of the individual to measure and regulate her own condition is the hallmark of Third Dimension wellness. Therefore, a society steeped in the Third Dimension should require a much-reduced system of medical administration. Indeed, a simplified and limited system of practitioners and hospitals would suffice to provide emergency trauma care and treatment for illnesses that can be addressed with First Dimension medicine's fundamental tools – pharmaceuticals and surgery. The goal of the Third Dimension is that individuals be able to lead a healthy life till the very end, without suffering from chronic diseases.

Even in the Third Dimension, though, medical research will continue at an unabated pace. Extensive research is required, for example, to measure the real intake of chemical toxins to which we are exposed on a daily basis as a result of living in urban, industrialised environments, eating foods treated with pesticides and preservatives, using electrical and electronic equipment that emits electromagnetic waves of various intensities and wavelengths, drinking chlorinated water from municipal water supplies, and daily using various chemicals, like paints and thinners, cleaning supplies, personal hygiene products, and insecticides. The long-term effect of this exposure and the interactions between different substances are not well understood and require research on an unprecedented scale, taking into account large numbers of variables, at the population level, in a variety of environments.

The same depth and breadth of research needs to be applied to a comprehensive analysis of all the essential processes occurring within the human body. The fundamentals of the body's infinitely complex functions, from how cells respond to external stimuli to how specific nutrients are broken down and absorbed by different tracts of the digestive apparatus, are only just beginning to be understood.

A focus of Third Dimension wellness will be on understanding bodily processes at cellular, sub-cellular, and genetic levels to find solutions for chronic illnesses and conditions related to Extremely Drug Resistant and Totally Drug Resistant pathogens, rather than trying to increase the potency of existing drugs. The Third Dimension treatment of a patient will also entail improving stem cell research and the ability to create new organs by cloning. While improving the sensitivity and performance of tests for pre-disease conditions, we must also study alternative medical traditions like Ayurveda and natural healing techniques in greater detail, which will allow them to be further refined and better understood.

Similarly, more research is needed into the effects of meditation. A recent article in *Scientific American* had this to say:[205]

> About 15 years of research have done more than show that meditation produces significant changes in both the function and structure of the brains of experienced practitioners. These studies are now starting to demonstrate that contemplative practices may have a substantive impact on biological processes critical for physical health [...] A comparison of the brain scans of meditators with tens of thousands of hours of practice with those of neophytes and non-meditators has started to explain why this set of techniques for training the mind holds great potential for supplying cognitive and emotional benefits. The goals of meditation, in fact, overlap with many of the objectives of clinical psychology, psychiatry, preventive medicine and education. As suggested by the growing compendium of research, meditation may be effective in treating depression and chronic pain and in cultivating a sense of overall well-being.

Ultimately, as we embark on our journey toward a higher level of consciousness, we awaken the body's incredible communication system. It is the best guide to our own health. As we become more present and enjoy higher levels of awareness, we will notice that our bodies have a very effective way of communicating with us via bio-feedback. For the aware person, following this communication about what to eat or not eat, do or not do, feel or not feel, will help us achieve a potent state of wellness, wherein the body's entire protective system – from its ability to heal itself to the calibration of the immune system to the regenerative capacities of our cells – will be fully directed to the process of keeping ourselves in a state of wellness. Developing meditation and mind–body techniques will help us analyse and interpret bio-feedback mechanisms, which will enable us to be better attuned to our bodies. As imbalances occur in our health, we will be the first to notice them, and using holistic healing techniques, especially those recommended in Ayurveda, we will be able to maintain our bodies in a state as close to wellness as possible. Research devoted to understanding and developing this awareness, and regular detox and cleansing programmes built into our daily lives will move large parts of the population from a state of being mildly diseased to a state of wellness.

Part VI

The Movement

23

The Third Dimension Movement: A Communitarian Revolution

While most calls for change focus on the external world, I propose a movement of personal transformation whose objective is to create conditions for the growth and evolution of higher forms of consciousness.

What I set out to do in this book was to create a coherent philosophy that can serve as a new logical system for the future, a system that will supersede the old and from which will emerge new paradigms for public administration, legislation, and economic exchange. In the central chapters of this book, I applied the framework of the Three Dimensions specifically to fundamental social structures like justice, governance, and the economy. To further demonstrate the scope of this endeavour, and how it could revolutionise all aspects of social organisation, I also applied it to a few key domains like education, agriculture, science, and medicine. Now, in the final section of the book, I will suggest how to promote this philosophy, its ideas and applications, and launch a movement for change that is built on this ideological foundation.

Fundamentally, the movement will be political in nature. Politics, despite its many flaws, remains one of the most powerful channels to effect significant change. However, the politics envisaged in this book entails none of the wrangling and scheming to which we are accustomed in the First Dimension. The movement's goal is to inspire, organise, and mobilise those who believe in human consciousness as a force for greater good. The movement, which I like to think of as a 'communitarian revolution', will be known as the Third Dimension Movement (TDM) and will be co-created by people across the world.

First Steps

The TDM's first step will be the creation of a Custodian Circle. This small body will consist of five members selected from among the movement's founders. The Circle will act, initially, as the gatekeeper for the creation of the first few Chapters of the TDM, and it will be the only authority empowered to settle any disputes arising in the creation or administration of early Chapters and of fledgling Areas and Regions. It will also have the authority to make changes to the movement's philosophy and guiding principles outlined in this book, based on feedback it may receive from early members and Chapters. The Circle, however, will be transitional and its existence may not exceed five years. As the TDM grows, the duties and responsibilities of the Circle will be taken over by the relevant National Secretariat (to be created for each country in which TDM Chapters exist), and by an International Steering Committee (ISC), which will consist of all national heads. These bodies will direct the further development of the movement's administrative structure and help turn it into a transformative force.

Formation of Local Chapters

The Circle's first endeavour will be to create, activate, and populate an information-rich and interactive website where users can do the following:

1. Learn about the movement;
2. Enrol as members of an existing Chapter;
3. Set up a new Chapter in a location where none exists;

4. Join forums and task forces set up to work on issues facing the organisation as it grows.

Anyone wishing to become involved in the TDM must first visit the website (www.thirddimensiontrust.org) and input her approximate address or general location. If there already exists a TDM Chapter in that area, the new user may apply online to join it, and her application will be evaluated by the relevant Chapter Leader. If no TDM Chapter exists in the applicant's area of residence, she may apply to set up a new Chapter and, if approved for membership, she will become, for the period of at least one year, its Leader. The leadership application can be submitted online and will be forwarded for approval to the Custodian Circle, initially, or to the National Secretariat if one already exists. (However, if a prospective member does not wish to take on a leadership role, she may opt to wait until a Chapter has been formed or join a neighbouring Chapter instead.)

In the early stages of the movement, the applications for membership in a Chapter and for leadership of a Chapter will be similar. In either case, the applicant will be asked to provide biographical details, with the addition of educational and professional details for Leader applications. Moreover, every applicant will be asked several questions about the movement's philosophy to ascertain whether she understands its precepts and the extent to which she agrees with them. This short survey will test her knowledge and understanding of this book, while giving her the opportunity to make suggestions and engage in discussion of key principles. Once completed, the application will be forwarded to the current Chapter Leader for evaluation for Chapter membership, or directly to the Circle or the National Secretariat for consideration as Chapter Leader.

Once the Circle or National Secretariat approves a new Chapter Leader, and thus the creation of a new Chapter, the Leader will receive training to prepare for the role. She will also receive a small sum as start-up funding and, most importantly, she will be assigned a goal-based scorecard by which her performance can be evaluated at the end of the first year, thus ensuring that the movement is a meritocracy from the very beginning. The scorecard will specify the Leader's responsibilities and goals for the first year. The system used to evaluate the success of a Chapter Leader will be similar, in concept, to what I discussed in Chapter 11 for Community Leaders in the Second and Third Dimensions. The measurement criteria will be far simpler, reflecting the fact that a Chapter Leader is, in the beginning at least, merely the organiser of a local campaign, not a governance officer. A first-year scorecard (Table 23.1), therefore, might contain as few as three line items.

Table 23.1: First-Year Scorecard of Chapter Leader

Responsibility	**Goal**	**Weight**	**Evaluation criteria**	**Assessed by**
Membership	Enrol at least 100 new members per year	50 points	1 point for each new member. No points below 50 members.	Database
Fundraising	Raise at least $100,000 per year	40 points	1 point for each $1,000 raised over $60,000; no single donor to exceed 20% of total amount raised.	Custodian Circle or National Secretariat
Administration	Set up physical Chapter office with all the necessary communication infrastructure	10 points	Full points if all items on admin checklist have been verified; none otherwise.	Custodian Circle or National Secretariat

A Chapter Leader who has managed to recruit only eighty new members but has successfully raised funds and set up her office operation diligently, would obtain a score of 90 per cent (40 out of 50 from membership, the full 40 from fundraising, and the full 10 from administration). To mirror the structure of future Community Leaders, a 90 per cent score will guarantee another year as Leader, whereas lower scores may bring about a new election among the current members of the Chapter. The tenure grid from Chapter 10 is reproduced in Table 23.2.

Table 23.2: Tenure Grid of Key Officers in TDM

Score range	Consequence
90% and above	Tenure renewed automatically due to high score.
80–89%	A new election may be called, but only if there is a motion, backed by majority vote of members.
70–79%	A new election is mandatory. The incumbent may run.
Below 70%	A new election is mandatory. The incumbent may not run.

Thus, the Custodian Circle or the National Secretariat would appoint the Chapter Leader only in the first instance. Thereafter, her continued tenure or replacement would be determined entirely by her score or the outcome of an election in which all full (paying) members of the Chapter may vote. In subsequent years, the Chapter Leader's scorecard will be modified: new responsibilities will be added and weighted, such as collaboration with other Chapters and organisation of ideological activities. Goals will also be adjusted as each Chapter grows. In the second year of the Chapter Leader's tenure, for example, the scorecard will have become more sophisticated (Table 23.3).

The most important goal of each Chapter will be to recruit new members. The first-year target for each Chapter is 100 full (paying) members. Chapters will also raise awareness and encourage involvement in the local community, perhaps by running meditation centres or helping meet community needs. The Chapter will hold regular meetings to read and discuss this book and the systems it lays out. As membership goals are met, Chapters will diversify into understanding and engaging with the political process at the local level.

The broad objectives of each Chapter are:

- To create a Community aligned with the principles of the movement and able to work on its own transformation through local forums;

Table 23.3: Second-Year Scorecard of Chapter Leader

Goal	Weight	Evaluation criteria	Assessed by
MEMBERSHIP			
Bring enrolment up to 300 members	20 points	Full points for achieving or exceeding the target. Minus 1 point for each 10 members below target. No points below 100.	Database
Renewal rate (Full Members) >80%	10 points	Full points for achieving or exceeding the target. Minus 1 point for each 5% below target. No points below 50%.	Database
Conversion rate (Observing Members to Full Members) >70%	10 points	Full points for achieving or exceeding the target. Minus 1 point for each 5% below target. No points below 20%.	Database
FUNDRAISING			
Raise at least $250,000	30 points	1 point for each $5,000 raised over $100,000; no single donor to exceed 20% of total amount raised.	Custodian Circle or National Secretariat
ENGAGEMENT			
Attendance at quarterly administration meetings 50%	5 points	Full points for achieving or exceeding the target. None otherwise.	Self-certified
Hold at least 8 events including community outreach, fundraising, recreational, meditation practice, etc. Attendance of at least 25 people at each event	10 points	Full points for achieving or exceeding the target. None otherwise.	Self-certified

Table 23.3: Second-year Scorecard of Chapter Leader (contd.)

Election of at least one Chapter member to an institution of local or regional governance	5 points	Full points for achieving or exceeding the target. None otherwise.	Custodian Circle or National Secretariat
ADMINISTRATION AND INTERNAL			
Achieve at least 80% score in end-of-year members' survey	10 points	Full points for achieving or exceeding the target. ½ point for 70–79%. None otherwise.	Member survey built into online management system
Satisfactory quality and timeliness of quarterly reports to Secretariat	5 points	Full points for achieving target. None otherwise.	Custodian Circle or National Secretariat

- To gather a large group of members and keep this number growing;
- To raise money to support the various tiers of the TDM – to support the area, regional and national tiers, once they have been formed; and
- To participate in the local electoral/political/governance process of its municipality.

Formation of National Secretariats and ISC

Once twenty contiguous, or at least neighbouring, TDM Chapters have been formed, they will be grouped by the Custodian Circle into an Area and will elect an Area Head from among their Chapter Leaders, subject to the usual eligibility criteria (having been a successful Chapter Leader for at least two years with a score of over 90 per cent for two consecutive years). The job of the Area Head is to promote the creation of the remaining eighty Chapters as quickly as possible, so that the Area may grow to a full complement of 100 Chapters. As soon as three neighbouring Areas are formed, they will be joined into a Region and elect a Regional Head, whose first job will be to form the remaining seven areas to make up the full complement of ten Areas necessary to constitute a Region, thus mirroring the governance structure envisioned for the Second Dimension.

As soon as there are sufficient Regions to cover 30 per cent of a country, a National Secretariat is formed. The Secretariat will consist of all Area and Region leaders. Its chairperson will be elected from among these members, with each Regional Head able to cast as many votes as there are Areas in her Region, while each Area Head will have a single vote.

The first job of the Secretariat will be to build up the Regions to cover the rest of the country. Similarly, once 30 per cent of the countries that comprise a Continent have national organisations, they may form a Continental Congress, whose primary task will be to encourage the formation of the remaining National Secretariats. And finally, once two Continents have Congresses, they will form an ISC, which will aim to complete membership in every country in the world.

The ISC will consist of all national heads and heads of the Continental Congress. Its chairperson will be elected from among these members, with Continental heads able to cast as many votes as there are participating countries in their respective Congresses, and the national heads able to cast one vote for every ten million people who inhabit their country.

Each Chapter will receive income through the collection of membership fees from its members, as well as from other fundraising activities. Sixty per cent of income from all sources will always remain in the Chapter, while the rest will be distributed among all the tiers of the TDM as follows:

- Chapter/Community: 60 per cent
- Area: 20 per cent
- Region: 10 per cent
- Nation: 5 per cent
- Continent: 3 per cent
- World: 2 per cent

What will officers in Areas, Regions, and higher levels do during the foundational phase of the movement? How will they utilise the funds at their disposal?

At each level of the pyramid, leaders will have goals that, while they remain in line with the overall objectives of the movement, are appropriate to the level at which they operate. As I shall discuss shortly, Area, Regional, and National levels especially will be thinking about how to connect with the current (First Dimension) political process and achieve representation, how to start more Chapters, and how to explore, communicate, and apply the TDM's philosophy. This will be done through extensive public outreach, using every available medium. In reaching out to the public, the aim is to create a grass-roots movement that can effect broad-based political change. Schedules would be drawn up for weekly Chapter meetings, monthly Area meetings, semi-annual regional meetings, and annual national conventions. Lasting for one or two days, these meetings will provide a forum for rigorous debate and decision-making among members.

The most important task of each level leader will be to support the leaders below her. Recall from Chapter 11 that in the Second Dimension every Area Manager's score – the same score upon which she relies for renewal of her tenure – is composed in part from scorecard line items for which she is responsible directly, but also and especially from aggregating the scores of the Community Leaders below her. (This aggregation is presented schematically in Figure 23.1, which repeats Figure 11.1.) Likewise, Regional Governors are awarded scores that are heavily reliant on the scores of the Area Managers below them, and so on up the pyramid. Therefore, each level leader's primary responsibility will be to support the leaders below him. This, too, will be a defining characteristic of the TDM from the beginning, and will be implemented even in the build-up stage, when the movement is under construction.

Area Heads will be engaged in growing membership indirectly. If they see that certain Chapter Leaders are struggling to meet their membership or fundraising goals, they may support their efforts by developing communication and awareness campaigns that are targeted to

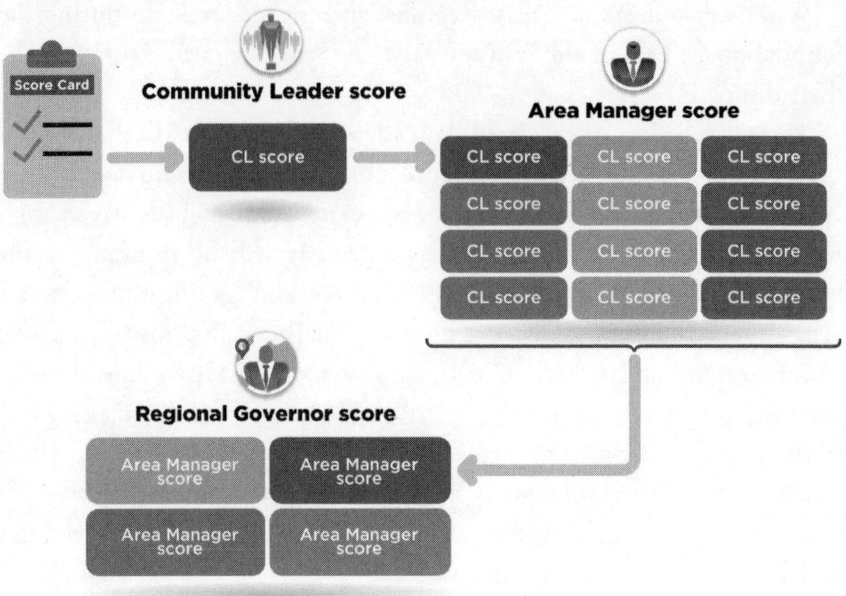

Figure 23.1: Aggregated Scorecards for Area Managers and Regional Governors

underperforming Chapters. Or they may organise training seminars for Chapter Leaders and other Chapter officers who lack the necessary skills in fundraising or public relations. Similarly, Regional Heads will have a strong and continuous interest in helping their Area Heads achieve their expected scores and will undertake whatever support activities they deem necessary toward achievement of the TDM's goals at every level of the organisation.

Committees at ISC and National Levels

At both ISC and national levels, the following committees will be formed:

- Election Committee – at the National Secretariat level, the Election Committee manages elections for Chapter Leaders.

At the ISC level, it runs elections for higher positions, such as Region and Continental Heads.

- Goals and Standards Committee – sets performance indicators for scorecard evaluation.
- Assessment Committee – assesses the performance of each leader in its purview via the scorecard system.

Engaging in the Political Process: Change from Within

As I hinted above, one of the goals of each Chapter will be to participate in local governance by supporting members who stand for election in local city councils as well as mayoral elections, and who take up duties in local task forces and committees – everything from membership in the local school board to a position in the mayor's advisory council. (I am referring to the First Dimension incarnations of these governance bodies and positions.) In other words, in the early phases of the movement it will be the duty of each TDM Chapter to engage fully – if discreetly – in the First Dimension political process. In the nascent stage of the movement, every Chapter member will be able to participate in mainstream politics alongside furthering the goals of the TDM. A TDM member who is a Chapter Leader, for example, would be encouraged to run for, say, a mayoral election. If the member attains the post of mayor, it would become necessary for her to temporarily renounce her Chapter Leader office in the TDM, because it would be untenable to continue in both roles effectively. However, the new mayor's governance philosophy would be informed by the principles of the movement and, hopefully, this would help bring about real change from the grass roots, and from within the First Dimension establishment.

The desire to participate in First Dimension structures of governance may seem contradictory at first. After all, in previous chapters (especially Chapter 10, on democracy) I proposed a new, meritocratic and professionalised system of governance that is, by definition, devoid of politics. The system is complete with new procedures for election, promotion, and renewal of tenure of government officials. And it specifically rejects the political nature of the First Dimension's democratic set-up and the way in which executive officers are currently elected. It seems counterintuitive now to argue that TDM members ought to become involved in First Dimension politics. As I explain below, however, it is necessary, albeit with certain adaptations.

Anti-Establishment Politics in the First Dimension

The nature of politics in most nation states today reflects and reinforces a low state of consciousness. This primitive state of awareness is evident in how politics concentrates power, money, and other forms of control, appealing to those who are deeply narcissistic. It is able to foster divisions in society and also self-select such individuals for positions of power and control. Can a system such as the one we have today, built on a low level of consciousness, produce leaders who inspire us and work for genuine change? If you were to think about all the world's leaders, could you pick five, or even three, who, in your opinion, are working toward a more just and equal world order with higher-quality rights and freedoms? In fact, the current interpretation of democracy seems to promote a particular type of individual – the likes of Donald Trump in the United States, Recep Erdogan in Turkey, Viktor Orban in Hungary, and Xi Jinping in China.

Fair, progressive, enlightened leaders fail to emerge because of the way the current system works in almost all nations of the world. This is not a problem confined to the United States, where a broken democratic structure is held hostage by big money and its lobbyists, or to India, where the callous politics of religion and caste keeps people divided. It is a problem repeated everywhere, because even though democracy is the best possible form of governance available today, it cannot address any of the pressing issues facing 21st-century society, or improve rights and freedoms, let alone help us determine the purpose of our existence.

Disenchantment with the establishment is an opportunity for fundamental transformation. Over the last half-century, frustrated citizens in many democratic countries have formed movements to protest against the inefficiency, corruption, ineptitude, and cronyism of existing governments.

They typically begin as populist, anti-establishment movements led by a charismatic personality, and soon become political parties. They are ignored at first, but then shock the system with remarkable results in an election. However, they often end up succumbing to the corrupt power structures that spawned them in the first place.

An exemplary case of this perversion of purpose is the rise and fall of the self-styled revolutionary Hugo Chávez in Venezuela. His dream was to reform Venezuela, especially the chronic corruption of its governing elites and the grinding poverty of many of its citizens, by toppling the political oligarchy that had ruled the country since the 1950s. After a failed military coup in 1992, Chávez turned to politics, founding the Fifth Republic Movement in 1997 to spearhead a 'Bolivarian revolution'. Chávez was a talented, compelling orator with a genuine ability to connect with the poor and offer them a tantalizing, ambitious vision of prosperity and social justice. His charisma, his connection to the under-represented classes, and his determination to stand up to the crooked old order swept him into power in 1998, and he immediately set about writing a new constitution, which was approved by referendum in 1999. He was re-elected president several times, remaining in power, with only short-lived interruptions, until his death in 2013.

Revenues from high oil prices allowed Chávez to funnel vast sums toward social programmes that ensured continued support from poor voters, especially his famous slum 'missions', which offered free healthcare and education, as well as heavily subsidised essentials like food and clothing. Yet his chaotic socialist interventions, such as the expropriation of rural estates and the nationalisation of much of the economy, also destroyed jobs and alienated foreign investors and local businesses. Skilled workers, professionals, and entrepreneurs began to leave the country in large numbers. Predictably, when the price of oil plummeted, so did the Venezuelan economy, burdened by heavy spending on social programmes and crippled by the absence of any real economic development.

By then Chávez's rule had become increasingly authoritarian and idiosyncratic, resulting, for example, in the mass firing of 18,000 employees of the state-run oil company, the undermining of other organs of state (especially the judiciary), and abuse of media channels. His most pressing preoccupation, during his entire time in office, was to force through constitutional amendments that would allow him to remain in office indefinitely. The legacy of Chávez's populism is a Venezuela where corruption is still rampant, crime rates have skyrocketed, the economy is in such disarray that basic necessities like medicines and food are in severe shortage, and millions of its citizens have fled to neighbouring countries in search of relief.

This example shows the typical trajectory of a political reform movement that starts as a well-intentioned effort to challenge the status quo and change things for the better, but is ultimately swallowed by the First Dimension's focus on power and self-aggrandisement. Many such movements and the political parties they spawn are devoid of a clear ideology and a comprehensive programme of policies to bring to fruition all their campaign promises, especially when it comes to managing an economy. They are usually overly reliant on the personal qualities of their founder who, true to the fashion of First Dimension democracy, is elected on the strength of his charisma, his ability to appeal to under-represented groups, his skill in public speaking, and his talent for taking advantage of the media. Once elected, however, the absence of a clear plan is exposed, as well as the leader's lack of experience in managing a system as complex and unwieldy as a nation. In most cases, his followers and closest collaborators are also political operatives, not professional managers who can succeed in roles of public administration. As the difficulties mount, the political party and its leader inevitably turn to the worst of First Dimension habits: remaining in power at all costs, distracting the citizenry with tendentious identity politics or convenient scapegoats, and finding ever more blatant ways to silence or co-opt the opposition.

Another recent example of the periodic manifestation of anti-establishment reform parties is Italy's Five Star Movement (*Movimento Cinque Stelle*, M5S). Founded in 2009 by comedian and social activist Beppe Grillo, M5S grew out of Grillo's extensive Internet and social media campaigns to shake up the political establishment with fresh ideas and unrelenting non-conformism with Italy's tired, corrupt and malfunctioning democracy. Though the movement lacked a clear manifesto, it was generally populist, anti-establishment, environmentalist, anti-globalist and Eurosceptic. (The 'five stars' in its name are a reference to five key issues, seemingly chosen at random: public water, sustainable transport, sustainable development, right to Internet access, and care for the environment.) Its leaders stressed that M5S was not a party but a social movement, and that, therefore, it could not be classified according to traditional left–right models. Nevertheless, M5S entered national politics in 2013 and garnered over 25 per cent of the popular vote in the general election. Once in parliament, however, it refused to enter into coalitions with other parties to form a government, thus continuing in its role as a disruptive force rather than a constructive one. It also focused more concretely on local governance, winning mayoral elections in several cities in Italy, including Turin and the capital, Rome. In national parliamentary elections held in March 2018, M5S emerged as the single largest party in Italy with over 32 per cent of the vote. In the wake of this success, it reversed its early stance against participating in coalitions in order to form a new, unorthodox government in collaboration with the *Lega*, a party also known for its populist, anti-establishment, Eurosceptic views, albeit with a markedly right-wing, anti-immigration ideology.

At the time of writing it is too early to say whether this new Italian government has managed to bring about meaningful reform or not. Progress toward a universal minimum income (one of M5S's main campaign pledges) has been slow, in part because of the European Union's opposition to the significant budget deficit that Italy would incur. Meanwhile, the new coalition has made international headlines for all the wrong reasons, such as denying port access to ships carrying migrants rescued in the Mediterranean Sea.

The verdict on M5S's performance in *local* governance of Rome, on the other hand, is undeniably negative. Almost three years in, the tenure of mayor Virginia Raggi is mired in controversy and dissatisfaction. Though youthful, photogenic, and a good debater, Raggi has shown all her own managerial limitations, as well as the limitations of her party's reliance on untested administrators. She has failed miserably to fix Rome's crumbling infrastructure, especially its public transport and waste disposal systems, which continue to be a source of much anger and embarrassment for Roman citizens. She is under continued scrutiny for alleged incompetence and was formally investigated for malfeasance in office, especially with regard to staffing decisions that reek of precisely the kind of cronyism that M5S ostensibly rejects.

The foregoing examples suggest that a realistic hope for systemic change cannot be built around a charismatic individual like Hugo Chávez or Beppe Grillo, nor can it hope to succeed without a carefully articulated and comprehensive policy platform. Most importantly, it cannot be brought about through the actions of a political party, because every such entity, so emblematic of the First Dimension, is doomed to be hampered in its efforts, and ultimately corrupted by the very system that created it.

For this reason, our movement is not a political one, and the TDM must never be constituted as a political party. Though it will encourage its individual members to participate in First Dimension governance whenever possible, and to stand for election, the TDM itself cannot morph into a political party intent on becoming part of a First Dimension government. This would be contrary to one of the main tenets of its philosophy, namely, that there can and must be a democracy without politics in the future. The Second Dimension democratic system that I have described elsewhere in this book will rely on the organisational skills, integrity, and commitment of *individual* administrators. They will manage all of society's needs on the strength of their own professional qualifications and track record, without having to belong to a political party. The very idea of a political party is obsolete and must be archived.

In the preceding paragraphs, I have commented briefly on failed attempts, in two countries, to bring about meaningful reform through anti-establishment political action. I cannot conclude this review without mentioning, at least in passing, what has happened in Delhi, the city where I have lived for most of my life.[206] At the time of writing, my home town is ruled by the 'Common Man Party' (Aam Aadmi Party, AAP). The AAP also has its origins in a popular grass-roots protest, namely, the India Against Corruption (IAC) campaign, which had been formed to mobilise mass interest in an anti-corruption bill. The bill, drafted and drawn up by civil society activists, sought the creation of an independent body to investigate corruption cases. Eventually, one faction of the IAC, led by Arvind Kejriwal, decided that the only realistic way to push through an anti-corruption agenda was to establish a political party around the IAC's goals and ideals. The newly created AAP contested the 2013 Delhi Legislative Assembly election, where it emerged as the second largest party, winning 28 of 70 seats. With no party achieving an outright majority, the AAP formed a minority government with support from the old Indian National Congress (INC) party, and Kejriwal became chief minister.

During his short tenure, however, Kejriwal and his party were continually at loggerheads with established powers, including the federal government, the INC and the Bharatiya Janata Party (the two parties that have controlled Indian politics since the late 1970s), and entrenched business and institutional interests. It became clear immediately that these groups would not support the AAP's anti-corruption bill, so Kejriwal resigned after a mere forty-nine days in office. The AAP seemed cut to size and defeated by the greasy machinery of First Dimension politics, but it came back stronger. When a new election was held for Delhi's Legislative Assembly in 2015, the AAP won a landslide victory, claiming 67 of 70 seats.

Despite the groundswell of support for the AAP and its leader, and widespread appreciation of the AAP's crusade against corruption and cronyism and in favour of transparent government, at the time of writing the jury is still out on whether the AAP will be able to maintain its momentum and achieve any lasting reforms. Thus far, the AAP administration has continued to squabble with the federal government over issues of jurisdiction, and it has had mixed results delivering the infrastructural and institutional changes it had promised to voters. It is also unclear whether the AAP can reach beyond the borders of Delhi and become a movement of national scale.

The problems these fledgling political players hope to fix (inequality for Chávez's Bolivarian revolution, political classism for M5S, corruption for the AAP) are not in themselves causes of modern society's malaise, but rather symptoms of an underlying, civilisation-level problem, that is, the flawed and irreparable paradigm for social organisation that I have labelled the 'First Dimension' in this book. Protest movements that turn into political parties fail to recognise the need to fundamentally reform not just certain institutions of government (including party-based electoral democracy), but the very way we think about ourselves and our civilisation. Only then should we go about making specific changes in legislation and governance.

Successful Social Movements in the First Dimension

If not a political party, then what ought the TDM to be? How else can fundamental, structural change – for which there is a deep desire among the people of almost every country – be brought about? If we look closely at civic developments in the last few decades, we can see that recent history offers many examples of movements that consistently and diligently tackled a flawed system from within, using all the legal, constitutional, and communication means that First Dimension democracy had put at their disposal, and eventually managed to bring about genuine, meaningful change. And they did so without forming political parties or participating in national government. Collective civic efforts of historical significance, such as the women's suffrage movement and the civil rights movement, could be cited in this regard, but I will focus instead on two examples, both from the United States, that are more recent.

The US gay rights movement can be said to have begun in 1924, when the Society for Human Rights – the country's first formal gay rights organisation – was founded in Chicago. It culminated in June 2015, when the Supreme Court ruled in *Obergefell v. Hodges* that same-sex couples have the right to marry and that states cannot interfere with this right. Though by this stage same-sex marriage was already legal in several states, the Supreme Court decision definitively put the matter to rest, paving the way for unconditional recognition of same-sex unions in every part of the country. This long-delayed acceptance of gay marriage represented the final and unequivocal attainment of full legal, social, and economic equality for gay and lesbian citizens.

The movement achieved this goal after ninety years of efforts by employing various means available in the contemporary legal and social environment. Societies, advocacy groups, and support organisations were formed. These groups brought legal challenges in district, federal, and supreme courts to fight attempts by conservative groups to criminalise or marginalise homosexuality in state legislation. Openly gay individuals (starting with Harvey Milk in the 1970s) began to seek election to representative and executive bodies at local and state level (mostly without party backing), and sought to influence legislation with the aim of outlawing discrimination on the basis of sexual orientation. They also directed their efforts increasingly to the court of public opinion, using established media networks and practices to sensitise the general population to liberal, progressive principles of tolerance. Gay and lesbian groups, in other words, worked within the bounds of the established social system to effect change. It was a long and arduous journey, but eventually they prevailed.

A different but analogous struggle (over environmental rather than civil rights) has been waged in the last decade by the Sierra Club's campaign against the coal industry across the United States.[207] Coal is America's top source of greenhouse gases, as well as its top source of mercury, sulphur dioxide, and other toxic air pollutants. To combat coal's environmental damage, the Sierra Club set up a campaign called Beyond Coal – the most extensive, costly, and effective campaign in the Club's 123-year history, and possibly in the history of environmental advocacy. Launched officially in 2010, Beyond Coal was able to secure strong financial backing from billionaire businessman Michael Bloomberg and set about fighting to shut down every coal-fired power plant in the United States. There were 523 such plants in 2010; by 2015, Beyond Coal had helped to shut down 190 of them.

How did Beyond Coal achieve this feat? It was not by using the tactics normally associated with environmental activism – hugging trees to prevent them from being felled, or obstructing whaling ships on the high seas. Beyond Coal also did not attempt to form a green political party to fulfil its aims. Instead, it relied on a persistent guerrilla warfare waged by 200 litigators in countless state and local hearings where utility commissions and other little-known governing bodies debated the viability of individual coal plants. With relentless determination, the Sierra Club's lawyers argued exclusively in the language of capitalist economics, bringing to these proceedings a barrage of spreadsheet models, financial scenarios, cost comparisons, and feasibility studies to demonstrate the sheer inefficiency of energy based on coal. They argued that refurbishing old and inefficient coal power plants to meet new environmental standards was too expensive, and much more expensive than adapting them to burn natural gas; that funding such renovations or new coal plants with large hikes in the price of electricity was a disservice to consumers; and that new electricity demand could be met if electrical utilities bought wind and solar power – the cost of which has fallen dramatically in recent years – instead of expanding coal plants or building new ones. In other words, they employed the First Dimension's own narrow-minded, capitalist logic (cutting costs and reducing inefficiencies in order to maximise profits) and the same tools (financial forecasts, statistics, cash flow analyses) to force the closure of 190 coal-fired power plants in under six years.

Just as the gay rights movement and Beyond Coal have achieved impressive results and lasting reforms, I hope that the TDM will be able to reshape society to fit a Second Dimension mould and, eventually, usher in the Third Dimension. This kind of momentous change cannot be achieved by imposing a top-down decree. It is the kind of change that must happen gradually and from within existing structures, so that the transition to higher dimensions can be brought about with minimal strain on the people of the world. TDM members will have to work at various levels to achieve goals in line with the philosophy of the movement while also advocating for political change. For example, a member could both lobby the local water utility to start a rainwater harvesting programme and work with the community to implement rainwater harvesting in individual homes. Achieving the first goal will give him political credibility, while the second will encourage better sustainability in line with the goals of the movement. In another example, a member could start a charter school that enacts the educational ideas of the movement, as laid out in Chapter 19, while also engaging with the local education board to implement reforms in the existing school system.

In this way members will be working within or alongside existing political and social structures to help move them toward the Second Dimension, while also gaining leverage to engage with the political process. Notwithstanding the risk of disappointment and distraction inherent in First Dimension politics, I urge adherents to TDM's ideology to engage in the representational process everywhere, by becoming involved in local governance; by seeking membership in local councils, boards of education, utility commissions, and safety committees; and eventually by standing for regional and national elections as independent candidates. Only by becoming part of the First Dimension system of governance can we hope to change it from within.

24

Moving Forward: A Call to Action

Dear Reader,

I feel we stand at the end of an epoch, as the age of duality, the age of cause and effect, begins to fade away. To employ a Marxian phrase, the nation state withers away and the futile concepts of 'I' versus the 'other', and 'us' versus 'them' have run their course in human development. In the 21st century, their time is up. Things fall apart, as the poet W.B. Yeats says in *The Second Coming,* when we feel that the underpinnings of civilisation have begun to lose their relevance. Yeats was writing in the wake of the First World War, which jolted the entire Western world. Nevertheless, a similar sentiment could be expressed today when taking in the dilapidated edifice of the First Dimension.

We should be proud of all that humanity has accomplished in the First Dimension. An improved understanding of human rights and governance, and especially the advances in science and technology that increasingly characterise the First Dimension, have brought us immeasurable improvements in quality of life, liberating many of us from the crippling constraints of the past – disease and heavy labour, gross injustice and hunger, isolation and constant violence. And yet we all know in our heart, perhaps without voicing this feeling aloud, that the vast First Dimension infrastructure that surrounds us, both physical and intellectual, is flawed. Increasingly, our efforts to fix its persistent evils – inequality and greed, environmental destruction and warfare, corruption and waste – feel like short-term, piecemeal fixes, no more effective than kicking an empty can down the street.

I remember going to the Soviet Union in 1983 as a high school student and having a profound sense of its hollowness. Talking about its demise at that time would have seemed, to most observers of that country, outside the realm of possibility. But my experience was reaffirmed when I read *The Long Telegram,* written in 1946 by George Kennan, then deputy chief of the United States embassy in Moscow. In the telegram, Kennan expounds on the internal contradictions of the Soviet Union. I realised then how his penetrating insight and deep understanding helped him see with certainty what was to come several decades later:

> We here are convinced that never since termination of civil war, have mass of Russian people been emotionally farther removed from doctrines of Communist Party than they are today. In Russia, party has now become a great and – for the moment – highly successful apparatus of dictatorial administration, but it has ceased to be a source of emotional inspiration. Thus, internal soundness and permanence of movement need not yet be regarded as assured.

I use this quote to illustrate my point that the components of the First Dimension logical system, as we know them, come out of an irrational mindset which we know upon deep examination to be hollow, not unlike a tree that has rotted from the inside, requiring only the slightest draught of wind to knock it down.

As I have shown in this book, the prevalent practices in various fields, such as governance, law, and economy, do not provide answers to the dilemmas posed by our rapidly changing world. We cling to old ideas and mental structures because they have served us well in our historical evolution and ushered in the age of modernity. The logical system of our First Dimension world is deeply entrenched because it is premised on a very reductionist interpretation of our humanity.

I hope I have been able to shed some light on what an alternative world might look like once we create conditions that help us move toward a higher level of consciousness. If we can begin this revolution in human thought, the old structures – those based on an understanding of ourselves as acquisitive, insecure beings who define their self-interest in the most limited terms – will cease.

This book is a call to those who have recognised the great contradictions, oppressive reductionism, and ultimate hollowness of First Dimension constructs. It is a call to act, because as an inveterate optimist I also believe that as human beings endowed with intellect and spirit, we possess a great capacity for change, for creative problem-solving in the face of adversity, and especially for personal development toward better ways to understand ourselves and the world around us. If we focus on this innate faculty for higher consciousness and apply ourselves to achieving it, then we will simultaneously bring about new logical frameworks to guide us in the future. For want of better terminology, I have labelled these frameworks 'Second Dimension' and 'Third Dimension'.

The Third Dimension Movement is a vehicle and an invitation to create a community of those seekers who work to understand, communicate, and ultimately create the paradigm shift that is necessary for us to attain these higher dimensions. It is my hope – and a bold one it is – that this book will lay the foundation for an alternative paradigm that will lead us to the full realisation of what it means to be human.

Please join me in this effort by becoming a member of the Third Dimension Movement. You may start by visiting our website at www.thirddimensiontrust.org.

Notes

1. T. J. Bouchard, Jr. *et al.*, 'Sources of Human Psychological Differences: The Minnesota Study of Twins Reared Apart,' *Science* 250, no. 4978 (October 12, 1990): 223–228.
2. Despina Archontaki, Gary J. Lewis, and Timothy C. Bates, 'Genetic Influences on Psychological Well-Being: A Nationally Representative Twin Study,' *Journal of Personality* 81, no. 2 (April 2013): 221–230.
3. Jerome H. Barkow, Leda Cosmides, and John Tooby, eds., *The Adapted Mind* (New York: Oxford University Press, 1992).
4. This summary of the basic assumptions of evolutionary psychology is based on Steven Pinker, *How the Mind Works* (New York: W.W. Norton, 1997).
5. Maslow's original paper on the subject was Abraham H. Maslow, 'A Theory of Human Motivation,' *Psychological Review* 50, no. 4 (1943): 370–396. He later refined and expanded his theory in Abraham H. Maslow, *Motivation and Personality* (New York: Harper, 1954). Maslow's hierarchy begins with basic needs: physiological needs (nourishment, shelter, energy) and safety needs (security, order, laws). Then come psychological needs: love and belongingness (family bonds, friendship, sexual intimacy) and esteem needs (dignity, independence, social status). Finally, at the top of the hierarchy, the need for self-actualisation and self-fulfilment.

6. Known as the 'Minnesota semi-starvation experiment', the study was later described and analysed in a hefty tome: Ancel Keys *et al.*, *The Biology of Human Starvation*, 2 vols. (Minneapolis, MN: University of Minnesota Press, 1950).
7. J.R. Galler *et al.*, 'Early Childhood Malnutrition Predicts Depressive Symptoms at Ages 11–17,' *Journal of Child Psychology and Psychiatry* 51, no. 7 (2010): 789–798.
8. This aspect of poverty is highlighted by historian Rutger Bregman in his best-selling *Utopia for Realists: And How We Can Get There*, trans. Elizabeth Mentone (London: Bloomsbury, 2017).
9. Katherine Harmon, 'How Important Is Physical Contact with Your Infant?' *Scientific American* (May 6, 2010), https://www.scientificamerican.com/article/infant-touch/
10. The first in this landmark series of studies was Albert Bandura, Dorothea Ross, and Sheila A. Ross, 'Transmission of Aggression Through Imitation of Aggressive Models,' *Journal of Abnormal and Social Psychology* 63, no. 3 (1961): 575–582.
11. Jason M. Cowell and Jean Decety, 'Precursors to Morality in Development as a Complex Interplay Between Neural, Socio-Environmental, and Behavioral Facets,' *Proceedings of the National Academy of Sciences USA* 112, no. 41 (2015): 12657–12662.
12. Bruce Lipton, 'What Are the Important Things to Know as a Parent?' *Bruce Lipton's Blog* (blog), (7 June 2017), https://www.brucelipton.com/blog/what-are-the-important-things-know-parent
13. Groupthink is a psychological phenomenon observed when a group of people make irrational decisions based on the urge to conform. Though the term was first used by Whyte, much of the pioneering research on the subject was carried out by Yale psychologist Irving Janis. See I.L. Janis, *Victims of Groupthink: A Psychological Study of Foreign-Policy Decisions and Fiascoes* (Boston: Houghton Mifflin, 1972).
14. A 1998 study showed that children of Holocaust survivors with post-traumatic stress disorder (PTSD) had a higher lifetime risk for PTSD and report more distress after traumatic events. Thus, these offspring may have a biological vulnerability to traumatic stress transmitted to them from their parents. See Rachel Yehuda *et al.*, 'Vulnerability to Posttraumatic Stress Disorder in Adult Offspring of Holocaust Survivors,' *American Journal of*

Psychiatry 155, no. 9 (1998): 1163–1171. Another study conducted in the same year reported intergenerational transmission of trauma in primates: S.J. Suomi and S. Levine, 'Psychobiology of Intergenerational Effects of Trauma: Evidence from Animal Studies,' in *International Handbook of Multigenerational Legacies of Trauma*, ed. Yael Danieli (New York: Plenum Press, 1998): 623–637.

15. See, for example, M.H. Teicher *et al.*, 'Developmental Neurobiology of Childhood Stress and Trauma,' *Psychiatric Clinics of North America* 25, no. 2 (2002): 397–426.
16. N.W. Hudson and R.C. Fraley, 'Volitional Personality Trait Change: Can People Choose to Change Their Personality Traits?' *Journal of Personality and Social Psychology* 109, no. 3 (September 2015): 490–507.
17. J. Krishnamurti, *The Book of Life: Daily Meditations with Krishnamurti* (New York: HarperCollins, 1995), 31 May observation.
18. This maxim is erroneously attributed to Albert Einstein. Its source is unknown. Nevertheless, it holds true both in general terms (solving a difficult problem often requires a new way of thinking) and in the specific case of my definition of levels of consciousness and the intellectual structures (dimensions) that they can engender.
19. For a concise review of the different interpretations of premodern friendship, see the Introduction in David Konstan, *Friendship in the Classical World* (Cambridge: Cambridge University Press, 1997).
20. Ray Pahl, *On Friendship* (Cambridge: Polity, 2000), p. 57.
21. E.H. Carr, *What is History?* (New York: Random House, 1961), p. 39.
22. *Ibid.*
23. This is, of course, an oversimplification. In fact, most psychologists and cognitive scientists would say that love is not an emotion. Emotions, such as joy, anger, fear, surprise, and sadness, tend to be short-lived. Moreover, they are usually connected to physical responses, especially facial expressions. At best, therefore, we can say that love is a long-lasting *combination* of emotions. Love has also been categorised as a drive (like, say, hunger), an act of the will, and a form of energy. In *The Language of Emotions*, author Karla McLaren argues that love belongs in a category of its own.
24. In English, 'to love' is also used as a superlative version of 'to like'. Thus, one might claim to love a song, or a food item, or a pair of shoes. These are purely idiomatic expressions, and need not be part of our discussion.

25. Lesbia's real name was probably Clodia Metelli, a libertine Roman aristocrat with whom Catullus had had a brief affair.
26. From a BBC article by de Botton that appeared on 22 July 2011. See https://www.bbc.com/news/magazine-14248803.
27. Huntington first proposed his thesis in 'The Clash of Civilizations?', an article published in 1993 in the magazine *Foreign Affairs*. He expanded on the theory in *The Clash of Civilizations and the Remaking of World Order* (New York: Simon & Schuster, 1996).
28. See https://www.adultdevelopmentstudy.org
29. From *The Essence of the Heart Sutra*, by His Holiness the Dalai Lama.
30. Our predecessors of the *Homo abilis* species, who lived about two million years ago, are known to have used tools. Recent archaeological discoveries in Kenya, however, suggest that even our more primitive ancestors of the *Australopithecus* genus, who lived about 3.3 million years ago, may have used simple stone tools.
31. Some readers may argue that this skills-based interdependence can be taught by capitalism as well – both by the interplay of diverse economic agents in free markets and more narrowly by the collaboration of diverse human resources in a corporate working environment. As I will argue in Chapter 14, however, capitalism's gravest limitation is its inability to bestow importance on anything that cannot be valued in monetary terms. Therefore, it cannot teach us the value of, say, good parenting, amicable mediation, or the ability to bring people together. Yet these are all qualities and skills that are vital to a healthy, productive society.
32. Putnam was not the first scholar to use the term 'social capital', but his definition of the concept has had a strong influence on academic thinking since the 1990s. Putnam's key contribution is *Making Democracy Work: Civic Traditions in Modern Italy* (Princeton: PUP, 1993), in which he argues that regional government in northern Italy was more successful (resulting in greater prosperity and order) than in southern Italy owing to a strong tradition of civic engagement and mutual trust dating back to the importance of guilds, associations, and clubs in medieval and Renaissance times. Also of note is his *Bowling Alone: The Collapse and Revival of American Community* (New York: Simon & Schuster, 2000), where he suggests that the decline of civic engagement in the United States is linked to the decline in membership in social organisations.

33. From a speech given by Ambedkar (in his role as chairman of the committee tasked with drafting India's constitution) to the Constituent Assembly in 1948. To put his words in the right context, we must note that Ambedkar is best remembered for his efforts to emancipate India's untouchables. What he found abhorrent about Indian villages, especially Hindu villages, was their unyielding segregation of untouchables, who suffered continual abuses at the hands of other castes. He was also reacting to Gandhi's romantic characterisation of the village as a place of equality and cooperation.
34. Ravish Kumar, 'A Sewing Machine, Murder, and The Absence of Regret,' NDTV (October 1, 2015), http://www.ndtv.com/blog/basehara-village-carries-no-shame-1225235
35. My concept of correct scaling is an elaboration of the principle of subsidiarity, which may be familiar to readers interested in political theory. Though it has origins in Catholic social thought, it is best known as a general principle of the European Union's legal framework. Subsidiarity holds that administrative, social, and commercial issues should be handled by the lowest, least centralised level of governance capable of doing so. My theory of correct scaling, however, implies a redefinition of what functions are appropriate to each jurisdictional level. As I argue in Chapter 12, for example, key functions like granting citizenship (normally handled by central authorities in the First Dimension) must be pushed down to the local level.
36. Mogens Herman Hansen, 'Democratic Freedom and the Concept of Freedom in Plato and Aristotle,' *Greek, Roman and Byzantine Studies* 50 (2010): 1–27.
37. The faculties model of the will has its origin in the writings of Plato and Aristotle, and it was the dominant view of the will in much of medieval and modern philosophy. What is distinct about free agents, according to this model, is their possession of certain capacities: intellect and volition. It is by virtue of having these faculties, and the interaction between them, that agents have free will.
38. https://en.oxforddictionaries.com/definition/law
39. The *Arthashastra* is traditionally ascribed to Kautilya (also known as Chanakya), an influential scholar at the university city of Takshashila and adviser to the first Mauryan emperor, Chandragupta. The treatise is more likely to be the work of multiple scholars over several centuries.

40. These absurd numbers apply only to federal tax issues. Most US citizens and corporations have to contend additionally with state-level taxation.
41. Many economies, including the European Union, India, Australia, South Africa, Singapore, and Turkey, have already adopted IFRS. It remains unclear, however, whether and when the United States will follow suit.
42. Philip K. Howard, 'Radically Simplify Law,' *Cato Online Forum* (12 November 2014), http://www.cato.org/publications/cato-online-forum/radically-simplify-law.
43. Lawsuits may target companies or associations, but this happens mostly in civil proceedings and the ultimate outcome is limited to financial punishment.
44. Nirbhaya lived with her parents and two younger brothers in a small house in the Mahavir Enclave II area of New Delhi, a very poor area. Her father worked as a baggage handler at the airport. He had sold a little plot of farmland in his home state of Uttar Pradesh to pay for his children's education. Nirbhaya was enrolled in a four-year physiotherapy training course and was doing an internship in a Delhi hospital at the time of her assault.
45. Measuring recidivism accurately is made challenging by two important characteristics. First, is recidivism defined as rearrest, reconviction, or reincarceration? Former convicts may be guilty of minor offences (such as parole violations, misdemeanours, and traffic fines) that trigger a rearrest but may not lead to a new prison sentence. Second, what is the appropriate follow-up period to be taken into consideration? National crime statistics may report two-year, three-year, or five-year recidivism. Recently, the US Bureau of Justice Statistics (BJS) reported a disturbingly high rate of recidivism in the United States of 83 per cent because, for the first time, it expanded the period of observation to nine years after release. (The analysis, based on 401,288 state prisoners released in 2005 in 30 states, is in: Mariel Alper, Matthew R. Durose, and Joshua Markman, *2018 Update on Prisoner Recidivism: A 9-Year Follow-up Period (2005–2014)*, BJS Special Report, May 2018.) Two earlier studies conducted by the Pew Center on the States in conjunction with the Association of State Correctional Administrators, on the other hand, found three-year recidivism rates of 45 per cent and 43

per cent for inmates released from prison in 1999 and 2004, respectively (see Pew Center on the States, *State of Recidivism: The Revolving Door of America's Prisons* [Washington, DC: The Pew Charitable Trusts, April 2011]). Examples of three-year reimprisonment rates in other developed countries where such statistics are available include Germany at 35 per cent, Chile at 50 per cent, and New Zealand at 44 per cent (see Seena Fazel and Achim Wolf, 'A Systematic Review of Criminal Recidivism Rates Worldwide: Current Difficulties and Recommendations for Best Practice,' *PLOSONE* 10, no. 6 [2015]: e0130390).

46. The original report by Bain & Company (India Philanthropy Report 2010) is no longer retrievable online. However, its main points were summarised by Bain & Company partner Arpan Sheth in a speech delivered in May 2010 and titled 'An Overview of Indian Philanthropy,' which is available at http://www.bain.com/bainweb/PDFs/cms/Public/India_Sheth_Speech.pdf
47. Charities Aid Foundation, CAF World Giving Index 2010 (Kent, UK: Charities Aid Foundation, 2010), https://www.cafonline.org/about-us/publications/2010-publications/world-giving-index
48. See Elisabeth Eaves, 'Who Gives the Most?' Forbes.com (December 26, 2008), https://www.forbes.com/2008/12/24/america-philanthropy-income-oped-cx_ee_1226eaves.html#764d63752a2f
49. Charities Aid Foundation, CAF World Giving Index 2017 (Kent, UK: Charities Aid Foundation, 2017), https://www.cafonline.org/about-us/publications/2017-publications/caf-world-giving-index-2017
50. See Dasra and Bain & Company, India Philanthropy Report 2017: The Individual Philanthropist's Path to Full Potential (Mumbai: Bain & Company, 2017), http://www.bain.com/Images/REPORT_India_Philanthropy_2017.pdf
51. Ram Singh and Rampur are not the real names and have been changed to protect the villagers' privacy.
52. See Pim Albers, 'The Assessment of Court Quality: A Breach of the Independence of the Judiciary or a Promising Development?' https://rm.coe.int/the-assessment-of-court-quality-a-breach-of-the-independence-of-the-ju/168078c569
53. In addition to the Singapore Subordinate Courts, the Consortium included the US National Center for State Courts, the US Federal Judicial Center, and the Australasian Institute of Judicial Administration.

54. See International Framework for Court Excellence, 'Global Measures of Court Performance: Discussion Draft Version 3' (9 November 2012), http://www.courtexcellence.com/~/media/Microsites/Files/ICCE/Global%20Measures_V3_11_2012.ashx
55. See Timothy McCorry, 'Alternatives to the Traditional Criminal Justice System: An Assessment of Victim-Offender Mediation and Neighborhood Accountability Boards in the United States,' *The New York Sociologist* 4 (March 2010) and Canadian Resource Centre for Victims of Crime, 'Restorative Justice in Canada: What Victims Should Know' (2011).
56. This system would lead, over time, to a homogenisation of legal norms and, by extension, of certain cultural values across the world. Rather than a loss of cultural diversity, this should be seen as a mechanism to cement everywhere the universal rights and freedoms upon which higher-dimensional laws and justice systems are based.
57. In contractual disputes the process by which an arbitrator is selected will have been defined in the contract already.
58. This judicial process will be managed by a small administrative department at the appropriate level of governance, subject to a scoring mechanism that will find its way to the scorecard of the Community Leader under the corresponding right to fair treatment under the law. (For more on how such scorecards will work, see Chapter 11.)
59. In the Third Dimension, incarceration would almost never be an option. Therefore, this limit must be defined as a maximum financial penalty or amount of community service.
60. A second body, the Council or Boule, consisting of 400 members, was tasked with drafting the deliberations for discussion and approval in the Ecclesia. Membership to the Boule was by election and was carefully vetted.
61. In its democratic heyday (the 5th century BCE) Athens, including its home territory of Attica, may have had as many as 250,000 inhabitants, but only about 30,000 of these were actual citizens. An even smaller subset (perhaps 5,000) regularly attended the meetings of the Ecclesia. Other Greek city states where some form of democratic government was in place were much smaller, typically including only a few thousand citizens. See Paul Cartledge, 'The Democratic Experiment,' http://www.bbc.co.uk/history/ancient/greeks/greekdemocracy_01.shtml

62. Throughout this chapter, I use the term 'democracy' to signify the general idea of governance by the people. This is a common misuse of the word. Strictly speaking, democracy is simply a polity in which everyone has a say in decisions that affect the commonwealth, but one in which only the will of the majority is executed. This means that, in theory at least, a democratic state could do anything at all as long as it enjoys the consent of the majority, including acting with impunity against the minority. In reality, when we speak of modern democracy we really mean the republic, that is, a democratic system in which the will of the majority is executed, but only within the bounds of a previously agreed set of written laws and statutes (the constitution), which safeguard the rights of everyone, whether they belong to the majority or the minority.
63. Even in smaller countries like Switzerland and Norway, however, this is beginning to change. Immigration has led to diversification of the population and, inevitably, more divisive politics.
64. The most common tool to assess inequality is the Gini coefficient, a statistical measure of family income distribution in a country. It can range from a value of 0 (perfect equality) to 1 (complete inequality). Thus, a low Gini coefficient indicates a low level of inequality and a more egalitarian society. Statisticians can compute the value of a country's Gini coefficient either before or after the application of taxes and government subsidies or welfare payments. Especially after considering the effects of taxation and other government programmes, the two countries mentioned here (Finland and Norway) have very low Gini coefficients (around 0.25).
65. In Chapter 15, I shall argue that all enterprises (public or private, for profit or non-profit, partnership or corporation, trust or association) can be evaluated and categorised according to the same system. The assessment of impact for what we now call a 'private' enterprise will be based on several factors, not just the number of people served by it.
66. The truncation at the top of the pyramid implies that there are higher, supranational levels of governance that supersede the National Council. These levels (Continental and Global) are discussed in Chapter 13.
67. There is no equivalence between governance and other spheres of activity at levels above 5, as no business, scientific or social enterprise can be said to have the same impact as a governance institution of national or international scale.

68. As the reader may recall from Chapter 10, the Community Leader level is the only level of governance in the Second Dimension where popular elections will be held. Whereas at higher levels (Area Manager, Regional Governor, and Head of State) candidates are chosen by their peers in the appropriate representative forum, Community Leaders will be elected by all adult citizens of the Community.
69. This number is realistic. According to the US Department of Justice's Office of Juvenile Justice and Delinquency Prevention, juveniles in the United States were involved in about 20 per cent of serious violent crimes annually between 1980 and 2016. There has been significant improvement in the last few years, however, with the 2016 rate at just 12.1 per cent.
70. MLM is a marketing strategy in which salespeople are compensated not only for sales they generate themselves, but also for the sales of the other salespeople whom they have recruited. This recruited sales force, who lie below the original recruiter in the organisational structure of the company, is referred to as the recruiting salesperson's 'downline'. As more and more salespeople recruit other salespeople, creating their own downline, the potential compensation flowing upward can increase rapidly. MLM has always received, and continues to receive, criticism on account of the fact that it can very easily be perverted into an illegal pyramid scheme that exploits members of the organisation. Amway, Herbalife, and Avon are examples of well-known direct sales companies that use multilevel marketing strategies.
71. According to the administrative structure I proposed in Chapter 10, Greater Delhi would be constituted as a Region because of its large population. The reader may recall that a Region can encompass up to 25 million inhabitants. The city would be subdivided into several Areas, each one of which would consist of 100 individual municipal entities labelled Communities.
72. To avoid confusion, recall that for leadership positions higher than Community Leader (that is, Area Manager, Regional Governor, and Head of State), the scorecard is composed of (*a*) an aggregation of the scores recorded by elected leaders below him; and (*b*) his performance in the delivery of those rights and freedoms for which he was directly responsible. For part (*b*), as we have just seen, he relies on the collaboration of Region-level executives that he appointed himself. These individuals have scorecards too, and although their scorecards are not used to determine eligibility for any

election, they are used by their superiors to evaluate their performance using the same rationale. For part (*a*), on the other hand, the leader will not have direct control of governance leaders below him, because they were elected, not appointed. For example, a Regional Governor does not appoint Area Managers. They are elected by their respective Area Caucuses. The relative independence of the Area Managers ensures a modicum of balance in the authority exercised by the Governor.

73. ttps://www.who.int/phe/health_topics/outdoorair/databases/AAP_database_summary_results_2016_v02.pdf
74. The report was co-authored by Greenpeace and software company IQAir AirVisual. See https://www.airvisual.com/world-most-polluted-cities?continent=&country=&state=&page=1&perPage=50&cities=/
75. Los Angeles data from https://www.epa.gov/outdoor-air-quality-data/air-quality-index-report. Delhi data collated from monthly reports issued by the Central Pollution Control Board at http://cpcb.nic.in/ambient-aq-data-delhi-ncr/. See also https://timesofindia.indiatimes.com/city/delhi/not-a-single-satisfactory-air-month-this-monsoon/articleshow/66112079.cms
76. ttp://english.cbcsd.org.cn/SDtrends/20130922/73436.shtml
77. ttps://www.theguardian.com/artanddesign/2018/oct/31/beijings-skyline-with-and-without-air-pollution-in-pictures
78. The first war against Saddam Hussein's regime was sanctioned by a resolution in the UN Security Council. In contrast, the second Iraqi war of 2004 was initiated by the United States and its allies without a mandate from the Security Council.
79. Quoted in Monica Kim,'The Everyday Psychology of Nationalism,' *The Atlantic,* March 5, 2014, https://www.theatlantic.com/health/archive/2014/03/the-everyday-psychology-of-nationalism/284188/
80. Daniel Druckman, 'Nationalism, Patriotism, and Group Loyalty: A Social Psychological Perspective,' *Mershon International Studies Review* 38, no. 1 (1994): 43–68.
81. The canton of Vaud – a relatively large canton – requires 12,000 signatures to put a referendum on the ballot, whereas a smaller canton like Aargau requires only 3,000.
82. This is the situation in Switzerland, where individuals see themselves as citizens of communities and cantons first, and of the nation next. Indeed,

even citizenship applications, though formally awarded by the federal government, must be processed and approved at the local level.

83. There will be no direct taxation in higher dimensions, such as income tax. The dues referred to here are primarily property taxes and usage fees. Taxation in the Second Dimension is discussed in Chapters 16 and 17.
84. In January 2018, the Doomsday Clock reappeared in the international news when the clock was moved to within two minutes before midnight, the closest it had ever been to a nuclear apocalypse.
85. Despite the central role played by Woodrow Wilson in the creation of the League, the United States did not join because of opposition from the US Senate. Russia joined only in 1934.
86. 2017 estimate by the UN Department of Economic and Social Affairs. See United Nations, Department of Economic and Social Affairs, Population Division (2017). *World Population Prospects: The 2017 Revision, Key Findings and Advance Tables*. Working Paper No. ESA/P/WP/248.
87. At the Continental Congress, the Heads of State are accompanied by their respective Regional Governors, who ensure that the needs and concerns of specific Regions are represented.
88. Oxfam International, 'Working for the Few,' *Oxfam Briefing Paper* 178 (January 2014), https://oxf.am/2FKRUWh
89. Oxfam International, 'An Economy for the 99%,' *Oxfam Briefing Paper* (January 2017), https://oxf.am/2FOD0hK
90. Organisation for Economic Co-operation and Development (OECD), 'An Overview of Growing Income Inequalities in OECD Countries: Main Findings,' in *Divided We Stand: Why Inequality Keeps Rising* (Paris: OECD, 2011), https://www.oecd.org/els/soc/49499779.pdf
91. István György Tóth, 'Time Series and Cross-Country Variation of Income Inequalities in Europe on the Medium Run: Are Inequality Structures Converging in the Past Three Decades?' *GINI Policy Paper* 3 (September 2013), http://www.gini-research.org/system/uploads/566/original/GINI_Policy_Paper_3.pdf?1384954508
92. Latin American countries have bucked the trend of rising Gini values by reducing their inequality measures significantly. That said, Latin America remains the region with the world's highest levels of inequality. These anomalies suggest an overall convergence of outlier countries toward a high

global average Gini value, possibly as a result of increasing globalisation of their economies. On Latin American inequality, see Nora Lustig, 'Most Unequal on Earth,' *IMF Finance & Development* 52, no. 3 (September 2015), http://www.imf.org/external/pubs/ft/fandd/2015/09/lustig.htm

93. Like other global indicators, the Gini coefficient has many flaws. It is usually applied to income, and less frequently to wealth, but it cannot measure the combination of both. Because its computation relies heavily on national income data, reliable time series of which are often not available for poor countries, most Gini analyses focus on OECD countries. For income, the Gini is often adjusted for taxation and welfare payments, which typically lowers the value, so one must be careful to specify whether the Gini value being discussed is for market incomes or post-tax incomes. Finally, because the Gini coefficient is a relative value, it can assign the same value to economies with very different average income levels. For example, a very poor country like Bangladesh can have the same coefficient as Switzerland (about 0.32). Despite the emergence of newer, better indicators (such as the Palma ratio), the Gini index remains a widely cited measure of inequality.
94. An externality is the effect an economic activity may have on unrelated third parties, that is, individuals or companies that are not directly involved in the production or consumption of the good in question. Pollution emitted by a factory is an example of a negative externality – it impacts the health of local residents and degrades their natural environment, even though they may not be consumers of the factory's products.
95. The Floor Space Index (FSI) or floor area ratio is the ratio of a building's total floor area to the size of the plot of land upon which it is built. For example, an FSI of 4.0 indicates that the total floor area of a building is four times the gross area of the plot on which it is constructed, as would be found in a multi-storey building. If zoning regulations allow for a higher FSI for a plot of land, its value typically rises because it could be developed into lucrative high-rise real estate.
96. See especially *Sacred Economics: Money, Gift, and Society in the Age of Transition* (North Atlantic Books, 2011).
97. For example, if a publisher prints a book and sells it to a bookshop for $15, and the bookseller, in turn, sells it to a customer for $20, it would be incorrect to add both amounts (totalling $35) to GDP. In fact, the publisher's

and the bookseller's combined contribution to GDP is $20, which is the price paid by the end user of the product. Alternatively, we could say that the publisher contributed $15 to GDP, and the bookseller only the value added of $20 – $15 = $5.

98. The corresponding formula is GDP = C + I + G + (X-M), where C is private consumption, I is investment by private firms in production equipment, and G is government expenditure on infrastructure, defence, social programmes, etc. The final variable, X-M, is the difference between the country's exports and imports. Imports must be subtracted because GDP measures the output of only the domestic economy.
99. An astute economist would point out that I have conveniently ignored the issue of opportunity cost. After all, one could argue that by taking a taxi you would arrive at work earlier and therefore your productivity would be greater. However, opportunity cost is very much a First Dimension concept. The notion that the usefulness of a project or activity must always be weighed against whatever alternatives exist for that same investment of time or resources is flawed in the same way that all First Dimension economic ideas are flawed, because it assumes that only activities or projects that are measurable in terms of monetary returns are worth pursuing. In this example, if your health or the savings in carbon dioxide emissions were given a monetary value, then the choice of walking over taking a taxi would make sense even by First Dimension standards.
100. For a good summary of this ongoing debate, see Michael J. Sandel, *What Money Can't Buy: The Moral Limits of Markets* (The Tanner Lectures on Human Values, 1998), http://tannerlectures.utah.edu/_documents/a-to-z/s/sandel00.pdf
101. See New Economics Foundation (NEF), *National Accounts of Well-being: Bringing Real Wealth onto the Balance Sheet* (London: NEF, January 2009).
102. We could use discounted cash flows, for example for certain assets with sustained value, like tourist-friendly landscapes or cultivable land. For non-renewable assets like petroleum, timber, coal, and iron ore, we could use the long-term average value of that commodity. For public goods like clean air and fresh water, more ingenious valuation methods would be required.
103. See Chapter 10, 'Democracy'.

104. Computing the value of the earth has already been attempted by scientists. In the 1990s, for example, Robert Costanza, an ecological economist at the Australian National University, led a team to assess the monetary value of environmental services provided by the earth, such as preventing soil erosion, producing food, purifying water and sequestering carbon dioxide. Costanza's team published their findings in 1997, estimating the earth's value at $33 trillion per year, equivalent to $50 trillion in current dollars (see Robert Costanza *et al.*, 'The Value of the World's Ecosystem Services and Natural Capital,' *Nature* 387 [1997]: 253–260). In 2014 they revised their estimate to over $140 trillion per year based on additional data and new findings about special ecosystems like coral reefs (see Robert Costanza *et al.*, 'Changes in the Global Value of Ecosystem Services,' *Global Environmental Change* 26 [2014]: 152–158). Other studies have attempted to quantify the value of the most important natural resources, such as fresh water and forest cover.
105. The Benefit Corporations or 'B Corps' in the United States put forward a positive example. They are for-profit corporations but hugely value the positive impact on the community, workers, society, and the environment. The directors of a B Corp play a role similar to that of a general corporation, but apart from considering the impact of their decisions on shareholders, they also assess environmental and social impacts. Similarly, the shareholders judge the company's performance based not only on financial reports but also on its contributions to the environment and to society.
106. The separation of stock into different classes with different voting weight is common in North American equities, but not elsewhere. In my country, India, differential voting right shares are still extremely uncommon, issued by only a handful of firms. Tata Motors was the first company to issue such shares in 2008.
107. Since 2000, these bonuses have amounted to between 6 per cent and 20 per cent of each employee's annual salary.
108. For companies with highly diversified holdings and/or product offerings, a balanced view of their utility score would have to be arrived at.
109. The general formula for calculating RoPDE is (GM – PDE)/PDE, where GM is gross margin and PDE is product development expense. See https://www.balancedscorecard.org/portals/0/pdf/howtomeasureinnovation.pdf
110. The concept of eco-efficiency was developed in the 1990s and brought into the mainstream of debate especially by the World Business Council

for Sustainable Development (WBCSD). See UN Economic and Social Commission for Asia and the Pacific (ESCAP), *Eco-efficiency Indicators: Measuring Resource-use Efficiency and the Impact of Economic Activities on the Environment* (Bangkok: UN ESCAP, 2009), https://sustainabledevelopment.un.org/content/documents/785eco.pdf

111. These two criteria would have to be assessed by independent third parties, such as Transparency International for transparency and a national antitrust watchdog for monopoly.
112. Karen Harris, Andrew Schwedel, and Austin Kim, 'A World Awash in Money,' *Bain Insights*, November 14, 2012, http://www.bain.com/publications/articles/a-world-awash-in-money.aspx
113. *Ibid.*
114. In most developed economies, the virtual or computerised money that exists only in banking records constitutes by far the largest portion of the overall money supply.
115. Throughout this chapter I will refer to the new financial instruments as 'meta-currencies' because, although they function very much like currencies, they are not genuine currencies for at least two reasons. First, they have limited uses. They cannot be used by all agents in the economy for all purposes, which is how a currency is usually defined. Second, their value is always measured using the relevant country's main cash currency (such as rupees for India and pesos for Mexico), and therefore they are ultimately convertible to that cash currency. They cannot circulate in the economy forever in their own right.
116. In *Making India Work*, both vouchers and TCs were described collectively as TCs. Here, I have refined the concept to distinguish between goods (redeemed with vouchers) and services (accessed with TCs).
117. Note that the distinction between government-run, parochial, and private educational institutions would probably be a thing of the past in the Second Dimension, and certainly in the Third Dimension. Just as the distinctions between private enterprise and public agency, and between for-profit and non-profit would disappear in higher dimensions (see Chapter 16), so too the difference in the ownership and management of schools will likely evaporate.
118. Like all subjective measurements, satisfaction surveys are prone to bias. In this case, parents would have an incentive to give their children's school

a higher rating than it deserves. A higher rating would secure a greater TC income for the school, resulting, in the parents' perception, in better education and better future prospects for their offspring. It is important, therefore, to balance subjective indicators with more objective performance measurements, such as graduation rates and independently administered testing.

119. Forest is a commodity, and as such its price is more or less the same on every exchange in the world. It is determined by the ceaseless interplay of supply and demand. Scarcity of forest can drive the price up, but so can an increase in population or population density in urban centres. Similarly, overabundance of forested acreage may lower its price.

120. This example is, of course, an oversimplification of how the system would work. For one thing, the assessment of the forest's value would have to be more sophisticated. The forest in question, for example, may not be virgin jungle, but rather a managed forest, sectors of which are logged periodically. So, an Area-level auditing mechanism would have to rate its environmental value carefully, perhaps assigning it one of several grades on a scale of A to D, where only Grades A and B qualify for use as EPCQ, and have different valuations.

121. The value of a natural resource is calculated over generations, as explained in Chapter 15. To briefly remind the reader, the depletion or destruction of the resource would trigger the debit, which will be allocated as a credit in the collective pool.

122. To simplify the calculation, I am ignoring the income potential of the portion of the population that requires support. Hence the calculation yields the maximum subsidy amount that the Community government is liable to pay, though the actual payout may in fact be lower in cases where families are able to contribute an income to their AEA.

123. The Leopard Conservation Reserve is quite extensive, straddling several local boundaries. As such it would qualify as an Area asset, or even a Regional asset. Therefore, any apportionments derived from it would be earned by the Area or the Region, not by individual Communities. However, Greater Sewari could opt to reforest an area contiguous with the Leopard Conservation Reserve, but entirely within the Community's boundaries, and therefore within its sole jurisdiction. This would allow the Community to claim apportionments for the newly developed annex, which would benefit

from the adjacent Reserve because it would attract endemic fauna from the Reserve.

124. Edgar L. Feige, Michele Boldrin, and Harry Huizinga, 'Taxation for the 21st Century: The Automated Payment Transaction (APT) Tax,' *Economic Policy* 15, no. 31 (2000): 475–511, http://www.jstor.org/stable/1344702
125. Will there still be individuals wealthy enough to engage in philanthropy in the Third Dimension, where higher levels of consciousness have lessened our desire for material wealth? Elsewhere in this book I argued for a continuation, indeed an intensification, of free-market economic practices to bring to life all segments of the Spectrum of Demand. Free markets, which rely on choices made by consumers (demand) and producers' ability to satisfy that demand as efficiently as possible (supply), lead by their very nature to disparities in income and wealth. Even in higher dimensions, there will still be entrepreneurs who are more successful than others and workers who are more industrious or talented than others. Wealth disparity will therefore persist in higher dimensions, although it will be drastically reduced compared to the First Dimension as a result of the economic measures I have described in this book.
126. Since its creation in 1999, the euro has emerged as a viable alternative as reserve currency. However, the dollar is still dominant, accounting for approximately 60–65 per cent of global currency reserves during the last decade, compared to 20–25 per cent for the euro.
127. See data published by the US Department of the Treasury at http://ticdata.treasury.gov/Publish/mfh.txt
128. https://www.treasurydirect.gov/govt/reports/pd/mspd/2018/opds102018.pdf
129. https://www.cbo.gov/publication/53651
130. The SDRs are an international reserve asset created in 1969 by the IMF to buttress the Bretton Woods system. They are assets created by fiat in order to keep pace with the rising demands of global trade. Countries are allocated SDRs in proportion to the IMF quotas they pay. As of December 2017, SDRs worth $204.1 billion had been issued and allocated to IMF's members. The value of an SDR unit is based on a basket of five currencies (dollar, euro, yen, pound sterling, and yuan). The SDRs do not amount to a genuine currency. They are not circulated and can be used only by government banks, not by private institutions or the public at large. Holders of SDRs may exchange them for currencies in the basket through deals with

other SDR holders. They can also use them to settle their debts to the IMF or to rebalance their reserves.

131. Since the creation of GUS presupposes an already established GNR value for each country, the initial GNR computation itself would have to be done in dollars. For the purpose of launching the GUS, the initial value of 1 GUS would be equal to $1.
132. Central banks would be able to adjust the exchange rate of their national currency to GUS in order to account for unexpected events occurring between periodic recalculation of GNR and population, such as a sudden loss of consumer confidence leading to hoarding of local currency, or the collapse of a particular industry. However, they would be able to do so only with approval from the global GUS regulator.
133. In this chapter, I have suggested that the calculation of GNR be redone every two years, so that each country's allocation of GUS can be either topped up or reduced accordingly. However, once Second Dimension statisticians have developed a methodology for calculating GNR and have reached a consensus on it, the computation could be done on an annual basis, or even on a quarterly basis, just as GDP is estimated currently.
134. See Matias Vernengo, 'Technology, Finance and Dependency: Latin American Radical Political Economy in Retrospect,' *Review of Radical Political Economics* 38, no. 4 (2006): 551–568. Also, Ricardo Hausmann, 'Currencies: Should There Be Five or One Hundred and Five?' *Foreign Policy* 116 (Autumn, 1999): 65–79.
135. Nepal is a small landlocked and extremely poor country bordering India to the north. According to World Bank data (https://data.worldbank.org/indicator/NY.GDP.PCAP.CD), in 2017 Nepal's GDP per capita was just $835, ranking it 163rd among the 188 countries surveyed.
136. 'Education: Latest Stories,' *UNICEF India*, accessed May 1, 2018, http://unicef.in/Story/1122/Education
137. For a quick and entertaining summary of Robinson's views on modern educational systems, see an animated adaptation of his well-known talk on this subject: Ken Robinson, 'Changing Education Paradigms,' talk at the Royal Society for the Encouragement of Arts, Manufactures and Commerce (RSA), London, RSA Animate video, 11:40, https://www.ted.com/talks/ken_robinson_changing_education_paradigms

138. Ivan Illich, *Deschooling Society* (Harmondsworth, UK: Penguin, 1973), p. 78.

139. Tony Wagner, *The Global Achievement Gap: Why Even Our Best Schools Don't Teach the New Survival Skills Our Children Need – and What We Can Do About It* (New York: Basic Books, 2008).

140. Gardner first outlined his theory of multiple intelligences in *Frames of Mind: The Theory of Multiple Intelligences* (New York: Basic Books, 1983). Since then, he has revisited the subject in many articles, books and interviews, including *Multiple Intelligences: The Theory in Practice* (New York: Basic Books, 1993) and *Multiple Intelligences: New Horizons* (New York: Basic Books, 2006).

141. See Hye Sun You, 'Why Teach Science with an Interdisciplinary Approach: History, Trends, and Conceptual Frameworks,' *Journal of Education and Learning* 6, no. 4 (2017): 66–77.

142. See, for example, S. Baijal *et al.*, 'The Influence of Concentrative Meditation Training on the Development of Attention Networks During Early Adolescence,' *Frontiers in Psychology* 2 (2011): 1–9; M. Napoli *et al.*, 'Mindfulness Training for Elementary School Students,' *Journal of Applied School Psychology* 21, no. 1 (2005): 99–125; and R.J. Semple *et al.*, 'A Randomized Trial of Mindfulness-based Cognitive Therapy for Children: Promoting Mindful Attention to Enhance Social-emotional Eesiliency in Children,' *Journal of Child and Family Studies* 19, no. 2 (2010): 218–229.

143. See C.N. Ortner *et al.*, 'Mindfulness Meditation and Reduced Emotional Interference on a Cognitive Task,' *Motivation and Emotion* 31, no. 4 (2007): 271–283.

144. See Michael D. Mrazek *et al.*, 'Mindfulness Training Improves Working Memory Capacity and GRE Performance while Reducing Mind Wandering,' *Psychological Science* 24, no. 5 (2013): 776–81.

145. Educational goals encapsulated in the Community Leader's scorecard would, of course, make their way into the scorecards of school administrators, especially school principals. As the reader may recall, positions of authority in Levels 16–20 (that is, below the level of Community Leader) are appointed directly by the Community Leader. The Community Leader would be free to evaluate the performance of his school principal(s) in any way he wishes,

but in order to ensure convergence of desired outcomes, he would be strongly encouraged to use a scorecard system similar to his own.

146. On Gross National Happiness (GNH), see Chapter 15.
147. Daniel E. Lieberman, 'Evolution's Sweet Tooth,' *The New York Times*, June 5, 2012, http://www.nytimes.com/2012/06/06/opinion/evolutions-sweet-tooth.html
148. It should be noted that this number can be misleading. Most cattle raised by industrial methods are not fed grain exclusively. They usually eat a mixture of hay, silage, and grain.
149. Michael Pollan, 'Farmer in Chief,' *The New York Times*, October 12, 2008, http://www.nytimes.com/2008/10/12/magazine/12policy-t.html
150. These hydrogenated fats are created by injecting hydrogen molecules into vegetable oils, thus changing the oil's chemical structure so that it has a longer shelf life and is solid at room temperature (think of vegetable shortening). Studies have linked artificial trans fats to cardiovascular problems, including heart disease. Consumption of trans fats is also associated with insulin resistance and type 2 diabetes.
151. HFCS contains marginally more fructose (which is sweeter) than glucose, compared to sugar, which contains them in equal amounts. More importantly, in sugar the two compounds are bound together, so our digestive system must work hard to break this bond before they can be absorbed into the bloodstream. The result is that we do not absorb much of the sugar that we eat. In HFCS, on the other hand, fructose and glucose have already been separated by the manufacturing process, so they can be absorbed much more readily by our digestive system. As a result, HFCS is closely linked to obesity, type 2 diabetes, and liver disease.
152. Eating large amounts of red meat has been linked to coronary heart disease, stroke, type 2 diabetes, and certain cancers.
153. Most predictions agree on this population level in 2050. They disagree, however, on what happens thereafter. According to one study, the population will peak around 2070 and decline slowly thereafter: see Wolfgang Lutz, William P. Butz, and Samir KC, eds., *World Population and Human Capital in the 21st Century* (Oxford: Oxford University Press, 2014), the executive summary of which can be found at http://pure.iiasa.ac.at/id/eprint/11189/1/XO-14-031.pdf. A more recent study by the UN's Population Division, on

the other hand, suggests that population will keep growing in the foreseeable future, exceeding 11 billion by 2100: see United Nations, Department of Economic and Social Affairs, Population Division, *World Population Prospects: The 2017 Revision, Key Findings and Advance Tables* (New York: United Nations, 2017), available online at https://population.un.org/wpp/Publications/Files/WPP2017_KeyFindings.pdf

154. For a valuable discussion of the food scarcity delusion, see Stephen J. Scanlan, J. Craig Jenkins, and Lindsey Peterson, 'The Scarcity Fallacy,' *Contexts*, February 17, 2010, http://contexts.org/articles/the-scarcity-fallacy/
155. See Emily S. Cassidy, Paul C. West, James S. Gerber, and Jonathan A. Foley, 'Redefining Agricultural Yields: From Tonnes to People Nourished per Hectare,' *Environmental Research Letters* 8, no. 3 (July–September 2013), article id. 034015.
156. Such a radical change would be difficult and slow to effect, but the study also noted that even small adjustments could be beneficial. Shifting most meat consumption from beef to pork and chicken, for example, would make a substantial difference because producing a kilo of those meats requires only half and a quarter, respectively, of the grain and water that it takes to produce a kilo of beef.
157. Frances Michaels, *What Is Permaculture?*, https://greenharvest.com.au/GreenGardenNotes/WhatIsPermaculture.html
158. Bill Mollison, *Permaculture: A Designer's Manual* (Tyalgum, NSW: Tagari Publications, 1988), p. *ix*.
159. *Ibid.*
160. For a pertinent example of how this is being done today, see http://altforest.org, which demonstrates how a 'rainforest micro-farm' can be created by replicating rainforest conditions in agriculture.
161. In periods of intense sunshine (between 11 a.m. and 3 p.m.) there is so much sunlight that a plant's process of photosynthesis shuts down temporarily. This is known as solar saturation. Some crops, therefore, benefit (that is, they grow faster and more abundantly) if they are partially covered by shade.
162. See Tomek de Ponti *et al.*, 'The Crop Yield Gap Between Organic and Conventional Agriculture,' *Agricultural Systems* 108 (2012): 1–9; and Lauren Ponisio *et al.*, 'Diversification Practices Reduce Organic to Conventional Yield Gap,' *Proceedings of the Royal Society B / Biological Sciences* 282 (2015): 20141396.

163. R. Lal, 'Enhancing Crop Yields in the Developing Countries through Restoration of the Soil Organic Carbon Pool in Agricultural Lands,' *Land Degradation & Development* 17 (2006): 197–209.
164. Dionys Forster *et al.*, 'Yield and Economic Performance of Organic and Conventional Cotton-based Farming Systems – Results from a Field Trial in India,' *PLOS ONE* 8.12 (2013): e81039.
165. David Blume, 'Food and Permaculture,' *Alcohol Can Be a Gas*, http://www.permaculture.com/node/1344
166. See Masanobu Fukuoka, *The Natural Way of Farming: The Theory and Practice of Green Philosophy*, trans. Frederic P. Metreaud (Tokyo and New York: Japan Publications, 1985).
167. The term 'micronutrients' denotes primarily vitamins (such as vitamins A, B, C, D, E, and K) and minerals (such as fluoride, iron, selenium, sodium, potassium, iodine, calcium, and zinc). Micronutrients are vital for many important functions in the body, including growth, immunity, and brain development. Macronutrients, on the other hand, include proteins, fats, and carbohydrates.
168. Michael Pollan, 'Unhappy Meals,' *The New York Times Magazine*, January 28, 2007, http://www.nytimes.com/2007/01/28/magazine/28nutritionism.t.html
169. In *Diet for a Small Planet* (Ballantine Books, 1971), researcher Frances Moore Lappé explains how essential amino acids can be obtained from complementary sources in vegetarian nutrition.
170. The results of various studies, including the ones mentioned here, are summarised in Diane M. Barrett, *Maximizing the Nutritional Value of Fruits & Vegetables*, http://www.fruitandvegetable.ucdavis.edu/files/197179.pdf
171. See H.S. Burr and F.S.C. Northrop, 'The Electro-Dynamic Theory of Life,' *The Quarterly Review of Biology* 10, no. 3 (September 1935): 322–333. Also, H.S. Burr and C.T. Lane, 'Electrical Characteristics of Living Systems,' *Yale Journal of Biology and Medicine* 8, no. 1 (October 1935): 31–35. In 1949, André Simoneton published *Radiations des aliments – Ondes humaines et santé*, reprinted in 1971 by Courrier du Livre. See also Peter Tompkins and Christopher Bird, *The Secret Life of Plants* (New York: Harper & Row, 1973), which documents controversial experiments that claim to reveal unusual phenomena such as plant sentience.

172. Food and Agriculture Organization (FAO), *An International Technical Workshop: Investing in Sustainable Crop Intensification – The Case for Improving Soil Health* (Proceedings), FAO, July 22–24, 2008, Integrated Crop Management, vol. 6 (Rome: FAO).
173. Markus Flury *et al.*, *Biodegradable Mulch: Performance and Adoptability* (biodegradablemulch.org, Report #SE-2015-01), August 2015, https://ag.tennessee.edu/biodegradablemulch/Documents/What_is_Soil_Quality_Aug5_2015.pdf
174. https://www.johnkay.com/2004/01/17/obliquity
175. Just how great a proportion of overall scientific research is carried out in the private sector is a subject of recurring debate. Looking at the United States only, the National Science Foundation (NSF) estimated that private businesses spent about $375 billion in research and development in 2016, with the pharmaceuticals ($65 billion) and electronics ($77 billion) sectors among the biggest spenders (https://www.nsf.gov/statistics/2018/nsf18312/). These figures include *all* spending, that is, basic/fundamental research, applied research, and product development, with the latter claiming the lion's share (77 per cent). For comparison, in 2018 the federal government provided only $177 billion of research funding (again, for all three types of research), as estimated by the American Association for the Advancement of Science based on the 'omnibus' spending bill signed by President Donald Trump in March 2018 (https://www.aaas.org/news/omnibus-would-provide-largest-research-increase-nearly-decade). Looking at basic research alone, data from NSF surveys show that federal agencies provided only 44 per cent of the amount spent on basic research in 2015, down from 61 per cent in 2004 and over 70 per cent in the 1960s (see Jeffrey Mervis, 'Data Check: U.S. Government Share of Basic Research Funding Falls Below 50%,' *Sciencemag.org* [March 9, 2017], https://www.sciencemag.org/news/2017/03/data-check-us-government-share-basic-research-funding-falls-below-50).
176. From an anecdote recounted by Mrs. Hedwig Born, wife of Max Born. The English translation is from Ronald W. Clark, *Einstein: The Life and Times* (New York: Avon Books, 2001), p. 243.
177. The study was first reported as *Use of Psychedelic Agents to Facilitate Creative Problem Solving*, a fifty-four-page report published in 1965 by the Institute for Psychedelic Research of San Francisco State College. The report was condensed into this paper: Willis W. Harman *et al.*, 'Psychedelic Agents in

Creative Problem-solving: A Pilot Study,' Monograph supplement 2-V19, *Psychological Reports* 19, no. 1 (August 1966): 211–227. Both are available at www.erowid.org

178. Mescaline is a psychedelic alkaloid known for its hallucinogenic effects similar to those of LSD. It occurs naturally in many plants and cacti, including the peyote cactus.
179. In some philosophical and religious traditions, the Third Eye has been associated with the pineal gland. Located in the very centre of the brain, the pineal gland is a small pinecone-shaped gland belonging to the endocrine system that produces the hormone melatonin. Melatonin is vital to the regulation of sleep–wake cycles; its production is regulated by the retina's detection of light and darkness – the brighter the light, the less melatonin is produced and released into the blood. Melatonin levels are highest at night, helping us to sleep, while low levels of melatonin during daylight hours help us to stay awake. The pineal gland's ability to 'see' light has led to its association with knowledge and clairvoyance.
180. Simon Singh and Edzard Ernst, *Trick or Treatment: The Undeniable Facts About Alternative Medicine* (New York: W.W. Norton & Company, 2009).
181. Ross DeVol and Armen Bedroussian, *An Unhealthy America: The Economic Burden of Chronic Disease* (Santa Monica, CA: Milken Institute, October 2007), http://www.milkeninstitute.org/publications/view/321
182. WHO, *Global Status Report on Noncommunicable Diseases 2010* (Geneva: WHO, April 2011), http://www.who.int/nmh/publications/ncd_report2010/en/
183. Debate over the true cost of drug development was sparked by a 2003 calculation performed by economists at the Tufts Center for the Study of Drug Development (see Joseph A. DiMasi, Ronald W. Hansen, and Henry G. Grabowski, 'The Price of Innovation: New Estimates of Drug Development Costs,' *Journal of Health Economics* 22, no. 2 [March 2003]: 151–185). The study estimated the cost incurred by a pharmaceutical company to develop a new prescription medication and bring it to market at $802 million, which amounts to over $1 billion in present-day dollars. Recently, the same authors revised their estimate to about $1.4 billion (in 2013 dollars), which they then capitalised to yield the much-discussed and controversial figure of $2.6 billion (see Joseph A. DiMasi, Ronald

W. Hansen, and Henry G. Grabowski, 'Innovation in the Pharmaceutical Industry: New Estimates of R&D Costs,' *Journal of Health Economics* 47 [May 2016]: 20–33). In both cases, critics were quick to point out flaws in the methodology, and that the Tufts Center is funded by the pharmaceutical industry. A rebuttal, for example, argued that the median cost of research and development of a new prescription drug during the same period analysed by the first Tufts Center study was only $43 million, equivalent to about $55 million in 2011 dollars (see Donald W. Light and Rebecca Warburton, 'Demythologizing the High Costs of Pharmaceutical Research,' *BioSocieties* 6, no. 1 [March 2011]: 34–50). In short, such cost estimates can differ by as much as two orders of magnitude.

184. Jack W. Scannell, Alex Blanckley, Helen Boldon, and B.H. Warrington, 'Diagnosing the Decline in Pharmaceutical R&D Efficiency,' *Nature Reviews Drug Discovery* 11, no. 3 (2012): 191–200.
185. Matthew Herper, 'The Cost of Creating a New Drug Now $5 Billion, Pushing Big Pharma to Change,' *Forbes.com* (August 11, 2013), http://www.forbes.com/sites/matthewherper/2013/08/11/how-the-staggering-cost-of-inventing-new-drugs-is-shaping-the-future-of-medicine.
186. James W. Mold, Robert M. Hamm, and Laine H. McCarthy, 'The Law of Diminishing Returns in Clinical Medicine: How Much Risk Reduction Is Enough?' *Journal of the American Board of Family Medicine* 23, no. 3 (May–June 2010): 371–375.
187. See, for example, J.Y. Chen *et al.*, 'Endometrial Cancer Incidence in Breast Cancer Patients Correlating with Age and Duration of Tamoxifen Use: A Population Based Study,' *Journal of Cancer* 5, no. 2 (2014): 151–155.
188. Alkylating agents attack the DNA of cancer cells to prevent them from replicating themselves. They are the oldest type of chemotherapy drugs. They are used to treat different types of cancer, including leukaemia, lymphoma, Hodgkin's disease, and sarcoma, as well as breast, lung, and ovarian cancer. Alkylating agents are known to cause myelodysplastic syndrome and acute myelogenous leukaemia.
189. The report, published in 2016, is available at http://www.who.int/diabetes/global-report/en/
190. According to WHO's *Global Report on Diabetes*, over 90 per cent of all diabetes cases around the world are type 2 diabetes. Studies have shown that type 2 diabetes is on the rise, with more than 60 per cent of all individuals

with the disorder now residing outside developed countries. India, China, sub-Saharan Africa, Oceania, and Latin America have all witnessed rapid rises in type 2 diabetes. See Ranjit Unnikrishnan, Rajendra Pradeepa, Shashank R. Joshi, and Viswanathan Mohan, 'Type 2 Diabetes: Demystifying the Global Epidemic,' *Diabetes* 66 (2017): 1432–1442. The disorder is also on the rise among children and adolescents. See Orit Pinhas-Hamiel and Philip Zeitler, 'The Global Spread of Type 2 Diabetes Mellitus in Children and Adolescents,' *The Journal of Pediatrics* 146, no. 5 (2005): 693–700.

191. See Diana Kwon, 'Does Parkinson's Begin in the Gut?' *Scientific American*, May 2018, https://www.scientificamerican.com/article/does-parkinsons-begin-in-the-gut/

192. Alpha cells produce glucagon, a hormone that has the opposite effect of insulin – it tells the liver to release stored glucose when blood sugar levels are too low.

193. Jeffrey De Fauw *et al.*, 'Clinically Applicable Deep Learning for Diagnosis and Referral in Retinal Disease,' *Nature Medicine* 24 (13 August 2018): 1342–1350.

194. Ryan Poplin *et al.*, 'Prediction of Cardiovascular Risk Factors from Retinal Fundus Photographs Via Deep Learning,' *Nature Biomedical Engineering* 2 (2018): 158–164.

195. 'BRCA Mutations: Cancer Risk and Genetic Testing,' National Cancer Institute, last reviewed January 30, 2018, https://www.cancer.gov/about-cancer/causes-prevention/genetics/brca-fact-sheet#q1

196. For a clear, succinct introduction to Ayurveda, see Vasant Lad, *Ayurveda: A Brief Introduction and Guide*, The Ayurvedic Institute website, https://www.ayurveda.com/resources/articles/ayurveda-a-brief-introduction-and-guide. Also, *Ayurveda: Life, Health and Longevity* (Albuquerque, NM: Ayurvedic Press, 2004) and *Prakriti: Your Ayurvedic Constitution,* 2nd edn. (Twin Lakes, WI: Lotus Press, 1998), both by Robert Svoboda.

197. For an overview, see Bethany E. Kok, Christian E. Waugh, and Barbara L. Fredrickson, 'Meditation and Health: The Search for Mechanisms of Action,' *Social and Personality Psychology Compass* 7, no. 1 (January 2013): 27–39.

198. Britta K. Hölzel *et al.*, 'Mindfulness Practice Leads to Increases in Regional Brain Gray Matter Density,' *Psychiatry Research: Neuroimaging* 191, no. 1 (January 2011): 36–43.

199. Manoj K. Bhasin *et al.*, 'Correction: Relaxation Response Induces Temporal Transcriptome Changes in Energy Metabolism, Insulin Secretion and Inflammatory Pathways,' *PLOS ONE* 12.2 (2017): e0172873.
200. Perla Kaliman *et al.*, 'Rapid Changes in Histone Deacetylases and Inflammatory Gene Expression in Expert Meditators,' *Psychoneuroendocrinology* 40 (February 2014): 96–107. Results of the study are summarised in Jill Sakai, 'Study Reveals Gene Expression Changes with Meditation,' December 2013, University of Wisconsin–Madison website, https://news.wisc.edu/study-reveals-gene-expression-changes-with-meditation
201. For an overview of the project, see Andy Fraser, 'The Shamatha Project,' Santa Barbara Institute for Consciousness Studies website, https://www.sbinstitute.com/sites/default/files/The%20Shamatha%20Project.pdf.
202. Tonya L. Jacobs *et al.*, 'Self-Reported Mindfulness and Cortisol during a Shamatha Meditation Retreat,' *Health Psychology* 32, no. 10 (October 2013): 1104–1109.
203. Helen Lavretsky *et al.*, 'A Pilot Study of Yogic Meditation for Family Dementia Caregivers with Depressive Symptoms: Effects on Mental Health, Cognition, and Telomerase Activity,' *International Journal of Geriatric Psychiatry* 28, no. 1 (2013): 57–65.
204. The existence of placebo effects has been questioned often by the scientific community. Recent clinical research has shown that such effects are indeed 'genuine biopsychosocial phenomena' that rely on complex neurobiologic mechanisms involving neurotransmitters and activation of specific areas of the brain. It should be noted, however, that while a placebo effect can provide genuine relief from the symptoms of a disease, it can rarely cure the disease itself. See Ted J. Kaptchuk and Franklin G. Miller, 'Perspective: Placebo Effects in Medicine,' *The New England Journal of Medicine* 373 (2015): 8–9.
205. Matthieu Ricard, Antoine Lutz, and Richard J. Davidson, 'Neuroscience Reveals the Secrets of Meditation's Benefits,' *Scientific American*, November 2014, https://www.scientificamerican.com/article/neuroscience-reveals-the-secrets-of-meditation-s-benefits/
206. By 'Delhi' I mean the National Capital Territory of Delhi (NCT), which is a union territory of India. The NCT is governed by its own judiciary, legislature (the Legislative Assembly), and executive. The latter is nominally headed by a lieutenant governor, but executive power rests in the role of

chief minister. Readers should not confuse the NCT with New Delhi, which is just one of the NCT's eleven districts. New Delhi also functions as the seat of India's federal government.

207. Michael Grunwald, 'Inside the War on Coal,' *Politico*, May 26, 2015, http://www.politico.com/agenda/story/2015/05/inside-war-on-coal-000002

Index